Cross-Cultural Psychology

Cross-Cultural Psychology
Understanding Diverse Communities

Jeffery Scott Mio

Saba Safdar

Lori A. Barker

Melanie M. Domenech Rodríguez

John Gonzalez

CANADIAN EDITION

OXFORD
UNIVERSITY PRESS

Oxford University Press is a department of the University of Oxford.
It furthers the University's objective of excellence in research, scholarship,
and education by publishing worldwide. Oxford is a registered trade mark of
Oxford University Press in the UK and in certain other countries.

Published in Canada by Oxford University Press
8 Sampson Mews, Suite 204, Don Mills, Ontario M3C 0H5 Canada

Copyright © Oxford University Press Canada 2023
Copyright © 2020, 2016, 2012 by Oxford University Press
Copyright © 2009, 2006 by McGraw-Hill

Adapted from a work originally published by Oxford University Press, Ltd.
This adapted version has been customized for Canada only and is published by
arrangement with Oxford University Press Ltd. It may not be sold elsewhere.

The moral rights of the authors have been asserted

Database right Oxford University Press (maker)

First Canadian edition published in 2023

All rights reserved. No part of this publication may be reproduced, stored in
a retrieval system, or transmitted, in any form or by any means, without the
prior permission in writing of Oxford University Press, or as expressly permitted
by law, by licence, or under terms agreed with the appropriate reprographics
rights organization. Enquiries concerning reproduction outside the scope of the
above should be sent to the Permissions Department at the address above
or through the following url: www.oupcanada.com/permission/permission_request.php

Every effort has been made to determine and contact copyright holders.
In the case of any omissions, the publisher will be pleased to make
suitable acknowledgement in future editions.

You must not circulate this work in any other form,
and you must impose this same condition on any acquirer.

Library and Archives Canada Cataloguing in Publication

Title: Cross-cultural psychology : understanding our diverse communities / Jeffery Scott Mio, Lori
A. Barker, Melanie M. Domenech Rodríguez, John Gonzalez, Saba Safdar.
Other titles: Multicultural psychology
Names: Mio, Jeffery Scott, 1954- author. | Barker, Lori A., author. | Domenech Rodriguez, Melanie
M., author. | Safdar, Saba F., author.
Description: Canadian edition. | Previously published under title: Multicultural psychology. New
York, New York: Oxford University Press, 2020. | Includes bibliographical references and index.
Identifiers: Canadiana (print) 20210333898 | Canadiana (ebook) 20210333995 | ISBN 9780199038176
(softcover) | ISBN 9780199038183 (EPUB)
Subjects: LCSH: Multiculturalism—Canada—Textbooks. | LCSH: Multiculturalism—Canada—Psychological
aspects—Textbooks. | LCSH: Ethnopsychology—Canada—Textbooks. | LCGFT: Textbooks.
Classification: LCC HM1271 .M56 2022 | DDC 155.8/2—dc23

Cover image: From Canadaland's *Return to Thunder Bay*, by Michah Dowbak & Blake Angeconeb, 2020
Cover and text design: Sherill Chapman

Oxford University Press is committed to our environment.
This book is printed on Forest Stewardship Council® certified paper
and comes from responsible sources.

Printed and bound in Canada
1 2 3 4 — 25 24 23 22

This book is dedicated to my students.
—Saba Safdar, Canadian adaptor

Brief Table of Contents

About the Authors   xv
Preface   xvi
Acknowledgements   xx
From the Publisher   xxi

1 What Is Culture and Cross-Cultural Psychology?   1

2 Cross-Cultural Issues Involving Research and Testing   30

3 Diversity and World Views   58

4 Cultural Differences in Communication   89

5 Immigrants, Refugees, and the Acculturation Process   121

6 Stereotyping, Prejudice, Discrimination, and Racism   147

7 Cultural Identity Development   181

8 Culture and Physical Health   208

9 Culture and Mental Health: Disorders and Treatments   236

10 Where Do We Go from Here? Building Cultural Competence   267

Glossary   294
References   301
Index   341

Detailed Table of Contents

About the Authors   xv
Preface   xvi
Acknowledgements   xx
From the Publisher   xxi

1   What Is Culture and Cross-Cultural Psychology?   1

Learning Objectives   1
- **1.1   What Is Culture?   2**
  - Scholarly Definitions of *Culture*   4
  - Culture and World View   6
- **1.2   What Is Race?   8**
  - The Biological Concept of Race   8
  - The Sociological Concept of Race   9
  - Ethnicity   10
- **1.3   What Is Cross-Cultural Psychology?   11**
- **1.4   What Is Cultural Psychology?   12**
- **1.5   What Is Ethnic Psychology?   12**
- **1.6   What Is Multicultural Psychology?   13**
  - Multiculturalism as a Philosophy   14
  - The Rise of Multiculturalism   16
- **1.7   Multiculturalism as the Fourth Force   19**
- **1.8   What Is the Biopsychosocial Model?   20**
- **1.9   Historical Background   24**
  - Dubious Beginnings   24
  - Gender Differences   25
  - Lesbian, Gay, Bisexual, Transgender, Queer, and Two-Spirit   26

Summary   28
Food for Thought   29
Critical Thinking Questions   29

2   Cross-Cultural Issues Involving Research and Testing   30

Learning Objectives   30
- **2.1   Research Methods in Psychology   31**
  - The General Research Model   31
  - The White-European Standard   32
  - Internal versus External Validity   32
- **2.2   Quantitative Research   34**
  - Quantitative Approaches   35
  - Experimental Designs   36

Detailed Table of Contents ix

- **2.3 Qualitative Research** 39
  - Qualitative Approaches and Gender 42
  - Qualitative Approaches and Older Populations 43
- **2.4 Biases in Cross-Cultural Research** 45
  - Construct Bias 45
  - Method Bias 45
  - Item Bias 46
  - Bias of the User 46
  - Bias in the Usage 46
- **2.5 Equivalence of Measures** 47
  - Language Barriers 47
- **2.6 Replication in Psychology** 48
- **2.7 Collaborative Problem Solving** 49
- **2.8 Intelligence Testing** 50
  - Intelligence and Context 52
  - Alternative Conceptions of Intelligence 53

Summary 56
Food for Thought 56
Critical Thinking Questions 57

3 Diversity and World Views 58

Learning Objectives 58

- **3.1 Different Approaches to Investigating Cultures** 59
  - Imposed Etics 59
  - Long-Term and Short-Term Orientation 60
  - Understanding Differences from Within 62
  - Male and Female Perspectives 63
  - Idiocentrism and Allocentrism 66
  - Guilt versus Shame 68
  - Face Saving, Face Giving, and Social Support 69
- **3.2 Are We WEIRD?** 70
- **3.3 Models of Value Orientation and World View** 70
  - Kluckhohn and Strodtbeck's Value Orientation Model 71
  - Schwartz's Theory of Human Values 72
  - Derald Wing Sue's World View Model 74
- **3.4 World Views of Different Ethnic Groups** 76
- **3.5 Social Expectations and World Views of Women** 79
- **3.6 World View of LGBTQ2+ Individuals** 80
- **3.7 World View Based on Social Class and Age** 84
  - Youth and World View 85

Summary 86
Food for Thought 87
Critical Thinking Questions 87
Note 88

x   Detailed Table of Contents

4   Cultural Differences in Communication   89

Learning Objectives   89

4.1   Conversational Rules: The Co-operative Principle   90
  The Maxim of Quality   90
  The Maxim of Quantity   91
  The Maxim of Relevance   91
  The Maxim of Manner   92
  Additional Maxims   94

4.2   Non-verbal Aspects of Language   95
  Proxemics   96
  Kinesics   97
  Paralanguage   100

4.3   High- versus Low-Context Communication   101

4.4   Direct versus Indirect Communication   102
  Ethnic Minority Patterns of Communication   104
    Afro-Caribbean and African Canadians   104
    Asian Canadians   105
    Further Cultural Examples   105
    Indigenous Peoples   106
  Communication Patterns of the Elderly   107
  Communication among Younger Adults   107

4.5   The Role of Social Media in Communication   108
  The Use of Social Media: The Negative Aspects   109
  The Use of Social Media: The Positive Aspects   110

4.6   Gender Differences in Communication   111

4.7   Bilingual Communication   113
  Cognitive Consequences of Bilingualism   114
  Social Consequences of Bilingualism   116

Summary   118
Food for Thought   119
Critical Thinking Questions   120

5   Immigrants, Refugees, and the Acculturation Process   121

Learning Objectives   121

5.1   Immigrants and Refugees   122
  Immigrants   123
  Refugees and Asylum Seekers   124
    The Syrian Refugee Crisis   124

5.2   Migration Phases   125
  The Six Stages of the Refugee Journey   126

5.3   Common Experiences of Immigrants and Refugees   128
  Language Barriers   129
  Support Networks   130
  Family Structure   131
  New Family Roles   133

Detailed Table of Contents   xi

    Employment 134
    Education 135
 5.4 Acculturation **137**
   Models of Acculturation 138
    Acculturation of Immigrants 139
    Acculturation of Diverse Populations 141
 5.5 Bronfenbrenner's Ecological Model **143**
Summary 144
Food for Thought 145
Critical Thinking Questions 145
Note 146

6 Stereotyping, Prejudice, Discrimination, and Racism 147

Learning Objectives 147
 6.1 Social Categorizations and Their Consequences **151**
   Stereotype 151
   Prejudice 151
   Discrimination 151
   Racism 151
   Distinction amongst Stereotypes, Prejudice, Discrimination, and Racism 152
 6.2 Stereotype Threat **153**
 6.3 The Development of Negative Stereotypes **155**
 6.4 Systematic Racism in Society **158**
   Indigenous Experiences with Racism 160
 6.5 Overt versus Covert Racism **163**
   The Grenfell Tower Tragedy: Was Socio-economic Status a Factor? 166
 6.6 The Complexities of Modern Racism **167**
   Aversive Racism 167
   Colour-Blind Racial Ideology 169
   Internalized Oppression 170
 6.7 Racial Microaggressions **172**
 6.8 Racism and the Biopsychosocial Model **174**
 6.9 White Privilege **176**
Summary 178
Food for Thought 179
Critical Thinking Questions 179
Note 180

7 Cultural Identity Development 181

Learning Objectives 181
 7.1 The Independent and Interdependent Self **183**
 7.2 Models of Personality **184**
   The Tripartite Model of Personal Identity 184
   The Five-Factor Model of Personality across Cultures 185

- 7.3 **Ethnic Identity Development** 186
  - Black Identity Development 187
  - White-European Identity Development 190
  - Chicano/Latino Identity Development 194
  - Asian/Filipino Identity Development 195
  - Indigenous Identity Development 196
- 7.4 **Multi-ethnic Identity Development Models** 196
  - Five-Stage Model of Biracial Identity Development 197
  - Banks' Typology of Ethnic Identity 199
  - Model of Bicultural Competence 199
- 7.5 **Sexual Identity Development** 200
- 7.6 **Racial and Cultural Identity Development Model (R/CID)** 202
- 7.7 **Critiques of Cultural Identity Models** 204
- 7.8 **Complexities of Multiple Identities** 205

Summary 206
Food for Thought 207
Critical Thinking Questions 207
Note 207

8 Culture and Physical Health 208

Learning Objectives 208
- 8.1 **Health and Health Disparities** 209
- 8.2 **Models of Health** 211
- 8.3 **Health Inequalities and Health Inequities Defined** 213
- 8.4 **A Look at National and Global Health Disparities** 214
  - Health Disparities in Canada 214
  - Health Disparities Globally 215
- 8.5 **Health Outcomes across Ethnic Groups** 216
  - Immigrants' Health 216
  - Indigenous Peoples' Health 217
- 8.6 **Causes of Health Disparities** 219
  - Poverty 220
  - Racism 221
- 8.7 **The Link between Racism, Poverty, and Health** 223
- 8.8 **Access to the Health-Care System** 224
  - Barriers to Health-Care Access among Indigenous Peoples 224
  - Barriers to Health-Care Access among Immigrants 225
  - Discriminatory Behaviours in Health-Care Systems 226
- 8.9 **Access to Health-Care Systems: A Global Review** 227
- 8.10 **Diverse Approaches to Medicine** 230
- 8.11 **Obscure Health Disparities** 231
- 8.12 **How to Bring about Change** 232

Summary 234
Food for Thought 235
Critical Thinking Questions 235

Detailed Table of Contents xiii

9 Culture and Mental Health: Disorders and Treatments   236

Learning Objectives   236

- **9.1 Culture and Diagnostic Manuals**   237
  - International Classification of Diseases and Related Health Problems   238
  - *Diagnostic and Statistical Manual of Mental Disorders*: A Classification System   238
  - Manuals of Mental Disorders: Examples from China, North Africa, and Latin America   239
- **9.2 Culture and the Expression of Symptoms**   241
- **9.3 Cultural Differences in Rates of Mental Disorders**   241
  - Psychiatric Epidemiology Studies across Countries and Ethnic Groups   243
  - Ethnic and Racial Groups Not Well Represented in Large Epidemiologic Studies   244
  - Critiquing Epidemiologic Studies   246
  - Conclusions from Existing Data   247
- **9.4 Utilization of Mental-Health Services**   247
- **9.5 Barriers: Access to Psychological Treatment**   248
  - Culture-Bound Values as Barriers   250
  - Class-Bound Values as Barriers   253
  - Language Variables as Barriers   253
- **9.6 Culturally Sensitive Therapeutic Approaches**   254
  - The Training of Mental-Health Professionals: Multicultural Competence   254
- **9.7 Gender Differences in Mental Disorders**   257
- **9.8 Culture-Specific Mental Disorders**   258
  - Eating Disorders: A Western Cultural Syndrome?   260
- **9.9 The Impact of the Pandemic on Mental Health**   263

Summary   265
Food for Thought   265
Critical Thinking Questions   266

10 Where Do We Go from Here? Building Cultural Competence   267

Learning Objectives   267

- **10.1 Cultural Competence**   268
- **10.2 Awareness of Your Own Cultural Attitudes**   269
  - The Four *F* Reactions: Freeze, Flee, Fight, and Fright   269
  - The Five *D*s of Difference   270
    - Distancing   270
    - Denial   271
    - Defensiveness   271
    - Devaluing   272
    - Discovery   274

10.3 Learning about Your Own Culture 276
10.4 Understanding Other World Views 279
   Learning Key Historical Events   279
   Becoming Aware of Socio-political Issues   279
   Knowing Basic Values and Beliefs of Other World Views   281
   Understanding Cultural Practices   282
   Knowing the Dynamics of Racism, Discrimination, and Stereotyping   282
10.5 Developing Culturally Appropriate Interpersonal Skills 283
   Participating in Education and Training   283
   Gaining Experience and Practice   286
   Saying "I Don't Know" and Asking Questions   286
   Travelling   287
   Speaking Up for Others: Being an Ally   287
   Speaking Up for Oneself: Comfort with Difficult Dialogues   288
   Developing an Attitude of Discovery and Courage   289
   Developing Empathy   290
10.6 A Change in World View 290
Summary   292
Food for Thought   293
Critical Thinking Questions   293

Glossary   294
References   301
Index   341

About the Authors

Dr Saba Safdar is a full professor of psychology at the University of Guelph, where she is Director of the Centre for Cross-Cultural Research. Safdar received her Ph.D. in 2002 from York University in Toronto, Canada, and has been a full-time faculty member since her graduation. Safdar has been a visiting professor in France, India, Kazakhstan, Spain, Russia, the UK, and the US.

Dr Safdar is an active researcher with scholarly publications ranging from books, book chapters, textbooks, journal articles, and research reports. Her first line of research is the examination of the psychosocial adaptation of immigrants in their country of settlement. In addition, she has examined experiences, barriers, and values of minorities and members of ethnic groups, including Muslims in and outside Canada. Dr Safdar's research has applicable components as it addresses social issues and involves both local and global communities. She has delivered two TEDx Talks with over 400,000 views by 2022.

Dr Jeffery Scott Mio is a professor in the Psychology and Sociology Department at California State Polytechnic University, Pomona (Cal Poly Pomona), where he also serves as the director of the MS in Psychology program. He received his Ph.D. from the University of Illinois, Chicago, in 1984. He taught at California State University, Fullerton, in the Counselling Department from 1984 to 1986 and then at Washington State University in the Department of Psychology from 1986 to 1994 before accepting his current position at Cal Poly Pomona.

Dr Lori A. Barker is a professor in the Psychology Department at California State Polytechnic University, Pomona (Cal Poly Pomona). She received her BA in psychology from Yale University and her Ph.D. in clinical psychology from the University of California, Los Angeles (UCLA). After receiving her degree, Dr Barker spent one additional year at UCLA as a National Institute of Mental Health postdoctoral research fellow. Dr Barker is a licensed clinical psychologist with a private practice in Riverside, California, called the Center for Individual, Family, and Community Wellness.

Dr Melanie M. Domenech Rodríguez is a professor of psychology at Utah State University (USU); she began her appointment at USU in 2000. Dr Domenech Rodríguez has been actively engaged in programs of parenting intervention research in Mexico, Puerto Rico, and Michigan, examining the effectiveness of GenerationPMTO. Her research has been funded by the National Institute of Mental Health and the National Institute of Child Health and Human Development.

Dr John Gonzalez is Ojibwe from White Earth Anishinaabe Nation and a professor of psychology at Bemidji State University in northern Minnesota, where he also received his undergraduate degree in psychology. He received his Ph.D. in clinical psychology from the University of North Dakota. Dr Gonzalez has taught multicultural psychology since 2005.

Preface

Throughout the years, the authors of this book have taught courses on cross-cultural psychology and multicultural psychology. They have attended conference presentations and workshops on this topic, and what has stuck with them are the stories people have been compelled to tell. Thus, they planned this book around stories (narratives or anecdotes) that illustrate important aspects of scientific studies and other professional writings in the field of cultural, cross-cultural, and multicultural psychology.

In general, the authors agree that anecdotes are not sufficient evidence to prove one's point. Although this is true from a scientific perspective and anecdotes are not substituted for scientific investigation, the authors use anecdotes as central points around which to build their case for cultural issues based on science. In addition, cultural and cross-cultural psychology emphasize the value of integrating quantitative and qualitative methods to accurately capture the richness of diverse cultures and communities. Thus, rather than substituting for science, the anecdotes are prototypes for scientific investigation. For example, science tells us that there are differences in the way in which men and women communicate. We illustrate those differences by presenting anecdotes highlighting the common experience women have of sometimes being shut out of conversations, particularly ones that are about "male" topics. Science tells us that there are various stages or statuses of ethnic identity, and the authors present some prototypical anecdotes that illustrate how those statuses of identity affect one's perceptions and life experiences. Science tells us that members of minority groups may have very different reactions to Anglo European therapists, and the authors present an anecdote that conveys a typical reaction to an Anglo European therapist who did not approach a family of colour in a culturally sensitive manner. Again, these stories are meant not to replace science, but to enrich science—to add texture to the clean (and sometimes sterile) lines of science.

Dr Safdar, in the process of adapting this textbook from the US to the Canadian edition, has replaced some of the US-focused stories. Instead, she has included stories with Canadian content or a more international focus. Furthermore, Canadian and cross-cultural research have been added to illustrate the range of studies that are conducted outside of the US. Many of the research findings have been updated to depict the most recent cultural understanding of psychological concepts.

Organization of the Book

This book is organized around the emphasis that we place in our undergraduate cross-cultural and multicultural courses and arose out of a perceived need we saw in the field.

In Chapter 1, we define relevant terms including *culture* and *race*. We discuss the overall importance of cross-cultural psychology and how it came into prominence. Historically, many researchers in the field have identified three forces in psychology: psychoanalysis, behaviourism, and humanism. Some feel that multicultural psychology is the fourth force in our field. Moreover, an understanding of the cultural context is essential as we view behaviour from the biopsychosocial perspective.

In Chapter 2, we explore issues involving research and testing. We build on the notion that the history of psychology was dominated by an Anglo European standard by explaining that sometimes such a standard is not relevant to communities of diversity and can even be damaging to them. There is also a preference for quantitative analysis in science because it is believed that qualitative studies introduce too much bias or are not generalizable enough.

However, bias can be introduced in quantitative analyses as well, through the choice of what to study, through the way in which one's measures are converted into numerical responses, through the interpretation of those results, and so on. Therefore, we discuss qualitative analyses, particularly as they apply to communities of diversity. Finally, we apply issues of research methodology to our understanding of psychological testing.

In Chapter 3, we discuss various kinds of world views. First, we discuss issues of etic versus emic perspectives. In cross-cultural psychology, the etic perspective attempts to develop theory by finding similarities across different cultures, whereas the emic perspective emphasizes meaningful concepts within cultures that may not translate across cultures. Among the most important distinctions in the cross-cultural literature is the distinction between individualism and collectivism. That is because these perspectives are infused in societies, so one's cultural context may be from an individualistic society or from a collectivistic society. Different cultural groups may also have different values, such as the importance of the past, present, or future. Again, we discuss how diverse communities can have very different world views from those of their Anglo European counterparts. We added a section on the world view of today's youth.

In Chapter 4, we examine differences in communication. We first present rules of conversation that have been identified by linguists and psycholinguists. There are some regularities in conversations within various groups, but there are many examples of differences among groups. For example, people in some groups feel more comfortable standing closer to their conversational partners than do people in other groups. Another key distinction in cross-cultural communication is the distinction between high- and low-context communication groups. In high-context groups, less is said because the context carries with it much of the communication, whereas in low-context groups, more must be said because there may be different rules governing contextual communication that may be applied to the situation. We explore differences in communication that have been identified in diverse communities. We pay particular attention to gender differences in communication: men tend to use more direct methods of communication, and women tend to use more indirect methods; women also use *softening* methods so that their opinions do not seem so harsh. We also present communication styles by older adults, and also communication styles by younger adults. We finish this chapter by discussing bilingual communication, including both cognitive and social consequences.

In Chapter 5, we discuss issues involving immigrants and refugees. Often, people do not make a distinction between these two populations. However, there can be some very important differences psychologically. For example, immigrants choose to leave their country of birth, and they prepare for that transition by studying this country and its traditions, learning a second language, deciding where to settle, and so on. In contrast, refugees come against their will. They often must escape from their countries of origin to save their lives, do not know where they will ultimately settle (often going from country to country until a final host country can be found), and encounter many hardships and even trauma in their transition. However, beyond those initial differences, immigrants and refugees can encounter many similar issues, such as language barriers, changing family roles, and problems with employment. We conclude this chapter by discussing models of acculturation.

In Chapter 6, we focus on issues involving racism. First, social psychologists make a distinction among stereotypes, prejudice, discrimination, and racism. All of these are forms of group categorization, but stereotypes relate to similarities we perceive within the categorized group, prejudice relates to our feelings about the categorized group, discrimination relates to our behaviours toward the categorized group, and racism relates to our institutional practices against the categorized group. Racism is also related to other *isms* (e.g., sexism, heterosexism, ableism) in that they all involve institutional practices that systematically disadvantage those who are on the downside of power. Although overt racism is largely a thing of the past, modern forms of racism still exist. We apply these issues of racism to contemporary socio-political issues in Canada and globally. One way to overcome racism and other *isms* is to understand issues of Anglo European privilege and other privileges of power. In so doing, one can become an advocate or ally for those who are unfairly disadvantaged by institutional practices.

In Chapter 7, we look at issues of identity. People who are familiar with developmental psychology know that this is one of the central questions that arise in adolescence. In cross-cultural psychology, one must explore not only issues of who one is and what aspirations one has, but also how those issues relate to one's racial/cultural identity. We discuss models of identity development, beginning with Black identity development, then White-European identity, Chicano/Latino identity, Asian/Filipino identity, and Indigenous identity development. We also discussed a general racial/cultural identity development model. This final model also includes other forms of identity, such as multi-ethnic identity development and gay/lesbian identity development. We conclude this chapter by discussing issues of multiple identities. At different times, one or a subset of these identities may come to the fore, and we need to understand how we can balance these different demands. Moreover, being secure within all our multiple identities means that when we emphasize one identity over another, we are not less of the other but rather are emphasizing the one identity in response to contextual demands.

In Chapter 8, we discuss physical health issues. Health and health behaviours are related to one's world view and the context within which one develops. For example, different groups of people of colour encounter differential care in a health-care system where policies and behaviours are still affected by remnants of racism. Much of that may be a result of poverty because in the absence of universal health care, people with better health insurance are treated better than are those who are compelled to use public assistance programs. To the extent that there remain differences in socio-economic status among different groups, there remain differences in health-care opportunities. However, even with the barrier of poverty removed, structural barriers remain, such as language and access. Change can occur if we increase the number of health-care providers for people of colour and address structural barriers in the health-care system.

In Chapter 9, we discuss mental-health disorders and treatments and describe different classifications that are used globally for mental-health diagnosis. We describe how many large-scale studies that have examined mental disorders have under-represented populations of colour. Also, some disorders may be specific to some cultures. These are called *culture-bound syndromes* and may be fundamentally different disorders or different expressions of similar disorders across cultural groups. We deal with issues involving mental-health treatment. In therapy, many people of colour either underutilize mental-health services or terminate treatment prematurely because of discomfort with their therapists. Their discomfort may be caused by various barriers to treatment, such as cultural (value) differences, class differences, and language problems. To overcome these barriers, we must develop culturally sensitive approaches to treatment.

Finally, in Chapter 10 we discuss general issues in increasing our cultural competence. We must be aware of our cultural attitudes and understand how they may be different from attitudes of other cultures. In coming to understand our differences, we may encounter what we call the "Five Ds of Difference": distancing, denial, defensiveness, devaluing, and discovery. The first four Ds of Difference involve negative reactions we might experience in an effort to hold on to our own more secure patterns of behaviour. However, the fifth D of Difference involves a positive reaction that we may experience by understanding how the difference expressed by the other culture may enrich our lives. When we prefer our own more secure patterns of behaviour to the different ones we might encounter in another culture, our secure patterns feel simpler, make us feel safe, and keep us sane as opposed to confused. We offer suggestions to help you improve your cultural competence, such as learning about other cultures before you encounter them; knowing about basic values, beliefs, and practices; not being afraid to ask questions; travelling to other places; becoming an ally; and making a decision to develop an attitude of discovery and courage.

We hope that you enjoy this book and learn a little bit more about yourself and others. We have certainly learned a little about ourselves in writing this book and are excited about that discovery. The field of cross-cultural psychology is relatively new, and it will undoubtedly change with the demographics of our country and the emergence of new and important issues. Our intention is to give you the tools to address and understand these emerging issues. The rest is up to you.

Acknowledgements

In adapting the textbook into the Canadian edition, I worked with a team of research assistants at the Centre for Cross-Cultural Research at the University of Guelph. In particular, two of my Ph.D. students, Saghar Chahar-Mahali and Elcin Ray-Yol, contributed significantly to completion of the textbook. They worked tirelessly and meticulously and led a team of research assistants who helped with each chapter. The research assistants in alphabetical order were: Sarah Dias, Amanda Harton, Jaiden Herkimer, Sara Hosseininezhad, Maria Reyes, Talia Rock, and Lareb Zahra. I am grateful to the team of students for their contributions, which ranged from identifying relevant sources, conducting literature reviews, attending meetings, and staying on schedule in order to deliver high-quality work.

In addition, I would like to give a shout-out to Lauren Wing (associate editor) and Tracey MacDonald (senior acquisitions editor) at Oxford University Press Canada for the support they provided throughout this process. Their guidance, feedback, and assistance are much appreciated. The adaptation of this textbook came with a good degree of freedom: the chance to illustrate the scholarly works that are conducted in Canada and introduce the tremendous research on cross-cultural psychology that is conducted outside of North America. This was a unique opportunity.

I would also like to thank the following reviewers for their helpful comments, along with those reviewers who chose to remain anonymous:

David Bourgeois
Saint Mary's University

Gustavo Gottret
University of Ottawa

Stacey McHenry
University of Saskatchewan

Wei Qi Elaine Perunovic
University of New Brunswick

From the Publisher

Oxford University Press Canada is pleased to present *Cross-Cultural Psychology*, a comprehensive introduction that combines qualitative and quantitative research with anecdotal material to examine multicultural issues and capture the richness of diverse cultures in relation to psychology. This first Canadian edition includes a wide variety of features guaranteed to interest readers and promote student learning.

Key Features

Experiences and Perspectives in Canada
Perspectives, experiences, policies, and examples from Canada—including discussions about racism, health care, Indigenous rights, immigration, LGTBQ2+ worldviews, and bilingualism in Canada—ensure the material is relevant to Canadian students while situating it within a global context.

Personal Stories from Canada and around the World
First-person narrative accounts by people of all ages and cultural backgrounds illustrate personal connections to topics such as communication, racial and cultural identity, development, racism, worldviews, and immigration within Canada's national context and beyond.

FOOD FOR THOUGHT

Whether multiculturalism truly is the fourth force in psychology remains to be seen. You are free to draw your own conclusions about that. We cannot deny, however, that culture is a critical factor in the way human beings think, feel, act, and interact. The field of cross-cultural psychology seeks to study that factor, with the ultimate goal of increasing our understanding of ourselves. We hope this chapter has whetted your appetite because in the following chapters we will introduce you to more specific areas of theory, research, and practice in the field of cross-cultural psychology.

Critical Thinking Questions

1. What were your early experiences with ethnic differences? What were your early experiences with other aspects of difference? How have those early experiences shaped you into the person you are now?
2. Have you ever been to foreign countries and felt out of place? Have you ever been to other regions of Canada or another country and felt out of place? Have you ever been to different areas of your own city that made you feel out of place? How have you handled those situations?

Extensive Pedagogical Features
A wealth of pedagogical features—including learning objectives, key terms, Food for Thought boxes, and critical thinking questions—enhance student comprehension and provide easy navigation of concepts.

Digital Resources

Cross-Cultural Psychology is supported by helpful digital resources for instructors, all available in OUP's online Oxford Learning Link (OLL).

- **An instructor's manual** includes learning objectives, key terms, classroom activities, additional resources, and essay questions.

- **A test bank** provides a comprehensive set of multiple choice questions to assess students' skills.

- **PowerPoint slides** summarize key points from each chapter.

Bing Wen/Shutterstock

1 What Is Culture and Cross-Cultural Psychology?

Learning Objectives

Reading this chapter will help you to:

1.1 comprehend the various definitions of *culture*;
1.2 recognize the difference between two related but distinct concepts: race (as a biological concept) and ethnicity (as a socio-cultural concept);
1.3 understand and describe cross-cultural psychology;
1.4 understand and describe cultural psychology;
1.5 understand and describe ethnic psychology;
1.6 understand multicultural psychology in relation to multiculturalism as a philosophy and the advancement of multiculturalism;
1.7 recognize how multiculturalism is the fourth force in psychology;
1.8 use the biopsychosocial model in explaining the effect of culture on behaviour; and
1.9 know a basic history of the field of cross-cultural psychology and its connection to gender research and lesbian, gay, bisexual, transgender, queer, and two-spirit (LGBTQ2+) issues.

Throughout this book you will read many unique stories. Motivated by these and other personal stories shared with us over the years by students, colleagues, family members, and friends, we have woven this material as illustrations into the fabric of theories, concepts, and research findings to create a textbook that uses a narrative approach to multicultural psychology. The use of oral history and personal life stories has a long tradition in the field of psychology. Personal narratives are particularly important in the study of people from diverse groups (Ponterotto, 2010). Atkinson says, "Telling our story enables us to be heard, recognized, and acknowledged by others. Story makes the implicit explicit, the hidden seen, the unformed, formed, and the confusing clear" (as cited in Ponterotto, 2010, p. 7). That is what we hope the stories included in this book will do for you: bring the relevance of culture to life. The book's topics include, among others, worldviews, communication, immigration, acculturation, racism, identity, and physical and mental health. We hope you enjoy this more personal approach.

> I am more convinced each day that telling our stories to each other is the way we learn best what our collective life is all about, the way we understand who we really are, how our stories are intertwined, what this reality means for us now, and what it portends for the future.
>
> —Dr. Terrence Roberts, psychology professor and one of the "Little Rock Nine" who integrated Central High School in Little Rock, Arkansas, in 1957 (Roberts, 2009, pp. 10–11)

1.1 What Is Culture?

Culture is a complex term and defining it is difficult. This is because we use the word *culture* all the time, and in so many ways. There are so many different aspects of a society that make up its culture. For example, people's shared behaviours, beliefs, and attitudes can reflect the culture of their society. Dana, an immigrant from Dubai, describes how Canada is considered to be a friendly and inclusive society. There are legislations and laws supporting equality and prohibiting discrimination based on gender, sexual orientation, age, disability, religion, and ethnicity:

> My family and I moved to Canada from Dubai about three years ago, and I have to say it was the best decision we have ever made. One of the first things we noticed and that surprised us was the fact that people are very kind and friendly here compared to how people were back in Dubai. Everyone tries to help you in every way possible.
>
> Another thing that really shocked me is how anyone can be hired here, especially people with disabilities, since everyone is considered the same no matter what. It's not to say that, back in Dubai, disabled people were not appreciated, but it's quite different how they are treated here. Even with the concept of LGBT [lesbian, gay, bisexual, and transgender] people—you're still considered a normal person, and no one judges you.
>
> —Dana, immigrant from United Arab Emirates (Kivanc, 2016)

When someone asks what culture you are from, how do you reply? Do you tell them your nationality (e.g., Chinese, El Salvadoran)? Do you tell them where your ancestors were from (e.g., "I'm Polish on my dad's side, but Swedish on my mother's")? Do you refer to your skin colour (e.g., "I'm Black")? Do you refer to your religion (e.g., "I'm atheist"), or do you use a specific ethnic label (e.g., "I'm Iranian-Canadian")? If you answer in one of these ways, you are like most people, who, when asked about culture, reply by stating their nationality, ethnicity, religion, or visible characteristics such as skin colour (Cohen et al., 2016; Hofstede, 2001; Markus & Kitayama, 2010).

Sometimes we use the word *culture* to mean various types of music, art, and dance. For example, when people refer to the cultural life of a city, they usually have in mind artistic opportunities, such as access to a good museum or symphony orchestra or the quality of the plays that come to town. At other times we use the term *culture* to refer to such things as food, clothing, and traditions. For example, in Canada, the term *Indigenous Peoples* is used to represent the original people of North America and their descendants (International Work Group for Indigenous Affairs, 2020). There are three main groups of Indigenous Peoples in Canada: Inuit, Métis, and First Nations. However, there are over 600 First Nations communities in Canada, each with their own culture and customs. Some Indigenous communities conduct powwows, sweat-lodge ceremonies, or talking circles. These activities represent traditions that Indigenous groups have passed down from generation to generation and are ways in which communities connect with their cultural heritage, express ideas, and solve problems.

At other times we use the term *culture* in reference to the regular or expected behaviours of a particular group. We might, for example, use the term *teen culture* to refer to the particular way adolescents act, talk, and dress. This term signifies that adolescents behave differently from people of other age groups. Kroeber and Kluckhohn (1952/1963) and Berry and associates (Berry et al., 1992) described six uses of culture in everyday language:

This painting by Métis artist Adam Paquette depicts a sweat-lodge ceremony and was shown in an exhibition at the Royal Alberta Museum.

Descriptive: the specific behaviours and activities associated with a culture
Historical: a group's heritage and traditions
Normative: the rules that govern the behaviour of a group
Psychological: behavioural processes, such as learning and problem solving
Structural: the organizational elements of a culture
Genetic: the origins of that culture

Let's use Mexican culture as an example. To talk about Spanish as the primary language is a descriptive use of culture. To talk about the holidays that people celebrate, such as Cinco de Mayo and El Día de los Muertos, is a historical use. To talk about traditional gender roles and machismo is a normative use. To talk about the process of learning a new language or adjusting to a new culture is a psychological use. To talk about the importance of the extended family is a structural use. Finally, to talk about the combined influence of Indigenous and Spanish (-European) people on Mexican physical appearance is a genetic use.

Sue, Ivey, and Pedersen (1996) gave the following broad definition of culture: "any group that shares a theme or issue(s)" (p. 16). Therefore, language, gender, ethnicity, spirituality, sexual preference, age, physical issues, socio-economic status, and survival after trauma all define cultures. Under this broad definition, we can have simultaneous membership in more than one culture.

Some psychologists argue that a broad definition of culture is not particularly helpful. Should something such as gender be included? Do men and women really have separate and distinct cultures? If this definition is taken to its extreme, anything could be considered a culture. Let us use the deaf community as an example. If we define a culture as a distinct group of people characterized by shared customs, behaviours, and values, would the deaf community fit that definition? Backenroth (1998) thinks so. She argues that deaf people share a common language (sign language); have their own schools, churches, and social organizations; have common experiences and a common way of interacting with one another and with hearing people; and therefore, have a distinct culture. Other authors agree that persons with disabilities, such as individuals who are hearing impaired, besides being distinguished by their physical impairment, share other psychological and sociological characteristics (Clymer, 1995; Rose, 1995).

Scholarly Definitions of *Culture*

So far, our discussion has covered how we use culture in everyday language, the subculture of particular groups (e.g., youth), and the various types of culture (e.g., art). But how do psychologists and other scholars define *culture*? Over time, different and sometimes contradictory definitions of the term have been suggested. One of the early definitions is provided by American anthropologist Melville J. Herskovits, who states that "Culture is the man-made part of the environment" (Herskovits, 1948, p. 17). According to this definition, culture is what people create and do in order to survive. Therefore, culture is a social structure and a system within which people interact.

Rohner (1984) defines *culture* as a learned system of meanings within a particular group of people that is transmitted across generations. Let us unpack this definition. First, culture is learned, and, therefore, we are not born with a particular culture. Second, we learn about our culture from the previous generation (e.g., from parents to children). Third, culture is defined with reference to a segment of people, signifying that human societies are differentiated by their culture. Fourth, culture is a system of meanings, such as beliefs, values, and norms, that is shared and understood by most members of the society. Although a system of meanings is shared by most members of a given population, it is by no means shared by all members. Variation and diversity exist within a culture. Additionally, no two members of a society have identical beliefs, values, and norms as people have individualized experiences that shape their thoughts and emotions. Therefore, there is no uniformity of behaviour within a particular culture.

Henry Triandis (1996), who is referred to as the grandfather of cross-cultural psychology, defines *culture* as "shared elements of subjective culture and behavioural patterns found among those who speak a particular language dialect, in a particular geographic region, during a specific historic period" (p. 408). In this definition, the shared cultural elements include both subjective culture (e.g., beliefs, norms, values) and shared behaviours. Geert Hofstede (2001), who developed the highly influential six dimensions model of culture, defines *culture* as "the collective programming of the human mind that distinguishes the members of one human group from those of another" (p. 9). Although the many definitions out there describe culture from different angles, they all emphasize that culture is learned, transferred from one generation to another, and shared within a specific population (see Table 1.1).

Schwartz (2014), however, challenges the notion of the "shared-ness" of culture. He defines *culture* as "the latent, normative value system, external to the individual, which

TABLE 1.1 Scholarly Definitions of *Culture*

Researcher	Definition of *Culture*
Melville Herskovits (1948)	The human-made part of the environment
Ronald Rohner (1984)	A learned system of meanings within a particular group of people that is transmitted across generations
Henry Triandis (1996)	The shared values, language, and behavioural pattern of a group of people who live in a geographical region during a specific period of time
Geert Hofstede (2001)	A shared collective programming of the human mind
Shalom Schwartz (2014)	A hypothetical construct that cannot be observed but manifests through symbols, norms, practices, beliefs, and values
Dwight Atkinson (2004)	Learned values and behaviours that are transferred from one generation to another, including symbols and artifacts
David Matsumoto and Linda Juang (2008)	A system of meaning and information shared by people that is transferred from one generation to another which helps the survival of the group and their well-being.

underlies and justifies the functioning of societal institutions" (p. 6). Note that in this definition, culture is neither a mental programming nor in the mind of individuals as was proposed earlier by several researchers. Rather, it is external, and it happens within the context of people's interacting with one another. In addition, Schwartz highlights that culture is a hypothetical construct that cannot be observed. Therefore, culture is not a behavioural pattern, as defined by Triandis (1996), but can be inferred from its manifestation through norms, symbols, values, and beliefs. None of these manifestations are culture itself, but they underlie culture. Furthermore, Schwartz argues that culture is expressed in practices, policies, and organizations. For example, if a culture emphasizes success and aspiration, the cultural value is then reflected in multiple domains, such as achievement-oriented child-rearing practices, a mastery-oriented educational system, and a competitive economic system (Schwartz, 2014). Because people are exposed to social institutions and policies that are organized to reflect the cultural expectation, behaviours that express cultural values are encouraged (Schwartz, 2014).

Atkinson (2004) suggests that culture "consists of values and behaviours that are learned and transmitted within an identifiable community . . . and also includes the symbols, artifacts, and products of that community" (p. 10). Matsumoto and Juang (2008) list several definitions of culture before presenting their own working definition. They define *human culture* as "a unique meaning and information system, shared by a group and transmitted across generations, that allows the group to meet basic needs of survival, pursue happiness and well-being, and derive meaning from life" (p. 12). In other words, culture usually refers to a particular group of people and includes their values, or guiding beliefs and principles, and behaviours, or typical activities. Those values and behaviours are symbolized in the things that the group of people produces, such as art, music, food, and language. All those things are passed down from generation to generation.

As Table 1.1 indicates, there are similarities in the ways that scholars have defined *culture*, as well as differences. All these definitions highlight that culture has an immense impact on people's emotions, cognition, and behaviours. As a result, we could define **culture** as the practices of a group of people, expressed through symbols, values, and beliefs and passed down from generation to generation.

culture The practices of a group of people, expressed through symbols, values, and beliefs and passed down from generation to generation.

Culture and World View

world view A psychological perception of the environment that determines how we think, behave, and feel.

Sue (1977) defines a **world view** as "the way in which people perceive their relationship to nature, institutions, other people, and things. World view constitutes our psychological orientation in life and can determine how we think, behave, make decisions, and define events" (p. 458). In other words, different cultural groups perceive, define, and interact with their environment in different ways based on their past learning experiences (Sue et al., 1996). People from different cultures may see or experience the same thing but interpret it in drastically different ways.

An example of how culture influences our behaviour is how people reacted to the COVID-19 pandemic that began in early 2020. Public health measures such as social distancing, travel bans, and washing hands are successful in protecting people from the pandemic to the degree that people believe they have some level of control over their lives. If people believe in faith, external control, or luck (all aspects of cultural values), they have little incentive to follow public

"My neighbor's house got TPed, and doubled in value."

The COVID-19 pandemic sparked toilet-paper hoarding in early 2020.

health measures, particularly severe measures such as quarantine (Ryder et al., 2020). Research has shown that when people accept personal responsibility for their well-being, they tend to have higher engagement with their health (Berry & Dalal, 1996, p. 58).

Similarly, hoarding behaviour sparked by the pandemic, such as panicked shoppers buying large quantities of toilet paper and flour, witnessed in the US and, to some extent, Canada, is a reflection of a broader cultural phenomenon. Gelfand (2020) analyzed Americans' chaotic and egocentric behaviour in response to COVID-19 with reference to loose versus tight cultures, which is a reflection of prioritizing freedom over rules in a society. Gelfand argued that in **loose cultures**, such as the US, people are not used to strict social action and therefore act in their own self-interest. Consequently, the US had one of the least effective approaches to the pandemic, with the highest number of deaths due to COVID-19 in the world. On the other hand, in **tight cultures**, such as Singapore, social punishments are in place for breaking the rules. Indeed, Singapore had one of the most effective responses to COVID-19.

loose cultures Those cultures with weak social norms where transgression of norms is permissible.

tight cultures Cultures with strict social norms where transgression of norms is punishable.

We can see another example of how culture influences our behaviour in the differing ways that rural people and Indigenous communities reacted when Gerald Stanley was acquitted of the second-degree murder of Colten Boushie in Saskatchewan (Hill, 2019). Boushie was a 22-year-old Indigenous man who was fatally shot on Gerald Stanley's farm in Saskatchewan on 9 August 2016. Stanley went on trial for the second-degree murder of Colten Boushie and was found not guilty. Reactions were wide-ranging. On the one hand, people living in rural areas thought the trial was justified and that Stanley should not be convicted; those in Indigenous communities, however, were outraged by the results of the trial (Hill, 2019).

Another case demonstrates the different worlds that people of colour live in. On 6 July 2016, in a routine traffic stop for a broken taillight, a White American police officer shot and killed Philando Castile, who was reaching for his driver's licence as the officer had instructed (Louwagie, 2016). Castile initially alerted the officer to the fact that he had a licence to carry a gun and did not want the officer to be alarmed if he saw one. This case gained national attention because Castile's girlfriend captured the immediate aftermath of the shooting and posted it to social media. Later, footage from a police dashboard camera revealed that Castile was indeed being calm and co-operative, yet the officer quickly escalated the situation and shot Castile to death. Moreover, the officer indicated by police radio before the stop that he was stopping the car because he thought that the driver looked like a robbery suspect (Mannix, 2016). Minnesota Governor Mark Dayton was shaken by this incident and said, "Would this have happened if the driver were White, if the passengers were White? . . . I don't think it would have" (Louwagie, 2016). The officer was acquitted in the ensuing trial, despite clear evidence that contradicted the officer's account of the incident (Stahl, 2017).

These differences in world view—whether between communities, between

A demonstrator at a rally in Edmonton, Alberta, in response to the acquittal of Gerald Stanley in the shooting of Colten Boushie.

A protestor holds a portrait of Philando Castile at a vigil honouring him on the fourth anniversary of his death.

individuals, or within an individual—all illustrate the need to study culture in psychology. We hope that further reading of this book will increase your understanding of these different perspectives and how they occur. World view will be discussed in more detail in Chapter 3.

1.2 What Is Race?

We have noted that most people use the word *culture* to refer to their race, ethnicity, or nationality. The terms *culture*, *race*, and *ethnicity* are often used interchangeably, but their meanings are distinctly different and their usage is often confusing. Atkinson (2004) calls them "three of the most misunderstood and misused words in the English language" (p. 5). Since they are vital to a discussion of cross-cultural psychology, we must try to define them and clear up some of the confusion. Let us begin by defining *race*. The term *race* is used in two main ways: as a biological concept and as a socio-cultural concept.

The Biological Concept of Race

biological definition of race A group of people who share a specific combination of physical, genetically inherited characteristics that distinguish them from other groups.

The **biological definition of race** was the first to emerge when scientists began to compare human groups. Zuckerman (1990) said, "To the biologist, a race, or subspecies, is an inbreeding, geographically isolated population that differs in distinguishable physical traits from other members of the species" (p. 1297). Biologically speaking, a race is a group of people who share a specific combination of physical, genetically inherited characteristics that distinguish them from other groups (Casas, 1984).

Social hierarchy is common in human history. For example, the Indian caste system goes back to 1500 BC. Similarly, in ancient Egypt, people were classified into categories ("Historical Definitions of Race," 2011). However, it was not until the Age of Enlightenment that the scientific notion of race as a biological construct was first developed. It became very popular during that time and in the centuries that followed to create taxonomies of the human species. By the late nineteenth century, several of these classification systems existed: the simplest, with only 2 categories; and the most complex, with 63 (Darwin, 1871).

Most of these early taxonomies placed humans in categories based on superficial phenotypic characteristics, such as skin colour, hair texture, shape of nose, shape of eyes, and size of lips. One of the most influential categorizations, which still influences conceptualizations of race today, came from Johann Friedrich Blumenbach (1752–1840), who placed human beings into five categories based on the shape of the skull: the Caucasian, or white race; the Mongolian, or yellow race; the Malayan, or brown race; the Ethiopian, or Negro or black race; and the American, or red race. Blumenbach believed that physical factors, such as skin colour and skull shape, interacted with environmental factors, such as geographic location, exposure to the sun, and diet, to produce the different racial groups (Blumenbach, 1775/1795/1865).

Today, results of genetic studies indicate that the physiological (biological) differences among racial groups are superficial and that as human beings we have far more genetic similarities than differences (Latter, 1980; Zuckerman, 1990). Variation within different racial groups is far greater than is variation among the groups (Jorde & Wooding, 2004). Indeed, estimates indicate that 88 to 90 per cent of genetic variation occurs within local populations, whereas only 10 to 12 per cent is between populations (Angier, 2000). This means that two people from different groups may share more similarities than two people from the same

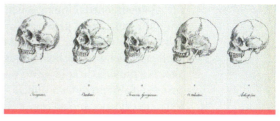

Blumenbach's five races, from *De generis humani varietate nativa* (*On the Natural Varieties of Mankind*, 1775).
Blumenbach, J. F. (1775/1795/1865). *The Anthropological Treatises of Johann Friedrich Blumenbach.*

group. Most respected scholars currently acknowledge that human beings came from the same beginnings in Africa and that genetic differences among groups can be explained by patterns of migration and adaptation as groups moved farther away from that point of origin (Angier, 2000; Begley, 1995; Diamond, 1997). The Canadian Race Relations Foundation concludes that "race is not intrinsic to human beings but rather an identity created, often by socially dominant groups to establish meaning in a social context" (Canadian Race Relations Foundation, 2015, para. 50). In other words, there really is only one biological race: the human race (Atkinson, 2004; Fish, 2002).

Although a biological definition of *race* has little evidence to support it, once the broad categories were drawn and the idea of significant genetic differences among groups was propagated, the term took on socio-cultural significance.

The Sociological Concept of Race

By the eighteenth century, scientists began to include behavioural and psychological characteristics in their classifications of race. The Great Chain of Being, an idea from Christian Western Europe in the medieval era, was the belief in a hierarchical structure of all life. Those nearest the top of the hierarchy were considered closest to perfection, or to God ("Great Chain of Being," 2011). This idea crept into racial categorizations in which Christian Europeans were placed at the top of the chain. Characteristics assigned to groups lower in the chain were often derogatory and demeaning. Thus, society assigned a value to these characteristics, which eventually led to notions of racial inferiority and superiority and to justification of the unfair treatment of different racial groups ("Historical Definitions," 2011), such as the enslavement of Black Africans. Such beliefs were widely spread and passed down from generation to generation, so that today, groups such as Black Canadians still struggle to combat stereotypes about their racial inferiority.

The inclusion of behavioural and psychological characteristics in the taxonomies, along with the value judgments placed on these characteristics and the resulting differential treatment of various human groups, led to the **socio-cultural concept of race**. The assignment of dispositional and intellectual characteristics to the racial groups was not completely arbitrary. It came from observations (albeit biased ones) of the behaviour of different groups. The socio-cultural meaning of the term *race* also came from the migration of various groups to different parts of the globe. Because of the resulting geographic isolation and inbreeding, these groups developed not only similar physical characteristics, but also their own unique set of values, beliefs, and practices—in other words, different cultures.

socio-cultural concept of race The perspective that characteristics, values, and behaviours that have been associated with groups of people who share different physical characteristics serve the social purpose of providing a way for outsiders to view another group and for members of a group to perceive themselves.

As mentioned, human genetic studies have found more differences between individuals from the same racial groups than between individuals from different racial categories (Saini, 2019). These studies lend support to the idea that race is a socio-cultural concept rather than a biological fact. Some scholars suggest that the modern term *race* exists due to its socio-cultural use, as it provides people with a way of organizing the world and reducing complexity. For some groups, it also provides a vehicle for identity and empowerment (Atkinson, 2004). Despite the existing evidence indicating its socio-cultural nature, misperceptions of race as a biological reality still continue among lay people and some psychology scholars (Morning, 2011). Hence, there has been much debate in the psychological literature about the appropriateness of its use (e.g., Helms et al., 2005; Richeson & Sommers, 2016).

Ethnicity

ethnicity A combination of race and culture.

The term **ethnicity** is often used interchangeably with *race*, *culture*, and *nationality*. Technically, ethnicity refers to a combination of physical, cultural, and national characteristics (Atkinson, 2004; Phinney, 1996). For example, Black people are all of African descent but now live all over the world in various cultures. Racially, they are Black, but depending on what part of the world they grew up in, they are from different cultures, leading to separate and distinct ethnic groups. Thus, we have Afro-Cubans, Afro-Brazilians, and Black Canadians. That is why racial categories can be confusing and, as discussed earlier, inaccurate. If a Black person from Cuba is filling out a survey in Canada and is asked about race, which box does that person check: Black or Latino? Both are correct. To select just one is misleading and inaccurate.

It should also be recognized that people have more than one identity. We have an identity related to each major demographic characteristic—ethnicity, social class, gender, age, religion, sexual orientation, and so on. We are simultaneously members of each of these groups, and each identity influences the others. For example, the experiences of a Black, gay male cannot be fully understood by examining each of these identities independently. As a male, he is in the

Although the modern understanding of race is that it is a social construction, previously the biological aspect of race was emphasized.

dominant group, but by being gay and Black he may experience both homophobia and racism. Navigating each of these identities constitutes a unique experience. Change one identity and you change the person's experience. To fully understand a person's experience, we must look at the interactions between these identities. This is known as the intersection of identities, or **intersectionality** (see Chapter 7) (Crenshaw, 1989; Gopaldas, 2013).

1.3 What Is Cross-Cultural Psychology?

Before discussing cross-cultural psychology, we must first define *psychology* more broadly. Most likely you have already had a class in introductory psychology, where **psychology** was defined as the systematic study of behaviour, cognition, and affect. In other words, psychologists are interested in how people act, think, and feel, and in all the factors that influence these human processes.

There are different fields when examining psychology from a cultural perspective, including cross-cultural psychology, cultural psychology, ethnic psychology, and multicultural psychology (Lonner et al., 2019). There is a considerable overlap among these sub-fields as they highlight the importance of culture in understanding the diversity of human behaviour, emotion, and thoughts. Notable differences also exist among these sub-fields. Although the focus of this textbook is cross-cultural psychology, a brief overview of cultural psychology, ethnic psychology, and multicultural psychology are provided in this chapter. Also, research that is conducted with the lens of these fields is discussed.

Cross-cultural psychology is essentially psychology but expanded globally, beyond national borders. This field is interested in cultural comparisons and searching for the universality of psychological processes, or what is similar or different across cultures (Heine & Ruby, 2010). However, as you might guess, there is no one accepted definition of *cross-cultural psychology* (remember that there is no one definition of *culture* that everyone agrees with, either).

Yet, the following definition is frequently cited: "Cross-cultural psychology is the study of similarities and differences in individual psychological functioning in various cultural and ethnocultural groups" (Kagitcibasi & Berry, 1989, p. 494). Accordingly, this definition states that cross-cultural research in psychology involves comparative investigating of psychological principles in other cultures and/or with people from different ethnic groups.

Because the majority of psychological research is done in industrialized Western nations, many psychological theories and concepts have not been tested for their robustness in other cultures, mainly non-Western nations. Moghaddam (1987) refers to this as first-world psychology. Considering that culturally oriented psychological research is relatively new and started to rise only in the late twentieth century, our psychological knowledge about the rest of the world is still limited. Therefore, psychology is still Eurocentric, individualistic, and decontextualized. The excerpt below by Gustav Jahoda, one of the pioneers in cross-cultural psychology, eloquently illustrates such ethnocentricity:

> ... When I mention a psychological subject, I mean a subject from a western industrialized culture; and not only from a western industrialized culture, but an American; and not only an American, but a college student. No doubt this is unfair, reflecting as it does on the amount of work that has been done in the United States. Nonetheless, the excessive concentration on such an odd (as far as humanity at large is concerned) population makes one wonder about the range of application of the "laws" experimentally derived in this manner. (Jahoda, 1970, p. 2)

intersectionality The meaningful ways in which various social statuses interact (e.g., race, gender, social class) and result in differing experiences with oppression and privilege.

psychology The systematic study of behaviour, cognition, and affect.

cross-cultural psychology The comparative study of psychological functioning in various cultural and ethnocultural groups.

Therefore, we need a field like cross-cultural psychology to help us understand the range of psychology functioning globally (Lonner et al., 2019). Recall that cross-cultural psychology is described as "psychology writ large." Thus, we must develop a psychology that is inclusive of humanity rather than based on an odd group of people.

1.4 What Is Cultural Psychology?

cultural psychology The study of human psychological processes within a cultural context based on the assumption that culture and psychological process are deeply connected together and cannot be studied in isolation.

Cultural psychology is the closest field to cross-cultural psychology and is concerned with human psychological processes within a cultural context. Cole (1996) describes several main characteristics of cultural psychology and states that cultural psychology emphasizes the importance of historical and everyday life events in understanding individual behaviour. Within this perspective, culture and psychological process are not independent of each other; rather, they are deeply connected and cannot be studied in isolation (Lonner et al., 2019). In other words, culture is not something that is out there and is the cause of psychological process. Overall, cultural psychologists strive to develop a deep understanding of the behaviours of human beings in the unique cultural context that they are grounded (Lonner et al., 2019).

Although both cultural psychology and cross-cultural psychology focus on the relevance of culture in understanding human behaviour, the two are different in their approach to culture. Cross-cultural psychology examines similarities and differences of individual behaviours across cultures and, therefore, is comparative in nature. The aim of cross-cultural psychology is to identify universal psychological characteristics that can be found in a large number of populations while highlighting cultural factors that impact psychological development and expression of behaviours (Berry, 2019). However, discovering universal psychological characteristics is not a goal of cultural psychology. Cultural psychology tends to use qualitative methods to capture the complexity of psychological phenomena (e.g., self-concept, memory, intimacy, emotional expression) that are embedded in the cultural context (Ratner, 2008). Qualitative methods allow for developing a deeper and a more comprehensive understanding of psychological concepts rooted in their specific culture. However, cross-cultural psychology tends to use quantitative methodology in order to make general statements about how cultural factors relate to psychological factors (Ratner, 2008).

1.5 What Is Ethnic Psychology?

ethnic psychology or ethnic minority psychology The study of social classifications and social opportunities of subordinate groups.

Ethnic psychology (or ethnic minority psychology) is the study of social classifications and social opportunities of subordinate groups with the aim of promoting social equality and social change (Leong et al., 2010). Ethnic psychology examines ethnic groups who were exposed to oppression and experienced colonization (e.g., Black Canadians) from the lens of cultural traditions and practices of the groups. One area of ethnic psychology is ethnic counselling. Comas-Diaz (2006) argues that through ethnic counselling, the specific needs of Latinos in the US, such as adaptation stress, cultural tension, identity conflict, and the loss of a social network, can be addressed. It is through restoring and validating one's heritage and focusing on cultural traditions and world views that ethnic psychology can promote emotional healing (Comas-Diaz, 2006; Early, 1996). From this perspective, the context in which ethnic groups are embedded and their circumstances are critical in understanding their thoughts, experience, and difficulties.

Although the term *ethnic psychology* is still used, there was movement in the field away from it sometime during the 1990s (Hall, 2014). One reason for this shift was to strengthen ties and develop allies across the various ethnic groups. Another was to move beyond ethnicity and be more inclusive of other identities related to gender, religion, sexual orientation, etc.

(Franklin, 2009). In addition, the term *minority* has come to have a negative connotation when referring to people of colour. In fact, when looking at the global population, people of colour make up a statistical majority. According to Statistics Canada (2017), by the year 2036, over one-third of Canadians (31–6 per cent) will be a member of a visible minority group.

1.6 What Is Multicultural Psychology?

The prefix *multi-* means "many," and the suffix *al* means "of" or "pertaining to." Therefore, the term *multicultural* means pertaining to many cultures. Those who study **multicultural psychology** tend to conduct research on different ethnic groups or on people with different cultural backgrounds who live in a pluralistic nation (Lonner et al., 2019). This includes the study of the perception of discrimination, prejudice, and aggressive behaviour of different groups within the border of a nation. If we put all that together, we can define *multicultural psychology* as the systematic study of all aspects of human behaviour that occurs in settings where people of different backgrounds interact. Multicultural psychologists are concerned with "the psychological reactions of individuals and groups caught up in culturally heterogeneous settings," including the "behaviours, perceptions, feelings, beliefs, and attitudes" that result from living in such conditions (Bochner, 1999, p. 21).

Almost all nations around the world are multicultural. Multicultural psychology focuses on cultural diversity and social cohesion (Berry, 2019). For example, Canada is a multicultural society, and the degree of its diversity has increased continuously over the years. In the first Canadian census in 1871, 20 ethnic origins were identified, while in the 2016 census, over 250 ethnic origins were identified, with almost half of the population reporting more than one origin (Statistics Canada, 2017). The World Population Review (2019) has indicated that the Canadian population continues to increase each year, mainly as a result of immigration, while natural population growth accounts for approximately 10 per cent of the population growth in Canada every year. As of 2019, approximately 22 per cent of Canada's population was born elsewhere. More than half of the immigrant population (60 per cent) comes from Asia, especially China and India. However, in the past, European immigrants were the more common immigrants settling in Canada (World Population Review, 2019). In addition to the increase in immigrants from Asia over the years, the Indigenous population in Canada has increased, with four per cent of the population being of Indigenous descent (World Population Review, 2019).

Our definition of multicultural psychology is concerned with **culture contact**, or what happens when people of different backgrounds interact with one another. Bochner (1999) defined *culture contact* as "critical incidents where people from different cultural, ethnic, or linguistic backgrounds come into social contact with each other" (p. 22) and described two broad categories of contacts:

1. contacts that occur between members of a culturally diverse society or between people of many different backgrounds who live and work together on a daily basis; and
2. contacts that occur when people from one society visit another country, for purposes such as business, tourism, study, or assistance (e.g., Canadian Red Cross).

multicultural psychology Refers to research conducted on different ethnic groups or on people with different cultural backgrounds who live in a pluralistic nation.

culture contact Critical incidents in which people from different cultures come into social contact with one another, either (a) by living and working with one another on a daily basis or (b) through visiting other countries on a temporary basis, such as for business, tourism, or study.

Ashley Callingbull is the first Canadian and the first Indigenous woman to win the Mrs Universe pageant.

Multicultural psychology is interested in both types of cultural contact, although it emphasizes the first type. One important line of inquiry within the field of multicultural psychology is the examination of adjustment of newcomers in the society of settlement (we will examine this concept later in the chapter).

Multiculturalism as a Philosophy

The idea of multiculturalism goes beyond the field of psychology. The term applies to settings in which more than one culture exists and represents a set of beliefs about how those groups should coexist (Heywood, 2007; Parekh, 2000). As a philosophy, multiculturalism has influenced a wide range of disciplines, including education (e.g., Banks & Banks, 2004), political science (e.g., Parekh, 2000), and medicine (e.g., Wear, 2003). It is a complex concept that has been discussed in many ways, without consensus about what it entails (Fowers & Davidov, 2006; Parekh, 2000). Nonetheless, the basic assumptions of multiculturalism can be summarized as tolerance, respect, inclusion, sensitivity, and equity (see Table 1.2).

Today, the term *tolerance* has come to mean a fair, open, and objective attitude toward people and ideas that differ from yours (Dictionary.com). This often refers to religious tolerance or allowing individuals of different faiths to practise their beliefs freely and openly. However, many people believe that simple tolerance is not enough and that there is a need to move beyond tolerance to other ideals. South African cleric and theologian Desmond Tutu expresses some of the limitations associated with using tolerance as a goal of multiculturalism:

> . . . [T]olerance to me seems like saying, "I do not like you, but . . . I just have to accept that you have the same right to your life choices as I do to mine." The word I think is a much better choice . . . is *understanding*. For me, understanding means that although I may not like or agree with everything you do or say, I get where you are coming from. (Tutu, 2012)

As Tutu points out, tolerance implies putting up with something we really do not like. What would the world be like if we simply tolerated one another? Tolerance should be the minimum goal, a starting point. Joseph White (2001) stated the goal should not be tolerance but mutual enrichment.

TABLE 1.2	Multiculturalism as a Philosophy: Basic Assumptions
Tolerance	A fair, open, and objective attitude toward people and ideas that differ from yours
Respect	To value, appreciate, and show regard or consideration for differences
Inclusion	Active efforts to reverse the historical exclusion of certain groups in society
Sensitivity	Awareness that cultural differences exist and taking these differences into account in our interactions
Equity	Equal access to opportunities and resources; this includes providing extra assistance to those who have historically not been given equal access
Empowerment	Helping members of marginalized and mistreated groups stand up for their rights
Social justice	Efforts aimed at providing equal distribution of rights, privileges, opportunities, and resources within a society
Social change	Widespread change in the institutions, behaviours, and relationships within a society

Inclusion refers to the realization that certain groups have historically been excluded from participation in mainstream society. Therefore, active efforts must be made to reverse this exclusion. For example, the Accessibility for Ontarians with Disabilities Act (2005) exists to prevent discrimination against individuals with physical disabilities, a law that requires all levels of the Ontario government, private sectors, and non-profits to follow standards that promote accessibility for persons with disabilities. Under this legislation, organizations are required to develop an accessibility policy in which barriers are identified that prevent people with disabilities from accessing their facilities, services, or goods. Organizations must then find ways to prevent or remove these barriers, with the goal of Ontario being fully accessible by 2025. For example, sensitivity to issues of gender means using gender-inclusive language, such as *chair of the board* instead of *chairman*.

Equity means that all people *should* have equal access to the same resources and opportunities by the creation of opportunities for those who have been historically disadvantaged. Equity and equality are not the same thing, although both are related to the idea of fairness. **Equality** is achieved when everyone has equal access to resources and opportunities and can take advantage of them if they choose. Equality assumes that everyone starts at the same level. Equity, however, recognizes that not everyone has equal access. Historically, some individuals have been excluded or lack the knowledge, finances, or training necessary to take advantage of these opportunities. Therefore, equity means providing remedies for the past injustices to level the playing field. Examples include providing classes in English as a second language in schools and targeting scholarships to students from poor families. Equality says that per-student funding at every school should be the same; equity says that students who come from less should get more to help them catch up. Equality is fairness as uniform distribution, whereas equity is fairness as justice (Kranich, 2005; Mann, 2014).

Multiculturalism as a philosophy goes beyond simple belief in concepts such as inclusion, sensitivity, and equity. It is also important to take action to ensure these ideas become reality. In other words, it is not enough to talk about the issues; we must actively work to reduce behaviours such as discrimination and oppression. From this action-oriented perspective, multiculturalism also involves the ideas of empowerment, social justice, and social change (Banks, 2010; Gorski, 2010).

> **equity** The state of all people having equal access to the same resources and opportunities.

> **equality** The state of all people having equal access to resources and opportunities and being able to take advantage of them if they choose.

Equality treats everyone the same, regardless of circumstances, whereas equity considers differing needs. We must have equity before we can achieve true equality.

Empowerment means helping individuals from marginalized, disenfranchised, and mistreated groups stand up for their rights and fight for equal treatment. It means putting pressure on people in power to share that power. *Social justice* means working toward equity, where every citizen is treated fairly and has equal access to the rights, privileges, opportunities, and resources available within society. Achieving these goals requires widespread *social change*. Gorski (2010) noted that social change occurs through transformation of the self, social institutions, and society. In terms of self, this means individuals work to reduce and eliminate personal prejudices and discriminatory behaviours. On a social institutional level, this means implementing policies and practices in schools, corporations, government, etc., to ensure everyone receives fair treatment. On a societal level, it means creating an environment that is inclusive, in which differences are valued and respected, where all members can live, work, and thrive side by side. In other words, multiculturalism is more than a philosophy: it is a "social, intellectual, and moral movement" (Fowers & Davidov, 2006, p. 581), where these basic values are seen as goals to be achieved.

These values—respect, inclusion, sensitivity, equity, empowerment, social justice, and social change—represent core values in the field of culture and psychology, and you will see them infused throughout this book. In considering these values, you might ask, as scientists, aren't psychologists supposed to be objective? If psychologists espouse certain values, doesn't that make them biased? Yes, as scientists, psychologist do their best to reduce the effects of bias on their research. However, most psychologists who focus on cultural issues acknowledge that complete objectivity is impossible and believe that scientists should be open about the values that drive their work (this idea is discussed further in Chapter 2). All fields of study are founded on a core set of values, but the values are not always explicitly understood or communicated. For example, physicians take the Hippocratic oath to do no harm. Lawyers in Ontario operate under the motto "Let right prevail." Even in science, the goal of being objective includes a value judgment. Therefore, multicultural psychology is explicit about the values it espouses and how these values guide theory, research, and practice in the field.

The Rise of Multiculturalism

As we have seen, the field of psychology has traditionally been dominated by European-American males in theory, research, and practice. Members of diverse groups, such as Black people, women, and sexual minorities, have traditionally been left out or viewed as inferior. The same can be said for other groups, such as people with disabilities and those of diverse religious backgrounds. The broader climate of social change, which addressed the issues of under-represented, oppressed, and disadvantaged groups during the 1950s, 1960s, and 1970s, also affected the field of psychology. Over time, psychology and psychologists have been pushed to become more inclusive.

The Canadian Psychological Association (CPA) is Canada's primary psychological organization. Since the CPA's founding in 1938 (Bhatt et al., 2013), multiculturalism within the association has advanced significantly. Culture was not made a formal sub-field of psychology in the CPA until 1980 when Section 10, "International and Cross-Cultural Psychology," was created (Bhatt et al., 2013). Since its establishment, the priorities of Section 10 were to embrace work with international psychologists and establish cross-cultural research as a legitimate area of psychology (Bhatt et al., 2013). The rise of multiculturalism in Canadian psychology is ongoing, but these series of events paved the way for present and future endeavours in cross-cultural research.

The importance of multiculturalism in psychology was not just being advanced in Canada during the twentieth century, but all over the world. The publication *History of the International Union of Psychological Science (IUPsyS)* (Rosenzweig et al., 2000) outlines the historical creation and recognition of psychology as an international profession. The Paris International Congress of Psychology in 1889 was the first mention of an international psychological organization. This led to the formation of the International Congress of Psychology, and, over the next 60 years, the International Congress of Psychology committee organized congressional psychology meetings all over the world, with the number of countries involved always increasing. It was not until 1948, at the twelfth congress, that the creation of an international psychology union was decided upon and the International Union of Psychological Science (IUPsyS) was established. As of 2000, the union represents 66 countries, involving approximately 500,000 psychologists. Today, the IUPsyS stands as a representation for psychology as an international discipline, with developers of the field originating from a diverse pool of unique cultures and perspectives. The importance of an international psychology union cannot be stressed enough, as the recognition of multiculturalism has grown immensely worldwide since the original committee was formed. Evidence for the rise of multiculturalism in psychology is seen in the various documents and policies adopted by IUPsyS, the Canadian Psychological Association (CPA), the American Psychological Association (APA), and other psychological organizations.

In 1996, the Canadian Psychological Association created a document based on the earlier version of the *Canadian Code of Ethics for Psychologists* (CPA, 2000), titled *Guidelines for Non-Discriminatory Practice*. Since its publication, the document has been updated twice, in 2001 and 2017. Ultimately, the goal of these guidelines has always been to "promote non-discriminatory care in therapeutic work with clients" (CPA, 2017a, p. 1). With the emphasis on sensitivity to culture and inclusion of diversity, these protocols (CPA, 2017a, 2017b) represent an ideal that all psychologists should strive for in practice (see Table 1.3 for a summary of the guidelines). As such, the document represents the rise and improvement of multicultural awareness in the psychological field over the past two decades.

Note that the multicultural movement has met serious resistance within the psychology field. Several authors cite reasons for such resistance. Sue and associates (1998) identify what they call "the seven deadly resistances" (p. 28). These are arguments raised by the power structure against integrating multiculturalism into training programs, such as the contentions that current theories are generalizable to all populations and that conceptually sound multicultural standards do not exist. Mio and Awakuni (2000) wrote a book titled *Resistance to Multiculturalism: Issues and Interventions,* in which their main premise is that resistance to multicultural issues is rooted in various forms of racism. They outline what they think are effective ways of addressing such resistance, such as self-awareness, openness, and self-examination; knowledge and understanding of European-American privilege; and knowledge and understanding of ethnic identity models. For example, the structure, policies, and publications of APA, as one of the world's largest psychological associations,

Codes of ethics help guide decisions based on moral values and principles.

TABLE 1.3 Guidelines for Ethical Practice with Diverse Populations

Guideline 1	"Recognize the inherent worth of all human beings regardless of how different they may be from oneself."
Guideline 2	"Be aware of one's own cultural, moral, and social beliefs, and be sensitive to how they may enhance one's interactions with others or may interfere with promoting the welfare of others."
Guideline 3	"Recognize the power differential between oneself and others in order to diminish the differences, and to use power for the advantage of others rather than unwittingly to abuse it."
Guideline 4	"Study group or cultural norms in order to recognize individual differences within the larger context."
Guideline 5	"Be aware that theories or precepts developed to describe people from the dominant culture may apply differently to people from non-dominant cultures."
Guideline 6	"Recognize the reality, variety, and implications of all forms of oppression in society, and facilitate clients' examination of options in dealing with such experiences."
Guideline 7	"Recognize that those who are subjected to physical or sexual assault are victims of crime and that those who assault are guilty of crimes."
Guideline 8	"Be knowledgeable about community resources available for diverse populations."
Guideline 9	"Respect, listen and learn from clients who are different from oneself in order to understand what is in their best interests."
Guideline 10	"Use inclusive and respectful language."
Guideline 11	"Share all relevant decision making with clients including goals of the interaction and the nature of proposed interventions in order to serve their best interests."
Guideline 12	"Ensure that consent is truly informed, keeping in mind diversity issues and cultural differences."
Guideline 13	"Be especially careful to be open, honest, and straightforward, remembering that persons who are oppressed may be distrustful or overly trustful of those in authority."
Guideline 14	"Assess accurately the source of difficulties, apportioning causality appropriately between individual, situational, and cultural factors."
Guideline 15	"Respect privacy and confidentiality according to the wishes of clients, and explain fully any limitations on confidentiality that may exist."
Guideline 16	"Evaluate the cultural meaning of dual/multiple and overlapping relationships in order to show respect and to avoid exploitation."
Guideline 17	"Constantly reevaluate one's competence, attitudes, and effectiveness in working with diverse populations."
Guideline 18	"Consult with others who may be more familiar with diversity in order to provide competent services."
Guideline 19	"Acknowledge one's own vulnerabilities and care for oneself outside of relationships as psychologists."
Guideline 20	"Make competent services available to disadvantaged groups by offering services at a lower cost in proportion to the client's income for a proportion of one's caseload."
Guideline 21	"Choose ways in which one can contribute to the making of a society that is respectful and caring of all its citizens."

Source: Adapted from "Multicultural Guidelines: An Ecological Approach to Context, Identity, and Intersectionality." https://cpa.ca/docs/File/Ethics/CoEGuidelines_NonDiscPract2017_Final.pdf, page 3.

illustrate a long and slow struggle toward the acknowledgement and inclusion of culture within psychology.

Comas-Díaz (2009) states that cultural psychology has "raised the consciousness of psychologists of all colours," "shifted the mainstream psychological paradigm" (p. 407), and better equipped us for the challenges of a global society. We look forward to sharing more with you about this exciting and vibrant field in the remainder of this book.

1.7 Multiculturalism as the Fourth Force

Pedersen (1990, 1991) proposes that multiculturalism is the **fourth force** in psychology. What does he mean? In psychology, the term *force* is used to describe a theory that has a huge influence on the field and precipitates a **paradigm shift**, or major change, in the way people think about human behaviour.

The notion that multiculturalism is the fourth force suggests that this perspective will have just as big an impact on the field of psychology as the first three forces: psychoanalysis, behaviourism, and humanism (Table 1.4). Pedersen (1990, 1991) does not see multiculturalism as replacing the other three theories, but as adding a fourth dimension to psychology to supplement and, ideally, to strengthen the other three. According to Pedersen, labelling multiculturalism the fourth force "explores the possibility that we are moving toward a generic theory of multiculturalism that recognizes the psychological consequences of each cultural context, where each behaviour has been learned and is displayed . . . and calls attention to the way in which a culture-centred perspective has changed the way we look at psychology across fields and theories" (1999, p. xxii).

In other words, calling multiculturalism the fourth force challenges us to acknowledge that

a) all behaviour occurs in and is impacted by a cultural context;
b) until recently, this fact has virtually been ignored by the field; and
c) once we understand the nature and contribution of culture, this understanding will dramatically alter and expand the way we study and understand behaviour.

Pedersen and other cultural psychologists believe it is no longer possible for psychologists to ignore their own culture or the cultures of their clients and research participants. A perspective grounded in cultural context makes our understanding of human behaviour clearer and more meaningful, rather than more obscure and awkward. According to Pedersen (1999), "The main goal of [multicultural psychology] is to convince general psychology that culture is an important contributor to the development of human behaviour, and to our understanding and study of it" (p. 6). Thus, identifying multiculturalism as the fourth force in psychology attempts to place it at the centre of the field.

fourth force Refers to the major influence that this perspective has on the field of psychology.

paradigm shift Refers to a major change in the way people think about human behaviour.

TABLE 1.4 Multiculturalism as a Fourth Force

Force	Name of theory	Key theorists
First force	Psychoanalysis	Freud
Second force	Behaviourism	Pavlov, Thorndike, Watson, Skinner
Third force	Humanism	Rogers
Fourth force	Multiculturalism	Sue, Pedersen, White, Ivey, Bernal, Trimble

1.8 What Is the Biopsychosocial Model?

One of the major tenets of culture and psychology is that all behaviour occurs in a cultural context. Therefore, to fully understand human behaviour, we must understand its cultural context. Culture influences everything.

The **biopsychosocial model** helps explain the effect of culture on behaviour. This model grew out of behavioural medicine and health psychology and focuses on an understanding of the psychological, social, and biological factors that contribute to illness and that can be utilized in the treatment and prevention of illness and the promotion of wellness (Engel, 1977; Schwartz, 1982). Although the model originally focused on an understanding of physical illnesses, it is also very useful in understanding psychological illnesses. Let us take a closer look at this model.

biopsychosocial model A model of human behaviour that takes into consideration biological, cognitive-affective, social-interpersonal, social institutional, and cultural factors.

> On the morning of 5 May 2004, David Reimer retrieved a shotgun from his home while his wife, Jane, was at work, took it into the garage, and sawed off the barrel. He then drove to the nearby parking lot of a grocery store, parked, raised the gun, and shot himself. He was 38 years old. What had led David to such despair that he decided to end his own life?
>
> Press reports cited an array of reasons for his despair: bad investments, marital problems, his twin brother's death two years earlier. Surprisingly little emphasis was given to the extraordinary circumstances of his upbringing. This was unfortunate because to truly understand David's suicide you first need to know his anguished history, chronicled in the book, *As Nature Made Him: The Boy Who Was Raised as a Girl,* by John Colapinto (2000).
>
> David Reimer was one of the most famous patients in medical history. He was eight months old when a doctor doing a routine circumcision accidentally removed his entire penis. David's parents were referred to a leading expert on gender identity, psychologist Dr John Money, who recommended a surgical sex change from male to female and the administration of female hormones to further feminize David's body. David became the ultimate experiment to prove that nurture, not nature, determines gender identity and sexual orientation. His twin brother, Brian, provided a perfect matched control.
>
> Dr Money continued to treat David and, according to his published reports through the 1970s, the experiment was a success. David, who had been renamed Brenda, was portrayed as a happy little girl. The reality was far more complicated. "Brenda" angrily tore off dresses, refused to play with dolls, beat up her twin brother, and seized his toy cars and guns. In school she was relentlessly teased for her masculine gait, tastes, and behaviours. The other children would not let her use either the boys' or the girls' restroom, so she had to go in the back alley. She complained to her parents and teachers that she felt like a boy. Brenda was also traumatized by her yearly visits to Dr Money, who used pictures of naked adults to "reinforce" Brenda's gender identity and who pressed her to have further surgery on her "vagina." Meanwhile, Brenda's guilt-ridden mother attempted suicide, her father lapsed into alcoholism, and the neglected twin brother, Brian, eventually descended into drug use, petty crime, and clinical depression.
>
> When Brenda was 14, a local psychiatrist finally convinced the parents to tell Brenda/David the truth. David later said about the revelation, "Suddenly it all made sense why I felt the way I did. I wasn't some sort of weirdo. I wasn't crazy."

David went through the painful process of converting back to his biological sex yet was still very troubled and attempted suicide twice in his twenties. He eventually married, but he was not easy to live with, given his explosive anger, fears of abandonment, feelings of sexual inadequacy, and continued depressive episodes. At about the age of 30, David received help from a rival psychologist of Dr Money, Dr Milton Diamond at the University of Hawaii, but he continued to have difficulties. In the spring of 2002, his twin brother died of an overdose of antidepressant medication. Then, in the fall of 2003, David was cheated out of $65,000 by an alleged con man. The last straw seemed to come on 2 May 2004, when, after 14 years of a difficult marriage, David's wife told him she wanted a separation. Two days later, David ended his own suffering.

(Adapted from Colapinto, 2000, and Associated Press, 2004)

Many factors contributed to David Reimer's suicide. The biopsychosocial model helps put those factors into perspective. The biopsychosocial model says that behaviour can be understood on many levels (see Figure 1.1). The first is the biological level. At the most basic level, our behaviour is influenced by our physiological and genetic makeup. When we lack certain nutrients, our body sends us signals that something is out of balance and must be corrected. For example, if we do not have enough fluids in our bodies, we feel thirsty and are motivated to drink. If our bodies lack fuel, we feel hungry and we eat. The behaviours of eating and drinking are linked to basic biological needs. Our behaviours are also influenced by our genetic makeup.

There was evidently a strong genetic component to David Reimer's depression. His mother and brother suffered from depression, and his father may have as well. It is possible that his father was self-medicating his depression through alcohol abuse. Perhaps David Reimer inherited a biological predisposition to depression from one or both of his parents. His unusual life circumstances brought it out for him and for his brother.

The second level of the biopsychosocial model is the cognitive-affective level. **Cognitions** refer to our thoughts but include all our basic mental processes, such as memories, perceptions, and beliefs. **Affect** refers to feelings or emotions. This level examines the effects our thoughts and feelings have on our behaviours. The connection between one's mental or psychological state and physical health has long been established. For example, we know that when we are stressed, our immune systems are weakened and we are more likely to get sick. You have probably had the experience of coming down with a cold during or immediately after a particularly stressful week at school.

The cognitive-affective level is the level at which most people understand and think about mental disorder because most of what we know and study in the field of psychology occurs at this level. Currently, the most

cognitions Thoughts and all basic mental processes, such as memories, perceptions, and beliefs.

affect Feelings or emotions.

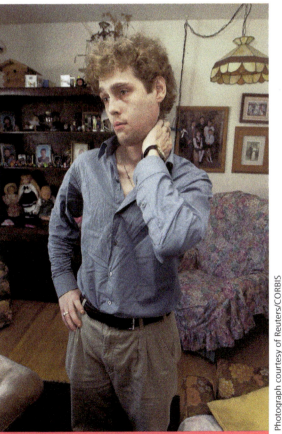

David Reimer was raised as Brenda after a botched circumcision.

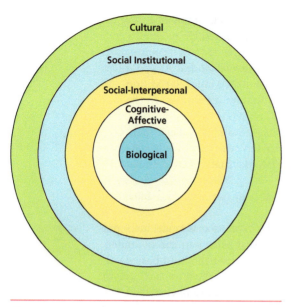

Figure 1.1 The biopsychosocial model.
Source: Adapted from Engel (1977) and Meyers (1986).

popular theory of depression is the cognitive theory, proposed by Aaron Beck (1967, 1970). Beck argued that depressed people make many cognitive errors, or distortions of reality. For instance, David Reimer may have concluded that because he did not have a penis, he was less of a man and would never be able to have a normal, happy, satisfying married life. According to Beck, such negative and distorted thoughts lead to negative or depressed feelings. Once people get caught in this negative cycle, it is very hard for them to get out. Even after David met and married Jane, he was still plagued by feelings of low self-esteem and sexual inadequacy.

The third level of the biopsychosocial model is the social-interpersonal level, which focuses on the impact of social relationships on our behaviour. This includes the interpersonal dynamics of the entire family system, or the unique pattern of interactions among family members. There was an interpersonal component to David Reimer's depression. His family relationships likely influenced his depression as he interacted with his alcohol-abusing father, his guilt-ridden mother, and his neglected brother. In addition, David was the recipient of relentless teasing and cruelty from his peers, which likely also had affected the development of his depression.

The fourth level of the biopsychosocial model is the social institutional level. Social institutions are large, complex, relatively stable clusters of social relationships that involve people working together to address some basic human or societal need (Sullivan & Thompson, 1994). Examples of social institutions include the military, the government, the educational system, and large corporations. At this level of analysis, psychologists try to understand how behaviour is influenced by our interactions with these large organizations. For example, workers may become depressed because their company downsizes and they lose their job or because they are juggling the demands of both career and family.

David Reimer's case was influenced by the family's interactions with the health-care system, first with the botched circumcision and then with the referral to and advice of Dr Money. At the time of the accident, David's parents were described as "teenagers barely off the farm" (Colapinto, 2004). It is not hard to imagine their fear and confusion and the influence that a powerful authority figure such as Dr Money, with the backing of the medical establishment, had on their decision-making. Anyone who has had a serious medical problem and had to navigate the health-care system can attest to how stressful this can be.

The final level of the biopsychosocial model is the cultural level. At last! You may have been wondering when culture would factor into this model. As we have discussed, culture reflects the values, beliefs, and practices of a group of people, and all behaviour occurs in a cultural context. For example, workers who have lost their jobs may feel that they were let go because of racism or sexism, issues which continue to pervade our society.

David Reimer's case was influenced by the cultural attitudes of the time. In the 1960s and 1970s, when David was growing up, traditional gender roles still predominated in our society. The belief was that David had to be either male or female, which could be dictated by his genitals and how he was treated. However, when Brenda/David did not fit the traditional ideas of how a girl ought to behave—wearing dresses, playing with dolls, walking and talking a certain way—he was ridiculed by his friends. As an adult, David equated masculinity, or being a "real man," with having a penis and being able to sexually satisfy his wife. Where did his ideas about masculinity and the proper husband role come from? They came from the larger society. What would have happened to David if he had been born into a different culture? Do you think his circumstances would have been different? What do you think would happen to him if he were born today?

Figure 1.1 depicts the biopsychosocial model as concentric circles, with the biological level in the centre and each level a larger ring until the last and largest, the cultural level. The biological level is the most basic level at which we can analyze and understand behaviour, and the levels become larger and more complex, with each level influencing the last. As the final level, culture influences all levels. Thus, the biopsychosocial model reminds us that all behaviour occurs within a cultural context. A complete analysis of David Reimer's suicide must consider all levels, from his biological predisposition to depression, to his negative thinking patterns, to his family dynamics and treatment by peers, to the health-care system and cultural beliefs about gender roles. All of these worked together, seemingly against David, to lead him to that moment when he raised a shotgun and took his own life.

After learning about the biopsychosocial model, a student shared the following:

> During the first two years of college, I was struggling with family issues as I found [it] hard to get along with my parents. The constant bickering had made me feel stressed and overwhelmed. I was not able to concentrate on schoolwork and was automatically put in a bad mood when I returned home from work or school. This got in the way of making time to do my assignments and readings as I would just want to go out and be with my friends instead of being at home. As time progressed, studying became less important to me and in a way I hated it as well. This would be an example of an effect on behaviour on a social-interpersonal level because I feel that a good relationship with my family and support would have had a more positive effect on my grades.
>
> Another reason why I feel I did poorly is because I was working more than thirty hours a week, and my work environment was stressful. I had problems with [other] employees and going to work became stressful as I was dealt more work. I feel like my progress in school was affected on a social institutional level as well because constant thoughts of work and stress would be on my mind while in school. Not only did family and work have an effect on [my] school grades but also my cultural background was an issue, as there were many pressures put upon myself for being born in a Korean family. Many Asian parents pressure children into hard work and good grades, and if these expectations were not met, you would be looked down upon. Being born in the States, it was hard for me to understand this type of mentality, but as I grew older, I began to understand more and more why many Asian cultures are this way. Sometimes I felt like if I wasn't pressured so much by my family and friends, I would have done better in school.
>
> —Lily, 20+-year-old Korean American student

Lily does a nice job of analyzing her academic struggles using the biopsychosocial model. She begins at the social-interpersonal level and then moves to the social institutional and cultural levels. The first two levels could also be used to explain her situation. From a biological point of view, some people would say perhaps she struggles in school because of a learning disability. At the cognitive-affective level, the difficulty she experiences studying for classes could be attributed to her internal feelings of stress, pressure, and being overwhelmed. Lily goes on to say that the biopsychosocial model increased her understanding of how behaviour is influenced by relationships with others, the institutions in which we function, and cultural attitudes. She says, "The next time I feel or do a certain thing, I think that this model will help me break down the reasons [for] my behaviours, and to become more positive within each level." We hope it does the same for you.

1.9 Historical Background

In this section, we highlight some historical events that influenced the field of cross-cultural psychology. This is not a comprehensive historical review but simply a description of a few key events to give you a sense of the way the field developed and the primary areas of theory, research, and practice in cross-cultural psychology. This section will give you a background for topics covered in more depth in the rest of the book.

Dubious Beginnings

The birth of psychology as a scientific field of study is traditionally regarded as having occurred in 1879 with the founding of the first psychological laboratory in Leipzig, Germany, by Wilhelm Wundt (Goldstein, 2005). Wundt's laboratory soon became a magnet for individuals wanting to become psychologists. Individuals who studied there went on to establish their own laboratories in countries around the world. Wundt and his colleagues studied psychophysiological processes they called **structuralism**. Through a process called **structural introspection**, research participants reported on their own mental experiences. The researchers measured things such as sensation, perception, reaction times, imagery, and attention (Wade & Tavris, 2003).

The intense examination of individual differences and quest for heritable traits leading to greater survival of the species eventually led to research on racial group differences. Early names for this area of research included ethnical psychology and racial psychology (Guthrie, 1998). Haddon (1910) defined *ethnical psychology* as "the study of the minds of other races and peoples, of which, among the more backward races, glimpses can be obtained only by living by means of observation and experiment" (p. 6). Robert Guthrie (1998), in his book *Even the Rat Was White*, argues that this research was highly influenced by the popular notion of racial superiority and an underlying desire by White Europeans to lend scientific credibility to such beliefs. Early studies compared racial groups not only on psychophysiological measures but also on intelligence and personality.

Guthrie (1998) described an early joint expedition by anthropologists and experimental psychologists sponsored by the Cambridge Anthropological Society to the Torres Strait in the South Pacific in 1889. The researchers used Wundtian methods of psychophysics to examine hearing, vision, taste, tactile acuity, pain, motor speed and accuracy, fatigue, and memory in Indigenous Peoples of that region. The (biased) researchers concluded that the inhabitants were far less intelligent than their examiners.

The interest in conducting cross-cultural research rose after World War II. There was a motivation to learn about human behaviour outside of national borders. At that time, however, there was no coherent research program for those who engaged in such endeavours. Lonner and colleagues (2019) describe those attempts as follows:

> "Sabbatical opportunism" and "jet-set research" prevailed for years. This usually meant that an inquisitive and energetic psychologist, typically from the United States or some other Western country, would travel to some exotic corner of the world during

structuralism The early formal approach to psychology that attempted to examine the contents of people's minds.

structural introspection The method that structuralists used to examine the contents of people's minds in which people reported on their own mental experiences.

an academic leave lasting a few weeks to several months and inter alia, "test" some principle or examine some theory of interest. Returning to the comforts of home, he (occasionally she) would characteristically write a report and submit to some accommodating if not enthusiastically welcoming journal and thus earn some credit in helping to expand psychology's vistas. (p. 9)

Not surprisingly, in the early days, there were many poor practices, including using theoretical models and tests that were developed in Euro-American contexts and applying them to different settings (Segall et al., 1998). Cross-cultural psychologists were criticized for their theoretical and methodological flaws. Their research was challenged because they compared populations that were very different, doing tasks that were unfamiliar and difficult to understand, which led to findings that fitted the stereotypes (Bond, 2019).

Gradually, better practices developed and advanced methodologies were established to address these challenges. During the period of 1966 to 1970, several psychological journals with a cross-cultural focus were established, including the *Cross-Cultural Psychology Bulletin*, the *International Journal of Psychology*, and the *Journal of Cross-Cultural Psychology* (Segall et al., 1998). Major handbooks were published in early 1980s, revealing large literature in the field. These include Triandis et al.'s (1980) *Handbook of Cross-Cultural Psychology*, Munroe, Munroe, and Whiting's (1981) *Cross-cultural Human Development*, and Pedersen's (1985) *Handbook of Cross-Cultural Counseling and Therapy*. In addition, the 1980s saw the monumental work of Geert Hofstede on cultural dimension in his book titled *Culture's Consequences*.

Since the 1980s, there has been a significant increase in research in cross-cultural psychology, with more journals and professional associations that embrace a cultural focus. There have been major handbooks indicating the large amount of research that has been conducted in the field, including three volumes of the *Handbook of Cross-Cultural Psychology* (Berry et al., 1997), *The Handbook of Culture and Psychology* (Matsumoto & Hwang, 2019), and *The Encyclopedia of Cross-Cultural Psychology* (Keith, 2013). All these highlight that cross-cultural psychology has expanded considerably since the early twentieth century and has matured respectfully.

Gender Differences

In psychology, the examination of gender differences usually revealed that women got the short end of the stick. In the early 1970s, during the resurgence of the women's movement in the United States, Carol Gilligan was a graduate student at Harvard University working with Lawrence Kohlberg. Kohlberg (1968, 1976) proposed six stages of moral reasoning based on research he conducted over a span of 12 years with 75 boys who ranged in age from 10 to 16 years old when the study began. Kohlberg used stories to test the boys' reasoning on several moral concepts. He was more interested in the reasoning behind his participants' answers than in what they would actually do. Based on his findings, Kohlberg concluded that children's moral reasoning changes with age and maturity, following his six stages in progressive order.

Women and men may have different ways of moral reasoning.

Gilligan (1982/1993) found that men tended to base their moral choices on abstract principles, such as justice and fairness, whereas women tended to base their choices on principles of compassion and care. In other words, women tended to be more relationship-oriented than men. According to Kohlberg's stages, this meant that women looked less moral than men because their responses did not fall into Kohlberg's higher levels of moral reasoning. Rather than concluding that women were not as moral as men, Gilligan suggested that women think and speak differently about relationships. Gilligan did not make strong claims about the cause of the differences but acknowledged that they "arise in a context where factors of social status and power combine with reproductive biology to shape the experience of males and females and the relations between the sexes" (Gilligan, 1982/1993, p. 2). In other words, factors at the biological, social-interpersonal, and cultural levels interact to result in the differing reactions of men and women to moral dilemmas.

Gilligan (1982/1993) criticized psychology for the "repeated exclusion of women from the critical theory-building studies of psychological research" (p. 1). Similarly, cross-cultural research on gender relations, specifically the monumental work of John Williams and Deborah Best (1990), highlighted the relationship between culture and gender. In their large-scale study of 30 countries, they found that gender roles and gender stereotypes are reflective of cultural patterns and beliefs. Their findings indicated the complexities of factors that influence masculinity and femininity and contributed to theories of gender and culture. Thanks to Gilligan, Best, and other leading women psychologists, research standards have changed. Women must now be included in studies, and gender differences must be examined for research to be considered good science. Another influence of Gilligan and others is that the psychology of women is a respected and growing field. We know that to truly understand the human condition, we must include humans from all backgrounds in our research samples. This was not always the case.

Lesbian, Gay, Bisexual, Transgender, Queer, and Two-Spirit

The lesbian, gay, bisexual, transgender, queer, and two-spirit (LGBTQ2+) movement is another important part of the history of cultural psychology and illustrates how psychology has handled another aspect of human diversity.

Variations in sexual identity were initially considered mental disorders. The *Diagnostic and Statistical Manual of Mental Disorders* (*DSM*) is published by the American Psychiatric Association and contains the diagnostic criteria professionals use to determine whether someone has a mental disorder. (See Chapter 9 for more discussion on the *DSM*.) The first edition of the manual (*DSM-I*) was published in 1952 and classified homosexuality under the broad category of personality disorders, as well as the subcategories of sociopathic personality disorder and sexual deviation. Other conditions in this category included transvestitism, pedophilia, and sexual sadism (American Psychiatric Association, 1952; cited in Drescher, 2015). In the next edition (*DSM-II*, American Psychiatric Association, 1968), homosexuality was no longer associated with being sociopathic but was still listed among the sexual deviations (Drescher, 2015).

Two years later, in 1970, gay activists protested at the American Psychiatric Association convention and demanded that homosexuality be removed from the

Prime Minister Justin Trudeau at the annual Vancouver Pride Parade in 2018.

DSM. These protests motivated various committees within the association to deliberate the validity of the diagnosis. At the annual convention in 1973, the debate came to a head, with both sides vigorously arguing their positions. In the end, the vote was swayed by a particular definition of *mental disorder*, which stated the condition must cause significant distress or be associated with significant impairment in social functioning. The majority concluded homosexuality did not fit these criteria and could therefore not be considered a mental disorder. In December 1973, the American Psychiatric Association Board of Trustees voted to remove homosexuality from the *DSM*. Dr Laura Brown, an out lesbian and one of the pioneers of feminist therapy, stated that on that day in 1973, she was "cured" of her "mental illness" (Brown, 2011). Members who opposed the decision of the Board of Trustees called for a vote from the entire membership of the American Psychiatric Association. Of the 20,000 members, 58 per cent voted to uphold the decision by the Board of Trustees to remove homosexuality from the *DSM* (Drescher, 2015).

Despite this victory, the belief that homosexuality was a mental disorder persisted. Subsequent printings of *DSM-II* did not list homosexuality specifically but did include the diagnosis "sexual orientation disturbance," which described homosexuality as a mental disorder if the individual was distressed by an attraction to the same sex and wanted to change. Eventually, these diagnoses were also removed.

The issue of gender identity is undergoing a similar transformation. A growing population of individuals identify as something other than the gender they were assigned at birth. Most well-known are those individuals who identify as transgender, or a different gender to the sex they were assigned at birth. Transgender identity has received substantial attention in the media recently through trans celebrities such as Caitlyn Jenner, Laverne Cox, and Alexis Arquette.

Transgender identity first came to the forefront in 1952 when an American, George Jorgensen, went to Denmark as a man and returned to the United States as a trans woman—Christine Jorgensen. Jorgensen underwent what eventually became known as gender reassignment surgery, and her case was published in the *Journal of the American Medical Association* (Hamburger et al., 1953). Most medical professionals, including psychiatrists, were critical of the procedure being performed on people they believed were mentally ill with disorders originally labelled "transsexualism" or "transvestitism." No such diagnoses appeared in the *DSM* until the third edition in 1980. The *DSM-III* and *DSM-III-R* (American Psychiatric Association, 1987) contained three diagnoses related to gender: gender identity disorder of childhood, transsexualism for adolescents and adults, and gender identity disorder of adolescence and adulthood, nontranssexual type. As with homosexuality, controversy surrounded these diagnoses and whether they should be considered mental disorders. Again, it was argued that variations in gender identity should only be considered mental disorders if the condition caused significant distress or interfered significantly with social functioning. Thus, in *DSM-V*, the name was changed to *gender dysphoria* with emphasis on the level of distress the individual experiences based on the discrepancy between assigned gender and experienced gender (Drescher, 2015).

The evolving controversy over whether sexual variations should be diagnosed as mental disorders illustrates that, unlike other medical diagnoses, mental disorders are social constructs and change as society changes. The controversy also illustrates the inherent tension in the diagnosis of mental disorders between the need for access to care, which requires a medical diagnosis, and trying to reduce the stigma associated with mental disorder (Drescher, 2015). In other words, an official diagnosis may be needed to determine, provide, and pay for the most appropriate course of treatment, but receiving a diagnosis may result in labelling, which can result in negative consequences that follow the individuals for the rest of their lives.

Although the field of psychology has not always been sensitive to the rights of the LGBTQ2+ community, the Canadian Psychological Association (CPA) has released a number

Gender dysphoria is discomfort or distress people may feel if their gender identity differs from their sex assigned at birth.

of statements regarding such issues in the past few decades. In 1982, it released a policy statement explaining that the CPA "endorses the principle that there be no discrimination on the basis of sexual orientation" (Canadian Psychological Association, 1982). In addition, the CPA endorsed a statement from the International Psychology Network (IPsyNet) for Lesbian, Gay, Bisexual, Transgender, and Intersex Issues in 2018, which is a commitment to provide inclusivity and advancement in psychological research in terms of the LGBTQ2+ community (Canadian Psychological Association, 2018). The current *Canadian Code of Ethics for Psychologists* also includes sections regarding LGBTQ2+ rights, which prohibit prejudice of any kind, including sexual orientation and gender discrimination (CPA, 2017c). Thus, Canadian psychology has made significant progress regarding these issues and continues to support LGBTQ2+ individuals in better and more informed ways.

Summary

Cross-cultural psychology is the comparative study of psychological functioning in various cultural and ethnocultural groups. Essential to an understanding of cross-cultural psychology are such terms as *ethnicity* and *culture*, as well as searching for the universality of psychological processes.

There are different fields when examining psychology from a cultural perspective, including cross-cultural psychology, cultural psychology, ethnic psychology, and multicultural psychology. There are similarities and differences among these fields.

It has been suggested that multiculturalism is the fourth force in psychology, meaning that it will have as big an effect on our understanding of human behaviour as did psychoanalysis, behaviourism, and humanism. The main premise of multicultural theory is that all behaviour occurs in a cultural context. Multicultural issues have gained greater acknowledgement and inclusion in the field of psychology over time.

FOOD FOR THOUGHT

Whether multiculturalism truly is the fourth force in psychology remains to be seen. You are free to draw your own conclusions about that. We cannot deny, however, that culture is a critical factor in the way human beings think, feel, act, and interact. The field of cross-cultural psychology seeks to study that factor, with the ultimate goal of increasing our understanding of ourselves. We hope this chapter has whetted your appetite because in the following chapters we will introduce you to more specific areas of theory, research, and practice in the field of cross-cultural psychology.

Critical Thinking Questions

1. What were your early experiences with ethnic differences? What were your early experiences with other aspects of difference? How have those early experiences shaped you into the person you are now?
2. Have you ever been to foreign countries and felt out of place? Have you ever been to other regions of Canada or another country and felt out of place? Have you ever been to different areas of your own city that made you feel out of place? How have you handled those situations?

SDI Productions/Getty images

2 Cross-Cultural Issues Involving Research and Testing

Learning Objectives

Reading this chapter will help you to:

2.1 understand research and testing issues in cross-cultural research;
2.2 identify basic tenets of quantitative research, including correlational and experimental research;
2.3 identity qualitative research and appropriate strategies for investigating diverse populations;
2.4 identify biases in conducting cross-cultural research;
2.5 distinguish among the different ways of equivalence of measures and the impact of language barriers in conducting cross-cultural research;
2.6 understand replication crisis in psychology;
2.7 know collaborative problem solving; and
2.8 explain intelligence testing and the challenge of using it cross-culturally.

Korchin (1980) noted that researchers tend to question the generality of findings only when the research involves ethnic minority populations. Korchin mentioned that once he and his colleague had conducted research on why some African-American youths had made extraordinary achievements. A paper from the research was submitted for publication and rejected. One reviewer had indicated that the research was grievously flawed because it lacked a White control group. Why was a White control group necessary if the interest was in African Americans? More critically, Korchin asked why we do not require studies of [White people] to have an African-American control group. In other words, we ask that ethnic minority research show its pertinence to other groups or more general phenomena, but we fail to make the same requests when the research involves White populations. (Sue, 1999, p. 1072)

As this quotation from Stanley Sue suggests, the scientific study of psychology is only as good as those who apply and interpret it. Researchers in psychology try to apply scientific methods in the attempt to be objective in discovery. As most researchers in the cross-cultural arena would agree, however, whereas our methods may aim for objectivity, our results and interpretations are laden with subjective values. In this chapter we examine cross-cultural issues relating to the ways in which psychological research has been conducted and relating to psychological testing.

2.1 Research Methods in Psychology

In the next section, we examine basic research methodology and concepts. These research designs, procedure, and analyses are relevant in understanding and critically examining studies that are conducted across cultures and across ethnic groups.

The General Research Model

The standard way of applying science to psychology is to have a pool of potential research participants and to assign each participant to either a control group or an experimental group. Each individual has an equal chance of being in either group. The control group either does not receive any treatment or receives a typical treatment, whereas the experimental group is given a regimen designed to make some significant difference (Figure 2.1). This difference is determined by comparing the results from the experimental group with the results from the control group.

To apply this general method to a concrete example, let us say that we are interested in finding out whether a new medication will relieve the symptoms of depression. The control group in this instance is given a placebo—typically a sugar pill—and the experimental group is given the experimental medication. No one knows whether they are receiving the sugar pill or the medication, and each individual has an equal chance of being in the control or the experimental group. After a period of time, we compare the groups to see whether those individuals who received the medication are measurably less depressed.

Although medical examples are the clearest form of experiments with people, let us explore an example more relevant to psychology. Suppose we are interested

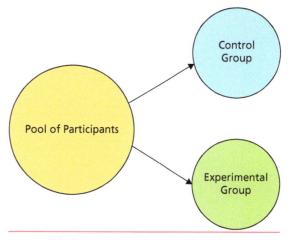

Figure 2.1 Assignment of research participants to a control or experimental group.

in finding out whether a new method of teaching history will result in students learning the subject better. With this new method, students act out historical events. The control group comprises the students learning history in the standard way, and the experimental group consists of the students acting out historical events. At the end of the academic year, students are tested about their knowledge of history, and we compare the scores from the two groups. If the new method is more effective for teaching history, the students in the experimental group will have higher scores on the history test than will the students in the control group. If the new method is less effective, the experimental group will have lower scores. If the new method does not make a difference, the students in the two groups will have approximately equal scores.

Now, what if we are interested in finding out whether students of colour, Indigenous students, and Black students learn as much as their White-European counterparts when both learn with the new method? We can compare the scores of ethnic minority students with the scores of White-European students to see whether their scores are higher, lower, or the same. That seems to be an easy comparison. However, a wealth of evidence from the modelling literature suggests that children learn more when they can identify with models displaying the behaviours (Bandura, 1977, 1986, 1997; Eron, 2000; Eron et al., 1996; Eron et al., 1971). Therefore, to the extent that history learned in North America is dominated by White-European events, what can we conclude if we find that White-European children have higher scores than their counterparts of colour? After all, the children will be portraying the European explorers, conquerors, and settlers in North American history.

The White-European Standard

J. Jones (1993) discusses that the dominant research paradigm in psychology is to see White European as the standard against which all others are measured. Thus, if people of colour are measured as different from the White-European standard, that difference is seen as deviant or deficient. For example, Derald Wing Sue had originally given his influential book the title *Counseling the Culturally Different* (Sue, 1981; Sue & Sue, 1990, 1999). However, *different* implied that those who were not in the majority were different from the standard in society, so by 2003 the authors changed the title of the book to *Counseling the Culturally Diverse* (Sue & Sue, 2003, 2008, 2013, 2016). As D. W. Sue and Sue (2003) put it,

> the phrase "culturally different" begs the question: "Different from what?" In almost all cases, the comparison standard is related to White Euro-American norms and has the unintended consequence of creating a hierarchy among different groups (race, culture, ethnicity, etc.) in our society. (p. xv)

In other words, the diverse groups that come closer to the White-European standard are considered higher in the hierarchy of groups and more acceptable to the majority, whereas the groups that are further from the norm are deemed less acceptable. In contrast, *diverse* implies that there are multiple perspectives or norms, with none being necessarily better or more desirable.

Internal versus External Validity

internal validity
When procedures in an experiment are designed to help make an inference that a change in procedure leads to a change in behaviour or outcome.

We began this chapter with a quotation from one of Stanley Sue's articles (S. Sue, 1999). The purpose of that article was to discuss the tension between internal and external validity. **Internal validity** refers to causal inference and how strong the research method is. If the research method includes random sample and takes into account confounding variables, then

The importance of internal validity.

a causal inference can be made. In other words, if it can be concluded that one independent variable rather than several confounding variables has caused the results of the experiment, the internal validity of the experiment is high. In the drug study, for example, a change in the medication (placebo versus medication) resulted in a change in depression; in the teaching study, a change in the method of teaching (standard teaching method versus students acting out historical scenarios) resulted in a change in student learning. In other words, internal validity suggests that our changes make a difference.

The reason researchers randomly assign potential research participants to experimental and control groups is to have more confidence that the changes in procedures *cause* differences in behaviour. Suppose we allow students to choose whether they want to act out history or to learn history the usual way. If we find differences in learning, can we infer that they result from the differences in teaching methods? Probably not. That is because those students who choose to learn by acting out history may be more extraverted, so we may be measuring differences between extraverts and introverts, not between acting out history and standard teaching models. Researchers expend substantial effort to ensure that studies are internally valid. If one cannot make any inference that one's changes result in differences, the study will be useless, no matter how interesting or important the topic is.

External validity refers to the generalizability of the results we obtain. There are two types of external validity: population validity and ecological validity. **Population validity** refers to the ability to generalize the results of the study to other populations. For example, in many psychological studies, introductory psychology students participate in studies and researchers conclude that "people" behave in similar manners. Is that inference justified? Sometimes yes and sometimes no. For example, if we were to study attraction and dating behaviour, introductory psychology students might be good research participants because they are at the age when such issues are very important, if not dominant. However, if we were interested in poverty or grief, introductory psychology students might not be the best population to study. **Ecological validity** refers to the ability to generalize the results of the study to other settings. If an experiment is conducted in a laboratory setting that has little resemblance to a real-life setting or is too complex or too simplified, then its ecological validity is low.

External validity may be—and often is—at odds with internal validity, as Campbell and Stanley (1963) indicated in their classic publication:

> Both types of criteria are obviously important, even though they are frequently at odds in that features increasing one may jeopardize the other. While internal validity is the *sine qua non*, and while the question of external validity, like the question of inductive inference, is never completely answerable, the selection of designs strong in both types of validity is obviously our ideal. (p. 5)

external validity The generalizability of the results to the study.

population validity The ability to generalize the results of the study to other populations.

ecological validity The ability to generalize the results of the study to other settings.

As Sue (1999) indicated, even though psychologists have recognized that both internal and external validity are important, the notions that internal validity is indispensable in experimental design and that external validity is "never completely answerable" have influenced the field to markedly favour internal validity over external validity. S. Sue called this "selective enforcement of scientific principles." As he so eloquently put it,

> The phenomenon of selective enforcement of scientific criteria is apparent. We criticize research for problems in internal validity. Yet, we pay relatively little attention to external validity. Whether in research papers submitted for publication or research grant proposals submitted for funding, ethnic minority research is primarily scrutinized for internal validity problems. This is appropriate. Yet much of research, whether or not it is focused on ethnics, is not criticized for external validity problems. In experimental studies, the discrepancies between internal and external validity are brought into bold relief. Rigorous and sometimes elegant experimental designs allow us to make causal inferences. However, because of their rigor and need to control for extraneous variables, they frequently involve small numbers of participants, foregoing issues of sampling and representativeness. (S. Sue, 1999, p. 1073)

Thus, when a researcher submits a study examining the effectiveness of a psychological treatment for depression, anxiety, or other forms of psychopathology, the study is typically reviewed for threats to internal validity and the proper application of statistical procedures, not for the degree to which the treatment can be generalized to all populations. Yet if you were in therapy for the treatment of one of these disorders, it would probably be more important for you to know whether the treatment will work for you than to know whether the study was conducted correctly. Scientifically, it is important that studies are conducted correctly, but practically, people want to know whether things will work.

2.2 Quantitative Research

Suppose you were given the following set of questions and were told to answer each one according to your preference:

At a party do you
a. interact with many people, including strangers?
b. interact with only a few close friends?

Do you
a. initiate conversations?
b. wait for others to begin talking to you?

Do you prefer to have
a. many friends but only a little bit of time for each one?
b. a few friends but more time to spend with each one?

Do you find it
a. easy to speak with strangers?
b. difficult to speak with strangers?

Are you
a. easily approachable?
b. somewhat reserved?

Note that all *a* answers are extraverted forms of answers and all *b* answers are introverted forms. If you were to answer 20 such questions, we would be able to calculate how introverted or extraverted you are. Thus, if you had 5 *a* answers, you would have an extravert score of 5, and if someone else had 12 *a* answers, they would have an extravert score of 12. From those scores, we could conclude that you are more introverted and that the other person is more extraverted.

Quantitative Approaches

The example on extraversion illustrates how a question can be turned into a meaningful number. You may have taken tests that ask you to circle a number to indicate what your preference is or what characterizes you best, such as the following:

Did you like this movie?
1   2   3   4   5   6   7
I did not like it at all   I liked it a lot

Do you consider yourself creative?
1   2   3   4   5   6   7
Not at all   Quite a bit

Research that involves turning questions into meaningful numbers that can be analyzed is called quantitative study. Our entire system of statistics is based on comparing numbers to make inferences about differences between groups or individuals and to identify patterns and relationships in numerical data (see Figure 2.2).

Thus, in our earlier example involving the effectiveness of an antidepressant medication, we can ask the individuals to rate on a scale from 1 to 10 how depressed they are after treatment, with 1 meaning *not depressed at all* and 10 meaning *deeply depressed*. If the medication (experimental) group yields an average score of 3.7 and the placebo (control) group yields an average score of 6.2, we can conclude that the medication was effective in relieving the depression. This general approach is known in science as **logical positivism** (Duarte, 2018; Stedman et al., 2016; Wilson et al., 2014).

logical positivism
Scientific approach that attempts to measure "truth" or real phenomena through methods of numbers and statistical analyses.

Correlational research is one type of quantitative study that examines the relation between two or more variables in order to establish their relationships. For example, education is positively correlated with income. Those who have higher levels of education tend to have high levels of income compared to those who have low levels of education. Furthermore, education is negatively correlated with fertility level (Meisenberg, 2008). Those who

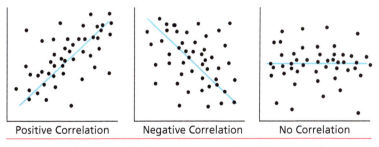

Figure 2.2 These graphs show patterns of positive, negative, and no correlation between two variables.

have higher levels of education tend to have lower fertility rates. As you see in these examples, correlational research, unlike experimental research, is descriptive. Its findings reveal relations between two or more variables without making any inferences. Not surprisingly, it is not possible to argue that education causes high income or low fertility because the influence of other factors (e.g., age, gender, religious ideology) are not examined in these studies.

Experimental Designs

To be able to predict the effect of one variable on another variable, experimental design is needed. An experiment is a type of research method in which one or more variables (referred to as independent variables) are manipulated to measure their effects on one or more other variables (referred to as dependent variables). A good experimental design must clearly define the variables that are going to be studied. For example, imagine you are interested in studying the self across cultures by using Triandis's (1989) conceptualizations of self: private, collective, and public. According to this theoretical framework, the private self refers to cognitions that involve ways you describe yourself (e.g., I'm funny; I run fast). The collective self refers to cognitions about group membership (e.g., I'm the youngest child; I'm a student). The public self refers to cognitions about how others view you (e.g., people think I'm honest; my friends think I'm a nerd). Triandis (1989) proposed that the degree to which private, collective, and public selves are emphasized varies across cultures.

Based on Triandis's (1989) theory, you develop your hypothesis and propose that people from individualistic cultures are more likely to emphasize private self-cognition and less likely to emphasize collective self-cognition than people from collectivistic cultures (Hypothesis 1). You also propose that when participants are primed with private self-concept, they make more idiocentric responses and fewer group responses than when participants are primed with collective self-concept (Hypothesis 2).

To test these hypotheses, you develop your experimental design by including participants who represent an individualistic culture (e.g., Anglo-European American students) and a collectivistic culture (e.g., Chinese students). This is exactly what Trafimow et al. (2009) did in their study in which 42 students (24 American native English speakers and 18 Chinese students) from an introductory psychology course participated.

An important procedure in an experimental design is random sampling. That is, all participants must be chosen randomly to ensure the sample represents the population (i.e., students in an introductory psychology course) in an unbiased way. In order to do this, the researchers asked all students in the course to submit their demographic information, including their names and whether they were native English speakers. Participants were selected randomly based on their names using a computer-generated procedure. In addition, participants were asked about their cultural background, which was used as an additional check for their selection.

Next, participants were randomly divided to receive private or collective priming. In the private self-priming condition, participants read a statement that asked them to think about how they were different from their family and friends. In the collective self-priming condition, participants read a statement that asked them to think about what they have in common with their family and friends (Trafimow et al., 2009).

Participants' responses to the priming condition were analyzed using content analysis. The responses were coded by two coders who were blind to the experimental conditions. The two coders agreed on 91 per cent of the responses they coded (Trafimow et al., 2009). This is referred to as **interrater reliability** (see Figure 2.3). The coders rated those responses that

interrater reliability
The degree to which coders agree on a rating system.

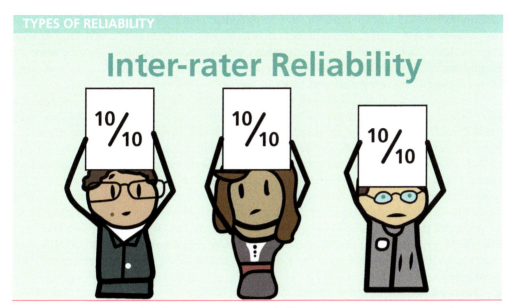

Figure 2.3 Interrater reliability is important in challenging measurement scenarios.
Source: Adapted from https://study.com/academy/lesson/the-reliability-coefficient-and-the-reliability-of-assessments.html

referred to personal beliefs, attitudes, and behaviours as idiocentric and those responses that referred to a group or group membership as group. The independent variable in this study is the cultural background of the participants (i.e., Anglo-European American versus Chinese), and the dependent variables are private and collective self-concept according to word count for idiocentrism and group-related responses.

The results of the study indicated that Anglo-European American participants give more idiocentric responses and fewer group responses than Chinese participants. This is consistent with Hypothesis 1. Furthermore, it was found that those who were in the private self-priming condition made more idiocentric responses and fewer group responses than those who were in the collective self-priming condition. This is consistent with Hypothesis 2. Overall, the findings indicate that culture has influence over the conceptualization of self: individualistic cultures emphasize the private self more than the collective self, while collectivistic cultures emphasize the collective self more than the private self. The study also highlights that regardless of cultural background, when the private or collective self is primed, all participants make idiocentric or group responses consistent with that prime (Trafimow et al., 2009).

The Trafimow and colleagues' (2009) study is a good example of using experimental design in conducting research with people from different cultural backgrounds. The use of random sampling and randomly assigning participants to experimental conditions are some of the safeguards that increase the internal validity of the findings. In addition, the study allows researchers to make predictions and causal inferences by manipulating variables in the experiment.

However, the study is not without limitations. One limitation is the lack of a control group. Control groups provide information about participants who do not receive any experimental intervention—in this case, a private versus collective self-priming condition.

Two common experimental research designs are cross-sectional and longitudinal designs. **Cross-sectional designs** gather data across different age groups. For example, if we wanted to know whether people become more conservative as they grow older, we might collect data

cross-sectional designs Research designs that gather data across different age groups.

from individuals in their twenties, thirties, forties, fifties, sixties, and seventies to see whether the participant responses are more conservative in later age groups than in earlier age groups. One problem with this kind of research, however, is that it may not accurately characterize the progression of political thought. Younger people may feel more liberal about some issues, and older people may feel more conservative about them.

The **longitudinal design** follows a certain set of individuals over time. Thus, to find out about liberal and conservative attitudes, we might want to collect data on 20-year-old individuals and then follow them for 60 years to see whether their attitudes become more conservative. A disadvantage of this research design is the length of time it takes to collect and analyze the data. Researchers must have the vision to design such a study when they are very young, the funding to sustain the research, and the patience to wait 60 years for the results. Over the course of the study, some participants may pass away, and researchers may also pass away. Another disadvantage of this research is that the cohort of individuals may be unusual. For example, individuals who grew up during war and political volatility (e.g., the Iraq War, the War in Afghanistan, or the refugee crisis) may have an entirely different world view than individuals who grew up during various pandemics, such as severe acute respiratory syndrome (SARS) and COVID-19.

Research in aging has long advocated sequential designs in studying elderly populations (Nesselroade & Labouvie, 1985). The **sequential design** is a combination of the cross-sectional and longitudinal designs. Researchers collect data on multiple cohorts of individuals and follow them over time so that by the end of the study, all age groups may be represented. For example, we might design a study collecting data on individuals in their twenties, thirties, and forties and follow those four cohorts for 30 years (Figure 2.4). Thus, individuals in the first group will ultimately represent ages from 20 to 50 (assuming some individuals were 20 years old when they first began the study), individuals in the second group will represent ages from 30 to 60, individuals in the third group will represent ages from 40 to 70, and individuals in the fourth group will represent ages from 50 to 80. Although this design still requires the researcher to actively collect data for a long time, it requires much less time (30 years) than a strict longitudinal design (60 years) in this example.

In the sequential design, the researcher will be able to compare data from multiple groups at similar ages. For example, if we want to see how liberal or conservative individuals are at age 45, we can look at three groups: the individuals whose data were collected in their twenties because, 20 years later, many of these individuals will have become 45 years old; the individuals whose data were collected in their thirties, all of whom will have become 45 years old 20 years later; and the individuals whose data were collected in their forties—this cohort will have many individuals whose data at age 45 will be available (see Figure 2.4). If a cohort is unusual, the data collected from it will differ from the data from other cohorts. However, if the data are more a function of age than of cohort, the results will be similar across the cohorts.

In sum, quantitative research involves collecting numerical data and conducting statistical analysis in order to find patterns of relationships between study variables. One type of quantitative research method is correlational research, which examines the relation between study variables without making a causal inference. In other words, in correlational research, the results indicate that A is related to B, but it cannot be established that A causes B. In order to make a causal inference, experimental research is conducted where an independent variable is manipulated in order to examine its effect on a dependent variable. In the next section, we examine an alternative methodology referred to as qualitative approaches to research.

---

longitudinal design Research designs that follow a certain set of individuals over time.

sequential design Sequential design refers to a combination of the cross-sectional and longitudinal designs.

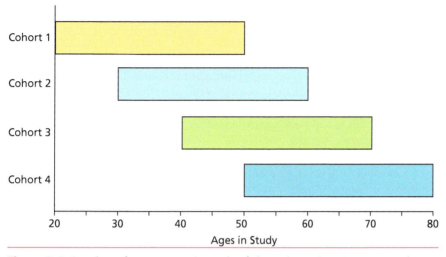

Figure 2.4 Overlap of age ranges in each of the cohorts in a 30-year study.

2.3 Qualitative Research

When people are asked whether they prefer to interact with many people at parties or just a few close friends, they often say, "Well, it depends on the party." If you looked at the extraversion–introversion questions at the beginning of this chapter, you likely felt that your answer would also depend on the situation. If the party was lively, with lots of interesting people, you would probably be more interested in meeting several people. However, if there were many people to whom you could not relate, you probably would hang out with your friends. If you were standing in a line and some strangers were engaged in a conversation about a topic that was of interest to you, it would probably be easier for you to be drawn into the conversation. If you were sitting in an airport in front of the gate and people were reading books around you, it would be difficult for you to talk to strangers.

These examples suggest that collecting only numerical data may result in the loss of some important information and/or may ignore contextual variables that could affect how we respond. Qualitative approaches to research can be employed when a researcher determines that gathering strictly numerical answers to questions results in the loss of essential information (Abdulla & Kasese-Hara, 2020; Beaird et al., 2020; Flynn et al., 2020; Funderburk et al., 2020). There are different kinds of qualitative data collection, such as case studies, structured interviews with open-ended questions, focus groups, and analyzing discourse (texts or narratives). Some people have used qualitative research to generate ideas for quantitative research, whereas others have used it as the goal of the research to give people an in-depth understanding of the phenomenon being examined. Our use of narratives in this book is a kind of qualitative application because we are trying to convince you of some underlying truths or themes experienced by people who have been touched by cultural issues.

Coles and Swami (2012) applied qualitative methods to investigate the adjustment of Malaysian international students in the United Kingdom. The authors conducted semi-structured interviews and identified key themes that explained the adjustment and integration of participants. They found that the Malaysian students described the strong support from their co-nationals as being essential in helping them with their adjustment. However, many of them explained that their large community and the strong in-group ties also isolated them from the British and other international students. They reported, though, that accommodation and classroom environment helped their integration with British and other international students. For example, the accommodation was an excellent way to integrate with British and other international students since they had an opportunity to connect during shared activities (e.g., watching movies, eating together, and cooking in the communal kitchen). Some students reported that they developed friendships with British and other international students during class hours when doing group work and assignments.

This example shows that the researchers were interested in examining the experience of participants as international students rather than measuring their adaptation as a group using numerical data. In general, in quantitative methods experiential data is lost because the focus tends to be on aggregating information. At the beginning of this section, we showed how context can play a part in people's responses to research questions. If the choice is between preferring to interact with many people at a party and preferring to interact with just a few, on the whole if you prefer interacting with many people, your answer would be classified as extraverted. You may know someone who always prefers to interact with many people (the life of the party), and that person's response would also be classified as an extraverted answer. Is it fair to give both of you one point for this question? Qualitative research methods can help us understand the degree to which a question is applicable to someone, or they can give a sense of the profound differences between two respondents.

Finally, qualitative methods are often used when it is difficult to convert a question into a numerical response. Aesthetic questions are difficult to convert into numerical responses, particularly when respondents are asked to compare objects that are markedly different. For example, how would you convert to a number the joy you experience when you see a very close friend for the first time in years? How does that joy compare with the joy you experience when you finish a lengthy project that involved many frustrations and obstacles? You may try to quantify those experiences, but are the numbers resulting from that conversion meaningful?

Researchers examining communities of immigrants and members of minority groups have increasingly employed qualitative techniques. For example, Yoon and colleagues (2017) examined how East Asian adolescents from immigrant families develop ethnic identities and integrate into the US mainstream society. They found that participants reported a discontinuity between their family and ethnic community and their school and larger society. Some participants noted that they were not comfortable with their ethnic identity and tended not to associate themselves with Asian culture, especially during their younger years. However, participants felt more comfortable with their cultural profile and being Asian as they became older (Yoon et al., 2017).

Similarly, Ndengeyingoma, Montigny, and Miron (2014) examined personal identity development of African adolescent refugees in Quebec. A combination of characteristics was identified as being influential on adolescents' identity development, including personal characteristics (e.g., religion), interpersonal relationships (e.g., peers), and environmental characteristics (e.g., cultural interactions). For example, even though the majority of the participants held Christian values, they reported that maintaining such values was challenging. Some reported that they "changed their religious practices in public" (e.g., going to Mass) when their friends did not hold the same religious commitments in order to retain their friendship ties (p. 5). Similarly, participants' perceptions of their national identity were influenced by their understanding of the Canadian culture and history and length of residency in the country. Furthermore, participants reported that the socio-environment in which they lived enabled them to have intercultural exchanges and receive support from other immigrants (Ndengeyingoma et al., 2014).

Overall, quantitative methodologies are important for several reasons, including to give voice to a particular group, to explore a topic, to develop an in-depth understanding of a phenomenon, and to collect experiential data, among others. This is not to say that quantitative techniques should be discarded. As Mio (2002) stated,

> As those of us in the multicultural arena know, measures on scales have helped us to understand elements of culture reasonably well, but this methodological approach has limited our understanding of culture, or at least the questions we can ask, for these questions must be reduced to quantifiable responses. Thus, in recent years, many multicultural researchers have drifted away from the logical positivistic methodology of numerical values that are statistically manipulated and analyzed and toward the more ethnographic and qualitative research methodologies used by our anthropology cousins. (p. 506)

A concept that is gaining interest in examining cultural differences is the intersubjective approach (Chiu et al., 2010). This approach treats individuals within societies as quasi-rational arbiters of societal norms, so their collective wisdom is most likely close to the norm of society. This approach has three premises:

1. people often act based on their perception of the beliefs and values of the wider society;
2. the immediate environment plays a role in one's perception of the broader society's beliefs and values, so not everyone in a society has the same intersubjective perception; and
3. intersubjective perceptions are sometimes distinct from one's personal beliefs and values.

Therefore, when people behave in a competitive manner, some may behave competitively because they feel that is what society dictates in their situation, even if they personally believe in co-operation. A researcher using the intersubjective approach would know by interviewing these individuals whether they were acting according to their personal beliefs or on the basis of how they perceived society expected them to behave.

One reason qualitative methods have not been widely employed is, frankly, that they are much more difficult to employ than quantitative methods. They typically use far fewer research participants and require more time to gather information because of the interview format of data collection. As noted in the section on quantitative approaches, our entire system of statistical inference is based on quantitative, logical, positivistic methods of inquiry. If we interview one or just a few individuals from a community, can we confidently generalize our results to the entire community or social group? How representative is that one individual or one community? A response from researchers who employ qualitative methods may be that we should not be confined only to questions that can be answered in numerical form. Moreover, how representative are the research participants in quantitative studies? We cannot be certain about the representativeness of our samples unless the samples cover the entire populations that we are attempting to make inferences about.

Clarke, Ellis, Peel, and Riggs (2010) feel that our Western bias toward the logical-positivistic approach unfairly places researchers who are challenging our existing knowledge in a defensive position while ignoring the limitations of logical positivism. They contend that qualitative researchers have had to justify their rejection of norms and standards in favour of alternative positions, yet quantitative researchers are never forced to justify their assumptions.

If quantitative researchers were forced to justify their assumptions as qualitative researchers are, there would be more open dialogue between the two camps.

Another reason qualitative methods have not been widely employed is that there is no agreement on the best ways to interpret the information we receive. For example, as we will see in the next chapter, meanings of words, phrases, concepts, and so on may change from culture to culture or even from subgroup to subgroup. Triandis and associates (Triandis et al., 1986; Triandis et al., 1988) discussed the difficulty in measuring self-reliance across cultures. In individualistic cultures, self-reliance is related to the pursuit of one's own goals and has a flavour of being in competition with others. In collectivistic cultures, self-reliance is related to not burdening others and there is no sense of competition. (We also discuss individualism and collectivism in Chapter 3.) The different meanings pose a difficulty in quantitative methods of inquiry because what does a 6 on a 10-point scale mean when respondents rate themselves on a scale measuring self-reliance in a collectivistic culture as opposed to self-reliance in an individualistic culture? In contrast, if we interview individuals in both cultures about the term and come up with a sense of how each culture can be characterized with respect to self-reliance, are we examining the same concept?

Qualitative Approaches and Gender

Qualitative approaches to inquiry are not limited to cultural issues. In fact, for years, research from the feminist literature has included qualitative methods. In her groundbreaking work, Carol Gilligan (1982/1993) discussed the differences between boys and girls based on interviews with them about their reasoning through moral dilemmas. Here is one such interpretation:

> Most striking among these differences is the imagery of violence in the boy's response, depicting a world of dangerous confrontation and explosive connection, where [the girl] sees a world of care and protection, a life lived with others whom "you may love as much or even more than you love yourself." Since the conception of morality reflects the understanding of social relationships, this difference in the imagery of relationships gives rise to a change in the moral injunction itself. To Jake, responsibility means not doing what he wants because he is thinking of others; to Amy, it means doing what others are counting on her to do regardless of what she herself wants. Both children are concerned with avoiding hurt but construe the problem in different ways—he seeing hurt to arise from the expression of aggression, she from a failure of response. (p. 38)

Much more depth can be derived from this analysis than can be obtained from an interpretation of quantitative differences in choices among alternative courses of action when children are given moral dilemmas to evaluate. Gilligan not only posits the reasoning behind the choices the children make in their course of action but also asserts what their different forms of imagery (or world views) are in guiding their choices. One might disagree with Gilligan's interpretations but would have to come up with an alternative set of interpretations of the meanings of children's world views, which again would require more depth of interpretation than can be derived from an analysis of different numerical averages. Other researchers have provided us with guidance on using qualitative methods in examining issues of gender (Ceballo, 2017; Hesse-Biber & Leavy, 2003; Hesse-Biber & Yaiser, 2003; Holder et al., 2015; Seale et al., 2004; ten Have, 2004).

Men and women can respond to research questions differently.

Qualitative Approaches and Older Populations

Because they have more life experience, older populations are more aware of contextual variables when considering questions. Hays (1996, 2007, 2009, 2016) developed a model of inquiry with older individuals of colour that she calls ADDRESSING:

- **(A)** Age and generational influences
- **(D)** Developmental and acquired
- **(D)** Disability
- **(R)** Religion
- **(E)** Ethnic and racial identity
- **(S)** Social status
- **(S)** Sexual orientation
- **(I)** Indigenous heritage
- **(N)** National origin
- **(G)** Gender

When developing research programs designed to measure older populations, researchers should include, or at least consider, all these variables. For example, many researchers lump all Asians together when conducting research comparing people of different ethnic groups with one another or with White Europeans. However, Asians from Hong Kong may respond quite differently than Asians from the Philippines.

> I was serving on a jury, and it was striking how much the individuals on the opposite side of the issue actually seemed to hate each other. I thought that farmers tried to help other farmers where they could, but this wasn't happening in this case. The suit that each was pressing against the other seemed rather trivial, but they were determined to make the other pay or at least suffer. Then it struck me—one of the guys was from Belgium and the other was from Germany. The Belgian was obviously not over World War II and wanted to extract all that he could out of this German farmer.
>
> —*Sam, 40+-year-old Japanese-American professor*

As this quotation indicates, the Hays model is not restricted to studying individuals of various ethnic groups. Here, national origin is an important factor along with generational influences, in view of the fact that many older Belgians still harbour resentment toward Germans. It is hard to imagine that 50 years from now, older Belgians will still harbour those feelings because their generation will have had a markedly different experience with people of German origin. Similarly, many older Koreans might still harbour resentment toward people of Japanese origin because of the hardships caused by World War II (Kim, 1997; Sung, 1991), whereas it is doubtful that Korean-Canadian adults will harbour such resentment toward Japanese Canadians 50 years from now.

Ejiade and Salami (2018) reported that conducting research with the elderly is difficult as elderly individuals are considered one of the most vulnerable populations. They reported that, in the Nigerian context, interviewer-administered questionnaires are more appropriate for the elderly than self-administered questionnaires. This is because interviewer-based questionnaires, which can take place in person or over the telephone, increase personal contact and provide an opportunity to ask for additional information (Ejiade & Salami, 2018). Similarly,

Older individuals may prefer different forms of data collection than those preferred by younger individuals.

Minocha et al. (2013) in their research with elderly participants in the UK found that the elderly preferred conversations through which they could connect with the events and stories rather than adhering to the protocols of the semi-structured interview. Thus, part of the advantage of these qualitative techniques of data gathering is the communal interaction with participants and engagement with participants.

2.4 Biases in Cross-Cultural Research

There are many methodological challenges in conducting cross-cultural research. Perhaps the most difficult question to address when applying tests and other measures to visible minorities and ethnic groups is the problem of **bias**. Biases are defined as factors that reduce the validity of the measurements that are used in different cultures (He & van de Vijver, 2012). A characteristic of bias is that it does not happen at random; rather, it is a systematic error in the measurement. A goal in conducting cross-cultural research is to reduce methodological bias and to increase equivalence of measures (equivalence of measures is discussed in the following section). Bias occurs when scores of different groups on a scale do not indicate a real difference between them. It has been suggested that there are three types of bias: construct bias, method bias, and item bias (He & van de Vijver, 2012; van de Vijver & Tanzer, 2004).

bias A factor that reduces the validity of the measurements that are used in different cultures.

Construct Bias

Construct bias means that the construct that is being studied across cultures is not identical. For example, although the meaning of *happiness* is different across cultures, when Oishi and colleagues (Oishi et al., 2013) compared the definition of *happiness* in dictionaries from 30 countries, the results indicated a similarity: in 24 out of the 30 nations, "luck" or "fortune" was part of the definition.

construct bias The construct being studied across cultures is not identical.

However, there are some notable *cross-cultural* differences. For instance, there are differences between countries that speak the same language. In Guatemala, the definition of *happiness* includes luck and fortune, but in Spain, Argentina, and Ecuador, the definition does not include luck and fortune. Similarly, while in Australia the definition of *happiness* also encompasses luck and fortune, in the US it does not. (Canada was not included in the study.) Therefore, sensitive measures that capture people's perspectives are vital when conducting cross-cultural research.

Method Bias

Method bias refers to three biases: sample bias, instrument bias, and administration bias (He & van de Vijver, 2012). **Sample bias** occurs when samples that are not equivalent and have different characteristics are compared (He & van de Vijver, 2012). For example, comparing university students in Culture A with farmers in Culture B is a sample bias, as the two samples have different characteristics and are not equivalent. Even when samples in both cultures are university students, sample bias may still occur. This is because going to university and gaining post-secondary education is a norm and more accessible in developed nations, such as Canada, than in developing nations, such as Malawi, where 85 per cent of the population live in rural areas and access to higher education is highly limited.

method bias Refers to three biases: sample bias, instrument bias, and administration bias.

sample bias A bias that occurs when samples that are not equivalent and have different characteristics are compared.

Instrument bias refers to the degree of familiarity with an instrument across cultures (He & van de Vijver, 2012). For example, university students in Canada are familiar with questions listed in multiple choice format. However, such a method of inquiry is rarely used among

instrument bias A bias that occurs when one cultural group has a larger degree of familiarity with an instrument over another.

students of a theological seminary in Iran. Therefore, the Canadian students have an advantage over the Iranian students if multiple choice questions are used as a method of investigation.

A type of instrument bias is **response style bias**, which refers to the tendency to agree rather than disagree with a statement and to use the endpoint of a scale (Dolnicar & Grun, 2007; Lentz, 1938). This means that participants' responses to items are not a reflection of the content of the items but rather a reflection of their cultural or other demographic backgrounds, which leads to biased results. Cultural differences in response style have been well documented (He & van de Vijver, 2012; Smith & Fischer, 2008). For example, Dolnicar and Grun (2007), in their study of a sample of university students, found that Australian students tend to use the extreme points of scales (i.e., strongly disagree or strongly agree) more than Asian students do.

The third type of method bias is **administration bias**, which refers to challenges at the time of data collection, such as ambiguous instruction and communication problems (He & van de Vijver, 2012). For example, it is possible that in one culture a short description of a survey is sufficient for participants to clearly understand what is expected of them. However, in a different cultural context, participants might be less familiar with the content of the survey, and a more detailed description of the study might be required. Participants' insufficient knowledge of a study or an instrument can have a negative impact on the quality of data collection.

> **response style bias** A bias that occurs when a culture has the tendency to agree rather than disagree with a statement and to use the endpoint of a scale.

> **administration bias** A bias that occurs when challenges during data collection, such as ambiguous instruction and communication problems, affect a group's response.

Item Bias

Item bias refers to the different meanings that an item could have across cultures. Van de Vijver and Meiring (2011) provide an example of item bias with this sentence: "I never [t]ake a long trip without checking the safety of my car." Although this item makes sense for Canadian university students, it does not apply to students who are in developing countries, as many do not have a car, and even if they do, public transport—mainly bus transport—is used for long trips. Using a car to compare the risk avoidance behaviour of Canadian students with students in a developing country is problematic as the response score of this item means different things in each culture.

> **item bias** A bias that occurs when an item has different meanings across cultures.

Bias of the User

Bias of the user refers to the introduction of bias into the interpretation of the test by the user of the test. If the user has a predetermined assessment of a group of individuals, then the test results may be interpreted to confirm that bias. In their systematic review of the literature, Ngaage and Agius (2016) found that Black Caribbean and Black African men in the UK had high rates of schizophrenia diagnoses. Even though various factors may account for such diagnoses among these populations (e.g., immigration status), it is important to recognize the limitations of the diagnostic tool, which skews these numbers (Ngaage & Agius, 2016). Hence, cultural and contextual factors need to be taken into account to decrease misdiagnoses among ethnically and culturally diverse populations.

Paniagua (2001) indicated that ethnic groups and visible minorities are seen by the majority group as being more pathological because the majority group does not value the lifestyles and norms of this group of individuals as much as they value their own.

> **bias of the user** A bias in the interpretation of a test when the test user has a particular perspective or bias that influences the interpretation of the test results.

Bias in the Usage

In contrast to bias of the user, **bias in the usage** of a test refers to how a test is used. For example, if a teacher uses a test of verbal fluency—which may be a good test for native English speakers—to determine who in a grade 1 class will be section leader, the use of that test may be

> **bias in the usage** A bias introduced when a test is used in an inappropriate manner that disadvantages the test taker.

biased if the test is administered in an area with many children whose parents are monolingual in a different language. Eventually, these children may become as fluent in English as their European Canadian counterparts, but at this very early age, most of them will not be. Thus, they will lose out on an early experience in leadership, not because they lack leadership ability, but because of another factor. Sometimes bias in the usage of a test is unconscious; sometimes, however, the bias is intentional and conscious.

2.5 Equivalence of Measures

Many researchers have discussed the problem of equivalence between measures developed in one culture and their translations to another culture (Brislin, 1986; Brislin et al., 1973; Cheung, 1985; Lin et al., 2020; Lonner, 1979). These issues involve the concepts of functional equivalence, conceptual equivalence, linguistic equivalence, and metric equivalence.

Functional equivalence refers to items that can be functionally instead of literally equated. For example, if we were to inquire about a child's knowledge of and conclusions about fairy tales, we might select *Beauty and the Beast* if we were testing children in Canada, whereas if we were testing children from a different background, we might select a well-known fairy tale from the child's country of origin.

functional equivalence The equating of items on a test or a survey functionally as opposed to literally.

Conceptual equivalence refers to terms or phrases whose meanings are culturally equivalent. For example, Marsella (1980) found that the term *depression* does not exist in some cultures, but if one were to describe a condition wherein an individual experiences fatigue and slowness of thought, the symptoms could be identified by those cultures. Thus, although the *term* "depression" does not exist in those cultures, the *condition* of depression does.

conceptual equivalence A term or phrase that has equivalent meanings in different cultures.

Linguistic equivalence refers to similarity of linguistic features of a text across two or more languages by evaluating grammatical accuracy and lexical similarity, which are broader than similarity of words. Most people have accepted the standard that measures must be back-translated instead of merely translated. Back translation is a procedure whereby the measure is translated into the target language and then translated back to the original language. If the back translation is the same or nearly the same as the original, then the translation is acceptable for study. However, sometimes the back translation is very different from the original phrasing, so a different translation must be sought. There is a joke from the Cold War about a computer that was designed to read every book in Russian to see whether any secret codes were being transmitted in the text. To test the computer, the American scientists had the computer translate "The spirit was willing but the flesh was weak." The computer whirred and translated the item into Russian and then back into English, and the result was "The vodka was good but the meat was rotten."

linguistic equivalence The translation of a term based on similarity of linguistic features by evaluating grammatical accuracy and lexical similarity.

Finally, **metric equivalence** refers to patterns of numerical scores and psychometric properties across cultures. Some cultures may be risk averse and not select the extremes of the possible answers. For example, in a culture that tends to be risk averse, research participants presented with a 7-point scale may select 6 as the highest score, so the researcher may have to make 6 in that culture the equivalent of 7 in a culture that uses the full range of the scale.

metric equivalence Patterns of numerical scores and psychometric properties across cultures.

Language Barriers

In addition to the problems of equivalence between measures, there is also the problem of language barriers. When conducting cross-cultural research or research with members of cultural groups whose first language is different from the researchers', language barriers can lead to miscommunication, misinterpretation, and inaccurate findings.

Researchers from Australia and Canada (Meuter et al., 2015) reviewed the negative consequences of miscommunications and language barriers in Australian health-care settings. They reported that even when a language barrier is not an issue, miscommunication can still take place because culturally diverse populations tend to describe their medical state and experience of pain and distress differently. Often, patients who do not speak the language of majority require an interpreter during their health-care encounters. This can further increase the potential for miscommunication of important medical information. Meuter and colleagues (2015) suggest that to overcome language barriers, it is important to identify the likelihood of occurrence of such barriers in medical settings. They further suggest that research must focus on determining specific aspects of language barriers to better train and prepare clinicians to meet the needs of their diverse patients.

Acevedo-Polakovich et al. (2007) further indicate that the clinical interview portion of the testing situation should determine the person's immigration history, contact with other cultural groups, acculturative status, acculturative stress, socio-economic status, and language abilities; as well, attention must be paid to measure selection and assessment planning and translation and the use of interpreters. Beyond language issues, Fields (2010) suggests that when conducting assessments about mental health, one must go beyond merely taking into account certain cultural beliefs an individual may have by engaging in a cultural exchange with the interviewee. To what extent might this render an instrument fundamentally different when going from one culture to another?

2.6 Replication in Psychology

Hales (2016) defines *replication* as verifying a previously conducted study by critically examining if the same results can be obtained. By using the methods that were used in the original study and replicating the original findings, the confidence in the accuracy of the findings increases. Replication is an important aspect of scientific activity as it increases internal validity, promotes unbiased and reliable scientific practices, decreases sampling error, and allows for the generalizability of findings (Hales, 2016; Milfont & Klein, 2018).

However, there are often inconsistencies in replicated findings. In particular, in 2015, a group of psychologists led by Brian Nosek from the University of Virginia published a report that provided evidence for replication crisis in psychology. These researchers tried to replicate 100 experiments published in top journals, but less than 40 per cent of the studies were replicated (Open Science Collaboration, 2015). This lack of confidence in research findings highlighted the replication crisis in psychology. There are a number of reasons for the replication crisis, and one of them is that, traditionally, researchers are rewarded for conducting original studies that reflect original thinking and not for replicating someone else's, or even their own, study (Diener & Biswas-Diener, 2020). Original studies with significant findings are also more likely to be published in scientific journals. Furthermore, there are many studies with small sample size and weak statistical analysis that have led to positive results, which are also more likely to be published than studies with negative results (i.e., no significant findings). In other words, there are many single studies with small samples that are published, and the findings of these studies are never revisited.

To resolve this problem, there is now a scientific movement in several disciplines, including psychology, that aims to increase the standard for published scientific work. Specifically, Open Science (2012) has adopted six principles for scientific research:

1. Open data
2. Open source

3. Open access
4. Open methodology
5. Open peer review
6. Open educational resources

It is now expected that researchers pre-register their study design, provide open access to data, share their methods and materials, pre-select the statistics that they will use to analyze their data, and publish in a peer-reviewed outlet that is available to the public. Such practice allows researchers to discover if their findings replicate, under what conditions they replicate, and how generalizable their findings are. Overall, only when the corpus of studies replicate the same results can we trust the findings; otherwise, we (both scientists and consumers of science) have to be skeptical about results of single studies.

2.7 Collaborative Problem Solving

As we move toward an interdependent world, the ability to engage in collaborative problem solving becomes more important. In the first report of its kind, the Organisation for Economic Co-operation and Development (2017) examined collaborative problem solving around the globe. Researchers examined 15-year-olds solving problems across 52 countries. The collaborative problem-solving tasks involved three types of problems:

1. a jigsaw problem, where individuals within a group are given different pieces of information and asked to put their information together to come up with a unified answer;
2. a consensus-building task, where the group must consider different points of view and avoid what social psychologists call *groupthink*; and
3. negotiation tasks, where group members have different opinions or perspectives but must come up with the best possible solution to their problem.

The researchers found that girls across all countries scored significantly higher than boys did, although the results of another study just a few years earlier (Organisation for Economic Co-operation and Development, 2013) indicated that boys individually had better problem-solving skills than did girls. It seems that the problem-solving skills of girls as a group far exceeded their individual problem-solving skills when such skills were used to conduct a collaborative problem-solving task. The researchers (Organisation for Economic Co-operation and Development, 2017) also discovered that disadvantaged children placed more importance on teamwork than did advantaged children.

In comparison to participants across the globe, children in Canada scored among the top-performing groups (Organisation for Economic Co-operation and Development, 2017). Overall, Canada ranked above average on collaborative problem-solving abilities, with 15–16 per cent of students achieving such abilities at a high level of complexity. There is also a correlation between problem solving and individual abilities in science, reading, and mathematics. Children in Canada tend to rank high in these subjects, as well.

Overall, collaborative problem solving is considered a fundamental skill for the twenty-first century (Neubert et al., 2015). In many large-scale assessments, such as comparing students' performance across countries, collaborative problem solving represents a range of skills that have connections to practice. Collaborative problem solving evaluates skills in settings where multiple problem solvers work on the same problem. This means that a shared understanding within the group is required where efforts and knowledge must be pooled in order to achieve a solution. In the twenty-first century, we are seeing a rise of collaborative tasks in education, work environments, and scientific efforts, which increases the importance of collaborative problem solving (Neubert et al., 2015).

2.8 Intelligence Testing

Psychologists have long been engaged in various types of testing. In this section, we discuss intelligence testing and cross-cultural issues and challenges that arise in its use. More than ever before, psychologists must be aware of these issues (Paniagua, 2014).

> When I was young, I remember being called to the school counsellor's office. Someone I had never met began giving me a test that I later recognized was an intelligence test. One of the items was "What is the Vatican?" I didn't know what it was. After the test, I asked the examiner what it was, and she told me. Since I was raised Buddhist and I was only a child, how was I supposed to know what the Vatican was? I remember thinking that the item was really unfair.
>
> —Jeremy, 40+-year-old Japanese-American professor

As this story indicates, the way in which we measure intelligence can be a reflection of cultural knowledge, not what Spearman (1904, 1927) would call *general intelligence*, or *g*. Many standardized intelligence tests, such as the Stanford–Binet Intelligence Scale (Thorndike et al., 1986) and the Wechsler Intelligence Scales for Children (Wechsler, 1991), use cultural knowledge as a part of the overall measurement of intelligence. This practice is based on Alfred Binet's long-held belief that such information was a direct measure of intelligence (Binet & Simon, 1905). This so-called direct measure contrasted with a movement headed by Sir Francis Galton to measure intelligence indirectly through sensory acuity (Galton, 1883). Galton measured intelligence by examining things such as visual acuity, how high a pitch people could hear, and how accurately people could detect different weights. Although the cultural knowledge method of measuring intelligence has proven to be much more successful and meaningful than the sensory acuity method, it is still vulnerable to subjective assessments of what is important to know and what is not.

Measuring intelligence has been a psychological pursuit at least since the time of Binet and Galton (late nineteenth century). We all have encountered people who we feel are smarter than or not as smart as we are, so this question seems to have some inherent interest. However, historically, people may have biases or assumptions about issues of intellect that influence the science they conduct. A famous case is that of Cyril Burt. Burt contended that Black people were intellectually inferior to Europeans as determined by his scientific investigations. Burt, a prominent figure in educational psychology, was influential in his day, and people accepted his findings without question. Part of the reason for that unquestioning acceptance may have been that his findings were consistent with the general racism of the time. Years later, however, many researchers determined that Burt had based his findings on his own assumptions and the genetic theory of intelligence that he was supporting, not on actual data analysis (Dorfman, 1978; Gillie, 1977; Kamin, 1974).

As the story at the beginning of this section indicates, there may be systematic reasons that some individuals do not score as high as others on an intelligence test. If a group of individuals not in the mainstream is asked about items that are common in the mainstream, should we be surprised that they do not score as high as people who are exposed to those items? The solution to this problem is not to simply add questions that are common to this subgroup and not to the mainstream but, rather, to try to find measures that truly get at some essence of intelligence. This pursuit is very difficult, however, because nearly every set of items is layered with cultural influence.

Another issue in measuring intelligence is that different cultures may value different contributions to what is called "intelligence." Cocodia (2014) reviewed perceptions and conceptualizations of intelligence across Asian, African, and Western cultures. Asians' perception of intelligence is influenced by their cultural traditions and philosophies. For example, according to Confucianism, character development, enhancement of knowledge, and maintenance of social interactions are among the characteristics of intelligent people. In Africa, among the Yoruba culture in Western Nigeria, intelligence relates to sensible behaviour, while among the Ibo culture, intelligence is associated with practical skills. In Western societies, however, intelligence is related to characteristics such as decision-making, planning, and problem-solving abilities (Cocodia, 2014).

Armour-Thomas (2003) posited this explanation:

> Although not ruling out other explanations, it is possible that the observed ethnic differences in intellectual performance may be attributed to different cultural values about what it means to be intelligent. If this is the case, an intelligence measure may be assessing different notions of valued intellectual abilities in different racial and ethnic groups and, in so doing, invalidating its results for these groups. (p. 363)

Overall, a great deal is at stake when measuring intelligence. In fact, intelligence tests, aptitude tests, achievement tests, and other forms of placement tests have been referred to as "high-stakes testing" because the results of the tests have real implications for getting into schools, applying for jobs, setting the tone for how people respond to you, and so forth. For example, many graduate programs require students to take the Graduate Record Examinations (GRE), which is a standardized test assessing analytical writing skills, verbal reasoning, quantitative reasoning, and critical thinking (Educational Testing Service, 2020). However, many have questioned the validity of GRE to truly indicate students' success in graduate studies. Miller and Stassun (2014) have argued that the GRE limits the number of minorities and women who are trying to pursue the sciences: "In simple terms, the GRE is a better indicator of sex and skin colour than of ability and ultimate success" (Miller & Stassun, 2014, p. 303). The following example is also an illustration of item bias, which we discussed earlier:

> For argument's sake, consider the following typical GRE analogies question: "Pitcher is to baseball as _____ is to football." To begin with, it would be very difficult for me to know what *baseball* is because I have never been exposed to the game. As regards "football," I would probably think about "soccer" because "football" refers to "soccer" to me. Clearly, this is not an issue of word ambiguity, but social exposure.
> —*An international graduate student at Louisiana State University (Mupinga & Mupinga, 2005)*

Intelligence tests have considerable impact. If you score high on intelligence tests, your teachers may give you more opportunities to succeed or may interpret some of your failures as a function of your not trying hard enough or of other factors getting in the way of your success. If you score low on intelligence tests, your teachers may assume that you do not know the answers, so why should they spend time on you? They may attribute your failures to what they perceive as your lesser abilities instead of other factors getting in your way. If you experience a lifetime of such assessments, you may tend to succeed or fail depending on expectations (Kearns, 2011; Roth et al., 2015).

Intelligence and Context

In considering intelligence and aging, Labouvie-Vief (1985) discusses how our Western view of mature intelligence resides outside context and observes that we regard consideration of contextual variables to be less mature or less intelligent. Labouvie-Vief notes, "According to such deficit interpretations, one might argue, of course, that the concrete bias of the uneducated and/or the old reflects an inherent restriction on abstract thinking" (p. 516). However, she cites an interaction reported by Luria (1976) to question the degree to which we cling to our own (or at least Luria's) conceptions of intelligence and ignore cultural and contextual variables:

> Subjects often assimilate the information presented in the problem to their own ways of conceptualizing reality; they construct new premises and correctly operate upon those. The following excerpt from Luria's study will serve as a good example. Three subjects were first shown a picture of a saw, an ax, and a hammer and then asked if a "log" belonged to the same category (i.e., tools).
>
> **Experimenter (E):** *Would you say these things are tools?*
> **All three subjects (S-1, S-2, S-3):** *Yes.*
> **E:** *What about a log?*
> **S-1:** *It also belongs with these. We make all sort of things out of logs—handles, doors, and the handles of tools.*
> **S-2:** *We say a log is a tool because it works with tools to make things.*
> **E:** *But one man said a log isn't a tool since it can't saw or chop.*
> **S-3:** *Yes you can—you can make handles out of it! . . .*
> **E:** *Name all the tools used to produce things . . .*
> **S-1:** *We have a saying: take a look in the fields and you'll see tools.*
>
> (Luria, 1976, pp. 94–95)
>
> If presented with the same task, city-educated subjects will almost inevitably exclude "log" from the category of tools, and from this fact Luria argues that the uneducated display a deficit in classificatory behaviour. Yet one also senses here a different dimension; these Uzbekistan peasants appear engaged in a bantering argument about the proper definition of "tool," rejecting any one concrete definition and arguing for a more flexible and perhaps even creative stance. And indeed, although the experimenter attempts to guide the subjects towards a "correct" definition of tools, one is hard put to judge who is more "rigid" or "concrete"—the subjects or the experimenter! (Labouvie-Vief, 1985, p. 517)

In other words, the experimenter had a conception of intelligence and was trying to measure that conception through a predetermined metric. When the elderly research participants brought their experience to bear on the situation, showing flexibility in their thinking, the experimenter rejected this flexibility in favour of an "objective" definition of *tool*. Which person is displaying more intelligence?

It has also been shown that information processing is different across cultures. For example, those from Asian cultures tend to place greater importance on contextual information, and their thinking patterns tend to be holistic. However, individuals with American-European backgrounds pay less attention to contextual cues, focus more on objects, and tend to have an analytical thinking pattern. These differences in their attention and information processing are learned in youth and carried on throughout their lives (Stern & Carstensen, 2000).

Alternative Conceptions of Intelligence

Sternberg (2002) related a research project by Cole, Gay, Glick, and Sharp (1971), who studied the Kpelle tribe in Africa. They were trying to sort objects conceptually:

> In Western culture, when adults are given a sorting task on an intelligence test, more intelligent people typically will sort hierarchically. For example, they may sort names of different kinds of fish together, and then place the word "fish" over that, with the name "animal" over "fish" and over "birds," and so on. Less intelligent people will typically sort functionally. They may sort "fish" with "eat," for example, because we eat fish, or they may sort "clothes" with "wear" because we wear clothes. The Kpelle sorted functionally—even after investigators unsuccessfully tried to get the Kpelle spontaneously to sort hierarchically.
>
> Finally, in desperation, one of the experimenters (Glick) asked a Kpelle to sort as a foolish person would sort. In response, the Kpelle quickly and easily sorted hierarchically. The Kpelle had been able to sort this way all along; they just hadn't done it because they viewed it as foolish—and probably considered the questioners rather unintelligent for asking such stupid questions. (pp. 503–4)

As you can see, our limitations in measuring intelligence may be limitations in both how we measure intelligence and how we understand intelligence.

Most of how we have measured intelligence in the past has been what Sternberg and his colleagues would call analytic intelligence (Chooi et al., 2014; Culross & Winkler, 2011; Momani & Gharaibeh, 2017; Sternberg, 2018). Sternberg's general model suggests that intelligence is not made up of a single factor, as Spearman (1904) suggested. Instead, it is made up of at least three components: analytic intelligence, creative intelligence, and practical intelligence. Intelligence tests and academic achievement tests have measured primarily analytic intelligence because it is the easiest component to measure. Analytic intelligence depends heavily on memorization and calculations based on learned formulas. Thus, individuals who excel in creative and practical forms of intelligence are not identified by our standard measures (Wagner, 2000).

As a test of this triarchic theory of intelligence, Sternberg and his colleagues (Sternberg, 2012, 2014; Sternberg et al., 1996; Sternberg et al., 1999; Sternberg et al., 2013) measured children who excelled only in analytic intelligence, only in creative intelligence, only in practical intelligence, in all three areas, or in none of the three areas. They then gave these children matching or mismatched instructions for performing a task. For example, children who excelled only in analytic intelligence performed better when given analytic instructions than when given practical instructions; children who excelled in practical intelligence performed better than did children who excelled in analytic intelligence when given practical instructions; and so forth. These results confirmed that differing forms of intelligence produce measurably different performances in different contexts.

A different conception of intelligence is proposed by Gardner (1983, 1993, 1999). Whereas standard intelligence tests generally measure a verbal component (with mathematical abilities subsumed under this verbal component) and a non-verbal component of intelligence, Gardner proposes that intelligence comprises seven intelligences:

1. Linguistic
2. Logical-mathematical
3. Spatial

4. Musical
5. Bodily-kinesthetic
6. Interpersonal
7. Intrapersonal

He later added an eighth intelligence: naturalistic intelligence (Gardner, 1999; Table 2.1). The following quotation is an example of one of Gardner's forms of intelligence (musical intelligence):

> Ellen is also blind, with an IQ of less than 50. She too is a musical genius. She constructs complicated chords to accompany music of any type she hears on the radio or television. She sang back the entire soundtrack of the Broadway musical *Evita* after one hearing of the album, transposing orchestra and chorus to the piano with her complex, precise chords including intense dissonances to reproduce mob and crowd noises. In addition, she has a remarkable spatial sense and a phenomenal memory. (Treffert, 2006)

Although intelligence-test purists might identify Gardner's linguistic and logical-mathematical intelligences as the only true measures of intelligence, classifying the other forms of intelligence as merely learned abilities, Gardner would hold fast to the notion that these are true forms of intelligence.

Creativity is seen as a type of intelligence.

TABLE 2.1 Gardner's Eight Types of Intelligence

Type of intelligence	Examples of intelligence
Linguistic	Reading and understanding a book; understanding oral presentations; writing term papers for a class
Logical-mathematical	Solving mathematical problems; understanding advanced calculus; logical reasoning processes
Spatial	Developing a cognitive map of a route; doing mental rotations; estimating whether objects will fit into certain spaces
Musical	Playing a musical instrument; composing music; appreciating the construction of music
Bodily-kinesthetic	Playing athletic events; learning new dance steps; being able to control one's bodily movements
Interpersonal	Being able to talk easily with others; detecting changes in emotional states of others; understanding others' motives
Intrapersonal	Being attuned to our own emotional states; understanding our own abilities; knowing how to change ourselves
Naturalist	Understanding patterns of nature; being able to survive in naturalistic settings

Source: Reproduced with permission from Gardner, H. (1999).

Gardner sees bodily-kinesthetic and musical abilities as distinct forms of intelligence.

Overall, performance on intelligence tests has been found to be associated with characteristics of the country rather than the intellectual abilities of people. This is consistent with the universalistic model that claims basic cognitive processes do not vary across cultures and cultural differences on cognitive test performance is a reflection of differences in cultural practices and educational differences (van de Vijver, 2015). In a meta-analysis of studies examining cognitive test performance across cultures, van de Vijver (2015) reviewed studies from 1973 to 1994 and identified 197 studies representing 48 countries. He found that cross-cultural differences in cognitive test performance were related to cultural variables, such as gross national product (GNP) and educational spending per capita per year, supporting the universalistic model for performance on cognitive tests.

Summary

Psychologists have conducted research with populations of colour in many ways, and challenges can arise in these research studies. Traditionally, cross-cultural studies were conducted by measuring differences between White European and comparison groups of people of different ethnicity or nationality. We discussed some of the limitations of such cross-cultural studies. We also described that sometimes comparing groups with each other does not make sense. For example, if we want to know why some Indigenous Peoples in Canada maintain a strong tie to their cultural background, there is no need to have a European Canadian comparison group.

Important differences exist between quantitative data and qualitative data. Quantitative data are data that can be transformed into numbers so that averages of one group can be compared with averages of another group. Qualitative data are more difficult to collect and to interpret. However, qualitative data may be more meaningful in studies of minorities and marginalized groups, comparisons between women and men, and studies of elderly populations.

One problem in studying different groups is the issue of equivalence. This problem is particularly important when the material in a study must be translated into a different language. There are at least four problems of equivalence: functional, conceptual, linguistic, and metric equivalence.

Research projects have differing designs. The two most common are cross-sectional and longitudinal designs. The cross-sectional design collects data all at once across age groups, whereas the longitudinal design collects data at one point in time and follows the original group across time to collect data across all age groups. A combination of these two designs is the sequential design, which collects data across age groups and follows the research participants over time. Because some research participants are older than others, data that are the equivalent of data from a longitudinal design can be collected in a much shorter period of time.

Researchers must be aware of different biases when conducting cross-cultural research. These include construct bias, method bias, and item bias. Method bias is a generic term for challenges associated with methodology consisting of sample bias, instrument bias, response style bias, and administration bias.

Finally, cross-cultural issues arise in psychological testing. For example, intelligence testing is subject to the same kinds of difficulties and challenges as other kinds of studies. Even if intelligence testing is constructed carefully, its use can be biased. An added challenge is that sometimes these tests involve high-stakes testing: the results of the tests may have a major impact on individuals' lives, so particular care should be taken when using such tests.

FOOD FOR THOUGHT

In Canada and several other Western countries, including Australia and the US, students who are interested in applying to a medical school must take the Medical College Admission Test (MCAT). The MCAT, which is a standardized computer-based test, measures students' critical thinking, problem solving, writing skills, and academic knowledge. Students are highly aware of the significance of the MCAT for their admission to medical school. They may or may not get into the medical school of their choice partly because of their MCAT score. As you can see, a test of this nature can have a major impact on a person's life and can even be a life-changing event. Think about how you might feel if you moved to a different country and were given a test that would affect your status in that country. You might gain some insight into the importance of psychological assessment.

Critical Thinking Questions

1. Have you ever been certain about something? If so, how did you know it was true? How did you go about proving its truth?
2. Have you ever been associated with a group that was the object of a research study (such as your gender, your ethnicity, your religious group)? If so, what did you think about the conclusions of the research? Did they apply to you or not?
3. In what ways have you been compared unfavourably with someone or with a group that had an advantage over you? How did that make you feel? What would a study that is more fair look like?
4. Did you ever perform poorly on a test and feel that if your teacher had just interviewed you, that teacher would have come away with a much better picture of your abilities? What happened?
5. In what ways have you ever felt that you were being unfairly measured against someone else's standards?

NumenaStudios/Shutterstock

3 Diversity and World Views

Learning Objectives

Reading this chapter will help you to:

3.1. understand different approaches in investigating cultures;
3.2. identify the components of a WEIRD population;
3.3. know models of value orientations and world view;
3.4. explain world views of different ethnic groups;
3.5. recognize how social expectations shape women's world views;
3.6. know the world view of LGBTQ2+; and
3.7. understand diverse world views based on social class and age.

She asked me if she took one pill for her heart and one pill for her hips and one pill for her chest and one pill for her blood how come they would all know which part of her body they should go to?

I explained to her that active metabolites in each pharmaceutical would adopt a spatial configuration leading to an exact interface with receptor molecules on the cellular surfaces of the target structures involved.

She told me not to bullshit her.

I told her that each pill had a different shape and that each part of her body had a different shape and that her pills could only work when both these shapes could fit together.

She said I had no right to talk about the shape of her body.

I said that each pill was a key and that her body was ten thousand locks.

She said she wasn't going to swallow that.

I told her that they worked by magic.

She asked me why I didn't say that in the first place.

(Colquhoun, 2002, p. 14)

Different people with different experiences often see the world in disparate manners. People who live in cold climates, for example, may see the world quite differently than those who live in warm climates; individuals who live in crowded cities may see the world differently than those who live in rural environments; people who are of one ethnicity may see the world differently than those of another ethnicity. The above prose was written by Glenn Colquhoun, a medical doctor from New Zealand, and this is a recounting of a real-life interaction he had with a Maori woman. The modern medicine model did not fit into her world view, and she was not satisfied with his explanations of how pills worked until he explained how they worked in a manner that she would understand—magic. In this chapter, we will examine some of the ways in which people have different world views, which reflect the ways in which the world is filtered through one's experiences and teachings.

3.1 Different Approaches to Investigating Cultures

The chapter-opening story illustrates a major topic in the cross-cultural arena: the distinction between the etic and the emic perspectives on cultures. These terms derive from the linguistic terms *phonetic* and *phonemic* (Pike, 1967). The **etic approach** attempts to find commonalities across cultures. It examines cultures from the outside to build theories that develop universal aspects of human behaviour. The **emic approach** examines only one culture from within that culture. This approach attempts to derive what is meaningful among group members (Bernal et al., 2014; Bernal & Domenech Rodríguez, 2012; Berry et al., 1992; Brislin, 1980; Jahoda, 1982; Mio, 2013). Kim and his colleagues (Kim & Berry, 1993; Kim & Park, 2006; Kim et al., 2006) call the emic approach the Indigenous and cultural psychology approach to investigation. Sue and Sue (2016) call the etic approach a culturally universal perspective, whereas the emic approach is a culturally specific perspective.

etic approach An attempt to build theories of human behaviour by examining commonalities across many cultures.

emic approach An attempt to derive meaningful concepts within one culture.

Imposed Etics

Although both emic and etic approaches are necessary in psychology, J. W. Berry (1969) cautions against **imposed etics**, by which he means the imposition of an outsider's world view on a different culture. Sometimes observers assume that behaviours or concepts are universal or have the same meaning they do in the observers' culture. For example, Colquhoun, in the opening story, initially demonstrated imposed etics when he tried to impose on the Maori woman

imposed etics The imposition of one culture's world view on another culture, assuming that one's own world views are universal.

his own value of modern medicine. He believed that the modern medicine notion of receptor sites should be understood by all, but instead, the Maori woman thought he was making something up. However, who is to say that our modern notions of medicine are correct? In the ancient Greek times of Hippocrates, after whom the Hippocratic oath is named, doctors believed that our personalities were determined by the bodily humours of blood, phlegm, yellow bile, and black bile. Currently, we talk about neurochemical transmitters and receptor sites. In the 2018 blockbuster film *Black Panther*, CIA agent Everett Ross is shot in the spine during a fight while attempting to save Nakia, a Wakandan warrior. In appreciation of this act, Nakia takes Ross home to Wakanda, a hidden country where technology is much more advanced than the rest of the world, to heal him. When Ross wakes up in Wakanda, he asks his doctor, Shuri, how long ago he was shot, and she tells him it happened the day before. He replies, "Bullet wounds don't just magically heal overnight," and Shuri says, "They do here" (Coogler, 2018).

The studies of Walter Mischel (1958, 1961) represent a historical example of imposed etics. Mischel was interested in studying the **delay of gratification**. He set up studies wherein children had a choice between a less desirable reward that they could have immediately (such as a small piece of candy or pretzels) and a more desirable reward that they could have if they waited until the next day (such as a large piece of candy or marshmallows). He found that European-American children at the Stanford Day Care Center predominantly chose to wait for the more desirable reward, whereas African-American children in the inner city of Oakland chose to take the less desirable reward immediately. Mischel concluded that African-American children in the inner city did not know how to delay gratification, but that if we could teach them to delay gratification, they could work themselves out of the inner city.

However, alternative interpretations suggest that the African-American children were behaving adaptively for a number of reasons based on their experiences: the experimenter could have been lying to them and would not show up the next day; the children may have been hungry, so the small piece of candy was more meaningful to them immediately; the experimenter could be robbed the next day; the experimenter's car could break down, so he might not show up; and so forth (Mio & Awakuni, 2000; Mio & Iwamasa, 1993; Mio & Morris, 1990). Therefore, even though Mischel's studies were well intentioned, they were still an example of imposed etics: Mischel thought he was studying delay of gratification (or lack thereof), whereas the more meaningful concept for the children was adaptive behaviour.

Next we examine another approach in investigating cultures. You may recall from Chapter 1 that Dutch psychologist Geert Hofstede (2001) developed a highly influential six dimensions model of culture in which he characterized national cultures based on values. These dimensions are as follows:

- Individualism/collectivism
- Power distance
- Masculinity/femininity
- Uncertainty avoidance
- Long-term/short-term orientation

The last dimension is relevant to our discussion.

Long-Term and Short-Term Orientation

Hofstede's (2001) sixth dimension of cultural values is called long-term versus short-term orientation. This dimension is linked to individuals' efforts to focus on the future (e.g., long-term orientation) versus the present and past (short-term orientation). Long-term-oriented societies

---

delay of gratification The ability to wait for a more desirable reward instead of taking a less desirable reward immediately.

value delayed gratification of needs, whereas short-term-oriented societies accept instant gratification of needs. East Asian countries such as China, Hong Kong, Taiwan, and Japan are more long-term oriented, and countries such as Canada, Australia, the United States, England, Germany, Sweden, the Netherlands, and Brazil are more short-term oriented (Hofstede, 2001).

In her book *Understanding Emotion in Chinese Culture: Thinking through Psychology*, Louise Sundararajan (2015) explains that in a collectivistic culture, "fitting in" is very important. For example, in Chinese society, people learn to suppress their feelings and strive to be in harmony with others. Similarly, children in Chinese culture learn to delay their gratification and learn the value of positive feelings associated with gratitude: "It is gratitude that will, later in adult life, facilitate the self-control necessary for delaying gratifications" (Sundararajan, 2015, p. 138). As a result, self-control and fitting in are associated with positive feelings among Chinese people; this is consistent with the long-term orientation value that emphasizes delayed gratification and a focus on the future.

The following quotation highlights Chinese long-term orientation cultural values:

In Western culture, academic achievement is largely seen as an individual endeavour. People are encouraged to formulate goals that focus on their own needs, interests, and preferences. In Chinese culture, by striking contrast, academic achievement is seen as a social endeavour. Individual academic achievement is not only a person's own quest for knowledge, but also a means to bring wealth, power, fame, and honour to the family. (Tao & Hong, 2014)

Even when there is some overlap or connection between ideas from different cultures, there may be cultural variations. A colleague told us of the connection between Freud's Oedipal complex and a Japanese variant of this story:

There was an old article . . . about the Ajase complex. It told of a Japanese psychiatrist in the 1920s or '30s who was pondering Freud's Oedipal complex. He concluded that the Oedipal complex was based on a Western family structure, and so, came up with the Ajase complex. Ajase is a mythical character, as was Oedipus. The story of Ajase speaks to the close mother–son relationship in an Asian family (especially a Japanese family). In fact, the myth does not even mention Ajase's father explicitly, just Ajase resolving his relationship with his mother (his mother did not have Ajase out of love for Ajase, but out of love for her husband and family duty as well—Ajase was torn apart when he realized this truth). This Japanese psychiatrist went to Vienna to present his thesis to Freud, himself. As I recall Freud's reaction, he found this cross-cultural variation of the Oedipal complex fascinating and read the thesis.

I think the Ajase complex speaks to the need for culture-specific assessment of Freudian theory and of Ericksonian theory, as well (Kohlberg could also be included).

—*Yasue, 60+-year-old Japanese-American professor*

At first blush, this Ajase complex seems similar to the Oedipus complex. However, the Ajase story does not include a jealousy of one's father, a fear that the father would cut off the boy's penis, or an underlying sexual connection between Ajase and his mother. Instead, the story seems to underscore the cultural value of not sticking out or being too prideful. Ajase thought he was special and central to the family structure, so he was devastated to discover that he was conceived as a result of family obligations. The Ajase complex may not resonate with those living in Western industrialized regions of the world, such as Canada, as family obligation may not be a top priority for them. Therefore, mythical characters such as Ajase are less likely to be fostered. Yet, in Japan and many Asian societies where family obligation and respect to tradition and the elderly are valued, the Ajase complex captures these cultural ideals. Indeed, the Ajase complex comes from stories found in Buddhist culture and in ancient Indian scripts (Okonogi, 1979).

Understanding Differences from Within

As discussed in Chapter 2, self-reliance is a good example of how different countries can conceptualize terms differently. Triandis and associates (Triandis et al., 1986, 1988) define individualistic and collectivistic countries based on multiple attributes. For example, in **individualistic countries** people tend to give priority to personal goals, they give more weight to personal attitudes, and the self is autonomous. In **collectivistic countries**, in contrast, people give priority to in-group goals, they give more weight to social norms, and the self and the group are interdependent. We will be discussing individualism and collectivism much more extensively later in this chapter, but, briefly stated, people in individualistic cultures tend to place individual rights over the rights of the collective whereas people in collectivistic cultures tend to place collective rights over the rights of the individual. Each culture has some elements of the other (i.e., individualistic cultures have some elements of collectivism, and collectivistic cultures have some elements of individualism), but, on balance, there are identifiable tendencies in most cultures (see Triandis, 1995). The emic definitions of self-reliance give completely different flavours to the term and an insight into the countries defining the term.

Sue and Sue (2000) give another example of emic differences between individualistic and collectivistic societies in defining a term:

> For example, one aspect of good decision-making in the Western [individualistic] cultures may be typified by an ability to make a personal decision without being unduly influenced by others, whereas good decision-making may be understood in Asian [collectivistic] cultures as an ability to make a decision that is best for the group. (p. 3)

Again, we see that the individualistic definition of the term *good decision-making* involves a reflection of individualism: independence. The collectivistic definition of the term *good decision-making* involves a collectivist value: paying attention to others.

A former student wrote about how *gayness* was understood in the Philippines before Western religious concepts took over the country:

> I believe also that lesbians, gays, and bisexuals have a connection with religion and spirituality. Beyond the privileges discussed in class, early shamans of almost every tribe and nation were almost always homosexual (though I have read that some were bisexual). In ancient Greece and Rome, many priests dressed in matron's gowns and paraded as women in certain festivals, and priestesses of certain deities wore belts that had a phallus shape in front for certain rites. The notion is that these are people who are in between norms of usual interaction or in between genders; they can be both. Thus, they were perceived also as being able to traverse in between the normal and paranormal worlds. In the Philippines, they were once called *babaylan* (priests, most likely gay men or wounded warriors and sickly men) and *catalonan* (priestesses, most likely lesbians or infertile women). It was not until the arrival of Christianity that these people were demonized and labelled as sinful. In many early societies, homosexuals are delegated the positions of spiritual

---

individualistic countries Countries that place individual rights and the pursuit of one's own goals over the rights of the collective and the goals of the group.

collectivistic countries Countries that place collective rights over the rights of the individual.

leaders primarily for two things: one, because they cannot or will not aid in the propagation of the tribe; and two, because they are seen to be not one, not another, yet both. This is a mysterious quality that was attributed to and associated with special abilities. In modern-day India, a special class of eunuchs who dress in feminine garb are believed to be able to curse or bless people because of this very reason. Thus, homosexuality has a long and intriguing yet hidden history.

—Trevor, 20+-year-old Chinese-Filipino student

Male and Female Perspectives

Some of the gender differences in world views are related to power differentials between men and women (Bendahan et al., 2015; Riggio, 2017). One striking illustration of this power differential was the Women's March of 2017 and the events leading up to it. The Women's March took place in countries around the world on 21 January 2017 and was spurred by the inauguration of Donald Trump as president of the United States. Trump's victory came in November 2016, just weeks after he admitted to abusing and harassing women by taking advantage of his privileged position as a celebrity. Since his inauguration was to be on 20 January 2017, organizers of the Women's March scheduled their protest for 21 January. Globally, there were an estimated 3.5 million to 5.6 million participants in the March, with over 120,000 in Canada; 10,000 estimated in Melbourne, Australia; over 600 in Tokyo; 700 in Cape Town, South Africa; hundreds in Mexico City; and more all over the world (Bridges, 2017).

Thousands of Canadians gathered in Toronto for the Women's March, protesting gender-based discrimination and advocating for female empowerment.

Since then, the Women's March has continued annually with over 700 marches on all seven continents (Boesveld, 2017). The march is considered one of the largest single-day protests that both Canada and the US have ever seen, with hundreds of thousands of people participating across North America and millions worldwide (Boesveld, 2017). The Women's March led to different reactions across countries. For example, in Pakistan, women's calls for reproductive rights and better education for women were met with considerable backlash (Toppa, 2019). The year ended with women around the world breaking their silence on being sexually harassed and being selected as *Time* magazine's "Person of the Year" (Felsenthal, 2017).

For years, women—and many men—have accused men of sexual abuse and harassment. As many in Hollywood had indicated, Harvey Weinstein's abuse had been an open secret (Zacharek et al., 2017). However, women were reticent to go public with these accusations for fear of ruining their careers or breaking settlement agreements. Finally, Ashley Judd told *The New York Times* of the abuse (Kantor & Twohey, 2017), and the newspaper uncovered a long history of Weinstein's abuse and paying off women in nondisclosure agreements. Action was swift, as Weinstein's own company, Miramax, fired him, and in March 2020, a court in New York City sentenced him to 23 years in prison. This was the dam breaking, with numerous women coming forward to give their accounts of abuse they had endured over the years. A #MeToo Twitter campaign had begun a couple of years before the Weinstein revelation, but the movement exploded when Hollywood stars began using it, prompting women of all professions to reveal abuse they had encountered. At the time of this writing, it appears that this movement will change how society treats victims of this kind of abuse and disciplines the abusers.

The #MeToo movement made headlines around the globe, prompting women from many different parts of the world to come forward and speak about their abuse. For example, in Canada, there has been a considerable increase in sexual violence support services (Canadian Women's Foundation, n.d.). Women in countries such as South Korea, Sweden, India, and Egypt, where perpetrators are routinely dismissed, have fought and won legal cases to ensure their attackers serve time for their crimes (Stone & Vogelstein, 2019). Most notably, Rania Fahmy, an Egyptian woman, was caught on camera fighting back against her attacker in 2017. Despite efforts to keep her silent, she filed charges against her attacker and won her case, making her one of the first Egyptian women to win a court ruling on sexual harassment charges. This victory set new legal paths for all Egyptian women who have suffered sexual harassment and abuse (Stone & Vogelstein, 2019).

In another example, a woman who was sexually assaulted on the streets of Cameroon discusses the common occurrences of gender-based violence in her country, and the particular caution women must practise on a daily basis:

> I didn't feel safe in Cameroon anymore. So many women have experienced violence in my country. . . . Women have to be careful to avoid danger here. When I'm alone on the street, I always feel panic. When people get aggressive and there is trouble, I get the same feeling as I did then.
>
> —*Virginie Laure, Cameroon woman seeking asylum in Greece*
> *(The UN Refugee Agency Canada, 2019)*

In addition to the issue of sexual harassment, men and women have very different experiences in the field of work. Cheung and Tang (2017) reviewed gender roles and stereotypes, marriage and family, paid and unpaid labour, violence against women, and mental health among women in Mainland China, Hong Kong, and Taiwan. The authors reported an increased rate of the women's labour force in these regions over time but with strong gender segregation in the labour market, both horizontally and vertically. The findings indicate that there are clear differences in job positions between genders: men tend to be at the top of occupational hierarchy and women at the bottom (vertical segregation). For example, there are more male CEOs than female, and there are more female administrative assistants than male. In addition, gender horizontal segregation in work settings means that men and women within the same occupational class tend to have different job tasks and experiences. For example, in occupations where women consist of less than 25 per cent of the workforce (also referred to as male-dominated occupations), women tend to receive less mentoring and have fewer career development opportunities than men, even if the women are working in the same job roles (Campuzano, 2019). In addition, women in male-dominated occupations tend to encounter more sexual harassment than those who work in non-male-dominated industries (Daley et al., 2018). In Canada, male-dominated industries include construction (12.1 per cent women); mining, oil, and gas extraction (17.7 per cent); manufacturing (21.6 per cent); and transportation and warehousing (23.5 per cent) (Statistics Canada, 2019).

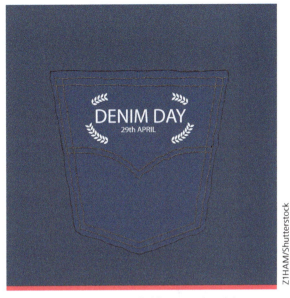

Denim Day has become a symbol for protesting violence against women.

The researchers also argue that family responsibilities can be seen as barriers for women to reach higher positions in the workforce (Cheung & Tang, 2017). Women spend more time doing household tasks than men, indicating the multiple roles that women play and the imbalance between work and family roles for women in Chinese society (Cheung & Tang, 2017). Halpern and Cheung (2008) found that working women often have to choose between having children or climbing the corporate/institutional ladder. In the popular press, the media describes this phenomenon as the "mommy track" versus the "career track." The women who choose to have children must be especially creative in being able to combine these two aspects of their lives. Traditionally, men did not have to make the same choices because they married women who were not in the workforce and stayed at home to raise their families.

The prevalence of traditional perspectives on women's roles can be heavily dependent on culture, with some societies adopting gendered institutions more than others. In a study conducted by Kelmendi (2015), women from Kosovo, a region that has a history of traditional and conservative family values, were interviewed. Participants stated they would experience domestic abuse if they began a career of their own, demonstrating that although professional institutions are generally more accepting toward women today, this is also culturally circumstantial. In other words, findings suggested that the patriarchal structure of Kosovan society and culturally defined gender roles may promote violence against women. In addition, a study conducted by Gigerenzer et al. (2014) examined the cultural differences between Germany and Spain. They found that although they vary in degree, gendered institutions still exist in both regions. Therefore, although there has been significant progress for women's rights, many "traditional" assumptions of what a man or woman should do are still very real and present around the world.

Idiocentrism and Allocentrism

Triandis (1995) made a distinction between idiocentrism/allocentrism and individualism/collectivism. Individualism and collectivism are ways of characterizing the dominant perspectives of societies, whereas idiocentrism and allocentrism are ways of characterizing individual values. **Idiocentric values** are based on personal achievement and giving priority to personal rather than group goals. Conversely, **allocentric values** focus on interpersonal values and collective goals. Thus, if individuals are idiocentric in an individualistic society, then their perspective will be in concert with society's perspective. However, if individuals are allocentric in an individualistic society, then their perspective will be at odds with society's perspective.

Because individualism and collectivism reflect a society's dominant modes of interaction, most people in societies are consistent with the society's perspective (i.e., individualistic societies have more idiocentric individuals in their respective societies, and collectivistic societies have more allocentric individuals in their respective societies). However, a certain percentage of people find themselves mismatched with respect to their society's perspective. Triandis (1995) calls these people **countercultural individuals**:

> Thus, in collectivist societies there are idiocentrics, who look for the earliest opportunity to escape the "oppression" of their ingroups, and in individualistic societies there are allocentrics, who reject individual pursuits and join gangs, clubs, communes, and other collectives. The idiocentrics reject conformity to the ingroup and are most likely to leave their culture and seek membership in individualistic cultures. They are also very likely to criticize and object to their culture. (p. 36)

In a widely cited study, Hofstede et al. (2010) examined individualism and collectivism across 79 countries. Western developed countries tend to be individualistic whereas Eastern developing countries are shown to be more collectivist. Japan was in the middle position of these two dimensions. The United States ranked highest in individualism, with Australia, England, Canada, the Netherlands, and New Zealand rounding out the top six countries. In a meta-analysis, Taras et al. (2012) examined individualism and collectivism across 49 countries. They reported that Sweden was ranked highest in individualism, followed by the Netherlands, New Zealand, Australia, Israel, and Spain. In fact, 15 of the most individualistic countries are what we would consider Western countries because all are in Europe or are predominantly White former British colonies (the United States, Canada, Australia, and New Zealand). Central America ranked lowest in individualism, which was closely followed by Arab countries and Malaysia.

Hofstede (1980; 2011), Mooij and Hofstede (2010), and Shi and Wang (2011) also categorize countries according to what Hofstede terms a **masculine–feminine dimension**, depending on the degree of power distance within the society. A country in which there is a great deal of power distance between people who are high in authority and people who are not in authority is labelled a masculine country; a country in which there is less power distance between these two points in the authority hierarchy is labelled a feminine country. Triandis (1995) describes this dimension as a horizontal–vertical dimension. Figure 3.1 depicts this dimension.

Triandis (1995) devised four statements on a scale to measure the degree to which people are horizontally individualistic ("One should live one's life independently of others"), vertically individualistic ("It is important to me that I do my job better than others would do it"), horizontally collectivistic ("My happiness depends very much on the happiness of those around me"), and vertically collectivistic ("I would sacrifice an activity that I enjoy very much

---

idiocentric values Values based on personal achievement and giving priority to personal goals and individualistic tendencies that reside within an individual.

allocentric values Values based on interpersonal achievement and collective goals and tendencies that reside within an individual.

countercultural individuals Idiocentric individuals residing in a collectivistic culture or allocentric individuals residing in an individualistic culture.

masculine–feminine dimension A continuum of authority from hierarchical (masculine) to egalitarian (feminine), also known as power distance by Hofstede (1980).

if my family did not approve of it") (Figure 3.1). In other words, the horizontal dimension places everyone at or near the same level, so the horizontally individualistic statement sees everyone as being equal and having an equal opportunity to live independent of others, whereas the horizontally collectivistic statement sees one person's happiness as being a shared (collective) experience. The vertical dimension deals with hierarchical structures of societies, so the vertically individualistic statement reflects competition, with each person trying to outdo others, whereas the vertically collectivistic statement reflects the requirement that the individual accede to the collective's desires and the belief that family is more important than the individual. A good example of these differences is how students greet others in different places. In Canada, we are more horizontal in our greetings, so students may say hello to professors by saying things like, "Hey there, Dr Safdar" or "How's it goin', Dr Safdar?" or simply "'Sup?" However, in Latin American countries, one might say to friends and peers, "¿Como estas?" or "¿Que tal?" but one would never greet an elder or a professor in such an informal manner, instead saying "¿Como esta usted?" which is a formal greeting.

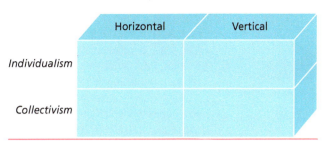

Figure 3.1 Triandis's (1995) individualism–collectivism and horizontal–vertical dimensions.

Many students are intrigued by the vertical dimension. Although it applies to their lives, they have never had a word to categorize their experiences. The following is a reaction we have received from a student:

> I am from a Filipino background where everything is centred on the family. For example, a family member's achievement in work, school, etc. can be looked at as the family's accomplishment. In other words, successes and failures from each family member are representative of the family as a whole. One way that I see this as an advantage is that because the family works together, each member encourages, supports, and helps the others. So in this type of family there is great social support. The disadvantage to this is that when one member of the family fails at something, the family as a whole is also seen as a failure, as well. So there is increased pressure to do well and accomplish goals. And this in turn may put a strain on the relationship between parent and child.
>
> A second advantage (vertical collectivism) is the fact that when parents become older and their own children grow up, their children take them into their homes and care for them, compared to other families where the parents are set up in retirement homes or their own homes (where they care for themselves) or convalescent homes (where other people care for them). The disadvantage to this is that when parents are living in the homes of the children, boundaries are unclear. The relationship changes from parent/child to parent/adult child. And when the transition isn't smooth, there could also be a strain on their relationship.
>
> —Ann Marie, 20+-year-old Filipina-American student

As Ann Marie indicates, there can be disadvantages to the collectivistic perspective, particularly the vertical collectivistic perspective. Because part of this orientation involves respect for one's elders and for individuals in authority, one may feel victim to the desires of people in authority. The following quote comes from a woman who spoke about how she hid her relationship from her parents because she strongly believed that her parents would not approve of her boyfriend.

> Being both Muslim and South Asian, it wasn't acceptable for a moderately religious girl to have a boyfriend. I had always been connected to both my culture and my faith, so when I did get a boyfriend, it was kind of like an identity shock. . . . He was Desi, but he wasn't Muslim. Even then, he still understood that I couldn't tell my parents anything and that we had to pursue our relationship in secret. . . .
>
> Fast forward a year and a half. . . . My dad began talking. . . . "Are you with a boy? Do you have boyfriend? Don't lie to me." . . . My dad started screaming and pacing around the room. . . .
>
> My boyfriend understood that it was time for us to part ways. . . . This relationship was hands down my biggest regret just because of the unnecessary pain and trouble it caused to my loved ones around me.
>
> —Anonymous, Desi Muslim–American immigrant (Anonymous, 2016)

Remember, individualism and collectivism are general terms that describe general feelings or choices when personal and collective choices are in conflict. The vertical collectivistic choices that the Muslim woman made were not without the anguish of her idiocentric feelings. If you were in her shoes and had selected a path that was more idiocentric, this would not mean that you did not feel allocentric tugs at your heartstrings.

Guilt versus Shame

guilt A negative emotion that involves an individual's sense of personal regret for having engaged in a negative behaviour.

In individualistic societies, **guilt** is a prominent negative emotion. In fact, psychoanalytic theory places guilt as one of the fundamental ways of punishing ourselves for violations of cultural expectations (Brenner, 1982). According to psychoanalytic theory, our behaviours are a result of the compromise formation. In this formula, the id wants to express a drive (sexual or aggressive), the ego employs a defence mechanism to express that drive, and the superego evaluates the defence mechanism. If the defence mechanism expresses the drive in a socially appropriate manner, then we feel good and fulfilled. If the drive is expressed in a socially inappropriate manner, then we are punished through depression or anxiety. Guilt is at the core of both depression and anxiety.

shame A negative emotion that involves an individual's sense of regret for having engaged in a negative behaviour that reflects badly on that individual's family.

Collectivistic (particularly Asian) societies tend to place more emphasis on **shame** as a motivating negative emotion (La Ferle et al., 2019; Sommers, 2012; Sue & Sue, 2016; van de Vijver et al., 2011). Whereas guilt is more of an individualistic notion in which someone does something wrong and feels guilty about it, shame is a more collectivistic concept wherein the offending behaviour is a reflection of one's upbringing or community. As Shon and Ja (1982) put it, "Shame and shaming are the mechanisms that traditionally help reinforce societal expectations and proper behaviour. The East Asian concept of *tiu lien* (loss of face) embodies the social concept of shame" (p. 214). This distinction between guilt and shame seems to resonate with many of our Asian students:

> Thinking about the concept of shame, I remember that we have a phrase that is similar to "shame on you," but the pronoun "you" is replaced with "people." It applies in situations where one has made a mistake. This phrase clearly indicates the notion that the mistake not only arouses guilty feelings but also brings shame to the family, and it is commonly used for children so as to let them know they should not make mistakes again and should prevent "loss of face" in the family.
>
> —Veronica, 20+-year-old Hong Kong–American immigrant student

Western cultures tend to emphasize guilt, whereas Eastern cultures tend to emphasize shame.

Face Saving, Face Giving, and Social Support

As the preceding discussion indicates, shame is related to a sense of regret for a behaviour that reflects badly on one's family. This is related to the concept of **losing face**, which is to lose respect and to suffer humiliation because of one's behaviour. An important social skill in collectivistic/Asian societies is the ability to help those with whom one is interacting to save face if they make a social mistake (Tao, 2017; Zane & Ku, 2014; Zane & Yeh, 2002). For example, Tao (2017) investigated the perception of face and politeness among Chinese and Japanese university students. Tao found that a majority of Chinese and Japanese students believe that **saving face** is very important when they interact with other people. In a study by Leong et al. (2011), the relationship between attitudes toward psychological help-seeking and loss of face, and conception of mental health was examined. Participants were American-Asian university students, including Chinese, Japanese, Korean, and Vietnamese Americans. The results indicated that concern about the loss of face and mental health conception are significantly related to participants' attitudes toward psychological help-seeking behaviour. Specifically, the researchers found that the higher concern over loss of face is negatively correlated with mental help–seeking behaviour among Asian-American students. Participants who scored high on shame and loss of face were not tolerant of the stigma attached to seeking psychological service and do not discuss their problems (Leong et al., 2011).

Most people are aware of the notion of losing face/saving face. One strategy to avoid losing face is to not stick out from the collective or otherwise leave oneself open to criticism from the group (Kitayama & Markus, 1999; Kitayama et al., 1997; Kitayama et al., 2004; Kitayama & Uchida, 2003; Markus & Kitayama, 1991).

In contrast, most people are not aware of the notion of **face giving/giving face** (Lim, 1994; Ting-Toomey, 2005; Ting-Toomey & Cocroft, 1994). Face giving is praising the virtues of another in public. In collectivistic societies, it is generally inappropriate or deemed to be overly drawing attention to oneself to talk about one's accomplishments. It is much more culturally appropriate to be humble about one's accomplishments and allow someone else to let others know about them. This allows one's self-esteem to be uplifted without seeming to toot one's own horn. For example, let's say that you have won a prestigious award but you are in a setting where most people do not know about the award. In Canada, you might say something like, "I was honoured and humbled to win this award." Even though you say that in a reserved

losing face To lose respect and to suffer humiliation because of one's behaviour.

saving face To avoid humiliation and losing respect by adopting social skills and strategies.

face giving/giving face Praising the virtues of another person in public.

Face giving is a common practice in Asian cultures.

manner, Asian groups still see it as inappropriate bragging. In Asian groups, it is much more appropriate to say nothing about your award, but because some people may know about it, someone else is expected to announce to the group that you have won the award. You can then express your humility about receiving it. This other person is engaging in face giving.

Notice that in face giving, your collective still knows about your award, your esteem is raised in the group, and your own self-esteem is increased. Kitayama and Markus (2000) discussed this in terms of how one gains happiness and subjective well-being through one's social relations. They suggest that in individualistic societies, good feelings are "owned" by individuals and people connect with others by discussing their good feelings with one another. This is seen as a personal property that the two interacting individuals may share with each other. In East Asian cultures, happiness and good feelings are the property of the interpersonal atmosphere, so the feelings are in the relationship between the two interacting individuals, not within each individual. Thus, one can see the importance of face giving in collectivistic societies. If one brags about one's own accomplishments, there is a bad feeling in the air; if one gives face to another, there is a good feeling in the air, and the two are drawn closer together through the process of empathy.

3.2 Are We WEIRD?

In examining cultures across the world, one must wonder whether the Western way of thinking is unusual. In a series of publications, some researchers concluded that we really are WEIRD, an acronym standing for Western, Educated, Industrialized, Rich, and Democratic (Henrich et al., 2010, 2016; Jones, 2010). To the extent that most psychologists, hence psychological researchers, are from Western-oriented countries—particularly the United States—the research that emerges from these countries is biased toward individuals who fit the WEIRD profile. In fact, Arnett (2008) calculated that 95 per cent of the empirical papers published in the six top journals in psychology were published in Western countries (68 per cent from the United States and 27 per cent from the United Kingdom, Canada, Australia, New Zealand, and the rest of Europe). However, the continents of Asia, Africa, and South America have a much larger population than the continents of North America, Europe, and Australia. Hence, much of our knowledge is WEIRD in that it has been conducted on a minority of people in the world—a minority that is predominantly individualistic as opposed to collectivistic in orientation. How do you think that this might affect the way in which we perceive the world?

3.3 Models of Value Orientation and World View

Values are important characteristics of human societies and culture (Hofstede, 1984, 2001; Rokeach, 1980, 1981; Schwartz, 1994). Early researchers (Rockeach, 1973; Rokeach & Cochrane, 1972; Rokeach & McLellan, 1972) argued that values are mechanisms that are socially developed and influence people's behaviour. For example, Rokeach (1973) found that when people's values are not aligned with values of their peers or of the broader society, they are more likely to change their values to match the society's values. The same finding has also been

Kluckhohn and Strodtbeck's Value Orientation Model

As Sue and Sue (2003) have pointed out, Kluckhohn and Strodtbeck (1961) present a model of world view based on value orientation. They identify four dimensions and examine how different groups responded to those dimensions. Table 3.1 presents these dimensions and value orientations.

Past, present, and future **time focus** are self-evident. However, the other value orientations probably need explanation. In the **human activity dimension**, *being* refers to being accepted for what you are. *Being and in becoming* means that you are motivated to become something more than what you are right now: you must nurture your inner self to realize your potential. *Doing* refers to the value of activity. If you work hard, you will eventually be rewarded.

In the **social relations dimension**, lineal orientation is related to our earlier discussion of a vertical relationship, in which there is a hierarchy of authority. Collateral orientation suggests that we should respect the opinions of our family and our friends when encountering problems, so this term is related to our earlier discussion of collectivism. Individualistic orientation is the same as individualism.

Finally, **people/nature relationship** refers to how people relate to nature. Subjugation to nature refers to one's submission to external forces, such as God, fate, and biology. Harmony with nature suggests that people should try to be in harmony with nature, allowing nature to be dominant in some circumstances and trying to overcome nature in other circumstances. Mastery over nature refers to trying to conquer and control nature.

These dimensions can differ across different racial/ethnic groups (Danylova, 2014; Jiang, 2015; Watkins & Gnoth, 2011). In a wonderful example of Indigenous value orientation, Trimble (2003) discusses a classroom exercise he conducted with his students. This exercise demonstrated to students that attachment to personally valued items is ephemeral for many Indigenous groups, particularly in the Pacific Northwest US. It also demonstrates how one might feel when left out of a collective activity. Because of the ephemeral (or permanent) nature of our attachment to objects, the exercise helps to demonstrate the time orientation dimension discussed in Kluckhohn and Strodtbeck's (1961) study.

> To demonstrate the value of sharing—and the nature of the Potlatch system of the northwest coast tribes in Canada and the United States—I ask students to bring something of value to the next class meeting and inform them that they may have to give it to someone else. At the beginning of that class, I arrange the students in a circle, and one by one I

time focus An orientation that values a particular time perspective. Some cultures value the past, some value the present, and some value the future. Although all cultures value all three, some cultures value one of these perspectives more than do other cultures.

human activity dimension The distinction among being, being and in becoming, and doing.

social relations dimension The distinction among lineal, collateral, and individualistic. Lineal orientation is a respect for the hierarchy within one's family. Collateral orientation is essentially the same as collectivism, and individualistic orientation is the same as individualism.

people/nature relationship Refers to how people relate to nature and includes subjugation to nature, harmony with nature, and mastery over nature.

TABLE 3.1 Kluckhohn and Strodtbeck's Value Orientation Model

Dimension	Value orientations		
1. Time focus	Past	Present	Future
2. Human activity	Being	Being and in becoming	Doing
3. Social relations	Lineal	Collateral	Individualistic
4. People/nature	Subjugation	Harmony with nature	Mastery over nature

Source: Kluckhohn and Strodtbeck (1961).

> have them place their valued possession in the circle's centre. Students then are asked to pick out their valued possession and give it to someone else in the circle, someone whom they respect and wish to honour for their value to the group (the instructor does not participate in the distribution process). Outcomes differ from one class to another. On some occasions, a few students do not receive recognition or gifts, and discussion can become spirited as they attempt to deal with being overlooked. Discussions invariably gravitate to the difference between the reciprocity norm and sharing one's possessions without expecting to receive anything in return. (Trimble, 2003, p. 230)

Can you imagine giving someone one of your prized possessions? Can you imagine doing this and not receiving anything in return? As these questions imply, people in Canada, the United States, and the UK seem to have an attachment to material possessions. Is this true throughout the world? Yes and no. As explained by Dominko and Verbič (2020), there is conflicting evidence on whether income has a positive or negative effect on happiness at a national level. Specifically, the Easterlin paradox, proposed by Richard Easterlin, a US economist, states that although happiness and income correlate positively, at a certain point, the increase in income does not lead to an increase in happiness.

It has also been suggested that, at a micro level, a higher income in a developed nation can slightly increase happiness over time. However, an important cultural factor that influences happiness is the political standing of a nation, since this determines the daily way of life for its citizens. For instance, for Europeans aged 50 and above, it was found that income may have an impact on subjective well-being based on the presence or absence of social and health-care benefits provided by the state (Dominko & Verbič, 2020). These benefits may include welfare and being able to afford proper physical and mental health care. The influence of social and health-care support on subjective well-being is particularly impactful for older people since these benefits become more and more crucial with age. This makes sense since the reliance on income for daily needs is more or less strong depending on the amount of help individuals are given. Moreover, some research suggests that nations that value leisure over intensive work (i.e., time over money) report higher subjective well-being (Macchia & Whillans, 2019). Such nations include the Netherlands, the UK, and Australia, where there is a high value on leisure and thus a high life satisfaction rate. All of this is to suggest that happiness is not only dependent on wealth when factors such as social relationships and support are also important determinants in most cultures.

Schwartz's Theory of Human Values

Shalom H. Schwartz proposed a universal set of values and described them as desirable goals that are important in guiding people's lives (1994). Societies and cultural groups play an important role in prioritizing which values are important (Schwartz, 2011). Consensus among cultural group members on the degree of importance of certain values increases group stability, co-operativeness, and functionality (Adair et al., 2013).

Schwartz's (1994) original value framework was tested in 44 countries from all continents, with a sample size of over 25,000 participants. Ten broad personal values were identified (Schwartz, 1994):

1. Achievement
2. Benevolence
3. Conformity

4. Hedonism
5. Power
6. Security
7. Self-direction
8. Stimulation
9. Tradition
10. Universalism

Achievement values are associated with ambition, competence, and success. Benevolence values are associated with helpfulness, enhancing welfare of others, and forgiveness. Conformity values are related to self-discipline, restraining impulses, and honouring parents/elders. Hedonism values are associated with pleasure and gratification for oneself and of life. Power values are related to social status, prestige, wealth, and authority. Security values are associated with safety, social order, and societal and family security. Self-direction values are related to independence, freedom, and creativity. Stimulation values are associated with excitement, novelty, and adventure. Tradition values are related to respect and acceptance of traditional customs and religion. Lastly, universalism values are associated with open-mindedness, appreciation, and tolerance of all people and environments (Calvez, 2014; Cleveland et al., 2011).

Schwartz's theory argues that these values have dynamic relations with one another (1994). That is, some values are compatible, while some are in conflict. For example, the hedonism value is compatible with the stimulation and achievement values, but it is in conflict with the tradition and conformity values. Figure 3.2 provides a schematic presentation of the 10 personal values. The values that are close to one another are compatible, as they share similar motivation. The values that are farther apart from one another are in conflict, as their underlying motivations are incompatible.

In Figure 3.2, the circumplex consists of two bipolar dimensions. One dimension captures the conflict between conservation values (i.e., security, conformity, and tradition) and openness to change values (i.e., self-direction and stimulation). This dimension highlights the distinction between values that emphasize order and self-restriction versus values that emphasize independence of thoughts and readiness for change (Schwartz, 2012). The second dimension captures the conflict between self-transcendence values (i.e., universalism and benevolence) and self-enhancement values (i.e., achievement and power). This dimension highlights the distinction between values that emphasize concern for welfare of others versus values that emphasize the pursuit of one's own interests (Schwartz, 2012).

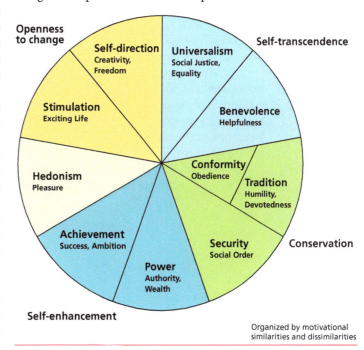

Figure 3.2 Schwartz's two dimensions position values in a circumplex value model.

Source: Reproduced with permission from Schwartz, S.H., Caprara, G.V. and Vecchione, M. (2010), Basic Personal Values, Core Political Values, and Voting: A Longitudinal Analysis. *Political Psychology*, 31: 421-452. https://doi.org/10.1111/j.1467-9221.2010.00764.x

The Schwartz value theory has been highly influential in psychology as he established the individual-level value framework. Other works, such as Hofstede's value framework (2001), were developed as a national-level phenomenon (Calvez, 2014). Schwartz's 10 broad values can be used to describe people's attitudes, beliefs, and behaviours. In a large national study of Canadian employees, it was found that participants endorse universalism, benevolence, and self-direction as top values (Lyons et al., 2005). Similarly, studies of university students in Ontario found that benevolence, achievement, and hedonism were rated as the most important values by participants (Cleveland et al., 2011; Lan et al., 2010). However, a survey of university students in Saskatchewan found that conformity, power, and tradition were highly endorsed by participants (Calvez, 2008). The results of these studies indicate that value priorities vary across Canada and across different age groups (Calvez, 2014).

Derald Wing Sue's World View Model

Derald Wing Sue, a professor of psychology at Columbia University in the US, is one of the most prolific and influential authors in the cross-cultural arena. In fact, he and his two brothers (Stanley and David) have all contributed heavily to this literature. Some time ago, Derald Wing Sue (1978) proposed a model of a person's world view that examined the intersection of **locus of control** and **locus of responsibility** (see Figure 3.3). Both dimensions vary along an internal–external continuum. Thus, a person can have an internal locus of control, an external locus of control, an internal locus of responsibility, or an external locus of responsibility. When crossed, these two dimensions yield four forms of world view.

People with an internal locus of control and an internal locus of responsibility (IC–IR) world view, or Quadrant I in the model in Figure 3.3, believe that they have control over their lives and that their position in life is based on their own attributes. This is the dominant view in Canada. We can control our own lives because of our own abilities. In investigating norms and behaviours around the world, such a view is often associated with people from individualistic cultures rather than collectivistic or group-oriented societies. As stated earlier, individualism tends to be a characteristic of Western populations. The popular belief is that individuals have freedom and autonomy over their own actions, and people are responsible for their own outcomes, whether they are positive or negative (Chen & Hong, 2015).

People with an external locus of control and an internal locus of responsibility (EC–IR) world view, or Quadrant II in the model, have little control over their lives, yet accept the dominant society's view that they are responsible for their position. D. W. Sue and Sue (2003, 2008, 2013, 2016) cite Stonequist's (1937) concept of the marginal man (person) to describe these individuals. They feel caught between two worlds, yet they do not see racism as having any relevance to their position in life.

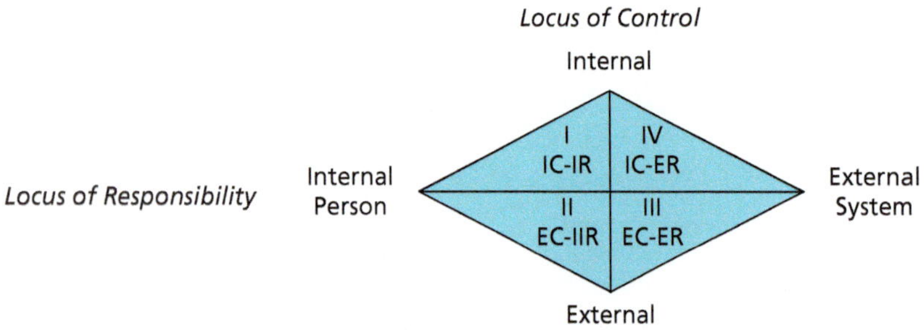

People with an external locus of control and an external locus of responsibility (EC–ER) world view, or Quadrant III in

locus of control A psychological concept referring to the perception of having control over outcomes of one's life, be it internal or external control.

locus of responsibility A psychological concept referring to the perception of having responsibility for one's position in life, be it internal feelings of responsibility or external, societal responsibility.

Figure 3.3 Derald Wing Sue's (1978) World View model.

Source: Reproduced with permission from Eliminating Cultural Oppression in Counseling: Toward a General Theory, by D. W. Sue, 1978, Journal of Counseling Psychology, 25.

the model, have little control over their lives and feel that the dominant societal system is against them. This is a recipe for disaster, and individuals often give up trying to succeed. Seligman's (1982) notion of learned helplessness is often associated with this quadrant. This concept suggests that people can become depressed because they have learned that no matter what they do, something bad will happen, or that they cannot predict their environment, so life seems meaningless. When a system of racism constantly assaults people, they often give up and develop a world view in which they are powerless to make changes.

Finally, people with an internal locus of control and an external locus of responsibility (IC–ER) world view, or Quadrant IV in the model, believe that they have strong personal abilities and could control their lives if the system of oppression and racism were not preventing them from realizing their full potential. Sue and Sue (2016) suggest that these individuals take pride in their ethnicities and strongly identify with their own ethnicity and those of others who see the injustices in the world.

One's experience with racism determines whether one develops an EC–ER world view or an IC–ER world view. Nagata and Takeshita (1998), in their examination of Japanese Americans who were interned during World War II, reported the reactions of some of their Nisei (children who were interned with their Japanese immigrant parents) research participants. After growing up, one participant volunteered for the US Army to fight in the war effort. He explains:

> It [the internment] affected me, my self-esteem, that they would think that of me. . . . You feel like "I'll show you that you're wrong!" That's part of what drove me to do what I did [volunteer for the army]. (p. 599)

Thus, his feeling of disempowerment from a racist system drove him to prove that he had some degree of control over his life.

Another example shows reliance on an internal locus of control instead of leading toward learned helplessness by an immigrant in response to racism:

> I came to Australia in my late twenties and during the days of bad racism. You saw it in lots of places—on the bus, train, at work. There was one woman at work, she always gave me a hard time, just always criticizing my work, and I know it's because I am Filipina. She thinks I'm inferior because I'm from a third-world place. You know what I did? I worked hard so I can get ahead of her. You use your brains with these people. I'm educated, you know. I graduated as one of the top of my college in the Philippines, and then I took courses here. You show your skills to them. She never said anything again once I was promoted above her. (Aquino 2016)

Thus, many individuals who had little exposure to racism seemed to take the internment experience very hard and developed an EC–ER world view. The people with this world view had the most difficult time adjusting to internment and may have even developed depression or other forms of difficulties at the time of removal from their homes. In contrast, many people who had actively experienced the racism around them seemed to understand that this was an oppressive system against which they had to resist, and they seemed to develop an IC–ER world view, knowing that they had their own abilities and that those abilities must be used to fight the system of oppression or to prove their worth to their oppressors. The effects of the Japanese-American internment experience can still be felt today (Mio et al., 2007; Nagata, 1990a, 1990b, 1993, 1998).

3.4 World Views of Different Ethnic Groups

We discuss issues of racism and related terms more extensively in Chapter 6, but here we address the issue of ethnic minority status in the development of an individual's world view. As D. W. Sue's (1978) model suggests, this issue is very important in shaping one's view of the world.

Although Canada is generally considered a multicultural nation, there is still a distinction between ethnic minority and majority groups across the country. Research conducted by Maiter et al. (2012) with minority youth revealed that many of them agree with the multicultural notion of Canada. However, they often undermine or fail to identify their own experiences of racism. While living in a majority-dominated nation, it is easier to accept the view of Canada as having no ethnic inequality (Maiter et al., 2012). Specifically, participants did not identify an experience as racism at first and had other explanations for the behaviour, but after further discussion, they tended to recognize the racist behaviour. Not recognizing racism encourages further silence on inequality (Maiter et al., 2012).

Although the ethnicities of the majority and minority group will differ around the globe (for example, Chinese are the dominant group in Hong Kong but a minority group in Canada), patterns of exclusion tend to be the same (e.g., the majority group marginalizes members of the minority group) (Kwan et al., 2018). Often, discrimination is amplified in times of extremism and political unrest, which can affect the well-being of minorities. In fact, many minority groups face inequality in accessing mental health services or find it difficult to be treated because of cultural or language barriers (Bhui et al., 2018).

Some individuals are referred to as **White ethnics**: individuals whose families have either recently emigrated from Europe or held on to their European origin identification. A good example of the latter use of the term can be seen in celebrations of St Patrick's Day in Canada and the US. People of Irish background "put on their Irish hats" and engage in more Irish activities and mannerisms than they normally display. What distinguishes European immigrants from visible minorities (e.g., Black Canadians, Chinese, Indigenous Peoples) is that European immigrants can blend into society and be indistinguishable from European Canadians who have been in this country for several generations. However, visible minorities cannot blend into the mainstream this way because their physical features (e.g., skin colour, hair texture, eye shape) distinguish them from the European-Canadian population. Therefore, visible minorities may experience racism or even just be thought of as different from the norm, which, in turn, can have a profound influence on their world views.

In a benign example of different world views, an African-American professor talked about her daughter's closest friend in her daycare school:

> It's interesting. . . Allie's best friend at her daycare is Rebecca. Allie is the only African American child in the daycare, and Rebecca is the only Asian American girl, and somehow they seem to know that they are the most different from the other children, so they have become close. I don't know if the other children or the daycare workers actually treat them differently, but they just seem to know that they are different.
>
> —*Linda, 30+-year-old African-American professor*

Another example shows an exchange between a woman of colour and her White doctor, illustrating subtle racism that exists due to skin colour (Hutcherson, 2017):

White ethnics Individuals whose families have either recently emigrated from Europe or held on to their European origin identification.

Woman of colour: *I need to send an immunization report to my college so I can matriculate.*
Doctor: *Where are you going?*
Woman of colour: *Harvard.*
Doctor: *You mean the one in Massachusetts?*

The same woman experienced a similar instance while she was in a store, picking up supplies for school.

Store employee: *Where are you going?*
Woman of colour: *Harvard.*
Store employee: *You mean the one in Massachusetts?*

A third instance happened at a United Parcel Service (UPS) store, where the woman was sending boxes to school. She stood in line behind a White male sending items to Princeton. There was also a White woman in front of her.

White woman (to the boy): *What college are you going to?*
Boy: *Princeton.*
White woman: *Congratulations!*
White woman (to the woman of colour): *Where are you sending your boxes?*
Woman of colour: *Harvard.*
White woman: *You mean the one in Massachusetts?*

These exchanges illustrate the underlying racism due to skin colour of the woman who was enrolled at Harvard University.

Some researchers have suggested that major motion pictures can have a huge influence on our perspectives and identities (Greenwood & Long, 2015; Tan & Visch, 2018; Young, 2012). Essentially, these authors indicate that such films invite audience members to co-create a world with the filmmakers in creating a vision of imaginary worlds with implications for real life. Greenwood and Long (2015) go so far as to say that movies can give adolescents life lessons and character role models and help them understand social relations. However, as Erigha (2016) points out, ethnic minority filmmakers have been systematically shut out of the world of science fiction. This has the dual effect of keeping such filmmakers from some of the most lucrative positions in Hollywood and failing to provide children with a representation in film of powerful African Americans.

Similarly, Indigenous artists in Canada have been excluded from the arts (McCuaig, 2012; Michelin, 2017).

A Reggae Lane mural by artist Adrian Hayles in Toronto's Little Jamaica neighbourhood.

The movie *Black Panther* is seen as a breakthrough in American cinema as it gave Black kids a superhero they could look up to who looks like them.

Michelin explains that not only were Indigenous Peoples wronged in the past by having their rights and land taken away from them, but they are also still being left out of art institutions in Canada. Results from a survey conducted in 2017 on the number of art professionals in Canada showed that Indigenous Peoples make up only a small proportion (Maranda, 2017 as cited in Michelin, 2017). Out of 184 art professional respondents, approximately 92 per cent identified as Caucasian, compared to only 4 per cent identifying as Indigenous (Maranda, 2017 as cited in Michelin, 2017). These findings suggest a lack of employment for Indigenous curators and a lack of funding for Indigenous art (Michelin, 2017). Conversely, curators and directors involved in decision-making for the display of art are mostly White, which means that Indigenous perspectives are missing in art institutions, resulting in a lack of Indigenous art (Dickenson & Martin, 2020). In addition, Indigenous artists are also frequently asked to work for free when creating art (Michelin, 2017).

Furthermore, Jamaican music in Canada is being left out of the music world, even though Toronto has one of the most populated Jamaican communities in the world (McCuaig, 2012). Specifically, Jamaican music in Canada has also been used by mainstream artists without recognition of its origins (McCuaig, 2012). This is frustrating for individuals with Jamaican heritage because music groups that were predominately White from the 1980s received large amounts of fame and money for their reggae music, whereas Black people today don't get nearly as many opportunities to succeed for their reggae music (McCuaig, 2012).

White privilege The socio-economical advantages that Caucasians receive in society.

As we will discuss in Chapter 6, there is a notion of **White privilege** in Canadian society. *White privilege* means that those who are Caucasian can assume that characterizations and images of them will appear widely in the society. People of colour—including Black people, Indigenous Peoples, and immigrants—cannot assume the same thing, particularly with respect to positive images. Ryan Coogler, the African-American director of *Black Panther*, indicated that when he was growing up and it came time to wear a costume for Halloween, there were no superhero costumes representing someone who was Black (Johnson, 2018).

It has been reported that the characters that children see on TV in terms of age, gender, and ethnic characteristics are out of sync with the real world (Dobrow, Gidney, & Burton, 2018). In particular, children see fewer female, Black, Chinese, and Hispanic characters. Researchers conducted a study on ethnic characters in children's television shows and found that bad guys in these shows tend not to be Americans:

> Stereotypes persist in both how characters are drawn and how they talk, with "bad guys" using non-American accents and dialects. We see this in characters like Dr. Doofenshmirtz from *Phineas and Ferb* or Nightmare Moon on *My Little Pony: Friendship Is Magic*.

It is important for children to see characters in movies that look and sound like themselves because without it, misrepresentation can lead to identity confusion amongst children who are from underrepresented ethnic groups. (Dobrow et al., 2018)

3.5 Social Expectations and World Views of Women

As we discussed earlier, women's world views are often different from men's, especially regarding safety and work expectations. We discuss sexism more in Chapter 6, but for now, let us examine how issues of sexism and other kinds of societal expectations can colour a woman's world views. This is particularly true for girls and women of colour:

> I think that shadeism is so real. It's such a real, real issue for . . . me and my family. . . . Because your lighter cousins are automatically the prettier cousins. And the darker cousins are automatically—they could be the most gorgeous person on the world, but they are not [considered] pretty, and you see that in the way they're treated, right? Like they obviously they don't get treated the same way. When guys would come around, the light-skin cousins would be ones that are pushed, like my grandma would always want to marry one of my cousins off to every single guy that came [over] because she was lighter skinned and she was considered to be . . . [the] beauty queen in our family. Like people would literally call her the beauty queen, right? And it's interesting, right? 'Cause she was light skinned, but she also dyed her hair blonde, so she looked very, very white, and I think that is one of the reasons that she was considered [a beauty queen]. But . . . for my other cousin, who was very dark skinned. . . you could see it in the way she was treated. . . . They treated her so badly, and . . . made her seem like she was not . . . suitable for anyone, right? So shadeism is such a real thing . . .
>
> —*Amrit, a 20+-year-old Indian-Guyanese-Canadian woman (Dhillon, 2016)*

Other issues also shape women's worlds. Iwamasa and Bangi (2003) discussed mental health issues related to women, including a higher incidence of depression, postpartum depression, and eating disorders. Eating disorders affect women more than men because thinness is considered an important component of feminine beauty. Research has shown that although the rates of eating disorders among women are higher than among men, men are also affected by eating disorders (Afifi et al. 2017; Mitchell et al., 2011; Sams & Keels, 2013). In addition, eating disorders, body dysmorphic disorder, and muscle dysmorphia have been increasing among men (Sams & Keels, 2013). As well, child maltreatment in relation to eating disorders and post-traumatic stress disorder (PTSD) are associated with developing eating disorders such as anorexia nervosa (AN), binge eating disorder (BED), and bulimia nervosa (BN) among men and women (Afifi et al. 2017; Mitchell et al., 2011).

Halpern et al. (2007) examined why science and mathematics fields are often not in women's world views. McLean and Beigi (2016) examined barriers to leadership roles for women. Eagly (2009) found that when engaging in prosocial behaviour, women differ from men in that their helping behaviours tend to be emotionally supportive and sensitive and mostly directed toward those who are close to them, whereas men tend to direct their helping behaviours toward the collective as a whole and use their strength and courage.

Mio and associates (Mio et al., 2003) discussed the impact that violence can have on women's views of the world. It is interesting that violence against men is more often perpetrated by other male strangers and that violence against women is more often perpetrated by their male partners. Thus, women encounter violence in settings where they would expect to find the most love and protection. Imagine how that can change one's world view. Moreover, women encounter sexual harassment in the workplace much more than men do. It has been suggested that there is no safe haven for women because violence against them can occur at home, in the workplace, and in the community (Koss et al., 1994; Rutherford, 2018). Furthermore, men tend not to have a concept of the feelings of vulnerability that women experience in their lives.

At the other end of the emotional spectrum are some gender differences in humour (Crawford, 2003; Ford et al., 2008; Martin, 2007; Mio, 2009; Mio & Graesser, 1991; Rappoport, 2005). One consistent finding is that men tend to prefer more aggressive forms of humour (Mio, 2009; Mio & Graesser, 1991; Rappoport, 2005). As well, a cross-cultural study comparing humour among British, Australian, and American participants found both gender and cultural differences (Martin & Sullivan, 2013). British participants reported a more negative view toward humour than Australians. Conversely, Americans were more likely to use humour in social settings compared to British participants. Gender differences in expression of humour were also found, with men being more likely than women to display humour (Martin & Sullivan, 2013).

Although psychologists often note the differences between men and women, it is important to note that there are more gender similarities than one would expect. In a study conducted by Batalha and colleagues (2011) with Australian and Swedish participants, for example, researchers found more gender similarities on social dominance orientation (SDO) than differences. SDO refers to the tendency of being dominant in group settings, which has been described as a male characteristic. However, the results indicated that depending on context and situation, women showed equal or even higher SDO than men. Similarly, research conducted by Ball et al. (2013) found that there were no significant gender differences in scores for the 13 years of Scholastic Aptitude Test–Math (SAT-M)—despite the perception that men and women are different in their mathematical ability. The researchers argued that many studies on gender differences often have small effect sizes, making it questionable if men and women are really so different after all (Ball et al., 2013).

3.6 World View of LGBTQ2+ Individuals

The world view of lesbian, gay, bisexual, transgender, queer, and two-spirit (LGBTQ2+) individuals still contains a large element of fear and danger (Herek, 2000). Because of heterosexism (discrimination by heterosexuals against non-heterosexuals), LGBTQ2+ individuals do not feel safe in the current environment:

> I first held hands with a boyfriend in public just this past year. I guess he was the first guy I felt strongly enough about to not be ashamed. It was scary. Perhaps it was growing up at a time where homosexuality wasn't talked about. Or maybe it was because it was the first time I felt so in love that I didn't care what anyone else thought.
>
> —Evan S., 28, lives in Madison, US (Phillip, 2018)

Some LGBTQ2+ individuals also feel that they are always on display or are a source of curiosity. This is a reflection of being aware that they are living in the context of a straight world:

> I've always been very comfortable with the fact that I'm gay, but the actual saying the word and wanting to avoid potential awkwardness from a conversation is something that I just . . . yeah, I dread it and I'm not good at it. If people carry on assuming that I'm straight and I don't say something straight away then it can start to feel a bit strange to have to bring it up later down the line.
>
> —Gay male vlogger (Lovelock, 2017)

Many LGBTQ2+ individuals report that others feel that their sexual orientation is their entire identity. It is easy to imagine that an Afro-Caribbean-Canadian woman might have an identity as a woman separate from her Caribbean-Canadian identity (and separate from her combined Caribbean-Canadian-woman identity), but LGBTQ2+ individuals often are seen only through the prism of their sexuality.

In recent years, it has been found that homophobia and discrimination based on sexual orientation and gender identity have shifted to become less overt in nature, but they still exist in society in the form of incivility and microaggressions, which are subtle forms of aggression or discrimination against an individual. A common microaggression that LGBTQ2+ individuals face is the phrase "That's so gay," where the discriminatory intent behind the term *gay* has become more implicit rather than explicit in its use (Nadal et al., 2016). Canada has a long history of LGBTQ2+ struggle and achievement and was the fourth country in the world to legalize same-sex marriage in 2005. However, although Canada may be a model now, it was not in the past.

Since the colonization of North America, the British have always held immense power over the policies that existed in their new colony. Due to this control, Canada's policies reflected those of Britain, including its stance on what was considered "the act of sodomy," which encompassed all same-sex relations that were sexual in nature (Rau et al., 2018). This was an act punishable by death or life imprisonment. As time went on, the laws became increasingly vague, allowing those in law enforcement to make their own discretionary decisions regarding what was considered a "homosexual act," making law enforcement officers constant predators of the LGBTQ2+ community. The individuals charged with these acts would then be considered "sexual predators" or "sexual psychopaths" (Rau, 2018). Eventually, in the mid- to late-1900s, a number of events began changing the public's perceptions of LGBTQ2+ individuals. The extensive punishments for "homosexual acts" were publicly criticized, and, in 1969, under Prime Minister Pierre Trudeau, gay sex was finally decriminalized (Rau et al., 2018).

This was not the end of discrimination, though, and a hard fight still had to be fought. After the Stonewall riots in New York City, where the patrons of a gay bar fought the New York Police Department's (NYPD) attempts to shut down their space, many cities took to protesting the discriminatory laws that still existed in legislation. In 1971, protests began in Ottawa and Vancouver against discrimination of LGBTQ2+ individuals, spreading to other cities like Toronto (Rau, 2019). Once the cause was in the public eye, more people came forth to call for equal treatment and create a community for LGBTQ2+ individuals across the nation, with the first gay publications being released in the early 1970s. Unfortunately, these publications were often victim to court charges for what was considered "advocating pedophilia" and were often in and out of publication (Rau, 2019).

On 5 February 1981, four bathhouses were raided by the Toronto Police, leading to the arrests of almost 300 men. The next day, almost 3000 people smashed windows and set fires in the streets of Toronto and Queen's Park, protesting the detainment of the 300 men, an event that would later be considered the Stonewall of Canada. These raids continued throughout the 1980s and caused very tense relations between the LGBTQ2+ community and the police (Rau et al., 2018).

The 1980s also faced the acquired immune deficiency syndrome (AIDS) crisis, which had a massive impact on the gay community, leading to countless unnecessary deaths from the disease due to the health services' discrimination against the LGBTQ2+ community. Many did not receive appropriate or proper care because health-care providers or health-care services in general were homophobic and held negative judgments toward LGBTQ2+ lifestyles. This led to more proactive protesting on the part of the LGBTQ2+ community to gain equal treatment from the government.

The AIDS epidemic was the cause of a number of discriminatory laws that still exist today. For example, the Canadian Blood Services continues to enforce major restrictions on gay men donating blood. Although the organization once completely barred gay men from donating blood, it revised its rule in 2019, announcing that gay men who have not had sex with another man for at least three months can donate blood (Canadian Blood Services, 2019). It is also important to refer to Canada's blood scandal in early 1980s when about 2,000 Canadians became infected with HIV and thousands were infected with hepatitis C due to tainted blood donation. The scandal led to the Canadian Red Cross Society to lose its control over the blood program in Canada and in 1998 the Canadian Blood Services was established as the new federal agency (CBC, 2013).

The 1990s and the new millennium brought a number of victories for the LGBTQ2+ community in Canada, including ending the ban against gay men and lesbians from joining the military in 1992, the inclusion of the LGBTQ2+ community in applications for refugee status from their origin countries in 1994, and—one of the biggest—the legalization of same-sex marriage in 2005 (Rau et al., 2018).

There are many nations in the world that still criminalize same-sex relations. Until 1934, Russia outlawed same-sex sexual relations, sending over 1000 people to prison annually, which was compounded by the law against sodomy, which was in place until 1993 (Buyantueva, 2018). Lesbian women were subject to psychiatric treatment, as homosexuality was classified as a mental illness. Even these numbers and facts were difficult to find, however, as the KGB (Committee for State Security) and the Russian police kept all LGBTQ2+ affairs top secret (Buyantueva, 2018). Near the end of the twentieth century, increased media attention and academic discussions and questions surrounding homosexuality led to an increased openness toward the subject. Many protests called for the decriminalization of homosexuality, but these protests were limited to few places and were quickly shut down (Buyantueva, 2018). Eventually, due to increased international pressure and awareness, the law banning sodomy was abolished in Russia, and some venues and areas were open for LGBTQ2+ individuals, though not many (Buyantueva, 2018). With the turn of the century, more and more advocacy groups for LGBTQ2+ rights emerged, urging for greater visibility and less discrimination. Unfortunately, even today Russia enforces laws against "gay propaganda," and same-sex marriage is still not recognized by the government (Buyantueva, 2018).

Even in Western developed nations, LGBTQ2+ individuals continue to face an incredible amount of discrimination. The US did not legalize same-sex marriage until 2015 and passed a bill in 2019 that barred trans individuals from joining the army although it was revised in 2021, under Biden's administration

Queer Eye's Jonathan Van Ness identifies as non-binary and has become a strong LGBTQ2+ role model and advocate in North America and beyond.

Kathy Hutchins/Shutterstock

(BBC News, 2021). Many roadblocks still stand in the way for LGBTQ2+ individuals, across cultures and countries, and many changes need to be made to make our cultures truly inclusive. Indeed, the lack of recognition of same-sex marriage has had serious and destructive impact on LGBTQ2+ individuals:

> I braced myself for a rant against same-sex marriage—about how LGBTIQ folk such as myself are terrible and "cruel" parents, and how our son sitting there drawing his dream farm was part of a "stolen generation." . . . People like me are simply not safe in a public space at the moment, especially in the virtual public space of social media. The attacks could come at any time, from anywhere, and so we're wary, on guard—even more than usual. . . . We all know that in some people's minds it's a referendum on whether LGBTIQ folks make good parents, whether we damage the moral foundation of society, whether we cheapen or corrupt revered institutions, whether we as people should be tolerated (or not). Whether we are abominations, crimes against nature—that old story. Marriage equality is just an alibi: we know exactly what this "survey" is about—it's a judgment of our very worth as humans. . . .
>
> —Adapted from *Sydney Morning Herald (Stead, 2017)*

Some LGBTQ2+ individuals must operate in an environment in which they do not know whether they will be accepted or rejected by their families (Hancock, 2003). On the one hand, if they are rejected by their families of origin, think of the world views that may result: because people whom they love and trust the most have rejected them, they may end up not trusting anyone or at least having a very difficult time doing so. On the other hand, those who do accept them may be considered a family of choice as opposed to their family of origin, and, as a result, they may be much more loyal to their family of choice.

Ever since Caitlyn Jenner (formerly Bruce Jenner) announced to the world that she was transgender (Bissinger, 2015), the topic of transgender individuals has been of interest in the broader society. However, there are still not many role models for females transitioning to males. Thus, transgender individuals are still searching for how to develop their respective world views, as Phoebe states:

> Ever since I was little, I was drawn to princesses and pink dolls, and I would pretend I was a female character when we played. My mum thought I was going to be gay: I would get mad when I was told I wasn't a girl. [Being trans before transitioning means] you aren't feeling like yourself. You're trapped. You just want to change your whole self. You lose part of yourself to find yourself again.
>
> Walking down the halls at school [after coming out], I sweat profusely. I would have people debate my gender in front of me, calling me "it," staring at me and posting stuff about me on online.
>
> I tried to keep my head high, though I crumbled really, but I didn't want to stop my transition. Everyone would like to say this is an accepting generation, but it's not. People will throw personal questions at me, expecting me to answer. They'll even ask what I have between my legs. I'm surprised I got this far on this path because it's going to be a rough path. I want to help people to be more confident and show them how to be themselves.
>
> —*Phoebe, 20+-year-old transgender girl from Kitchener, Ontario (McKeon, 2015)*

3.7 World View Based on Social Class and Age

The world view based on social class can vary widely depending on how many resources people have. You might recall from your introductory psychology courses that Abraham Maslow had a theory based on a hierarchy of needs (Maslow, 1970), where one must address one's basic needs (e.g., food, water, safety) before addressing higher needs, such as self-esteem, aesthetics, and self-actualization. People who are in the upper class and are financially secure can feel freer to pursue ways to self-actualize—or realize their highest potential as a person—whereas those who are in the lower classes necessarily are concerned with putting food on the table and a roof over their heads. Such pursuit of very different needs necessarily will lead to different views of the world.

Poverty can have a lasting effect on one's world view. According to the United Nations Report on Poverty, there are 1.3 billion people from a number of first-, second-, and third-world countries who are multi-dimensionally poor. This suggests that their indicators of poverty include decreased health, threat of violence, and low quality of work, taking the concept of poverty further than just wealth (UN Refugee Agency, 2019). A third of these people are children under the age of 10, meaning that poverty will have a massive impact on their lives during critical times in their development (UN, 2019).

People in poverty live with much more daily stress, mainly because they do not have the resources to address these stressors. They have a higher probability of dealing with crime in their neighbourhoods, and they do not have the resources to be able to move to safer neighbourhoods. Moreover, the well-known phenomenon of low-income neighbourhoods being food deserts (Dubowitz et al., 2015), where there are no stores that sell nutritious food, can lead to obesity (because of the consumption of high-fat, processed foods, such as potato chips and cookies) and other health-related problems. Such conditions lead to decreased life expectancy (Chetty et al., 2016) and poor subjective well-being (Clark et al., 2016). Indeed, poverty coupled with race (Boylan et al., 2016; Matthews et al., 2017) can lead to decreased life expectancy because of cardiovascular stress.

Mio and Fu (2017) discuss how poverty colours a person's world view throughout life. Even when people are able to get out of poverty later in life, they may still feel that spending any amount of money is extravagant or wasteful. Lott and Bullock (2007) discuss how teachers might have low expectations for students who they know live in poverty, and how they might discount the opinions of these students and/or their parents, or apply other kinds of stereotypes. To the extent that elementary school has a lasting impact on one's development, these experiences cannot help but impact these children's world views.

At the other end of the spectrum, Joseph Stiglitz (2012), who received the Nobel Prize for Economics, warned against the trend toward widening the wealth gap between the upper and lower levels of economic social class. This gap has widened to the point where "the top .1 per cent receive in a day and a half about what the bottom 90 per cent receives in a year" (Stiglitz, 2012, p. 4). As Stiglitz points out, when people who are poor have even less disposable income, they will no longer be able to purchase the products that the people who are rich and who own companies are trying to sell. An oft-quoted statement from Henry Ford (Ford & Crowther, 1922) declares that he raised the minimum wage of his workers to $5.00 per day—an amount that was extremely generous for that era—so that his workers would have enough money to buy his cars.

An example of different world views from people of substantially different economic classes comes from Paul Krugman (2012), another Nobel Laureate of Economics. He reports that when people protested against the upper 1 per cent of wage earners and the bottom 99 per cent wanted more economic justice, rich investors at the Chicago Board of Trade unsympathetically yelled at the protestors to get jobs and threw applications for McDonald's restaurants at them. This highlights the lack of apparent understanding by some investors of structural barriers that prevent a large segment of the society from having access to resources.

Youth and World View

In the 1980s, nuclear war between the United States and the Soviet Union was a real possibility. The world was viewed as dangerous, and drop drills were routine. In a drop drill, a teacher would say, "Boys and girls, drop!" and children were to duck under their desks, face away from the window, and cover their eyes and the backs of their heads. This drill was to protect children from a nuclear blast in the hopes that some would survive an atom bomb dropped in their proximity, far enough away that they would not be killed by the initial blast but close enough that the concussive wave caused by the nuclear weapon might cause the building to collapse and/or the windows to blow into a classroom.

Youth tend to have a different world view than older generations. Around the world, youth activism is an important part of creating change and re-examining policy and norms. The 2012 Idle No More movement in Canada sparked Indigenous youth to seek reconciliation and solidarity from the Canadian government through a series of political rallies and protests (Friedel, 2015). The activism resulting from this movement is ongoing. First Nations, Métis, and Inuit youth have begun a dialogue across Canada, speaking out about the daily impacts of the colonialism, trauma, and social injustices that they face, both on and off reserves (Freeman, 2019; Friedel, 2015).

There has also been an overwhelming global movement among youth demanding action on climate change policies, most notably through the Fridays for Future campaign. This

Greta Thunberg has emerged as one of this generation's most prominent voices against climate change.

campaign was founded by Greta Thunberg, a teenage Swedish activist who has gained recognition across the globe for her efforts to stop climate change (Hagedorn et al., 2019). Protests such as these have united young people from opposite sides of the world who advocate for the future of the earth and environmental sustainability by putting pressure on politicians. The movement has already raised enormous awareness of the issue and, hopefully, with more time and empowerment, today's youth can encourage changes at an international level. After all, when discussing any type of social movement, the impact of young people can be tremendous. In addition, because the issue affects their future, theirs is a vital and necessary perspective to consider.

Yet a different reality exists for American youth, who live in a world where there is a real possibility that a shooter could roam the hallways of their schools. Cameron Kasky, a student at Marjory Stoneman Douglas High School in Parkland, Florida, who survived the mass shooting that occurred on that campus on 14 February 2018, called his generation "the mass-shooting generation" (Alter, 2018). Alternatively, this generation has also been called Generation Columbine (Toppo, 2018) because the Parkland, Florida, shooting was the 208th shooting since Columbine[1] (Roberts, 2018). Thus, the world of these students involves routine locker searches, bulletproof backpacks, and active-shooter drills (Toppo, 2018). The 208 school shootings occurred in 41 different states and Washington, DC, and they have touched every region of the US except Alaska.

Summary

World views come in many forms. The world looks different depending on whether a person is looking at behaviour and concepts from within a culture or from without. The emic perspective is the perspective from within a culture, and this perspective seems to be more important than the etic perspective, or the perspective from outside the culture being examined. Although both perspectives are important in advancing our scientific knowledge of cultures, often those who view a culture from without impose their own world views on the behaviours of the culture being observed. This can lead to wildly different (and wrong) interpretations of the behaviours.

Perhaps one of the most important distinctions between cultures is the individualism–collectivism dimension. Individualistic societies place more importance on individual rights, whereas collective societies place more value on the desires of the collective. This dimension also exists in conjunction with the horizontal–vertical distinction. Thus, a society can be horizontally individualistic, vertically individualistic, horizontally collectivistic, or vertically collectivistic, depending on the degree to which it is hierarchically structured. The individualism–collectivism distinction has important implications for how one experiences some negative emotions. Individualistic societies tend to place more importance on guilt, whereas collectivistic societies place more importance on shame. Collectivistic societies also tend to place more emphasis on face saving and face giving.

Kluckhohn and Strodtbeck (1961) present a model that examines various dimensions of viewing the world. In combination, cultures, groups, or subgroups can be understood in terms of these value orientations. According to Kluckhohn and Strodtbeck's model, racial/ethnic groups seem to have world views that are much more similar to one another than they are to the middle-class European-Canadian or -American world view. This situation is perhaps a result of similar experiences with racism. Derald Wing Sue's (1978) model of world view seems to combine Kluckhohn and Strodtbeck's model with racism. Women and men develop differing world views because of their experience with sexism and other issues that affect women more than men. However, there are also many similarities between men and women. The world views of LGBTQ2+ individuals may differ from those of non-LGBTQ2+ individuals, particularly about issues of safety. People who are in fundamentally different social economic classes see the world in fundamentally different ways. Finally, the youth of today engage in social justice activism, such as environmental issues and the Idle No More movement in Canada.

FOOD FOR THOUGHT

When one of the authors of this book, Jeffery Scott Mio, attended a conference for deaf people, he felt uncomfortable and out of place. All around him, people were using Sign Language, and although he knew some signs and phrases, the deaf people were signing so fast that he could not keep up with them. As he described this situation, "The silence was deafening." Obviously, these people had no intention of harming him—they were merely communicating with one another. Still, he felt out of place and even a little frightened because his world view was so different from that of the people around him; or, rather, the dominant world view was so different from his own. In thinking about the issues raised in this chapter, recall a situation in which you had a markedly different view of the world from those around you. You probably felt a little uncomfortable or afraid. That is a normal feeling until one begins to understand and appreciate the dominant world view. If you did some reading about this situation or the people in it, you probably felt a little more comfortable and less afraid the next time you encountered it. Did you gain some insight into someone who has entered your world?

Critical Thinking Questions

1. Have your actions ever been misconstrued by another person or a group of people because their assumptions differed from yours? If so, how did that make you feel? What steps did you take to correct their misconception?
2. Have you ever misperceived someone else's actions because you applied your own assumptions, which were different from the other person's? If so, how did you resolve the problem?
3. Would you characterize yourself and your family as allocentric (collectivistic) or as idiocentric (individualistic)? Why? Do you fulfill society's expectation regarding this dimension?
4. What advantages and disadvantages does your world view on collectivism and individualism have when you interact with the society at large?
5. Describe a situation when you engaged in face giving or someone else has given you face. What kind of connection did you feel with that person after the face giving?
6. If you are a person of colour, do you feel you stand out because of your ethnicity/race in certain situations? If you are European Canadian, do you tend to notice when a person of colour is around? How do you feel about this dynamic?

7. Have you ever pretended that you were a superhero of a different race? How did that make you feel?
8. If you are a woman, to what extent is your view of the world markedly different from that of men? If you are a man, to what extent is your view of the world markedly different from that of women?
9. If you are an individual who is LGBTQ2+, how does your world view differ from that of people who are straight? If you are straight, how does your world view differ from that of LGBTQ2+ individuals?
10. If you are an individual who is economically very well off, have you ever tried to live among poor people or volunteered at a soup kitchen? Explain your experience and what you learned.
11. To what extent has Greta Thunberg and her activism affected the way you view the world and climate change?

Note

1   The US Columbine shooting occurred in April 1999 at Columbine High School in Columbine, Colorado. Two students shot and killed twelve fellow students and one teacher.

Azami Adiputera/Shutterstock

4 Cultural Differences in Communication

Learning Objectives

Reading this chapter will help you to:

4.1 understand conventions of conversation;
4.2 identify non-verbal components of communication;
4.3 recognize the differences between high- and low-context communication;
4.4 understand which strategies are appropriate for communicating with diverse populations;
4.5 identify the positive and negative impacts of social media on communication;
4.6 know gender differences in communication; and
4.7 explain cognitive complexities between monolingual and bilingual communicators.

4 Cultural Differences in Communication

Communication, which includes both verbal and non-verbal communication, is an important life skill. It helps us to transfer information and maintain relationships. There are many different ways of communicating. In some societies, overt, direct communication is required. Although most people can understand or interpret implications and other forms of indirect communication, some contexts or some people require direct communication. In this chapter, we discuss issues of communication that can differ across cultural groups and genders.

4.1 Conversational Rules: The Co-operative Principle

British philosopher Paul Grice (1975) proposes a set of conversational rules that guide people's conversations (see Table 4.1). Grice suggests that we all engage in what is called the **co-operative principle**, that is, we strive to communicate with one another sincerely and effectively. He proposed four maxims that guide such conversations: quality, quantity, relevance, and manner.

Kheirabadi and Aghagolzadeh (2012) indicate that the four maxims of quality, quantity, relevance, and manner are considered important linguistic criteria or "news values" for editors and journalists. News values are a set of criteria that impact the selection of a news story as worthy for publication. These four maxims help editors and journalists to decide whether a news story is valuable enough to be published or broadcasted. The scholars present examples from newspapers to support that Gricean maxims (i.e., quality, quantity, relevance, and manner) can be presented as criteria for reporting news. For example, one of the news values criteria is the presentation of statistics or figures, which indicates the accuracy of the news. When journalists present statistics, they are demonstrating that their news has the maxim of quality. A news value related to the maxim of quantity requires the news to be sufficiently informative: neither too short nor too long. A news value related to the maxim of a relation represents news that reports relevant news stories for the target readers. Finally, news values related to the maxim of manner reflect the news that is transparent and lacks ambiguity in the content (Kheirabadi & Aghagolzadeh, 2012).

> **co-operative principle** A psycholinguistic term that assumes that we strive to communicate with one another sincerely and effectively when we engage in a conversation.

The Maxim of Quality

The **maxim of quality** suggests that whenever we engage in a conversation, we strive to be truthful. Because you and I are engaged in a co-operative conversational relationship, you expect me to tell you the truth or give you my honest opinion on the topic we are discussing.

> **maxim of quality** A communicative presumption that suggests that we tell each other the truth when we engage in a conversation.

TABLE 4.1 Grice's Conversational Maxims with Norman and Rummelhart's Additions

Maxim	Brief definition
Quality	Tell the truth.
Quantity	Say about as much as is appropriate for the situation.
Relevance	Stick to the topic.
Manner	Speak to your partner in an appropriate manner.
Relations with conversational partner	Take advantage of your past relationship with your conversational partner; fill in others who may not be privy to your mutual understandings.
Rule violations	Identify when you are breaking one of the conversational maxims.

Source: Grice (1975); Norman and Rummelhart (1975).

If you can never be certain that I am telling you the truth, you may choose to break off our conversation. Alternatively, if you do not know that I am telling you a lie, we are not engaged in a co-operative relationship: I am manipulating you.

The Maxim of Quantity

The **maxim of quantity** suggests that each of us should contribute an appropriate amount to our conversation. In normal conversations, two speakers are generally expected to contribute equally. Have you ever tried to talk with a partner who dominated the conversation, never allowing you to contribute? Did that irritate you? If so, you were irritated because your conversational partner violated the maxim of quantity. However, in some contexts, it is appropriate for one person to dominate the conversation. For example, on talk shows or in television interviews, the interviewee often contributes more to the conversation than the host or interviewer, who asks only brief questions to move the conversation forward. This is also true in therapy, where the client is expected to contribute more to the conversation than the therapist, who mostly listens. What other contexts can you think of in which one partner is supposed to dominate the discussion?

maxim of quantity A communicative presumption that suggests that we contribute an appropriate amount of talk when we engage in a conversation.

The Maxim of Relevance

The **maxim of relevance** suggests that we strive to remain on topic. If we suddenly start talking about baseball during a discussion of cross-cultural psychology, we are violating the maxim of relevance because our utterance does not relate to the topic, even though it may be truthful and of an appropriate length. Some people may go into long digressions when talking, and you may wonder whether they are being relevant. Often these people get back on track and say something that ends up being relevant to the topic, but by the time they get there, they have violated the maxim of quantity. The excerpt below from an interview between Syrian President Bashar al-Assad and German public broadcaster ARD shows how the maxim of relevance can be violated:

maxim of relevance A communicative presumption that suggests that our discussion remains relevant to the conversation.

> **Todenhöfer (T):** *Mr. President, members of the opposition and Western politicians say that you are the main obstacle for peace in Syria. Would you be ready to step down as president if this could bring peace to your country and stop the bloodshed?*
> **Bashar al-Assad (BA) [The Syrian leader]:** *The president shouldn't run away from challenge and we have a national challenge now in Syria. The president shouldn't escape the situation, but from the other side you can stay as president, stay in this position only when you have the public support. So, answering this question should be answered by the Syrian people, by the election not by the president. I can nominate myself, I can run for the election or not run, but to leave or not to leave, this is about the Syrian people.*

The excerpt above shows how Assad flouted the maxim of relevance. Todenhöfer implied that Assad's immediate step-down would bring peace and stop bloodshed in the country. His question was not about the presidential election but, rather, about Assad resigning as president. However, Assad replied that the one to decide the fate of a leader would be the Syrian people through election, not the president himself. However, in order to follow the maxim of relevance, Assad should have indicated whether he would step down. Instead, he consciously made his answer irrelevant to the topic (Ayasreh & Razali, 2018, p. 45).

White (2010) tested a newer model based on Grice's (1975) co-operative principle, but since its development, it has become its own independent framework. White's conversational model is based on relevance theory, which states that in order for the maxim of relevance to be fulfilled, the conversation must have positive cognitive effects (i.e., information must be useful and contribute well to the conversation as a whole) and be relatively easy to understand. Thus, not only does this theory affirm the findings of the co-operative principle, but it creates a whole new level for the model, displaying just how complex everyday communication is between people.

The Maxim of Manner

The **maxim of manner** suggests that people should be clear in their communication and pay attention to normal standards of conduct. This is the broadest maxim and can include a wide range of issues. For example, you would not discuss quantum mechanics with a three-year-old, nor would you speak in a disrespectful manner to someone in a position of authority. You would not talk in an intentionally obscure manner, nor would you shout to someone standing less than a metre in front of you. In Canada and many other Western countries, the appropriate distance between two people engaging in a typical conversation is about half a metre, or arm's length. It would violate the maxim of manner to stand 10 centimetres from that person's face, and it would also be a violation if you were to stand 3 metres away.

Sorokowska et al. (2017) conducted a study with 8943 participants across 42 countries within South America, North America, Southern Europe, Northern Europe, the Middle East, and Asia to examine variability in personal space preferences. Each participant was shown a graph of two figures: A and B. The researchers asked participants to imagine themselves in the position of Figure A and indicate how close Figure B should stand to them. Results revealed that respondents from South America, the Middle East, and Southern Europe required less personal space than their counterparts from Northern Europe, North America, and Asia (Sorokowska et al., 2017). The researchers also found that people preferred different distances across countries depending on gender, age, and the country's temperature (Sorokowska et al., 2017). In particular, women and people residing in colder climates (e.g., Canada) demonstrated a preference to maintain a greater distance with strangers. Older individuals and women were inclined to have more distance with acquaintances. Additionally, people in warmer countries (e.g., Saudi Arabia) and older individuals preferred to keep a greater distance with those they were close to (see Figure 4.1).

The researchers also examined how people from different countries differ in their preference for three types of interpersonal distances: social, personal, and intimate (Figure 4.2). **Social distance** is the distance between individuals during formal interactions; **personal distance** is maintained in interactions with friends; and **intimate distance** is observed between individuals in close relationships. It was found that of the three interpersonal distances, social distance was the longest, while intimate distance was the shortest, with personal distance in between. Overall, the results indicate that a combination of gender, age, and the country's temperature are influential factors on preferred social distances (Sorokowska et al., 2017).

An American professor, James, describes an interesting formality when he made a presentation in Germany:

> I went to Germany the summer after I served as the interim department chair. After my talk, there was a question–answer period. The director of the institute began this period

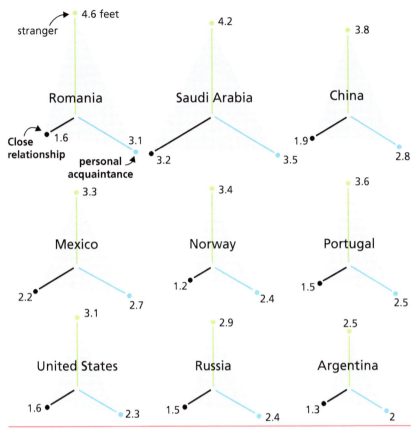

Figure 4.1 Preferred space in interactions with acquaintances, strangers, and close persons across countries.

Source: Sorokowska A, Sorokowski P, Hilper P, et al. 2017. Preferred interpersonal distances: A global comparison. *Journal of Cross-Cultural Psychology, 48*(4), 577–592. © 2017. Reprinted by Permission of SAGE Publications, Inc.

by asking me a question. This guy and very few others asked me questions. After a while, I noticed that some of the other professors were passing notes down the aisle, but they never asked me any questions. When my talk was over, I asked the director of the institute why it was that the other professors were not engaged in the question–answer period. He told me that they actually were engaged, but in Germany, only people at the same level or higher could ask questions, and since I was the director of my institute, only he and a few other directors could ask me questions. The younger professors were writing questions they wanted asked, and they passed these questions down to those who could address me.

—James, 40+-year-old American professor

Such a formal system may not exist in Canada, but we often have informal rules similar to the one described by James. If you work in a large corporation, you may have been told that you must take any questions to your supervisor because the manager or director of the organization cannot be bothered by every question from every employee. In Canada, however, there is more of an egalitarian tradition. People are considered equal, so asking people of different

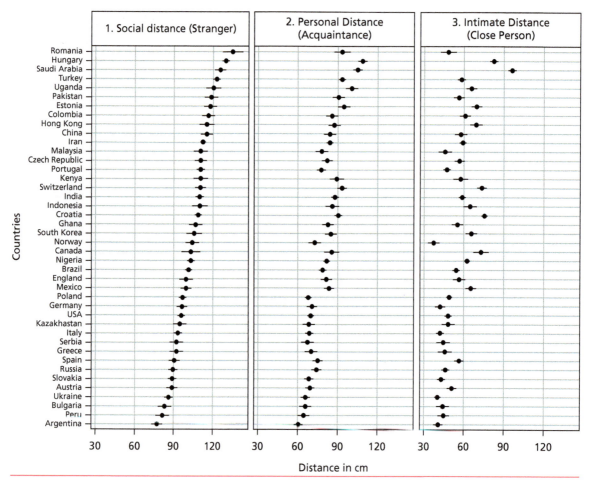

Figure 4.2 Those from Asian countries tend to stand farther away from one another while talking than their North American counterparts.

Source: Sorokowska A, Sorokowski P, Hilper P, et al. 2017. Preferred interpersonal distances: A global comparison. *Journal of Cross-Cultural Psychology*, 48(4), 577–592. © 2017. Reprinted by Permission of SAGE Publications, Inc.

hierarchies is not violating the maxim of manner. In fact, at the University of Guelph, regular Board of Governor meetings are held, and these meetings are open to the public. At open meetings, students can discuss their concerns when granted speaking privileges. Such meetings are a great way to fill the gap between higher authority and the student body, as they allow for more personal conversation between the two groups. Does your campus conduct events that equalize the power between students and your campus's president or chancellor?

Additional Maxims

Norman and Rummelhart (1975) added two maxims to Grice's (1975) conversational rules: *relations with conversational partner* and *rule violations*. The maxim of **relations with conversational partner** suggests that we should rely on our previous experience with our partners in our conversations. If we were talking to you about cross-cultural psychology, we would know

relations with conversational partner A communicative presumption that suggests that we use our previous relationship with our conversational partner so that we do not have to repeat shared experiences.

that you know something about the topic, so we could talk about something within the area knowing that you would be able to follow what we are saying. However, if we were talking with someone who knew nothing about cross-cultural psychology, we might have to give a brief sketch of the subject before we could discuss a specific topic. If you had an inside joke with a friend, you could use telegraphic language to refer to the inside joke and apply it to the present situation, but if you were with people unfamiliar with the inside joke, you should fill them in before making the comments or let them know later why the situation was so funny.

The maxim of **rule violations** suggests that when violating one of the other maxims, one must signal that violation. For example, if we want someone to interpret a comment as ironic, or the opposite of what the literal comment means, we must signal it with a voice inflection or some other means. We are sure that you all have been in a boring lecture or at a boring party when someone has said, "This is *really* interesting." The emphasis on *really*, said with a voice inflection or stress, signals that you should interpret the comment not literally but ironically. Some people draw quotation marks in the air when they want others to interpret a comment ironically instead of literally or to disregard the comment. For example, someone might say "The 'experts' say you should do this…" and draw quotation marks in the air with their fingers when they say "experts," which means that you should disregard the advice that the experts are giving. You may be aware of this joke:

> An English professor says, "Some people mistakenly believe that double negatives always mean the opposite. For example, if I were to say, 'This is not unlike the situation last week,' I mean by the double negatives of 'not' and 'unlike' to mean that the current situation is exactly like the situation last week. That is well and good, but sometimes a double negative can be an intensifier. Thus, if I were to say, 'One should never, never stick one's finger into a light socket,' I really mean that one should not do this under any circumstance. However, there is never an instance where a double positive is anything but an intensifier. In other words, double positives always intensify the positive meaning of something and never mean the opposite or something negative."
>
> A student in the back of the room says, "Yeah, right!"

rule violations A communicative presumption that suggests that we signal our conversational partners when we are about to engage in a violation of one of the other maxims.

We might note that this is a humorous violation of the maxim of manner, but it is also an illustration of how in many English-speaking countries (e.g., Canada, the US, the UK, Australia) we allow such violations of hierarchies, and under many circumstances students and their professors can be at the same level of hierarchy.

As one can imagine, different cultures can have different conversational rules, but they likely have similar general maxims that guide their behaviours. The greatest variation occurs in the maxim of manner because different rules govern what is an appropriate or inappropriate manner. This is particularly true for many cultures that attend to hierarchical communications, such as the German culture that Professor James encountered. We turn next to these non-verbal aspects of language.

4.2 Non-verbal Aspects of Language

One of the greatest differences among cultures is the way in which non-verbal communication is used. Sue and Sue (2003, 2008, 2013, 2016) categorize non-verbal communication into *proxemics*, *kinesics*, *paralanguage*, and *high- and low-context communication*. Because high–low context communication is such an important issue in the cross-cultural literature, we present it in the next section.

Proxemics

proxemics Personal space in conversations.

Proxemics deals with personal space. When people interact with one another, they maintain a standard range of distance between them. The range of distance varies depending on the context, such as a close, intimate relationship or a public lecture (Hall, 1966, 1976). As we noted earlier, in normal conversations the distance between two conversational partners is usually about half a metre (1.5 feet). According to Hall, the acceptable distance is half a metre to over one metre (1.5 to over 3 feet). However, numerous researchers have found that conversational partners in other cultures tend to stand or sit closer to one another when interacting than do those in Canada and other Western countries (Dolphin, 1999; Matsumoto, 2000). For example, a close distance is maintained between individuals from Arab countries. Those from Spain and Italy also tend to have a close proximity during conversational interactions. However, greater personal space is preferred among those from Britain (Ramlaul & Vosper, 2013).

One of this book's authors, Jeffery Scott Mio, recalls being at a sporting event and feeling uncomfortable when he saw two sports reporters standing extremely close to each other. He remembers thinking how interesting it was that *he* was the one who was feeling uncomfortable in just observing these two people standing so close to each other when they were talking. He then realized that in the context of televised sporting events, they had to stand close to each other in order to both be in the camera shot on television. After he realized the context, he felt much more comfortable about their distance from each other.

contact cultures Cultures that encourage touching and closer proximity.

Cultures that encourage touching and closer proximity are considered **contact cultures**. Middle Eastern and South American cultures fall into this category. Cultures that do not encourage physical contact, and whose members tend to stand farther apart when interacting are considered non-contact cultures (Andersen et al., 2013). Non-contact cultures can be found in Central and East Asia, which are considered some of the most touch-avoidant regions in the world (Andersen et al., 2013).

In addition to cultural characteristics, there are many other factors that influence social proximity, including ethnicity, gender, and religious ideology. A group of Russian researchers, Menshikova et al. (2018), investigated non-verbal communication and its manifestation between cultures, specifically in proxemic behaviour. In their procedure, they used the CAVE automatic virtual reality system to create three different avatars that each had either Slavic, North Caucasian, or Central Asian features. These avatars would then interact with the self-identified Russian participants in the virtual reality environment. The interpersonal distances between the participants and the avatars would then be measured by the virtual reality system. The results revealed that participants had the smallest interpersonal distance between themselves and the avatar when the avatar's ethnic features matched their own (Menshikova et al., 2018).

Similarly, Mahmoud and Hussein (2019) conducted a study to analyze the non-verbal behaviour habits of 100 Arab and Kurdish refugees over three Iraqi refugee camps. In this study, they interviewed both men and women of various ages and religions in the camp. The results revealed several differences between the Kurdish and the Arab populations residing in the camp. For example, the Kurdish populations were considerably less enthusiastic and expressive than their Arab counterparts and tended to stay together within their communities. When asked whether they wanted to participate in the study, the Arab participants were considerably more enthusiastic and willing to do so, while the Kurdish participants were less willing to take part in the study, to the point that it was difficult for the researchers to find male Kurdish participants. The researchers related this hesitancy to the minority status of Kurdish people in Iraq in comparison to the majority status of Arabs in Iraq. Due to their minority and often discriminated status, Kurdish people would be less trusting and, therefore, less willing to participate. The patterns in proxemics between the two cultures were largely based on religion, as there were 73 Muslim participants and 27 Yazidi participants in the group of 100 individuals involved in the study. Muslim participants would often stand farther apart from one another and avoid touching if they were of the opposite sex, as per religious guidelines, but this was not as evident in the Yazidi participants.

When talking with someone from a different culture, a person can find it difficult to determine a comfortable talking distance. Sue and Sue (2003, 2008, 2013, 2016) gave a practical reason that proxemics is an important topic in cross-cultural studies. When an individual from a culture that prefers smaller distances between speakers comes in contact with an individual from a culture that prefers larger distances, the first individual might misinterpret the second one's warmth, sincerity, or motive. Imagine a person from a close culture trying to stand closer to a person from a distant culture, who keeps moving away. The person from the close culture may feel that the other individual is not a warm person or is trying to hide something, whereas the person from the distant culture may feel that the other individual is trying to become overly personal or invasive.

Kinesics

Sue and Sue (2003, 2008, 2013, 2016) define **kinesics** as aspects of communication that deal with bodily movements. This is a wide-ranging category that includes "facial expressions, body movements, gestures, and conversational regulators" (Andersen, 1999, p. 245). One kinesics aspect that has been studied extensively is eye contact or gaze duration. Matsumoto (2000) reported that eye contact can be an indication of either aggression or nurturance, depending on the context. He cites the animal literature as a suggestion of a genetic, animalistic basis for the relation between gaze duration and dominance (see also Matsumoto & Juang, 2012). Eye contact has been suggested as being a powerful mode of communication, and gaze is picked up at a young age because children use it as a means of communication with their caregivers (Matsumoto, 2006). However, rules regarding non-verbal communications, including gaze, vary across cultures. Cultures that use physical contact during social interactions were found to gaze more than cultures with members who do not usually engage in close physical proximity when interacting with one another (Matsumoto, 2006; Matsumoto & Juang, 2012). For example, Japanese people tend to look at the throat of the other person during social interactions (Jackson, 2020).

Most of us can remember being told as children that it is impolite to stare at someone. However, equally embedded in our minds are phrases such as "gazing lovingly into someone's eyes" or "casting a loving glance," which indicate that eye contact or gazes can also indicate affection or care. Moreover, there is even evidence that love can be distinguished from lust by evaluating eye gazes (Bolmont et al., 2014).

As one might expect, people of different cultures seem to engage in varying levels of eye contact. Some early researchers found that people from Arabic cultures tend to gaze longer and more directly than people from North America do (Hall, 1963; Watson & Graves, 1966). Across the world, expectations for eye gaze are different. For example, a direct gaze is considered respectful in North American cultures, while it is considered rude and can even be perceived as threatening in East Asian cultures (Adams & Nelson, 2016). In addition, in East Asian cultures, the proper gaze would not be at the other person's eyes but, rather, downwards, away from the other person's face (Adams & Nelson, 2016). A friend and colleague of the authors, Joseph Trimble, once said this:

> When I am interacting with my White colleagues, I sit or stand across from them and interact with them in a manner that is comfortable for them. However, when I visit my friends on the Lakota reservation, I find myself standing side by side with them, looking at

kinesics Bodily movements in conversations, including hand gestures, facial expressions, and eye contact.

Bodily movements, or kinesics, are important forms of expression in conversation.

> my feet and kicking at the ground. We rarely look at each other, but we have very good and deep conversations.
>
> — Joseph Trimble, personal communication, January 1999

However, not having a great deal of eye contact is different from avoiding eye contact. According to van Meurs and Spencer-Oatey (2010), there are cultural differences in eye contact avoidance during conflict. Many researchers (e.g., Bond & Hwang, 1986; Ohbuchi & Takahashi, 1994) label this as a neglect style of dealing with conflict. East Asians tend to have less eye contact under conditions of conflict than their counterparts in North America. We say *tend to have* because there are large variations in both populations, and among those in the West. For example, van Meurs and Spencer-Oatey (2010) report that British managers had a more avoidant style of managing than their Dutch counterparts.

In North America, direct eye contact tends to be considered respectful during conversation.

Sue and Sue (2003, 2008, 2013, 2016) discuss smiling as an important part of kinesics. In general, smiling is an indication of happiness, liking, and other positive feelings. However, Asian cultures may also use smiling as a way of discharging uncomfortable feelings. Ekman (1972) conducted early experiments in which he showed American and Japanese students highly stressful videotapes (e.g., of a surgical operation) and secretly videotaped their facial expressions. Half of the time the research participants watched the stressful videotapes alone, and half of the time they watched the videotape with an older, high-status experimenter. The American participants showed facial expressions of disgust, fear, and other negative affects when they watched the film alone or with the experimenter. However, the Japanese participants displayed these negative expressions when watching the videotape alone, but they smiled in the presence of the high-status experimenter; they did not want to offend the experimenter by seeming to disapprove of the task the experimenter was asking them to perform. Thus, although facial expressions of emotion may have some universal application, as evidenced by the similar expressions of the American and Japanese participants when viewing the videotapes alone, the social setting may be an important determinant of the kinesics displayed in a particular situation. Overall, it has been reported that Asians, including Japanese people, Chinese people, and Koreans, tend to smile when expressing negative emotions.

Kinesics may be determined by the general influences of individualism and collectivism. They tend to be more synchronized in collectivistic cultures (Andersen, 1999; Argyle, 1975), whereas in individualistic cultures, people are allowed to do their own thing and not coordinate their movements with others as much. Matsumoto (1991) speculates that "collective cultures will foster emotional displays of their members that maintain and facilitate group cohesion, harmony, or cooperation, to a greater degree than individualistic cultures" (p. 132).

Paralanguage

paralanguage
Non-verbal vocal cues in conversation, such as loudness of voice, silences, and rates of speech.

Sue and Sue (2003, 2008, 2013, 2016) refer to **paralanguage** as a category that involves the use of non-verbal vocal cues in communication, such as loudness of voice, silences, and rate of speech. Perhaps the aspect of paralanguage that lends itself to the most cultural variation of meaning is silence.

Hall (1966, 1976) found that silences mean different things in different cultures. For example, some cultures (Russian, Spanish) view silence as agreement among the conversational partners. Asian cultures view silence as a sign of respect for elders. In Canada and many Western societies, silences are often signals for the receiver of a message to contribute to the conversation. When silences last too long, however, people in these societies often become uncomfortable as there is a preference for individuals to keep talking throughout conversations with minimal pauses (Lemak, 2012). On the other hand, many Northern European and Asian cultures prefer to speak only when there is verbal information to be passed on and, therefore, do not see silence in the same negative light as members of Western cultures (Lemak, 2012). It is interesting to note that the Western Apache Indigenous Peoples have rules with regards to the use of silence. For example, if the social status of the one they are speaking to is unknown, the elongated pauses and silences between sentences reflect this lack of knowledge (Lemak, 2012). For some Indigenous communities, silences are a way of gathering one's thoughts, so breaking the silence merely disrupts their train of thought.

Many of you have probably heard the expression "pregnant pause," which indicates the discomfort one feels when the conversation has come to a halt and there is an extended period during which neither conversational partner contributes to the conversation.

Many people in Western cultures feel most comfortable when there are no silences during conversation.

The forms of non-verbal communication we have mentioned are important contributors to conversations between partners, but one of the most important and underappreciated aspects of non-verbal communication is the distinction between high- and low-context communication, which we will now examine.

4.3 High- versus Low-Context Communication

> A daughter from a higher-class family [in Malaysia] fell in love with the son of a lower-class family. The son approached his parents and told them that he wanted to marry the girl from a higher-class family. His mother said she would approach the girl's family to see if it were acceptable to them. She made an appointment with the girl's mother and went to the home on the proper day. She was greeted by the mother and was shown into the sitting room. Refreshments were brought in consisting of tea and bananas. The two mothers talked about the weather and other things, but they never mentioned their children. After a period of time, the boy's mother thanked her hostess politely and left. Upon returning home she told her son that the marriage was unacceptable and, therefore, not possible. (Shon & Ja, 1982, p. 216)

How did the mother from the lower-class family know that the mother from the higher-class family disapproved of the marriage? It is because she used the context of the situation to understand the other mother's wishes. In Malaysia, tea and bananas do not go together, so the mother from the higher-class family was giving the other mother the message that their children should not go together. Hall (1976, 1999) calls this **high-context communication (HC)**, which means that much of the communication is carried either by the context of the situation or by societal rules that are internalized. Conversely, **low-context communication (LC)** is language dependent: the language itself is the crucial aspect of the communication, and context does not carry as much meaning. Hall (1999) explains:

high-context communication (HC) Communication in which the context conveys much of the meaning.

> A high-context (HC) communication or message is one in which most of the information is either in the physical context or internalized in the person, while very little is in the coded, explicit, transmitted part of the message. A low-context (LC) communication is just the opposite; i.e., the mass of the information is vested in the explicit code. (p. 47)

low-context communication (LC) Language-dependent communication in which the words carry most of the meaning and context plays a lesser role.

Although no culture is exclusively HC or LC, cultures fall on a continuum between high and low context. Communication in Canada and many Western Europeans countries (e.g., Germany, Switzerland, Scandinavian countries) tends to be at the low-context end of this continuum and many Asian countries tend to be at the high end (Hall, 1976; Singh & Pereira, 2005). Hall (1976) connects the Asian dependence on context to the Chinese written language, which is over 3500 years old and has not changed much in the past 3000 years. Thus, other countries whose written languages are derivations of the Chinese language (e.g., Japan, Korea) are HC countries.

One advantage of HC is that it allows individuals to avoid confrontations. In the example of the Malaysian mothers, notice how the mother from the higher class does not have to directly state her wish that their two children not marry. Also, the mother from the lower class does not have to be embarrassed by being told to her face that her son is not acceptable to the other family. Although in many Western countries people might prefer clarity in communication, direct questioning in HC countries is considered a sign of immaturity because it causes both parties to lose face (Andersen, 1999). Incidentally, although we do not know how this situation was ultimately resolved, it is possible that in the long run, the mother from the upper-class family gave her consent to the marriage. As Elliot and associates (Elliot et al., 1982) found, people who talked less and allowed context to communicate more were seen as more attractive in collectivistic cultures. Merkin (2015) found supporting evidence that people from collectivistic cultures find direct communication to be face-threatening and instead communicate in a high-context manner. Allowing context to drive conversation is seen as harmonious communication in which face is protected and the risk of humiliation is avoided. Communicating in such a way is more likely to build trust between individuals (Lovell et al., 2012), whereas direct communication is seen as a threat or disrespect. Thus, if these mothers had additional contact in the future, the mother from the upper-class family may have come to see the mother from the lower-class family as more attractive because she could read contextual cues. For those of you who are romantics, there is hope that love conquered all in this case.

As indicated earlier, HC helps one to save face. As we discussed in Chapter 3 and according to Ting-Toomey (1994), "Face involves the claimed sense of self-respect or self-dignity in an interactive situation" (p. 3). Thus, saving face is preserving one's dignity when interacting with another person or when being viewed or evaluated in a public context.

With respect to HC communication, a joke among Japanese immigrants is that when they visit non-Japanese families for dinner, they go home hungry. That is because of the Japanese concept of *enryo*, a term meaning "to hold back or to suppress one's desires." Thus, in Japanese families influenced by *enryo*, if one is hungry and is offered more food, one must say no. The food must then be offered again, and again the answer must be no. If the food is offered a third time, it is appropriate to accept the food while also complimenting the cook on how tasty the food is. However, when Japanese immigrants or visitors visit the homes of people from other cultures and are offered food, when they refuse the food the first time, the food is taken away, even though the visitor may still be hungry.

The concept of *taarof* in Persian culture (i.e., among Iranians) is similar to the notion of *enryo*. *Taarof* is a ritual practice of over-politeness, which includes both genuine and insincere offers, invitations, and suggestions (Izadi, 2016). For example, Iranians may offer to pay for the dinner of their friends to demonstrate their politeness. In return, it is expected that the friends decline the offer, recognizing that it was merely a polite offer. Additionally, by declining the offer, the friends do not appear greedy and impolite. Only if the person persists on the offer is it acceptable for the friends to accept the offer. Non-Iranians perceive *taarof* as confusing during their interactions with Iranians (Izadi & Zilaie, 2014).

A co-author of this book, Lori A. Baker, is an African-American woman whose brother is married to a Japanese-American woman. She used to get irritated when her sister-in-law continued to offer her food even when Lori had said she was full and did not want any more to eat. Lori's thought was, "I just said no—why are you offering me food again?" However, after some time, she came to realize that her sister-in-law was just following the Japanese tradition of offering the food multiple times just in case she (Lori) was holding back and being polite in the Japanese tradition. Thus, Lori has now learned how to be definitive in saying no the first time she refuses the food.

4.4 Direct versus Indirect Communication

direct communication Blunt communication that is literal and to the point.

indirect communication Communication that relies on context and the receiver's ability to draw inferences.

Related to high- versus low-context communication is direct versus indirect communication. Most people know that **direct communication** is literal and assertive communication. It is related to low-context communication in that the message is contained in the language used. **Indirect communication** relies on both context and the receiver's powers of inference. To illustrate the difference between these two forms of communication, let us say that someone wants a window closed. Direct speech would say, "Close the window." Indirect speech would say, "Are you cold?" Brown and Levinson (1978) indicate that indirect speech acts are used because they convey a degree of politeness in communication. As such, they are universal.

Both indirect communication and high-context communication resonated with a student. She related this rather amusing anecdote:

> I come from a culture that values indirectness. I remember when I was getting married; it is customary for the bride to look sad and depressed. She should let her family feel that she is not happy leaving home. If a bride smiles and shows that she is happy it is an indirect way of saying she does not value her family and she would forget them if she leaves home. I cried and acted so sad. My younger sister however took it a step further; she ran away from home the night before her wedding. I remember my father huffing and puffing and screaming, "If she does not want to marry we would just cancel it—nobody is forcing her." I laughed so hard secretly because I knew she wanted so badly to get married but she was trying to show that she was a "good girl." I always resented the indirect way of doing things because we always have to refuse things and gifts when it is offered to us for the first time and luckily people would continue to insist. God knows how difficult it was for me when I migrated to the USA. I kept insisting my friends eat more or take something I offered them when they said no. They resented it and thought I had no boundaries.
>
> —Adjoa, 40+-year-old Ghanaian immigrant student

Smith (2011) acknowledges that indirect communication may be a universal component of all languages. However, she cites wide cultural variations in preference for direct or indirect communication styles. As we discussed in Chapter 3, people in many Asian countries are concerned with saving and giving face. Therefore, it should not be surprising to find that indirect speech is prevalent in Asian countries (Khalib & Tayeh, 2014; Kim, 2010). Lebra (1976) indicates that this level of indirect communication can be extremely subtle. Lebra reports that a woman communicated discord with her mother-in-law based on slight irregularities found in the mother-in-law's flower arrangement. Chinese people use modifiers, such as *maybe* and *perhaps* when communicating with others, which implies their indirect communication style. This is often confusing for people from Western cultures (Fang & Faure, 2011). When a Chinese person states, "Maybe I will come with you," or "Perhaps it is too far for you to walk," they mean "I'm coming" (Fang & Faure, 2011). Table 4.2 summarizes Yum's (1999) comparison of North American and East Asian forms of communication (p. 83).

TABLE 4.2 Comparison between North American and East Asian Orientations to Communication Patterns

East Asian orientations	North American orientations
1. Process orientation: Communication is perceived as a process of infinite interpretation.	Outcome orientation: Communication is perceived as the transference of messages.
2. Differentiated linguistic codes: Different linguistic codes are used depending on the persons involved and situations.	Less differentiated linguistic codes: Linguistic codes are not as extensively differentiated as in East Asia.
3. Indirect communication emphasis: The use of indirect communication is prevalent and accepted as normative.	Direct communication emphasis: Direct communication is a norm despite the extensive use of indirect communication.
4. Receiver centred: Meaning is in the interpretation. Emphasis is on listening, sensitivity, and removal of preconception.	Sender centred: Meaning is in the messages created by the sender. Emphasis is on how to formulate the best messages, how to improve source credibility, and how to improve delivery skills.

Ethnic Minority Patterns of Communication

Researchers have conducted a great deal of research comparing Asian and East Asian forms of communication with Western forms of communication because of the general interest in collectivistic versus individualistic cultures. Most of the foregoing information deals with this comparison. A few other researchers have examined differences in communication patterns among other ethnic minority populations in one country. Sometimes generalizations cannot be applied to all people in a group, but the following are general trends identified by some researchers.

Afro-Caribbean and African Canadians

It is important to be aware of stereotypes as they create strain between ethnic groups. For example, many Afro-Caribbean and African Canadians experience negative stereotypes and racism in their daily lives (Madibbo, 2016). This may include racial profiling and difficulties advancing their career as a result of their efforts being underappreciated or undervalued. Often, there is a false association of violence and crime with people of African or Caribbean descent. Not only does this affect these communities in terms of further exclusion, but it creates an incorrect notion of what a Canadian should look like (i.e., White and of a European heritage), thereby excluding anyone who does not fit that stereotype of what it means to be Canadian (Madibbo, 2016). Additionally, even though most African Canadians speak English, there is a substantial number of African immigrants and Afro-Caribbeans who speak French in Canada. This can create even more of a struggle for them because there is already a stigma involved with being an immigrant, and many Africans in Canada feel they are not considered genuine Canadians to begin with (Madibbo, 2016). Additionally, those immigrants who speak only French become a part of yet another minority, since English is the majority language spoken in Canada. Thus, it can be difficult for French-speaking African immigrants to feel a sense of belonging in not only the general community but also in the Canadian Francophone community. In general, whether stereotypes involve English- or French-speaking Afro-Caribbean or African Canadians, it is essential that such stereotypes be challenged because perpetuating them creates marginalization and unhealthy power dynamics between the majority and the Afro-Caribbean community (Madibbo, 2016). As Canada becomes increasingly diverse in its population, normative ideas of what it means to be a Canadian or a Francophone will become less relevant.

Mensah and Williams (2015) conducted a study with African immigrants in Canada to investigate how they identify with their home country and Canada while interacting with Anglo-Canadians. It was found that immigrants who thought racism to be high in Canada identified less with Canada and were less likely to consider themselves as simply Canadian. For example, they tended to identify themselves as Ghanaian Canadian instead, or just Ghanaian. Therefore, those who are fearful and misinformed about immigrants are making new Canadians feel less and less connected to the already unfamiliar society they now call home. Although it is possible for those coming to a new country to feel a strong connection with their ethnicity while still feeling a part of their host nation, such an outcome is not only dependent on the individual but also on those around the individual.

More generally, however, the initiation of intercultural communication is dependent on many factors. Logan et al. (2015) found that sometimes anxiety can result from communication between two different cultural groups, which can inhibit their willingness to interact with each other. This anxiety could be a result of fear or uncertainty but needs to be addressed since it can lead to the negative appraisal of any given group. Thus, when it comes to any minority group, including African immigrants, interaction must be encouraged in order to challenge notions of ethnocentrism (i.e., the evaluation of other cultures from the view that one's own cultural standards and beliefs are superior).

Asian Canadians

Fang and Huang (2020) investigated the power dynamics that exist within first- and second-generation Asian Canadians and examined their experiences and world views. Frequently, the participants discussed their confusion regarding their identity as Asian Canadians, especially if they did not have many friends of the same ethnicity. Many participants described their later experiences with other individuals in their ethnic group as negative due to the accusation that they had become "White-washed." These individuals then had to find their own identities, which were often self-described as "in-between" as they incorporated their traditional Asian cultures surrounded by Canadian society. The study revealed that ethnic groups are not uniform, and there are differences between individuals. Such differences are reflected in the language the community members use with one another and can even be a cause for developing hierarchies within the group, leading most often to stereotyping and discrimination within that group.

Further Cultural Examples

One study by Min (2013) examined communication styles and greetings by analyzing both a South Korean and a Chilean television drama to compare Chileans and South Koreans in their interpersonal contact, particularly their greetings. Min (2013) compared greetings depicted between two male friends, two female friends, male and female friends, two teachers, and between a teacher and a student. The results revealed that among two male friends, Chileans' greetings involved handshaking and touching of the shoulder. However, in Koreans' greetings, physical contact was absent, and the two male friends merely exchanged eye contact. The greetings between two female friends in the Korean drama usually involved hand waving and exchanging eye contact, while in the Chilean drama, the greetings involved hugging and kissing. In the Chilean drama, greetings between male and female friends included a kiss on the cheek or a hug, while in the Korean drama, touching was not involved. In their greetings, Chilean teachers tended to maintain more intimate distance. However, Korean teachers had more social distance. When greeting their teachers, Korean students tended to bow before them to express respect. This study illustrates that greeting expectations vary across cultures. Awareness of such expectations can promote intercultural interactions and prevent misunderstanding.

A bicultural student who read about contact culture was struck by the difference between him and his biracial friend. The student was raised mostly by his European-American mother and said that his Mexican-American father did not really retain the Mexican part of his culture. However, his friend was raised mostly by his mother, who was Latino:

> When I first met my friend [Chaz] I noticed that when he would be engaged in a conversation that he would always be all "touchy feely" with the person who he was talking to; I always thought it was just the way he was. I didn't realize that it was this way for his entire family and his culture. Most of the time I just noticed him being "touchy feely" with females who he was engaged in a conversation with, so I just assumed that he was flirting with them, but then I noticed that he was like that to males that he was engaged in a conversation with. . . . I learned that most Latino/na are "touchy feely" when they are engaged in a conversation because that is their culture. Chaz is half Mexican and half White. He was brought up by his mom who is one hundred per cent Mexican, and therefore he grew up in the Latino culture.
>
> —*Denny, 20+-year-old biracial (Mexican/European) student*

Latino people tend to touch each other more than people from many Western cultures do.

Indigenous Peoples

The term *Indigenous Peoples* is used to describe the original peoples of the land now known as Canada and their descendants. As previously discussed in Chapter 1, there are multiple terms that are used to categorize Indigenous Peoples in the Americas. In Canada, Indigenous Peoples are split into three distinct groups: Métis, Inuit, and First Nations (Government of Canada, 2017). In the US, *Native American* is the most widely accepted terminology for Indigenous Peoples.

It has been argued that different conceptualization is one of the biggest contributors to miscommunication between Indigenous and non-Indigenous peoples. While investigating the miscommunications between Aboriginal Australian English and Australian English, Sharifian (2010) found that some Aboriginal Australian groups use methods of communication that are not typically seen in Western society. For example, in August of 1990, an Aboriginal Australian man was sentenced to two years of probation for setting fire to bushland in fear that a *pulypart* would come in to steal his child. In his culture, a *pulypart* is a mystical creature that steals babies but is afraid of fire. Although the man acted according to his Aboriginal beliefs, it is not a belief that is widely accepted in Western culture, and, therefore, it came with consequences (Sharifian, 2010).

Perhaps a far less recognized Indigenous group is that of the people in Papua New Guinea, who are commonly referred to as Melanesians (Minority Rights Group International, 2007). Melanesians are one of the few groups left in the world in which Western culture has had little impact. In Melanesian culture, music and dance are used to express important life events, such as birth, death, and economic transactions (Standish & Jackson, 2019).

Communication Patterns of the Elderly

Few researchers have examined how elderly individuals differ from non-elderly individuals in communication styles. Because of the increased use of the health-care system, many researchers have examined how medical professionals must communicate with the elderly (Christenson et al., 2011; Moberg & Rick, 2008). For example, Pennbrant (2013) found that the involvement and acknowledgement of elderly patients' relatives during a medical meeting increase the ability of relatives to convey the treatment-related information to the elderly patient. Ballantyne, Yang, and Boon (2013) found that in dealing with patients with limited English abilities, medical professionals needed to ask what the patient heard when receiving medical instructions. Non-medical studies have involved factors such as the amount of respect given to elderly individuals when interacting with them (Giles et al., 2012) and examining how elderly individuals interface with new electronic devices and applications (Bruder et al., 2014). Moreover, Underwood (2010) found that normal-functioning elderly individuals did not differ in the sophistication of their conversational interactions compared to their younger counterparts.

Some interesting studies have concentrated on how grandparents interact with their grandchildren. Much of the interest in this area has been stimulated by the relatively recent increase in grandparents taking responsibility for the care of their grandchildren for various reasons: child abuse or neglect in the parents' home, divorce, and/or working parents (Backhouse & Graham, 2011; Doley et al., 2015; Hayslip et al., 2019; McKay, 1999). The major motivation for grandparent–grandchild interaction is the desire by the grandparents to transmit knowledge based on their lives and family history (Nussbaum & Bettini, 1994). This is in keeping with Erik Erikson's (1950/1963, 1964) notion that a life-stage motivation in older ages is to pass on wisdom to subsequent generations. Nussbaum and Bettini note that grandchildren are quite interested in this kind of knowledge as well. Mokuau et al. (2015) found that it was important to Native-Hawaiian grandparents to teach their grandchildren life skills (e.g., social interaction) and provide them with life guidance (e.g., being a good citizen). Moreover, Native-Hawaiian grandparents discussed some of the cultural values and family histories that they passed on to their grandchildren. For example, they discussed the importance of *ohana* (family), suggesting that "You have to take care of one another, love each other, help each other out. That's why you have *ohana*, to help each other out" (Mokuau et al., 2015, p. 9). McKay (1989, 1993, 1999) found that grandchildren also enjoyed hearing stories about their parents when their parents were children.

Communication among Younger Adults

One rising difference in communication patterns between younger adults and older adults is the use of social media. Justin Trudeau knew the power of the internet and used it not only to raise campaign contributions but also to motivate his supporters to work in his favour.

Similarly, Catherine McKenna, the former minister of environment and climate change (2015–2019), has been known to use social media extensively (Marche, 2019). For example, through #YouthClimateAction she has called on Canada's youth to take action on climate. However, she is also accountable for supporting the Trans Mountain pipeline, a project that many environmentalists oppose (Marche, 2019). Therefore, her posts on social media have led

Grandparents often have a desire to pass on wisdom and knowledge to their grandchildren.

to confusion among some Canadians who believe she is contradicting herself by degrading the environment with the production of a pipeline while urging youth to develop solutions for a clean and sustainable energy, economy, and food system.

Why do modern politicians engage in so much social media? Perhaps it is because it is how younger adults communicate. As many people who have studied politics have understood, younger adults are the most difficult class to motivate to vote (Brennan & Cook, 2015). Because young adults use social media so much more than older adults do, using this form of communication is an attempt to reach younger adults.

4.5 The Role of Social Media in Communication

Social media has changed the way people communicate and has become a platform for communication. Indeed, most people use some form of social media, ranging from Twitter and Snapchat to Facebook and Instagram. These platforms are used to share information, personal stories, pictures, and moments. Young people are the main users of most social media platforms. For example, teenagers spend nearly nine hours per day consuming media (Kaiser Family Foundation, 2013; Tsukayama, 2015), including watching online videos, listening to music, and engaging in other forms of technology. However, the study by the Kaiser Family Foundation (cited by all researchers in this area, such as Coyne et al., 2018 and Zhao et al. 2012) was conducted in 2010, before the existence of Snapchat and Instagram. More recently, MTM Jr (2020) published a report on Canadian teenagers aged 12 to 17, which stated that 72 per cent use some sort of social media platform. For these teens specifically, Instagram, Facebook, and Snapchat were the most commonly used. Additionally,

Popular street artist Banksy has created art commenting on the rising need for "likes" on social media.

for Canadian adults (aged 18+) who use social media, at least 50 per cent of users visited Facebook, messaging apps, Instagram, YouTube, TikTok/Douyin, Snapchat, Reddit, and Twitter daily, in that order of frequency (Gruzd & Mai, 2020). Facebook is the most popular of all social media platforms, with 74 per cent of Canadians using it on a regular basis (Kunst, 2019).

The Use of Social Media: The Negative Aspects

Why do young people use so much social media? As Bayer et al. (2016) indicate, college and university Snapchat users enjoyed being able to share mundane experiences with individuals whom they trusted. Although Snapchat was not designed for in-depth social support, the platform allows people to share parts of their lives with others, such as what they are eating, something that made them laugh, or something that caught their interest. These students felt that this form of social media was more enjoyable than other forms of communication.

A criticism of today's social media usage is that such forms of communication can cause shallow thinking, called the *shallowing hypothesis* (Annisette & Lafreniere, 2017). Annisette and Lafreniere found that individuals who texted or used social media frequently were also less likely to be reflective. This does not mean that people who are on social media are incapable of being reflective; rather, it underlines the characteristic of situations that tend to be fast-paced and require less prolonged attention. This has implications for lowering moral standards because people are less likely to understand the implications of their actions if they are less likely to reflect on their thoughts.

One of the most negative aspects of social media can be the bullying that some children receive online. In a study that included over 1000 middle and high school students aged 10 to 17 years old from all Canadian provinces, Beran et al. (2015) investigated cyberbullying. They found that 14 per cent of participants had been cyberbullied once or more in the past month. Additionally, one in seven Canadian children in this age range was a victim of cyberbullying (Beran et al., 2015). Likewise, another Canadian study found that adolescents have the highest cyberbullying victimization rates compared to any other age group (Kim et al., 2017). Cyberbullying was also strongly associated with mental health struggles, drug use, and binge drinking in adolescents (Kim et al., 2017).

Because social media is a peer-to-peer form of communication and because nearly anyone can start a blog or plant information on the internet, information coming from any online communication could be without an editor (Prado, 2017). Prado asserts that this serves to render consumers of this form of information gathering indifferent to any evidence in support of the information. Thus, opinions are placed on equal footing as evidence. Pingree et al. (2018) posit that the use of social media has led consumers of news to be complacent because news and Twitter are considered trivial.

The Use of Social Media: The Positive Aspects

Because of limitations associated with social media, it is easy to discount this form of communication as shallow and trivial. However, major social movements have been organized through social media. For example, the grassroots protest Idle No More (INM) commenced in December 2012 as a result of four women from Saskatoon, Saskatchewan, initiating a fight for Indigenous rights in Canada (Raynauld et al., 2017). These rights include being involved in political decision-making, keeping Indigenous land safe from new construction and pollution, and abolishing Bill C-45, which takes away Indigenous Peoples' treaty rights (Raynauld et al., 2017). By using social media, this social movement (#IdleNoMore) raised awareness all over the world (Raynauld et al., 2017). By educating those who are not Indigenous on Indigenous struggles, movements such as Idle No More recruit more advocates for policy changes in Canada that better serve Indigenous Peoples (Raynauld et al., 2017). In 2020, the Idle No More movement continued to be involved in various campaigns across Canada, including the Six Nations land claim of "1492 Land Back Lane," the fight for Mi'kmaq fishing rights with "Wet'suwet'en Strong," and with the Black Lives Matter and #DefundthePolice movements (Idle No More, 2020).

Similarly, the #BlackLivesMatter (BLM) campaign represents another positive impact that social media has had on social justice movements. In June 2020, BLM demonstrations erupted across the United States in response to the death of George Floyd, who was killed by a police officer in Minneapolis (Oborne & Cooke, 2020). The movement spread to numerous regions around the world in protest of police brutality against Black people. In Canada, the BLM campaign has drawn attention to the existence of systematic racism and the disproportionate number of Black Canadians who are killed by police (Bridges, 2020). Although BLM was first formed in 2013, this resurgence of the movement gained enormous traction in 2020 globally (Oborne & Cooke, 2020).

Bogen et al. (2018) credit Twitter's #NotOkay campaign with bringing sexual victimization to the forefront of public consciousness and changing long-standing policies—almost overnight. Another arguably better-known hashtag movement is the #MeToo movement, which started in 2017 and made international headlines. The movement was a powerful platform prompting women to talk about their experiences of sexual assault and harassment in society.

Idle No More is a protest movement for Indigenous rights and has been ongoing since 2012.

Gleason (2018) contends that teenagers now think in terms of effective hashtags for national campaigns. Thus, great social movements can be influenced by current social media technology.

4.6 Gender Differences in Communication

Studies focused on women's communication, or even gendered communication more broadly, often occur within a context of sexism. In a 2011 study of undergraduate business students, for example, a combination of 92 descriptive terms from the 1973 Schein Descriptive Index (SDI) was used to examine what characteristics students believed a successful business manager should possess (Holtzen, 2011). Participants were asked to describe women in general, men in general, and successful business managers using the SDI. The top 10 characteristics used to describe each individual group (women, men, and successful business managers) were examined. Of the top 10 characteristics associated with female characteristics, none overlapped with successful manager characteristics. However, three descriptors—*leadership ability*, *self-confident*, and *ambitious*—were used to describe both men and successful managers, therefore indicating that successful managerial characteristics are more commonly attributed to men than to women.

A cross-cultural study of university students by Williams and Best (1982, 1994) found that in 30 countries—including those from Asia, Africa, Oceania, the Americas, and Europe—there was a remarkable agreement about "male" and "female" characteristics. Participants (on average 100 university students per country) were given a 300-item Adjective Check List and were then asked if each of these adjectives were associated with a certain gender in the participants' respective culture. These associations were then analyzed to produce cultural world views about gender-specific characteristics. The results indicated that although assessments of these characteristics varied to some degree from country to country, overall across cultures, men were perceived as active, aggressive, individualistic, loud, rational, and tough, whereas women were perceived as affectionate, dependent, gentle, sensitive, submissive, and weak. In other words, gender stereotypes were found to be pancultural, and women are often said to be emotional, while men are often said to be rational. These stereotypes provide social models for young children and create expectations about how men and women should behave.

Lakoff (1975) found that women used **tag questions** more often than their male counterparts. Tag questions are questions added to a statement of assertion asking for confirmation. An example of a tag question is "This class is interesting, don't you think?" The tag question ("don't you think?") allows the conversational partner to agree or disagree with the assertion ("This class is interesting"). Traditionally, tag questions have been interpreted as an indication of weakness or passivity on the part of the speaker (Paludi, 1998). However, Paludi indicates that another interpretation of tag questions is that they connote warmth by inviting the other individual to engage in a conversation.

Hanafiyeh and Afghari (2014) did an analysis of gender differences in communication, particularly of the claims made by Lakoff (1975). The results indicate that many of the previous findings hold true. This includes female participants' more frequent use of intensifiers (e.g., "very" or "so"), hedges (e.g., "sort of" or "kind of"), and tag questions (e.g., "aren't you?" or "you think?"), indicating a less assertive style of communication.

Although research on gender and communication tends to focus on the differences between men and women, there are many similarities in their communication. For instance, the use of adverbs (e.g., *badly* or *slowly*) in order to answer questions of how or when seems to be fairly consistent between genders (Hanafiyeh & Afghari, 2014). In addition, it has been shown that males and females often have a great deal of non-verbal behaviours in common, including finger pointing and head nodding (Yang, 2010). Furthermore, these stereotypes of feminine versus masculine communications (for example, that women are worse at negotiating or that women are quieter than men) may actually be perpetuating the opposite communication style in women. A study by Von Hippel et al. (2011) demonstrated that when women are faced with these stereotypes about communication (e.g., men are more assertive leaders), they will sometimes adopt a more "masculine" communication style as a response (e.g., being more self-reliant, confident, and decisive). Therefore, it is difficult to tell what is truly so different in the communication of men and women when communication is such a dynamic and changing process.

Similarly, it was previously argued that women use more tentative language, including **qualifiers** such as "I think" or "It seems to me," than men (Carli, 1990; Wood, 1994, 1999). Qualifiers are words or phrases that soften statements and affect the certainty of the statement. For example, "I may be wrong, but I think this class is interesting." The phrase "I may be wrong" is a qualifier. However, women use qualifiers less than before. Bongiorno et al. (2014) argues that this is a reflection of a shift in women's roles over time. In fact, women who are more assertive tend to experience less prejudice than women who are less assertive. This is possibly because women are treated more as equals in conversation than they were in previous decades. For these reasons, the use of hesitant language by women, including

---

tag questions Questions added to a statement of assertion, such as "This is good, don't you think?"

qualifiers Words or phrases that soften statements and affect the certainty of a statement.

qualifiers, may have become less and less rewarded and, thus, has been diminishing in frequency (Bongiorno et al., 2014).

Carol K. Goman (2016), in her research conducted in Canada, Europe, and the US, found that men tend to be more decisive, while women tend to be more collaborative. In addition, men tend to be better at monologue, and they signal dominant behaviour such as standing tall, expressing anger, and spreading their materials on a table while sitting. On the other hand, women tend to be better at dialogue, and they signal warm behaviour such as smiling, leaning forward, nodding their head, and orienting their body toward the listener. Goman (2016) also reported that, overall, men and women recognize similar competence and incompetence not only in themselves but also in each other and that sometimes they engage in behaviours that are in the opposite direction that these comparisons suggest. Therefore, it is important to note that these findings are about general differences between men and women, and they do not apply to every man and every woman. Indeed, differences in communication style are also a reflection of different preferences that people have.

Wood (1999) emphasizes that gender differences in communication are more a product of socialization than of biology. In other words, communication isn't gendered at all but, rather, a product of how you grew up. There seem to be two sources of such socialization: family communication and communication between playmates. Paludi (1998) suggests that this socialization occurs very early because parents respond measurably differently to boys and girls. Will et al. (1976) found that differences in socialization happened even when people only *thought* they were interacting with a boy or a girl. They dressed an infant in pink and referred to it as *Beth* and dressed the same infant in blue and referred to it as *Adam*. The research participants played with the infant measurably differently—for example, offering Beth a doll and Adam a toy train.

Similarly, Basu et al. (2017) argue that gender is not solely based on one's sex but that it is also a product of socialization. Stereotypical male and female behaviours are learned through this socialization process, and everything from culture, family, school, and peers can influence a person's gender identity. Basu et al. (2017) found that boys and girls are treated differently once they enter adolescence, when gender norms become much more apparent. For example, in India, the place of a girl is expected to be in the home, whereas boys learn they have much more autonomy in their life. Therefore, it is possible that communication differences between genders are also shaped by gendered socialization since this socialization affects so many aspects of a child's psychological development and behaviour.

4.7 Bilingual Communication

Most people in the world are bilingual or multilingual (Coulmas, 2017; Grøver et al., 2019; Matsumoto, 2000; Matsumoto & Juang, 2012; Romaine, 2017). There are various ways in which people can become bilingual. Some people grow up in societies in which two or more languages are pervasive and in which one must know multiple languages to survive (e.g., Switzerland and Quebec); some are bilingual because their native language is not the official language of the country (e.g., Zulu speakers in South Africa who needed to learn English and Lithuanian speakers who needed to learn Russian before the fall of the Soviet Union); some are bilingual because they immigrated to a country that speaks a different language (e.g., Spanish or Cantonese speakers who immigrate to Canada); some are bilingual because of colonization (e.g., Cree speakers in Canada, where English was imposed on them); some are bilingual because of education and extensive travel (e.g., those in Canada who learn Spanish and have the opportunity to travel to Spain); some are bilingual for economic or professional reasons (e.g., Korean businessmen who learn English to do business with American companies); and some are bilingual because they grew up in households that spoke two languages. When the second language does not replace the native language, this is called **additive bilingualism** (Berry et al., 1992; Lambert, 1977). When the second language replaces the native language, this is called **subtractive bilingualism** (Berry et al., 1992; Lambert, 1977). Subtractive bilingualism is also called **language attrition** (Snow, 1993). Language attrition occurs when a language is used infrequently, even when the first language is well ingrained.

The following story highlights the challenges and the benefits of growing up in a bilingual family:

> My daughter is nearly 2, responds to both languages and, as my son did at her age, has started to say words in each language. The trickier part is later when words are strung together to make sentences. My son also understands everything in Polish but as to be expected, English is his dominant language. It is the language his father speaks to him, the language his father and his mother speak to each other and the language of his peer group in London, where we reside. Even though most of our close friends speak second languages—Icelandic, Spanish, Swedish, Portuguese, French—the common one among most of us is English. If prompted, my son will say a short sentence in Polish, but more often will code-switch, substituting one English word for a Polish one in an otherwise English sentence.
>
> After having two children of my own, I now know what an uphill battle it is to raise bilingual children, especially in a home with only one multilingual parent speaking the minority language. It is an anxiety-ridden, often soul-crushing, arduous feat not for the faint of heart. There are monumental highs and colossal lows, tears, frustrations and small victories that would, to an outsider, seem inconsequential, but are everything to me.
>
> —Malwina Gudowska, a Polish-Canadian mother (Gudowska, 2019).

When two languages are used in the household so that people become bilingual from birth, this is called **native bilingualism** (Snow, 1993). There are both cognitive and social consequences of bilingualism (Lambert, 1967, 1977, 1980).

Cognitive Consequences of Bilingualism

Early studies indicated that bilingual children performed more poorly than their monolingual counterparts did (see Lambert, 1977, and Matsumoto, 2000, for reviews of these early studies). However, Lambert and colleagues criticized those early researchers for not controlling for social class or educational opportunities (Lambert, 1977; Lambert & Anisfeld, 1969; Peal & Lambert, 1962). When studies were controlled for these factors, Lambert and Anisfeld (1969) and Peal and Lambert (1962) found that bilingual children performed better on various measures of intelligence. Price-Williams and Ramirez (1977) suggest that this performance might be the result of increased levels of cognitive flexibility among bilingual individuals.

Bialystok and Craik (2010) examined the advantages and disadvantages of being bilingual. They found some costs of being bilingual, such as having smaller vocabularies, having more tip-of-the-tongue experiences, and generating slightly fewer words in a timed task (called *semantic fluency tasks*) than did individuals who are monolingual. However, bilingual individuals demonstrated better performance in non-verbal tasks that required conflict resolution. For example, most people are familiar with the Stroop effect, in which it is difficult to name the colour of the ink if the word is the name of a colour different from the colour of the ink. People who are bilingual demonstrate less interference in Stroop tasks. Put another way, bilinguals

---

additive bilingualism The acquisition of a second language that does not replace the native language.

subtractive bilingualism The acquisition of a second language that replaces the native language.

language attrition Equivalent to subtractive bilingualism.

native bilingualism The ability to speak two languages from birth, acquired because both languages are spoken in the household.

perform better than their monolingual counterparts. A surprising and significant difference, however, is that being bilingual seems to give some degree of protection against cognitive decline. In examining 91 monolingual and 93 bilingual individuals who had been diagnosed with dementia, Bialystok and Craik found that bilingual individuals contracted the dementia more than four years *later* than those who were monolingual.

C. Baker (2013), Kroll et al. (2014), and Verkoeijen et al. (2012) also examined aspects of bilingualism. C. Baker concluded that knowing two languages is a benefit to individuals if both languages are well learned. However, problems can occur in the classroom if the second language is not as highly developed as the home language. Verkoeijen et al. (2012) found that studying in the language of origin and testing in the second language helped students learn material more deeply as opposed to learning only surface features of the list of words to be remembered.

There is evidence that acquiring a second language changes the brain location of certain concepts or at least causes a change in category clustering of concepts. Kroll et al. (2014) also concluded that bilingualism changes brain structure. In a study by Garcia-Penton and colleagues (2014), the connectivity differences in the brain were investigated between two groups, each comprising 13 individuals. One group contained only Spanish-speaking monolinguals, and the other group had Spanish- and Basque- speaking bilinguals who learned both languages at an early age. These individuals were between 20 and 40 years of age. Using an MRI (magnetic resonance imaging) to scan each individual's brain, the researchers found that bilingual individuals had greater connectivity in the subnetworks of the language processing and the frontal regions of the brain than their monolingual counterparts. They concluded that this increased connectivity in these brain regions impacts the entire functioning of the brain and that there are critical differences in the neuroanatomy of bilingual and monolingual individuals.

Researchers in neuroimaging studies that have examined the brain when bilingual and monolingual individuals are engaged in general cognitive tasks revealed that bilingual individuals seem to be able to think more efficiently than their monolingual counterparts. For example, when viewing a non-verbal conflict, although the anterior cingulate cortex areas are activated in both types of individuals, bilingual anterior cingulate cortex activation is more focused in its activation. These researchers speculated that this efficiency may be behind the protection against dementia that Bialystock and Craik (2010) discovered previously. Subsequent research (Rossi et al., 2017) confirmed changes in brain structure through magnetic resonance imaging analysis.

> When I try to figure out words that I don't know in English, I think of Spanish words that are written similarly. This happens quite a bit when I see a word in English that is spelled the same way in Spanish. If I am thinking in English I sometimes don't know the word. However, if I switch to Spanish, the meaning of the word often comes to me right away. My brain is wired to think in Spanish first and then English. Like I count in Spanish and spell in Spanish.
>
> —*Andres, 30+-year-old Mexican-American professor*

Although popular wisdom has it that children acquire second languages faster than adults do, systematic investigation proves otherwise (Snow, 1993). This is true for both formal and informal acquisition of the language (Huang, 2015; Llanes & Muñoz, 2013; Muñoz, 2008; Snow, 1983, 1987). However, older learners may be more "fossilized" in their native languages, so accents from their first language will persist into their second language (Birdsong & Vanhove, 2016;

DeKeyser, 2013). Thus, an older learner's mastery of the second language may be inferior to that of a younger learner.

Garcia and Kleifgen (2010) suggest that the political debate has disadvantaged individuals who are not quite bilingually fluent. They are often referred to as being of "limited English proficiency." Even the less judgmental "English-language learner" label has a somewhat negative connotation in that it suggests that these people are in the process of learning English but will not become fluent. Garcia and Kleifgen prefer the term "emergent bilinguals" because these individuals will ultimately become proficient in two languages. In this global economy, bilingual abilities will become increasingly important.

According to Statistics Canada (2017), from 2011 to 2016, there was about a 14.5 per cent increase in the number of people speaking languages other than English or French at home, accounting for 7.6 million Canadians. In 2016, 22.3 per cent of the Canadian population (7.7 million people) reported that they use a language other than English and French as their mother tongue. In 2016, 49.5 per cent of those with an immigrant mother tongue resided in Ontario, and the most common immigrant languages were (in order) Arabic, Persian, Urdu, Tagalog, Chinese languages, and Punjabi (Statistics Canada, 2017).

Garcia and Kleifgen reviewed the positive aspects of being bilingual beyond what Bialystok and Craik (2010) did, and they concluded that bilinguals have a greater analytic orientation to language (called *metalinguistic awareness*); have a greater flexibility of perceptions and interpretations to describing the world, resulting in greater creativity; and are better at gauging communicative situations, such as if someone is hesitant about a suggestion or merely thinking through the suggestion. This creative flexibility can lead to playfulness with languages:

> As a consequence of speaking more languages, I always feel that my native language is more of a playground than a prescriptive canvas. I like to play with words, and change things according to what I like. For example, in Italian (my native language) the verb for "to meow" is *miagolare* . . . so many vowels!! It seems almost impossible to pronounce. One day, while addressing my very vocal cat, I wanted to tell it in Italian "Can you meow less"? Very spontaneously, I decided to change the verb *miagolare* into *miagare* thus eliminating a bunch of sounds from it. . . . To me it sounded perfect! And so much easier to pronounce. The nice thing is that I introduced the new verb to my parents who found it funny enough. To date, they also started using *miagare* instead of *miagolare*.
>
> —Emilia, 30+-year-old Italian immigrant professor

Social Consequences of Bilingualism

Research conducted by Clément et al. (2001) demonstrated that learning a second language can have effects on group dynamics and determine the groups that individuals belong to. This is especially true for minorities and immigrants because in order to fit into a new society, learning the majority language is often a necessity. The researchers found that, particularly for the minority group, learning the majority language may lead to quicker assimilation; and the more confidence individuals have speaking the new language, the more they will identify with that group. Thus, language can be viewed as a binder of societies as it creates relationships and social structure between people.

Speaking multiple languages has an effect on one's identity (Berry et al., 1992). In fact, ability to speak the language reflective of one's racial/ethnic group is a dimension or a component of some racial identity models (Adaobi, 2014; Chen, 2014; Freynet & Clément, 2015;

Kouhpaeenejad & Gholaminejad 2014; Leeman, 2010). If you speak a particular language, you may feel an instant connection with someone else who speaks that language, or you may have observed people who seem to have such a connection with one another when they are speaking their native language. There is a Czech proverb that goes, "Learn a new language and get a new soul." Consistent with this proverb, and as you see from empirical studies, there are many benefits in learning a new language as doing so corresponds with learning about another culture and world view.

Christina Higgins and Kim Stoker (2011) conducted a qualitative study to examine a sense of social inclusion and belonging to Korea among four Korean-born women who were raised as adoptees in the US and had recently returned to Korea. The participants reported that they felt disconnected from Korean society in their daily interactions and were better able to connect with other Korean adoptees and marginalized groups than with Korean citizens. Participants pointed to the pressure they felt from Koreans to speak Korean fluently. The Koreans' acculturation expectation for them resulted in "a mismatch with the identities the[se] women projected for themselves" (p. 404).

In the short run, giving up one's language of origin may make it easier to fit into one's social environment when that environment does not support the language of origin. You may remember from your childhood that anyone who deviated from the predominant group was teased and ridiculed. One student, Judy, wrote about how she tried to eliminate any evidence of her difference from her peers:

> The issue of acculturation is extremely interesting to me, especially since I am not an American citizen. I was born and raised in Munich, Germany, and didn't set foot on American ground until I was eleven years old. . . . My quick assimilation into the new Californian life supports the fact that children adapt very quickly to their new environment. In my case, this was primarily driven by the fact that I just wanted to fit in!
>
> In Germany I had stood out my entire life for being Eurasian (my father is Japanese, my mother German), and the taunting and constant questions were still too fresh in my mind. I was relieved to see that being Asian was of very little consequence in my Arcadia elementary class, since the majority of the other children stemmed from an Asian background. Hence, I was determined to fit in and appear "American" in every way. I asked my mother to pack me sandwiches instead of the Tupperware dishes filled with German or Japanese leftovers. I refused to wear some of the clothes I had brought over, simply because they didn't quite look like everyone else's. I learned to speak English (accent-free) over the next year, achieved primarily by watching countless episodes of *Full House* and *I Love Lucy*. The end product resulted in my mother scolding me for "becoming completely Americanized" and trying to hide the parts of me that were the most special.
>
> —Judy, 20+-year-old German/Japanese student

In other reaction papers, Judy indicated that she wished she knew more about her background, particularly her Japanese background. Her mother imparted much of her German knowledge, but her father was not very communicative about his Japanese background. Thus, while Judy was in Germany, even though her classmates knew she was Eurasian and identified her as Japanese, her lack of knowledge about her Japanese heritage left her with a sense of loss. Had she known more about her Japanese heritage and had she known some Japanese words, her teasing classmates might have expressed interest in her instead of taunting her. When she came to America, she tried to eliminate all aspects of her German heritage so that she would fit in with other Asian and Eurasian children in her school.

Maintaining one's native language can be a source of connection with others who also speak that language.

Summary

Grice (1975) identified some conversational conventions that make face-to-face communication a co-operative endeavour. These conventions go beyond the content of the communication and to extra-verbal issues, such as turn taking, politeness, and relationships between the two conversational partners. In this chapter, we dealt with many of these extra-verbal issues. Sue and Sue (2003) identified some of these areas as proxemics, kinesics, paralanguage, and high- and low-context communication factors. We discussed some aspects of proxemics, kinesics, and paralanguage, but much of this chapter dealt with high- versus low-context communication.

Communication is more than just language. Words constitute much of the basis of our communication with one another, but they do not make up the entirety of what is being communicated. Societies that depend more on words than on the context within which the words are transmitted are called low-context communication societies. Alternatively, societies that depend more on the context to convey a message are called high-context communication societies. In general, Western societies tend to be LC and Asian societies tend to be HC. Connected with the LC–HC distinction is the distinction between direct and indirect communication. HC societies in particular use indirect communication. Part of this connection is that indirect communication in conjunction with contextual messages allows people to avoid conflict. In Asian cultures, this form of communication also allows people to save face.

There are many specific cultural differences in communication. High-context communication is associated with Asian cultures. African Caribbeans vary in their communication styles, primarily in ways that examine the authenticity of their conversational partners, particularly when their partners are White Europeans. Thus, they are attuned to issues such as stereotyping, honesty, and power. Latinos tend to be from contact cultures. Thus, they touch their conversational partners more and are more emotionally expressive. Indigenous groups appreciate silences more and are governed by a time orientation of eras as opposed to chronology. Moreover, side-by-side conversations and less eye contact are more common among some Indigenous groups.

Elderly individuals may use language in ways that vary from the ways in which young and middle-aged adults use language. Most of the research in this area has been on grandparent–grandchild communication and has revealed how knowledge is transmitted through this kind of communication. Grandparents are particularly interested in telling the story of the family, and grandchildren are particularly interested in hearing these kinds of stories.

Gender differences and similarities in communication are particularly interesting. Women, more than men, tend to use qualifiers and other forms of communication that indicate tentativeness. However, recent studies find that women use fewer qualifiers in their speech in recent decades compared to the past. It is important to note that women's conversations occur within the context of general societal sexism.

Researchers in earlier studies indicated that bilingualism reduces one's ability to function in society. However, more recent studies have demonstrated that a second language seems to add to cognitive flexibility and ability. Snow (1993) pointed out that bilingualism can be achieved in many ways, such as learning a second language beyond one's native language, having a second language imposed on one, and learning two languages from birth because two languages are spoken at home. It is surprising that being bilingual may help protect people from cognitive decline, and Bialystok and Craik (2010) found that age of onset of dementia is later for individuals who are bilingual than for those who are monolingual. Moreover, there has been an increase in emergent bilinguals in Canada. Lambert (1977) indicated that there are at least two consequences of bilingualism: cognitive and social. Besides cognitive flexibility, one cognitive consequence of bilingualism seems to be that clusters of concepts are influenced such that these clusters are a combination of the native language and the acquired language. Social consequences seem to be connections with others who also speak the language, contributions to one's identity, and ethnic pride.

FOOD FOR THOUGHT

We all have a sense of the conventions of everyday speech. Although we cannot really verbalize what conversational rules are, we can certainly recognize when they are violated. On situation comedy shows, such violations are funny; in our everyday lives, they make us feel uncomfortable. Think about times when you may have violated conversational conventions—for instance, talking louder to a person who does not understand English. After reading this chapter, you may be more conscious of how you interact with others in conversation.

Critical Thinking Questions

1. Have you ever been in a conversation with someone who violated one of the co-operative principles (e.g., the person kept talking and did not let you join in the conversation or stood uncomfortably close to you)? If so, how did that make you feel?
2. Can you recall ever being in a conversation with two (or more) people who seemed to have some inside information to which you were not privy? Did their conversation seem to leave you out of their discussion? If so, how did you signal to them that you did not know what they were talking about?
3. Do you consider yourself a high-context or a low-context communicator? How have your conversations gone with those who tend to be your context opposite?
4. Do you tend to have a direct or an indirect communication style? How does it feel when you are in a conversation with someone who uses the opposite style of communication?
5. When you are in a conversation with someone from a different racial or ethnic group, are you aware of different styles of communication?
6. Do you maintain physical contact with your conversational partners, or do some conversational partners physically touch you when they talk with you? How does this make you feel?
7. When interacting with elderly individuals, do you notice that they tend to like to transmit information about the past? When interacting with your grandparents, do they pass down family stories, particularly about your parents?
8. How does your use of social media differ from that of your parents or even from that of your older siblings or cousins?
9. Have you studied different languages? How fluent are you in those other languages?
10. Seek out people who have learned English as a second language. To what extent did they feel that English replaced their native language, or to what extent did they feel that they were able to retain their native language?

Janossy Gergely/Shutterstock

5 Immigrants, Refugees, and the Acculturation Process

Learning Objectives

Reading this chapter will help you to:

5.1 understand the distinction between immigrants and refugees;
5.2 describe phases of migration and stages of refugees' journey;
5.3 identify common experiences of immigrants and refugees;
5.4 recognize the differences among models of acculturation; and
5.5 distinguish among the different contexts in Bronfenbrenner's ecological model.

In 1604, the first European colony was established by French explorers Samuel de Champlain and Pierre de Monts at Saint Croix Island (present-day Maine), and another was built at Port-Royal in Acadia (present-day Nova Scotia) (Immigration, Refugees and Citizenship Canada, 2011). After the American Revolution in 1776, more than 40,000 Loyalists arrived in Canada from the United States to settle in Nova Scotia and Quebec. The Loyalists had German, Scandinavian, Dutch, and British origins and various religious denominations, such as Baptist, Presbyterian, Anglican, Jewish, Quaker, Methodist, and Catholic (Immigration, Refugees and Citizenship Canada, 2015).

In the mid-nineteenth century, there was a massive wave of Irish immigrants into Canada. They quickly established Irish hubs within Canadian cities and brought economic benefits to the country. However, their settlement into working-class neighbourhoods resulted in negative majority attitudes toward them. It was clear that Irish immigrants were a visible minority group, as their social, religious, and cultural values did not align with the Canadian majority (Troper, 2013).

In the late nineteenth century, English-speaking Canadians described ideal immigrants as British or White English-speaking American farmers who were independent. Despite increased pressures to select outside of these ideals in order for Canada to benefit economically, preferences remained strong; as a result, Syrian, Jewish, Asian, Roma, and Black people were seen as the least preferred immigrants. For a period of time, Asian women were not allowed to immigrate to Canada due to the belief that their immigration would encourage Asian labour workers to permanently reside in Canada (Troper, 2013).

Between 1901 and 1914, 750,000 immigrants were welcomed into Canada from the United States, and about one-third had European heritage. Through Pier 21 (in Halifax, Nova Scotia) alone, one million immigrants entered Canada between 1928 and 1971 (Immigration, Refugees and Citizenship Canada, 2011). Today, Canada's population continues to grow and is largely driven by immigration. In 2016, Canada admitted 323,192 permanent immigrants, the highest level in Canadian history. Not long after, in 2019, 313,580 more immigrants were allowed entry into Canada.

This high rate of migration is not unique to Canada. In 2019, the United Nations released a report describing global migration trends. In the last decade, the total number of migrants had increased by 13 million. Most migrants came from India, followed by Mexico, China, Russia, and the Syrian Arab Republic, with the majority settling in Europe, followed by North America, Northern Africa, and Western Asia (UN, 2019a). People may decide to migrate for many different reasons, but the most common are to seek refuge or asylum, to work internationally, and to reunite with family members.

What is certain is that immigration continues to play an important role in human behaviour. Moreover, immigration affects us all, from our own families or personal histories to the transformation of our communities.

5.1 Immigrants and Refugees

migration The movement of persons away from their place of usual residence.

Migration can be described as "the movement of persons away from their place of usual residence, either across an international border or within a State" (International Organization for Migration, n.d., para. 46). This definition does not specify the reason for movement but instead focuses on the action of moving from one geographical location to another. As you will read in this chapter, people migrate for different reasons, ranging from economical and educational purposes to family reunion and to escape from war and environmental disasters. According to How et al. (2018), *refugees* and *immigrants* have very different experiences when they arrive in their new settling country. Their stories of acculturation and stress may differ because of the differences in how they decided to migrate to a new country.

According to the UN Refugees and Migrants report (2020), *refugees* are those who flee from their birth country due to conflict, fear of persecution for their political opinion, ethnicity, religion, sexuality, and membership of a particular social group. Although there is no legal definition of *migrants*, it is generally accepted that *immigrants* are those who leave their country of birth or residence voluntarily and settle in another country either temporarily or permanently.

Immigrants

According to the United Nations definition, **international immigrants** are individuals who move into a country other than that of their nationality or usual residence so that the country of destination effectively becomes their new country of usual residence (International Organization for Migration, n.d., para. 25). Immigrants usually have some time to consider their migration. Their decision may be based on their desire to improve the lives of their families. Adult immigrants may be employed in their own country and want to apply their knowledge, expecting that their new settling country will be able to provide them a higher salary and more success than their country of origin can afford them. Other adults may have trade or professional skills and are eager to be employed. Immigrants may have a job waiting for them or at least have some assistance in finding a job (How et al., 2018).

Social support networks may be more readily available to immigrants than to refugees, both in the host country and in their country of origin, so that contacts are maintained with family members from their own country even after they leave. In that sense, immigrants may have consistent social and economic support so that they do not feel completely alone in a new host country. With their migration usually planned, immigrants tend to seek out other support systems within their own cultural group, which serve as additional safe havens and extended families.

Immigrants are more likely than refugees to have opportunities to plan their exit from their host country, arrange for orderly transportation to their chosen place of residence, pack their belongings, and say goodbye to family and friends. They may be able to ship items to their arrival place if family members or friends will be there to receive them. Family and friends may be present to welcome immigrants to their new home and to help them learn to function within their new society (Hong & Ham, 2001; How et al., 2018).

Some immigrants will have the opportunity to return to their home country periodically for visits. They may even choose to return home if the host country is not what they thought it would be. In their elderly years, immigrants may return to their home countries, remain settled in their host country, or exercise the third option of spending significant time between the host and native countries (Bolzman et al., 2006).

However, immigration experiences vary widely. Some immigrants may flee because of extreme social insecurity resulting from drug trafficking or high rates of interpersonal violence in their native countries. These immigrants may experience harsh trauma during migration, which has lasting effects for individuals and their adaptation to a host country (Sládková, 2014). Immigrants may not feel completely at home with either their host culture or their original culture.

Globally, immigrants are increasingly moving to countries that are not only far away from their home countries, but also very different culturally. **Culture shock**—the experience a person has when moving to a country in which the culture is very different from their own

international immigrants People who move into a country other than their country of origin and become residents of the new country.

culture shock The experience individuals have when moving to a country in which the culture is very different from their own.

(Tartakovsky, 2013)—may result. Some countries, such as the US and Israel, have begun building walls to keep out illegal immigrants and have even enacted policies that encourage "culturally similar" immigrants to enter and discourage "culturally different" immigrants from entering, while others, such as Canada, actively reject such policies. These policies and attitudes make immigrants feel unwelcome in their host countries (Tartakovsky, 2013).

In recent years, there have been a number of changes to immigration due to globalization. First, the number of immigrants in developed countries is continuously rising. A larger foreign population gives immigrants more electoral power and representation in policy-making and government. Their needs are being considered, which means acceptance is increasing (Tartakovsky, 2013). Furthermore, with the advent of the internet and social media, immigrants are capable of connecting with other immigrants and creating their own networks. This makes them less reliant on the host society to assimilate and also decreases the amount of control that the host society has on the immigrant population (Tartakovsky, 2013). In sum, the immigrant experience is not only varied but also ever changing in the face of global shifts and development.

Refugees and Asylum Seekers

refugees Those who are forced to flee from their birth countries due to conflict, environmental disaster, or fear of persecution.

asylum seekers A special class of refugees whose refugee claims have not been decided on by the country in which the claim is submitted.

Refugees are individuals that are forced to flee their country due to persecution, war, or violence (United Nations High Commission for Refugees, 2018). They are unable to return home or are too concerned for their safety to do so (UN High Commission for Refugees, 2018). **Asylum seekers**, a special class of refugees, are individuals who request international protection but whose refugee claims have not been decided on by the country in which the claim is submitted (UN High Commission for Refugees, 2018).

In contrast to most immigrants, not all refugees want to leave their home countries. Often, family members who leave together do not stay together. Some die during flight, and their bodies are left behind without proper burial. According to the UN Refugee Agency (2019), approximately 2275 refugees and migrants were found dead or went missing in the Mediterranean Sea in 2018. In addition to the exposure to trauma or violence in their countries of origin, refugees experience significant distress in the process of applying for refugee status (Kirmayer et al., 2011; Schock et al., 2015). This stress is added to the already high risk for post-traumatic stress disorder (PTSD), depression, chronic pain, and other somatic complaints (Kirmayer et al., 2011). Because refugees' flights are often unplanned, during their migration they may experience resistance, and sometimes violence, from individuals who are not welcoming and who are ignorant about refugees' cultures. Syrian refugees are a prime example.

The Syrian Refugee Crisis

The Syrian refugee crisis was considered one of the largest humanitarian crises of the 2010s, with over 6.6 million individuals displaced. Most refugees ended up in Europe, but many other countries accepted more over time. In 2015, during the heaviest point of the crisis, the Canadian Liberal government announced that it would be taking in 25,000 Syrian refugees. By 2017, Canada had resettled 40,000 Syrian refugees (Hynie, 2018).

The integration of so many new individuals was not an easy process, regardless of where in the world they were being taken in. Mass migration from a specific country often leads to racism and xenophobia against that ethnic group (Louis et al., 2013). In Germany, many members of the public spoke out against refugees. Media agencies began representing Syrian refugees as "others" and not part of the German identity, so much so that they were seen as threats to the social fabric of the country. The media began focusing on attacks perpetrated by refugees and painting them as threats in disguise or people who would deteriorate the Western culture and way of life (Hynie, 2018). Similarly, in Slovenia, the refugee crises were depicted as an out-of-control catastrophe. The refugee situation as a whole was denoted as a threat to society (Hynie, 2018). Glăveanu and colleagues (2018) studied memes on Reddit, a large online social platform. They found that refugees—in particular, Muslim refugees—tend to be portrayed as violent and disrespectful to women. Perhaps not surprisingly, the majority of people living in Poland (73 per cent), Greece (69 per cent), Hungary (69 per cent), and Italy (65 per cent) claim that people leaving countries such as Syria and Iraq to seek asylum are a major threat to their countries (Stokes et al., 2016). This was a common reaction across Europe, as tensions flared at the thought of millions of foreigners entering European countries.

In Canada, the media painted an empathic view of the crisis, particularly after the death of Alan Kurdi, a three-year-old Syrian boy whose boat capsized in the Mediterranean Sea as his family tried to reach Greece (Hynie, 2018). A viral photo of Kurdi was shared around the world, showing the true consequences of this crisis. Globally, Canada showed that it was more accepting of refugees and created resettlement programs like Welcome Refugees and provided considerable social assistance as the refugees arrived (Hynie, 2018). Under Welcome Refugees, the government provides essential services, such as shelter, food, and income, to refugees with the aim of facilitating their settlement in Canada. In 2021, *The Globe and Mail* interviewed several Syrian refugees in Canada on the 10-year anniversary of the beginning of the civil war in Syria. Reflecting on their experience, all of the refugees were grateful for having a chance to rebuild their lives in Canada, and they shared many heartwarming stories (Robbins, 2021). This positive experience is reflective of the favourable views that most Canadians have of Syrian refugees. A national survey reported that 48 per cent of Canadians are comfortable with the number of Syrian refugees in Canada and 10 per cent think we can welcome even more (Environics Institute for Survey Research, 2016). This is compared with 36 per cent of Canadians who think there are too many Syrian refugees, indicating that, overall, Canadians are generally supportive of the high number of Syrian refugees that Canada accepted (Environics Institute for Survey Research, 2016).

5.2 Migration Phases

There are three phases of migration to consider when speaking of immigrants and refugees: *pre-migration, migration,* and *post-migration* (Hong & Ham, 2001). The **pre-migration phase** refers to the time before individuals leave their country of origin. We must consider the established set of values, beliefs, and familial relations imposed on individuals by the norms of their culture. Disruption of set patterns and norms can affect each person differently, sometimes depending on that person's age at the time of departure to another country. Immigrants' experiences during the pre-migration period determine how readily they will be able to tolerate outside experiences and, at times, an imposed set of norms. In the pre-migration period, we must also consider rituals that are looked on as *abnormal* in the host country; after migration, individuals often do not feel that they have the freedom to practise rituals that have been an important part of their lives. These individuals usually must re-establish their rituals in certain diverse communities where they are welcome.

The **migration phase** refers to the experience of leaving the country of origin. This phase includes the feelings of the migrating individuals when they are close to departure, saying goodbye to family members and friends, and then travelling. While they are departing, they have the opportunity to really think about the decision they have made, finalized by their departure. Some people may feel fear and apprehension, and others may avoid having expectations

pre-migration phase The time before individuals leave their country of origin.

migration phase The period when individuals are migrating from their country of origin to a host country. This includes the period immediately before the migration and the process of departure.

for fear of disappointment. The separation from what is known, safe, and comfortable may bring about feelings of isolation, loss, trauma, and sometimes suicidal ideation (Hovey, 2000). Still, people who leave their countries of origin often do so in search of something better than what they have had, so they are somewhat prepared for the unknown. Immigrants have usually been prepared by social networks of people who already reside in the host country, thereby lessening the shock of relocation.

The **post-migration phase** refers to the continued stress that immigrants experience, specifically related to new societal and cultural contexts. Individuals may experience feelings of ambiguity and confusion because of the desire to hold on to their own cultural beliefs while living in a country that holds different and sometimes opposing cultural views. The post-migration period is when language, new roles and hierarchies, education, and employment begin to change. Individuals who are unable to adjust during the post-migration period may suffer financially, emotionally, and/or mentally.

The phases of migration become an important aspect to consider in predicting the outcome of immigrants' lives. Generally, the differences in the outcomes of their stories are rooted in the way immigrants left their native countries and the resources they had when settling into their host country. Unfortunately, when we talk about adaptation of immigrants, no single concept can explain how some people end up living here successfully, whereas others continue to struggle for the rest of their lives.

> **post-migration phase** The continued stress experienced by immigrants, specifically related to new societal and cultural contexts.

The Six Stages of the Refugee Journey

John W. Berry (1988, 1991), a professor emeritus of psychology from Queen's University in Canada, discusses the notion of "refugee careers" (Table 5.1) and identifies six stages:

1. Pre-departure
2. Flight
3. First asylum
4. Claimant
5. Settlement
6. Adaptation

Pre-departure refers to the conditions that force refugees from their homelands, such as wars, revolutions, and natural disasters. *Flight* refers to the period of transit away from a refugee's home country. This is a period of maximum uncertainty, during which refugees do not know where they are going. They know only that they must flee their homes and

TABLE 5.1 Berry's Six Stages of Refugee Careers

Stage	Brief description
Pre-departure	Conditions that force refugees to flee their homelands
Flight	The period of transit away from the homeland
First asylum	First place where refugees settle
Claimant	The first country of potential resettlement
Settlement	The country of settlement
Adaptation	Adjustment to the new country of settlement

Source: Berry (1988, 1991).

communities. Whereas immigrants plan their departures over the course of months or years and know where they are going, refugees often make their decision to leave in a matter of days or even hours.

First asylum refers to the first place the refugees settle where they feel safe. Conditions in these places of asylum vary widely, however, from safe and relatively good to woefully underfunded and unhealthy. According to the UN Refugee Agency (2018), in 2017 alone, 68.5 million individuals were displaced, which is equal to 44,500 people displaced every day and an individual being displaced every two seconds. Of the 68.5 million people displaced, 25.4 million were escaping their countries of origin to avoid punishment. Also in 2017, 2.9 million more refugees escaped their countries to avoid punishment than in 2016 (UN Refugee Agency, 2018). The UN Refugee Agency (2018) claims this is the biggest increase in one year, with Turkey being the top country of origin for these individuals, even though it also hosts 3.5 million refugees itself. Of all refugees displaced in 2017, 53 per cent were young, with a large number of them not living with their families. To put these numbers in perspective, the amount of people who were intentionally displaced in 2017 is almost equivalent to the entire population of Thailand. In total, one out of 110 people is an individual displaced. Overall, refugees have a high likelihood of being unemployed and getting incarcerated, and they also have lower education opportunities (UN Refugee Agency, 2018).

Claimant refers to a country that grants asylum. At this point, there is a possibility that the refugees can be deported or repatriated. Often, refugees are permitted to stay in the initial country for only a limited time. If they exceed the time limit, they are subject to deportation. *Settlement* refers to a country's formal acceptance of refugees who want to settle there. Finally, *adaptation* refers to the adjustments that refugees make to live in their new host countries. This process is referred to as *acculturation* later in this chapter.

Because refugees generally flee extremely difficult circumstances, they often experience post-traumatic stress disorder (PTSD) (Kirmayer et al., 2011; Nasiroglu & Ceri, 2016; Wulfes et al., 2019). Frequently, refugees experience deaths in their families, threats of violence or death, separation from important family members, and other forms of trauma. Trauma and adaptation intersect in complex ways. Refugees exposed to trauma and loss can experience symptoms of post-traumatic stress disorder and prolonged grief disorder, which vary according to adaption to the new culture. For example, for Mandean refugees in Australia, disruptions in social support and cultural practices predicted symptoms of post-traumatic stress disorder. Adaptation difficulties since relocating predicted prolonged grief disorder, and exposure to traumatic loss predicted post-traumatic stress disorder/prolonged grief disorder comorbidity (Nickerson et al., 2014).

Furthermore, unaccompanied minors experience developmental disruptions that threaten their educational, economic, social, and psychological well-being. There are well-documented impacts on mental health for such minors (Reavell & Fazıl, 2017; Sanchez-Cao et al., 2013). For instance, research indicates that refugee minors show high incidents of post-traumatic stress disorder and depression (Reavell & Fazil, 2017). Age and gender of refugee minors (i.e., those who are younger than 18) are associated with mental well-being (Reavell & Fazil, 2017). Specifically, older children are at a higher risk of experiencing depression symptoms as they are more likely to internalize their reactions to previous experiences because of their developed cognitive ability (Reavell & Fazil, 2017). With respect to gender, girls are more likely to experience symptoms of PTSD because they tend to score higher on intrusion and avoidance (Reavell & Fazil, 2017). In 2017, 174,000 unaccompanied children were reported fleeing alone to seek refuge in other countries (United Nations High Commission for Refugees, n.d.).

Many unaccompanied refugee children run away from camps and reception centres to find their families.

Refugees often hope to return to their country of origin. However, a lack of financial and social resources as well as the perceived threat in their own country make return an unattainable dream for most of them. For the most part, they are left in the host country with other people of their ethnic group, as a type of extended family. They usually live in neighbourhoods that are ethnically homogeneous so that they are able to fulfill their needs without having to go too far outside their respective communities. This arrangement represents a double-edged sword. On the one hand, living within their communities allows them to settle in their new land with relative ease. On the other hand, it may delay the acculturation process in the long run (Tartakovsky, 2013). According to Ryan et al. (2008), the overwhelming majority of research about refugees has not been about culture learning, ethnic identity, or economic integration but, rather, about mental health issues.

5.3 Common Experiences of Immigrants and Refugees

We have seen that there are many differences between immigrants and refugees, even when we only consider the reasons behind their migration. Just as important, however, are the potential similarities in the experiences of these groups once the individuals begin their lives in their new country.

People in a host country often do not distinguish between immigrants and refugees and use a convenient label to support a discriminatory stance. In other words, if it is convenient to label the targeted group as *immigrants*, then immigrants and refugees are lumped together under that label to support the stance that we should curb immigration. If it is convenient to label the targeted group as *refugees*, then immigrants and refugees are lumped together under that label to support a person's stance that tax dollars should not go toward supporting people fleeing from their countries of origin—freedom should be their payment.

Asian immigration to Canada has had a difficult and troubled history of exclusion and xenophobia. Asian immigrants first began moving to Canada to find work, and often they were used for cheap labour. This migration was the beginning of tensions between White Canadians and Asian immigrants, as White Canadians believed that Chinese immigrants were taking their jobs. In 1886, in an effort to stem migration from China, the Canadian government implemented a $10 head tax (equivalent to about $300 in today's worth) on every Chinese immigrant attempting to enter the country. As the years went on, this head tax continued to increase, culminating in a total of $500 per Chinese immigrant in 1903 (Man, 2013). Regardless of this tax, Chinese immigrants continued to come to Canada in search of a better life; as a result, from 1923 to 1947, the Chinese Exclusion Act was implemented. This act effectively barred any Chinese immigrant from entering Canada (Man, 2013).

Chinese immigrants were not the only Asian population the Canadian government discriminated against. All Japanese immigrants who arrived after 1922 had to report to the Royal Canadian Mounted Police (RCMP) on a regular basis (Roy, 2011). This greatly increased fear of the Japanese in Canada and caused a stir of anti-Japanese rhetoric. Newspapers called for removal of Japanese immigrants and spread hate and fear among their readers. During the Second World War, Japanese Canadians faced immense institutional discrimination from the government following the attacks on Pearl Harbour in 1941. After this attack, Prime Minister William Lyon Mackenzie King called for the deporting or detaining of all Japanese individuals, even those who were Canadian born, from the coast of British Columbia. This decision was seen as a military necessity and was the government's key justification for the institutional racism that continued against Japanese Canadians throughout this era. Japanese Canadians were fingerprinted and identified, and some were even incarcerated (Roy, 2011). After much propaganda and concern, in mid-February of 1942, Canada began moving military-age Japanese-Canadian men inland to Yellowhead to work in camps, far away from the Vancouver coast (Roy, 2011). Although Canada has a reputation for being an accepting country, there are, sadly, many examples of discrimination.

Now let us take a closer look at some of the common experiences that immigrants and refugees face in their host countries. Foremost among these experiences are problems with language barriers, support networks, changing family hierarchies, new family roles, employment, and education.

Language Barriers

People who come from other countries encounter language barriers that are sometimes hard to overcome. Differences in how individuals deal with communication problems are apparent within the older and the younger generations. As if the words were not hard enough to learn, directness in some countries (e.g., Canada, Australia, the Netherlands) clashes with indirectness in other countries (e.g., Japan, India, Iran) to create an awkward and guarded relationship between people. Generally, younger generations adapt more readily to the direct ways of certain cultures, but older people may find the directness rude and insensitive, which increases their dependence on the younger generation for communication.

Even people who can communicate reasonably well in English may experience some sort of loss. Many individuals who migrate from one country to another have little or no exposure to the host country's language. This is especially true of people from developing countries who migrate to more developed countries. How can we expect a person to succeed when that person does not know how to speak effectively with other people on a daily basis? Older immigrants may have a harder time acquiring a new language (Chiswick & Miller, 2008). They may rely on their children or the younger generation to communicate with people outside their community, a dependence that affects both older people and younger ones. Older people may feel alienated, insecure, distrustful, and useless, whereas the youth may feel overly responsible for their parents. Some young immigrants begin to lose a sense of the importance of their native tongue. Fluency in the English language becomes the mark of "a better person" within these groups, and whether someone is a refugee or an immigrant, the less pronounced the accent, the more privilege that person achieves.

Derwing and Waugh (2012) investigated the relationship between official-language (English or French) proficiency and the social integration of adult newcomers to Canada. They reviewed a variety of research findings, one of which included a longitudinal study that examined the linguistic proficiency of two groups (Mandarin speakers and Slavic-language speakers) of adult immigrants upon arrival, two years after arrival, and seven years after arrival. Derwing and Waughn (2012) found that a lack of language proficiency impacted immigrants' ability to integrate successfully socially and limited their opportunities in the workplace. Importantly, they noted that inadequate access to cultural knowledge also played a critical factor in the social integration of immigrants to Canada. For instance, some international workers had difficulty understanding the communication norms of Canada, such as the expectation that one should admit when they have made a mistake in their work. Not admitting the mistake to their superiors would be an example of a lack of cultural knowledge.

Whenever individuals feel unsuccessful within the mainstream society because of language barriers, they move into the part of the country, town, or city where most of "their own" live. This trend is apparent when we see that specific ethnic groups occupy certain towns or cities. These areas become safe havens for most immigrants or refugees and others who might be experiencing **acculturative stress**. Acculturative stress refers to behavioural and psychological reactions, characterized by uncertainty, anxiety, and depression, resulting from contact between different cultures (Sam & Berry, 2010).

Whereas immigrants, who are usually prepared to migrate, may have some knowledge of the host country's language, refugees, who had no plans to migrate, are thrown into confusion and burdened with humiliation. This situation is a result not only of their inability to speak the new language but also of the lack of social support networks willing or able to translate so that they can function and live in the new cultural context.

acculturative stress
Behavioural and psychological reactions, characterized by uncertainty, anxiety, and depression, resulting from contact between different cultures.

Support Networks

Whether an individual is an immigrant or a refugee, support networks become one of the most important factors within a societal context to assist the acculturation process. Although employment, language, roles, and education may be important, lack of support networks can be the greatest source of stress.

As we have noted, immigrants usually have more ready-support networks than refugees do. Although that is the case, we must further consider the country from which the immigrant comes and the generation travelling to the new host country. Researchers (Chadwick & Collins, 2015; Hong & Ham, 2001; Jiménez-García et al., 2011) suggest that the lack of a support network leads to social isolation and stress for many immigrants, particularly when they encounter difficult situations. We may assume that the farther one's country of origin is from the host country, the harder it is to maintain contact with family members left behind. Whenever problems of any kind arise, the isolation and stress caused by the lack of support systems may lead to anxiety, depression, and marital conflict.

Although community resources are available, immigrants and refugees fear being turned away or humiliated because of their difficulty speaking English (or the host country's language) and their different ways of behaving; as a result, they rarely reach out for help. In Canada, because limited community resources target individuals who speak English as a second language, most immigrants and refugees remain isolated. They may spend the rest of their days alone and unaware of available help. This lack of desire to reach out may stem not from total ignorance of available resources, but from previous experiences of alienation from the majority population. Technology and social media have played an important role in supporting the integration and well-being of refugees (Alencar, 2017; Díaz Andrade & Doolin, 2016).

Among immigrants and refugees, *perceived* quality of social support may be a more accurate predictor of psychological distress than the quantity of social support (Sierau et al., 2019). Therefore, larger social networks may not offer more support than another resource that the person believes can offer better support. Immigrants, who usually have a more positive view of their move, will have a more positive perception of support than will refugees, who did not want to migrate in the first place. These perceptions are an extra factor that should be considered within the context of supportive networks.

Social support has important benefits for immigrants and refugees and has an impact on their psychological and physical health and their adjustment in their country of settlement (Makwarimba et al., 2013; Morling et al., 2003; Safdar et al., 2003). Social support has been studied in terms of in-group and outgroup support.

In-group social support refers to support provided by members of a person's community, cultural group, and family (Safdar et al., 2003; Safdar et al., 2009). In-group support decreases the levels of loneliness and depression that newcomers often face when they come to a new country (Makwarimba et al., 2013). In-group support also increases community involvement and political consciousness later on (Ysseldyck et al., 2014).

Outgroup social support refers to support provided by members of the larger society and includes both informal (e.g., having friends from the mainstream society) and formal support (e.g., social services that guide the newcomer in the new host country). In general, the presence of social support contributes to the newcomer's overall happiness and satisfaction in the new country.

in-group social support Support provided by members of a person's community, cultural group, and family.

outgroup social support Support provided by members of the larger society, including both informal and formal support.

Family Structure

While migrating individuals struggle with language and maintaining social contact, changes are also taking place within their family structures. Decision-making power and the family hierarchy may dramatically shift after migration.

In many Western nations, including Canada, primarily individualistic and egalitarian principles prevail. That may cause problems in the realm of family hierarchies and organization for immigrants and refugees entering the country. Although Canada is known as a country driven by individualism, patriarchy still exists in many ways within the family, if not within the society as a whole. People from Western cultures tend to share a Canadian view of hierarchy and individualism, but some revere the mother most within the family and consider the mother the head of the family. Meanwhile, individuals from the Eastern societies tend to be collectivistic, but some are still very patriarchal.

Young Indian boys bear the burden of patriarchy in India.

Studies make a distinction between horizontal (emphasizing equality) and vertical (emphasizing hierarchy) cultural orientations within individualistic and collectivistic cultures (Triandis, 2001). In other words, there are many variations in collectivistic and individualistic countries. For instance, in vertical-individualistic societies (e.g., the UK, the US, and France), individuals gain their personal status and impress others via competition, achievement, and surpassing others (Shavitt & Cho, 2016). In contrast, in vertical-collectivist societies (e.g., Korea, Japan, and India), individuals give priority to complying with authority figures, so they emphasize the value of meeting duties and obligations (Shavitt & Cho, 2016). In horizontal-individualistic societies (e.g., Canada, Australia, Norway), individuals value equality and self-expression and disregard hierarchy. In horizontal-collectivistic societies (e.g., Brazil and several Latin American countries), individuals disregard hierarchy; instead, they value interdependence and sociability in an equalitarian manner (Chirkov et al., 2005; Shavitt & Cho, 2016). In light of all these differences, how can we begin to understand changes that take place in an individual's life after they move or flee to a host country?

For example, although Mexican families emphasize affiliation and co-operation (Falicov, 2005; Killoren et al., 2015), those values are supported with clear hierarchies. Parents and children try to achieve smooth relationships that avoid conflict. Respect for parents is a must, but in Mexican families, the mother commands much authority. For these groups, the status of the children is low and the status of the parents is high. Although a patriarchal view persists, more complex dynamics exist in a wide range: from patriarchal to egalitarian and many combinations in between (Falicov, 2005; Lam et al., 2012).

The process of acculturation disrupts this hierarchy for most families, as the children begin to command equal time and independence from parental decisions. The parents' views of how things were in the old country begin to conflict with the children's views of how things should be now that they are residing in a country that values individualism and egalitarianism. Women, who traditionally are lower in the hierarchy than their husbands and partners are, begin to demand equality, particularly after they gain employment. (Dual incomes are often necessary for the family to survive.) Daughters demand the same treatment as sons after learning about feminism and equal rights.

Many migrant families include grandparents who are regarded as the "root of the oak," commanding as much respect as the parents, if not more. Yet elderly people who migrated or fled to a new host country must also endure the changes in hierarchy. Outside responsibilities, the necessity that all members of the family be employed, and less respect for the old ways combine to lessen the importance of the elderly within Western cultures (Hossain et al., 2018). Within many Western societies, elderly individuals are encouraged to remain independent regardless of ailment, whereas in other countries, elders are viewed as part of the nuclear family.

Within the hierarchy are roles in the family subsystems that usually change. Many family members resist those changes, if only to maintain some stability, and find that other members rebel and eventually leave the system.

New Family Roles

Along with changes in the family hierarchy come changes in roles. Men who are used to being the breadwinners may be exposed to a society that allows for stay-at-home dads. Though fathers who decide to stay home are still somewhat underappreciated in Canadian society, in other countries this role *cannot* exist. Furthermore, men must give up their role as sole breadwinner in the household when their wives must enter the workforce to meet the family's needs. Women's role of housewife and mother changes to that of "supermom," who cleans the house, cares for the children, and works 40-hour weeks. Sometimes, the father must accept additional roles in childcare and housekeeping, sharing those responsibilities with his partner.

Grandparents who migrate in their later years can become strangers in the home. Their children and grandchildren are busy with their own lives, so the grandparents often begin to associate with other seniors who share their values and circumstances and with whom they feel comfortable. Although they sometimes assume the role of babysitter for the younger children while parents work, they are often not as revered as they once were in their country of origin.

Children of immigrant families have more household responsibilities than they did in pre-migration days because both parents are now working (Getrich, 2019; Hong & Ham, 2001). They also become translators for their parents publicly, especially if the parents struggle with the language of the host country.

If the family has boundaries that are too rigid to adapt to the demands of their new situation, dysfunction can occur and relationships can break down (Everri et al., 2016; Hong & Ham, 2001). Role changes between partners and their children may cause marital conflict. Children as family translators have too much power, and from a family-therapy perspective (Hayashino & Chopra, 2009; Hoffman, 1981; Nichols & Schwartz, 1998), there is a violation of generational boundaries. What this means is that adults *should* be at a higher level in the family hierarchy than children, but because the children have more power around language issues, they enter into the adults' level of power.

For most families, the demands of changing roles present difficulties that eventually modify the family system. If families cannot adjust to these changing roles, they may face dissolution.

For most of us, it is easy to say that change is necessary to maintain co-operation and avoid conflict, but for families who migrate with deeply rooted beliefs, such change is not an easy process. In a sense, it is impressive that so many families *are* able to adapt to these changes.

Employment

Reasons for immigration are clustered into four main categories:

1. Economic
2. Social
3. Political
4. Environmental

Within these broad areas, there are many factors that push people away from their countries of origin and others that pull people into a new host culture. Employment opportunities are considered a pull factor. Within these four categories, an immigrant must make a number of decisions.

It is important that immigrants have an established community in their new country to ensure that they are not isolated and have support. As described earlier, in-group support leads to better overall health for immigrants. The presence of an established cultural community in an immigrant's new country of residence is a social pull factor (Weeks et al., 2012). However, discrimination and the current political climate in individuals' home country may be a push factor, as immigrants may face discrimination they never have before; furthermore, if the political climate is not stable, this could prove to be problematic for immigrants (Chen, 2017). Economic security of the new country is a major factor for immigrants, as economic stability means a higher likelihood of finding employment, better conditions of work, and higher income. These contribute to immigrants' well-being and promise a secure future in the new country (Weeks et al., 2012).

Once immigrants are settled in Canada, prolonged low-income employment or underemployment can take its toll. Lacking English-language skills and enjoying only limited social support, most immigrants and refugees are forced to find employment in diverse communities that are also limited in growth and income. Immigrants who have sufficient financial resources attempt to establish local businesses but must do so in high-crime neighbourhoods. Some groups have financial assets tied up in their small businesses, which prevents them from moving into more favourable businesses or neighborhoods. Other groups settle into factory jobs and other low-paying, intensive manual labour that requires many working hours.

Not only do these individuals face limited employment opportunities, but once they do find employment, their pre-migration experiences, limited English, and physical characteristics become reasons for employers to discriminate against them. Promotions are nearly impossible, even for those who have held prestigious positions in their countries of origin. Degrees held by immigrants before their move are not as marketable in the settling society, and they are forced to accept jobs with much lower status. Decline in status lowers self-esteem and increases disillusionment, and these factors can eventually cause family distress. For some individuals who have some social or familial support, further education to obtain equivalent credentials is possible. For others, the necessity of making ends meet makes such opportunities impossible. Most people migrating to Canada recognize that they must attend English or

French classes to move forward with employment, but they cannot always do so. Although both immigrants and refugees suffer downward mobility as a result of limitations in employment opportunities, immigrants may suffer more because of the significant differences between their employment in their home country and their lack of ability to attain similar status in their new settling society (Gans, 2009; Vinokurov et al., 2017). For refugees, migration to another country involves issues dealing more with their survival and personal freedom than with simply trying to pursue a better life. They most likely lost their jobs and social status before leaving their host country (Gans, 2009; Heelsum, 2017).

Individuals who are unable to master the English language are easily taken advantage of and discriminated against by employers and other employees. These individuals may be forced to accept conditions that do not meet minimal legal standards, but their lack of education and their need to feed their families force them to tolerate such treatment and working conditions. Some immigrants who are able to establish businesses are leery of taking their businesses outside of smaller ethnic communities because they know that thriving within a bigger cosmopolitan setting is nearly impossible. Although some do dream that their established businesses within smaller, diverse communities are only a stepping-stone to a well-accepted and profitable venture, such dreams rarely become reality. To clinicians and other laypeople, these people present a picture of resilience, determination, content, and noble self-sacrifice (Creese & Wiebe, 2012; Hong & Ham, 2001). Yet beneath such external appearances can lie severe stress, doubt, and frustration (Hong & Ham, 2001; Morita, 2017).

Education

Immigrants in Canada and around the world are proving to have higher education than their native counterparts. For example, according to the Canadian census (Statistics Canada, 2017), four in ten immigrants in Canada have received a bachelor's degree or higher, while only under one-quarter of Canadian-born individuals can claim the same level of education. Over half of immigrants who came to Canada in the five years prior to the 2016 census have a bachelor's degree or higher (Statistics Canada, 2017). Regardless of this, immigrants' levels of poverty are still higher than Canadian-born individuals', especially chronic poverty, where an individual or family is in poverty for five or more consecutive years (Picot & Lu, 2017).

Higher levels of education do not always guarantee good economic outcomes for first-generation immigrants. Degrees may not transfer between the country of origin and the settling society, relegating highly trained professionals to menial positions, either short-term or permanently. Although this can affect the mental health and well-being of immigrants, it is important to understand that one of the primary reasons that immigrants move is to provide their children with greater opportunities.

Data show that immigrants today, much like their European counterparts from earlier generations, bring with them ambition, an extraordinary work ethic, and a willingness to sacrifice for the benefit of future generations. The educational attainment of the children of immigrants is very strong and occurs regardless of their parents' educational preparation (Waters & Pineau, 2015). According to Statistics Canada (2019b), the second generation of immigrants on average has an educational level that surpasses that of third-generation Canadian-born individuals and beyond. Unfortunately, not all immigrant groups benefit from educational opportunities in their country. For example, in Canada, many Muslim immigrants face discrimination based on Muslim stereotypes. Not only are they discriminated against by their peers, they are also judged negatively by teachers who evaluate them based on historical events, especially 9/11 (Guo, 2012). In addition, the school curricula in Canada lack sufficient cultural diversity and tend to focus on European values and practices (Guo, 2012). These prejudiced attitudes, as well as discrimination against immigrant Muslims in all domains of society, have led to low self-esteem among many Muslim Canadians, especially school-age children (Guo, 2012).

Parental involvement in academic achievement is an interesting construct to consider as researchers study cross-cultural psychology. Parental involvement in Canadian schools is considered good when parents attend parent–teacher conferences, reach out to teachers at other times, check their children's homework, and volunteer at school. But for some immigrant parents, parental involvement appears to mean something different. For Latino parents, parental involvement may be more tied to communication of parental expectations for educational attainment and monitoring of their children's activities and their parenting styles than to specific activities to advance academic achievement.

The reasons for differences in how immigrant parents versus teachers and schools understand good parental involvement may be complex. One of the authors of this book, Melanie Domenech Rodríguez, lived in Puerto Rico for a year, and her young children attended school there. She vividly recalls being stopped at the gate and being asked to leave her children there because parents were not welcome in the school. This was in sharp contrast to her experience in the United States as an active parent volunteer in the classroom and a school board member. Such differences in local practices may profoundly shape the behaviour of first-generation immigrants who may not even know the rules in North American schools. Furthermore, it is also difficult for parents with a limited or different education to support their children in completing homework. Melanie has repeatedly attempted to help her children complete math homework over the years, but the instruction practices are dramatically different in the United States today than they were in Puerto Rico in the 1970s and 1980s. Despite holding a doctoral degree, Melanie was only able to successfully help her children in mathematics when doing multiplication. Imagine what the experience must be for a parent with much less educational attainment.

Although we highlight the preceding issues as major considerations in attempting to comprehend the experiences of immigrants and refugees, they are only some of the many issues that relate to the process of acculturation. How individuals adapt to the differences between their country of origin and their host country may determine their success. In defining the success of immigrants and refugees, we should not look at the success of non-immigrant individuals who have lived all their lives in one country.

Immigrants are substantially beneficial to their society of settlement as they play a key role in population growth and economic growth. According to Statistics Canada (2018), in 2017–2018, international migration accounted for 80 per cent of the population growth. This is especially important due to Canada's ageing population and low fertility rates. Immigrants, then, make certain that Canada's population continues to flourish, which in turn ensures that the labour force continues to grow (Immigration, Refugees and Citizenship Canada, 2019). It is estimated that by 2036, the worker-to-retiree ratio will be 2:1 (Immigration, Refugees and Citizenship Canada, 2017). However, since immigrants are typically younger, they can help lessen any further decline of this ratio. In addition, immigrants help fill the labour gaps of those who are retiring, stimulating economic growth. Also, when a person migrates to Canada, they become part of the consumer market, entailing that they pay taxes and may invest in property, again contributing to Canada's economic growth.

In the next section, we apply the process of acculturation to *natural citizens,* as well as to immigrants and refugees.

5.4 Acculturation

Acculturation, the process by which groups and individuals change as a result of intercultural interactions (Redfield et al., 1936), can indeed be difficult—spanning myriad experiences across people and over time that have important social, economic, and psychological impacts.

Acculturation is clearly evident in immigrants and refugees because of the sharp differences in language, beliefs, values, and practices between groups. Acculturation is also seen within national groups, as is the case in cross-ethnic interactions within a country (e.g., Anglo-Quebecers). We focus our discussion on immigrants and refugees to help us make meaningful comparisons involving the acculturation process and facilitate further examination of cross-cultural topics.

We are all aware of how difficult it is to grow up and face developmental, societal, and economic changes in our own multicultural society. Can we, then, begin to imagine how hard it is for people who grew up in a different country with different norms? Can we imagine the acculturation process that occurs in a new host country? We must consider language, norms, education, family systems, and more, as well as the confusing and sometimes heartbreaking experiences immigrants and refugees must endure. Some might argue that people can stay where they are and avoid this process, but that defies our human history, which is one of constant motion. From the first humans to inhabit the earth, people have been migrating to new lands in search of better living conditions.

Tseng and Yoshikawa (2008) reported acculturation was most often conceptualized, measured, and analyzed at the individual level; acculturation measures are used to assess individuals' levels of acculturation, and then individuals' acculturation levels are analyzed in relation to individual-level outcomes such as physical and mental health status, social and emotional well-being, and educational achievement. Depending on the changes people go through, their stress levels will differ.

Note that acculturation is a *process* as opposed to an *outcome*. In other words, people who immigrate to a new society are acculturating—or adjusting—to their new host country, as opposed to trying to achieve a certain level of acculturation as an end point. Moreover, the host country is also undergoing a process of adjusting to immigrants. For example, Markham, Ontario, is described as a "majority-minority" city, in which 78 per cent of the city's population is a visible minority (Statistics Canada, 2017). With the vast majority of visible minorities being of Chinese descent (46 per cent), it is no surprise that the city has adapted certain practices. Notably, most signs in Markham are in Chinese, and even the bank serves customers in Cantonese and Mandarin (Ansari, 2018). Also, large grocers, such as FoodyMart, aim to serve the Chinese population by providing traditional Chinese cuisine.

It is critical for psychologists to note that nearly all research on acculturation treats the variable as a static predictor or outcome. There is very little longitudinal research on acculturation, so little is known about how individuals acculturate over time and how these patterns of change relate to health and well-being. This presents a great opportunity for psychology students who are looking for topics to research.

Acculturation is a bi-directional process (Schwartz et al., 2010). While groups are trying to acculturate to the host culture, the success of their adjustment is at least partially dependent on how the host culture reacts to them; that is, when new immigrants arrive, they undergo a process of change, but so do the people who come in contact with them. If

acculturation Experiences and changes that groups and individuals undergo when they come in contact with a different culture.

a group experiences discrimination, the acculturation process is impeded. According to John Berry, who is considered the father of psychological research on acculturation, "There is evidence that discrimination is often the most powerful predictor of poor psychological and sociocultural adaptation" (Sam & Berry, 2010, p. 479). This is also the position taken by Schwartz et al. (2010).

Enculturation can be considered the other side of the acculturation coin. Through enculturation, individuals retain or deepen their learning of their own cultural norms (B. S. Kim & Abreu, 2001). There is much less research into enculturation, yet researchers in one meta-analysis reported that enculturation did not predict negative mental health outcomes such as depression, anxiety, psychological distress, and negative affect. On the contrary, enculturation predicted positive mental health outcomes, specifically self-esteem, satisfaction with life, and positive affect (Yoon et al., 2013). This finding is important because individuals connecting with their culture of origin may build important resilience in the process.

> **enculturation** When individuals retain or deepen their learning of their own cultural norms.

Models of Acculturation

Traditionally, researchers in the field have identified the process of adjusting to a new culture as being assimilated into that culture. These researchers contend that immigrants or refugees maintain their original cultures for the most part, then their children begin to transition to acquiring the norms and values of the host culture while they lose their connection to their parents' culture, and then the grandchildren of the immigrants or refugees lose almost all connection with their grandparents' culture. By the third or fourth generation, there is

Immigrant parents are often conflicted as to how traditionally they should raise their children versus how Westernized their children should be raised.

TABLE 5.2 Berry's Model of Acculturation

Status	Brief descriptions
Assimilationist	An individual who has given up the identity of origin in favour of identifying with the host culture's values and beliefs
Separationist	An individual who identifies with the identity of origin and rejects all of the host culture's values and beliefs
Marginalist	An individual who does not identify with either the original culture or the host culture
Integrationist	An individual who combines (integrates) aspects of the original culture and the host culture

Source: Reproduced with permission of Sam & Berry (2016).

almost no hint of the original culture in favour of the norms and values of the host culture (Gordon, 1964; Warner & Srole, 1946). However, most researchers now feel that there are different ways of acculturating. They have examined models of acculturation to foster understanding of the processes that individuals undergo before, during, and after their move to a new country. (Keep in mind that the classifications in this model [and others] are processes rather than end points.)

Acculturation of Immigrants

John Berry laid the foundations for research on acculturation within psychology (Brislin, 2000; Kim, 2009; Leong, 2001; Schwartz et al., 2010). Berry's (1990, 1997) original model is presented in Table 5.2.

Uzma Jalaluddin, an Indian-Canadian writer and high school teacher, discusses her experience observing her children's acculturation in Canada:

> My kids have never visited India. They don't know how to speak Urdu, the language I grew up with, or Malayalam, the south Indian language of my husband's family. They also have no spicy Indian food game, and any time I make biryani or rajmah or palak paneer, they ask what else they can eat for dinner. They do like butter chicken, but when a curry is also a pizza-and-poutine topping choice, it loses its cultural authenticity. . . . Culture is about more than food or colourful clothing. It is a mindset, a way to experience the world and navigate one's place within. Culture is family and history tradition. . . . Every parent marvels at how much things have changed since they were kids. For immigrants, and the children of immigrants, this feeling is magnified by their dislocation of place, or the echo of that dislocation in their children's lives. In contrast, my kids don't struggle with the same identity issues. They don't feel the tug of war between the culture of "back home" and here. For them, "back home" is a historical fact, not a living reality. While I'm happy for their firm foothold in Canada, their lack of cultural knowledge also makes me sad.
>
> —Uzma Jalaluddin, Indian-Canadian high school teacher (Jalaluddin, 2018)

According to Berry's model, although Uzma may still feel very close to her culture, her sons seem to be representative of the **assimilationist** in Canadian society. Her sons do not partake in any cultural traditions or beliefs as they have grown accustomed to the Canadian culture. As Uzma describes, home to her is India, but to her sons it is, and always will be, Canada. The children have essentially become Canadian, and, possibly in their own minds,

assimilationist An individual who accepts the host society values but rejects the values of their heritage culture.

that has made their transition easier. The sons may believe that they will be more accepted if they are like everyone else. Assimilationists can also be said to believe in guilt by association, in that they think that they will increase their level of privilege if they are closely associated with the majority culture. However, is that true?

> My wife and I are very traditional, and we stick to all Sudanese customs. This is very important to us. We have sent our children to school back in Sudan, so they know what it is to be Sudanese. Otherwise, they might become too Australian. I want them to be able to have a good future in their own country. I hope when my daughter grows up, she will want to marry a Sudanese man. It is very important, culturally, that she does. If I want to socialise with friends, I prefer to go to the Sudanese Club. I am always welcome there and the people have similar values to mine. I often find that Australians are very forthright, and I find it difficult to relate to Australians about anything. I do not want to become Australian. It is important that my family and I maintain Sudanese citizenship.
> —Sadiq, Sudanese immigrant in Australia (Makwarimba et al., 2013)

separationist An individual who rejects the host society values and only accepts the values of the heritage culture.

Some of us may applaud Sadiq's strict commitment to pursue and follow his own beliefs and his refusal to assimilate into the majority culture. However, some may wonder how Sadiq can ever become successful in Australia if he refuses to follow any of its traditions, especially if he intends to stay. According to Berry's model, Sadiq's case is representative of the **separationist**. Separationists refuse to observe any traditions of their host country. They strongly maintain the beliefs and values of their country of origin and are unwilling to identify with any other culture, even though they are confronted with the values of the host country on a daily basis. Sadiq and others like him may have observed and experienced discrimination because of their ethnic and cultural backgrounds. Whereas others prefer to join the majority to avoid the wrath of society, Sadiq chose to stay separate from the majority as much as he could for the same reason. Although Sadiq belongs in a different group than others who assimilate, hate and fear exist within both groups because of the experiences that they have been through.

> Growing up, I got punched . . . robbed for my clothes, was jumped on multiple occasions, fought back, and broke knuckles . . . I was too scared to tell my parents what was happening.
> My Ecuadorian father would have slapped some machismo into the side of my head and told me to defend myself. That's what he had been taught by his father before him and, likely, what drew me to crave the acceptance of other men his age.
> I had to survive—so I joined a gang. . . .
> It's now 22 years later and I am a federal offender, ex-gang member, and an ex-drug dealer. For my crimes, I have served more than 11 years of my life behind bars. . . .
> Upon my release, I began a non-profit initiative that aimed at helping the marginalized in my community improve their mental health with fitness, as it had helped me when I was incarcerated.
> I am now the executive director of a non-profit organization that works with youth. . . . Additionally, I mentor various youths who are trying to escape the street life and transition into a life of normalcy.
> —Jose Vivar, former gang member turned advocate (Vivar, 2019)

marginalist An individual who rejects the host society's values and also rejects the heritage culture values.

Jose is representative of Berry's **marginalist** category. Marginalists are alienated individuals who neither adopt values of the host culture nor hold on to the values of their own culture.

These people, as shown by Jose's story, must create their own group, with separate norms and a different value system, which some of us may not completely understand. This group paints the classic picture of rebellion. They turn their backs on society, just as they feel that society has turned its back on them. They choose a family that accepts them regardless of where they come from. Although marginalist groups are considered the outcasts of society, they still come together by having something in common. Besides the common experience of not belonging, they may share common ethnic backgrounds, religion, beliefs, and so on.

The last group is the **integrationists, or biculturals**. These individuals are able to make the best of both worlds. They hold on to their own values, beliefs, and culture while learning about and adapting to their host culture. Integrationists are the individuals who are deemed most likely to succeed (David et al., 2009; Thomas et al., 2010). They also seem to be the most well-balanced and the happiest of the four main groups. Although they can function in the host society, they are still able to relate to their own people without difficulty. We could suppose that integrationists are more readily able to deal with people from other ethnic groups because they have adopted a flexibility of association. Research reveals that integration is advantageous to an immigrant's psychological and social well-being (Safdar et al., 2012; Ward, 2013). Integration is associated with higher levels of well-being and less acculturative stress (Scottham & Dias, 2010; Ward, 2013). In addition, integrated immigrants generally have higher self-esteem than those who are not integrated (Berry & Sabatier, 2010; Ward, 2013). Finally, integration is also associated with low levels of identity conflict, which further enhances the integrated individual's overall well-being (Ward, 2013; Ward et al., 2011).

integrationists or biculturals Individuals who hold on to their original values while also learning and adopting the values of the host culture.

It could be that these acculturation groups are not necessarily stable, meaning there may be fluidity in a person's status. More specifically, at age 14, someone may be grouped with marginalists, who choose to give up their own cultural beliefs while refusing to adopt those of the host culture. The changes that this same person experiences can later allow that person to go from being a marginalist to being an integrationist. It could also be that a person is associated with more than one group over the course of the lifetime. This fluidity suggests that there are more variables to consider when looking at the processes that immigrants and refugees must go through to appropriately acculturate into their host culture.

Acculturation of Diverse Populations

LaFramboise proposes a model of acculturation from her Native American perspective (LaFramboise et al., 1993). Similar to J. Berry's model, LaFramboise's model (Table 5.3) includes *assimilationists,* who are also defined as people who completely absorb the dominant

TABLE 5.3 LaFramboise and Associates' Model of Acculturation

Status	Brief description
Assimilation	Absorption into the dominant culture
Acculturated	Competence in a second culture without complete acceptance
Fusion	The process of combining one's culture of origin with the host culture, creating a somewhat new culture
Alternation	The process of alternating between one's culture of origin and the host culture depending on what the context dictates
Multicultural	Distinct cultural identities are maintained with a single multicultural social structure

Source: Reproduced with permission from LaFramboise et al. (1993). Copyright © 1993, American Psychological Association.

culture. Although assimilationists believe that complete absorption into the dominant culture ensures acceptance, they may experience rejection from the members of their own cultural group. Assimilationists also lose their original cultural identity, which may later cause guilt and isolation.

LaFramboise and associates (LaFramboise et al., 1993) define individuals who are competent in a second culture without completely accepting it as being acculturated. This group seems to mirror integrationists in that people are able to show competence within the dominant culture. The difference is that individuals who are classified as acculturated are always identified as members of the minority culture, and they are relegated to a lower status and not completely accepted, even given their capabilities. Chao et al. (2007) might call these individuals *bicultural essentialists*, people who believe that there is an essential quality to their ethnicity. Such individuals may experience more difficulties in switching between cultures than they consciously realize.

Another group defined by LaFramboise and associates (LaFramboise et al., 1993) is characterized by fusion. This idea is similar to the melting pot theory, wherein individuals come together to form a new, homogenous culture from parts of the different cultures. The opposite of the melting pot approach is multiculturalism, where it is recognized that many cultures are accepted and encouraged to thrive without promoting any one culture as dominant or the norm.

Fusion differs from Berry's assimilation group because aspects of multiple cultures are integrated into a new culture. Cultures of origin are not distinct and identifiable (LaFramboise et al., 1993). Fusion can sometimes be used as an excuse to "not see colour" or other differences among people, which some people may argue is the perpetuating principle behind continuing racist acts. In Chapter 6, you will learn about colour-blindness.

A group that seems to have similarities with Berry's (1990, 1997) integrationist model is the alternation group (LaFramboise et al., 1993). This group regards two cultures as equal. Individuals do not have to choose between the two cultures and can alter their behaviour to fit the context. LaFramboise et al. (1993) see this group as the optimal one, just as Berry (1990, 1997) describes the integrationist group as his most positive one. Though the alternation group is optimal and many people would like to be able to adjust themselves according to context, this kind of life is not easy. It is not always possible to maintain positive relationships, even when an individual can adapt and adjust accordingly. However, there does seem to be some evidence that individuals can master this process (Devos, 2006).

The **multicultural model**, according to LaFramboise et al. (1993), involves cultures with distinct identities joined together within a social structure. Individuals from one culture co-operate with those of other cultures to serve common needs. This is different from the melting pot notion in that each subculture can maintain its identity while living among others without necessarily assimilating or completely adopting the others' cultures. This group may be more accurately described by Jesse Jackson's[1] pluralistic quilt idea, in which each culture can be seen apart from the others, yet they are all joined within the same blanket. This is the optimal and most extreme definition of the multicultural model. When there is interaction, however, there also tends to be mutual influence, and cultures of origin tend not to be distinctly maintained. Thus, the multicultural group is difficult to achieve in practice (LaFramboise et al., 1993).

The Berry and LaFramboise models of acculturation help us to determine the ways that people adapt to this society. These models could apply not only to immigrants and refugees but also to members of minority cultures who are trying to adapt successfully. However, as stated

---

multicultural model The multicultural model involves cultures with distinct identities joined together within a social structure.

previously, the process of acculturation and the success of immigrants who are attempting to adjust to a new culture can be determined by their experiences before, during, and after their arrival in the host country.

5.5 Bronfenbrenner's Ecological Model

As one approach, consider some researchers' suggestions of a necessary ecological fit for migrating individuals (Falicov, 1998, 2005; Hong & Ham, 2001). By **ecological fit or ecological context**, we mean the degree to which there is a match between the sociocultural environment in the migrant's culture of origin and the country to which the migrant is immigrating. Tseng and Yoshikawa (2008) suggest that an ecological perspective opens up our conceptualization of acculturation to include process of change at the social setting; social network; and organizational, institutional, community, and policy levels. Several layers of ecological context must be considered, and we cannot stress enough how important an individual's context is as the individual moves from the smallest layer or system of ecological context to the largest. Modified from Bronfenbrenner's (1979) model, the layers are as follows:

- Microsystem
- Mesosystem
- Exosystem
- Macrosystem (Figure 5.1)

ecological fit or ecological context Similarity of the social and cultural environments between an immigrant's country of origin and new host country.

microsystem A layer of context that includes relationships among family members living within one household.

mesosystem A layer of context that includes relationships in the immediate area outside the family, such as schools, work, the extended family, and the community in which one lives.

exosystem A layer of context that includes major societal institutions, such as the media and the government.

These layers are relevant to acculturation because of possible stressors that exist within each layer and because they may dictate an individual's degree of acculturation.

The **microsystem** includes relationships among family members. These relationships primarily involve the immediate family living in the same household. The **mesosystem** extends to relationships outside the family but is limited to the school, the workplace, extended families, and the community in which one lives. The **exosystem** involves the major societal institutions, such as the media, the government, and laws. Finally, the **macrosystem** encompasses the cultural norms and societal rules that determine the overall exchanges and interactions of the society in which we live. These four systems are interrelated, which means that things occurring at the smallest level of context can affect what occurs in the largest context (Hong & Ham, 2001).

When we observe the migration process, we can imagine how a person's ecological fit is disrupted. Immigrants and refugees are moved from a familiar environment in which the rules of the government and their communities are well defined. During their flight or migration, their context changes, and all that they are familiar with becomes unknown. As they go

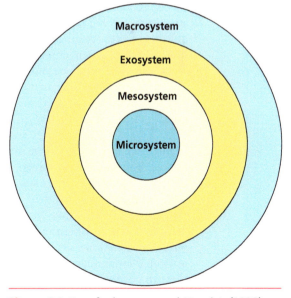

Figure 5.1 Bronfenbrenner and Morris's (1998) ecological model.

Source: Reproduced with permission from Bronfenbrenner and Morris (1998).

macrosystem A layer of context that includes the cultural norms and societal rules that determine rules of conduct.

through the different stages of migration (pre-migration, migration, and post-migration), they will experience changes within the different layers or systems. Such changes are inevitable because of the different belief systems and cultural norms that exist in their host country.

We can begin to see how the different systems are composed of a person's family, language, roles, and beliefs, but the geographical context also becomes an issue. In considering individuals outside the majority culture, intersecting layers of issues must be discussed within the same context. We cannot describe the reasons individuals have for leaving their country of origin without describing the changes that individuals must endure. Additionally, the changes come from imposed rules within the host culture and affect rules learned from the country of origin. The changes that take place during and after migration, sometimes drastic, result in culture shock and acculturative stress. Most minority culture members must make a choice between holding on to their own culture and adopting the majority culture.

More specifically, certain migrating groups experience more culture shock and acculturative stress than others do. How can we explain that? Again, we go back to the question of which variables are to be taken into consideration when looking at a healthy acculturation process.

In consideration of the acculturation process, we should begin with the reason behind the need to migrate to another country. Although we noted earlier that the acculturation process is not limited to immigrants and refugees, most of our discussion related to the issues of migrating individuals. Individuals who undergo the process of acculturation and are natural citizens of Canada do not experience the stressors of pre-migration and migration. They may share some post-migration experiences of immigrants and refugees, mainly involving stereotypes, prejudice, and discrimination.

Immigrants and refugees face the challenge of holding on to their own beliefs while they attempt to succeed in their host country. They must learn a different language and adapt to different roles to remain physically and mentally healthy. They must also deal with the changes that their children undergo and how those changes modify their family structure. They learn to accept their limitations and sharpen their skills so that they can maintain a certain lifestyle most befitting a Canadian context.

Summary

Immigrants and refugees have much in common, but they also have important unique experiences. Both come from foreign lands and face challenges adapting to a new language and customs. However, there are some important psychological differences. Immigrants decide to migrate for economic, political, and/or personal reasons. Thus, the acculturation process starts before immigrants arrive. They learn about the culture and norms of their settling society, decide whether those norms are consonant with their view of the world, and carefully decide where in the new society they will settle. Often, they have family and friends here who can assist in their immigration process or at least help them with the kinds of norms and services that can be of assistance.

In contrast, refugees have very little time to decide to leave their homelands, often only a few hours. They may not want to leave but perhaps oppose those in power and must flee political upheaval or the threat of death. They do not know where they will finally settle because their overriding motivation to leave is to save their lives. After they leave their homelands, they typically are held in refugee camps that are overcrowded and unsanitary. Throughout the process of leaving (before, during, and after), refugees often experience a great deal of trauma, such as seeing family members and friends die or going through extreme hardships of transit. As a result of these circumstances, the acculturation process cannot begin before the refugees arrive in their host countries.

Once in their host countries, both immigrants and refugees must acculturate to their new surroundings; that is, they must adjust to the new country, with its unfamiliar customs and values. Among the challenges they face are language barriers, new family roles, employment opportunities, and educational opportunities. Often, children learn the new language much faster than their parents do and are able to interact with the social agencies of the new country. This gives the children more power than their parents have and leads to a disruption of the family hierarchy.

Researchers have developed models of acculturation that identify various resolutions of acculturation, such as maintaining two cultural competencies, holding on to the traditional culture, blending the two cultures, or being confused about cultural issues. The degree to which immigrants and refugees successfully adjust to their host culture depends on the degree to which they can successfully negotiate the blending of their traditional values with the new values of their host cultures.

FOOD FOR THOUGHT

Most of you attend colleges and universities with immigrants and refugees who have recently settled in Canada. Colleges and universities may have special offices that support cross-cultural and/or international students and offer specific programs, such as guest speakers or movie events. Take advantage of these offerings. If you know any immigrants or refugees, ask them whether they might be willing to tell you why their families came to Canada. Were they immigrants or refugees? Note that some people came to Canada as small children and might not know all the circumstances that brought them here. If you engage in a conversation with immigrants or refugees, you might want to ask them whether their parents feel a need to talk about their reasons for coming to Canada. More often than not, people want their stories heard, and you might be able to learn something from their parents.

Critical Thinking Questions

1. What is the history of your family in Canada? What hardships did your family experience when coming to Canada? What were the conditions of your family's ancestral homeland before they arrived?
2. If you are an Indigenous person, what hardships did your family encounter when members came in contact with European Canadians? What were the conditions of your family's ancestral home before your family came in contact with European Canadians?
3. If your family immigrated to Canada, did family members settle in an area known for immigrants from your family's country, or did they settle in an area that was widely integrated?

4. If your family immigrated to Canada, did your ancestors speak English, or did they have to learn English after arriving here? If they spoke a non-English language, what issues did they encounter?
5. What roles within your family changed after your family arrived in Canada?
6. How would you characterize yourself according to the acculturation models? Are you different from others in your family? If so, what are the differences?

Note

1. In his 1988 US presidential campaign, Jesse Jackson described "a quilt of many colours" sewn by his grandmother. He said that a single patch of colour was not large enough to provide warmth, but that when it was combined with other patches of colour, the result was a quilt that could keep someone warm and safe.

Shawn Goldberg/Shutterstock

6 Stereotyping, Prejudice, Discrimination, and Racism

Learning Objectives

Reading this chapter will help you to:

6.1 understand the differences among stereotyping, prejudice, discrimination, and racism;
6.2 describe stereotype threat and conditions under which it occurs;
6.3 explain the processes that lead to the development of negative stereotypes;
6.4 recognize the characteristics of systematic racism in the criminal justice system and politics;
6.5 identify components of overt versus covert racism;
6.6 recognize the characteristics of aversive racism and colour-blind racial ideology;
6.7 know the three categories of racial microaggressions and strategies that are appropriate for combating them;
6.8 explain the five levels of the biopsychosocial model and its relevance to racism; and
6.9 distinguish between White-European privilege and allied behaviours.

There's an old story about an elementary teacher. Her name was Mrs Thompson. And as she stood in front of her fifth-grade class on the very first day of school, she told the children a lie. Like most teachers, she looked at her students and said that she loved them all the same.

But that was impossible, because there in the front row, slumped in his seat, was a little boy named Teddy Stoddard. Mrs Thompson had watched Teddy the year before and noticed that he didn't play well with the other children, that his clothes were messy, and that he constantly needed a bath. And Teddy could be unpleasant. It got to the point where Mrs Thompson would actually take delight in marking his papers with a broad red pen, making bold X's and then putting a big F at the top of his papers.

At the school where Mrs Thompson taught, she was required to review each child's past records, and she put Teddy's off until last. However, when she reviewed his file, she was in for a surprise.

Teddy's first-grade teacher wrote, "Teddy is a bright child with a ready laugh. He does his work neatly and has good manners . . . he is a joy to be around."

His second-grade teacher wrote, "Teddy is an excellent student, well-liked by his classmates, but he is troubled because his mother has a terminal illness and life at home must be a struggle."

His third-grade teacher wrote, "His mother's death has been hard on him. He tries to do his best, but his father doesn't show much interest, and his home life will soon affect him if some steps aren't taken."

Teddy's fourth-grade teacher wrote, "Teddy is withdrawn and doesn't show much interest in school. He doesn't have many friends and he sometimes sleeps in class."

By now, Mrs Thompson realized the problem, and she was ashamed of herself. She felt even worse when her students brought her Christmas presents, wrapped in beautiful ribbons and bright paper, except for Teddy's. His present was clumsily wrapped in the heavy brown paper that he got from a grocery bag.

Mrs Thompson took pains to open it in the middle of the other presents. Some of the children started to laugh when she found a rhinestone bracelet with some of the stones missing, and a bottle that was one quarter full of perfume. But she stifled the children's laughter when she exclaimed how pretty the bracelet was, putting it on, and dabbing some of the perfume on her wrist.

Teddy Stoddard stayed after school that day just long enough to say, "Mrs Thompson, today you smelled just like my mom used to." After the children left, she cried for at least an hour. On that very day, she quit teaching reading and writing and arithmetic. Instead, she began to teach children.

Mrs Thompson paid particular attention to Teddy. As she worked with him, his mind seemed to come alive. The more she encouraged him, the faster he responded.

By the end of the year, Teddy had become one of the smartest children in the class, and, despite her lie that she would love all the children the same, Teddy became one of her "teacher's pets."

A year later, she found a note under her door from Teddy, telling her that she was still the best teacher he ever had in his whole life.

Six years went by before she got another note from Teddy. He then wrote that he had finished high school, third in his class, and she was still the best teacher he ever had in his whole life.

Four years after that, she got another letter, saying that while things had been tough at times, he'd stayed in school, had stuck with it, and would soon graduate from college with the highest of honours. He assured Mrs Thompson that she was still his best and favourite teacher he ever had in his whole life.

Then four more years passed and yet another letter came. This time he explained that after he got his bachelor's degree, he decided to go a little further. The letter explained that she was still his best and favourite teacher he ever had. But now his name was a little longer—the letter was signed Theodore F. Stoddard, M.D.

The story doesn't end there. You see, there was yet another letter that spring. Teddy said he'd met this girl and was going to be married. He explained that his father had died a couple of years ago, and he was wondering if Mrs Thompson might agree to sit in the place at the wedding that was usually reserved for the mother of the groom. Of course, Mrs Thompson did.

And guess what? She wore that bracelet, the one with several rhinestones missing. And she made sure she was wearing the perfume that Teddy remembered his mother wearing on their last Christmas together.

They hugged each other, and Dr Stoddard whispered in Mrs Thompson's ear, "Thank you, Mrs Thompson, for believing in me. Thank you so much for making me feel important and showing me that I could make a difference."

Mrs Thompson, with tears in her eyes, whispered back. She said, "Teddy, you have it all wrong. You were the one who taught me that I could make a difference. I didn't know how to teach until I met you."

This story has been used repeatedly and in a wide variety of settings to inspire people—especially teachers—with the power of a single individual's influence on others' lives. Although the story is fictional, it illustrates what can happen when we help individuals in need and open them up to a world of possibilities. This version of the story travelled around the internet several years ago and has been published on Barbara and David Mikkelson's website (Mikkelson & Mikkelson, 2005). In sum, the essence of the Teddy Stoddard story is true.

As mentioned, this story is used primarily as a poignant way of motivating teachers to inspire their own students. It appears in various forms on tens of thousands of websites. Why has the story become so popular? What is it about this story that resonates with people?

Besides demonstrating that teachers can make a difference (or, more broadly, that people can make a difference) in other people's lives, this story also demonstrates how wrong we can be when we make judgments about others without knowing their stories or personal histories. Let us explore this notion further.

One of the more important theories in social psychology is **attribution theory** (Kelly, 1967, 1973), which describes how people explain the causes of human behaviour. Attribution theory suggests that we use two primary dimensions to develop judgments (attributions) about others' behaviours: the internal–external dimension and the stable–unstable dimension. When combined, these two dimensions yield four possible explanations of another's behaviours: internal–stable, internal–unstable, external–stable, and external–unstable. For example, if you were to see Bobby hit Alejandro, you might say that Bobby is an aggressive child (an internal–stable attribution), that Bobby was in a bad mood (an internal–unstable attribution), that everyone hits Alejandro (an external–stable attribution, since this is external to Bobby), or that Alejandro just hit Bobby, so Bobby reciprocated (an external–unstable attribution; Table 6.1).

According to Ross (1977), we have a tendency to overuse dispositional (internal–stable) attributions and to underestimate external causes for behaviours. Thus, of the four attributions, we tend to believe that Bobby is an aggressive child before we believe any of the other

attribution theory A theory that attempts to determine the cause of a behaviour. Two major dimensions are internal–external and stable–unstable.

TABLE 6.1 Attribution Theory: Four Kinds of Attributions for Bobby Hitting Alejandro

	Internal	External
Stable	Internal–stable: Bobby is an aggressive child.	External–stable: Everyone hits Alejandro.
Unstable	Internal–unstable: Bobby was in a bad mood.	External–unstable: Alejandro just hit Bobby.

fundamental attribution error or correspondence bias The tendency to overestimate dispositional (internal, stable) causes of behaviours and to underestimate external causes of behaviours.

three possible explanations of his behaviour. This tendency is called the **fundamental attribution error or correspondence bias** (Ross, 1977). Our assessment may or may not be an error, but if we ignore possible external reasons for certain behaviours, then we may be committing this error. For example, Bobby may be an aggressive child, so our attribution of him as an aggressive child may be accurate. However, if he is *not* an aggressive child and we fail to take into account that Alejandro just hit him, we would be committing dispositional bias if we were to assume that Bobby is aggressive. The tendency to commit the fundamental attribution error may be more of a Western error because there are some indications that Eastern Asians do not have this tendency (Choi et al., 1999). Therefore, the term *fundamental* is not accurate as this error is not fundamental to all people. Rather, it is an error or a bias that is identified more among people in some cultures than others.

Let us consider the Teddy Stoddard story once again. How many of you automatically thought that Teddy Stoddard was a child with European background? That was our immediate reaction, too. Mrs Thompson (whom we might also have assumed to have a European background) turned this child's life around and made him a productive member of society. However, let us engage in a thought experiment: suppose that Teddy Stoddard was an African-Caribbean child and Mrs Thompson had a European background. What might have been the result? Mrs Thompson might have responded in a different manner, still compassionate and caring, but different. She might have thought, "Oh, what a shame that this child has had such a hardship! I should not be so hard on him. Maybe I will grade his papers with a bit more leniency."

We bring this up because in the story, Mrs Thompson reacted to Teddy as an individual, and she gave him a kind of encouragement that resulted in his blossoming into a success story. Alternatively, in our thought experiment, Mrs Thompson sees Teddy as a representative of a particular ethnic group. As a result, her caring for him might have resulted not in his flourishing but, rather, in his recognizing that not all people with European background are bad and that some will treat him with more kindness than others do. He might have been more forgiving toward those with a European background who treated him with less compassion. One of the challenges that people of colour face is that others, including those with a European background, tend to engage in another kind of attributional error: the **ultimate attribution error**. Thomas Pettigrew (1979) coined this term to mean that when attributions are directed toward individuals who represent a particular group, the internal and stable attributions are ascribed to the group members instead of just to the individual. Again, in the case of Bobby hitting Alejandro, if Bobby were an African-Caribbean child, an ultimate attribution error would be to say, "Children with African-Caribbean background are so aggressive," instead of limiting the aggression to Bobby.

ultimate attribution error The tendency to ascribe the cause of a behaviour to dispositional characteristics of the group rather than to an individual member.

The ultimate attribution error can be applied to any group that can be targeted for discrimination. Have you ever heard one woman's behaviour attributed to all women? One LGBTQ2+ person's behaviour attributed to all LGBTQ2+ persons? One person's behaviour from a religious minority attributed to all people from that religion? This is how the attribution error can undermine entire groups of people.

6.1 Social Categorizations and Their Consequences

> If you are Jewish, you are teased. They call you stingy. They throw five cents at you. Or they throw money on the ground and call out "Who is the Jew?" Or they will say, "That's a Jew nose." They say something about *payot* [sidelocks]. Then they have a *brit* [circumcision] set. Or they take scissors and go like this [demonstrating scissors cutting with his hands]: "Do you want another *brit*?"
>
> —A Jewish male high school student in Sydney, Australia (Gross & Rutland, 2014, p. 318)

Is this student's story one of stereotyping, prejudice, discrimination, or racism? Most social psychologists make a distinction among these forms of racial/ethnic categorization. Myers (2013) describes the differences in the headings that follow.

Stereotype

A **stereotype** is a generalization about a group or its members based on categorization. It can be an accurate reflection of a group's norm; an overgeneralization, applying the norm to every member of the group or not allowing for variation about this norm; or simply inaccurate. Stereotypes are cognitive categorizations of people based on some demographic characteristic and do not necessarily convey positive or negative evaluations. For example, to say that Asians tend to be more collectivistic than English Canadians is an accurate stereotype. To insist that all Asians are collectivistic is an overgeneralization. However, to say that Asians are collectivistic is not to make a positive or a negative assessment of Asians based on this categorization. Stereotypes are considered the cognitive component of categorization.

stereotype An overgeneralization about a group or its members based on their categorization.

Prejudice

A **prejudice** is a judgment about a group or its members based on their categorization. Prejudice may be positive or negative, but it is typically thought to be negative. For example, someone may be prejudiced against Asians because they are collectivistic and tend to suppress individual freedoms or not express individualistic creativities. Prejudices are considered the evaluative component of categorization.

prejudice (Mostly) a negative judgment about a group or its members based on their categorization.

Discrimination

Discrimination is a negative behaviour toward a group or its members based on their categorization. For example, an Asian individual may not be selected for an assignment because it is assumed that this individual's collectivistic tendencies will not allow this person to be creative enough. Discrimination is considered the behavioural component of categorization.

discrimination A negative behaviour toward a group or its members based on their categorization.

Racism

Racism is a discriminatory behaviour that has institutional power behind it. This applies to people with institutional backing (those on the upside of power) who discriminate against individuals on the downside of power. For example, an individual may discriminate against an Asian individual and be backed by institutions of power. Most social psychologists feel that racism is a routine mistreatment of individuals on the downside of power, meaning that the

racism Discriminatory behaviour that is backed by institutional power.

mistreatment is part of institutional practices. Racism is considered the institutional component of categorization.

Distinction amongst Stereotypes, Prejudice, Discrimination, and Racism

Did you notice that stereotyping and prejudice are internal activities? For example, if people held a stereotypic attitude toward you, or even a prejudicial one, but kept that attitude or feeling to themselves, you are not hurt. It is not until their attitude is expressed either behaviourally (discrimination) or institutionally (racism) that you get hurt. It is difficult to get stereotypic or prejudicial attitudes out of our system because many of them are products of years of "learning" or exposure. However, if we can become aware of such attitudes and work to counteract them, we will not hurt others. Once we act on them, we have crossed the line into discrimination and/or racism.

As a humorous example of categorization and assumptions based on the status of an individual, our author Jeffery Scott Mio asked his students to imagine that he had some thoughts and feelings about students who sit in the front of a class (front-sitters) versus students who sit in the back of the class (back-sitters). He told them that he thought front-sitters ask more questions during lecture and that back-sitters ask fewer questions during lecture. However, students did not know whether he felt positively toward front-sitters and negatively toward back-sitters or if it was the other way around. On the one hand, if someone were to ask more questions during lecture, he may feel that they are more involved in class and the topics they are covering; thus, he may have a more favourable opinion of them. On the other hand, he could feel that the questions get in the way of his lectures, and he would not be able to get through all the material that he wanted to cover. In this case, he may feel more negatively toward students who ask a lot of questions. Students simply did not know whether he felt more positively toward front-sitters or more negatively toward front-sitters. Jeffery pointed out that his assumptions about front-sitters and back-sitters—that they ask more and fewer questions, respectively—are stereotypes and that his opinions of front-sitters and back-sitters are prejudices. However, unless he acted on them, students would never know what his stereotypes and prejudices are with regard to where they sit in the class, so his opinions of them do not hurt (or advantage) them. They are not hurt by his categorizations until he actually acts on them, which is discrimination. If students complain to his department chair, his dean, and/or the president of his university that they are being disadvantaged because they are front-sitters (or back-sitters), and if those leaders all support his discrimination, then this becomes an *ism* where there is institutional support for his discriminatory behaviour.

The description of racism also applies to other *isms*, such as sexism, ageism, ableism, heterosexism, and anti-Semitism and other forms of religious discrimination. Institutional practices of the dominant society tend to suppress members of the non-dominant parts of society.

The practice of *isms* may not always be intentional, and once it is exposed, members of the dominant group may be motivated to change the behaviour to be fairer. However, until exposure takes place, the practice may have an element of suppression. For example, most universities heavily weigh teaching and research productivity for the purposes of making tenure decisions. Members of the dominant group may feel that this emphasis is fair because it applies to all individuals equally. However, many Indigenous faculty and faculty of colour may have been hired to help recruit and advise Indigenous students and students of colour and engage those respective communities. Furthermore, many Indigenous scholars engage in Indigenous community-based research, which requires additional protocols in the research process and adds substantial time to the review and dissemination of research findings. As such, these activities necessarily take away from their ability to publish as much as their European-Canadian colleagues or publish in more "prestigious" journals—because many Indigenous scholars tend to publish their work in journals that are more likely to be read by practitioners and providers in the Indigenous community. Therefore, when compared with their European-Canadian colleagues, they may not be evaluated favourably. However, if such inequities are pointed out and if the institution is motivated to be fair, community activities may be given some value in the tenure process, and articles published in some ethnically focused journals should be considered to be as scholarly as those in more prestigious journals.

6.2 Stereotype Threat

Claude M. Steele (1997) has written extensively about what he terms **stereotype threat**—the threat that individuals belonging to a group that is negatively stereotyped will confirm that stereotype when confronted with a difficult task that purports to measure differences in abilities. For example, Steele and Aronson (1995) reported on freshman African-American students who were extremely accomplished in English, as measured by their verbal scores on the Scholastic Aptitude Test, who were given the Graduate Record Examination subject test in English. The subject test was four years beyond their education level, but the students did not know that it was designed for students who were far more advanced than they were at the time. Still, these students performed just as well as their European-American counterparts when both groups were led to believe that the test was simply a very difficult test that was being administered because they had previously proven how accomplished they were. When the students were led to believe that the test would measure differences between African Americans and European Americans, however, African-American student performance decreased.

> **stereotype threat**
> A fear that one will confirm the negative stereotype of a group to which one belongs.

The same pattern was demonstrated for women taking mathematics tests. Freshman women who had received extremely high quantitative scores on their Scholastic Aptitude Test were given the Graduate Record Examination subject test in mathematics. Again, these women performed as well as their male counterparts did when they were led to believe that the test was simply a very difficult one. However, when they were led to believe that the test might measure gender differences in mathematics, the women's scores decreased. This pattern also seems true with respect to gender differences in political knowledge (Hyde, 2016; McGlone & Neal, 2003).

Steele (2001) states that stereotype threat occurs under specific circumstances. First, an individual must excel in an area that is contrary to the stereotype. In the areas examined in C. M. Steele's earlier studies, African Americans are not stereotypically considered to excel in English in comparison with their European-American counterparts, women are not considered to excel in math in comparison with their male counterparts, and women are not considered as interested in politics as men are. And Asians—especially Asians who are learning English as a second language—are not considered fluent in written or oral English skills.

Second, the stereotype must be negative. Verbal and mathematical skills are highly valued, and deficits in those areas are considered negative; politics are important in that they relate to how the country is run. For example, Derald Wing Sue, one of the most respected researchers in multicultural psychology, jokes about his inability to dance, saying that Asians are not really expected to dance well. Thus, although that is a negative stereotype about Asians, deficits in dancing are not threatening because dancing is not a highly valued skill in mainstream Canada or the US. However, if one does not speak English well in these countries, they may be considered less intelligent.

Elizabeth Eckford, one of the first Black students to attend Little Rock Central High School in Arkansas, ignores hostile screams from fellow White students.

Third, the area in which the individual excels must be important to that individual. The African-American and female research participants in C. M. Steele's earlier studies excelled in English and mathematics, respectively, in high school, and the students valued those skills. They were at the top of their high school classes and received much recognition for their accomplishments. The Asian student taking the writing test was in a graduate program learning to become a therapist, an occupation in which verbal fluency skills are important.

Finally, the test of the individual's skills must be challenging. Clearly, tests four years beyond one's current training would be challenging. In the example of the Asian student, the writing test was not difficult and merely involved developing a written argument about a topic, but because failing the test would mean not receiving a degree from the university, it was a high-stakes test.[1]

Steele (2001) reasoned that the internal dialogue of victims of stereotype threat goes something like this: "Oh, no! I thought I was bright in this area, but now I am not performing well. I wonder if the stereotypes are true. Could it be that I have hit the limits of my abilities? Is my failure in this area only confirming the negative stereotypes that people have about me and people like me?" Contrast this internal dialogue with that of someone who is not threatened by such a negative stereotype: "Gosh, this test is hard!" The internal dialogue for the latter individuals is not as complex as the internal dialogue for those who are threatened by negative stereotypes. The internal dialogue for such threatened individuals adds a greater amount of stress, which interferes with their ability to perform.

Steele (2001) suggests that no one is immune from negative stereotypes. He cites a study conducted at a major university on European Americans and African Americans. The negative stereotype for European-American athletes is that they are not as naturally athletic as their African-American counterparts, and the negative stereotype for African-American athletes is that they do not think as well as their European-American counterparts. The researchers of this study told half of the group of athletes that a certain miniature golf course measured one's true athletic abilities, and they told the other half that the course measured one's ability to engage in complex planning. As predicted by the stereotype threat theory, the European-American athletes performed worse than their African-American counterparts when told that the course measured true athletic abilities, and the African-American athletes performed worse than their European-American counterparts when told that the course measured complex planning abilities.

In an amusing example of how Steele himself fell victim to stereotype threat (Steele, 2012), he discussed a meeting he had with the dean of his college. Steele was the chair of the Psychology Department at Stanford, and Stanford had just restructured so that the college that had previously included psychology, humanities, and social sciences had merged with the College of Sciences to form the College of Humanities and Sciences. The dean of the new college was a scientist, and Steele was well aware of the history of psychology and its struggle to be recognized as a real science. The Psychology Department had requested a new magnetic resonance imaging machine for the study of areas of the brain that are activated under different conditions. The dean was curious about how psychologists use magnetic resonance imaging and, out of intellectual curiosity, asked Steele how psychologists use this piece of very expensive equipment. Steele laughingly recalled his somewhat tongue-tied attempt to explain how, in psychology, scientists really do conduct sophisticated studies using magnetic resonance imaging. He noted that his performance was inhibited by his perceived inferiority as a psychologist trying to explain science to someone whose discipline was in the "hard" sciences.

What kinds of negative stereotypes apply to you? How would you respond? Have you ever been in a situation in which you were performing an activity that might support a negative stereotype about a group to which you belonged? Did your fear of confirming the stereotype interfere with your performance? If so, then you have first-hand experience of stereotype threat. According to Steele and his colleagues (Murphy et al., 2007; Steele, 1997, 2001; Steele & Aronson, 1995), the signal of the threat can be subtle. For example, Murphy et al. (2007) signalled the threat subtly by showing women students of math, science, or engineering courses videotapes of such courses with either a balance of men and women or the number of men far outnumbering that of women. Remember, stereotype threat happens only if you have high ability in a particular area, performing well is part of your identity, and the task you are doing is difficult (or there is pressure on you to perform exceptionally well on the task).

In recent years, the focus of stereotype threat has been on how to eliminate or at least minimize this effect on performance (e.g., Alter et al., 2010; Casad & Merrit, 2014; Forbes & Schmader, 2010; Regner et al., 2010; Sawyer et al., 2012; Shapiro, 2013; Shapiro et al., 2013; Walton & Spencer, 2009). For example, Alter et al. (2010) replicated the stereotype threat effects when testing Black grade school children and college students in mathematics. However, when they reframed the task as a challenge, as opposed to a threat, students' performance was not negatively impacted. Have you ever encountered a difficult task, but when you reframed it as a challenge you performed better than you thought you would? Armenta (2010) discovered that positive stereotypes can boost performance under stereotype threat conditions. He also found that individuals who had high ethnic identities were positively or negatively affected by the stereotype, depending on whether the stereotype was positive or negative, whereas people with low ethnic identities were not affected by the stereotype. Walton and Spencer (2009), in their extensive evaluation of numerous studies totalling nearly 18,000 research participants across five countries, found that under conditions of reduced psychological threat, students who were stereotyped performed better than non-stereotyped students. Have you found a positive stereotype about your groups to give you the confidence to perform better?

6.3 The Development of Negative Stereotypes

Over a year after 11 September 2001, a young, working-class male from Niagara Falls crossed the border into the US. He recounts his experience with the White customs officer:

> When we got close to the actual [US] border . . . there was a customs officer walking down the aisle between the cars, looking in everyone's car. He passed our car, but I did see in the case of any people of colour [or] someone wearing a religious headdress, he would stop at their window and ask them questions.
> —*Canadian male residing in Niagara Falls (Helleiner, 2012, p. 123)*

How do negative stereotypes develop? Why do people hold such views? There are at least two ways in which such stereotypes can develop. One is somewhat benign and the other is somewhat malicious.

Hamilton and his colleagues have discussed how negative stereotypes can develop from normal cognitive processes (Hamilton, 1981; Hamilton et al., 1985; Hamilton & Gifford, 1976; Hamilton & Rose, 1980; Hamilton & Sherman, 1989, 1994, 1996; Hamilton & Trolier, 1986). Essentially, this perspective suggests that people of colour (and other numerical and identifiable minorities) are labelled with negative stereotypes because of an overestimation of negative behaviours that occur with their minority status. Hamilton says that when two minority events co-occur, there is a natural cognitive process that takes notice of that co-occurrence. Because special note is taken, the overestimation occurs. Hamilton states that negative events are not as frequent as positive events in our lives. If a person of colour—who is in the statistical minority and by definition is less frequently encountered by the majority population—engages in a negative behaviour, the observer sees two minority events happening together and registers that co-occurrence. Hamilton calls this overestimation **illusory correlation** because the observer sees a correlation between the two events that does not really exist. Thus, if, for example, people with European and African-Caribbean background living in Canada have engaged in the same percentage of shoplifting in the past, store managers and workers may feel that people with African-Caribbean background engage in a greater amount of shoplifting (illusory correlation) because the co-occurrence of the minority group (African-Caribbean) and the minority behaviour (shoplifting) in the past had a greater impact on perception.

As evidence for this stance, Hamilton and his colleagues conducted several studies that demonstrated the relative ease with which illusory correlation can occur (Hamilton, 1981; Hamilton et al., 1985; Hamilton & Gifford, 1976; Hamilton & Rose, 1980; Hamilton & Sherman, 1989, 1994, 1996; Hamilton & Trolier, 1986). They conducted these studies even without using people of colour as experimental stimuli. Research participants received descriptors of two groups of people (Group A and Group B). Participants received 16 descriptions of positive behaviours and attributes and 8 negative descriptors for Group A. They also received 8 descriptions of positive behaviours and attributes and 4 negative descriptors for Group B. Thus, the participants received half as many descriptions of Group B as they did of Group A, and there were half as many negative descriptions as there were positive descriptions. In other words, both Group B and negative behaviours/attributes were minority events. Later, when the participants were asked to recall all the positive and negative events for both Groups A and B, they recalled about twice as many positive descriptors as negative descriptors for Group A (an accurate recollection), but they recalled about equal amounts of positive and negative descriptors for Group B (an overestimation of negative descriptors). Illusory correlation has been confirmed by other researchers in the field (Ratliff & Nosek, 2010; Risen et al., 2007; Sherman et al., 2009; Smith & Alpert, 2007; Van Rooy et al., 2013).

Castelli and Carraro (2011) examined how politically conservative females created a biased perception of numerical minority groups. Similar to studies by Hamilton and colleagues (Hamilton & Gifford, 1976; Hamilton & Rose, 1980; Hamilton & Sherman, 1989, 1994, 1996), participants received 18 positive behaviours and 8 negative behaviours for Group A (majority group) and received 9 positive and 4 negative behaviours for group B (minority group). Participants' political ideology was also assessed using a self-report measure. When asked to recall behaviours of Group A and Group B, the researchers found that there was an illusory correlation between Group B and negative behaviours. It was also noted that participants who demonstrated conservative ideologies accentuated the illusory correlation between Group B and negative behaviours compared to their liberal counterparts. The findings provide further evidence for illusory correlation and illustrate that conservatives tend to pay higher attention to negative information (Carraro et al., 2011).

---

illusory correlation
A false perception of associating two events together.

One way of understanding Hamilton's series of studies is to view illusory correlation as a form of Tversky and Kahneman's well-known **availability heuristic** (Tversky & Kahneman, 1973). A heuristic is a mental shortcut or rule of thumb used for making calculations or assessments of sometimes complex circumstances. Availability is a specific kind of heuristic in which the perception of frequency, importance, or probability of an event is based on the ease with which the event comes to mind. In their original study, Tversky and Kahneman asked their research participants whether there were more words that began with the letter k or words with the letter k in the third position. Many more participants said that there were more words that began with the letter k even though there are three times as many words with k in the third position. Tversky and Kahneman suggest that because our minds are organized in something of a lexicon (dictionary-like) manner, it is easier to "look up" words that begin with the letter k than it is to look up words that have k in the third position. This relative ease in coming to mind was therefore translated into an assessment that there were more words that began with the letter k. If the co-occurrence (illusory correlation) of two minority events is noticed or registered more, it will come to mind more easily than the co-occurrence of two majority events or a majority and a minority event, so the co-occurring minority events will be judged to be more numerous or probable. Risen et al. (2007) suggest that illusory correlation can occur with a single co-occurrence if the group is rare and the behaviour is unusual enough. Incidentally, Daniel Kahneman received the Nobel Prize for Economics in 2002 for his work with Amos Tversky because their work helped us understand how people allow heuristics to interfere with their economic decisions. Unfortunately, because Amos Tversky passed away in 1996, he was not able to share the honour with his friend and colleague.

As Tversky and Kahneman's (1973) study on the letter k demonstrates, sometimes the availability heuristic can lead us to wildly disparate conclusions. Could it be that stores and shops are overlooking a number of shoplifters because they are overly focused on customers of colour? Quite possibly. Canadian studies illustrate that racial profiling openly exists in the stop and search practices of the Canadian police force. In a study by Wortley and Owusu-Bempah (2011), White, Black, and Chinese participants were asked about their experiences being stopped by Toronto police while they were driving, walking, or standing in public places. The results revealed that in the two years prior to the study, 34 per cent of Black respondents were stopped by police, in comparison to 28 per cent of White respondents and 22 per cent of Chinese respondents. Black respondents also reported to be more likely to experience multiple and repeated stops, with 14 per cent of them reporting that they had been stopped multiple times in the past year, compared to 5 per cent of White and 3 per cent of Chinese respondents. This trend holds true for police searches as well. The results revealed that 12 per cent of Black respondents reported being searched by police in the past two years, while only 3 per cent of White and Chinese respondents had the same experience. The authors argued that racial stereotyping was a practice within the Toronto Police Department and that it was harming the police department's relationship with the Black community (Wortley & Owusu-Bempah, 2011).

Again, racial profiling is inefficient because the police must spend some amount of time with an innocent person while the person who committed the crime is allowed more time to escape. An Indigenous man describes his experience of racial profiling:

> There [were] three of us, and we decided we were going to walk to the park just over here and go and sit down on the park bench. And the park was full of people. . . . It was warm; it was nice. And as I walked into the park, there was a policeman and a policewoman,

availability heuristic A mental shortcut whereby the importance, frequency, or credence of something is exaggerated because it comes to mind easily.

and the policeman came up to greet us and he asked me for my ID. And I just said to him, "Is there a reason why you want my ID?" And he said, "Well, we have to check everybody's ID." I don't know what he said, but I said "Why don't you ask that woman over there? Have you asked that woman over there for her ID? . . . If you give me a good reason to give you my ID, then, you know, I could do that for you. But until you do that, I can't do that for you. . . ." He said, "Well, we are trying to establish good community relations." That was his answer to me.

—*Ontario Human Rights Commission, n.d.*

The less benign and more malicious reason for the development of negative stereotypes is the need of people in power to justify the suppression of those who do not have power (Aronson, 1990; Mio, 2003). This stance is based on **cognitive dissonance theory** (Festinger, 1957). According to Festinger, attitudes follow behaviour. Cognitive dissonance theory suggests that when two cognitions are in conflict (dissonance), people are motivated to reduce that dissonance, just as they would be motivated to reduce hunger or thirst. Thus, if we were to observe ourselves behaving badly toward another person or a group of people, we might engage in the following internal dialogue: "I am a good person, but I behaved badly toward that other person. That person must have deserved such bad treatment." This reduces the dissonance and leaves us feeling justified in engaging in such negative behaviour. As Aronson (1990) stated in his presidential address to the Western Psychological Association Convention, psychoanalytic theory suggests that if we feel hostility toward another individual, we should get the hostility out of our systems; thus, the process of catharsis would reduce our hostility toward that individual. However, cognitive dissonance theory predicts the opposite (and more correct) result: "If we hurt someone, it does not produce a release of hostile energy—on the contrary, it causes us to try to justify our actions by derogating our victim; this impels us to feel more hostility toward him, which opens the door for still further aggressions."

cognitive dissonance theory When two cognitions are in conflict, a person will be motivated to change one of them to reduce the unsettled feelings caused by the discrepancy.

6.4 Systematic Racism in Society

Stories about racism have always been present in our society as part of the news cycle. However, with the advent of social media, the voices of social activists are more difficult to ignore and society is becoming more aware of racism. For example, for communities of colour, police brutality has long been considered a problem and a form of racism. Over the decades and in recent years, several incidents have received national attention, primarily involving the beating and/or killing of unarmed Black and Indigenous men and women by police. They include the stories of Clayton Donnelly in British Columbia (Killer Cops Canada, 2019a), Nicholas Gibbs in Quebec (Killer Cops Canada, 2018), Kyle Schriver in Alberta (Killer Cops Canada, 2020), and Machuar Mawien Madut in Manitoba (Killer Cops Canada, 2019b), to name a few. Clayton Donnelly passed away from a taser-induced cardiac arrest in 2019 from a police officer who claimed he had been driving erratically and would not pull over (Bregolisse, 2019). Nicholas Gibbs was unarmed and did not speak French when police shot him five times after shouting at him in French (Killer Cops Canada, 2018). Kyle Schriver died in 2020 from gunshot wounds from police officers after allegedly being held at gunpoint (White, 2020). Machuar Mawien Madut was a South Sudanese migrant who struggled with mental health (Killer Cops Canada, 2019b). At the time he was shot, he had a hammer in his hand and appeared to be breaking into a suite (Killer Cops Canada, 2019b).

Most of these incidents were recorded on video; these recordings show that the person was unarmed and not a threat at the time. Why are we discussing police brutality and shootings in terms of racism? Remember, the definition of *racism* is discriminatory behaviour that is backed by institutional power. In this instance, law enforcement is part of the criminal justice system (institution) that engages in the mistreatment of people of colour. Furthermore, this mistreatment occurs at disproportionate rates relative to the overall population. In other words, ethnic minorities, particularly visible minorities, are more likely to be incarcerated and/or on probation and parole than are European Canadians.

In addition, police tend to target minority groups when searching for suspects (Neil & Carmichael, 2015; Wortley, 2003; Wortley & Owusu-Bempah, 2011). Research indicates that, compared to White people, Black people are more likely to be pulled over and searched when driving or walking (Neil & Carmichael, 2015; Wortley, 2003; Wortley & Owusu-Bempah, 2011). Not only are minorities singled out by police and sent to prison at higher rates than the majority, they are also more likely to be denied bail requests and punished with longer sentences in prison in comparison to White people (Commission on Systemic Racism in the Ontario Criminal Justice System, 1995).

International rates of imprisonment indicate that minorities make up the majority of prison populations (Penal Reform International, 2018). The number of people currently imprisoned around the world is approximately 10.35 million, and most of them are adult men who are typically from impoverished backgrounds and who are members of minority groups (Rope et al., 2018). For example, Aboriginal and Torres Strait Islander women make up only 2 per cent of the adult female population in Australia but 34 per cent of the women in prison (Rope et al., 2018). And although 18 per cent of Australia's population are people with disabilities, they make up 50 per cent of the total number of individuals entering prison in the country (Rope et al., 2018).

Two series of events provide striking examples of racism in Western society. This first example of racism was observed after the 2015 terrorist attacks in Paris, France. A study conducted by Goodwin et al. (2017) found that people who were especially nervous after the attacks were more likely to show racism and exclusion toward the Muslim community, which happens to be a sizable portion of the French population, at 7.5 per cent. An undeniable "us versus them" mentality emerged that pegged Muslims as a homogenous group of people who were dangerous. Consequentially, many Muslims became subject to violence and hate crimes, but these were often underreported because of the incorrect assumption that Muslims are always the perpetrators of crimes, not the victims (Britton, 2015). Thus, racism can come in many forms, and certain world events may shift the social climate dramatically, sometimes in very negative ways.

A Black-Canadian mother explains the difficulties her sons face with frequently being stopped by the police:

> There's no doubt in my mind that [my son's friends] were arrested because they were Black. Whenever you complain, [the police] behave as if you're making a mountain out of a molehill. I have decided that I am not going to keep quiet because I'll be damned if I go through it again with Andrew [her younger son]. All the young, Black men I've talked to, they've resigned themselves to the fact that getting stopped by police is a way of life.
> —*Donna Wallen, mother of Mark Wallen, who was a victim of police brutality in Kingston, ON, Canada (Marshall, 2017, p. 76)*

A second example of overt racism in society was displayed by a British conservative politician, Enoch Powell, in 1960s England (Hickson, 2018). In a speech referred to as the "Rivers of Blood," Powell spread fear and racist sentiments about immigration, and it became one of the most controversial addresses in political history. The speech portrayed falsities of how those who are White would become the minority and subjected to abuse from immigrants and that being "British" was all about someone's ethnicity and skin colour. Powell notified the press himself,

After Australia's Christchurch Massacre by a White supremacist, the true impact of White supremacy groups across the world was realized, and White supremacists became more vocal, causing more protesters to call for an end to the White supremacy movement.

in order to ensure the speech would reach as many people as possible, and he used openly racist language. The purpose of the speech was to evoke conflict and tensions among majority and minority groups while gaining the vote of those who agreed with his sentiments (Hickson, 2018).

A more recent example of overt racism was displayed by another British politician, Nigel Farage. He was the leader of the populist libertarian United Kingdom Independence Party (UKIP) from 2006–2009 and 2010–2016. In 2019, Farage launched the Brexit Party and became its leader. Durrheim et al. (2018) have explained how Farage launched his "Breaking Point" poster in 2016, just before the European Union (EU) referendum. The poster was captioned "Breaking Point: The EU has failed us all. We must break free of the EU and take back control of our borders." The picture depicted a lineup of migrants entering Slovenia, a country that had previously joined the EU. The campaign was quickly labelled as discriminatory for two reasons: the poster fostered a racial bias and hatred toward a specific group, and the propaganda was likely to influence public views of immigrants negatively as a result of scaremongering and condoning racism. The purpose of Farage's message was to create fear that if Britain remained part of the EU, then the country would be overrun with illegal immigrants. As you can see, these fear-induced messages are not limited to one country, one time, or against one ethnic group.

Indigenous Experiences with Racism

The relationship between Indigenous Peoples in Canada and the White settler population has been a long and often troubled one, ever since the arrival and subsequent colonization of North America by Europeans. Upon arrival, Europeans perceived Indigenous practices to be inferior to their own and therefore began a long history of enforcing colonial ideology and attempting to eradicate Indigenous beliefs (Anderson & Robertson, 2011). Indigenous communities were destroyed by the ongoing racism and discrimination they faced at the hands of the European settlers, who later formed the Canadian government. Colonizers then created governments and hierarchies that recognized Indigenous Peoples as far inferior to their European counterparts. Such historical oppressions have resulted in the loss of traditional culture, language, beliefs, knowledge, and teachings from ancestors (MacDonald & Steenbeek, 2015).

Indigenous communities were also forced to endure the residential school system. Indigenous children were taken away from their homes and placed in residential Catholic schools to unlearn their cultural heritage and to absorb European culture. There, they faced neglect and abuse, leading to the death of many children and lasting impacts on generations to come (Miller, 2012). These residential schools existed well into the late twentieth century, and the discovery of previously unknown graves of children attending these schools continued in the first half of the twenty-first century.

The Sixties Scoop was an event in Canadian history in which Family Service agencies took Indigenous children from their parents and their Indigenous way of life and placed them with White Canadian and American families in an attempt to force these children to lose their cultural identity (Niigaanwewidam & Sinclair, 2016).

Throughout Canada's history, Indigenous communities have been discriminated against and forced to change to suit European needs. This treatment has had a massive impact on the well-being of Indigenous communities: today, Indigenous communities are four times more likely to live in poverty than their non-Indigenous counterparts. As well, the immense assimilation pressure Indigenous Peoples have faced has negatively impacted their traditional

Protesters march in Ottawa for Indigenous Peoples' Day of Rage against Colonialism.

healing practices and medicines (MacDonald & Steenbeek, 2015). The traditional practices that were once in place are no longer part of the lives of many Indigenous Peoples today. Moreover, over half of Indigenous children on reserves live in poverty (Gadacz, 2006).

Around the world and in Canada there are various laws that were explicitly designed to advantage a group of individuals over others. One example of overt racism in Canada is the 1876 Indian Act. As demonstrated by Borrows (2016), this federal document was created in order to forcefully assimilate Indigenous Peoples into European culture. This act made it possible for the establishment of residential schools and the placement of the First Nations communities onto reserves, stripping them of their rights. The inherent discrimination that underlies this document paved the way to extreme racism toward Indigenous Peoples and destroyed their traditions, culture, and families in the process. Although the act was conceived well over 100 years ago, the repercussions are still felt today.

Furthermore, research in Canada has revealed that Indigenous and Black Peoples are disproportionately represented in federal and provincial prisons compared to their White counterparts (Neil & Carmichael, 2015; Wortley, 2003). Although Indigenous Peoples comprise only 4.3 per cent of Canada's total population, 18 per cent of federal and 25 per cent of provincial prison admissions in Canada are Indigenous Peoples (Neil & Carmichael, 2015; Statistics Canada, 2010, 2012, 2013). Furthermore, evidence suggests that a higher Indigenous population per capita correlates with increased admission of individuals to federal prison (Neil & Carmichael, 2015). Specifically, with every 10 per cent increase in Indigenous Peoples per capita, approximately 26 more people per 100,000 are incarcerated in federal prison (Neil & Carmichael, 2015). Additionally, provinces with high rates of minorities generally have higher rates of prison admissions (Neil & Carmichael, 2015).

Many people across Canada came to the support of the Wet'suwet'en peoples at the time of the Alberta protests.

The following example further illustrates racism in the criminal justice system. It begins in 2014 in Manitoba, Canada, with the death of a missing Indigenous girl, Tina Fontaine, with more deaths to follow. As Palmater (2016) explains, this tragedy illustrates how severe the crisis of missing and murdered Indigenous women and girls is in Canada to this day. Although they make up only 2 per cent of Canada's population, Indigenous women account for 16 per cent of women who are murdered or missing. The magnitude of this statistic is often attributed to societal and structural racism, especially since many cases have led to victim blaming and a lack of priority on the part of both government and criminal institutions. Thus, the fight to protect Indigenous women has since become a social movement, but mistreatment of all Indigenous Peoples has been a long-standing issue in the criminal justice system. An article written for the *UN Chronicle* (Gorelick, 2013) stated that besides the over-representation of Indigenous Peoples in prisons, Indigenous Peoples are also often subjected to racial profiling and limited parole opportunities, and are more likely to be accused of homicide by both the police and the courts. These statistics show how racism can be structurally ingrained in society and also show the negative consequences that follow the internalization of such discrimination.

6.5 Overt versus Covert Racism

Overt racism is "old-style" racism, in which those in the majority openly engage in hostile and aggressive acts against people of colour without fear of reprisal. Such acts include slavery, lynchings, residential schools, and legal segregation (Jones, 1997). Although overt racism may be thought of as a thing of the past, many people have reported being the victim of overt racism or seeing it first-hand.

For example, Henry (2019) states that in Ontario in 1850, the Common Schools Act made it legal to segregate schools in terms of race, leading to the establishment of all-Black schools. Although that may seem like a long time ago, the last racially segregated school did not close in Ontario until 1965. In many cases, if an area did not have a separate school for Black children, those children were denied access to an education altogether. Racism was also evident in the sectors of employment, transportation, commercial businesses, and everyday life in general. The perpetuation of such policies was reinforced by the common notion that Black people were somehow inferior, and stereotypes of primitiveness were strongly believed. Fortunately, many Black activists, protests, and demonstrations emerged in the twentieth century, but the system is still far from perfect.

In the early 1990s, Toronto schools proposed the creation of "Africentric" education. The goal was to give children a learning environment that featured Black teachers, role models, and history lessons (Thompson & Wallner, 2012). It was an attempt to mitigate potential challenges for Black children in school. The hope was that if the children identified more with their environment, then they would have a better social and academic life. However, the Black community was divided on the idea. On one hand, the program was seen as a temporary fix for a long history of institutionalized racism, while others thought it was a good way for children to develop a sense of identity. In 2008, the Toronto District School Board revisited the concept and finally progressed with "Africentric" schooling. There are such schools today that operate according to these principles, including the Africentric Alternative School in Toronto (Webb & Gulson, 2015). This is one example of ongoing policy changes in which Canada is trying to better address the needs of minority groups.

Ridley (1995) identifies covert racism as a modern form of racism that seems subtle and even deniable. According to Ridley, covert racism can be either intentional or unintentional.

overt racism Discriminatory behaviour in which people in the majority engage in open, hostile acts of aggression against racial minorities.

covert, intentional racism Discriminatory behaviour that is intentional but is covered up so that people can deny their racism.

Covert, intentional racism occurs when individuals are aware that they are acting in a racist manner but try to disguise their true intent with a plausible story.

Many people believe that affirmative action draws covert, intentional racists. Certainly, there are individuals who want to eliminate affirmative action for principled reasons, such as the ideal of equality for all and the belief that favouring one group over another necessarily discriminates against the group not being favoured. However, other individuals oppose affirmative action as a covert, intentional way of impeding the progress of people of colour. For example, the election of Barack Obama as president of the United States, twice, was not proof that racism no longer exists in the US (Ifil, 2009; Mio, 2016). Instead, the seeds of a "Whitelash" were sown that culminated in the election of Donald Trump eight years later (Coates, 2017).

symbolic racism An attempt and affect that is not overtly racist but is motivated to reject others based on their ethnicity and skin colour.

Sears (1988) refers to **symbolic racism** as an attempt to resist someone on the basis of ethnicity, but ethnicity and skin colour are not technically discussed. Symbolic racism can infiltrate many institutions in our society and can impact individuals on a massive scale. Canada has always accepted immigrants and refugees, but the process of selection has never been immune to societal biases. For example, refugees who come from particular countries or are members of a particular group can be refused based solely on the perceived "risk of danger." With the increasing emphasis on security in refugee screening, the number of individuals who can be considered dangerous has grown. The determination of who is considered dangerous then intersects with a person's nationality and social class, and often the decision is made based on these factors (Bryan & Denov, 2011). As a result, being in the same group as or having similar features to those who are dangerous is enough to be categorized as dangerous.

There has always been a history of correlating problems with those who are newest to a group, such as migrants. In 1959, Klapp explained the concept of vilification as a moral choice to label an individual as a villain and treat that person as such. This extends further, not only to the individual but also to the people associated with that individual, thereby vilifying a whole group (Bryan & Denov, 2011). This type of vilification is then implemented by society, as well as the system that chooses who gets to be a part of that society. Canadian immigration policies that attempt to market certain immigrants and protect the country from certain refugees have created a hostile environment for certain types of individuals (Bryan & Denov, 2011). The symbolic racism that is evident and that is driving decision-making in the immigration and refugee system is detrimental not only to those who come to the country for shelter and a better life but also to the well-being and social environment of the country itself.

From 1989 to 1990, a national public debate regarding the inclusion of turbans in the RCMP uniform swept Canada and exposed the true mindsets of many across the country. This debate began when a new Sikh RCMP recruit, Baltej Singh Dhillon, was forced to choose between becoming an RCMP officer and his Orthodox Sikh

Baltej Singh Dhillon poses for a photo after being granted the right to wear a Sikh turban in the RCMP in 1990.

Chuck Stoody/Canadian Press Images

religious requirement of wearing a turban. According to the RCMP dress regulations, the RCMP work cap was the only head gear permissible for an officer to wear. When Dhillon made a request to be allowed to wear his turban instead of the work cap, a national debate regarding the sanctity of the uniform ensued (Mann, 2020). Many believed that the RCMP uniform was a Canadian symbol and was representative of the country's identity. Therefore, making any changes to this uniform would be seen as compromising the Canadian way of life (Mann, 2020). Others believed that the dress code should not be altered for newcomers and immigrants, but instead they should change to adapt to the Canadian way of life and give up their previous beliefs (Mann, 2020). An Alberta-based group called the Defenders of the RCMP Traditions even went as far as circulating a petition across Canada to oppose the change to the RCMP uniform. This petition gathered over 200,000 signatures (Mann, 2020). This simple change to the RCMP uniform to make it more inclusive was seen as a threat to the Canadian identity, and it fostered a swell of anti-immigrant sentiment and overt racism toward new immigrants to Canada, specifically Sikh immigrants (Mann, 2020). This event exposed the symbolic racism that still exists in many Canadian institutions that bar minorities from integrating with the Canadian identity. Although refusal based on ethnicity or religion was not mentioned in the RCMP guidelines, the strict dress code that was in place effectively rejected all individuals who wore headdresses as a religious garment (e.g., Sikh men wearing turbans, Muslim women wearing hijabs, and Jewish individuals wearing kippahs) and discriminated against them based on nothing more than their religious requirements. Eventually, the dress code regulations were changed, and Dhillon was able to join the RCMP, but his struggle was one that defined and changed the public's view on Canadian identity (Mann, 2020).

covert, unintentional racism Discriminatory behaviour that is unintentional or well-intended but serves to perpetuate ongoing racist acts or traditions.

Ridley (1995) felt that **covert, unintentional racism** is much more insidious and pervasive than covert, intentional racism. Such racism may be expressed by anyone—even people who would consider themselves enlightened. However, covert, unintentional racism is generally expressed by individuals who are unaware of racist traditions or have good intentions, but they perpetuate such racism without thought.

The story of lawyer Hadiya Roderique from Toronto is another example of how common covert racism is. In an interview with CBC News (Sciarpelletti, 2020), Roderique discussed why she left her profession in law. She is the daughter of two Caribbean immigrants but has lived in Canada her whole life. Roderique's career path followed that of any other law student in Canada, except for the unnecessary obstacles she's had to face because of her skin colour. This was especially apparent once she left law school and became a practising lawyer. She explained that there would be a "look you get when you walk over to the defence counsel side," and often people mistook her for an assistant instead of a lawyer, even though she was wearing a full suit (Sciapelletti, 2020). In the interview, Roderique raised the question, "How do you report someone's raised eyebrow when they find out that you're their lawyer, or that you're the junior that's assigned to their file?" highlighting the frustration that comes with racism that is so covert that it does not

Many people hoped that the election of Jagmeet Singh as the leader of the New Democratic Party (NDP) in 2017 would signal the acceptance of a visible minority leader among the majority in Canada, but detractors use modern forms of racism to oppose him.

necessarily read as racism to many people. As a result, Roderique left law because of the unhappiness that resulted from this discrimination.

Ridley (1995) argues that covert, unintentional racism is perhaps the most damaging of all forms of racism because it is practised by well-intentioned individuals who do not see themselves as racist at all. They are not motivated to change their behaviours or perceptions because they do not equate themselves with obvious, overt racists of the past or the present.

In general, overt forms of racism are not as common as they used to be. Modern forms of racism are much more subtle and difficult to detect. To stop it, we must be able to identify these forms of racism and make others aware of the ways in which they perpetuate it. Before we examine the complexities of different forms of modern racism, let us consider a tragic event that highlights racism in society.

The Grenfell Tower Tragedy: Was Socio-economic Status a Factor?

The Grenfell Tower fire that occurred in London, UK, in 2017 is considered an example of gross disregard for not only the safety of London's working class but also their lives. The Grenfell Tower was a 24-storey residential apartment building that housed 350 people, mainly made up of working-class families and migrants, most of whom were ethnic minorities (MacLeod, 2018). On 14 June 2017, a small fire was reported to the fire department on the fourth floor of the building. Within minutes, this fire began to engulf the external walls of the building and travel higher. As the fire department began entering the building to evacuate people, the safety policy of the building remained in effect, a "stay put" policy that advised residents to stay in their flats during a fire. Despite the fire department's attempts to evacuate people, the fire grew too fast and the stay put policy was lifted. By this time, people above the fire on higher floors had become trapped, some waving and screaming in the windows, other jumping out of their flats to the ground below (MacLeod, 2018).

Safety officers found jarring deficits in safety precautions, such as firefighting equipment in the building that was well outdated and had not been checked for four years. Residents had been experiencing concerning events that amounted to safety hazards, such as electrical surges and appliances emitting smoke. Furthermore, the materials used to build and renovate Grenfell Tower were found to be sub-standard in quality and, therefore, unsafe for use (MacLeod, 2018). These concerns and precautions were not properly acted upon by the management of the building. These cost-cutting measures were major contributors to the 72 casualties and 70 injuries that resulted from the fire (MacLeod, 2018).

Questions also were raised regarding the nature of the fire as it had spread incredibly fast and burned for

The Grenfell Tower fire spread incredibly quickly and burned for days, leaving many questioning whether poor structure and safety precautions had contributed to the scale of the catastrophe.

Daniel Leal-Olivas/Getty Images

days. It was found later that the residents of Grenfell had consistently raised concerns in 2013 over the fire safety precautions that existed in the tower and the need for them to be updated. This blatant disregard for the lives of lower-income tenants and minority families who lived in Grenfell Tower exposed a dark and dangerous side of London's management and council. If the residents of the tower had been affluent, White Londoners, would management have allowed this tragedy to occur? Was the reason the victims were overlooked and denied safety because of their socio-economic status and race? These are all questions that had to be grappled with in the wake of the calamity, questions that would expose and alter how communities manage ethnicity and wealth differences in their residents.

6.6 The Complexities of Modern Racism

In the next section, we examine different types of racism and the psychological underlying of these behaviours and their consequences.

Aversive Racism

Gaertner and Dovidio (1986) discuss **aversive racism**, a form of modern racism practised by individuals who believe that they are not racist and who would find it offensive or aversive if they were thought to be racist. When their unconsciously racist views surface, these individuals cite logical or common-sense reasons for their views and thereby deny that they are racist. Therefore, a characteristic of aversive racism is that the individual endorses both egalitarian values and negative views toward minorities groups.

Dovidio (2001) and Dovidio and Gaertner (2000) report support for their aversive racism concept. For example, when making hiring decisions between Black and White candidates, individuals who scored high on the authors' aversive racism scale hired White candidates rather than their Black counterparts. When given the opportunity to discuss their decisions, aversive racists focused on the strengths of the White candidates and the weaknesses of the Black candidates. Another group of aversive racists hired more White candidates than Black candidates, but although the candidates' qualifications were opposite to those of the first set of candidates, the second group's reasoning also focused on the strengths of the White candidates and the weaknesses of the Black candidates. In other words, hiring decisions were based on the opposite qualifications, yet the two groups always favoured the White candidates and had "logical" reasons to back up their decisions. Figures 6.1 and 6.2 show Mio's (2003) depictions of data from Dovidio and Gaertner's (2000) study.

In a Canadian study by Son Hing and colleagues (2008), employment and college admission were examined and it was found that when both White applicants and applicants belonging to minority groups have strong qualifications, White people are not chosen over ethnic minorities. However, when there is moderate or more ambiguous qualifications for both groups, White people are consistently chosen over ethnic minorities (Son Hing et al., 2008). In fact, aversive racism has been repeatedly found to be a useful conceptualization for many modern forms of racism (de França & Monteiro, 2013; Dovidio & Gaertner, 2008; Dovidio et al., 2009; Henkel et al., 2006; Pearson et al., 2009; Penner et al., 2010; Rodenborg & Boisen, 2013). Dovidio et al. (2009) concluded that this form of modern racism is so pervasive that it behooves us to educate people about its effects and to find ways to combat such discrimination from otherwise well-intentioned individuals.

Some aversive racists may excuse racist symbols as meaningless or part of tradition, with no intent to create a hostile racist environment. A study by Maeder et al. (2015) illustrated

aversive racism Covert, unintentional discriminatory behaviour practised by individuals who hold both egalitarian values and negative views toward minority groups.

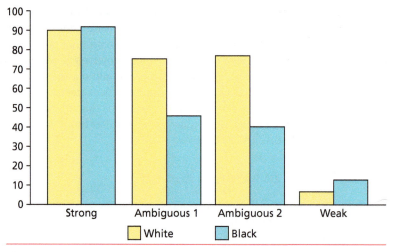

Figure 6.1 Representation of Dovidio and Gaertner's (2000) data on aversive racism—probability of being hired. In Ambiguous 1, the European-American (White) candidate was strong on Criterion A and weak on Criterion B, whereas the African-American (Black) candidate was weak on Criterion A and strong on Criterion B. In Ambiguous 2, the White candidate was weak on Criterion A and strong on Criterion B, whereas the Black candidate was strong on Criterion A and weak on Criterion B. However, the White candidate had a higher probability of being hired in both ambiguous situations.
Source: Adapted from Dovidio & Gaertner (2000).

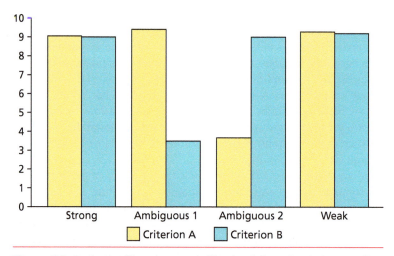

Figure 6.2 Ratings of importance of both of the criteria in Dovidio and Gaertner's (2000) study.
Source: Adapted from Dovidio & Gaertner (2000).

aversive racism by examining the influence of ethnicity on jurors' decisions in a Canadian court, using White, Black, and Indigenous defendants. They conducted two studies where they established race-salience (which they defined as the degree that racial and ethnic issues are made prominent in a trial). In Study 1, the jurors received a detailed mock-trial transcript, but in Study 2, the jurors received a shorter and more ambiguous mock-trial transcript. The transcript depicted a fake robbery case. It was found that in Study 1 the jurors gave more not guilty verdicts, while in Study 2 the jurors gave more guilty verdicts for the Indigenous and Black defendants but not for the White defendant. Consistent with aversive racism theory, which proposes racism can occur under particular ambiguous conditions, the jurors relied more on ethnic bias to make decisions when the situation was ambiguous and the ethnicity of the defendants was salient (Study 2).

Although the following story is an example of aversive sexism rather than aversive racism, the principle is the same. The story was told by a professor in an academic department with two different disciplines. One division had a gender balance, whereas the other division was all male. The names of the colleague and the department have been withheld to protect both from reprisal.

> My department was conducting searches a few years ago. The other division had two positions for which it was searching. One of the positions was a "generalist" position, and the other position was a "specialty" one. The top two candidates for each position were a man and a woman. The generalist candidates differed in that the woman was finishing up her dissertation and the man had a post-doctoral position. The woman had one publication and several conference presentations, and her references said that she was a very promising candidate. The man, who had received his Ph.D. several years before, had a few publications and a contract for a book. The specialty candidates differed in that the man was finishing up his dissertation. Although he did not have any publications, he had several conference presentations, and his references said that he was a very promising candidate. The woman, who had received her Ph.D. several years before, had a few publications, had already published a book, and had received two fairly substantial grants. Amazingly, the chair of the search committee recommended that we offer the generalist position to the male candidate because he was a proven individual, and he also recommended that we offer the specialty position to the male candidate because he was a promising individual. Despite the fact that all of the women from my division of the department voiced their opposition to this ranking of candidates, the chair of the search committee stood his ground, feeling that he had made the right choices. It wasn't until a man from our division voiced his opposition to this ranking that the chair of the search committee agreed to reconsider the rankings. Sexism is alive and well in modern academia.
>
> —Lonnie, 30+-year-old European-American woman

Colour-Blind Racial Ideology

Since 2000, the concept of a **colour-blind racial ideology** has gained attention (Apfelbaum et al., 2010; Apfelbaum et al., 2008; Awad et al., 2005; Bonilla-Silva, 2003; Bonilla-Silva & Dietrich, 2011; Chao et al., 2011; Guinier & Torres, 2007; Holoien & Shelton, 2012; Knowles et al., 2009; Neville & Awad, 2014; Neville et al., 2013; Neville et al., 2006; Plaut et al., 2009; Tynes & Markoe, 2010; Worthington et al., 2008). This ideology essentially suggests that people often attempt to pretend that race and racism will not exist if people ignore race or ethnicity. According to Neville et al. (2013), colour-blind racial ideology contains two dimensions: colour evasion and power evasion. The colour evasion dimension asserts that there are no differences in the way that people are treated based on the colour of their skin. The power evasion dimension asserts that any differences in accomplishments are completely based on the individual's own work and not due to any advantages of skin colour built into the system.

colour-blind racial ideology An attempt to pretend that race and racism will not exist if people ignore race or ethnicity. This ideology has two components: colour evasion and power evasion.

When people engage in colour evasion, they often say things such as "I don't see colour" and "We are all the same." Part of the motivation behind this stance is a discomfort in discussing racial or ethnic issues. As a result, these individuals may choose to have fewer interracial interactions to avoid their discomfort. However, people cannot help but notice the race or ethnicity of other people with whom they engage.

When people engage in power evasion, they often say things such as "Racism is not important in today's society," "Everyone has an equal chance to succeed," and "Reverse racism is more prevalent than racism in today's society." Such attitudes fuel more racial hostility in these individuals, and they are less competent in interacting in today's multicultural society Have you encountered individuals who do not believe that racism exists in today's society? You may even have had these kinds of ideas yourself because you were told that being "colour-blind" was the correct way to think.

Internalized Oppression

> **internalized oppression** People who are colonized and/or oppressed may automatically accept the superiority of the oppressor.

For many years, E. J. R. David has been writing about **internalized oppression** (David, 2008, 2009, 2010, 2014; David & Derthick, 2014; David & Okazaki, 2006, 2010). This concept is not new; various researchers have discussed it dating back to the classic study by K. B. Clark and Clark (1939; also see Bailey et al., 2011; Bearman et al., 2009; Brown, 1986; Duran & Duran, 1995; Freire, 1970; Gainor, 1992; Hanna et al., 2000; Lipsky, 1977, 1987; Padilla, 2001, 2004; Parmer et al., 2004; Poupart, 2003; Prilleltensky & Laurier, 1996; Pyke, 2010; Rosenwasser, 2002; Ross et al., 2007; Szymanski & Kashubeck-West, 2008; Tappan, 2006; Thomas et al., 2005).

Internalized oppression is implicit in the first stage/status of racial identity development models (see Chapter 7). When individuals are trying to fit in with the majority population or the population in power (as is the case for countries that have been colonized), their first stage/status of identity development is to suppress their cognitive, behavioural, and emotional tendencies that may differ from those of the population in power in favour of the tendencies of those in power.

Many South Asians countries, such as India, were ruled by the British for many years, and being White was deemed a symbol of the ruling class (Nagar, 2018). For decades, the use of skin-whitening products in India has been heavily advertised, portraying Whiteness as a desirable goal (Jha, 2016). In India, fair skin is often considered a social marker of class, whereby people of darker complexion are more likely to be rejected and disregarded. The implication of the caste system in India has put this notion into action, where lower-caste members are perceived as dark and inferior; and upper-class members, as fair and superior (Nagar, 2018). This form of internalized oppression has been severely influenced by colonialism, globalization, and, as mentioned, the caste system (Nagar, 2018).

> My name means "wish," but over the years I have been called many other names that mean "black." This is because I'm a dark-skinned woman from India. . . . Even members of my own family made jokes about the way I look. A popular one was that the electricity went out in the hospital when my mother was about to deliver me and that's how I got my dark colour. At school, one of my teachers once asked me, with a smirk, "Are you from Africa?"
>
> As I grew older, I was pressured to change the way I look, to become lighter-skinned. Desperate measures were taken. From homemade—turmeric, curd, gram—to store-bought,

many cosmetic products were applied on my skin to make me fairer. . . . Once, an elderly relative approached my parents with a proposal from a young man. My father declined, and I heard the relative tell him, "How can you decline? What does your daughter possess that makes you think she could get a better proposal? Have you not seen her? She is dark!"

I never responded to people's cruel comments or jokes. I never shared my insecurities or feelings of resentment with anyone. I just became numb and shut down. Soon, I was not comfortable being in photographs or attending social functions. I wanted to be invisible.

—Muna Beatty, an anti-colourism advocate based in India (Beatty, 2018)

Similarly, Indigenous communities frequently encounter discrimination and stereotyping, not only in Canada but also in other parts of the world, including the US and Australia. The Canadian media have constantly shown Indigenous communities and their way of life to be inferior to that of Europeans, portraying them as lacking sophistication and knowledge. This type of propaganda against Indigenous Peoples was used to justify the colonization of their land. As most media outlets were run by White Europeans, the media took the side of the Government of Canada over the voices of Indigenous Peoples (Anderson & Robertson, 2011). Similarly, Native Americans struggle to navigate in a society where the oppressor is still in power, which leads to the rejection of their values, knowledge, beliefs, and ceremonies (Gonzalez et al., 2014). The dominant image and message about Indigenous Peoples tends to be negative: they are portrayed as alcoholics living on government handouts and as a vanquished people of the past, forever defeated in Western movies. For Indigenous Peoples, this portrayal has resulted in their identities being stolen. These internalizations and stereotypes have been detrimental to Indigenous populations.

One of the authors of this book, John Gonzalez, shares part of the story of his own internalized oppression:

I remember growing up on White Earth in the 70s. My dad, Jim "Ironlegs" Weaver taught us how to sing and dance—we went to powwows every summer. We had sweats behind our house. But, back then, hardly anybody was doing sweats or ceremonies, it seemed like nobody was singing or dancing and going to powwows, except our family and maybe a few others. I looked around the Rez and started to wonder why. When I would go hang out with cousins and friends, they would tease me. I started to question my own identity. Instead of going to powwows and doing ceremonies, it seemed like being Indian meant partying and doing drugs. I strayed from the sacred Circle. I wanted to be like the other Indians on the Rez. I had to go through some rough times and learn the hard way before I freed myself and found my way back to our Anishinaabe ways so that I could heal.

—John Gonzalez (David, 2014, p. 14)

The extreme levels of poverty, unemployment, and lack of opportunity in Indigenous communities in North America, particularly in rural reservation communities, reinforce these ideas for Indigenous youth, which may contribute to the high levels of suicide among this group (Whitbeck et al., 2014).

Thus, just as many forms of modern racism affect people who are European Canadians unconsciously and/or implicitly, internalized oppression affects people of colour unconsciously and/or implicitly, even when people are sophisticated about issues of racism. Moreover, such oppression directly hurts people who engage in it.

6.7 Racial Microaggressions

As we have been discussing throughout this chapter, modern forms of racism are subtle and sometimes unconscious. Certainly, Ridley's (1995) conception of covert, unintentional racism, Gaertner and Dovidio's (1986) aversive racism, and Neville and Awad's (2014) colour-blind racial ideology are unknown to those who engage in such forms of racism. When these forms of racism are pointed out to the individuals engaging in these practices, they will either deny that they were being racist or strive to adjust their behaviour immediately.

Derald Wing Sue and his colleagues have examined these forms of modern racism and come up with what they call racial microaggressions (Burrow & Hill, 2012; Jones & Galliher, 2015; Nadal, 2011; Nadal et al., 2014; Owen et al., 2014; Sue, Bucceri, et al., 2007; Sue, Capodilupo, et al., 2007; Sue et al., 2009; Sue et al., 2008; Sue & Sue, 2008, 2013; Torres-Harding et al., 2012; Wang et al., 2011). A racial **microaggression** is a small slight or offence that may be intentional but is mostly unintentional and does not harm the target of the offences in any major way; however, the offence can accumulate and become burdensome over time.

A study conducted by Houshmand et al. (2014) investigated microaggressions in the lives of South and East Asian international students in Canada. The results indicated that these students do indeed face racist microaggressions on campus, but there were also specific themes of racism that participants experienced. For example, they commonly felt excluded and avoided by White peers, as well as experiencing the stereotype that Asians are especially intelligent when it comes to math and science. Many of the international students thus felt a pressure to conform to these stereotypes, showing just how powerful microaggressions can be. Other frequent themes included being mocked for having an accent, feeling invisible, and experiencing a disregard of their values and needs on the part of other students. Although many students coped with the discrimination in a positive way (e.g., by seeking comfort from members of their own cultural group or multicultural environments), others tended to withdraw from social situations. Therefore, although microaggressions may not seem particularly apparent or harmful in the moment, they can lead to distress for minority individuals.

Sue and colleagues categorized racial microaggressions into three categories: microassault, microinsult, and microinvalidation. A **microassault** is similar to our conceptions of "old-fashioned" racism. These are "blatant verbal, nonverbal, or environmental" attacks that are intentionally discriminatory or biased (Sue & Sue, 2013, p. 154). Racial epithets and discriminatory hiring practices fall into this category. If people who engage in microassaults have any sense of conscience, they engage in such behaviour only when there is some degree of anonymity, when they are in the presence of like-minded individuals, or when they simply lose control and blurt out their underlying feelings. Another example of a microassault is when people want to tell a racist joke but then check to make sure that someone who could be the target of the joke is not around to hear it. Because of its anonymity, the internet is a fertile ground for such behaviour.

A **microinsult** is an unintentional behaviour or verbal comment conveying rudeness or insensitivity. For example, a Blackfoot Piikani First Nations woman recalls an incident she experienced while working as a bank teller in a small Mormon community. A customer refused her service simply because he did not want her to have access to his bank account. Although she explained to the customer that she was well equipped for the job and assured him that she had no control over his bank account, he still continued to refuse her service and was eventually looked after by her supervisor instead (Canel-Çınarbaş & Yohani, 2019).

Sahar Ibrahim, a staff member at the Centre for Race and Culture in Edmonton, describes her experiences with microaggressions as a non-White individual in Canada:

---

microaggression A small slight or offence that may be intentional but is mostly unintentional and does not harm the target of the offences in any major way but can accumulate to be burdensome over time.

microassault A blatant verbal, non-verbal, or environmental attack that is intentionally discriminatory or biased.

microinsult An unintentional behaviour or verbal comment conveying rudeness or insensitivity.

> I was born and raised in Treaty 7 territory in Calgary, I was an Air Cadet, I speak French and English, and I love hiking and snowboarding; but because my skin is brown, I am constantly asked where I'm from. I don't mind the curiosity, but it does bother me when answering "Calgary" is never satisfactory. And even stating that my parents are from East Africa isn't satisfactory, because I'm Brown and not Black. We haven't lived in South Asia for well over 100 years, and yet, that's always the answer that satisfies people. But if I was White, even if I was an immigrant, Calgary would be a good enough answer, or I would just never get asked that question.
>
> —Sahar Ibrahim, Centre for Race and Culture, 2020

Here, we see that Sahar, despite being born and raised in Calgary, is constantly questioned about her identity. Due to her Brown skin, she is always assumed to be a foreigner or an outsider, and when she explains that she is from Calgary, the answer is never satisfactory (Center for Race and Culture, 2020). This lack of sensitivity is an example of microaggression, even if it is unintentional.

A **microinvalidation** is related to a microinsult in that it is generally unintentional while also dismissive of the experience of people of colour. A microinvalidation excludes, negates, or dismisses the perceptions of the target person. For example, Dene, a First Nations person in Canada who was adopted by a White family, recalls being told as a child that his teachers' racist remarks were of no concern to him because he was adopted by a White family, which meant that he too was also White (Canel-Çınarbaş & Yohani, 2019). His family's reasoning for disregarding racist remarks is an example of microinvalidation. Similarly, an African-Canadian girl studying at a high school in Newfoundland and Labrador had her African heritage questioned by her White peers. They claimed that she was not truly Black because she had light-coloured skin. Her peers' assumption that there is an "appropriate" dark tone associated with Blackness is an indication of microinvalidation (Baker, 2017).

One of this book's authors, Jeffery Scott Mio, once encountered a microinvalidation that he will never forget. He found a recipe for spanakopita (Greek spinach and cheese pie). When he was in Chicago as a graduate student, he loved spanakopita, so he was excited to try the recipe. He went to the grocery store and looked for two items that he had never bought before: phyllo dough and feta cheese. After looking around the store for a while trying to find the items on his own, he asked a grocery store worker where the phyllo dough was. When she did not understand him, he said, "I'm not sure if it is pronounced 'feel-o' or 'file-o,' but it is a dough to make spinach cheese pie." When she still did not know what he was looking for, he then asked where the feta cheese was. It was obvious to him that she did not know what phyllo and feta were, but instead of admitting to her own ignorance, she said, "You have a funny accent. I can't understand what you are saying."

Hernandez, Carranza, and Almeida (2010) examined people of colour who were mental health professionals. These professionals were aware of the concept of microaggressions and discussed their ways of coping with them. Although confrontation with the perpetrator was one method, it was only one of eight such measures. In fact, confrontation was fourth on the list of most commonly used coping strategies.

The first strategy was to identify the key issue involved and decide how to respond. If the perpetrator was simply naive, then education might be the best strategy. If the perpetrator was more abusive, then confrontation might be needed. This strategy, along with self-care and seeking mentoring, was employed by all participants in the study.

The rest of the strategies used, from most used to least used, were as follows:

---

microinvalidation An action that excludes, negates, or dismisses the perceptions of the target person.

- Organizing public responses
- Practising spirituality
- Keeping records and documenting experiences tied with confrontation
- Seeking support from European allies

The authors did not suggest that one should ignore microaggressions but, rather, that one should find ways to cope with them.

Note that the previous examples of microaggressions are racial microaggressions. However, microaggressions can be perpetrated against any group on the downside of power, just as the concepts of general racism can be applied to any group that can be targeted. Thus, sexism, heterosexism, ageism, ableism, and the like can be subtly expressed in the form of microaggressions. For example, when someone constantly refers to an indefinite person as *he*, that person is engaging in a sexist microaggression. When someone assumes that people are either married or single and does not consider gay or lesbian partnerships, that person is engaging in a heterosexist microaggression. When someone does not believe that a person in a wheelchair has career aspirations and should be content to work in a repetitive job with no future advancement, that person is engaging in an ableist microaggression. What other examples of non-racial microaggressions can you think of?

6.8 Racism and the Biopsychosocial Model

As we have demonstrated, racism is not just one thing; it exists in several forms. Many arguments about race occur because of misunderstandings about its different forms. The biopsychosocial model discussed in Chapter 1 can help with understanding the different types of racism (see Figure 1.1).

Remember, the biopsychosocial model has five levels:

1. Biological
2. Cognitive-affective
3. Social-interpersonal
4. Social institutional
5. Cultural

With regard to racism, let's begin at the cognitive-affective level, which addresses thoughts and feelings. Stereotyping and prejudice exist at the cognitive-affective level and are the building blocks of racism at the individual level. As mentioned previously, stereotypes are expectations or generalizations about a person's behaviour based on that person's membership in a group. Therefore, stereotypes reflect beliefs one holds regarding individuals who belong to different groups. When evaluations are added to stereotypes, they become prejudice, which refers to judgments—positive or negative—about someone based on their membership in a particular group. More specifically, racial prejudice or racial bias involves attitudes toward a particular person or group because of race. So, an individual person can harbour racist thoughts and feelings.

When an individual acts on negative thoughts and feelings, racism becomes interpersonal. The social-interpersonal level of the biopsychosocial model examines the dynamics of social relationships. Generally, when people use the term *racism*, they are referring to interpersonal racism, or the negative treatment of someone simply because they belong to a particular racial group. As mentioned previously, this is the definition of *discrimination*. When a landlord refuses to rent an apartment to a family because of its race, an employer decides not to hire an applicant because of that person's race, or a sales associate follows a customer around a store because of that customer's race, this is discrimination or racism at the social-interpersonal level.

Racism also exists at the social institutional level. In Chapter 1, social institutions were defined as complex networks of social relationships designed to fulfill a function in society. Examples of social institutions include the educational system, law enforcement, government, organized religion, and corporations. Institutional racism occurs when the policies and practices of a social institution result in the differential treatment of particular ethnic groups. Examples of institutional racism include racial profiling by law enforcement, biased sentencing by the criminal justice system, and bias in educational standardized tests. Institutional racism also occurs when interpersonal racism is backed by institutional power. For example, when an individual landlord refuses to rent an apartment to an individual family, that is interpersonal racism (discrimination). However, when social institutions—such as government housing policies and bank lending practices—support landlords, homeowners, and real estate agents who engage in such practices, thereby making it more difficult for people of colour to live in certain areas, it becomes institutional racism.

Racism has existed since humans began to divide themselves into categories and became engrained in the fabric of the Western world during more than 400 years of the Atlantic slave trade. Racist ideologies continue to exist, despite scientific evidence that as humans we are more genetically similar than different (see Chapter 1). Because such beliefs have been around for so long, they have become the norm—like the proverbial water to the fish. Practices that have roots in racism go unnoticed because they are so commonplace. This is **cultural racism**. Blaut (1992) defines *cultural racism* as the belief that one's own culture is inherently superior to another. He argues that although most people no longer believe in biological racial superiority, they still believe in cultural superiority—more specifically, European cultural superiority. In this view, other racial/ethnic groups are seen as having the *capacity* to be equal in terms of intelligence, appropriate social behaviour, etc.; they just have not had the *opportunity* to do so. Therefore, Europeans feel justified in their discrimination against other racial/ethnic groups until those groups develop to the same "level" as Europeans. From this perspective, the differences between groups are based on culture, not biology. It is argued that this type of thinking has gone beyond the individual level and is so widespread that it has moved to the cultural level.

Similarly, the term *culturally deprived* was used to describe children of colour from the inner city. This term was used by well-meaning liberals, mainly White people with a European background, who did not realize they were perpetuating the belief that the White middle-class environment was the "correct" environment, and anything different was deprived. A similar problem occurs with the terms *developing countries* and *third-world countries*. These terms are used in everyday language with White/European culture as the standard without awareness of their implications, illustrating the concept of cultural racism.

Cultural racism is similar to **implicit racial attitudes**, or ideas and opinions individuals hold about race, of which they are unaware. People can harbour racist attitudes that are outside their conscious awareness but that still impact their behaviour. For example, employers who refuse to hire an applicant of colour may genuinely believe that the applicant is less qualified and may not realize that the applicant's skin colour influenced their decision (Craig & Richeson, 2014; Dovidio & Gaertner, 2004; Schmidt & Nosek, 2010). A large body of research supports the idea of implicit bias (see Fazio & Olson, 2003; FitzGerald & Hurst, 2017; Holroyd, 2015; Levy, 2017).

cultural racism The belief that one's own culture is inherently superior to another.

implicit racial attitude An idea or opinion about race that people hold but are unaware they hold.

Understanding that racism occurs on different levels helps explain some of the arguments people have regarding racism. For example, when people use their personal lack of prejudice ("I'm not a racist!") as evidence that racism is dead, they are talking about racism at the cognitive-affective and social-interpersonal levels. In other words, they do not believe they harbour any racist beliefs, and they do their best to treat everyone equally. People also argue that racism is dead because they have never experienced racist treatment, nor have they witnessed anyone else being treated that way. Even some people of colour will say, "I've never experienced any racism." However, just because you are not racist, have not experienced racism, and have not witnessed racism does not mean it is gone. In addition, social, institutional, and cultural racism have been apparent in recent news stories, such as the Grenfell Tower tragedy described earlier and #StopAsianHate, the movement in response to attacks, harassment, and racism that Asians living in Western nations, particularly Asian Americans, experienced during the COVID-19 pandemic.

6.9 White Privilege

One of the most powerful works on the depth of unconscious European North American racism was proposed by Peggy McIntosh (1988, 1995). Earlier in this chapter, Lonnie's story about how the all-male search committee ranked the female candidates second in both searches clearly illustrates **male privilege**, which refers to systematic advantages that society provides to men based on their gender. This includes men getting paid more at work and having more power in organizations and politics than women. *White privilege* is similar to male privilege in that many unearned advantages are given to individuals with White-European background without examination. If society truly is fair, such advantages should not exist. McIntosh (1995, pp. 79–81) presented many instances that might otherwise be unexamined but that underscore the advantages of being a White European in society, such as turning on the television or looking at the front page of the newspaper and seeing people of one's ethnicity and skin colour widely and positively represented. For example, unless one is viewing a martial arts movie, one rarely sees an Asian male on a television program or in a movie. Asian females are typically presented as the girlfriends of White-European male protagonists, but Asian males are almost never seen with White-European females and are rarely seen with Asian females. It is telling when

male privilege Systematic advantages that society provides to men based on their gender. It also refers to the unearned advantages associated with being male.

Asians and Indigenous Peoples have traditionally not been in positions of power in Canada. However, there are exceptions, such as Theresa Tam, the Chief Public Health Officer of Canada in 2021 (left) and former MP Jody Wilson-Raybould (right).

BOX 6.1 Shades of Beauty

For a wonderful discussion of skin colour and beauty, search online for Lupita Nyong'o's speech at the 2013 Essence Awards. Nyong'o won the Academy Award for best supporting actress for her role as Patsey in the film *12 Years a Slave* (McQueen, 2013). In her speech, Nyong'o talks about how desperately she wanted to be lighter skinned. However, once Alek Wek, a dark-skinned supermodel, was acclaimed by all as beautiful, Nyong'o began gaining confidence in herself. She said that her mother told her that she "could not eat beauty." What her mother meant was that beauty cannot sustain someone, but inner beauty and compassion can.

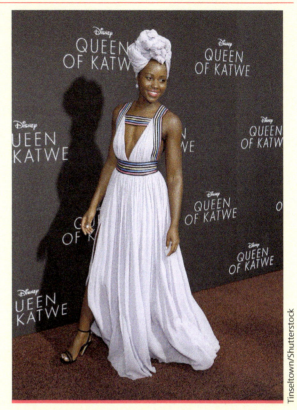

Lupita Nyong'o began to gain confidence in herself when she saw a dark-skinned supermodel gain acclaim.

students have to rack their brains trying to remember the last time they saw an Asian man in a relationship with a White European or an Asian woman on television.

Articles such as McIntosh's (1995) help us to understand how White-European people can assist in eliminating racism. Her insights help other people see how society is set up to give an advantage to one class of individuals over other classes of individuals. Thus, the basis of our form of government—that all people are created equal—is not true unless we help make it true and form "a more perfect union." One step in helping to form a more perfect union is to produce more people like McIntosh—individuals who have power merely by their status but who are willing to give up some of their power to help those on the downside of power gain more equality, what writers in the field call a development of **allies** (Kivel, 1996; Mio & Roades, 2003; Roades & Mio, 2000; Rose, 1996; Tatum, 1997; Wise, 2008, 2013). Allies are those individuals on the upside of any form of unearned power and privilege—such as White privilege, male privilege, heterosexual privilege, and ability privilege—who are willing to work for social justice in giving those on the downside of power and privilege equal status. According to Tatum (1997), many of her White-European students feel powerless when they study racism, but when

allies Individuals who are on the upside of power who cross a demographic boundary to advocate for those on the downside of power.

she talks about allies and how allies can help eliminate racism, her students suddenly feel empowered because this mindset helps them understand how they can confront this otherwise daunting issue.

Being an ally can be a learning process, as illustrated in the experience of this student:

> My experience in the engineering college was very stereotypical . . . I indulged in sexist and homophobic jokes . . . I policed the sexuality of women through my words and behaviour, I was possessive of the ones I dated . . . I had built a masculine (toxic) culture around myself. . . . The privilege of being a cis-gendered upper-caste Hindu man was built around me. In the first few days of my fellowship, I "casually" cracked a premenstrual syndrome (PMS) joke, wherein I assumed a peer of mine was responding in a particular way because of her period and was then told by her that what I had done was wrong. . . . [She] made me more reflective about the privilege I had and what I was doing because of it. . . . I started questioning who the ones in power are and who dominates high social positions. And when I did that, I could see how dominated it was by upper-caste men. I saw how institutions could be patriarchal. . . . It is almost as if all the notions that I had within me crumbled, and a new set of notions started forming. . . . I am a feminist. A feminist who is going to continuously read, listen, and understand, and not stop calling myself a feminist because I make mistakes.
>
> —Sudhamshu Mitra, Young India Fellowship student, India (Mitra, 2017)

Not only can *being* an ally be difficult, but also *teaching* about White privilege and social justice issues can be difficult (Boatright-Horowitz & Soeung, 2009). Boatright-Horowitz and Soeung found that professors (one European American, one Black) who taught about White privilege to European-American students were rated significantly lower than the same professors who taught about social learning theory. For those of us who are committed to a just world, the consequences of teaching about these matters are worth the benefit of exposing people to such issues.

Summary

Bias comes in many shapes and sizes. Some forms of bias are subtle and some are quite striking; some are unintentional and some are intentional. One of social psychology's basic theories—attribution theory—explains how bias can be revealed in our categorization of events. Ways of categorization can lead to stereotyping, prejudice, discrimination, and racism. Stereotyping and prejudice occur within ourselves and do not hurt others, whereas discrimination and racism are actions against others and consequently cause damage. This damage can be as minor as a mild irritation or a strained relationship or as serious as blatant unfairness or even death.

Ultimately, however, racism hurts everyone. The targets of racism are hurt by the racist comments or actions. The perpetrators are also hurt because they live in fear of those whom they categorize negatively, and when someone's racist attitudes become public, that person may even lose a prestigious position. Racism can be overt and intentional and thus easily identified, but it can also be covert and unintentional and difficult to identify.

Many modern forms of racism are difficult to detect. Most individuals who hold racist views are unaware that their views are racist and would even vigorously deny that they are racist. These modern forms of racism are often unintentional, but they cannot be eliminated unless people are willing to examine their own contribution to a racist atmosphere. Racial microaggressions are forms of modern racism. They do not overtly hurt targets of racism because of the relatively minor injury they cause, but an accumulation of microaggressions can become burdensome. These microaggressions can also be applied to sexism, heterosexism, and other kinds of *isms* that target individuals on the downside of power. Peggy McIntosh (1995) identified the various advantages of her White privilege. These privileges are unearned and unconscious unless they are brought to light. For example, McIntosh knows that White-European people will be characterized positively in almost any newspaper or television show, whereas most people of colour may never see characters of their ethnicity portrayed as part of life in their society. By identifying these privileges, she makes herself aware of the advantages that come with her skin colour and the special burden such privileges place on her to make her work harder for social justice.

FOOD FOR THOUGHT

You can extend Peggy McIntosh's concept of White privilege to privileges of all kinds. Men are privileged in our society over women, heterosexuals are privileged over gay and lesbian individuals, and able-bodied individuals are advantaged over individuals with disabilities. Men often think nothing of staying in their offices late at night and then walking to their cars to go home. However, women are often concerned about doing the same thing. On campus, they can use the escort service the police department provides at night, but it is inconvenient. This is just one example of male privilege. We encourage you to think of other kinds of privileges from which you have benefited. In so doing, you will begin to think like an ally in working toward social justice.

Critical Thinking Questions

1. Have you ever attributed something to someone's personality but later found out it was the context that determined the person's actions? Have you ever felt that someone else unfairly attributed something you did to your personality or character when it was the situation that determined your action? Did you get the chance to talk with the other person in either of these situations so that you could develop a better understanding of each other?
2. If you have ever seen a television news report that a person of colour has engaged in some criminal action, have you immediately attributed that action to others in that person's ethnic group?
3. What institutional practices can you identify that unfairly disadvantage people of colour? What institutional practices can you identify that unfairly disadvantage women? What institutional practices can you identify that unfairly disadvantage people of non-dominant sexual orientations? What institutional practices can you identify that unfairly disadvantage people of non-dominant religions? What institutional practices can you identify that

unfairly disadvantage people who have physical disabilities? What institutional practices can you identify that unfairly disadvantage someone of a non-dominant group?
4. What negative stereotypes can be attributed to a group to which you belong? Have you experienced stereotype threat based on these negative stereotypes?
5. What kinds of covert forms of racism can you identify around you?
6. Did you think that being colour-blind to race was something positive? If so, has your opinion changed after reading this chapter?
7. Can you think of times when you may have committed a microaggression against someone else? If so, how might you respond now?
8. What kinds of dominant group privilege can you identify that benefit you?
9. What kinds of things related to your dominant group privilege can you do to intervene on someone else's behalf?

Note

1 Students are allowed to take this written test multiple times to pass it and receive a degree. However, failure on this test even once is a blow to the self-esteem of a student who is bright, so even the brightest students feel pressure when taking the test.

Brocreative/Shutterstock

7 Cultural Identity Development

Learning Objectives

Reading this chapter will help you to:

7.1 explain the distinction between the independent and interdependent self;
7.2 compare two different models of personality: the tripartite model and the five-factor model (FFM);
7.3 understand the importance of ethnic identity development, including Black, White, Latino, Asian, and Indigenous identity;
7.4 discuss models of multi-ethnic identity development;
7.5 explain sexual identity development;
7.6 examine stages of the racial and cultural identity development model;
7.7 explain critiques of cultural identity models; and
7.8 recognize the complexities of having multiple identities.

Who am I? All human beings, at some point in their lives, face that question. Erik Erikson (1950/1963) stated that one of the major developmental tasks for human beings is the establishment of an identity. Our search for an identity takes place across many domains: physical appearance, personal interests, career plans, religious beliefs, gender roles, and so on. An important characteristic of identity is that it is fluid and therefore changes across time and context. We construct our identity or identities in relation with others (Hall, 1991; 2000). In other words, identity is not static and does not naturally exist. Rather, there is a process of identity formation and identity construction (Reicher, 2004). Although every individual struggles with identity questions, individuals from culturally diverse groups face a unique challenge. They must also resolve conflicts related to their minority status, whether that is based on ethnicity, gender, sexual orientation, physical ability, or some other trait that makes them different from the mainstream society. Society reacts to those differences, often in negative ways, and individuals must come to terms with the prejudice, discrimination, marginalization, and oppression based on their membership in that group. Women experience sexism, people of colour experience racism, and LGBTQ2+ people experience heterosexism. There are many more *isms* (e.g., ableism, classism, ageism). Individuals who hold marginalized identities struggle to make meaning of the fact that some aspect of their being is not accepted by society.

In Canada, the group labelled as Black accounts for 3.5 per cent of the Canadian population (Statistics Canada, 2016). It has been suggested that the Black-Canadian population consists of ancestors of those who fled the US during slavery and the American Civil War and migrants, mostly from Africa and the Caribbean (Mensah, 2010). Overall, the label of "Black" does not refer to a homogenous group of people, and it is important to consider historical and societal context when we refer to Black people or Black identity.

Daniel Tatum (1997) explains that when adolescents of African and African-Caribbean descent experience society's negative reactions to their Blackness, they are more likely to internalize the negative perception. For them, colour is often not perceived to be an issue during early childhood, growing up in predominantly White or mixed neighbourhoods. They may make friends and interact easily with children from other ethnic backgrounds. Black children often have not had negative experiences associated with their skin colour because the larger society does not yet see them as a threat. However, as they get older, things start to change. The Black adolescent girl who goes shopping at the mall with her White friends sees the salespeople follow her around to make sure she does not shoplift, but they do not do this to her friends. She may also notice that the salespeople rush to help her friends but ignore her. The Black adolescent boy might notice that White women clutch their purses more tightly when he walks by, look nervous when he enters the elevator, or cross to the other side of the street to avoid him. Young Black people might also notice that their friends' parents do not mind if their children have Black friends but draw the line when it comes to dating.

> Why do Black youths, in particular, think about themselves in terms of race? Because that is how the rest of the world thinks of them. Our self-perceptions are shaped by the messages that we receive from those around us, and when young Black men and women enter adolescence, the racial content of those messages intensifies. (Tatum, 1997, pp. 53–4)

When Black youths try to discuss their thoughts and feelings about racially motivated incidents with their White friends, they may receive little support. Their friends may respond, "Oh, I'm sure they didn't mean it like that!" or "Just forget about it. It's not a big deal." But their African or African-Caribbean friends might say, "The same thing happened to me!" or "I know just how you feel." From their White friends they tend to get denial and minimization; with their Black friends, they find similarity, understanding, and support. Therefore, they gradually drift away from their White peers and toward their Black peers.

> When feelings, rational or irrational, are invalidated, most people disengage. They not only choose to discontinue the conversation but are more likely to turn to someone who will understand their perspective.... Not only are Black adolescents encountering racism and reflecting on their identity, but their White peers, even when they are not the perpetrators (and sometimes they are), are unprepared to respond in supportive ways. The Black students turn to each other for the much-needed support they are not likely to find anywhere else. (Tatum, 1997, pp. 59–60)

These perceptions are complicated. For example, starting at age 10, Black boys are likely to be seen as less innocent than children of other ethnic/racial groups (Goff et al., 2014). They are also more likely to be seen as older by both the general public and police officers (Goff et al., 2014). The latter has real implications for police actions. Black children living in predominantly White society must cope with the reality of dramatically higher incarceration rates and differential treatment within the justice system (National Council on Crime and Delinquency, 2007). They also have a greater likelihood of dying at the hands of law enforcement; one report estimated that African-American teenagers were 21 times more likely to be shot dead by a police officer than their European-American counterparts (Gabrielson et al., 2014). According to the Ontario Human Rights Commission (2018), between 2013 and 2017, a Black person in Toronto was 19.5 times more likely to be shot dead by the Toronto Police Service compared to a White person. However, although the likelihood of deadly shootings of Black people is relatively similar between the United States and Toronto, the rate at which fatal shootings occurs is much greater in the United States (Lartey, 2015).

Differential treatment within the justice system also applies to other minority groups living in most societies around the globe. For example, Aboriginal peoples in Australia have consistently been shown to be victims of police brutality and are subject to racist remarks, harsh treatment, harassment, and excessive sentences (Korff, 2020). Furthermore, Aboriginal youth in Australia are 26 times more likely to be in detention on an average night, compared to the non-Aboriginal youth population (Australian Institute of Health and Welfare, 2018). In general, young people from cultural minority groups in Canada (e.g., Black, Asian, Indigenous) must cope with society's reactions to their "otherness." This is an important part of their identity development process.

7.1 The Independent and Interdependent Self

A foundational aspect of our personalities and our identities is how we describe ourselves. For example, if you were asked, "Who are you?" what would you say? Your self-description illuminates your personality (e.g., I'm introverted), your cultural background (e.g., I'm Canadian), your religion (e.g., I am a practising Muslim), and more. Markus and Kitayama (1991) theorize that depending on which hemisphere of the world you inhabit, you are likely to have developed either an independent or interdependent self. People from the Northern hemisphere and Westerners tend to have an independent self: they value autonomy and being unique. People from the Southern hemisphere and Easterners tend to have an interdependent self: they value harmony in social contexts and fitting in (Markus & Kitayama, 1991; Wang, 2011; Zhu et al., 2007). These differences are evident at a neurological level, as shown in a study by Zhu et al. (2007). The same area of the brain was active when independent and interdependent participants described themselves, but when asked to describe their mother, only the interdependent participants activated that same region of the brain (Zhu et al., 2007). This implies that interdependent individuals' self-representations are closely linked to their representation of others. Additionally, Markus and Kitayama (1991) hypothesize that independent individuals' identities are heavily based on their personal attributes and abilities, but interdependent individuals' identities do not rest so heavily on these qualities. This theory has been supported in a number of studies. For example, a study conducted by Markus et al. (2006) examined the Olympic media coverage related to American and Japanese athletes. It was found that American coverage allocated attention to the athlete's personal attributes (i.e., skill, talent, and strength), whereas Japanese coverage allocated attention to the athlete's background experiences (i.e., how long they had been competing), emotional states, and reactions to their performance.

7.2 Models of Personality

tripartite model of personal identity The understanding that personal identity is made up of three components: individual, group, and universal levels.

An old Asian saying goes something like this: All individuals, in many respects, are (a) like no other individuals, (b) like some individuals, and (c) like all other individuals (Murray & Kluckhohn, 1953). Sue and Sue (2003) note, "While this statement might seem confusing and contradictory, Asians believe this saying to have great wisdom and to be entirely true with respect to human development and identity" (p. 11).

The Tripartite Model of Personal Identity

D. W. Sue (2001) proposed a **tripartite model of personal identity**. The model is illustrated as three concentric circles (see Figure 7.1), which describe the individual, group, and universal levels of personal identity.

According to the adage mentioned above, on the individual level, "all individuals are, in some respects, like no other individuals." Each person is unique in genetic makeup, personality characteristics, and personal experiences. Our individual uniqueness sets us apart from all other human beings and is an important part of our identity.

The second part of the adage says, "All individuals are, in some respects, like some other individuals." This is the group level of personal identity, which focuses on similarities and differences among individuals. As mentioned earlier, society divides people into groups based on demographic characteristics (e.g., gender,

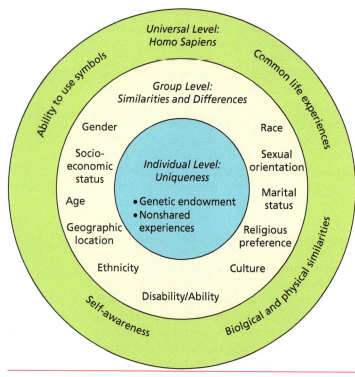

Figure 7.1 The tripartite model of personal identity.

Source: From "Multidimensional Facets of Cultural Competence," by D. W. Sue, 2001, *The Counseling Psychologist, 29.* (p. 793).

ethnicity, socio-economic status, religious preference). Therefore, a part of our identity is based on our membership in these various groups. The third part of the saying reflects the universal level of personal identity: "All individuals are, in some respects, like all other individuals." We all share some characteristics as members of the human race, such as biological and physical similarities, common life experiences (e.g., birth, death, love, fear), and common practices or behaviours (e.g., language).

In this chapter, we focus on the second level of personal identity development: the group level. Membership in groups shapes the way we see ourselves, others in our group, and others outside our group. As we mentioned earlier, membership in some groups is valued over membership in others—men over women, Christian over Muslim, able-bodied over disabled, and White over Black. Society's reactions to our group membership influence group identity formation. A large body of literature exists on the cultural identity process, and there is no way to cover all of it, but in this chapter we will introduce you to it. The majority of this literature focuses on racial identity development, so that is where we begin.

The Five-Factor Model of Personality across Cultures

The five-factor model (FFM) of personality can be remembered using the word OCEAN as an acronym. It is made up of the following factors:

- (O) Openness to experience
- (C) Conscientiousness
- (E) Extraversion
- (A) Agreeableness
- (N) Neuroticism

People who are open to experience tend to have a wide range of interests and seek creativity and novelty rather than routine and habitual experience. Individuals who are high on conscientiousness tend to be thoughtful, task-focused, and detail-oriented. Those who are extraverted tend to be sociable and outgoing. People who are agreeable tend to be polite, affectionate, and helpful, and those who are high on neuroticism tend to have low emotional stability, high anxiety, and high depression. These personality traits tend to be stable, and individuals may be low or high on any of these traits (Digman, 1990; Goldberg, 1993; McCrae & Oliver, 1992). The model has been tested cross-culturally, and there is evidence for its universality. In other words, these factors capture variability in individual personalities across different cultural contexts.

A study by Church and Katigbak (2002) examined the FFM in the Philippines. The researchers discovered that the FFM replicates well in the Philippines and that personality traits are not culture specific. However, some cultures may just be higher naturally on one dimension than another, and subgroup differences, such as gender and age, are probably associated with the wide range of personality traits found within individual cultures. Similarly, McCrae (2002) found that as a person ages, there is often a decrease in neuroticism, extraversion, and openness, and an increase in agreeableness and conscientiousness. The findings did not only apply to Western cultures but appeared relevant to most people around the world. It was also found that traits are generally geographically specific. For example, Germany and Switzerland are similar in their average trait expression because they are close in location. The FFM and the majority of personality models have been found to pertain to cultures all over the world (Sarbescu & Boncu, 2018), implying that there may be a structure to the way personality traits are expressed universally.

7.3 Ethnic Identity Development

Deana, a Filipina/African-American woman, describes several phases she went through in her own identity development.

> My memory may be a bit tainted, but I think my daughter was about 5 years old, shortly after entering kindergarten, when she began to talk about race and features. I guess before that, she was exposed to very few children. She was always with my family, wherein the subjects of race, identity, discrimination, and such topics were never discussed. When she was 5, I believe that I was still struggling with my own identity, so I really never talked about her multiracial identity. She came home and asked me why her friend's hair looked different from hers. She said that she touched it and everything, and it felt different too. I asked her "what her friend" was and she told me her friend's name. "No," I said, and I proceeded to ask about where she was from, and the colour of her skin, but my daughter just concentrated on the texture of her hair, while she answered that she was from the same school and that her colour was dark brown. This is going to sound amazing, but although I never had conversations with my daughter, prior to that day, about race, I thought she knew Black people from White people, Asian people from Hispanics, Whites from Asians, and so on and so forth. I believe that my assumptions were based on my own world view and knowledge base, and I may have been projecting some feelings onto my daughter. The contradiction was that even though in my mind, I assumed that she knew the differences among different ethnic groups, I was not surprised that she couldn't tell between the racial features! How then did I think that she would know the differences between ethnic groups if she had no basis for that knowledge? I think because I assumed that a person's identity would be determined by how they looked alone, and that's how I went about defining my own ethnicity, then I assumed that my daughter and everyone else would think the same way. It was also because many people assumed that they knew exactly "what I was," based on how I looked, and for the most part, they were wrong! I was annoyed at my daughter for not knowing what I meant when I asked "what her friend was." I hated having to explain more about the one thing that I avoided all of my life. To define myself, my family, and my daughter was to justify many things that I didn't feel I should have to explain. Nowadays, I talk freely to her about ethnicity, discrimination, and such issues, because now that she is older, she too has experienced being "the other." Seeing who her friends are and how she has evolved now that I have educated myself, in turn increasing my ability to educate her, makes me feel confident that although she will continue to face obstacles along the way, she is better equipped to do so, as I am now.
>
> —Deana, 20+-year-old Filipina/African-American woman

At first, Deana saw her mixed racial background as negative; she denied it and avoided dealing with it. However, her daughter's questions about racial differences forced Deana to become comfortable with and understand her own identity. Through educating her daughter and herself, Deana gained more confidence in dealing with issues of racial identity. Although not everyone has the same experience as Deana, all individuals from diverse backgrounds face similar questions about their identity and go through similar phases in addressing those questions.

Black Identity Development

Research on cultural identity can be traced back to a landmark experiment conducted by the husband-and-wife team of Kenneth and Mamie Clark (Clark & Clark, 1939), two African-American psychologists, in 1939. In their study, the Clarks presented African-American children with Black and White dolls and asked them a series of questions, such as which doll was the prettiest, smartest, or dirtiest. They found that African-American children consistently attributed more positive traits to the White dolls and negative traits to the Black dolls.

The Clarks concluded that the results demonstrated the low self-esteem and negative self-image of Black children and attributed this to the racism, oppression, and discrimination experienced by Black children in White America. The Clark study had widespread influence in the field of psychology and beyond, and it was used as evidence in the 1954 *Brown v. Board of Education* decision by the Supreme Court that segregated schools were unconstitutional (Clark et al., 2004; Pickren, 2004).

William Cross (1971) was another major influence on the study of cultural identity development. Cross outlined stages that Black individuals go through in moving from self-hatred to self-acceptance. He called this process "nigrescence," or the process of becoming Black. The model contains four (originally five) stages. They are as follows (Worrell et al., 2001):

1. Pre-encounter
2. Encounter
3. Immersion/Emersion
4. Internalization

At the **pre-encounter stage**, individuals are programmed to think of the world as non-Black or anti-Black. They think and act in ways that devalue their Blackness and idealize Whiteness. In other words, they have internalized society's attitudes about European superiority.

In the **encounter stage**, individuals experience some significant or startling event that forces them to re-evaluate their previous ideas about race. Cross (1971) mentions the assassination of Dr Martin Luther King Jr as an event that forced many people to re-evaluate their attitudes about ethnicity and Blackness.

In the third stage, **immersion/emersion**, a reversal occurs wherein people start to idealize Blackness and immerse themselves in Black culture. The full Black identity is not developed at this stage as a sense of confusion and excitement mark this stage. An individual may also reject Whites and act confrontational. Cross's final stage is **internalization**, wherein people feel positive and secure about their Black identity. There is an abandonment of feelings of hate toward Blackness and an increased comfort with and acceptance of other cultures. Although Cross (1991, 1995) made some revisions to the original theory on the basis of subsequent research, the basic structure of the model remains the same.

Deana, who was discussing racial identity with her five-year-old daughter earlier in the chapter, was in the pre-encounter stage when she avoided dealing with her multi-ethnic background. Her daughter's questions about racial differences moved her into the encounter stage. In the end, she appears to achieve some positive resolution about her racial identity and reach the internalization stage.

Since Cross first published his stages of "nigrescence" in 1971, racial identity development has become one of the most widely researched topics in cross-cultural psychology (Parham,

pre-encounter stage The stage or status in which one is influenced by the dominant Eurocentric values of Blackness and may devalue one's own Blackness.

encounter stage The stage or status in which one encounters experiences that lead to re-evaluating one's own beliefs about Blackness and race.

immersion/emersion The stage or status in which a group begins to immerse themselves in and focus on their own identity and culture.

internalization The stage or status in which one feels comfortable with one's identity. This allows one to express acceptance of other cultures.

Racial identity development models suggest that a sense of pride about being of African descent is psychologically healthy.

2001). Several new theories have been introduced regarding racial identity development among Black individuals. For instance, the Black Identity Development Model introduced by Bailey W. Jackson in 2001 and updated in 2012 details five stages of development (Jackson, 2012). The updated model exhibits Black identity as more than simply a consequence of discrimination and racism but also integrates the impact of the Black heritage and culture as a source of further identity development. This theory, similar to Cross's nigrescence theory, has five stages:

1. Naive
2. Acceptance
3. Resistance
4. Redefinition
5. Internalization

In the naive stage, children do not have an understanding of race and the social differences that arise from it and therefore feel unaffected by race. After this stage comes acceptance. During the acceptance stage, individuals internalize the concept of racial dominance that is being reinforced by the society they are living in and will often seek approval from the White community and reject their Black community to fit this model of racial supremacy. This stage is then followed by the frustrating and often painful resistance stage, where individuals begin to recognize racism everywhere it exists and reject and unlearn the racial supremacy that is evident in their lives. This stage may be one of the longest stages an individual experiences, but it eventually transitions into redefinition. During the redefinition stage, individuals find their identity independent of the expectations placed on them by society and become more in touch with their Black community. Here they learn from their community to understand their culture and heritage and how it impacts them. The final stage, internalization, is a cumulation of everything learned in the previous stages. Here, individuals know who they are and understand their identity as a Black person without having to defend or explain it. This is also the stage where a multi-ethnic person may choose to investigate the intersections between Black identity and their other identities (Jackson, 2012).

Scholars also developed theories and models that emphasize intersectional identity development. For instance, Patricia Hill Collins (2000) studied the intersection between Black identity and feminist theory. She created a model of Black feminist thought by taking the tenets of feminism that were historically applied only to middle-class White women and inserting the experiences and knowledge of Black women (Collins, 2000). This theory integrated different identities that often were studied separately, thereby effectively renewing interest in the intersections of identity development. Parham and Helms (1981) constructed the Racial Identity Attitude Scale to measure Cross's stages (see Box 7.1 for sample items). The Racial Identity Attitude Scale has been used to explore the relationship between racial identity and a wide variety of other variables, such as self-esteem (Parham & Helms, 1985a), demographic factors (Parham & Williams, 1993), affective states (Parham & Helms, 1985b), and the counselling process (Helms, 1985). There has also been a proliferation of other cultural identity models. Similarly, Cross's model and its revisions (Cross, 1991, 1995; Cross et al., 1999; Cross & Vandiver, 2001) have stimulated a great deal of research, particularly testing the psychometric properties (see Chapter 2) of the model (Telesford et al., 2013; Vandiver et al., 2002; Vandiver et al., 2001; Worrell & Gardner-Kitt, 2006; Worrell et al., 2011; Worrell et al., 2004; Worrell et al., 2006; Worrell & Watson, 2008).

BOX 7.1 The Racial Identity Attitude Scale

Many measures have been developed to capture cultural identity. One of the most widely used, the Racial Identity Attitude Scale, was developed by Parham and Helms (1981) to measure Cross's stages of Black racial identity development. Other widely used scales include the Multidimensional Inventory of Black Identity (MIBI), which was developed in 1997 by Sellers and colleagues. More recently, the Cross Racial Identity Scale (CRIS) was developed by Cross and Vandiver in 2001 as a complement to Cross's nigrescence theory. Here are some sample items from the Racial Identity Attitude Scale. Although the scale was originally designed for African Americans, we have left the race blank so that you can fill it in with your own race.

Pre-encounter
I believe that large numbers of _____ are untrustworthy.
I believe that White people look and express themselves better than _____ do.
I feel very uncomfortable around _____ people.

Encounter
I feel unable to involve myself in White experience, and am increasing my involvement in _____ experiences.
I find myself reading a lot of _____ literature and thinking about being _____.
I feel guilty and/or anxious about some of the things I believe about _____ people.

> **Immersion/Emersion**
> I have changed my style of life to fit my beliefs about _____ people.
> I believe that everything _____ is good, and consequently, I limit myself to _____ activities.
> I speak my mind regardless of the consequences (e.g., being kicked out of school, being imprisoned, being exposed to danger).
>
> **Internalization**
> People, regardless of their race, have strengths and limitations.
> I feel good about being _____ but do not limit myself to _____ activities.
> I am determined to find my _____ identity.
>
> ---
> From *Black and White Racial Identity: Theory, Research, and Practice*, by J. E. Helms, 1990, (pp. 245–7). Westport, CT: Praeger.

There are also models for Asians/Filipinos (e.g., Chang & Kwan, 2009; Cheryan & Tsai, 2007; Kitano, 1982; Nadal, 2004), Indigenous Peoples (e.g., Gonzalez & Bennett, 2011; Horse, 2012; Trimble, 1987, 2000; Trimble et al., 2002), Latinos (e.g., Ruiz, 1990), and White Europeans (e.g., Corvin & Wiggins, 1989; Helms, 1984, 1990, 1995; Ponterotto, 1988), as well as for other identities such as gender (Kohlberg, 1966) and sexual orientation (e.g., Cass, 1979).

White-European Identity Development

> We had one biological child and wanted a family bigger than one child, so we had applied to adopt, and after two years of waiting, we got the call. This child, we were told, had treaty status, and he was one month old. This was our introduction to a culture other than what we had grown up in. We joined a group of families who had also adopted children of [Indigenous] background and attempted to raise our youngest son with an awareness of [Indigenous] cultures in our province. . . . When he was about 14 years old, one day he asked me to come into the grocery store with him. "Mom, when you come in, they don't look at me and follow me." The first time he said that, I looked up at him (he was already taller than me), dumbfounded. I thought, "Why on earth would anyone in the store be looking at you, much less be following you? Your brother never asked me this or told me that anyone in a store followed him. What is this all about?" I didn't say any of this, I just said "Sure, OK," and went into stores with him. . . . For me, it has been a learning experience: I am White, with a capital *W*, and I do not and never did have to deal with these subtle, upsetting experiences. I do not have to live my life, as my son does still, with a seemingly never-ending series of experiences that point out that it is still a "White" world.
>
> —*Marie, the White mother of an Indigenous son (Syed & Hill, 2011, pp. 4–5)*

Most often, cultural identity development is discussed as a minority phenomenon, in which members of minority groups struggle with the negative attitudes of and treatment by the dominant culture. What about those in the dominant group? Do they struggle with such questions as well?

The story of Marie demonstrates the lack of awareness she had about her privilege and how much she learned when she adopted her son. In doing this, she was confronted with the realities of discrimination and her place in that social system. Many cross-cultural psychologists have addressed the issue of White-European identity (Carter, 1995; Corvin & Wiggins, 1989; D'Andrea, 2003; Helms, 1984, 1990, 1995; Ponterotto, 1988). They believe that members of the dominant group must confront racism and oppression from the other side—as perpetrators rather than as recipients. Several models of White-European identity development have been proposed (Hardiman, 1982; Ponterotto, 1988; Rowe et al., 1994), but the most cited and most researched was developed by Janet Helms (1984, 1990, 1995).

White identity theories, like Black identity theories, have experienced much change in recent years. After Helms's initial study, many models have reflected and updated the stages detailed in her theory. One of these models was proposed by Rowe et al. (1994), who first criticized the original theory for several reasons, including its focus on White attitudes about other racial outgroups rather than their own, as well as the fact that the theory is originally based on other minorities' identity development and the oppression and discrimination they face (Rowe et al., 1994). In response to these criticisms, Rowe and colleagues developed an alternative model of White racial consciousness.

Rowe and colleagues' model of White racial consciousness consists of a number of achieved and unachieved attitudes that reflect an individual's understanding of their own White identity, their social dominance, and their awareness of their privilege within the society. Achieved attitudes exist in individuals who have gained understanding of their White identity, while unachieved attitudes exist in individuals who have not explored their White identity (Rowe et al., 1994). Within the achieved mental attitudes, several mentalities exist:

- Dominant
- Conflictive
- Reactive
- Integrative (Rowe et al., 1994)

The dominant-type mentality is one in which individuals understand that they are White and, due to their ethnicity or skin colour, think they are superior to others. Conflictive-type mentalities exist in individuals who oppose overtly racist policies but also oppose policies that are meant to minimize racism (Rowe et al., 1994). The reactive-type mentality is where individuals are aware that the current society benefits White people above all other ethnicities and can identify and oppose racist acts and policies wherever they appear in the society (Rowe et al., 1994). Lastly, integrative-type mentalities exist when individuals have a deep-rooted understanding of minority issues and see the need to change the current society as their moral responsibility (Rowe et al., 1994).

Conversely, unachieved racial attitudes include the following mentality types:

- Avoidant
- Dependent
- Dissonant

Avoidant-type mentality exists in individuals who find minority and ethnic issues to be inconvenient or anxiety-inducing. Therefore, they actively refuse to explore their ethnicity and the impacts of their ethnicity on others (Rowe et al., 1994). Dependent-type individuals have developed an understanding of their White identity at some point in their lives, but since this understanding has been developed, they refuse to change it by exploring further or considering new information. Lastly, dissonant-type mentality is attributed to individuals who do not have a committed idea of what it means to be White and are uncertain of their identity. They may accept new information but will not commit to any ideas (Rowe et al., 1994).

These different attitudes and types are not considered as stages, however, because individuals do not have to move through each attitude. Instead, we can simply consider them as categories in which each individual's mindset can be placed. To move between attitudes, individuals would have to alter their mental schemas by understanding new perspectives and new information to change their mindsets (Rowe et al., 1994).

Helms assumes that racist attitudes are a central part of being a White European and that the development of a healthy White-European identity requires abandoning racist ideas and defining oneself as non-racist. She delineates six statuses (originally stages) that White Europeans go through in this process:

1. Contact
2. Disintegration
3. Reintegration
4. Pseudo-independence
5. Immersion/Emersion
6. Autonomy

Helms now uses the term *statuses* instead of *stages* to reflect the fact that individuals may exhibit attitudes and behaviours of more than one stage at the same time and that identity development is a dynamic process rather than a static condition that a person achieves or a category to which a person is assigned (Helms, 1995).

In Helms's first status, **contact status**, White-European people are unaware of and uninformed about racism, discrimination, prejudice, and privilege. They have minimal experience with people from other backgrounds and may profess to be **colour-blind** (as we discussed in Chapter 6), making such statements as "I don't see colour," "People are people," and "We're all the same under our skin." Individuals in this status hold two opposing beliefs: one, that everything White European is superior and everything minority is inferior; and two, that racial and cultural differences do not matter. Referring to Marie's story, all her life, she never had to think about issues such as skin colour or minority status because, being White, such things never pertained to her in any negative way. Her son's daily struggles allowed her to become aware of her status, but she acknowledges that she will never fully be able to relate to what her son has to deal with as a racial minority.

Increased exposure to people from different backgrounds moves individuals into the second status, **disintegration status**, the status in which White-European people are in enough contact with people of colour that their naïveté about racism is shattered. Increased experience with people of colour leads to information that is incongruent with a person's previously held notions; the contradiction causes dissonance. For example, working with an African-Caribbean colleague on a project and seeing what a good job that person does contradicts the belief that Black people are incompetent. Seeing that same colleague passed over for promotions challenges the belief that everyone has an equal chance of success, regardless of colour. Discovering that a loved one had to confront issues of racism challenges the idea that such things do not still happen in today's society. The struggle to make sense of those contradictions may result in feelings of guilt, depression, anxiety, and helplessness. To reduce that conflict, White Europeans may avoid members of diverse groups, try to convince others that people of colour are not inferior, or convince themselves that racism does not exist or at least is not their fault.

contact status The status in which White Europeans are uninformed about the realities of racism and privilege.

colour-blind The stance that everyone is the same and that there is no need to acknowledge ethnic or skin-colour differences.

disintegration status The status in which White Europeans have enough contact with people of colour that their naïveté about racism is shattered.

Most likely, according to Helms (1995), White Europeans resolve their racial conflict by retreating to the comfort and acceptance of their own ethnic group and, either passively or actively, supporting European superiority. This is the defining characteristic of the third status, **reintegration status**.

The fourth status in Helms's model is **pseudo-independence status**. This status marks the first phase in the development of a non-racist White-European identity. They begin to acknowledge some existence of racism but see the solution in changing Black people, not White Europeans. They may reach out to Black people, wanting to help, but do so by imposing European standards. They struggle to find a new White-European identity but lack positive examples for how to do so.

The next status, *immersion/emersion status*, includes the formation of a more positive White-European identity. Individuals take time to explore their own culture, learning what it means to be White European in a diverse society. They no longer focus on changing Black people but instead focus on changing White Europeans and understand that a central part of White-European identity is letting go of one's own racist attitudes and actively fighting the racist attitudes of others.

The final status, **autonomy status**, represents the accomplishment of a positive White-European identity. In this status, White Europeans feel good about their group but also find contact with individuals from other groups mutually enriching. They expand their sensitivity beyond racism to include other forms of oppression, acknowledge their privilege, and act as allies who actively seek to combat discrimination.

> Nick was 15 when he joined The National Front, a far-right, fascist political party in the UK.
>
> "On the surface of it all it looked, you know, like normal guys; they come around and introduced themselves in suits. It didn't seem to have a thuggish element," he said. "But once I got involved, I found out that underneath there was a lot of violence."
>
> "There was lots of immigration in London, and a lot of people had lost their job[s], including my father," Nick said. "I felt like where I lived in the East End of London [in public housing] when refugees were coming over, they went in front of the people who were living there for a long time. It made me really angry."
>
> "In Britain, we had *Searchlight* magazine, an anti-fascist magazine, and they would pick out right-wing people, and they would put in their address, telephone numbers, and you would get attacked. And [our neo Nazi group] Combat 18 started to do the same thing back to the Left, picking out left-wingers, and it got to the stage where we were going to people's houses and attacking them, and that's one of the reasons why I drew away from them, because I don't agree with that at all.
>
> "To me it was a mob-on-mob mentality."
>
> Finally, and like many other "formers," Nick was inspired to [do] a complete about-face when a person he least expected to show him compassion did just that. This was during the birth of his first child by emergency C-section. As it turned out, a Pakistani doctor saved the lives of Nick's wife and newborn daughter.
>
> "When I walked out of that room, I felt like a weight had been lifted off my shoulders," Nick said. "I was a changed person. It was that quick for me. I realized that without these people, who I hated for no other reason than the colour of their skin, they just saved my wife and daughter's [lives]. . . . And it made me realize that everyone, no matter the colour of their skin, has got a value in the world."
>
> Nick and his wife had two more children, and they eventually settled in British Columbia. While very few people knew of Nick's past, it wasn't long before he became involved with

---

reintegration status The status in which White Europeans retreat to their comfort zone within their European communities, which actively or passively support European superiority.

pseudo-independence status The status in which White Europeans begin to acknowledge the realities of racism but believe that it is Blacks who should change, not Europeans.

autonomy status The status in which White-European people are comfortable with their European identity, understand that racism is connected with other forms of oppression, and work to address all forms of oppression.

> a local human rights group, Inclusion Chilliwack, which focused on LGBTQ rights group and anti-bullying in schools.
>
> He also became an active member of Cycling4Diversity. And when he began opening up about his past, his friends urged him to speak publicly about his reformation.
>
> —Nick Cooper, reformed White supremacist (Rangel, 2019, paras. 6, 7, 9, 11, 13–17)

Nick's story reflects a number of statuses in Helms's model of White identity development. He exhibits his status overtly, such as his progression to the reintegration stage in which he joined Combat 18 to retreat back into his White community, in which he was comfortable. It was not until a Pakistani doctor helped with the delivery of his child that he reached the immersion status, where he began to understand his place in a multiracial society and accept individuals from other backgrounds. Later, when he moved to British Columbia, he began his autonomy status, where he understood his identity, and respected, learned about, and helped other individuals with different racial identities.

Although some White Europeans struggle with the issues around their own race and racial identity, sadly, many White Europeans remain in the contact and colour-blind statuses of Helms's model.

Lund and Carr (2010) worked to investigate the systemic nature of racism in Canada through their Great White North project. They were particularly interested in determining whether White people in Canada in fact recognized themselves as White. Reactions to their project suggested that many did not use the term *White* to describe themselves and were even quite hostile to the idea. The project provided evidence that many White people do not acknowledge their Whiteness, which questions the ability of White Canadians to truly understand their privilege.

The work and writings of several other experts (e.g., Bonilla-Silva, 2017; DiAngelo, 2016; Neville et al., 2016) further demonstrate this common narrative that many White Europeans have in relation to their identity. Although research is often interested in the formation of identity for racialized minorities, there is also importance in discovering how White-European identities develop. Studies concerning this topic (Britton, 2013; Loftsdottir, 2011; Walton et al., 2018) provide valuable cross-cultural knowledge and give insight into the perspectives of majority groups. For instance, Britton (2013) explains the overlooked struggles of White mothers who have multi-ethnic children, and Loftsdottir (2011) demonstrates how White identities are often rooted in the social history of colonialism. Additionally, Walton et al. (2018) describe how daily life, such as children going to school and being taught a particular way, may shape White identity. These authors argue that a goal of White identity development should be more than being non-racist; rather, the goal should be to be *anti*-racist, which involves being active instead of passive.

Chicano/Latino Identity Development

Ruiz (1990) proposes a Chicano/Latino identity development model based on four assumptions: marginality has a high correlation with maladjustment; forced assimilation produces negative experiences, which are destructive to an individual; pride in one's own ethnic identity has a positive correlation with mental health; and pride in one's own ethnic identity results in freedom of choice, especially in the acculturation process.

Delgado-Romero (2001) reports that Ruiz's model was derived from case histories of Chicano, Mexican, and other Latino university students. We can then assume that the model may not be representative of other Latinos, with consideration to their country of origin, socio-economic status, acculturation, and so on. Ruiz (1990) proposes five stages of Chicano/Latino identity development: causal, cognitive, consequence, working through, and successful resolution.

In the **causal stage**, negative messages from the environment and other individuals, which may be humiliating and traumatizing, can cause individuals to negate, deny, or ignore their Latino heritage. Persons may fail to identify as Latino or with the Latino culture. During the **cognitive stage**, because of the negative and erroneous messages from the previous stage, ethnic group membership is associated with prejudice and poverty, and the only means of escape and the only road to success is to assimilate into the dominant society. In the **consequence stage**, individuals may reject their Chicano/Latino heritage because of ongoing and intensifying fragmentation of their ethnic identity. Individuals may feel significant pressure to assimilate given the negative messages and desire for acceptance from the majority culture. A Chicano/Latino identity development model can be applied to other cultural identities as well.

In the **working-through stage**, the individual begins to struggle with the ethnic conflict, and this stage marks the beginning of a healthier and integrated Chicano/Latino identity. Individuals increase their ethnic consciousness and reintegrate and reconnect with their ethnic identity and ethnic community. In the final **successful resolution stage**, the individual attains a greater sense of self-acceptance and acceptance of cultural and ethnic identity, believing that ethnic identity is positive and can lead one to be successful. Increased/improved self-esteem is also attained in this stage.

Ruiz's (1990) model is a stage model and follows the structure of other published models. It is also pan-ethnic, covering many subgroups that are subsumed under the umbrella of Latino. We can assume that the model may not be representative of other Latinos, with consideration of their country of origin, socio-economic status, acculturation, and so on. A model that takes into account the multiple Latino subgroups and the complexities of intersecting identities was put forth by Ferdman and Gallegos (2001). The authors stressed the importance of the way Latinos view themselves through "lenses" that capture how the individuals see themselves, how they see the broader context in which Latinos reside, and how much they keep in or out.

An additional model that is widely used when discussing Latino identity is by Torres (2003). In their Hispanic identity development model, identity is said to be influenced by two factors: socio-environmental factors and cognitive and psychological factors. Both of these will interact to determine whether an individual of Latino ethnicity develops one of the following:

- a bicultural orientation (meaning they identify with both the Latino and majority culture),
- a Latino/Hispanic orientation (they identify more with the Latino culture than the majority culture),
- an Anglo orientation (they identify more with majority culture than the Latino culture), or
- a marginal orientation (they identify with neither the majority nor the Latino culture).

Asian/Filipino Identity Development

In examining the literature, there is a lack of Asian-specific identity development models. Instead, most studies on this topic use more general ethnic identity models. One of the models that is widely used in Asian identity research is by Phinney (1989). This model suggests that there are three stages to identity development:

---

causal stage An emotional stage when the individual accepts the negative labels attached to a Latino identity and feels humiliated and traumatized by these labels.

cognitive stage The belief that maintaining a Latino identity necessarily means being poor and the assumption that success in life can be attained only through assimilation to the mainstream culture.

consequence stage Rejection of Latino heritage because of the sense that negative attributes are associated with being Latino.

working-through stage A stage when individuals feel distress because of alienation from their Latino community and are therefore motivated to integrate their Latino identity into a sense of self.

successful resolution stage The final stage, when the Latino identity is integrated into one's own identity and there is a sense of acceptance and positive Latino identity.

1. diffuse/foreclosed (before exploration of ethnicity),
2. moratorium (active exploring of ethnicity), and
3. achieved (explored and now has a clear understanding of ethnicity).

Specifically, the diffuse/foreclosed stage is characterized by no or little ethnicity exploration, usually with a general positive or negative perspective of an individual's ethnicity based on past social experiences. The moratorium stage is where individuals start to investigate and question their ethnicity, while being unsure of the meaning of their identity. Finally, the achieved stage is when individuals feel a clear sense of what their ethnic identity is and find acceptance because of prior ethnic exploration. As such, this model has been applied to many cultural groups, including those of Asian descent.

Nadal (2004) explains some Asian identity development models, but he also points out that certain models were based on Chinese people (Sue & Sue, 1971), Japanese people (Kitano, 1982), Asian college students (Suinn et al., 1992), Filipino people (Nadal, 2004), and the racial and cultural identity development model (R/CID) (addressed later in this chapter). Nadal reported that Asian models, although they make an essential contribution to Asian ethnic identity literature, fail to address intragroup differences.

As much as different Asian identity development models attempt to examine and explain ethnic identity development, there is much to say about the fact that such models cannot fully explain Asian identity as a whole given the heterogeneity in the Asian/Pacific Islander community. Current Asian identity development models cannot seem to describe identity development that encompasses all Asian/Pacific Islander individuals; therefore, the R/CID is most typically utilized to describe the ethnic identity development of Asian/Pacific Islanders.

Indigenous Identity Development

As with the discussion on Asian identity models and the great heterogeneity in the Asian/Pacific Islander community, the diversity and histories of each Indigenous group make it difficult to develop an all-encompassing identity development model for Indigenous Peoples in North America. Having said that, a few unique characteristics in the identity development for Indigenous groups are common. First, a primary consideration in the identity development of Indigenous groups is political, not ethnic. The Canadian Constitution Act of 1982 recognizes three Indigenous groups: First Nations, Métis, and Inuit. First Nations are further split into "Status" and "non-Status Indians" (Statistics Canada, 2019). A legal definition of Indigenous status (or, officially, "Indian status") is dependent upon several factors, such as bloodline, ethnic origin, and, most importantly, signed treaties between Indigenous groups and the Government of Canada. Another common factor in Indigenous identity is related to time and space; in other words, becoming aware or gaining consciousness of one's Indigenous history and connection to the land. These two aspects profoundly shape the identities of Indigenous groups, regardless of whether they live on reservations or in urban settings, because they are reminded of their history every day while living in a colonized state.

7.4 Multi-ethnic Identity Development Models

All of the racial identity development models discussed thus far apply to individuals from one ethnic background. What about people from multi-ethnic backgrounds? What challenges do they face in their identity development processes?

With the diversity of people and ethnicities in Canada, inter-ethnic group marriages are becoming increasingly common (Statistics Canada, 2018). In 2011, 4.6 per cent of all marriages in Canada were mixed unions, in which at least one partner was a member of a visible minority group (Statistics Canada, 2018). Compared to the 2006 report, the number of mixed unions was up from 3.6 per cent. This has also partly been the cause for the increased number of people reporting multi-ethnic origins. Around the world, mixed unions are being influenced by immigration rates. Increases in migration and immigration lead to increased mixed marriages in most European countries. Across Europe, 1 in 12 married individuals are in a mixed marriage (Lanzieri, 2012). For instance, in the United Kingdom, the 2011 census found that almost 1 in 10, or 9 per cent, of couples were mixed unions, an increase from 7 per cent in 2001 (Potter-Collins, 2014).

As the number of multi-ethnic people in in the world has risen, increased attention has been paid to their unique identity development process. Individuals from multi-ethnic backgrounds face a more complex identity process than do those from mono-ethnic backgrounds (Kerwin & Ponterotto, 1995). These individuals must reconcile the heritage of parents from two ethnic backgrounds and decide where they fit in a society that likes to pigeonhole people into a single category (Keerdoja, 1984). In addition, they may face discrimination from both groups because they are not seen as full members of either one (Johnson, 1992; Sue & Sue, 2003). Multi-ethnic individuals may feel pressured to identify with one group over the other. Often, society's reactions are based on a person's appearance—that is, what ethnic group they look like. In 2016, Statistics Canada conducted a study that revealed that 41.1 per cent of the population reported multi-ethnic origins. Long-established ethnic groups, such as Indigenous Peoples and Europeans, identified as multi-ethnic, while groups that had only recently settled in Canada (i.e., Asian and African people) identified as having one ethnicity (Statistics Canada, 2016). Additionally, it was found that those who were born in Canada were more likely to consider themselves multi-ethnic than those who were not born in Canada (Statistics Canada, 2016). There are varied reasons for this, but one has to do with pressure in society to identify with a single ethnicity.

We also see many of the conflicts related to multi-ethnic identities in David's story:

> I don't identify as German because of my dark skin colour. German history [hesitates], I don't know. It is hard to explain. I've learned a lot about German history. . . . For me, a German person is White and has blue eyes and blond hair. That's how I see Germans. I have nothing against them, but that's how I see them. Of course, there are a lot of people that are Black and have a German passport, but they're not German either. They were born and raised in Germany and have some German traits, but I don't see them as German. I see them as people that have a German passport, but not as Germans.
> —David, 20+-year-old biracial German citizen (Hubbard & Utsey, 2015, p. 102)

David does not want to be associated with a country's history, struggles to identify with its stereotypes, and views himself as an outsider. Such confusion and conflict about identity has been a topic of interest among researchers in recent years (Charmaraman & Grossman, 2010; Cheng & Lee, 2009; Shih & Sanchez, 2009; Suyemoto, 2004).

Five-Stage Model of Biracial Identity Development

Many models of multi-ethnic identity development have been proposed (Jacobs, 1992; Kerwin & Ponterotto, 1995; Kich, 1992). The first was W. S. C. Poston's (1990) five-stage model of biracial identity development. At the **personal identity stage**, a young child's sense of self is

personal identity stage The first stage of identity development in which children base their identity on personal factors, such as self-esteem, instead of on ethnicity.

choice of group categorization stage The stage in which a young person is forced to choose one identity over another.

enmeshment/denial stage The stage or status in which a young person feels guilty about choosing one ethnicity over the other because of the implicit rejection of the parent whose ethnicity was not chosen.

appreciation stage The stage or status in which young people begin to broaden their perspective to include the ethnicity not initially selected for their identity.

integration stage The stage or status in which a child/adolescent/adult sees the benefits of embracing both ethnicities.

independent from that child's ethnic group. Identity is instead based primarily on personal factors, such as self-esteem, that develop within the context of the family. In the second stage, the **choice of group categorization stage**, the young person feels pressure to choose one identity over the other. That pressure may come from family members, peers, physical appearance, or society (Hall, 1980, 1992). In the next stage, the **enmeshment/denial stage**, feelings of guilt and self-hatred arise from choosing one group over another. A positive multi-ethnic identity begins to emerge in the **appreciation stage**, when individuals begin to broaden their perspective and begin to explore the previously rejected side of their ethnic heritage. Finally, in the fifth stage, the **integration stage**, the person sees the benefits of embracing both identities.

In his model, W. S. C. Poston (1990) suggests that healthy resolution of the multi-ethnic experience entails integration of and appreciation for both or all ethnic backgrounds. There is an implicit assumption in his model that all individuals with more than one ethnicity follow the same path. Root (1990, 1998, 2004) agrees that multi-ethnic individuals must come to

The number of biracial and multiracial individuals has increased in recent years.

terms with both sides of their heritage but describes five possible resolutions for this process. Root says that a multi-ethnic person may choose to

1. accept the identity society assigns,
2. identify with both ethnic groups,
3. identify with a single ethnic group,
4. identify with a new *mixed-race* group, or
5. identify with the ethnicity considered the one with the higher-status culture in this country (hyperdescension as opposed to hypodescension).[1]

Banks' Typology of Ethnic Identity

A widely used model was proposed by James Banks in 1994, called Banks' Typology of Ethnic Identity (McAllister & Irvine, 2000). The model is not specific to an ethnic group, making it quite applicable to a variety of people, including those with multi-ethnicity. There are six stages in total, and the model describes how an individual comes to terms with multiple cultures and identities.

The first is called *ethnic psychological captivity*, where people internalize stereotypes of different ethnicities. However, majority culture members may not experience this stage as strongly as minority groups. The second stage is called *ethnic encapsulation*, where conflict of ethnic identity begins, and individuals of majority and minority groups become somewhat ethnocentric. For the dominant group, this usually comes from a feeling of superiority, and for marginalized groups it comes from fear of discrimination from other cultures. However, in stage three, called *ethnic identity clarification*, people begin to see the pros and cons of all cultures, and this is often where ethnic identity acceptance occurs. Stage four, titled *bi-ethnicity*, is where individuals finally feel competent enough to function in more than one culture; that is, cross-cultural contact. In stage five, *multi-ethnicity and reflective nationalism*, individuals feel comfortable in a range of cultures and begin to understand the more complex aspects of groups, such as their values and traditions. Finally, the sixth stage of *globalism and global competency* marks people's confidence in their identity. As such, they find balance between their ethnic, national, and global identity and can function with different groups (whether they are a part of those cultural groups or not).

Model of Bicultural Competence

There is another theory, developed by LaFromboise et al. (1993), proposing a model of bicultural competence, which was created from the alternation model of bicultural identity. The premise of the model is that individuals can be competent in more than one culture without sacrificing their functionality in either one or having to choose between them. Essentially, their model proposes that to develop bicultural competence, individuals must maintain a degree of individualism, while still being substantially integrated into society. When this occurs, it prevents any of the negative outcomes, such as retreating from the dominant culture or psychological stress. The theory also states that in order for someone to gain bicultural competence, they should also have a basic understanding of both cultures they are in contact with (this way they feel more confident in their ability to function in a bicultural environment; LaFromboise et al., 1993). Thus, there are many theories concerning the formation of cultural identity, and they all bring different perspectives to the debate.

7.5 Sexual Identity Development

As we have mentioned, ethnic identity has dominated the field of cultural identity development. However, several models address other minority identities. In this section, we present a model of sexual identity development as an example.

Coming out, or the process by which non-heterosexual individuals come to terms with their sexuality and share that orientation with others, is a unique aspect of their identity development. The gamut of non-heterosexual identities is broad. One current acronym is LGBTQQIP2SAA, which stands for lesbian, gay, bisexual, transgender, queer, questioning, intersex, pansexual, two-spirit, asexual, and ally, but these vary across various groups and countries. For practical purposes, the label *non-heterosexual* is used in this section, although it is important to note that the length of the acronym is intended to be inclusive of the wide array of sexual identities and that an ethnic gloss such as *gay* would be inaccurate to capture the complexity of people who are not heterosexual.

Rudy's story describes the phases he went through in his coming-out process:

> I knew that I was gay at the age of 14, but I didn't have the confidence to tell anyone at that time. I was scared what people might think, and at the time I was being bullied, so I thought it would only make it worse. At 15, I told one of my best friends that I was gay and nothing changed between us at all, which was great! Then throughout [grade] 11, I started to tell more and more of my good friends, until I finally told my mum at the end of the year. She completely accepted me, although my dad was a lot harder to tell and unfortunately, he still feels uncomfortable with it. I'm now 17 and in college, and I couldn't be happier in my life! I'm also trying to get involved in LGBT support for my area, to help other youth who are going through what I did.
>
> —Rudy, 17+-year-old English gay man (Stonewall Cymru, 2017, p.11)

Non-heterosexual individuals face heterosexism in that everyone is assumed to be heterosexual. Coming out is also not a one-time event. It happens over time and in different contexts. Whenever non-heterosexual individuals meet someone new, they must decide whether to divulge their sexual orientation (Israel, 2004).

Cass (1979) proposed a series of six stages that help to explain some of the thoughts and feelings Rudy had about his sexual orientation. According to Cass, the first stage that young people go through when questioning their sexual identity is **identity confusion**. This is when the first awareness of being different from same-sex peers occurs. During childhood or adolescence, these young people begin to recognize feelings, thoughts, and behaviours that are outside the norm for how their gender is socialized, such as preferring activities or having interests typical of another gender. Rudy noticed that he liked hanging out with his female cousins, playing with dolls, and admiring male television stars. At first that was acceptable, but soon others made fun of him because of it. Feelings and thoughts of attraction toward same-sex peers may not be apparent at this stage, but the feelings of being *the other* or different are enough to cause the child or adolescent to withdraw from family members and peers.

The next stage is **identity comparison**. In this stage, the differences are more pronounced, and non-heterosexual children recognize how they are different. Thoughts and feelings about same-sex peers become more conscious. A girl who finds herself attracted to another girl sees that other girls talk about boys. This creates incongruence because the girl knows she's a girl and has most likely been socialized as a girl. Suddenly, things change and she has feelings that are not part of the accepted social guidelines for being a girl. She may question why she is so

---

coming out The process by which non-heterosexual individuals openly express their sexual orientation.

identity confusion The stage or status in which gay, lesbian, or bisexual individuals begin to question their sexual identity.

identity comparison The stage or status in which non-heterosexual individuals recognize their differences from most same-sex individuals.

different. When Rudy heard the comments and questions by his family members and friends about his behaviour, he began to question himself and asked, "Am I weird?" In grade 6, he consciously noticed himself admiring another boy in his class.

The third stage of sexual identity development in Cass's (1979) model is **identity tolerance**. In this stage, individuals learn to walk a tightrope. They are now fully conscious that they have sexual feelings toward others of the same sex but keep the feelings hidden. Others most likely remain unaware that the individual has this orientation. This is what we typically describe as *being in the closet*. These individuals may work very hard to keep their orientation a secret, but that results in feelings of guilt, pain, anger, and self-hatred. Individuals are in constant turmoil because they must constantly internally justify their actions. They also hold out hope that this may just be a phase. Rudy confirmed his same-sex attraction when he made out with another boy in the bathroom in grade 8. However, he then became the "stud" that his father wanted him to be and that all the girls desired. He even got a girlfriend and worked hard to fit in with the other boys, all the while being careful not to stare at other boys too long.

The fourth stage is **identity acceptance**. In this stage, the individuals move one step closer to coming out. In acceptance, they can no longer deny their same-sex attraction. Nonetheless, these individuals continue to live in a secret world where same-sex sexual relationships occur "underground" in limited, specific environments (e.g., gay clubs) and infrequently for fear of being discovered. They continue to internalize society's negative views of same-sex attraction as evil, sinful, and unacceptable. This may lead to feelings of hopelessness and even suicide. The suicide rate is high for individuals who come to accept their same-sex sexual attraction as a fact but lack the social support needed to assume pride in their orientation. Approximately three per cent of the Canadian population identifies as lesbian, gay, or bisexual (LGB) (Statistics Canada, 2017). A Canadian study found that LGB youth are at a considerably higher risk of suicide compared to their heterosexual peers and are approximately 14 times more likely to attempt suicide (Benibgui, 2010). Further, an Ontario-based survey within the transgender community revealed that 77 per cent of transgender individuals had seriously considered suicide (Bauer et al., 2010). Hatzenbuehler (2011) also reported that the risk of attempting suicide increased by 20 per cent among LGB persons living in unsupportive environments. Support from family and friends is incredibly important and has been found to help promote positive mental health and reduce stress in LGB individuals (Benibgui, 2010).

The next stage in Cass's model is **identity pride**. In this stage, individuals formally come out of the closet. They now feel pride in their orientation and find causes (e.g., rallies, clubs, walk-a-thons) to explore, express, and celebrate their newly found voice. Yet there is not a complete association of personal identity with same-sex attraction. For example, a man may come out to his parents and begin to join marches and rallies for gay pride, yet he may still not be out at work or with some of his friends, and he may expend a great deal of energy maintaining these multiple identities.

In the final stage, **identity synthesis**, people are able to integrate their sexual identity with their other identities (e.g., woman, lesbian, Black Canadian, student). Individuals are comfortable with their orientation and no longer feel the need to justify their being. Self-acceptance provides people with the coping mechanisms needed to endure and fight the ignorance and discrimination they will face in embracing their diverse selves. This positive self-acceptance is most possible when the individual has a strong social support system to help them withstand societal pressures. However, that support may be difficult to obtain from family members and friends who are unwilling to accept the person's sexual orientation. It may take some time and effort to build a new support system, and this may include relocation to an environment that is more supportive (e.g., moving to a city with a large, visible non-heterosexual population).

---

identity tolerance The stage or status in which non-heterosexual individuals fully recognize their non-heterosexual feelings but attempt to hide them from others and from themselves by trying to believe, for example, that it is just a phase they are going through.

identity acceptance The stage or status in which a non-heterosexual individual fully accepts their sexual orientation but expresses those values in limited, specific environments.

identity pride The stage or status in which a non-heterosexual individual openly expresses their sexual orientation and takes pride in that identity.

identity synthesis The stage or status in which a non-heterosexual individual is able to integrate all aspects of their identities, including ethnicity and gender.

Leticia, a Latino lesbian woman, describes the struggles she faced in her coming-out process:

> I wanted to be straight for a long time, but I've known that I was a lesbian for an even longer time. Anyway, when I came out to my parents, I guess I was hopeful. My dad said that he would pray for my salvation, and my mom didn't say a word. After 8 years, you'd think that one of them knew that I was not straight (I brought home my first girlfriend when I was 12). I knew I was queer before that, but I was too afraid to make any moves toward any girls. Then I turned 18, and I met the most beautiful girl in the world. I wanted to let everyone know that she was my girl. Her parents were really cool and she had been "out" for a long time. I thought it was time to come out of the closet after many years of feeling like crap and being and staying invisible. Anyway, I [had] told my parents that I was queer, but they really reacted more violently after they found out about Michelle. I guess it was okay to say I was queer, but it wasn't okay to have proof that I am.
>
> Nowadays, Michelle and I live together. . . . I'm not really sure what to call us, or myself for that matter. I know that I love her, that I'm queer, but there still feels like something's missing. I remember having to write a paper in college recently, [answering] the question, "Who are you?" I wasn't sure how to answer it because being a lesbian is the most predominant identity that "rules" my life right now, but I know that I'm more.
>
> —*Leticia, 20+-year-old Latino lesbian woman*

Leticia's story highlights the complexities of family interactions and sexual orientation but also invites questions about intersecting identities. What are the unique complexities of being both lesbian and Latino? Strong arguments have been recently advanced for the importance of understanding the intersection of identities in reducing health disparities (Bowleg, 2012).

7.6 Racial and Cultural Identity Development Model (R/CID)

At this point you might be thinking, "I'm confused. There are too many of these identity models and they all sound alike!" It is true. There are many cultural identity development models, and we have covered only a few. They sound similar because of the influence of the original model proposed by Cross (1971) and because all people in minority groups have the shared experience of oppression. A group of multicultural psychologists proposed a comprehensive model of cultural identity development that pulls together the common features of all the models for different groups. The first was presented by Atkinson, Morten, and Sue (1979, 1989, 1998), who called it the *minority identity development model*. The model was later revised by Sue and Sue (1990, 1999, 2003, 2008), who called it the **racial and cultural identity development model (R/CID)**. Each stage in the R/CID addresses how individuals feel about themselves, others of the same group, others of another minority group, and members of the majority or dominant group (Sue & Sue, 2003, 2008). The model is summarized in Table 7.1.

The first stage of the R/CID model is the **conformity stage**. In this stage, individuals show a strong preference for the values, beliefs, and features of the dominant culture over their own. They have incorporated society's view that the dominant culture is superior. Individuals have strong negative attitudes toward the self, their own group, and other minority groups. Members of the dominant groups are respected, admired, and emulated.

Next is the **dissonance stage**. At some point, individuals encounter information that contradicts their cultural values and beliefs. For example, a closeted gay man who thinks all gay men are "fairies" may meet a gay man who is very masculine. An Asian-Canadian person who

---

racial and cultural identity development model (R/CID) A general model that covers all forms of cultural identity and addresses how one relates to oneself, to others of the same culture, to others of different cultures, and to the dominant cultural group.

conformity stage The stage in which individuals show preference for the values, beliefs, and features of the dominant culture over their own values and beliefs.

dissonance stage The stage in which there is a sudden or gradual occurrence that challenges one's belief of inferiority of one's own group and superiority of the dominant group.

TABLE 7.1 The Racial and Cultural Identity Development Model

Stages of minority development model	Attitude toward self	Attitude toward others of the same minority	Attitude toward others of a different minority	Attitude toward the dominant group
Stage 1: Conformity	Self-depreciating or neutral because of negative attitudes toward self	Group-depreciating or neutral because of negative attitudes toward own group	Discriminatory or neutral	Group appreciating
Stage 2: Dissonance and appreciating	Conflict between self-depreciating and group appreciating	Conflict between group-depreciating views of minority hierarchy and feelings of shared experience	Conflict between dominant held and group depreciating	Conflict between group appreciating
Stage 3: Resistance and immersion	Self-appreciating	Group-appreciating experiences and feelings of culturocentrism	Conflict between feelings of empathy for other minority	Group depreciating
Stage 4: Introspection	Concern with basis of self-appreciation	Concern with nature of unequivocal appreciation	Concern with ethnocentric basis for judging others	Concern with basis of group depreciation
Stage 5: Integrative awareness	Self-appreciating	Group appreciating	Group appreciating	Selective appreciation

Source: From *Counseling American Minorities: A Cross-cultural Perspective*, 5th ed., by D. R. Atkinson, G. Morten, and D. W. Sue, Eds., 1998, (p. 41). Dubuque, IA: Brown; and *Counseling the Culturally Diverse*, 4th and 5th eds., by D. W. Sue and D. Sue, 2003 and 2008, (p. 215). New York, NY: Wiley.

thinks racism does not exist anymore may experience a racist incident. Although movement into the dissonance stage may occur suddenly with a traumatic event (as discussed in Cross's model), the developers of the R/CID model believe it also occurs slowly through a gradual breakdown of denial as individuals question their attitudes from the conformity stage. In dissonance, individuals are in conflict between positive and negative views of the self, members of their own group, members of other minority groups, and members of the majority.

In a study conducted on the experience of being an ethnic minority while practising clinical psychology, Meera, a participant, revealed her transition from conforming to society to appreciating her ethnic identity and using it in her practice:

The third stage of the R/CID is the **resistance and immersion stage**. In this stage, individuals accept minority views and reject the dominant culture. Individuals feel guilt and shame about previously being a sellout and contributing to the oppression of their own group. There is anger, distrust, and dislike for the dominant group. Individuals are motivated to discover more about their own culture and build a stronger sense of connection to their own group. Relationships with people belonging to other minority groups tend to be transitory and superficial.

In the **introspection stage**, individuals begin to let go of some of the intense feelings of anger toward the dominant culture and redirect that energy into greater understanding of themselves and their own group. They move away from total immersion in their own group toward greater autonomy, but there is some conflict. There is also more of an attempt to

---

resistance and immersion stage The stage in which individuals become immersed within their own cultural group and reject the dominant culture with feelings of anger and guilt for their initial preference of the dominant culture and rejection of their own culture.

introspection stage The stage in which individuals tend to educate themselves about their own identity, appreciate their own and other cultural groups, and become less angry at the dominant group.

From the early racial identity development models arose more general racial and cultural identity models, encouraging cultural pride across many groups.

integrative awareness stage The stage in which individuals find a greater sense of cultural security, become aware of themselves as individual and cultural beings, and recognize differences among cultural groups, both positive and negative.

understand the attitudes and experiences of other groups, including a struggle to sort out the positive and negative aspects of the dominant group.

The final stage of the R/CID is the **integrative awareness stage**. In this stage, individuals achieve an inner sense of security and appreciate the positive and the negative aspects of both their own culture and the dominant culture. They have a positive sense of group pride but are also able to question group values. Individuals see themselves as a unique individual, a member of a cultural group, and a member of the larger society. They now reach out to members of other minority groups to gain a greater understanding of their attitudes and experiences and express support for all oppressed people. They also distinguish between people in the dominant group in deciding whom to trust and in determining who also actively seeks to eliminate oppression.

The R/CID attempts to pull together the common characteristics of all the stage models. Do you think it is useful to have one comprehensive model of cultural identity development, or do you think each group has unique characteristics and experiences that must be taken into account? Try going back to previous stories in the chapter and applying the stages of the R/CID.

7.7 Critiques of Cultural Identity Models

Although cultural identity models have made a huge contribution to the field of cross-cultural psychology, our understanding of human behaviour, and our diverse society, they are not without limitations. Most models of cultural identity development suggest a linear progression through each of the stages. In other words, it is assumed that all individuals begin at the first stage and gradually work their way through all the stages in the order described. However, that is not necessarily the case. Parham (1989) suggests that people may cycle back and forth through the stages across the life span. For example, in Cross's (1971) model, individuals who have reached the final stage of internalization might have an experience that throws them back into the encounter or immersion/emersion stage. As mentioned earlier, Helms (1995) herself changed the term *stages* to *statuses* to reflect the idea that these identities are not static categories but represent a dynamic developmental process.

Another observation is that not all minority individuals begin their developmental process in a stage where they idealize Whiteness and denigrate their own racial minority background. For example, in Cross's (1971) model, not all Black people begin at the pre-encounter stage. Children who grow up in predominantly Black environments or in homes where they are taught to have a sense of pride in their racial identity may begin at a later stage. However, negative racial experiences during adolescence (such as those described in Tatum's 1997 book) can cause them to have attitudes and behaviours more characteristic of the pre-encounter, encounter, and/or immersion/emersion stages of Cross's model.

Another criticism of the cultural identity models is that they assume one definition of mental health, judging the final stage of the model as the healthiest. In the final stage of most of the models, individuals achieve pride in their own group but also reach out to other groups and incorporate positive aspects of the dominant group into their identity. However, for some individuals, immersion in their own group may be an adaptive response for their situation. The R/CID assumes that a healthy identity includes some degree of autonomy, but in some instances, sublimation of one's individual needs for the sake of the group may be a healthy choice. We must be careful in assuming that one identity outcome is the healthiest for all members of a particular group and under all circumstances (Barker-Hackett, 2003). Some critics of the stage models question the relevance of such models for different generations (Krate et al., 1974). Others criticize the models for overemphasizing reactions to racism and oppression (Akbar, 1989; Nobles, 1989) and lacking empirical evidence to support some of the stages (Behrens, 1997; Cross, 1995; Helms, 1989).

7.8 Complexities of Multiple Identities

Remember Leticia, the Latino lesbian woman who told her story earlier in this chapter? When faced with the question "Who are you?" she was not sure how to answer. She felt that her lesbian identity dominated at the time, but she also felt that she was more than that. Leticia is Latino, but she does not specifically mention her ethnic identity in her story. We may wonder where she is in her ethnic identity development and how that is related to her sexual orientation identity. The emotional turmoil of the sexual identity process is painful enough, but people of colour who are non-heterosexual face even more oppressive consequences. They face a unique challenge—integrating two identities, one pertaining to their ethnicity and the other to their sexual orientation—in a society that does not fully accept either one. Lesbian women of colour face triple jeopardy, since they must cope with oppression occasioned by their ethnicity, their gender, and their sexual orientation (Akerlund & Cheung, 2000; Greene & Boyd-Franklin, 1996).

We may also wonder about the reaction of Leticia's family members to her sexual orientation. Was it because of their culture? Their religion? We all have multiple identities. We are not just a gender, sexual orientation, or religion; we are all of these things. Membership (or lack of membership) in each of these groups shapes our experiences and our world views. It has a powerful influence over how society views us, how we view ourselves, and how we view others (Atkinson et al., 1998; Sue & Sue, 2003, 2008).

All of us belong to more than one group (e.g., Leticia is a woman, a lesbian, a Latino), but one of those identities may be more important to us than the others (e.g., sexual orientation over ethnicity). Characteristics of the person and characteristics of the situation interact to determine which identity is most salient at a particular time (Sellers et al., 1998). For example, if Leticia is at a club with all lesbian women but is the only Latino in the room, her race may become more salient than her sexual orientation.

The complexity of identity formation and modification has been extensively examined with immigrants. For example, Ibrahim (1999, 2008) studied Francophone-African immigrant youth who had to negotiate and understand their identity as a Black person after moving to Canada. Ibrahim argues that one is not born Black but becomes Black. The African youth were not Black in Africa but became Black once they settled in North America. Blackness, then, is beyond just the colour of one's skin. It becomes a code, a bodily expression, a language, a style of clothing, and, most importantly, an experiential memory (Ibrahim, 2008). The product of Blackness that the African youth undertake is a result of both their experience and cultural and linguistic mannerisms they bring from their native land and the Canadian context. Similarly, Litchmore (2019) examined the identity of Black high school students in the Toronto District School Board. She demonstrated that schooling and broader Canadian contexts contributed to students' understanding of what it means to be Black and the academic expectations of them as Black students. Specifically, Litchmore (2019) reported that students were aware that being Black was associated with academic under-performance, and although some students resisted this deficit discourse, others took up the dominant view of Black students that exists within the schooling context and the broader Canadian context.

The work of Sellers and colleagues (Sellers et al., 1997) helps to explain this shift in the salience of identities. They examined the significance of race in the overall self-concept and defined **racial salience** as the extent to which one's ethnicity is relevant in self-concept in a particular situation. In other words, the significance of one's ethnicity varies across individuals and across situations. For example, being the only Black person in a class may make race salient for one person but not have an impact on another Black student in the same situation because of that student's own attitudes and beliefs about their ethnic identity.

What groups do you identify with the most? Which group identity is most salient for you? Why? Does the salience of your identities ever change? If so, how? Why?

racial salience The extent to which one's ethnicity is relevant in self-concept in a particular situation.

Summary

The study of identity development is one of the most popular studies in the field of cross-cultural psychology. Psychologists have proposed two models of self-concepts: independent and interdependent self. These views of self capture variations of self-concepts across cultures. Additionally, cross-cultural psychologists have examined the five-factor model of personality across cultures and have found that these factors explain variability in individual differences cross-culturally. Psychologists attempt to understand how personal, social, political, and cultural factors interact to shape individuals' identities. These models began with ethnic groups. Cultural minorities face unique identity challenges because of the racism, discrimination, and oppression from a society that does not value their differences. We also examined identities of sexual minority groups and multi-ethnic groups. The chapter highlights that many models of cultural identity development exist, reflecting the unique situations of the various groups.

The models share some common characteristics. Most assume that cultural minorities begin in a stage where they devalue their own culture and idealize the dominant culture. However, life experiences challenge that perspective and force them to re-evaluate their beliefs. This moves them into a status where they immerse themselves in their own culture and devalue the dominant culture. Resolution is achieved when individuals have a positive view of their own group but also identify with and incorporate positive aspects of other groups.

All people have multiple identities, such as woman, student, daughter, and member of an ethnic minority group. At times, one of those dimensions becomes more important, and at other times another dimension becomes more important. Sometimes these dimensions can conflict. For example, if you are a woman who is a member of an ethnic minority group and the discussion turns to physical abuse, as a woman you might feel it important to speak out to put an end to the abuse, but as a member of an ethnic minority group, you might feel that your discussion of the topic may unfairly lead others to conclude that all male members of your group engage in abuse. The more secure you are in all your identities, the less these conflicts will interfere with your ability to speak your mind with confidence.

FOOD FOR THOUGHT

The cultural identity development models have made a huge contribution to our understanding of human behaviour and our society as a whole, but perhaps the most important contribution is an increased understanding of ourselves. If you have not explored your own cultural identities, we strongly suggest that you begin such an exploration. Some people tell us, "I'm a Heinz 57—I am a mix of so many different cultures that I don't know what I am other than a Canadian." We tell them to go home and consult with their parents and/or grandparents. They will discover that they do have some identifiable ethnicities that can be a source of interest and understanding. These students soon come back to us and say, "I was wondering where this particular characteristic came from, and then my grandmother told me that when she was growing up, she learned to behave in this manner. I guess I just picked it up from my mother, who had picked it up from my grandmother. I then looked up the country where my grandmother's parents came from, and everything began to make sense." By completing this kind of examination, you might discover how enriching exploring your cultural identity can be.

Critical Thinking Questions

1. How are you like everyone else? How are you like a group of identifiable people?
2. How are you unique?
3. How are you like others in your ethnocultural group? What similarities do you see among people of other ethnocultural groups?
4. When interacting with people of different racial and ethnic groups, have you noticed that some seem to be more connected with their groups than others are?
5. Have you noticed that some seem to reject interactions with you, whereas others seem open to interacting with you?
6. If you are someone with a multi-ethnic background, with what group or groups do you feel most comfortable? What group or groups seem to be most accepting of you? If you know people who are multi-ethnic, with what group or groups do they feel most comfortable?
7. If you are non-heterosexual, how comfortable are you with your sexuality? If you know people who are non-heterosexual, how comfortable are they with their respective sexual orientation?
8. What other identities do you have? Do they ever come into conflict with your ethnic identity? If so, how have you resolved those conflicts?

Note

1. Root (2004) added this fifth resolution, which she called symbolic identity. There is typically a hypodescension of identity wherein individuals identify with the lower-status culture in their country. For example, if someone is an offspring of one Black and one White parent, the person's identity is generally considered Black. In symbolic identity, there is a hyperdescension of identity. In other words, the person identifies as being White and consciously knows that this is a nonstandard identity. Being half-Black is only symbolic to the person; the person knows they are half-Black, but it does not have much relevance in their life. This is akin to the situation of someone with Irish ancestral roots who may become more aware of their Irish heritage on St Patrick's Day but for whom being of Irish descent does not have much bearing on their day-to-day life.

FatCamera/Getty Images

8 Culture and Physical Health

Learning Objectives

Reading this chapter will help you to:

8.1 define *health* and *health disparities*;
8.2 identify components of the common-sense model and the health-belief models;
8.3 recognize the distinction between health inequalities and health inequities and how to create health equity;
8.4 identify characteristics of health disparities at national and global levels;
8.5 understand health characteristics among immigrants and Indigenous Peoples;
8.6 describe the causes of health disparities;
8.7 recognize the link between racism, poverty, and health;
8.8 discuss barriers in accessing the health-care system among Indigenous Peoples and immigrants;
8.9 examine barriers in accessing the health-care system from a global perspective;
8.10 understand different approaches to medical practices;
8.11 identify health disparities amongst LGBTQ2+ populations; and
8.12 explain how to move forward to reduce health disparities.

This chapter examines factors such as ethnicity, poverty, and racism that are associated with health outcomes and the use of health care. Health-care disparities both nationally and globally are discussed. In addition, general health problems that are more common to minority groups than to White Europeans are examined. The chapter aims to help you develop a more elaborate view of health disparities, the definitions involved, possible causes, and their impact on health outcomes.

As you read various discussions in the chapter, keep in mind that the WHO (World Health Organization, 2017) recognizes health as a fundamental human right whereby everyone should have access to affordable health services as needed. Unfortunately, violations of this human right are far too common. According to a joint report from the WHO and World Bank (2017), at least half of the world's population is unable to secure essential health services. The report states that approximately 800 million people spend more than 10 per cent of their household budget on health care. Even more devastating, many households are being pushed into poverty each year due to out-of-pocket health-care expenses. As a result, one billion people live with uncontrolled hypertension, and more than 200 million women do not have adequate coverage for family planning (WHO and World Bank, 2017).

8.1 Health and Health Disparities

The World Health Organization (WHO) defines **health** as "a state of complete physical, mental and social well-being and not merely the absence of disease or infirmity" (1946, p. 1). Therefore, a person is not necessarily healthy just because there is an absence of symptoms. We can argue that different people of colour suffer from illnesses that do not afflict the majority population as much, and the ways in which such illnesses are treated may be defined by looking at people's health behaviours. Those health behaviours are influenced by people's beliefs about their health and its treatment.

health A complete state of physical, mental, and social well-being, not merely the absence of disease or infirmity.

Health is a state of physical and mental well-being.

Thoughts about health and the treatment of health issues influence how people behave or seek treatment to maintain or improve their health. For example, if you feel that your health problems are caused by a chemical imbalance of some sort, you will tend to seek out a healer who will prescribe a medication. However, if you feel that your health problems are caused by a dietary imbalance, you will seek out a healer who will map out a diet program for you. Your thoughts about health may also be influenced by those from whom you seek treatment, such as Indigenous healers, who have markedly different world views about the nature of disorders compared to more Western-oriented healers.

Health behaviours are behaviours undertaken by people to enhance or maintain their health. Health behaviours differ according to demographic factors. Younger, affluent, better-educated people under low levels of stress and with high levels of social support typically practise better health habits than do people under higher levels of stress with fewer resources, such as individuals in lower socio-economic classes (Taylor, 2009). What is considered a healthy lifestyle and suitable health care could be different for people from different cultures. For example, in *The Spirit Catches You and You Fall Down*, Anne Fadiman (2012) tells the story of a Hmong family and their many miscommunications with Western medical providers. Lia, a child, suffered from epilepsy seizures. In a poignant example, Lia's parents discarded the medications she was prescribed and instead used coining, a practice that prompted a call to Child Protective Services. Coining is a technique that has a long history amongst Asians, particularly Chinese and East Asians and is aimed at removing negative energy in the body. This practice is documented in medical literature (Tan & Mallika, 2011) but may not be easily accessible to physicians because the information may not be found in traditional medical books or Western-based journals. It is important to be thoughtful about people's belief systems and the ways in which these beliefs influence their health behaviours.

In examining health behaviours, it is evident that health-care disparities exist around the world and among people of colour and marginalized groups. **Marginalized groups** are people who are disadvantaged because of their ethnicity, socio-economic status, disability, age, gender, sexual orientation, geographic location, special health-care needs, or need for end-of-life care. **Health disparities** are systematic differences in health, such as illness, mortality, disability, and injury, that affect disadvantaged groups (Dehlendorf et al., 2010). **Health-care disparities** are defined as differential access to health care and health insurance, which can be at the institutional level or at the patient–provider level. Institutional-level health-care disparities result from structures within the health-care system, including rules and regulations. Patient–provider-level health-care disparities result from discriminatory behaviours that affect care (Smedley et al., 2003). Although we may not be able to address the specific health and health-care requirements of each group, we will elaborate on health-care needs more broadly so that we begin to explore ways to make improvements in meeting those needs.

Access to health care is not the same for all people. Indeed, in some parts of the world, people still die from preventable diseases. Equally distressing is that even in rich and developed countries, some people do not receive optimal care for illnesses. For example, in Canada, Indigenous Peoples receive suboptimal care. Is this because they do not seek medical attention or "ignore" their illnesses, or do they choose to deal with their illnesses on their own because they have continually received suboptimal care? In examining people's health, questions about health go hand in hand with questions about health care. We cannot discuss health without discussing health care, especially as it relates to health disparities for people of colour. Let's start with psychological models of health.

---

health behaviours Behaviours undertaken by people to enhance or maintain their well-being.

marginalized groups People who are disadvantaged because of their ethnicity, socio-economic status, disability, age, gender, sexual orientation, geographic location, special health-care needs, or need for end-of-life care.

health disparities Systematic differences in illness, mortality, disability, and injury that marginalized groups experience in comparison with their privileged counterparts.

health-care disparities Differential access to health care or treatment by health-care providers at the institutional or patient–provider level.

8.2 Models of Health

Health psychology is devoted to understanding psychological influences on how people stay healthy, why they become ill, and how they respond when they do become ill. For example, a health psychology researcher may be interested in why people continue to smoke even though they know that smoking increases their risk of cancer and heart disease (Taylor, 2009). On the positive side, a health psychology researcher may be interested in the factors behind why some people engage in strict regimens of good diet and exercise.

Two models are often used to predict health outcomes: the common-sense model, which taps into illness perceptions, and the health-belief model. The **common-sense model** was developed specifically for medical illnesses and addresses patients' cognitive and emotional representations of illness. The **health-belief model** was originally developed for preventive medicine and has been deeply studied in communications for its applicability to media and other health interventions.

The common-sense model is linear (Figure 8.1). In this model, perceptions of illness predict coping, and coping predicts the evaluations that patients use to revise their perceptions and coping. The model has been supported by individual and meta-analytic research within the United States, United Kingdom, Australia, and the Netherlands (Dempster et al., 2015). A recent systematic review has also identified studies in Canada, Germany, Italy, Israel, South Korea, China, Sweden, and Oman that support the common-sense model (Breland et al., 2020).

For example, people's perceptions of their illness explain their emergency department visits (i.e., coping) regardless of the symptoms experienced (Ninou et al., 2016). Knowing this can help providers reach out to patients who either underutilize or overutilize emergency rooms. Providers can help patients adjust their coping strategies, thereby reducing health disparities. More recently, the common-sense model has been useful in understanding mental health outcomes for patients with significant health conditions. For example, in a systematic review of 21 studies of coronary heart disease patients (including Canadian patients), illness perceptions predicted quality of life and mood (Foxwell et al., 2013).

The health-belief model includes four main areas of analysis: **susceptibility**, **severity**, **benefits**, and **barriers** (Carpenter, 2010). This model has been updated to specify self-efficacy, motivation, and cues to action, but these areas have little empirical support (Carpenter, 2010; Jones et al., 2015).

In simple terms, the health-belief model explains that when individuals perceive a health outcome to be severe (e.g., cancer), believe that they are susceptible (e.g., because they have a family history of lung cancer), perceive interventions as beneficial (e.g., smoking cessation reduces mortality), and think the barriers to adopting the new behaviour are surmountable (e.g., their home was smoke-free already because their partner is allergic to

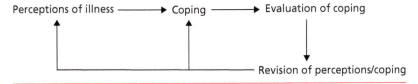

Figure 8.1 The mediational common-sense model.

---

health psychology The study of psychological influences on how people stay healthy, why they become ill, and how they respond when they do get ill.

common-sense model A theoretical framework used to explain how patients perceive an illness, cope with that perception, evaluate their coping, and integrate feedback and experiences into revising their perceptions and their coping.

health-belief model A set of assumptions that suggests that one's health behaviour is affected by one's perception of a personal health threat, as well as by how a particular health practice would be effective in reducing the personal health threat.

susceptibility One of the areas of analysis of the health-belief model that refers to the likelihood of acquiring a disease or being impacted by an illness-producing stimulus.

severity One of the areas of analysis of the health-belief model that refers to intensity of negative outcome.

benefits One of the areas of analysis of the health-belief model that refers to advantages gained from a behaviour.

barriers One of the areas of analysis of the health-belief model that refers to obstacles that reduce the likelihood of engaging in a new behaviour.

smoke), then the positive behaviour is more likely to occur. Researchers have not clearly established what the optimal order of these variables should be (Carpenter, 2010; Jones et al., 2015). However, the health-belief model, like the common-sense model, provides important points of intervention for engaging patients in behavioural change that is likely to improve health.

BOX 8.1 Canadian Contributions to the Health-Belief Model

Canadian researchers Orji and colleagues have proposed an extension to the health-belief model to include concern for appearance, consideration of future consequences, self-identity, and perceived importance (Orji et al., 2012). They examined healthy dietary behaviour to validate the new model since healthy eating is associated with many health benefits (e.g., preventing or delaying the onset of type 2 diabetes, obesity, etc.). They found that perceptions of susceptibility were the best predictors of healthy dietary behaviour in the baseline health-belief model, which was in line with the original model. However, the researchers reported that the variables in their proposed extended model (i.e., concern for appearance, consideration of future consequences, self-identity, and perceived importance) were better predictors of healthy behaviour compared to the previously proposed variables (i.e., susceptibility, severity, benefits, barriers, motivation, and cues to action) with the exception of self-efficacy. Compared to the original health-belief model with just four determinants, Orji and colleagues (2012) reported that their extended model led to a 78 per cent increase in predictive capacity. Although this report suggests the addition of more variables to the health-belief model, further research must be conducted to determine the validity and reliability of such claims.

People's health behaviours depend on their health beliefs.

Cultural beliefs and values are paramount to health beliefs, beliefs about relevant or appropriate coping/intervention strategies, and beliefs about susceptibility and severity. Indeed, medical anthropologists Kleinman, Einsenberg, and Good (1978) documented these relationships decades ago. They recommended five key questions that continue to be used today by culturally competent health providers:

1. What do you think has caused your problem?
2. Why do you think it started when it did?
3. What do you think your sickness does to you? How does it work?
4. How severe is your sickness? Will it have a short or long course?
5. What kind of treatment do you think you should receive?

It is easy to see how the tenets of the health models above map onto these questions.

> Health personnel do not listen to all our problems. My daughter had some problems but a temporarily employed doctor attended to her. He kept insisting that there is no problem and the condition got worse and worse.
> —*Pakistani woman in Oslo, Norway (Gele et al., 2017, p. 492).*

8.3 Health Inequalities and Health Inequities Defined

If a Canadian suffers from a cardiovascular disease and an Ethiopian suffers from the same illness, will they be given equal treatment in their respective countries? If one treatment is superior to the other, then **health inequality** is in place. Health inequalities are defined as "differences in health between groups of people. These differences might be due to non-modifiable factors such as age or sex, or modifiable factors such as socioeconomic status" (WHO, 2010, p. 34). The International Federation of Red Cross and Red Crescent Societies (2011) states that "[health inequities] usually affect particular groups of people, and they occur across the social gradient. The most vulnerable people have the least access, not only to health services, but also to the resources that contribute to good health" (p. 5).

Health inequities are "the subset of social inequalities that are systematic, socially produced (and therefore modifiable) and unfair. They are not distributed randomly, but rather show a consistent pattern across the population, often by socioeconomic status or geographical location" (WHO, 2010, p. 34). Health inequities exist in every part of the world and along a social gradient, meaning that the lower individuals are on the gradient, the more they will be affected by inequity (WHO, 2010). For example, there is a negative correlation between infant mortality rates and household wealth. The poorest have the highest infant mortality rates, and the wealthiest have the lowest rates. Moreover, social factors—including wealth, education, and the discrimination and marginalization of an individual's unmodifiable identity (i.e., sex, ethnicity, sexual orientation)—determine the health inequities that individual is subject to.

To reduce health disparities, WHO's Commission on Social Determinants of Health (CSDH) have outlined three courses of action (WHO, 2013):

1. Improving the quality of life (i.e., where people are born, grow, work, and age)
2. Changing how power, wealth, and resources are distributed at a local, national, and global level
3. Developing an action plan based on research and knowledge to tackle problems, and raising public awareness

health inequality Health differences that are associated with age, gender, and socio-economic status.

health inequity Systematic differences in health inequalities that stem from social and economic inequalities.

Historically, health inequality research has mainly focused on the relationship between economic status and health. However, factors such as education, social class, sex, gender, age, ethnicity, place of residence, and geography may account for health inequalities and therefore should be taken into consideration (WHO, 2013). Although it is not an exhaustive list, the WHO has an acronym, PROGRESS, which summarizes some of the equity stratifiers (WHO, 2013, p. 7):

- (P) Place of residence (rural, urban, etc.)
- (R) Race or ethnicity
- (O) Occupation
- (G) Gender
- (R) Religion
- (E) Education
- (S) Socio-economic status
- (S) Social capital or resources

The characteristics of the population determine which equity stratifiers are most relevant to them. For example, in some cultures, religion may heavily influence health-related behaviours and accessible health-care services, while in other cultures, religion may not play any role.

Before we discuss more specific causes of health disparities, let us consider some of the more common health issues faced by minority groups. Some of these health issues can be seen by comparing the health problems of minority groups with the health problems of the majority population, and others can be seen by comparing the health problems of ethnic minority groups.

8.4 A Look at National and Global Health Disparities

Health Disparities in Canada

Even though it may appear that health inequalities are less of an issue in developed societies today, they are still present and affect people's daily lives. Within Canada, one disparity that affects health care is the level of income inequality within each province. Hajizadeh et al. (2016) point out that inequalities in health care due to education and income are relevant across all Canadian provinces (the Atlantic provinces, Quebec, Ontario, the Prairies, and British Columbia). The researchers report that although health disparities due to income and education stayed the same in the Atlantic provinces, Ontario, and British Columbia, they increased over time in Quebec and the Prairies. Therefore, the socio-economic inequality gap in Canadian health care has not decreased; rather, it has increased in some provinces and stayed the same in others. These results indicate that little has been done to provide easier access to services or create better policies (such as policies in education and public safety) to reduce health inequalities in the provinces.

In addition to socio-economic inequality in health care across the provinces, there is also health-care inequality in terms of ethnicity. For instance, Martin et al. (2018) indicate that recent immigrants in Canada struggle twice as much as Canadian-born people in accessing health care and, in general, utilize fewer health resources. For refugees, these issues are exacerbated, and language barriers are commonly noted as one of the biggest barriers to health care. Similarly, in more rural provinces, such as Nunavut, residents often have to travel long distances to reach hospitals for the treatment of more serious health concerns (Martin et al., 2018). It is estimated that 85 per cent of Nunavut's population is Inuit, creating a large ethnic inequality gap in simply accessing health care in the first place. In addition, many Indigenous Peoples in Canada face wage gaps up to 50 per cent when compared to non-Indigenous Canadians, so the money needed to travel these long distances may not always be available (Martin et al., 2018).

Health Disparities Globally

Health disparities are not only apparent in Canada but also around the world. For instance, researchers (Beckfield et al., 2013) report that although health inequalities are found across societies, the nature and causes of inequalities can vary across countries. Their study used survey results from 48 countries (e.g., Canada, Brazil, Vietnam, Trinidad and Tobago, and Malaysia), which accounted for 74 per cent of the world population. Specifically, they found that within a country, a large income inequality increases the amount of inequality within its health systems. Low income reduces people's access to preventive health strategies. A large income disparity is also associated with greater education-based health inequalities in a country. With more education, people are more aware of positive health behaviours that promote healthiness. Education also gives people more resources to improve their health (e.g., money, power, and social networks).

Furthermore, Razzak et al. (2011) examined health disparities across 190 countries, 48 of which were considered to contain a Muslim majority. They found that in countries where the majority of the population is Muslim (e.g., Pakistan, Morocco, Lebanon, and the United Arab Emirates), funding for health-care systems is one-fifth that of non-Muslim majority countries (e.g., Canada, Kenya, Fiji, Mexico, and New Zealand). The researchers attributed the differences in health between Muslim and non-Muslim majority countries to four main factors:

1. Gross national income
2. Literacy rates (low literacy is associated with poor health)
3. Access to clean water (in terms of spreading communicable diseases)
4. The level of corruption, which is defined as the level of perceived abuse of power in a health-care system for private gain

The researchers (Razzak et al., 2011) argue that while religion is not a direct cause of the health inequalities between countries, religion does affect where someone stands in a society: religion can produce social stratification in terms of what groups or religious sects have more power than others. These results demonstrate that there are several factors that can create disparities in health care, including ethnic, cultural, religious, economic, gender, social, or environmental.

Table 8.1 outlines health disparities around the globe (WHO, 2019b). It shows the many dimensions of health that must be considered when examining health disparities and access to health care.

Overall, it is important to understand that health disparities are multifaceted, ranging from life expectancy and serious diseases to access to health care and maternal care. In the following sections, we examine characteristics of health disparities among immigrants and Indigenous Peoples.

TABLE 8.1 Major Health Disparities around the World

Area of care	Differences across countries
Life expectancy	In low-income countries (e.g., African regions and Southeast Asia), life expectancy is less than that of wealthy countries, with the most at-risk group being children under five years old. Low-income countries expect only 21 per cent of their population to reach 70+ years of age, whereas high-income countries expect 72.5 per cent of their population to reach 70+ years of age.
Maternity and pregnancy	Women in low-income countries have a much higher chance of dying of maternal causes. For instance, the chance in Africa is 1 in 37, whereas women in Europe have a 1 in 3400 chance of dying due to maternal causes. Rates of births attended by a skilled health professional are lowest in the African, Eastern Mediterranean, and Southeast Asian regions. Needs are met for family planning (i.e., access to modern contraceptive methods, high-quality pregnancy, and childbirth care) most often in the Western Pacific region and least often in the African regions.
Obesity in children	The prevalence of obesity in children is the highest in the Americas (i.e., the United States and Canada), where 1 in 14 children are overweight. In low-income countries (i.e., most African and Southeast Asian countries), it is the lowest, where only 1 in 32 children are overweight.
Human immunodeficiency virus (HIV)	The highest rates of HIV infection are in the African regions.
Infectious diseases	Low-income countries (e.g., most African and Southeast Asian countries) have much higher mortality rates from infectious diseases, such as malaria and hepatitis B, than high-income countries (e.g., North American and European countries).
Non-communicable diseases	The highest risk of death from a non-communicable disease (e.g., cancer, diabetes, chronic respiratory disease) is seen in the Southeast Asian regions for men and the African regions for women (i.e., low- to middle-income countries). The lowest risk is seen in the Americas, Western Pacific regions, and Europe.
Suicide	Rates of death from suicide are highest in European regions for men and Southeast Asian regions for women. The lowest rates are seen in the Eastern Mediterranean region for both men and women.
Air pollution mortality	The lowest rates of deaths attributed to air pollution are seen in the Americas, whereas the African regions are the highest, where rates are six times higher than in the Americas.
Number of health-care workers	The African regions have the lowest number of medical doctors and midwifery personnel in relation to their population. The highest density is seen in the European regions.

Note: These data were obtained from the WHO (2019b).

8.5 Health Outcomes across Ethnic Groups

Immigrants' Health

immigrant health paradox The paradox where immigrants tend to have better health than the native-born despite the fact that they have a lower socio-economic status compared to non-immigrants. (See also *healthy immigrant effect*.)

It has been found that first-generation immigrants (i.e., those who were born outside their country of residence) tend to have better health than a native-born population, despite their lower socio-economic status compared to non-immigrants. This phenomenon is referred to as the **immigrant health paradox** (Abraído-Lanza et al., 2005; Beiser, 2005).

In Canada, immigrants are less likely than their Canadian-born counterparts to be at risk of obesity, cardiovascular diseases, and mental health disorders (De Maio, 2010). There are several explanations for this paradox in this context. For example, immigrants go through extensive health and medical screening as part of their immigration selection process prior to entry to their destination country (Islam, 2013; Kobayashi & Prus, 2012). It has also been suggested that destination countries such as Canada are more likely to accept younger and highly educated immigrants, and this demographic is likely to be healthier than older and less educated Canadian-born individuals (Islam, 2013). The paradox has also been found with respect to the mortality rates of new immigrants. Wallace and Kulu (2014) examined the differences in the mortality rates of new immigrants to England and Wales from various countries, including Ireland, Pakistan, Bangladesh, the Caribbean, and China. Immigrants' mortality rates were then compared to the mortality rates of those native to England and Wales. Overall, most immigrants, with the exception of Irish and Scottish immigrants, had lower mortality rates than those of native individuals from England and Wales, further reinforcing the existence of the immigrant health paradox around the world (Wallace & Kulu, 2014).

The health paradox has also been seen in the psychological health of immigrants. A study conducted on Muslim immigrant children in the Netherlands found that although the children were of lower socio-economic status, they reported a decreased amount of behavioural and psychological problems (e.g., depression and anxiety), as well as increased self-esteem compared to their non-immigrant counterparts (Van Geel & Vedder, 2010). Despite this, evidence suggests that immigrants' advantage of better health does diminish over time (De Maio, 2010). The longer immigrants remain in their new country, the more they adopt the host country's lifestyle and culture, which influences their health behaviour. For example, in a study, Black immigrants were asked how their lifestyles had changed when they came to Canada, and how this impacted their diet and health. Angela, a Ugandan immigrant woman, stated the following:

> When I came here, I liked eating out, that was my favourite thing to do, which I did not do back home. . . . I went to Harvey's [a Canadian burger chain], mostly the cheap places. . . . Those fast foods, they don't exist at home. So here, it is even better, you feel like you elevated yourself. (Blanchet et al., 2018, para. 24)

The different lifestyle and fast-food culture in Canada mean a change in behaviour for many immigrants and a driving factor for their eventual decline in dietary health (Blanchet et al., 2018). In a longitudinal study, Kim and colleagues (2013) examined the health of immigrants to Canada over the four years after they had immigrated. They found differences in the progressive health of immigrants depending on their length of stay, culture, and country of origin (Kim et al., 2013). Over the four years, every immigrant group showed signs of decreased self-reported physical health, but the decreasing rates varied among ethnicities (Kim et al., 2013). On average, upon immigration, immigrants had better health than their native-born counterparts. However, their health diminished the longer they stayed in Canada, as they adapted to the host country's lifestyle (Kim et al., 2013). As well, immigrants from West Asia, South Asia, China, Africa, and Arab countries were more likely than European immigrants to have decreasing self-reported health over time (Kim et al., 2013). This was attributed to the similarity of the European and Canadian cultures, making the adjustment to Canadian culture easier for the European immigrants compared to other immigrants from very different cultural backgrounds (Kim et al., 2013). In particular, those who came from cultures that were very different from that of Canada, such as India or China, would experience more prominent health decreases than Europeans (Kim et al., 2013).

Indigenous Peoples' Health

Indigenous Peoples around the world suffer poorer health than non-Indigenous people. According to a United Nations report, over 50 per cent of Indigenous Peoples who are over 35 years old have type 2 diabetes (UN, 2019). A common history of colonization and marginalization has profoundly affected Indigenous Peoples' health (National Collaborating Centre for Aboriginal Health, 2013). Globally, Indigenous Peoples face comparatively higher rates of lifestyle diseases, malnutrition, infant mortality, infectious disease burdens, disease caused by environmental contamination, and illnesses and deaths linked to the misuse of alcohol and other drugs (NCCAH, 2013). Additionally, poor health is associated with poverty, malnutrition, poor hygiene, overcrowding, environmental contamination, and prevalent infection (Gracey & King, 2009; NCCAH, 2013).

The life expectancy of Indigenous Peoples globally is also lower than that of the general population, with that gap being up to 20 years in some countries (e.g., Australia, Nepal). In Canada, on average, Indigenous Peoples die 17 years younger than non-Indigenous Canadians. For comparison, the life expectancy gap in Guatemala is 12 years; in Panama, 10; in Mexico, 6; and in New Zealand, 11 (UN, 2019). Malnutrition is among the top health issues that affect Indigenous Peoples worldwide and is a result of environmental degradation, contamination, loss of land, and the decline in accessibility of traditional food sources (UN, 2019). Due to the decline in accessibility of traditional food, Indigenous communities are forced to depend on commercial foods. Traditional foods, however, hold many core values for Indigenous Peoples, and it has been shown that the quality of the Indigenous diet is improved when traditional food is included (Chan et al., 2019).

The First Nations Food, Nutrition, and Environment study reported that Canadian First Nations face extremely high rates of food insecurity (48 per cent), which is defined as "the inability to acquire or consume an adequate quality diet or sufficient quantity of food in socially acceptable ways, or the uncertainty that one will be able to do so" (Government of Canada, 2020). Such food insecurity is therefore a contributing factor to the malnutrition that many Indigenous communities face.

Although malnourishment is a pressing issue, lifestyle diseases, such as type 2 diabetes, obesity, hypertension, and cardiovascular diseases are quickly emerging, especially in the Americas and Australia, where Indigenous communities are highly influenced by urbanization (Gracey & King, 2009; Phipps et al., 2015). According to a UN report, over 50 per cent of Indigenous Peoples who are over 35 years of age suffer from type 2 diabetes (UN, 2019). Indeed, diabetic rates have reached epidemic proportions in some Indigenous communities, and diabetic rates in Indigenous communities in Canada are three to five times higher than rates among non-Indigenous populations (Harris et al., 2011). Studies have revealed that the prevalence of diabetes among First Nations children and youth in Canada is rapidly increasing (Halseth, 2019).

In addition, Indigenous Peoples are disproportionately affected by diseases that are caused by poverty, including tuberculosis, malnutrition, and malaria (UN, 2019). Many Indigenous communities live on unproductive land, surrounded by environmental health hazards (Gracey & King, 2009; Knibbs & Sly, 2014). These communities also face overcrowding and inadequate housing and often live in homes with mould, bug infestations, and insufficient heating. Exposure to infection is increased by poor housing, lack of proper hygiene, and overcrowding (Sawchuk, 2018). These poor living conditions mixed with inadequate nutrition and high rates of infection are significantly burdensome to Indigenous children. Furthermore, the rates of Indigenous infant deaths are comparatively much higher than those of the general population, with mortality rates approximately 1.5 times higher than the national Canadian average. In Nunavut, the rates are triple the national rate (Sawchuk, 2018).

Additionally, many Indigenous communities face water contamination. In fact, a 2015 CBC report revealed that, between 2004 and 2015, two-thirds of First Nations communities in Canada lived under a public notice that their water was contaminated (Levasseur & Marcoux,

2015). Lack of access to clean water exposes Indigenous communities to harmful environmental hazards, which in turn increases the rate of infectious disease. Although many diseases are treatable and interventions have been put into place in the general health system, many Indigenous communities do not receive the proper care they need.

Indigenous Peoples face an enormous amount of pressure to assimilate into mainstream society, which encourages them to abandon important concepts of Indigenous culture and traditional healing practices. Traditional healing promotes health and wellness using a holistic model of health, whereby the use of ceremonies; plant, animal, or mineral-based medicines; energetic therapies; and hands-on techniques encourage the balance of the physical, mental, emotional, and spiritual aspects of a being (First Nations Health Authority, 2020).

8.6 Causes of Health Disparities

Before we review some of the causes of health disparities, we should point out that people's perceptions of a health threat cannot completely influence them to change health behaviours in a positive direction. This is because we should also consider whether a person believes that a health measure could reduce a health threat, which involves the individual's perception of the effectiveness of the treatment, the cost of the treatment, and trust in the health care system. For example, an individual must place a large degree of trust in the diagnosing health professional to believe that a health threat exists. The individual must also believe that treatment costs are valid and worthwhile.

A Canadian study conducted by Ahmed et al. (2016) found that multiple ethnic groups valued having a physician that understood their cultural and religious beliefs. For example, it is common among women from South Asia, Eastern Europe, Africa, and Central and South America to be reserved and to dress modestly. Therefore, even when a physical exam is done by a female physician, these women are shy and uncomfortable about exposing their bodies. Asian, South Asian, and Muslim women especially value having a physician of similar background and gender. They believed that it helps the physician to understand their circumstances and be able to relate to them. In the study, the notion of respect was emphasized in senior patients from Asia and the Middle East, particularly immigrants from Vietnam and China. They felt disrespected by medical staff when they were addressed by their first names. All minority groups valued reliable information from the health-care system but were cautious of the form it came in. For example, Iranian immigrants did not trust informational pamphlets or brochures because they are not seen as reliable in their home country (Ahmed et al., 2016).

It may be hard to imagine anyone distrusting a medical professional who is supposedly trained to diagnose correctly and treat effectively, but we must look at the issue of trust from a different point of view. Through the eyes of a minority group member, health professionals may not appear as reliable as they do through the eyes of a majority group member:

> I compare the way [the doctors] treated my granddaughters; the brunette was not treated the same as [those of visible Asian descent]. Even in the way [the doctors] talk to them. I've seen that in the private clinic too. I've seen it happen, and with the same doctor she talked to one of my granddaughters in one way and to the other one in a very different way. I always paid much attention to them and I didn't like this way of treating my granddaughters so I said to myself I will change this doctor.
> —*Woman of Japanese ancestry in Brazil (Chauhan et al., 2020, pp. 445–6).*

In the above story, the grandmother notices the different ways in which the doctor speaks to her granddaughters based on their ethnicity. It illustrates the implicit racism that is still prevalent in public and private health care. Although the doctor's actions are not explicitly discriminatory, such actions create distrust and resentment between the patients and the physician. It is important to look at the differential treatment that ethnocultural minorities receive in the health-care system and how such treatment contributes to health disparities.

Poverty

Although, in general, life expectancy has increased globally, health disparities still exist between groups of different socio-economic status. Socio-economic status is, in fact, a strong indicator of many health outcomes (Commission on Social Determinants of Health, 2008; Wang & Geng, 2019) and can be measured by income, education, or occupational status (Chen & Miller, 2013). An overwhelming amount of research has associated low socio-economic status to poor health outcomes, including diabetes (Suwannaphant et al., 2017), cardiovascular disease (Mestral & Stringhini, 2017), and adverse birth defects (Blumenshine et al., 2010). As well, people of lower socio-economic status suffer from more chronic conditions, have lower life expectancies, and are more likely to report poor health (Arpey et al., 2017).

Several studies in countries including Canada, Belgium, Denmark, Norway, and the United States have indicated that people with lower income or less education are underprivileged in terms of health and life expectancies (Bushnik et al., 2020). In particular, a recent Canadian study reported that people with higher income or with higher levels of education have longer life expectancies and are expected to live in good health for more years compared to those with less income or less education (Bushnik et al., 2020). These findings are in accordance with previous literature that has associated income inequalities with poorer health (Lago et al., 2018).

But why exactly are people of low socio-economic status more likely to suffer poorer health? The reasons are plentiful. For instance, the cost of health care is a major barrier for people of low socio-economic status, especially in countries in which universal health care is not available. The cost limits their access to health care and diminishes the number of diagnostic tests and medications made available to them (Arpey et al., 2017). Researchers have also suggested that physicians' perceptions of patients of low socio-economic status impact their clinical decisions, affecting the quality of care that such individuals receive. For example, a physician may decide to delay diagnostic testing, prescribe more generic medication, or avoid referral to specialists when needed (Arpey et al., 2017). By doing so, patients' options are limited, and their health will be negatively influenced. Overall, the quality of and access to health care is severely impacted for low socio-economic status groups compared to their high socio-economic status counterparts.

One of the authors of this text, Melanie Domenech Rodríguez, had a mammogram in 2017. While she was waiting in line, she was speaking on the phone in Spanish. She overheard the nurse offering a European-American patient a higher quality mammogram. When it was her turn to check in, she was not offered the same test. Melanie asked the nurse about it. The nurse said it would cost extra. Melanie handed the nurse a credit card and asked to obtain the higher quality assessment. The nurse was friendly and probably did not consider that she was perpetuating health disparities, but her likely implicit biases kept her from providing equitable care across patients (e.g., she perceived Melanie as Spanish-speaking and assumed she must be poor). Yet the actions of one nurse do not have the power to predict disparities at the rate at which they are evidenced. Structural racism may be implicated, for example, in the form of little or no training in cultural competence in health care.

Poverty is related to poor health. This rally by health-care providers in Peterborough, Ontario, was in response to provincial health-care cuts.

Racism

It is challenging to achieve an understanding of health disparities when they are so complicated. Structural issues such as poverty play a large role in where people live, what environmental hazards they are exposed to, and what life experiences they are more likely to have. However, individual-level factors also contribute to health disparities, and bias on the part of medical providers features prominently among these factors.

Implicit bias refers to attitudes that are unconscious or involuntary but nonetheless influence how people feel, think, and behave. In contrast to **explicit bias**, which refers to conscious attitudes, implicit biases are hard to measure because people do not know they hold such attitudes. A clever measure for implicit bias is the Implicit Associations Test (IAT) (Greenwald et al., 1998). The IAT measures implicit bias through response times to word–picture pairings. For example, a picture of a Black man could be presented alongside a picture of a White man with the words *good* and *bad* over each picture. Test takers must follow an instruction in which they pair the word *good* with the Black or White man picture. The ability of respondents to follow the cues as they change results in a score that provides an assessment of implicit attitudes.

The IAT developers created Project Implicit, an online platform that allows individuals to take the IAT and learn what their response times suggest about their attitudes across social groups (e.g., ethnicity, gender, sexual orientation), even intersectionally (e.g., gender and ethnicity). Although Project Implicit has been operating since 2005, the first publications about implicit bias in health-care providers did not appear until 2007. Thus, this area of knowledge is relatively new. We also believe it is very exciting.

implicit bias Attitudes that are unconscious or involuntary but nonetheless influence how people feel, think, and behave.

explicit bias Conscious attitudes that are deliberate and that influence how people feel, think, and behave.

In a recent systematic review of implicit bias in health-care providers, Maina and colleagues (2018) synthesized the available knowledge gathered from 37 published reports. Health-care providers included physicians across varied areas of medicine (e.g., pediatrics, trauma surgery, emergency medicine), other providers (e.g., nurses, physician assistants, psychologists), and participants at varied levels of training (professionals, students). Most researchers (31 studies) used the Race IAT and found that health-care providers showed pro-White and anti-Black bias that ranged from slight to strong. In contrast, researchers in studies that used the Race/Quality Care IAT showed that providers had a positive implicit association between superior quality health care in Black patients compared to White patients. While bias was observed against people of colour, the perceptions among providers was that people of colour received better care.

Attitudes can be tricky. Over many years teaching cultural and cross-cultural psychology, we have learned that students respond negatively to feedback that their implicit attitudes may be biased. In our teaching, we often stress that the nature of our automatic assumptions is not necessarily something to be ashamed of but, rather, that there is power in bringing the unknown into known awareness so that we can pay attention to how our unconscious attitudes may shape our behaviours and then take steps to be more intentional about how we interact with others. Implicit attitudes matter not for their existence in someone's head, but for the impact they have on actual outcomes.

In health-care settings, implicit attitudes can result in poorer care. Indeed, in the review of the IAT literature, a striking finding was that researchers in 25 studies examined outcomes. Of the 25 studies, 12 were studies in which providers responded to vignette rather than real-world situations. Most of those 12 studies (8) did not indicate a relationship between implicit attitudes and a medical outcome. Yet of the 11 studies that involved either simulation (2) or real-world patient care (9), all but one documented the significant impact of implicit attitudes on outcomes, especially patient–provider communication. Although most studies have involved adult participants, the few studies with children have demonstrated the same pro-White bias (Johnson et al., 2017; Maina et al., 2018). These are powerful findings because most people do not want to appear racist and will work diligently to project values of equality. However, many of us have been culturally programmed (Domenech Rodríguez, 2018) to hold biased attitudes, and we have been shaped to respond in ways that are biased. These realities are not personally shameful; rather, they are social realities that can be altered (see the vignette below).

What is important is what each of us does after we become aware that we hold biased attitudes and after we become aware of the potential such attitudes hold for shaping our actions. Few interventions to reduce implicit attitudes in medical providers exist, but some studies (Castillo et al., 2007; Chapman et al., 2018) show promise in reducing implicit attitudes.

> Biases and racist attitudes not only have an impact on the quality of health care that one receives; they also influence the health outcome of the individual seeking health care. According to Brondolo, Gallo, and Myers (2009), racism has resulted in inequitable access to social, educational, and material resources, which have both direct effects on health status (i.e., through access to healthy diets and appropriate medical care) and indirect effects on health status (i.e., racism's influence on stress, psychosocial resources, and positive and negative emotions). In their meta-analysis, Lee and Ahn (2011) included 23 studies conducted in a variety of settings in North America and Europe. These studies examined East Asian participants' experiences with racism and discrimination and the impacts of such experiences on their health. Those who experienced racism and discrimination demonstrated higher overall distress and

were more likely to develop anxiety and depression than those who did not experience racism. However, those with stronger individual resources (e.g., better coping mechanisms) and positive personal constructs (e.g., self-confidence and sense of belonging) were found to have fewer negative health outcomes. In particular, such participants reported fewer instances of depression and anxiety.

In a similar meta-analysis, Harris and colleagues (2018) examined the prevalence of racism and its impact on the self-reported health of Maori, Pacific Islander, Asian, and European individuals in New Zealand. The results indicated that Asian immigrants and Maori and Pacific individuals experienced the most self-reported racism compared to Europeans (Harris et al., 2018). Increased experiences of racism in the last 12 months by these demographics were also found to be associated with negative health consequences as determined by health surveys and self-reported health data (Harris et al., 2018).

8.7 The Link between Racism, Poverty, and Health

Strong evidence indicates a relationship between racism and stress associated with low socio-economic status and health disparities. The WHO (2008) suggests that people who experience economic and social disadvantage experience greater stress and have fewer resources to respond to it. For example, in the UK, the 20 to 25 per cent of people who smoke or are obese are concentrated among the 26 per cent of the population that lives in poverty. Consequently, this 26 per cent of the population has the highest rate of anxiety (Friedli, 2009).

Socio-economic status as been found to heavily influence people's stress levels (Burton, 2010; Friedli, 2009). Low income can decrease people's quality of food and shelter, further increasing their levels of anxiety (Burton, 2010). In turn, individuals with increased levels of stress are more likely to engage in negative health-impacting behaviours (Burton, 2010). To cope with stress, people may engage in frequent smoking and drinking, causing more health problems, such as lung cancer and liver disease (Burton, 2010). Stressors can be chronic, and their chronicity leads to more permanent changes, both psychologically (e.g., cognitive appraisals of threats) and physically (e.g., allostatic load).

One source of stress is lack of employment. People with foreign-sounding names are less likely to be called for interviews compared to English-sounding names, which constitutes a threat to newcomers' livelihoods and financial stability. To test this, Philip Oreopoulos (2011) sent out 12,910 mock resumés via email to various job openings in the Greater Toronto Area. The resumés were designed to represent recently arrived immigrants from China, India, Pakistan, and Britain. To form a comparison, Oreopoulos (2011) also sent out mock resumés that represented non-immigrants. There were four different types of resumés that were constructed:

1. English-sounding name, Canadian education, Canadian experience
2. Foreign-sounding name, Canadian experience, Canadian education
3. Foreign-sounding name, foreign education, some foreign experience
4. All foreign experience

One of each type of the resumés was sent in random order to each employer of interest. Resumés from applicants with non-English-sounding names were less likely to get a callback for an interview. Oreopoulos (2011) reported that employers preferred and valued English-sounding names and Canadian experience. Employers seemed to discriminate by name, even when Canadian education and Canadian experience were listed.

However, conditional upon the fact that four to six years of Canadian experience was displayed, there was no significant difference in callback rates on resumés with foreign names when either Canadian education or foreign education was listed. This implies that employers do not seem to care whether a candidate has Canadian or foreign education but, rather, place emphasis on Canadian experience. Overall, the study indicated that resumés with English-sounding names, Canadian education, and Canadian experience received more callbacks for interviews (15.7 per cent) compared to resumés that listed a foreign-sounding name, foreign education, and foreign experience (6 per cent). The tendency for employers to dismiss immigrant applicants therefore reduces the labour market for newcomers and limits their economic growth.

Similarly, Branker (2017) reported discrimination of Caribbean immigrants in the Toronto labour market. Participants reported that they believed that Canadian employers held negative opinions about their skills and work ethic, despite possessing high levels of education and work experience (Branker, 2017). Several participants also felt that Toronto employers were hesitant to hire immigrants, pushing some to hide that they were immigrants to avoid being disregarded too early in the application process. Furthermore, more than half of the participants expressed that Caribbean immigrant women face more severe labour market discrimination compared to immigrant men. Such discrimination not only reveals a barrier to hiring processes but also to promotions and management positions and, therefore, threatens economic opportunities and financial stability. More important, the accumulation of stressors that result from racism and discrimination creates an exponential risk for people who experience them.

8.8 Access to the Health-Care System

Barriers to Health-Care Access among Indigenous Peoples

For a country like Canada, a developed first-world nation with a renowned health-care program, the expectation would be that all Canadians would have readily accessible health care across the nation. Unfortunately, this could not be further from the truth. For decades, Indigenous Peoples in Canada have suffered from exclusion and rejection from the services that most other Canadians enjoy freely—particularly access to health care.

Canada's North falls desperately short in terms of primary health-care accessibility. Although Northern Canada claims some of the highest national health expenditures per capita, it still faces considerably lower health-care quality and health outcomes than anywhere else in Canada (Oosterveer & Young, 2015). There are many examples of shortcomings and barriers to proper health-care access, such as the issue of transportation between communities and hospitals. Due to the number of small remote communities in Northern Canada, moving patients from their communities to nearby hospitals becomes very difficult and most often requires a helicopter or plane escort. It can take up to six days for a plane to be available to pick up a patient depending on the location and the conditions of travel (Oosterveer & Young, 2015). In emergency situations, the speed of a helicopter or plane can mean the difference between living and dying.

The number of health professionals in these remote communities is also incredibly low, and emergencies must often be handled by underqualified personnel (Oosterveer & Young, 2015). The health professionals that do work in these communities are on alternating schedules and do not stay in one community for long. In some areas, there is often only a nurse in the community for two weeks in every six weeks, and a physician arrives for three days every six weeks (Oosterveer & Young, 2015). The turnover rate for health professionals in the North is also very high, leaving its communities more unprepared than ever (Oosterveer & Young, 2015). Furthermore, the health professionals that do work in Indigenous communities are usually non-Indigenous. This presents a lack of cultural sensitivity and a language barrier between the doctor and patient, leading to a lack of trust or understanding that could further decrease the quality of care available (Oosterveer & Young, 2015). Due to both the lack of health professionals and the difficulty of treating those who are sick in these communities, there is very little time to produce and run preventive health measures. The nurses and caretakers are constantly busy with those who are ill, so the larger community has no programs to encourage preventive measures and reduce the number of people who are getting sick (Oosterveer & Young, 2015). This leads to an increased influx of preventable cases into the already rushed schedules of the health-care workers in these areas.

In addition, the current biomedical approach to health care is not appropriate for Indigenous health because traditional healing practices and beliefs are ignored. An Australian study focused on cancer treatment in Indigenous populations noted that better health outcomes were observed when health-care providers were willing to incorporate elements of Indigenous health treatments into the medical plan (Shahid et al., 2010). Therefore, it is important that health-care providers acknowledge and understand the importance of traditional healing practices in order to provide appropriate care. Moreover, studies have shown that Indigenous Peoples are sensitive to power imbalances in health-care interactions, ultimately affecting their communication with health-care professionals. To address such power imbalances, health-care interactions should be focused on building trust, reciprocity, and shared decision-making in order to reduce the gap in health outcomes (Peiris et al., 2008; Walker et al., 2010). Moreover, models of health care must take into account the Indigenous concept of health and consider the cultural importance of traditional healing practices (i.e., smudging, healing circles, ceremonies, traditional diets, herbal medicines, and sweats) (UN, 2019).

Barriers to Health-Care Access among Immigrants

One of the challenges that some immigrants face when accessing the health-care system is language difficulties. It is common that newcomers bring friends or family members to appointments to assist with communication. These **language brokers** have no translation or interpretation training and support communication between two or more people (Kam et al., 2017). It is common for minor children of immigrant parents to serve as language brokers. Some theories predict negative outcomes for children who broker, focusing on the negative effects when children are exposed to inappropriate material (e.g., a physician telling a parent through a child that they have a terminal illness). Other researchers point out that brokering places children in an adult role and can negatively impact family dynamics by shifting power roles between parents and children or giving children developmentally inappropriate responsibilities. Some scholars look at the positive impact of brokering, citing an increased sense of self-efficacy and language mastery for children who broker. Another possible positive impact is that language brokering allows children to make meaningful contributions to their family, supporting interdependence.

Language brokering occurs across ethnic groups, although not much is known about the frequency with which it occurs. Research is limited—meaning that many opportunities to conduct research in this area exist for interested students! Wong (2019) conducted a study in Toronto to examine the effects of language brokering among immigrants aged 17 to 25 from China, Taiwan, and Hong Kong. Findings indicated that the participants felt a range of

language brokers People who support translation or interpretation without formal training for this task.

emotions when language brokering for their families in different situations, such as stores, schools, doctor's offices, and when translating emails, letters, and texts. Participants reported feeling confident, independent, stressed, and frustrated. Overall, Wong (2019) found that there were some benefits to language brokering. In this vein, most of the participants stated that they felt more mature and responsible and able to enhance their bilingualism and biculturalism when being of assistance to their family.

The case of language brokering is an interesting addition to our discussion on health disparities. Children may step in as language brokers to increase access of care for their parents, and this act can have important consequences for their own future health. In fact, Kam and her colleagues studied 120 mother–adolescent pairs with varied Latino heritage and found that both mothers and adolescents experienced benefits to language brokering—specifically, greater perspective taking and empathic concern (Kam et al., 2017). This finding was supported regardless of whether the participants had positive or negative feelings about language brokering, suggesting that the brokering itself had positive effects. Indeed, when children language broker for their parents, they also shape the parent–child relationship. In a study of 4- to 11-year-old children using direct observations of 60 parent–child pairs, Straits (2010) found that language brokering was positively related to the quality of the parent–child relationship. She also examined the impact of brokering on the parent–child power dynamic and found that the two were not significantly related.

Regardless of outcomes, it is important in health settings to have access to trained interpreters. Children have many opportunities to language broker and garner the benefits of this activity in less risky or delicate settings (e.g., working on homework together).

Discriminatory Behaviours in Health-Care Systems

According to Du Mont and Forte (2016), both cultural minority and majority group members within Canada report being discriminated against in the health-care system (i.e., in a hospital, doctor's office, etc.) at one point or another. While the most common form of discrimination is based on the ethnicity of minorities, some majority and minority culture members also experience discrimination based on disability, weight, gender, and/or income. The researchers reported that even the psychological perception of discrimination, and the stress and anxiety that comes along with it, is enough to trigger physical health problems in a person in the future.

Similarly, Pollock et al. (2012) conducted research within four Canadian cities in Southern Ontario: Hamilton, Guelph, Cambridge, and the Kitchener-Waterloo region. The goal was to interview immigrants and refugees (Middle Eastern, African, Latin American, South Asian, Eastern European, and Caribbean) in these regions about their experiences with the health-care system and identify where the issues of discrimination and racism were occurring. The results indicated that although participants' experiences of discrimination were often isolated events, such experiences were usually enough to impact participants' utilization of the health-care system. For example, their use of the health-care system decreased overall, especially in regard to preventive health care, which could affect their general health in the long term. Furthermore, the participants found that the quality of care they received was lower in light of these experiences. They also reported increased stress because they did not know how to respond to the discrimination that they faced in the medical system. Much of this uncertainty stemmed from the ambiguity of the situation: many questioned whether they could even label their experiences as discriminatory, which made their experiences even more vague and unsettling. Pollock et al. (2012) note that reported discrimination does not mean health-care workers were necessarily trying to be discriminatory. Instead, such behaviours are often a product of the health system as a whole because the way it is built creates barriers for certain ethnic groups, often in subtle but significant ways. As such, there needs to be a way to create cultural competency within health-care facilities so better service can be provided to the growing immigrant and refugee population in Canada.

Although some people of colour who have directly reported discrimination and racism continue to utilize medical services, others refuse to entertain the idea of seeking medical help as a result of their discrimination, as the following example illustrates:

> Mary was wearing a head scarf when she presented at the hospital with severe pain following a surgical procedure. "The moment the nurse saw me, listened to my accent, the nurse cursed me and said the F-word . . . she said, 'F— you. I know you guys very well.' In response to the nurse's verbal abuse, Mary started to cry and said, "Please don't be aggressive." The nurse apologized, and when Mary later spoke with hospital management to report the incident, the manager responded, "What do you want more than an apology?" Mary said the incident "left me with a very bitter experience . . . I wouldn't want to go to a hospital . . . still don't feel safe." Since that time, Mary explained that she stopped wearing a head scarf so as not to appear "visibly Muslim" because she felt that "Muslim women who leave home and go into the community become targets."
>
> —"Mary, who described feeling vulnerable and threatened by a nurse's response to her, recounts an example of outright discrimination" in Ontario, Canada (Pollock et al., 2012, p. 68)

In Mary's story, she was a victim of outright discrimination by the nurse merely because of her accent and religious beliefs. The hospital management failed to recognize the severity of the situation and did not properly address the issue. Therefore, such incidences can reoccur, further contributing to minorities not feeling safe in the community, especially in health-care settings. Such negative and unjust experiences can create a barrier for ethnocultural minorities to access health care. This, in turn, can deteriorate their mental and physical well-being.

8.9 Access to Health-Care Systems: A Global Review

Access to health care is a prevalent problem in the global society. Every country has a different health-care system, and each system has its own set of problems. In 2017, the Commonwealth Fund released a set of rankings for the health-care systems of the 11 countries in the Commonwealth, including Canada, the US, Australia, the UK, New Zealand, the Netherlands, Sweden, Switzerland, Norway, France, and Germany, with the UK ranking at the top (Schneider et al., 2017). The countries at the top, such as the UK, Australia, and the Netherlands, have superior health-care systems for several reasons, including the increased affordability of their programs and the efficiency of the care (Schneider et al., 2017). Canada was ranked ninth of the eleven countries, as it has deficiencies that could be improved upon (Schneider et al., 2017). For example, although Canada has a universal health-care system, there are still major disparities between the health care that high-income individuals versus low-income individuals receive. The results revealed that low-income individuals frequently avoid dental or vision care because they are not covered in the Canadian health-care system (Schneider et al., 2017). It was also found that many low-income individuals don't fill prescriptions due to their cost (Schneider et al., 2017). Alternatively, high-ranking countries have programs that provide coverage for every citizen regardless of class or status and do so while keeping the quality of care high (Schneider et al., 2017).

The study by the Commonwealth Fund also found that health-care expenditures did not reflect the access to health-care that existed, especially in low-ranking, high-income countries like the US (Schneider et al., 2017). In the US, health-care expenditures are higher than most other developed countries, yet the number of people who cannot access health-care is also incredibly high (Schneider et al., 2017). The high costs of health care in the US makes it unaffordable for most of the population and, therefore, leaves most low-income individuals without coverage or access (Schneider et al., 2017). Administration efficiency is also a problem, as the US lacks a universal health-care system. As a result, the time spent filing health insurance claims slows the process of receiving the actual care (Schneider et al., 2017). In the study, lower-ranking countries fell short when it came to the organization, implementation, and accessibility of their health-care programs. The results of the study indicate that although health expenditures may be an indicator of a good health-care program, the accessibility of that care and the administration efficiency of the care are also factors to be considered.

More recently, the business-oriented news agency Bloomberg released its "World's Healthiest Country Index" for 2019, which placed Spain in the top spot from a pool of 169 of the world's economies (Miller & Lu, 2019). This decision was made based on factors such as life expectancy, obesity, and drug use rates, as well as the public's access to clean water and other health-care necessities (Miller & Lu, 2019). It is interesting that despite the high ranking on the health index, Spain was among one of the worst-hit countries in the COVID-19 pandemic. This indicates that there are other factors that are crucial during a pandemic, such as population density and close-contact cultural practices.

On the World's Healthiest Country Index, Canada ranked sixteenth, as its almost universal health-care system weighed as a considerable advantage in the overall health of the population (Miller & Lu, 2019). Spain (first) and Japan (in third place) were ranked high due to their high national life expectancies, compounded with the advantages of their cultural diets, which have been shown to allow their populations to have lower cardiovascular disease and obesity rates than other countries (Miller & Lu, 2019). Cuba, ranked thirtieth, was a high-ranking country due its emphasis on preventive measures in its universal health-care system, making it the highest-ranked country that was not considered a high-income country (Miller & Lu, 2019).

Another study published in *The Lancet*, a peer-reviewed journal, ranked 195 countries on their health-care access and quality. The results illustrated that most of the highest-ranking countries, such as Iceland and Sweden, were located in Europe or nearby. Exceptions to this trend included Canada, Australia, Japan, and New Zealand. Canada ranked fourteenth out of the 195 countries (Global Burden of Disease, 2018). The countries with the lowest rankings were usually located in sub-Saharan Africa (Global Burden of Disease, 2018). The highest-ranking countries, such as Iceland and Norway (ranking first and second, in that order), were placed on top due to their low prevalence of diseases, low infant mortality rates, and long life expectancies, all of which could be attributed to the smooth functioning of their health-care systems (Global Burden of Disease, 2018). High-ranking countries had low disease infection rates due to a properly functioning vaccination program and disease prevention system, both of which are components of a good health-care system (Global Burden of Disease, 2018). Lower-ranking countries, such as Somalia and the Central African Republic, were often ranked lower due to the inaccessibility or variance in accessibility of their health-care systems, as well as their lack of investment in disease prevention.

The Commonwealth Fund's international program conducts annual surveys of clinicians and patients in 11 high-income countries (Canada, the US, Australia, France, Germany, the Netherlands, New Zealand, Norway, Sweden, Switzerland, and the UK) to assess various aspects of health care, such as financial barriers to care, satisfaction with care, and management of chronic diseases (Commonwealth Fund, 2020). All 11 countries, with the exception of the United States, possess universal health care. Table 8.2 displays data from the 2016 Commonwealth Fund International Health Policy Survey (Osborn et al., 2016), which compares the percentage of adults that reported problems in cost and access to health care across the 11 countries. The United States ranked highest (33 per cent) in terms of reported cost-related access problems within the past year. Many US residents depend on insurance to cover their medical bills. As a result, the cost of health care is a great concern in countries like the US, in which health care is privatized.

TABLE 8.2 Health Disparities around the Globe: Percentage of Adults in 11 Countries That Reported Problems in Cost and Access to Health Care

	CAN	US	AUS	FR	GER	NET	NZ	NOR	SWE	SWIZ	UK
Had any cost-related access problem to medical care in past year	16	33	14	17	7	8	18	10	8	22	7
Skipped dental care or checkup because of cost in past year	28	32	21	23	14	11	22	22	19	21	11
Did not see a doctor or nurse on same or next day, last time they needed care	53	42	31	44	47	19	22	50	41	43	41
Did not "always" or "often" hear from regular doctor on same day, when contacted doctor with a medical concern	32	27	14	14	13	13	17	22	24	12	21
Said it was "somewhat" or "very" difficult to obtain after-hours care	37	51	44	64	64	25	44	40	64	58	49
Used emergency department in past two years	41	35	22	33	11	20	23	26	37	30	24
Waited two months or longer for specialist appointment	30	6	13	4	3	7	20	28	19	9	19
Reported regular doctor did not "always" or "often" spend enough time with them and explain things in a way they could understand	26	23	11	36	22	9	17	29	34	18	19
Low-income adults who reported cost-related access problems in the past year	30	43	24	30	16	23[a]	28	20	16	31	8[a]
Low-income adults who reported waiting six days or more to see a doctor or nurse, last time they needed care	37	35	11	27	38	5[a]	7	29	32	14	27[a]
Low-income adults who reported regular doctors did not "always" or "often" spend enough time and explain things in a way they could understand	31	28	13	39	34	12[a]	33	29	39	20	19[a]
Low-income adults who reported coordination problems in delivery of health care in past two years	33	36	28	48	24	25[a]	36	39	36	25	37[a]
Low-income adults who reported using emergency department in past two years	44	50	27	46	11	23[a]	31	35	39	35	31[a]

Data collected from Commonwealth Fund International Health Policy Survey, 2016
Countries: Canada, United States, Australia, France, Germany, the Netherlands, New Zealand, Norway, Sweden, Switzerland, United Kingdom
Note: *a* indicates sample size was less than 100 (Commonwealth Fund, 2017; Osborn et al., 2016).

Although Canada spends a significant amount of money on health care, access to primary care is still an important issue that must be addressed. Thirty per cent of Canadian adults reported waiting two months or longer for a specialist appointment, the highest percentage among all 11 countries. Knowing that cost of care is a barrier to access, what do you think this means for low-income adults? Take a look at Table 8.2 and try to identify any possible trends. In what countries are low-income adults heavily impacted? In what countries are low-income adults comparable to moderate-income adults? Do you see a difference in reports from countries with privatized versus universal health care, and if so, why? We see that overall, low-income adults experience greater difficulty in accessing care compared to the rest of the population.

8.10 Diverse Approaches to Medicine

The medical information and practices most commonly seen today are based on scientific evidence but still have roots in traditional Western and North American healing practices. Due to this deep-rooted background in Western tradition, our medical practices vary from those practices in other parts of the world. For example, East Asian medical practices are based mainly in the philosophy that the human body and nature are interconnected, as are the mind, the soul, and the body. The Primordial Qi theory, which sees the entirety of the physical world as a unity of Qi, similar to energy, can be considered as the basis of East Asian sciences (Sun et al., 2013). Qi is regulated by eating and breathing. Therefore, much of the medical diagnoses and emphasis are placed on these two biological functions, as they are predictors of Qi levels (Sun et al., 2013). This holistic way of understanding health integrates the Yin-Yang theory into medical practices, a theory that states that even seemingly opposite parts of the body function together in a balance that is necessary for the whole body (Sun et al., 2013). Illness or disease, therefore, is seen as a disruption of this balance, and the goal is to return the balance to the normal state.

Western medicine, on the other hand, is based mainly on the knowledge of the natural sciences and the studies of cells and the body. The culture of research that has been developed in the West is the division and understanding of each component of an organism (Sun et al., 2013). Beginning with atomic theory, the ideal is that each small component of an organism should be understood. The reductionist way of thinking separates each part of the body with organs and layers and tissues, seeing diseases as microscopic forms that attack specific areas, and those areas specifically will be in need of treatments (Sun et al., 2013).

Apart from these views of medicine, each culture has its own specific belief systems and practices, some that have lasted years. For example, northern Vietnamese medicine is heavily based on Chinese and East Asian medical practices, but the southern folk practices remain that are traditional to the region and have been practised for many generations (Lundberg & Thu, 2011). These are visible in the cultural birth giving and midwifery practices, such as the common practice of sleeping by a fire after giving birth as doing so allows heat to re-enter the body after much of it was lost with the blood loss during childbirth (Lundberg & Thu, 2011). This allows the mother to regain her Yin-Yang balance, called *am* and *duong* in Vietnamese (Lundberg & Thu, 2011). Similarly, in Native American and Canadian Indigenous birthing practices, expecting mothers are encouraged to stand near the drums during ceremonies so that the baby can hear the vibrations and the beating of the drum, replicating the beating of Mother Earth (Best Start Resource Center, 2010).

Some old folk traditions from different cultures have even been rekindled and have made a return to common practice. For example, the use of aromatherapy and herbs as alternative and natural forms of medicine is an old medical practice, prominent in many cultures. North American Indigenous groups often use sage and other herbs for medicinal purposes, such as getting rid of bad energy and easing headaches and pains (Best Start Resource Center, 2010). Chinese medical practices have long used herbal concoctions to cure common ailments by boiling them to make tea or creating salves for topical use (Lilly & Kundu, 2012). Similarly, illnesses and discomforts, such as constipation, were easily treated with flowers, fruits, and seeds in ancient Iranian medical books dating back all the way to the tenth and eleventh centuries (Masoomi et al., 2016). Even the use of sounds for healing purposes has a rich history, especially in Turkish folk medicine, as the sounds of running water were said to ease troubled minds, such as those with anxiety or schizophrenia (Uğurlu, 2011). Today, people use the sounds of rain and running water to help them calm down and fall asleep, reflecting and reviving these ancient practices. An increasing number of the population is turning to alternative forms of medicine, such as herbal medicines, for their natural properties (Lilly & Kundu, 2012).

8.11 Obscure Health Disparities

It is important to note that there is a marginalized group of people for whom little information exists regarding health disparities: LGBTQ2+ populations. There are no adequate measures for assessment of sexual orientation and/or gender identity. Hughes and colleagues (2016) provide a good model, but it's very much just a start. Indeed, students and even professors are often still confused about the difference between sexual orientation and gender identity. Sexual orientation refers to a person's sexual attraction to others, and its labels include lesbian, gay, bisexual, and pansexual. Gender identity refers to a person's sense of self in relation to gender. When people identify with their biological sex, they are considered to be cisgender. When people are born with sex organs different from their internal sense of self, they may use the label *transgender*. For example, a person born with female sex organs who identifies as a man may identify as transgender male. These distinctions are important in health care, where approaches to treatment may be informed by biological sex characteristics and result in the invalidation, marginalization, or shaming of those who do not identify with their biological sex.

Available data paint a bleak picture of disparities for LGBTQ2+ groups. A recent review of health disparities among lesbian, gay, bisexual, and transgender (LGBT) youth revealed that LGBT youths were at higher risk for negative health outcomes, such as substance use, sexually transmitted diseases, cancers, cardiovascular diseases, anxiety, depression, and obesity. These youths were also at higher risk than their non-LGBT counterparts of experiencing bullying, isolation, and rejection (Hafeez et al., 2017). LGBT youths were also at higher risk of suicide (Hafeez et al., 2017), and when LGBT youths have attempted suicide, they have been found to be at dramatically higher risk for a repeated attempt (Mustanski & Liu, 2013).

In their systematic review, Lewis and Wilson (2017) found that in Canada and Europe, HIV and the associated risk factors were more prevalent among ethnic minority men (Latino, Black, and Asian men) who had sex with men than among ethnic majority men. This may be because when minority men migrate within or between countries (something majority culture men usually experience less of), there is an increased prevalence of high-risk sexual activity occurring. This is likely because it is a way to release stress and it helps create social connections in an unfamiliar place. As such, post-migration is an especially vulnerable time for men to contract HIV because of risk factors such as isolation, depression, and increased substance abuse that could lead to unsafe sexual activity.

Additionally, Gunaratnam et al. (2019) conducted a study in Australia on HIV prevalence for men who have sex with other men and for men engaging in sex with women. They found that HIV rates in Australian men who have had sex with men decreased between 2006 and 2015. However, HIV rates were significantly higher for men who were born in Southeast Asia,

Northeast Asia, or the Americas and engaged in male-to-male sex compared to heterosexual men born in Southeast Asia, Southern and Central Asia, and sub-Saharan Africa. Additionally, their HIV rates were also higher than rates of women born in Southeast Asia and sub-Saharan Africa. As a result, the authors concluded there was a disproportionate risk of contracting HIV for men in Asia and the Americas who have sex with other men. Overall, these results indicate an elevated and unequal health risk for ethnic minority men within the LGBTQ2+ community.

8.12 How to Bring About Change

If you receive relatively good health care or if you have reasonably good access to the health-care system, you might be tempted to ask, "Why should I care about other people not receiving adequate health care?" First, because you are reading this book on cross-cultural psychology, you probably already care somewhat about this issue. Second, on a broad level, persistent disparities in health care are inconsistent with human values. As noted earlier, the WHO (2017) describes health as a human rights issue. Labelling health as a human right ensures that everyone has equal access to health care, that health justice (i.e., health care that is timely, acceptable, and affordable) applies to all, and that the obligation to provide health care is on states. If there are systematic disparities in health care that are caused by correctable factors, we should be motivated to address those problems.

On a more pragmatic level, continued health disparities will ultimately strain our health-care system. To the extent that such persistent disparities will ultimately cause a rise in the cost of health care in our society, we will all pay for such disparities. For that reason, we must address these problems before they strain our economy beyond our capacity to pay for them.

An example of why devoting resources to health care is so important has been demonstrated by the novel COVID-19 outbreak, which began in late 2019. As one media article by Travers (2020) discussed, some countries have done a better job than others in dealing with the COVID-19 pandemic. Public opinion polls show that people from Vietnam, Canada, and New Zealand, to name a few, are the most supportive of their government's pandemic approaches. These places also have relatively low mortality rates compared to those ranking near the bottom, which includes the United States, Spain, and Japan. In particular, over half of Americans believe their government has been too slow in handling the pandemic. Although there could be many reasons for certain countries having experienced less public satisfaction with their emergency measures, a lack of universal health care in the United States is an important factor in higher fatality rates and questionable preparedness. To support this argument, countries that have been supporting people with paid sick leave, wage support, income support, and free health care, such as Canada, Singapore, and New Zealand, have seen better outcomes with COVID-19 than those without such supports (International Trade Union Confederation, 2020).

With everything being said, there are some health-care challenges people will be faced with in the coming decade. An article from the WHO (Ghebreyesus, 2020) discusses how public health ultimately needs to be at the forefront of social and political agendas. This means providing better services to more vulnerable regions of the world, fixing the gaps in the system, and investing time and money into protecting people's future health. More specifically, the WHO (2019c) released a list of threats that face the world today and in the foreseeable future. The list includes air pollution and climate change, non-communicable diseases (e.g., diabetes), pandemics and high-threat pathogens, antimicrobial resistance, weak primary health care, vaccine hesitancy, and HIV, to name a few. These are all issues that people need to allocate resources and attention to as soon as possible. Overall, the general theme is that there needs to be greater response to these issues from sectors other than health care; the efforts also need to include government and policy-level changes, as well as changes in individuals and communities.

It appears that global health matters have become more prominent on political agendas over the years, as people have begun to recognize how health issues can impact security, economics, and social justice (Kickbusch, 2013). In terms of security, it is now understood how a virus can impact the world, spreading to countries in a matter of hours and causing damaging outcomes for people in all areas of life. Additionally, there is a vital global market in relation to health, as something like a pandemic could have long-term impacts on the world's economy. More and more people are also recognizing that health care is not a privilege; it is a human right. However, because it has become clearer that health is an issue of inequality, countries must work together to address such a complex problem. Of course, this is easier said than done. But if resources are better allocated and funds are distributed appropriately into fixing health-care systems, people around the world will benefit. Ultimately, health needs must be considered less as a national affair and more as an international and global issue.

Focusing more on the health system is not only beneficial for reducing disparities for minority groups, but it is crucial for the entire global population. For instance, preventing a pandemic may not have seemed to be a priority at one time, but we now know the devastating impacts that result when countries are not prepared. As such, changes need to be made to mitigate potential global health issues, including making preparedness plans publicly available, doing regular virus testing in population samples, developing a resiliency plan for low-income countries, and ensuring medical facilities and hospitals have all the necessary equipment to handle the worst possible scenarios (WHO, 2019d).

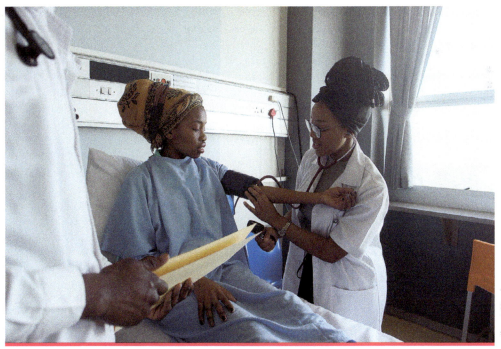

Increasing the number of people of colour in the health-care profession can help to overcome the distrust of the system that many people of colour have.

How would we like to see things change? What goals should we set to improve global health? Are there easy answers? It seems that institutionalized racism is the underlying theme in health and health-care disparities and that much work must be done to reduce such disparities. The time to act is now.

Summary

Health disparities exist among people of colour, between groups, and between minority group members and European Americans. A look at ethnic minority groups as a whole, however, makes it easier to pay close attention to what might be involved in eliminating disparities in health and health care.

Health beliefs involve individuals' perceptions of their illnesses, how susceptible they are to both illness and discrimination based on their trust in the health professional who makes the diagnosis, and the cost of treatment. Health beliefs dictate the ways that minority groups maintain their health. Because health behaviours contribute to the continuation of healthy or unhealthy lifestyles, people of colour who typically seek care less often and receive suboptimal care compared with European Americans have a lower quality of life.

The health of minority group members depends on their ability to access care. Accessing health care in Canadian society has proven to be more difficult for people of colour than for European Canadians. Gaining entry into the health-care system, structural barriers (such as transportation and obtaining appointments with doctors), patients' perceptions of the care they may receive or have received, and utilization of care are all categories of difficulties to consider in accessing health care. These difficulties ultimately determine the quality of care that people of colour will receive and occur within the context of mistrust of the health-care system given the racism that people have experienced in this domain.

Because access to care and quality of care seem to go hand in hand, and may also be independent of each other, a common theme in both is institutional racism. Institutional racism in the health-care field occurs when health professionals remain incompetent in cultural issues (e.g., communicating with patients, understanding cultural norms when it comes to treatment, providing appropriate information and diagnoses). Racist beliefs on the part of health professionals also disempower people of colour because they are reliant on health professionals' decisions about their treatment.

Changes in laws and policies that govern health and health-care agencies have led to some improvements in health disparities, but disparities are still evident. Continued monitoring and improved research and practice are needed. At a broad social level, people of colour are at higher risk for encountering stressors in social determinants that are tied to health outcomes. They are less likely to be insured and more likely to experience negative outcomes in access to and quality of care. When the health-care workforce is socio-demographically different from the population of patients, opportunities for cultural misunderstandings abound. And while some strides have been taken in advancing cultural competence, there is room for much more.

FOOD FOR THOUGHT

Our goal is to undo discriminatory practices within the health-care system. Because we know that such a goal is vague and idealistic, at this time we think it best to target incremental policy changes. These changes involve additional research and more training for both health professionals and people of colour in order to increase awareness of cultural issues, improve communication surrounding the treatment of illnesses, create a system to ensure that such changes are made, and enlist more minority group members and leaders in the effort to bring about change. The apparent limitations are that to begin change, we need policy changes, which would involve getting our political leaders to take a closer look at current policies and to vote for better health care for the entire society. Are you ready to work for those changes?

Critical Thinking Questions

1. What kinds of healthy behaviours happen around you (e.g., jogging, going to the gym)? What kinds of unhealthy behaviours happen around you (e.g., smoking, drinking alcohol)? Do friends with different ethnicities have different kinds of health behaviours around them?
2. Do you have a family doctor? How easy is it for you to see your family doctor? How easy is it for you to get to a local hospital? Does your family speak the same language as your doctor, or do you need an interpreter?
3. How much do you trust your family doctor? How much do you trust other elements of the health-care system?

Monkey Business Images/Shutterstock

9 Culture and Mental Health: Disorders and Treatments

Learning Objectives

Reading this chapter will help you to:

9.1 recognize different diagnostic classification of mental disorders, including the *International Classification of Diseases and Related Health Problems* (*ICD*), the *Diagnostic and Statistical Manual of Mental Disorders* (*DSM*), and region-specific manuals;
9.2 identify diverse cultural expressions of symptoms of mental-health issues;
9.3 understand the impact of culture on the rates of mental disorders;
9.4 explain the pattern of mental-health service use among minorities and immigrants in Canada;
9.5 identify barriers to the utilization of mental-illness treatment;
9.6 understand characteristics of multicultural counselling;
9.7 understand gender differences in mental disorders;
9.8 recognize mental disorders specific to different cultures; and
9.9 understand the impact of COVID-19 on mental health.

A study in the United Kingdom investigated barriers to mental-health services experienced by Black and minority ethnic communities in Southeast England (Memon et al., 2016). A major barrier to seeking help due to cultural stigma was the inability to recognize and accept symptoms as mental illness. The study found that individuals who had spent less time in the UK were less likely to identify mental-illness symptoms and seek help (Memon et al., 2016). One participant reported, "Our people cannot go to mental health services because . . . [they] think it is only crazy people going there" (Memon et al., 2016, p. 4). Another participant explained how a diagnosis could stigmatize the entire family: "In our country, if you hear about somebody in [a] family [being] sick, is mental, you lose trust in this person and [the] whole family, maybe [their] relative[s], as well. And . . . they whisper about the whole family and maybe talk about [their] grandmother, grandfather, and they lose respect" (Memon et al., 2016, p. 4). The study also revealed that Black and minority ethnic communities struggled to find health-care professionals who could understand the realities they experience as ethnic minorities: "They do not want to be aware of what we are trying to say. So, they just put us in a category. [It's] just [the] White British way" (Memon et al., 2016, p. 6).

The study by Memon and colleagues (2016) illustrates the impact of culture on perceptions of mental health. A major premise of cultural psychology is that all behaviour occurs in and is shaped by only a cultural context. Therefore, mental health is influenced by culture. We can see the effect of culture on mental health in many ways, including the types of symptoms experienced, the manner in which those symptoms are expressed, and the meaning those symptoms have for the individual, their family, and their community. Culture influences how clients cope with their troubles, whether they seek help, and from whom. Culture also plays a role in the causation of mental disorders, their **prevalence**, and their treatment.

In addition, culture influences counsellors and therapists and the institutions that provide mental-health treatment. Mental-health professionals bring their own culture, including their attitudes and beliefs, to the setting, which can influence their diagnosis and what strategies are used to help the client (US Department of Health and Human Services, 2001). There is growing evidence that cultural competence is an effective approach in improving health-care experiences and compliance with therapy (Kolapo, 2017). In a multicultural nation, such as Canada, it is crucial that mental-health-care providers recognize the importance of cultural perceptions to adjust their care to fulfill the needs of their patients. Cultural naïveté and insensitivity from health-care professionals may limit the effectiveness of mental-health interventions. In this chapter, we discuss these and many other aspects of culture's impact on mental health and the diagnosis and treatment of mental-health problems.

prevalence The rate of a particular disorder at a given point in time.

9.1 Culture and Diagnostic Manuals

We cannot discuss culture and the diagnosis of mental disorders without talking about the *International Statistical Classification of Diseases and Related Health Problems*, currently in its eleventh version (*ICD-11*) and the *Diagnostic and Statistical Manual of Mental Disorders* (*DSM*). The *ICD-11* is an international classification system for all diseases and health problems, not just mental disorders. The *DSM* is the primary manual used by health and mental-health professionals in Canada. It has gone through several revisions; the most current version is the *DSM-5*, the fifth edition (American Psychiatric Association, 2013). The developers of the *ICD-11* and the *DSM-5* worked closely together to make the two manuals compatible.

International Classification of Diseases and Related Health Problems

The first version of the *International Classification of Diseases* (*ICD*) was developed in 1853 by William Farr and Marc d'Espine, when they created the *International List of Causes of Death* (Clark et al., 2017). The document was revised every decade in the twentieth century until 1938, when, it was proposed that a more integrated classification system was needed. Thus, in 1944, international representatives from the Canadian and British governments, the American Psychological Association (APA), and the Health Section of the League of Nations (an intergovernmental organization) came together to create the *Statistical Classification of Diseases, Injuries, and Causes of Death*. This was also around the time when the World Health Organization (WHO) was formed, not long after World War II.

From the creation and revision of these three documents, the WHO published the *International Classification of Diseases, Injuries, and Causes of Death* in 1949, which became known as the *ICD-6*. The document combined mortality and morbidity data for the first time in history and also included mental illness classification. Additionally, the *ICD* influenced the creation of the APA's *Diagnostic and Statistical Manual of Mental Disorders* (*DSM*) in 1952, and since then, the histories of the *ICD* and *DSM* overlap considerably.

As we are writing this textbook (in 2021), the *ICD-11* is in use. The goal of the *ICD-11*, especially in terms of mental health, was to modify its classification system for better clinical use that can easily be used by the public and a variety of professionals, including researchers, patients, and governments (Gaebel et al., 2017). The *ICD-11* contains 23 sub-chapters related to mental health, ranging from neurodevelopmental disorders and schizophrenia to bodily distress disorder and mental or behavioural disorders associated with pregnancy, childbirth, and the puerperium (Gaebel et al., 2017). There are many applications for the *ICD-11* (Gaebel et al., 2020). For instance, it was designed to be more globally applicable than the *ICD-10*. That is, there is less need for country-specific versions of the *ICD-11* because it was made with the intent to be used in a wide range of settings (such as research, clinical, and academic settings) around the globe. Thus, a major application of the *ICD-11* is providing more accurate diagnoses, which can lead to better, faster treatment of mental disorders. This is especially helpful in lower- and middle-income countries. Furthermore, the *ICD-11* serves an important purpose within the scientific and research communities.

Diagnostic and Statistical Manual of Mental Disorders: A Classification System

Diagnostic categories in the *DSM* are based on empirical research and focus on behavioural descriptions of symptoms. Specific diagnoses represent clusters of symptoms that typically are seen together and that have some defining feature. A diagnosis is made on the basis of a set of behavioural criteria. If the person exhibits a minimum number of symptoms in the list, then a specific diagnosis is made.

The *DSM-IV* (American Psychiatric Association, 1994) was the first version of the *DSM* to systematically include cultural issues. Now, a section on cultural issues is included with each of the diagnostic categories. In addition, there is an "Outline for Cultural Formulation," which is a guide that helps mental-health professionals systematically review the client's cultural background, the role of culture in the expression of the client's symptoms, and the role that cultural differences may play in the relationship between the client and the therapist.

The *DSM-5* identifies three types of cultural concepts. **Cultural syndromes** are clusters of symptoms that tend to occur only in specific cultural groups. These used to be referred to as culture-bound syndromes. Second, **cultural idioms of distress** are specific ways of expressing troubling thoughts, behaviours, and emotions. Finally, **cultural explanations or perceived causes** refer to when certain cultural groups attach unique meanings to symptoms or have particular explanations for the etiology of illness or distress. *DSM-5* also includes a glossary of cultural concepts of distress. We will give some examples later in the chapter (see section 9.8).

Although the *DSM* strives to be an objective diagnostic tool, research studies repeatedly demonstrate clinician bias in applying diagnostic criteria. That is, clients reporting the same symptoms are given different diagnoses. Many studies have confirmed clinician bias in applying diagnostic criteria. For example, Jarvis and colleagues (2011) conducted a study that included psychiatric inpatients from hospitals in Montreal, Canada, and Padua, Italy, determining the likelihood of patients with different ethnicities receiving a diagnosis of psychosis. The study found that most Black patients, independent of any other factors, were more likely to receive a diagnosis of psychosis than any other ethnicity (Jarvis et al., 2011). Specifically, about three-quarters of Black patients were diagnosed with psychosis compared to only half of White patients (Jarvis et al., 2011). Similar results were found in a study by Tortelli and colleagues (2014), who measured the differences in psychosis diagnoses between ethnicities of individuals in Paris, France. The results from this study showed that the number of migrants, specifically those from sub-Saharan Africa, being admitted for psychosis was considerably higher than for any other ethnicity (Tortelli et al., 2014).

In their study of Chinese and South Asian Canadians in relation to the general Ontario population, Chiu et al. (2016) found that mental illness severity was the greatest among those of Chinese background. Notably, Chinese patients were more likely to undergo involuntary hospitalization, present more positive symptoms, and exhibit aggressive behaviours than South Asians and the general Ontario reference group. More specifically, there was an excess of schizophrenia diagnoses among Asians in their sample. The researchers suggested that these high rates of illness severity seen in the Asian-Canadian population are likely a consequence of barriers to health-care access and the underutilization of health services. Thus, Asian Canadians may not necessarily experience more mental-illness symptoms than the average Canadian, but their delay in seeking and accessing help may progress the symptoms further into a full diagnosis (which may explain the excess of mental illness diagnoses in this population).

Manuals of Mental Disorders: Examples from China, North Africa, and Latin America

Individual countries also have their own diagnostic manuals. For example, in China they use the *Chinese Classification of Mental Disorders*, third edition. This manual is also written to correspond with both the *DSM* and the *ICD*. However, it includes some cultural variations on the main diagnoses and approximately 40 culture-specific diagnoses. It is published in both Chinese and English (Lee, 2001; Surhone et al., 2010).

Another example of an alternative diagnostic manual is the *Manual for North African Practitioners*, a psychiatric diagnostic manual used in countries like Algeria (Scull, 2013). This manual is based on both traditional North African psychiatric practices and illnesses as well as the French psychiatric classification system because Algeria is a former colony of France and French medical practices still have an influence on Algerian medicine (Scull, 2013). This manual serves as a more culturally appropriate classification system for individuals in the region (Scull, 2013). The *DSM-5*, on the other hand, is based on Anglo-Western diagnostic

---

cultural syndromes Clusters of symptoms that tend to occur only in specific cultural groups.

cultural idioms of distress Specific ways of expressing troubling thoughts, behaviours, and emotions.

cultural explanations or perceived causes When certain cultural groups attach unique meanings to symptoms or have particular explanations for the etiology of illness or distress.

criteria and does not contain certain diagnoses that are specific to other cultures (Scull, 2013). For example, the *Manual for North African Practitioners* includes disorders such as *bouffés délirantes*, also known as short-lived psychosis, where an individual experiences hallucinations, delusions, and mood changes (Scull, 2013). This disorder is one that has been seen in North Africa but is not outlined in the *DSM-5*. Psychosis is a common area in which Western and Arab/North African individuals differ in the way the illness manifests (Dwairy, 2006). In the *Manual for North African Practitioners*, for example, the symptoms of schizophrenia and other psychotic diseases include fewer malevolent manifestations and decreased likelihood of becoming withdrawn in comparison to the *DSM-5*'s description of symptoms (Dwairy, 2006). One psychotic illness specific to Arab culture that is mentioned in the North African manual but not in the *DSM-5* is erotomania (Dwairy, 2006). This illness is filed under "psychosis of passion" and is an illness in which individuals believe they are deeply loved by someone else (Dwairy, 2006). These examples of culturally specific illnesses and diagnoses emphasize the necessity of culturally specific diagnostic manuals (Scull, 2013).

Similarly, in Latin America, the concept of person-centred medicine (PCM) is well known and well-practised (Mezzich et al., 2016). This approach to medicine requires the medical professional to take a whole-body approach when treating an illness (Mezzich et al., 2016). This means illnesses are not singular beings, and the body cannot be reduced to certain organs or systems (Mezzich et al., 2016). Instead, the care and attention are placed on the person as a whole, rather than reducing them to certain parts (Mezzich et al., 2016). PCM is at the core of the diagnostic manual commonly used in Latin America, the *Latin American Guide for Psychiatric Diagnosis* (*GLADP*) (Mezzich et al., 2016). Although this manual is based upon the *ICD-11*, it incorporates the local cultural understanding of PCM to create a diagnostic manual better suited for the regions of Latin America (Mezzich et al., 2016). As opposed to the *DSM* or the *ICD*, the *GLADP* also adds a cultural and environmental basis for the illnesses it describes (Hofmann, 2018). Overall, as you see, illnesses can be diagnosed differently around the world due to a difference in the understanding of those illnesses (Mezzich et al., 2016).

The World Psychiatric Association and the World Health Organization conducted a survey of almost 5000 psychiatrists across 44 countries regarding the cross-cultural utility of diagnostic classification systems like the *DSM* and *ICD* (Reed et al., 2011). Most of the participating psychiatrists (70.1 per cent) reported using the *ICD-10*, and most of the remainder (23.0 per cent) used the *DSM-IV* (the study was conducted before the publication of *DSM-5*). A small percentage (5.6 per cent) reported using another system (e.g., the *Chinese Classification of Mental Disorders*). The survey also included the statement, "The diagnostic system I use is difficult to apply across cultures, or when the patient/service user is of a different cultural or ethnic background from my own." Overall, about 75 per cent of the worldwide participants somewhat, mostly, or completely agreed with this statement. However, when the responses were divided by region, some differences appeared. Nearly 30 per cent of the participants in Latin America, East Asia, and Southeast Asia mostly or completely agreed with this statement, whereas only 10 per cent of participants from the United States mostly agreed (Canada was not included in the study). For European respondents (comprising 21 different European countries, including the UK, Germany, and Romania), just over 25 per cent of psychiatrists mostly or completely agreed with the statement. Many psychiatrists from countries such as Cuba, Russia, China, India, Japan, and France also felt there was a need for classification systems specific to their nations. In other words, a significant number of psychiatrists around the world questioned the applicability of global diagnostic systems like the *DSM* to the patients they serve.

9.2 Culture and the Expression of Symptoms

An accurate diagnosis depends on both the client's ability to describe their symptoms and the clinician's ability to observe and accurately interpret those symptoms. Culture influences the way that individuals express the symptoms of various disorders. People from different cultures may have the same disorder but may experience and describe their symptoms in very different ways. The manifestation of these symptoms can vary with age, gender, race, ethnicity, and culture.

Let us again use the example of depression. Certain cultures might experience and express more physical symptoms of depression than mood symptoms. This is known as somatization, or the expression of psychological symptoms through physical disorders. For example, individuals from Latino and Mediterranean cultures may complain of nerves or headaches, those from Middle Eastern cultures may complain of problems of the heart, and Asians may talk about weakness, tiredness, or imbalance. It is important for clinicians to be aware of such cultural differences in expression to avoid misdiagnosis. For example, some individuals may express a fear of being hexed or bewitched or may report vivid feelings of being visited by someone who has died. These may be acceptable and understood experiences in some cultures but could be mistaken by a traditional Western therapist for symptoms of psychosis.

In addition, the expression of depressive symptoms can change with age. The symptoms listed in *DSM-5* criteria typically describe how depression is experienced by adolescents and adults. Children may have somatic complaints as well as irritability and social withdrawal, and their depression often coexists with other behavioural problems, such as disruptive behaviour, hyperactivity, and inattention. In contrast, depressive symptoms in the elderly may include disorientation, memory loss, and distractibility.

9.3 Cultural Differences in Rates of Mental Disorders

In the field of public health, *prevalence* is defined as the rate of existing cases of a disorder at a given point in time. An example would be the number of people currently diagnosed with schizophrenia. Another term used when reporting rates of various disorders is **incidence**, which refers to the number of new cases of a disorder that occur during a given period of time, such as the number of people who are diagnosed with schizophrenia this year. *Lifetime incidence* refers to the number of cases of a disorder that occur during one's lifetime. Therefore, if an individual was diagnosed with schizophrenia two years ago and continues to suffer from this disorder, that person would be included in the prevalence rate, would not be included in the incidence rate in the past year, but would be included in the lifetime incidence rate.

A report from the World Health Organization (2017) stated that globally the number of people diagnosed with common mental disorders (e.g., depressive and anxiety disorders) is increasing. More specifically, their statistics (gathered in 2015) indicated that an estimated 4.4 per cent of the world population has depression, which translates to approximately 322 million people. The rate of people living with depression increased by 18.4 per cent between 2005 and 2015. According to the results, the highest number of cases is seen in the Southeast Asia region and the Western Pacific region. These regions include both India and China. On the other hand, the smallest number of cases of depression is seen in the African region. Furthermore, the World Health Organization (2017) article reported that an estimated 3.6 per cent of the global population, or 246 million people, are living

> **incidence** The number of new cases of a disorder that occur during a given period of time.

with anxiety disorders. This represents a 14.9 per cent increase in diagnosed anxiety from 2005 to 2015. The report identifies the Americas (North and South America) as having the most cases of anxiety. Africa and the Eastern Mediterranean (including countries such as Kenya and Pakistan, respectively) were identified as regions with the fewest cases of anxiety. A study from the Global Burden of Disease (2018) reported that mental disorders have greater than 10 per cent prevalence rates in the majority of countries. As such, there is an increasing need for mental-health services globally. Unfortunately, the prevalence of depression and anxiety increased even more during the global pandemic. Based on data that was completed in July 2020, it was found that during the COVID-19 pandemic global prevalence of depression was 24 per cent; anxiety, 21 per cent (Castaldelli-Maia et al., 2021). Similar to the pattern reported earlier, the prevalence of depression and anxiety was lower in Asia (18 per cent for each disorder) compared to other regions of the world (29 per cent for each disorder).

Overall, there is a great deal of interest in comparing the incidence and prevalence rates of disorders in the different ethnic groups. The literature is mixed, with some studies showing lower rates of mental disorders in populations of colour and some showing greater rates, making it difficult to draw conclusions about ethnic group differences and mental disorders. However, the results of a few large epidemiologic studies reveal some trends.

Mental-health treatment and experiences vary across different ethnic groups.

Psychiatric Epidemiology Studies across Countries and Ethnic Groups

Bromet and colleagues (2020) analyzed 18 countries participating in the World Health Organization (WHO) and World Mental Health (WHM) Survey Initiative to investigate the prevalence of major depressive episodes (MDE). Bromet et al. (2020) examined WHO-WMH survey data from 10 high-income countries—France, Germany, Belgium, Israel, Italy, Japan, the Netherlands, New Zealand, Spain, and the United States—and eight low- to middle-income countries—Brazil, China, India, Colombia, Lebanon, South Africa, Mexico, Ukraine—for the prevalence of MDE. Overall, they concluded that lifetime MDE prevalence varied substantially between countries, with the highest estimates in high-income countries (14.6 per cent) compared to low-income countries (11.1 per cent). In fact, the lowest prevalence (<10 per cent) of MDE was represented by Mexico, China, India, and South Africa. In contrast, the highest rates (>18 per cent) were present in the Netherlands, France, and the United States (Bromet et al., 2020). It is argued that income inequality, which is experienced more heavily in high-income countries, perhaps plays a significant role in the prevalence of depressive disorders (Kessler & Bromet, 2013).

At the national level, a study conducted by Chiu et al. (2018) investigated mental-health factors across the four largest ethnic groups in Ontario: White, South Asian, Chinese, and Black. The data were based on a sample from Statistics Canada's Community Health Survey (CCHS) from 2001 to 2014. The researchers measured mental-health factors such as the sense of belonging, self-rated mental health, past-year and lifetime suicidal ideation, and the prevalence of diagnosed anxiety and mood disorders within each ethnic group. The detailed findings for mental disorder prevalence in the four ethnic groups are shown in Table 9.1.

The results indicate that White individuals have higher rates of lifetime suicidal ideation, mood disorders, and anxiety disorders. The researchers attribute these results to possible differences in mental illness reporting, help-seeking behaviours, and barriers to accessing health services between the four ethnic groups examined. The South Asian group had the strongest sense of belonging, as well as one of the lowest prevalence rates of fair or poor self-rated mental health. Since South Asians are the largest visible minority in Ontario and studies show that mental illness is lower when immigrants and minorities are surrounded by others of the same ethnicity, this may be a reason that South Asian mental health results were mostly positive.

The findings show that Black Canadians also have a good sense of belonging ratings, as well as relatively positive self-rated mental health. Studies have found that the rationale used to explain the better mental health of South Asians (i.e., that mental health is good when around others of the same ethnicity) is not as strong or relevant for Black individuals. As such, the

TABLE 9.1 Prevalence of Mental Disorder in Ethnic Groups in Ontario, Canada

	White	South Asian	Chinese	Black
Past-year suicidal ideation	1.9%	0.9%	1.6%	1.1%
Lifetime suicidal ideation	8.7%	3.6%	4.6%	3.6%
Mood disorder (e.g. depression or bipolar disorder)	7.9%	3.4%	2.5%	4.3%
Anxiety disorder (e.g. obsessive-compulsive or panic disorder)	6.4%	2.5%	1.5%	3.0%

Source: (Palay et al., 2019).

researchers propose that the positive mental health observed in Black Canadians may be due to their living in racially diverse regions, like Ontario, which has been shown to increase one's sense of belonging to Canada as a whole.

Additionally, Chinese participants had the worst self-rated mental health and the weakest sense of belonging. However, this group did not have the highest number of cases of mental illness. The researchers propose that this disparity (the worst self-rated mental health but not the highest number of cases of mental illness) could be due to differences in traditional beliefs about mental health. The study found that Chinese individuals have the highest rates of not seeking help, despite mental health issues, which supports their claim surrounding mental-health beliefs.

In the United States, Breslau et al. (2006) reported that ethnic minority groups display lower rates of mental disorder than non-Hispanic European Americans. This phenomenon runs counter to the expectation that minority groups would experience higher rates of mental disorder because of the social disadvantages and stressors they experience. The observation that immigrants, despite the stress associated with the experiences of being an immigrant, have health advantages over members of the host society is referred to as the *immigrant health paradox* or the **healthy immigrant effect (HIE)** (Kwak, 2016; Markides & Rote, 2015; Straiton et al., 2014). Different explanations have been offered for this unexpected health advantage, including a sense of belonging to one's own community, ethnic identification, religious participation, and living in regions with a high immigrant/minority population, all of which lead to a decrease in psychological distress (Breslau et al., 2006; Caron & Liu, 2010; Markides & Rote, 2015; Stafford et al., 2010).

Importantly, the immigrant health paradox deteriorates over time so that immigrants' health converges to the level of health of those who did not migrate (Kwak, 2016; Straiton et al., 2014). For example, a nationwide Canadian study found that recent immigrants (arrived 0 to 9 years prior) exhibited lower rates of anxiety disorders (1.85 per cent) compared to their Canadian-born counterparts (6.44 per cent) (Aglipay et al., 2013). Furthermore, it was also noted that longer-term immigrants (those who have lived in Canada for 10 or more years) reported higher rates of anxiety disorders (3.95 per cent) compared to recent immigrants (Aglipay et al., 2013), suggesting that length of residency in the host country plays a factor in health outcomes.

Ethnic and Racial Groups Not Well Represented in Large Epidemiologic Studies

When studying and reporting on mental illness and substance abuse, it is imperative to understand the impact of the culture and environment in which an individual is living (Haque, 2010). Most diagnostic criteria for these illnesses are based on research in North American or European societies, where the largest portion of the population is Caucasian (Haque, 2010). Minorities are not often included in research due to factors such as language barriers between researchers and their participants or a lack of culturally sensitive measures to correctly gather information from these populations (Haque, 2010). This dramatically decreases the generalizability of this information to other ethnic groups with different cultures and creates a massive gap in research regarding minorities (Haque, 2010).

For example, although there is an abundance of research on Indigenous Peoples in Canada, there is still a lack of proper representation in literature. Nelson and Wilson (2017) conducted a nationwide review of studies that addressed mental illness in Indigenous populations in Canada and found significant gaps in the literature. For example, the scholars reported that Métis peoples and urban or off-reserve Indigenous Peoples are drastically under-represented

---

healthy immigrant effect (HIE) The paradox where immigrants tend to have better health than the native-born despite having a lower socio-economic status compared to non-immigrants. (See also *immigrant health paradox*.)

Indigenous communities in Canada suffer disproportionate rates of poor mental health.

in mental-health studies. Given the complexity of different Indigenous groups, it is difficult to completely generalize results if only a few populations are being examined. Furthermore, much of the research on Indigenous mental health has centred on substance abuse and suicide and often disregards other mental illnesses (e.g., anxiety, bipolar disorder, eating disorders, schizophrenia) that are consistently examined in the general Canadian population (Nelson & Wilson, 2017). As a result, it appears that substance abuse and suicide are overemphasized. The emphasis on certain mental illnesses in research on Indigenous populations has devastating effects in terms of access to care. Prevalent themes of substance abuse and suicide in research add an additional layer of stigmatization to Indigenous Peoples. This can cause a shift in health-care providers' perceptions of Indigenous Peoples and may lead to inaccurate diagnoses, delays in treatment, and, at its worst, denial of health care (Nelson et al., 2016; Nelson & Wilson, 2017).

Another example is Arab Canadians, who are one of the fastest-growing demographic groups in Canada are severely under-represented in the psychological literature and in data on mental health. The number of studies that exist regarding mental illness with a specific focus on Arabs is very limited, and the research that does exist is not entirely generalizable to all Arabs (Gearing et al., 2013). Gathering mental-health data from marginalized populations like Arabs can be very difficult for a number of reasons, but one of the main barriers to collecting this information is the considerable negative stigma that exists among Arab communities regarding mental illness (Dardas & Simmons, 2015). Even when diagnosed, Arabs are unlikely to disclose the fact that they have a mental illness, leading to a considerable lack of information regarding mental illness among Arab individuals (Dardas & Simmons, 2015).

In general, when demographics like Arabs are excluded from the literature on mental health, the quality of treatment available for these individuals decreases, putting whole ethnic groups at risk (Dardas & Simmons, 2015).

On a global scale, collecting reliable information from every country can be a very difficult task. Most North American and European countries have a solid infrastructure in place to collect research and data from their populations on topics such as mental illness and substance use, but this is not the case in all countries (UNODC, 2018). Many developing countries experiencing political turmoil either do not have stable governments in place to collect this type of data or the governments are not capable of collecting this data from the population due to a lack of research funding (UNODC, 2018). For example, in the 2018 United Nations Report on Drugs and Crime, data regarding statistics on drug use and deaths in many countries were uncertain, as regions such as the Caribbean only have data from one area: Puerto Rico (UNODC, 2018). The data collected from many Central African countries only contained responses from 58 per cent of the population; from Middle Eastern countries, that number was 17 per cent (UNODC, 2018). As a result, the wealth of data comes from North American and European countries and therefore allows them to be better represented in research than most other ethnic minorities.

Critiquing Epidemiologic Studies

The question of ethnic group differences in the prevalence of mental disorders may be a natural one to ask, but it is a complicated one to answer. The epidemiologic studies previously cited in this chapter are among some of the largest, most rigorous studies to date. As mentioned, the WHO-WMH Survey Initiative conducts representative surveys around the world using the Composite International Diagnostic Interview (CIDI). As a result, the WHO-WMH Survey Initiative has been able to expand across 29 countries, allowing for multiple comparisons between different groups of people from around the world. For example, WHO-WMH surveys have allowed researchers to examine and compare data on the prevalence of anxiety (Stein et al., 2017), major depressive episodes (Bromet at al., 2020), and PTSD (Karam et al., 2014). Moreover, questions integrated into the CIDI cover a variety of demographic topics, such as childhood experiences, marital status, socio-economic status, and presence of children. Including such topics allows for a deeper investigation of risk factors and the social consequences of mental disorders (WHO WMH-CIDI, 2020). Given the structure of this diagnostic tool and the cultural flexibility it attains, the WHO-WMH Survey Initiative allows for a more accurate representation of populations around the world.

Chang (2002) discusses a number of concerns with epidemiologic studies. As mentioned previously, one problem is the lack of representation, or small sample sizes of some groups (e.g., Indigenous Peoples, Muslim Canadians), which leads to a limited ability to make meaningful comparisons. A second problem is within-group heterogeneity. Aggregate data that combine all members of an ethnic group ignore the large variation that exists within groups. For example, among immigrant groups such as Asians and Latinos, there is considerable variation based on generation, acculturation, linguistic ability, and socio-economic status. Many authors call for research that examines particular groups in more detail to examine within-group differences (Chang, 2002). A third concern with epidemiologic studies has to do with diagnostic accuracy. Diagnoses in many large studies were based on *DSM* criteria. The *DSM* is based on Western diagnostic concepts that may not fully recognize cultural variations in experience and expression of psychological symptoms, such as the tendency for somatization. In addition, questions may not be fully understood, respondents may not answer in a completely honest manner, and interviewers may not accurately interpret participants' responses. The fourth concern is that available diagnostic categories may not fully cover the range of symptoms or disorders experienced across cultural groups, such as cultural syndromes (see the discussion later in this chapter). Williams and Harris-Reid (1999) also discuss the difficulties in generalizing the findings on ethnic group differences in mental health. They cite limitations related to different research methodologies, different criteria for identifying mental disorder and minority status, the heterogeneity of minority groups, and the lack of research available on some groups.

Conclusions from Existing Data

What conclusions can be drawn from the existing data on mental disorders and ethnic group membership? Research indicates, with some exceptions, that members of minority groups tend to have lower rates of mental disorders and that there is significant within-group variation based on characteristics such as gender, age, educational level, and socio-economic status.

In general, if we look at the prevalence of mental disorders globally, certain disorders appear with relative consistency. Schizophrenia, for example, occurs at a rate of about 0.03 per cent; bipolar disorder, at 0.06 per cent; and panic disorder, at 0.4 to 2.9 per cent (Global Burden of Disease, 2018). The consistency in the occurrence of these disorders across different countries, combined with the results of family and genetic studies, suggests that there is a strong genetic component to these disorders and that cultural factors play less of a role (US Department of Health and Human Services, 2001). Differential rates across cultures suggest that culture does play a greater role in other disorders, however (U.S. Department of Health and Human Services, 2001), such as depression, for which the rates range from 2 per cent to 19 per cent across countries (World Health Organization, 2017). This result suggests that cultural factors, such as poverty and violence, may play a greater role than genetics does in the causation of major depression (Herba et al., 2016; U.S. Department of Health and Human Services, 2001).

9.4 Utilization of Mental-Health Services

In 2009, the Diversity Task Group of the Mental Health Commission of Canada (Hansson et al., 2009) released a report highlighting that immigrant, refugee, ethnocultural, and racialized populations face more barriers to accessing mental-health services in Canada than those outside these groups.

> When I first started showing symptoms of depression, my mother thought that I was just being lazy, or a "bad girl." My dad was working abroad at that time. I can remember every time she talked to my dad, she would yell, "This girl is being so lazy for no reason, we've given her too much love and spoiled her." However, when I refused to go to school for weeks rather than days, refused to eat, go out with friends, watch movies, or do anything I used to enjoy, my mom's concerns deepened. I think she did not know what to do or whom to go to. . . . "She can't have any mental health problem. We have given her everything she needs. I don't understand what is wrong with this girl." My mom was scared and confused. I think more than anything, she was scared to tell friends and family that her daughter was suffering from depression. I have to say, in a culture like mine, having mental health problems such as depression and anxiety was taboo. It is not something you frequently hear about or talk about.
>
> —*Sudarshini, 20+-year-old South Asian student*

As you see in Sudarshini's story, depression is attributed to cultural factors and the strong pressure from parents to excel academically. Sudarshini expresses concern about the cultural stigma attached to mental health and does not seek professional help. The story illustrates several of the cultural factors that serve as barriers to mental-health treatment for diverse populations.

Even with Canada's universal health-care system, Canadians still face barriers when accessing mental-health care. Approximately half of Canadians experiencing a depressive episode report receiving treatment and care for their mental illness (Patten et al., 2016). Globally, we see the same trend. Mental illnesses make up a large part of the global burden of disease and are the leading cause for disability worldwide, but many of those in need of mental-health services are not receiving adequate care (Wainberg et al., 2017). This lack of access to mental-health services and care is a barrier faced by many, but particularly by Black people, Indigenous Peoples, and people of colour (BIPOC).

In an Ontario-based study regarding the utilization of mental-health services by ethnic minorities, Chiu and colleagues (2018) reported that, compared to White Canadians, South Asian, Chinese, and Black participants were significantly less likely to have used mental-health services within the previous year. Additionally, despite reporting mental-health disturbances, less than half of individuals across all four ethnic groups sought help. Unmet needs for care were particularly higher among ethnic minorities, especially those of Chinese heritage. The researchers mentioned that differences in mental-health-service utilization between ethnic groups may be due to differences in mental illness reporting, help-seeking behaviours, or accessibility to services (Chiu et al., 2018).

Decreased utilization of mental-health services was highlighted in a study conducted in British Columbia by Chen and colleagues (2010). The results revealed that Chinese Canadians with severe and persistent depression had considerably lower rates of usage of mental-health services than non-Chinese individuals with depression (Chen et al., 2010). When they did access mental-health services, it was usually only after the symptoms had become severe and all other options had been exhausted (Chen et al., 2010). Some reasons for this trend included a lack of information and education regarding mental health and a lack of mental-health services that were accessible to minority groups.

Researchers have also identified cultural incompatibility to be one of the main reasons South Asian Canadians, specifically from Calgary, do not seek mental-health services (Lai & Surood, 2010). Most participants expressed the desire to speak in languages they were comfortable with and felt that the therapists and psychiatrists who were treating them did not understand their culture (Lai & Surood, 2010). It is this lack of cultural sensitivity in mental-health-care providers and the inaccessibility of mental-health care for ethnic minorities that discourage such individuals from receiving proper mental-health care.

In general, BIPOC experience considerably more difficulty accessing mental-health services than their non-minority counterparts. Some of these barriers include inadequate outreach programs, a lack of language accommodations for newcomers, and a lack of culturally sensitive care for people of different cultures. Such barriers lead to decreased trust of mental-health professionals and, therefore, less mental-health-service use (Chen et al., 2010).

9.5 Barriers: Access to Psychological Treatment

As we have pointed out, research consistently shows that people of colour tend to underutilize mental-health services. What are some of the barriers that prevent them from getting the services they need? Is it that they have negative attitudes toward seeking help? Toward psychotherapy? Or is it that they have negative experiences once they go to therapy? The answer is multifaceted and includes the perception that help is not needed, people's negative attitudes toward psychotherapy, and, as mentioned, a lack of trust of mental-health services.

Mojtabai et al. (2011) explored barriers to seeking mental-health treatment in the general population. They found that the majority of people with common mental disorders (e.g., anxiety, depression, substance abuse) did not seek help because they did not think they needed help. Among those with a perceived need, a large portion did not seek help because they preferred to deal with their problems on their own. These attitudinal and evaluative factors served to prevent help-seeking more than structural barriers, such as lack of transportation, finances, or inability to get an appointment. Mojtabai et al. (2011) found the effects of these barriers differed based on the severity of the disorder and recognized they can also differ based on socio-demographic characteristics, such as ethnicity, gender, and socio-economic status.

It has been suggested that the negative attitudes that ethnic minorities have toward psychotherapy prevent them from seeking help in the first place. These negative attitudes can impact the way that ethnic minorities interact with health-care providers and can even be the reason for a decreased level of trust in mental-health-care professionals. Negative attitudes and a lack of trust of mental-health services are evident in Canada, especially among Black Canadians. Black Canadians are less likely than other demographics to access mental-health care due to a variety of reasons, including the lack of knowledge of resources for Black communities, racism, and discrimination. One prominent barrier is the lack of trust they have in health-care professionals and the system (Ottawa Public Health, 2020). This lack of trust stems from the institutionalized racism that has become embedded in the health-care system, making it considerably harder for Black Canadians to seek care (Taylor & Richards, 2019). Most treatments and research are based on mainly White participants in North American settings and therefore cannot be generalized to minority groups. The exclusion of Black participants in research compounded with the lack of culturally sensitive care available for Black and other ethnic minority groups creates major barriers in their access to health care (Taylor & Richards, 2019). Furthermore, when Black individuals do receive treatment, they are often treated by non-Black professionals who do not understand the cultural differences or experiences of those within the Black community (Daley et al., 2012). This leads to a lack of understanding of symptoms and behaviours exhibited by Black patients and often completely de-contextualizes their experiences, leading to misdiagnoses (Daley et al., 2012). In turn, misdiagnoses further decrease the level of trust that Black individuals have in mental-health-care professionals (Daley et al., 2012).

Studies have also found that when Black individuals in Canada are taken to hospitals for psychotic episodes and mental-health emergencies, they are more often taken there forcefully by police or ambulance rather than by community members (Jarvis et al., 2005). This was reiterated in a study carried out in the UK, which revealed that Black individuals were more likely than White individuals to be referred to mental-health services through the criminal justice system (Morgan et al., 2006). Forceful admission into mental-health treatment by the police or justice system also contributes to the lack of trust in the mental-health-care system and decreases the likelihood of Black communities seeking mental-health services (Morgan et al., 2006).

> I had never really heard a Black person say that they were depressed or had anxiety. I was so ignorant myself that I thought it was something White girls got.
> — *Stacy-Ann Buchanan, Jamaican-Canadian mental-health advocate and actress*

Stacy-Ann Buchanan immigrated to Toronto from Jamaica when she was 14. She has been vocal about her experiences with anxiety and depression and the way that, to a large degree, mental illness was not talked about in Jamaica.

Sue and Sue (2016) articulated what they saw as the three major barriers to effective multicultural counselling and therapy: (1) culture-bound values, (2) class-bound values, and (3) language variables (see Table 9.2).

Culture-Bound Values as Barriers

Psychotherapy is directly influenced by the culture within which it was developed. Psychotherapy was originally developed by Western Europeans (e.g., Freud). Therefore, it reflects a Western perspective, and some of the central values of that perspective may be in direct conflict with the values of clients from other cultures. Sue and Sue (2016) describe some of the European values embedded in psychotherapy that may conflict with values of clients from other cultures. They refer to these values as culture-bound values. Culture-bound values in counselling and psychotherapy include individualism, verbal/emotional/behavioural expressiveness, insight, openness and intimacy, scientific empiricism, clear distinctions between mental and physical functioning, ambiguity, and communication patterns between client and counsellor.

In Chapter 3, we discussed the differences between individualism and collectivism. Psychotherapy tends to be a very individualistic process. If we look at

TABLE 9.2   Sue and Sue's Barriers to Multicultural Counselling and Therapy

Culture-bound values
Focus on the individual
Verbal/emotional/behavioural expressiveness
Insight
Self-disclosure (openness and intimacy)
Scientific empiricism
Distinctions between mental and physical functioning
Patterns of communication
Class-bound values
Bias toward White middle- to upper-class values
Bias against people who are poor
Lack of understanding of the stressors of poverty
Language barriers
Need for professional interpretation
Lack of bilingual therapists
Use of standard English

Source: Reproduced with permission from Sue, D. W., & Sue, D. (2016). *Counseling the culturally diverse: Theory and practice* (7th ed.). Hoboken, NJ: Wiley

the most popular theories of human development, such as those of Piaget and Erickson, we see that they emphasize individuation—the development of an autonomous, independent self—as healthy development. If we look at the goals of some of the main orientations to psychotherapy, we also see this focus on the individual. For example, Carl Rogers emphasized self-actualization, or the development of one's full potential. Alfred Adler emphasized the concept of self-esteem: how individuals feel about themselves is seen as a critical component of mental health, and individuals' self-esteem is greatly influenced by their personal accomplishments. These concepts are not as important in collectivistic cultures, however, where people have an interdependent sense of the self. In some cultures, too much emphasis on the self is seen as unhealthy. For example, in North America "The squeaky wheel gets the grease," but in Japan, "The nail that sticks out gets pounded down." In North American culture, in other words, the loud, assertive person gets positive attention, but in Japanese culture, assertiveness is seen as being selfish and against group standards.

The second culture-bound value described by Sue and Sue (2016) is verbal/emotional/behavioural expressiveness. Based on work by his mentor, Josef Breuer, Freud developed the talking cure, or talk therapy (Freud, 1909/1977). This therapy formed the basis for practically all modern approaches to counselling and psychotherapy (Corey, 2017). Therefore, it is expected that clients are able to verbally express their internal thoughts and feelings and engage in active dialogue with the therapist. This is viewed as an essential ingredient in effective therapy. However, not all cultures value this type of verbal expression. Different cultures place varying emphasis on acceptable ways to express emotion. Western cultures tend to value open and outward expression of emotions, whereas other cultures, such as Asian cultures, value emotional restraint (see our discussion of direct versus indirect expression in Chapter 4). People of colour, because of mistrust, may withhold true feelings in situations in which they feel threatened. In the Western tradition, in which outward emotional expression is valued and expected, clients who do not express enough emotion are labelled resistant, restricted, and repressed by their therapists.

With the vast popularity of cognitive behavioural approaches, behavioural expressiveness has become more valued in counselling and psychotherapy (Sue & Sue, 2016). Clients are expected to be assertive, stand up for themselves, and complete assignments aimed at directly confronting problems or changing problematic behaviours. Again, some cultures value a more indirect, subtle approach (Sue & Sue, 2016). Murphy-Shigematsu (2014) explains the Japanese concept of *shikata ga nai*, which means, "It is out of my control; nothing can be done." He gives the example of Japanese Americans placed in internment camps during World War II. Rather than resist, they chose to make the best of a bad situation. Inside the camps, they planted beautiful gardens, wrote poetry, formed baseball leagues, and so on. Some of the younger generation criticized this attitude and wondered why their elders did not fight back. Murphy-Shigematsu reframes this passivity and, rather than seeing it as a sign of weakness, interprets it as a sign of strength. He says that acceptance of one's vulnerability and helplessness takes courage and leads to new hopes and new meanings. A culturally insensitive therapist could easily misinterpret such an attitude as negative.

The third culture-bound value described by Sue and Sue (2016) is insight. Many traditional forms of counselling and psychotherapy (e.g., psychoanalytic, humanistic) believe that the path to wellness lies in insight, or the client's understanding of the underlying dynamics of their problems. Other cultures do not see the need for such in-depth self-exploration. In fact, some Asian cultures believe that thinking too much about something can make the problem worse. Asian elders advise children not to think about the problem because then they are thinking about themselves too much, instead of thinking about the family. The following story, involving a Mexican-American family, illustrates a conflict over this value of insight:

> My family went to therapy once because my teenage sister was getting into a lot of trouble, and my mother didn't know how to handle her anymore. We were assigned to a White male therapist. In the first session, the therapist asked my mother a lot of questions about her own feelings and actions. I could see my mother was getting a bit irritated. She didn't understand why the therapist was focusing on her and not my sister. At the end of the session the therapist suggested that my mother keep a journal, record her thoughts and feelings for the week, and bring them back to the next session. We never went back.
> —Belen, 20+-year-old Mexican-American student

In this story, we can see the factors that resulted in this family's terminating therapy after the first session. One main factor was the clash in the culture-bound value of insight. This mother wanted practical advice on coping with her daughter's behavioural problems. Instead, the therapist told the mother to keep a journal. We can assume that the therapist had good intentions, believing that the problems lay with the interactions between the mother and the daughter and that the mother needed to become more aware of those interpersonal dynamics. However, this was not a culturally sensitive intervention, and the family never went back.

The fourth culture-bound value is self-disclosure, or intimacy and openness. In therapy, clients are supposed to share the most intimate details of their lives. In many cultures, such personal disclosures are reserved for only the closest family members and friends. Intimate relationships are developed over time, not once a week in a 50-minute session.

The fifth culture-bound value is scientific empiricism. Psychology patterns itself after the physical sciences, which emphasize objective, rational, linear thinking. In Western approaches, a therapist is supposed to be neutral, rational, and logical, like a scientist. Mental-health concerns are approached through linear problem solving and quantitative evaluation through the use of tools such as psycho-diagnostic tests (e.g., intelligence tests, personality tests). Instead, many cultures take a more circular, holistic, harmonious approach to the world. For example, instead of breaking nature down into its components to study it, control it, and exploit it for profit, as Western cultures do, many Indigenous cultures emphasize harmonious living with the world. Instead of emphasizing rational, reductionist problem solving, they believe in the value of intuition. (Remember the differences in world view discussed in Chapter 3.)

Sixth, Western philosophy also draws a distinction between mental and physical functioning. In other words, the mind and the body are seen as two separate entities, and there is a distinction between mental and physical health. That distinction is not made in other cultures. Thus, in seeking help for an emotional problem, there is no difference in going to your regular physician or your priest. Just as the doctor prescribes a specific, tangible solution to the problem (e.g., medication), the counsellor or therapist may be expected to do the same.

Finally, patterns of communication differ from one culture to another. As described earlier, in some cultures, such as Chinese and Japanese, children are reared to respect their elders and authority figures, and they do not speak until they are spoken to. A therapist may be viewed as an authority figure, and a culturally different client may come in and wait for the therapist to speak first and take the lead in running the session. However, in many traditional Western therapies, the client is expected to do most of the talking and take responsibility for directing the session while the therapist takes a less active role. Therapists may misunderstand and misinterpret the behaviour of a culturally different client who comes in and does not say much. In fact, the silence may be misjudged as the client's being dependent, inarticulate, or less intelligent.

Class-Bound Values as Barriers

Effective cross-cultural therapy can also be hindered by class-bound values. According to Sue and Sue (2016), the values that underlie typical mental-health practices are decidedly White-European middle class, and practitioners often fail to recognize the economic implications for the delivery of such mental-health services. For example, poor clients may not have transportation to get to sessions and may not have the money or the insurance coverage to pay for services. A therapist who wants poor clients to openly express intimate parts of their lives, to introspect, and to gain insight into the underlying dynamics of their behaviour may be in direct conflict with clients who are more concerned about finding a job, putting food on the table, or finding adequate care for their children. Clients who are in survival mode, just trying to make it from day to day, may expect more tangible advice and suggestions from a therapist. It is also often difficult for a therapist who comes from a middle- to upper-class background to relate to the circumstances and hardships affecting a client who lives in poverty.

The inferior and biased treatment of clients of lower socio-economic status is well documented in the literature and globally (Aarts et al., 2010, Kumachev et al., 2016, Rahman et al., 2011). For example, Olah and colleagues (2013) investigated how socio-economic status affects physicians' responses to patients. To explore this effect, a male and female researcher made calls to a random sample of family physicians and general practices in Toronto. The callers presented themselves as patients seeking a primary care physician and followed a script that suggested that they were either patients of high socio-economic status (i.e., bank employee) or low socio-economic status (i.e., recipient of social assistance). Results illustrated that callers were significantly more likely (50 per cent) to receive an appointment when they presented themselves as an individual of high socio-economic status. These findings illustrate some of the class-bound variables that affect the provision of mental-health services for members of minority groups.

Language Variables as Barriers

The third barrier to effective cross-cultural therapy described by Sue and Sue (2016) is language variables. Because psychotherapy is a "talking cure," the client and the therapist must be able to accurately and appropriately send and receive both verbal and non-verbal messages for therapy to be effective.

Ohtani and colleagues (2015) examined the impact of language proficiency on access to and utilization of mental-health services in the general population as well as among those with psychiatric disorders. In this systemic review, the researchers included studies from Canada, the United States, the Netherlands, and Australia. Across all countries, insufficient language proficiency was found

"My tattoo was a lot cheaper than therapy."

Mental-health services can be prohibitively expensive for many people.

to be significantly associated with the underutilization of mental-health services in both the general and psychiatric patient populations. Importantly, the researchers reported inconsistent findings of the association between ethnic background and access to health care, suggesting that language proficiency may play a greater role in access to care than one's ethnic background. For example, among Chinese-Canadian men, English proficiency was associated with a higher rate of mental-health visits, whereas in Chinese-Canadian women, English proficiency was associated with reduced mental-health service use (Ohtani et al., 2015).

9.6 Culturally Sensitive Therapeutic Approaches

With all these barriers to minority groups seeking and receiving appropriate mental-health services, it might seem like an impossible task for members of these groups to get the help they need. Several approaches have been developed to overcome these obstacles and provide services that are more appropriate for culturally diverse groups. Multicultural counselling has received the most attention as a culturally sensitive therapeutic approach. Sue and Sue (2016) summarized the key elements of multicultural counselling and therapy (MCT). First, MCT sees therapy as both a helping role and a process, where the role of the therapist and repertoire of helping skills are broadened to include teaching, consulting, and advocacy and are tailored to fit the cultural values and life experiences of clients. MCT recognizes that client identities are composed of individual, group, and universal dimensions. It advocates the use of both universal and culture-specific modes of helping strategies. In other words, there are universal features of helping that cut across cultures, but clients also need strategies that incorporate the values, practices, and beliefs of their particular group. Multicultural counselling and therapy incorporates both individualistic and collectivistic perspectives and strives to balance attention to unique individual characteristics with consideration for the impact of contextual factors on these individuals. This may involve a shift in focus from individual client change to altering systems (e.g., education, employment, government, business, society).

In the following sections we will discuss some of the approaches developed to provide effective mental-health services to diverse populations.

The Training of Mental-Health Professionals: Multicultural Competence

One way to overcome barriers to effective multicultural therapy is to increase the ability of mental-health professionals to work with culturally diverse populations. Sue and Sue (1999) argue that the way to effective multicultural therapy is through the training and education of mental-health professionals. That leads us to the issue of **multicultural competence**. In general, multicultural competence refers to effectiveness in working with people who are different from you. More specifically, Mio and colleagues (2012) defined *multicultural competence* as multidimensional, consisting of awareness of one's own culture and its biases, the ability to learn about other cultures and values, and the application of that knowledge to a culturally appropriate set of skills.

Multicultural competence utilizes a broad definition of culture (see Chapter 1) whereby any kind of difference between the therapist/counsellor and client is considered a cultural encounter. This includes a male therapist working with a female client, a straight therapist working with a gay client, a European-Canadian therapist working with an Asian-Canadian client, a Protestant therapist working with a Catholic client, and so on. Because every individual, including every therapist and client, brings a unique set of cultural identities to the therapy office, all therapy could be considered multicultural therapy (Comas-Díaz, 2014; Pedersen, 1988). There are three

multicultural competence The awareness of one's own culture, the ability to learn about other cultures, and the development of a culturally appropriate set of skills to work effectively with diverse groups.

primary domains of multicultural competence (Arredondo et al., 1996; Sue et al., 1982; Sue et al., 1992; Sue et al., 1998):

1. the counsellor's awareness of his or her own cultural assumptions, values, and biases;
2. an understanding of the client's world view; and
3. the development of culturally appropriate intervention strategies and techniques.

One of the primary aspects of multicultural competence is self-awareness. In other words, counsellors and therapists cannot be effective in working with individuals from different backgrounds unless they first understand themselves. That includes an understanding of their own cultural heritage, the impact it has on their attitudes and behaviours, and an understanding of the attitudes they have toward other groups, such as biases, prejudices, and stereotypes.

Second, effective counsellors and therapists must be able to see the world through their clients' eyes. They must have basic information about the various groups they encounter, such as the history of the group, current issues they are facing, typical values, and typical practices. That knowledge should not be used to formulate stereotypes or to make hasty judgments about members of particular groups but instead should be used to formulate hypotheses that can be explored with the client. For example, if you are a therapist with a Latino client, you might assume that your client is Catholic and subscribes to traditional gender roles. These things may exemplify Latino culture in general but may not hold true for an individual Latino client in your office. These are issues that must be explored with that client to see whether they apply.

Third, therapists and counsellors must develop a repertoire of culturally appropriate strategies, such as the ability to assess level of acculturation and ethnic identity, comfort discussing difficult topics such as racism and sexism, and collaboration with other institutional, community, and Indigenous sources of help.

The tripartite model of multicultural counselling competencies (Sue et al., 1982) plays a significant role in multicultural counselling research (Sinacore et al., 2011). For example, Canadian researchers Collins and Arthur (2010) propose a model for culture-infused counselling and identify three core competency domains:

1. cultural awareness of self,
2. cultural awareness of others, and
3. establishment of a culturally sensitive working alliance.

As seen in Figure 9.1, a culturally sensitive working alliance is impossible to effectively establish without recognizing the first two core competencies: awareness of cultural self and cultural awareness of others. The working alliance allows for cultural awareness of self and cultural awareness of the client to be translated into a purposeful collaborative process. Subsequently, decisions about therapy tasks and goals are determined jointly with the counsellor and the client to optimize end results. Furthermore, within each core competency exist a set of specific attitudes and beliefs, knowledge, and skills. For instance, actively pursuing cultural self-awareness is a skill that belongs to the first domain: awareness of cultural self (Collins & Arthur, 2010). Emerging developments in the field and changes in the world at large highlighted the need for an update, such as increased understanding about the impact of intersecting identities (e.g., ethnicity, gender, sexual orientation, religion, socio-economic status) (see Chapter 7) and of the larger context (e.g., communities, institutions, social climates) on mental-health outcomes and health disparities.

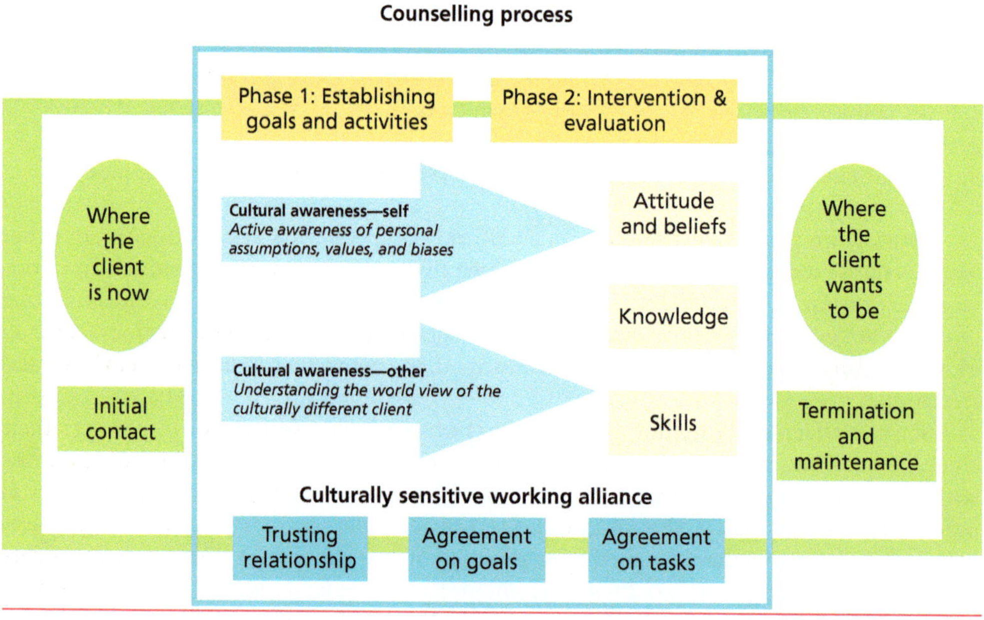

Figure 9.1 The culturally sensitive working alliance as the foundation for multicultural counselling.

Source: Reproduced with permission from Collins, S., & Arthur, N. (2010). Culture-infused counselling: A fresh look at a classic framework of multicultural counselling competencies. *Counselling Psychology Quarterly, 23*(2), 203–216. https://doi.org/10.1080/09515071003798204.

In the following quote, three second-generation Asian-Canadian women discuss their perspectives on mental-health services and care, such as therapy and counselling:

> **[Person 1]:** For me, [counselling] is just . . . one of many resources you could use to better yourself. . . . [I]t doesn't necessarily mean that . . . you're weak. . . . [I]t's not something that should be, like, feared, I guess. And it's not something that only serious cases can use, as well, like if you are just struggling with anxiety, you could go to counselling . . . to . . . get more practice on . . . how can I learn to deal with this, how can I get some better tactics to tackle it.
>
> **[Person 2]:** . . . [Although] I think on my mom's end, she just never really thought about mental health . . . but more so that, like, okay it's important to talk about what happens during your day, it's important to let someone know about what's going on in your life. So, in a sense like she was promoting mental well-being . . . without really talking about mental well-being. I never thought about counselling, either. For me, I always sought out different ways to deal with it, so, like, my mom said . . . exercising, meditation . . . anything that I can do to deal with my stress . . . and I think that not being exposed to the topic of mental health with . . . my family or anything, I think it did play a part.
>
> **[Person 3]:** I think that our generation, we are more open to seeking out these new, you know, new things, so counselling is one of them. . . . I don't even think that counselling is an option for the older generation. It's more . . . it's not even like a last resort. It's not even an option at all. I think that [my family] would see me as a weak person, that I didn't know how to handle um my own mental health. . . . [I]f I were to seek out counselling, I think they would kind of even ask, like, "Why do you need that?

> Why—like, there's nothing wrong with you physically, [so] why would you need to seek out counselling?" . . . [T]hey wouldn't understand.
> —Second-generation Asian-Canadian women discussing their perceptions
> of therapy and mental-health services (Yeung, 2018, pp. 43–8)

The women discuss how they view psychotherapy and mental-health services on a personal level. Some note that it is simply a resource available to use to improve their own personal health. They then go on to explain the generational differences that they have seen regarding the perception of mental-health services between themselves as second-generation immigrants and their parents as first-generation immigrants. They note that although they may be open to the idea of counselling and therapy, their parents still do not entirely understand the need for it and will often encourage them to pursue other methods of coping, such as meditation and exercise. This was attributed to the lack of access their parents had to information regarding mental-health services and their benefits. This lack of access also created a barrier for them to access these services and led them not to completely understand the purpose and potential that mental-health services had on an individual's overall health. Lastly, the women describe their community's perception of mental-health services and the stigma that still exists around the services themselves and the people who use them. They explain that these services are seen as something that is not necessary and that the physical needs of the body are seen as more important. This stigma also serves as a barrier for individuals to access mental-health care.

9.7 Gender Differences in Mental Disorders

We cannot leave a discussion of group differences in mental disorders without talking about gender. Gender differences in the prevalence of mental disorders are fairly robust, with women reporting higher lifetime rates of mood and anxiety disorders and men reporting higher rates of substance abuse and impulse control disorders (Kessler et al., 2015).

The differentiation has been described as women having higher rates of internalizing disorders and men having higher rates of **externalizing** disorders. What this means is that women tend to focus their feelings on the self, whereas men project their feelings outward and express them through overt behaviours. According to Rosenfeld (1999), this means that, generally, women live with more profound feelings of sadness, loss, low self-esteem, guilt, hopelessness, and self-blame than men. They suffer more anxiety, ranging from fears of specific objects or situations, to panic attacks, to free-floating anxiety and constant worry. In contrast, men consume more alcohol and drugs and do so more frequently than women. Abuse of alcohol and drugs leads to more negative physical consequences for men, such as blackouts and hallucinations, and it interferes with their lives more often, causing more problems at work, at school, or in the family. Men are more likely to exhibit aggressive and violent behaviour (Mio et al., 2003). They are also more prone to criminal behaviour, deceitfulness, impulsivity, irresponsibility, and recklessness.

Researchers (Kvrgic et al., 2013; Rosenfeld, 1999; Sikka et al., 2010) believe these differences are more accurately explained by life circumstances, such as women traditionally having less power (e.g., women earning less than their husbands), having greater responsibility for taking care of the home and raising children, and having stronger social ties. Decreased power and control and increased social responsibility and their different interpretations of those circumstances, combined with different coping strategies, have often led women to have higher rates of depression and anxiety than men. Unfortunately, despite many legal and social rights that women have gained in the past 100 years, gender relations

externalizing Projecting feelings outward and expressing them through overt behaviours.

There is gender imbalance in health-care leadership.

across the world indicate that men tend to have higher status and power than women, although the degree of this difference varies across cultures (Safdar & Kosakowska-Berezecka, 2015).

There is also discussion about whether the different disorders exhibited by men and women are really in response to different circumstances or whether they are different reactions to the same circumstances. Norms for the acceptable expression of emotions differ drastically between men and women. These norms are socialized into boys and girls from a very young age. How many men reading this book were told, "Stop crying; boys don't cry," "Don't be a sissy," or "Suck it up and be a man"? Men are often discouraged from expressing feelings, especially feelings that are defined as feminine or weak, such as worry, fear, and helplessness—all emotions associated with anxiety and depression. Feelings such as anger are typically more socially acceptable for men. Thus, it seems that men and women have different disorders because they express different symptoms, encounter different social experiences, and have different kinds of reactions to circumstances.

9.8 Culture-Specific Mental Disorders

Earlier in the chapter we mentioned that the *DSM-5* includes a section on cultural concepts of distress, defined as "ways that cultural groups experience, understand, and communicate suffering, behavioural problems, or troubling thoughts and emotions" (American Psychiatric Association, 2013, p. 758). We also defined the three types of cultural concepts: cultural syndromes, cultural idioms of distress, and cultural explanations or perceived causes.

One example of cultural syndromes in *DSM-5* is *ataque de nervios*. This condition is typically reported among Latinos, especially those from the Caribbean (Durà-Vilà et al., 2012; Guarnaccia et al., 2010; Lewis-Fernández et al., 2010; Moitra et al., 2018). Symptoms include uncontrollable shouting, attacks of crying, trembling, heat in the chest rising to the head, fainting spells, and verbal or physical aggression. Generally, the victims report feeling out of control, and the experience often occurs in response to a stressful event, such as news of a close loved one's death. The episodes are usually discrete, with the individuals quickly returning to their usual level of functioning (American Psychiatric Association, 2013).

Another example of a cultural syndrome is *kufungisisa*, or "thinking too much." This is an expression used by the Shona in Zimbabwe to explain anxiety, depression, and somatic complaints. For example, the person might say, "My heart hurts because I'm thinking too much." It is used as a way to express distress regarding interpersonal and social difficulties, such as marital problems or having no money to take care of one's children. Typical symptoms include excessive worry, panic attacks, depression, and irritability. Thinking too much is believed to cause damage to the mind and the body and symptoms such as headaches and dizziness. Similar expressions are used in other African cultures, such as "brain fag syndrome" in Nigeria, which is when high school and university students complain that their brains are fatigued from too much studying (American Psychiatric Association, 2013; Ebigbo et al., 2015; Kidia et al., 2015).

A culture-bound illness specifically classified in the *ICD* is the Indonesian illness *amok* (Loue & Sajatovic, 2012), in which an individual exhibits unprovoked yet extreme destructive behaviour (Loue & Sajatovic, 2012). This behaviour can be homicidal and is entirely indiscriminate, with no prior organization or intention (Loue & Sajatovic, 2012). Once the violent episode ends, the individual often experiences amnesia or fatigue, with no memory of the episode (Loue & Sajatovic, 2012). Many people who have experienced *amok* commit suicide during their episode (Loue & Sajatovic, 2012). *Amok* can occur in individuals after they have experienced a long period of anxiety, but most episodes occur without warning (Loue & Sajatovic, 2012). Within Indonesian culture, extreme violence such as the type exhibited in *amok* is often reserved for warfare, and within war, soldiers may often commit suicide if unsuccessful or defeated (Loue & Sajatovic, 2012). This cultural practice is likely the reason for the extreme violence and suicidal behaviour seen in patients with *amok* (Loue & Sajatovic, 2012). It may also explain why it only exists within Indonesian cultures (Loue & Sajatovic, 2012).

In general, the inclusion of cultural concepts of distress in diagnostic manuals accomplishes a number of goals. First, it helps to avoid misdiagnosis. Cultural variation in the presentation and explanation of symptoms can lead clinicians to draw inaccurate conclusions. Awareness of these differences can help prevent this. Second, exploration of these cultural concepts can yield useful information and increase our understanding of the impact of culture on mental health. Third, use of these concepts can help build rapport and improve relationships between mental-health providers and consumers. Clients may feel more comfortable if therapists "speak their language." Fourth, understanding and use of these cultural concepts can improve the effectiveness of treatment, allowing clinicians to target specific problems and apply appropriate interventions. Fifth, these concepts help guide research. As mentioned earlier, research led to the inclusion of specific cultural concepts in the *DSM*. Further research will allow expansion of this. Finally, by distinguishing these syndromes, idioms, and explanations, we can gather more accurate epidemiologic data, learn more about their incidence and prevalence, and track changes over time. All of these are reasons why the *DSM* includes the section on cultural concepts of distress (American Psychiatric Association, 2013).

Eating Disorders: A Western Cultural Syndrome?

Eating disorders present an interesting example of some of the issues regarding culture and mental disorder discussed earlier. The most common eating disorders include **anorexia nervosa**, **bulimia nervosa**, and **binge-eating disorder**. Anorexia nervosa is characterized by extreme weight loss, the intense fear of gaining weight, and a distorted body image. Bulimia nervosa is characterized by bingeing and purging. Individuals have episodes during which they consume excessively large amounts of food; afterward, they engage in extreme activities to avoid gaining weight, such as vomiting, excessive exercise, and the use of laxatives or diuretics. Binge-eating disorder is characterized by eating a larger than normal amount of food during a discrete period of time. The amount is larger than what most people would eat during that same period and under similar circumstances. For example, eating 20 hot dogs within 30 minutes would not be unusual if you were participating in a hot dog–eating contest. However, sitting at home by yourself and eating 20 hot dogs within 30 minutes would likely be considered a binge.

It is a commonly held belief that eating disorders are most prevalent in Western, European, and North American female populations (Chisuwa & O'Dea, 2010; Murray et al., 2017). Most research studies focus on this population (Balhara et al., 2012; Nakai et al., 2014), but a large number of studies examine the prevalence of these disorders in different cultural groups. Some of these studies suggest that eating disorders are less common among people of colour living in Western societies, but the results are inconclusive (Pike et al., 2014; Shuttlesworth & Zotter, 2011).

Research suggests Black women tend to be more satisfied with their body weight, size, and appearance than White women and therefore Black women experience a lower prevalence of eating disorders (Ristovski-Slijepcevic et al., 2010). These lower rates may be because of a higher tolerance of larger body types in the Black community. Ristovski-Slijepcevic et al. (2010) carried out a qualitative study on body image and eating habits with a sample of Black and White Canadians from Halifax and Vancouver. One of their findings was that the Black women showed the most resistance to the dominant, Westernized ideal of beauty and thinness, supporting the previous literature that positive views of body image among Black-Canadian women result in their lower risk of developing an eating disorder.

Solmi et al. (2016) conducted a study with a multi-ethnic sample in London, UK, to examine the prevalence and distribution of eating disorders among individuals from different ethnic backgrounds. Their results indicated that Black Britons accounted for one-third of all bulimia nervosa (BN) cases identified in the study, but for all other eating disorders (e.g., binge eating, purging), the prevalence rates were relatively similar across ethnic groups (e.g., White, Black, Asian). The other exception was for White participants, who had the highest prevalence of binge-eating disorder. Similarly, a study conducted by Boisvert and Harrell (2012) examined the roles of culture and ethnicity in eating-disorder development among a sample of Canadian women of varying ethnicities (Indigenous,

---

anorexia nervosa An eating disorder marked by extreme weight loss, intense fear of gaining weight, and a distorted body image.

bulimia nervosa An eating disorder marked by the consumption of a large amount of food in one sitting—called a binge—followed by the purging of that food, most typically through vomiting but also through extreme exercise or the use of laxatives.

binge-eating disorder An eating disorder marked by consumption of large amounts of food in one sitting, accompanied by feelings of lack of control, embarrassment, disgust, depression, and guilt, along with rapid eating, eating until uncomfortably full, and eating large amounts when not hungry.

Are eating disorders a "White woman's problem"?

Hispanic, Asian, and White) on dimensions that are considered to be predictors and symptoms of eating disorders, such as high body mass index (BMI) and high body shame. In the Asian sample (consisting of women from Chinese, Indian, and Southwest Asian backgrounds), the researchers found that although Asian women had low BMIs, they also reported having higher body shame than both Indigenous and White women. The finding of low BMIs indicates Asian women have a lower risk of eating disorder development, but their high levels of body shame simultaneously increase that risk, creating a complicated relationship with eating disorders. Thus, there is a modifying factor of ethnicity in the risk of developing an eating disorder.

Similar findings were reported by Latner et al. (2011), who conducted a study comparing differences in body image between Asian, Pacific Islander, and White individuals in Australia and Hawaii. The results indicated that body image scores for male and female Asians in Australia and Hawaii were quite low, indicating more body dissatisfaction in Asians than Pacific Islanders and similar body dissatisfaction compared to White individuals. Again, this was complicated by the fact that Asians also had the lowest BMI scores of the three groups. It was speculated that body dissatisfaction occurred among Asians because of a stricter cultural standard or norm of thinness, which could put them at a higher risk of developing eating disorders.

Qian et al. (2013) conducted a review of the literature on the global prevalence of eating disorders. The authors investigated the lifetime prevalence of anorexia, bulimia, and total eating disorders for Western countries (e.g., the Netherlands, Germany, Spain, Mexico, and

New Zealand) and South Asia. Overall, the results indicate that, globally, eating disorders are common. Notably, the prevalence of eating disorders in Western countries was significantly higher than in Asia. However, because only one study from Asia was included, it is important to note that research continues to expand on the topic of eating disorders around the world.

As you can see, the results are mixed. Although most studies suggest lower rates of eating-related problems for women of colour, a few indicate the rates are higher. To settle the controversy, Wade et al. (2011) examined major studies in eating disorder prevalence from Australia, New Zealand, Europe, and North America. It was found that the lifetime prevalence of anorexia nervosa across all regions of interest ranged from 0.9 to 2.2 per cent. In North American studies of non-Caucasian women (Black, Latino, Asian), the prevalence was significantly lower (0.12 to 0.14 per cent). Although lower rates of anorexia nervosa in women of colour were reported, the same cannot be said for bulimia nervosa and binge-eating disorders. The researchers found that the prevalence of these disorders was similar for all women, regardless of ethnicity. Furthermore, when subclinical levels of eating disorders were taken into account, the prevalence of all disorders increased across the board. It is important to note, however, that studies included in this meta-analysis were all from developed Western countries; therefore, it is unclear whether similar findings would be reported in countries where thinness is less emphasized (Wade et al., 2011).

Nevertheless, the most consistent finding in the literature is that symptoms related to eating disorders are more prevalent in Western European/North American populations than in non-European populations. Therefore, some researchers describe eating disorders as cultural syndromes because culture clearly plays a role in their development (Chisuwa & O'Dea, 2010; Pike et al., 2014). However, some finer distinctions may need to be made. Keel and Klump (2003) reviewed the literature, looking at incidence rates and historical evidence as well as the genetic heritability of anorexia nervosa and bulimia nervosa and concluded that bulimia nervosa seems to be a cultural syndrome but anorexia nervosa does not. They attribute this to there being a seemingly greater genetic base for anorexia nervosa.

Why do you think eating disorders might be more common in Western culture than in other cultures? Most authors relate this phenomenon to cultural differences in standards of beauty, with the Western ideal being a very thin body type. Some authors believe that eating disorders are on the rise in non-Western cultures because of increased exposure to Western standards of beauty through the media and the adoption of those standards through acculturation (Pike & Dunne, 2015; Smink et al., 2012; Thomas et al., 2010).

Some researchers argue that there is now adequate documentation that eating disorders are no longer exclusively a Western phenomenon. Eating disorders do exist in other countries and cultures and so should not be considered a cultural syndrome (Kolar et al., 2016; Musaiger et al., 2013; Pike et al., 2014; Smink et al., 2012). As mentioned, many people surmise that this is a result of increased exposure to Western culture around the globe. However, Nasser et al. (2001) indicate that this view is oversimplified. In their interdisciplinary critique of the issue, they examined other cultural, social, political, and economic forces that may influence the increased incidence and prevalence of eating disorders in non-Western cultures. For example, they noticed a rise in the rates of eating disorders in countries and groups in transition, such as among Black women in South Africa after the dismantling of apartheid and women in Russia after the fall of the Soviet Union.

Whereas eating disorders have been primarily associated with Western women, Asians are increasingly suffering from eating disorders as they are exposed to Western standards.

9.9 The Impact of the Pandemic on Mental Health

On 30 January 2020, the World Health Organization (WHO, 2020) declared that COVID-19 (coronavirus disease 2019) was a public health emergency at an international level and, therefore, a pandemic. China was already in lockdown, and within weeks, countries shut down one after another. In early March 2020, most Canadian cities went into lockdown. Businesses, banks, companies, factories, community centres, schools, universities, and government offices closed. People were urged to stay home and avoid social contact. Crowded cities became empty. There are eerie photos capturing the world in standstill.

As we write this textbook, the pandemic continues, and its full impact on mental health is not well understood. However, there is evidence of the negative consequences of the pandemic and social distancing on people around the world. The Canadian Psychological Association (2020) has already released several fact sheets examining the impact of COVID-19 on mental health, on relationships, on parenting, and on work. In addition, it has been suggested that the way individuals experience the pandemic is highly dependent on their culture (Ryder et al., 2020). For instance, the extent to which people follow rules of social isolation, quarantine, and health authorities' advice on better hygiene is a reflection of societal tightness and looseness. In tight societies, people are expected to follow the rules, and there are harsh punishments for violating the societal norms (e.g., China, Japan, Pakistan). In loose societies, in contrast, there are fewer expectations, and people are forgiven if they violate the norms (e.g., Australia, Canada, the US) (Gelfand et al., 2011). This distinction played out clearly and powerfully during COVID-19. The Chinese government put more than 50 million people under

An aerial view of usually crowded Bernard Avenue in Kelowna, British Columbia, in spring 2020.

mandatory quarantine and monitored their movement through their smartphones (Gelfand, 2020). Chinese people largely co-operated and came together to protect themselves and their fellow citizens. In North America, on the other hand, there was a sense of panic and egocentric behaviours. Perhaps you witnessed in your community that people were hoarding supplies, such as toilet paper, food, drinks, and even hand sanitizer. Some refused to wear face masks and did not follow strict social distancing rules. North Americans are not used to having their social behaviours tightly controlled (Gelfand, 2020).

A study conducted in Spain found that feelings of loneliness during the quarantine were common, and being in quarantine was a predictive factor for the development of depression, anxiety, and post-traumatic stress disorder (González-Sanguino et al., 2020). Interestingly, spiritual well-being was the most important protective factor against developing a mental-health issue. Shapiro et al. (2020) surveyed people in Israel on their mental health in April 2020, about a month after COVID-19 had reached the country. The study indicated that although participants reported high levels of anxiety and depression, they did not seek care for their mental health. Some participants reported barriers to access (e.g., financial challenges) of mental-health-care services. However, 87 per cent of the sample stated they did not think mental health services were needed, even though 25 per cent reported high or very high anxiety and worry. Overall, it has been suggested that the prevalence of depression during the pandemic was seven times more than the worldwide prevalence rate of depression in 2017, which was 3.44 per cent (Bueno-Notivol et al., 2021).

Furthermore, it has been found that vulnerable populations, including ethnic minorities, individuals with disabilities, and those in low socio-economic status were disproportionately impacted by the COVID-19 pandemic (Goldin & Muggah, 2020; The Lancet Public Health, 2021). The pandemic has exacerbated inequalities everywhere (Baroud, 2020). For example, those who worked in low-paid occupations, such as store attendants, garbage removal, and bus drivers, were considered essential workers and were more likely to come into contact with infected people. Adding to this was the fact that poor neighbourhoods became pandemic hotspots. Low-paid occupations also do not have the option of working from home, which tends to be available for high-paid occupations. Moreover, low-paid occupations were concentrated in the service, tourism, hotel, and restaurant sectors, which were hit hard during the pandemic, and their activities were suspended (Goldin & Muggah, 2020). In fact, millions of individuals lost their jobs globally due to COVID, yet there was a rise in the stock market and within only 12 weeks (18 March to 11 June 2020) US billionaires' wealth increased more than $637 billion. To put this into perspective, the wealth of the top five billionaires (Jeff Bezos, Bill Gates, Mark Zuckerberg, Warren Buffett, and Larry Ellison) grew 26 per cent or $101.7 billion, while over the same period 44 million Americans lost their jobs due to COVID-19 (Goldin & Muggah, 2020; Rushe, 2020). Inequalities such as these damage societies and have psychological consequences for people that make the process of recovering from the pandemic that much more difficult (Baroud, 2020; Pizzigati, 2021).

Summary

Many issues are related to culture and mental health, including the prevalence of disorders in different groups, how symptoms are expressed, and how disorders are diagnosed. In this chapter, we discussed the *ICD-11*, the *DSM*, and region-specific manuals to illustrate examples of classifications of mental disorders. Although there are many similarities in disorders across the world, there are also some cultural syndromes. These syndromes seem to be specific expressions of disorders that are connected to cultural values and traditions. We discussed epidemiologic studies, such as WHO-WMH, and illustrated some of their limitations, such as the small sample sizes of some groups and their diagnostic accuracy. We also discussed barriers to mental-health treatment and examined multicultural treatment as efforts at overcoming those barriers. These efforts include training mental-health professionals to be multiculturally competent. We also looked at the psychological impact of COVID-19. Overall, in this chapter we illustrated that, like every other aspect of human behaviour, culture influences mental health.

FOOD FOR THOUGHT

Most of us have encountered mental-health difficulties in our lives. Have you ever been so anxious before taking a test that you could not sleep the night before or concentrate on your studies for the test? Have you ever broken up with a partner and become very sad about it, making it difficult for you to enjoy things you usually enjoy? These are common forms of mental-health difficulties, called anxiety and depression. When people encounter issues such as these, they usually can get through a brief period of discomfort and then begin feeling back to normal. Think about a mental-health difficulty that you or someone close to you had to deal with. What were its characteristics? How did that make you feel? How did it impact your life?

Critical Thinking Questions

1. What do you think are the reasons for ethnic group differences in the rates of mental disorders? Why do you think ethnic groups often have lower rates of mental disorder than European Canadians?
2. Which approach do you think is more important: looking for common mental disorders across cultures or looking for cultural syndromes? What are the pros and cons of each approach?
3. What are the benefits of large-scale epidemiological studies? What are some of the challenges?
4. Have you or anyone in your family ever needed the services of mental-health professionals? If so, what was your/their experience like? Would you/they ever go again? How comfortable did you/they feel with the therapist? Was the therapist of the same ethnic group as you or your family member, or was the therapist from a different group?
5. If you have ever needed to see a mental-health professional, how easy or difficult was it to find such a professional? How easy or difficult was it to find a professional who spoke your preferred language? How easy or difficult was it to find transportation to this professional?

urbazon/Getty Images

10 Where Do We Go from Here? Building Cultural Competence

Learning Objectives

Reading this chapter will help you to:

10.1 define *cultural competence*;
10.2 identify how to increase your cultural awareness;
10.3 explain how to learn about your own culture;
10.4 recognize the differences between your own and others' world views;
10.5 describe how to develop culturally appropriate interpersonal skills; and
10.6 distinguish between a stagnant approach to cultural competence and a dynamic approach to increasing your cultural skills.

Our main goal for this book is to increase your knowledge and understanding of cultural issues and to bring those issues to life by sharing the personal stories of real people. By now you should have a good understanding of the theories, concepts, and methods of cultural and cross-cultural psychology, and you are probably more aware of how these issues affect you and those with whom you live, study, and work every day. We hope that you are now motivated to continue learning and growing as a person living in a diverse world and that this is just one step in your journey toward cultural competence.

10.1 Cultural Competence

What is cultural competence? As we discussed in Chapter 9, **cultural competence** means effectiveness in interacting with people who are different from you. It is the ability to have positive, productive, and enriching experiences with people from different backgrounds.

The concept of cultural competence originally related to the training of professional psychotherapists and counsellors to work with clients from diverse backgrounds. However, cultural competence is not just for people in the helping professions. Everyone can benefit from increasing their level of cultural competence. In Chapter 1, we described the growing diversification and globalization of all societies, including Canada. Such diversity affects almost every aspect of life and increases the chances that you will interact with people who are different from you in many ways.

Right now, if you are studying in a library or some other public place, chances are you will see someone of a different background—a different ethnicity, gender, age, sexual orientation, religion, or physical ability. As you sit in your classes each day, most likely you are in rooms with people of different backgrounds. At work, there are probably co-workers, customers, clients, and supervisors from different backgrounds. What about in the building or neighbourhood where you live? The stores you shop in every day? The point is, we live in a multicultural society and in an increasingly diverse world.

Have you heard the term *global village*? It refers to the fact that the world is getting smaller and smaller every day because of increased mobility and technology that allow us to travel and communicate with people all over the world in an instant. We live and work in a world full of many kinds of people, and it is important to learn to interact with them effectively. For example, if you go to school with people from different backgrounds, it would benefit you to be able to study and do projects with them more effectively. When you are job hunting, it looks good to potential employers if you have skills in working with diverse groups of people. Cultural competence, therefore, is a vital skill for everyone today. Cultural competence is the ability to understand and interact with people of diverse socio-cultural backgrounds in order to effectively provide relevant, high-quality care in culturally appropriate settings (Betancourt & Green, 2010).

In Chapter 9, we discussed the specific areas of cultural competence for professional psychologists. The four general areas of professional cultural competence are as follows:

1. Counsellors' awareness of their own cultural values and biases
2. An understanding of the client's world view
3. The development of culturally appropriate intervention strategies and techniques
4. Counselling and advocacy interventions

Each of these areas is further broken down into attitudes and beliefs, knowledge, skills, and actions (Ratts et al., 2015).

> **cultural competence** The ability to interact effectively with individuals who are of a culture different from one's own.

Although these competencies were developed for professional counsellors and therapists, they can be applied to your everyday life. In other words, each person can use these guidelines to improve relationships and interact effectively with people of different backgrounds. If we apply these principles to everyday interactions, they could read as follows:

- Awareness of your own cultural attitudes
- Understanding other world views and developing culturally appropriate interpersonal skills

Let us explore each of these areas further and see how they can be used to develop personal cultural competence.

10.2 Awareness of Your Own Cultural Attitudes

Cultural competence begins with awareness of your own attitudes and beliefs. An African proverb says, "Know thyself." Most cultural psychologists would agree that understanding your own beliefs, values, perceptions, feelings, reactions, and so on is critical in effective interactions with others. One way to increase self-awareness is to know how you react in cultural situations. In other words, how do you think, feel, and behave in situations with people who are different from you?

We can all think of times when we felt different. Perhaps as a child you were the last person picked for a dodgeball team, or were teased about being overweight, or were the only person of your ethnicity in a class. Maybe you have been to a party where you felt out of place because you did not know anyone there. Maybe you were the target of taunts and prejudiced remarks for being gay. Often experiences with being different are tied to a range of negative emotions, such as fear, humiliation, rejection, alienation, sadness, and anger. Our natural tendency is to avoid such painful and uncomfortable experiences and to minimize or hide the differences.

Often, having friends from different countries can increase one's cultural competence. People may have preconceived ideas about individuals from other countries. However, after meeting a variety of individuals with different backgrounds, one becomes more aware of cross-cultural similarities and differences, which could have a positive impact on their attitudes toward diversity (Jon, 2013).

The Four *F* Reactions: Freeze, Flee, Fight, and Fright

Our natural human response to a situation that is unfamiliar is to interpret it as a potential threat. This activates the **freeze**, **flee**, **fight**, or **fright** response. When we interpret a situation as a potential threat, our natural instinct is to first stop and evaluate the situation (freeze). The next reaction is to try to escape the danger (flee). If escape is not possible, we may become aggressive and try to fight off the danger (fight). If none of these strategies works, the next reaction may be to freeze up because we do not know what to do, because we hope we will not be noticed, or because escape is not possible and we are just waiting for the situation to be over (fright) (Bracha et al., 2004). These strategies may work for a zebra being preyed upon by a lion, and they may have also worked for human beings being chased by saber-toothed tigers in the prehistoric era, but when we are talking about relationships between human beings today, these strategies may not be as effective.

freeze To stop and try to interpret a situation that may be a potential threat.

flee An attempt to escape an uncomfortable or potentially dangerous situation.

fight If escape is not possible, we may attempt to be aggressive to defend against the danger we perceive.

fright Feelings of anxiety about a potentially dangerous situation.

TABLE 10.1 Harrell's Five *D*s of Difference

D term	Definition
Distancing	Avoiding situations in which one feels different
Denial	Pretending that differences do not exist
Defensiveness	Defending or protecting oneself from pain and fear
Devaluing	Evaluating a difference from oneself as unimportant or deficient
Discovery	Embracing differences and seeking opportunities to gain familiarity

Source: Reproduced with permission from Harrell, S. P. (2014). Compassionate confrontation and empathic exploration: The integration of race-related narratives in clinical supervision. In C. A. Falender, E. P. Shafranske, & C. J. Falicov (Eds.), *Multiculturalism and diversity in clinical supervision: A competency-based approach* (pp. 83–110). American Psychological Association. https://doi.org/10.1037/14370-004

The point is, it is natural to feel some stress, tension, or discomfort when we encounter people or situations that are different. It is even natural to feel afraid, to want to escape, to freeze up, or to even become angry and aggressive. Let's take a closer look at how people respond in situations in which they feel different.

The Five *D*s of Difference

Harrell (1995) uses the Five *D*s of Difference to explain people's reactions to situations in which they feel different. They are distancing, denial, defensiveness, devaluing, and discovery (Table 10.1).

Distancing

The first *D* of Difference is **distancing**, or avoiding situations in which we feel different. If we do not get too close to the difference, the possibility of negative experiences is minimized. Distancing can occur physically, emotionally, or intellectually. We may avoid going into situations in which we know we will be different. Many people do this by always spending time with people of similar backgrounds. Or, once we are in a situation in which we feel different, we may leave as soon as we can. If we are unable to leave the uncomfortable situation immediately, we may turn to various coping mechanisms.

Harrell (1995) suggests that pity is a form of emotional distancing. The person feeling the pity may feel superior to the people in the other group, and the recipient of the pity may feel ashamed or deviant. This emotional distancing prevents meaningful, sincere, honest interaction between the individuals as equals. People can also distance themselves intellectually and take a more scientific or objective approach to the situation:

> I am taking a sociology course right now . . . and we talked pretty briefly about [Indigenous] health and I was kind of disappointed that it was [only] one lecture. I felt [the professor] just kind of lacked. It was . . . rushed, and I think she just didn't address it enough considering it's such a big thing in Canada and it's a class about health in Canada. I felt like it was just brushed over.
>
> I'm sitting there [in class] and they're telling me about [Indigenous Peoples] and I'm like, "That doesn't sound right." And, it sounds a little weird to be taught by, I hate to say this, but a White person. I don't want somebody who's White to tell us how we lived, you know? 'Cause I'm sure they're experts and they know they're talking about, but it just

distancing The first of Harrell's Five *D*s of Difference; avoiding situations in which one feels different. Distancing can occur physically, emotionally, or intellectually.

> seems that sometimes the information isn't from what we know is correct and it seems more like a miseducation of the others. I know what's correct because I live it, you know. I've learned it from when I was born, but you have people who I find in my classes who are being miseducated on various issues.
> —*Indigenous student in Canada (Clark et al., 2014, p. 119)*

In the quote above, an Indigenous student discusses the way that their peers and teachers distance themselves from Indigenous issues and Indigenous-related education in their classes. They discuss how the lack of Indigenous consideration in academics has led to the distancing of Indigenous issues in many fields, including health, history, and sociology. It has also caused misinformation and miseducation in classrooms regarding the Indigenous experience.

Denial

When we encounter people and situations that are different or unfamiliar, our tendency may also be to deny the difference. This involves pretending not to see the difference, minimizing its importance, or ignoring it altogether. A common **denial** statement is, "People make too much out of differences. Aren't we all human beings? Don't we all have the same red blood running through our veins?" Some people say, "Oh, I don't see colour. I see a person." Often, people who use denial statements are well intentioned and believe they are paying a compliment to the person they are interacting with, but these statements are more harmful than helpful. Recipients of such a comment might feel an important part of their identity is denied, minimized, or ignored. The implication of the denial statement is that it would be somehow negative to notice that someone is Black, Indigenous, or a member of a particular ethnic group. Although it is true that many common experiences bind us together as human beings, there are also things that make us different and unique. Remember the tripartite model of personal identity (Sue, 2001) in Chapter 7? It describes the three parts of personal identity: individual, group, and universal. Although everyone has things in common, denying the differences may make others feel invisible, ignored, discounted, and unimportant, and that limits the ability to have meaningful, enriching interactions with one another.

denial The second of Harrell's Five *D*s of Difference; pretending that there is no difference between oneself and another, minimizing the difference's importance, or ignoring the difference altogether.

Defensiveness

The third *D* of Difference is **defensiveness**. Being defensive means trying to defend or protect oneself. Remember, unfamiliar situations are often perceived as threatening, which leads to feelings of discomfort, tension, and fear. Therefore, people react by trying to protect themselves from the perceived threat. People who get defensive maintain that they are not bothered by the difference.

A classic example of a defensive statement is "I'm not a racist!" Instead, the negative feelings associated with the difference are externalized and attributed to those other "bad, racist people." Another classic defensive statement is "I have lots of friends who are [minority group]." People making such a statement are trying to prove that they are not bothered by the difference. This attitude may even be seen among people who are very involved in working with oppressed groups. Their involvement may be their defence against the discomfort they feel with the difference.

It is often hard for people to admit that they are bothered by difference. To admit that they do have some racist or heterosexist ideas would be a threat to their self-image as an unbiased, fair, caring individual in a society where a high value is placed on equality. These people would be classified as aversive racists (see the discussion in Chapter 6); that is, they consciously feel that racism is aversive, yet they unconsciously hold racist views. To confront their discomfort with the difference would reveal a conflict of values. Those individuals who become involved

defensiveness The third of Harrell's Five *D*s of Difference; trying to protect oneself from acknowledging the difference between oneself and another to avoid feelings of discomfort or anxiety.

in diverse communities may feel hurt, rejected, disappointed, and confused when confronted with this contradiction.

Jodi, a Black woman, describes her experiences in her workplace that exemplify the defensiveness of White people when faced with racism:

> . . . While explaining [to colleagues] why a particular act might be perceived as racist or offensive, I've had White folks refuse to look at me and instead look at another White person with whom they agreed. White people have become visibly upset and have excluded me from meetings after I called out racist behaviours. . . . And then there were the fair-weather allies—the White folks who toed the party line in front of our White colleagues but would tell me in private that they agreed with me. . . . These acts of White fragility were ways for White people to avoid responsibility for how they contribute to racism and inequitable workplaces, ways for them to remain comfortable while preserving the illusion of honest and open dialogue.
>
> —Jodi M. Savage, Black woman, New York City–based writer and attorney
> (Savage, 2020, para. 12, pp. 14–16)

Jodi's description of White fragility and fair-weather allies emphasizes biases that White people may have despite their good intentions. Jodi also highlights that once she called out people on their biases, they reacted with hurt, shock, and feeling that their good intentions were not appreciated. The relationships between Jodi and her White co-workers illustrate the fourth *D* of Difference: devaluing.

The Black Lives Matter (BLM) movement has demonstrated how such distancing dynamics can manifest. This was especially illustrated in the activism and protests that stemmed from George Floyd's murder by a police officer in May 2020 in Minneapolis, US. Many Canadians, both Black and non-Black, attended protests in support of the BLM movement across the country (Juric, 2020). However, as an article by Undi (2020) from CBC News reported, many Black Lives Matter activists in Canada have had concerns with some White and non-Black allyship dynamics. As the movement spread, many people tried to show their support on social media. This kind of support left some wondering whether online actions would translate into actions offline, particularly after the momentum died down and it was no longer trendy to show daily, public support of BLM. As the article states, raising awareness performatively or just because others expect you to rather than actually caring about fixing injustices is not an effective allyship. One criticism is that non-Black activists should be listening, learning, and amplifying Black voices, rather than speaking over or for Black people (Juric, 2020). Attending protests is also not the only way non-Black people can combat racism; education and action in daily life can make a huge difference, but the concern is that this is not necessarily happening often. Thus, tensions can actually increase between some activists and allies despite having a common goal, which demonstrates just how complex social issues can be.

Devaluing

As mentioned earlier, one of the first things we do when we encounter something different is evaluate it. Unfortunately, we often have the tendency to see things that are different or unfamiliar as strange, weird, or even scary. This reflects the tendency toward **devaluing**, which is the fourth *D* of Difference. Thomas Parham, coauthor of the book *The Psychology of Blacks* (Parham et al., 1999), calls this the *difference equals deficiency* logic. In other words, we tend to see things that are different as deficient, or less than.

Think about your initial reaction when someone wants you to try a new food. You may turn your nose up at it before you have even tried it. The automatic assumption may be, "I'm

devaluing The fourth of Harrell's Five *D*s of Difference; assessing the difference between oneself and another as deficient or less important.

A Black Lives Matter mural by artist DENIAL is displayed in Montreal's Plateau Mont-Royal neighbourhood.

not going to like that!" What about when you meet someone, such as a new roommate or co-worker? On one level, you may be excited about meeting the new person, but on another level you immediately begin to form a social hierarchy (you may recall this from your social psychology course in terms of social comparison). Is this person taller than I am? More attractive? Smarter? Wealthier? You want to see how you measure up. Our natural tendency as human beings is to preserve and increase our self-esteem, so we naturally want to place ourselves higher on the scale than the other person. In other words, we find ways to devalue things about the other person to help ourselves feel more comfortable.

Another way to look at it is that to devalue is to maintain a feeling of superiority. We feel better about ourselves when we see others who are different as deviant, primitive, immoral, lazy, stupid, and so on. When we devalue people who are different, it is easier to justify our negative feelings. The fear and threat may then become anger and rage. We can justify our negative feelings about "those people" because of their bad or immoral behaviour. Examples of devaluing statements are "AIDS is God's punishment on gay people for their immoral behaviour" and "If Black people would just work harder, they could find jobs, do better in school, and get ahead in this world."

People tend to devalue what they see as different, such as an accent. This devaluation can exist in the workplace, as some employers devalue accents because they hold the false belief that people with accents have inadequate communication skills. Similarly, sometimes we devalue things that are different and do not realize it. For example, people may describe something or someone from a different culture as exotic. Often they mean that as a compliment, but to the intended recipient, it can be an insult. Whereas some might see it as positive, the word *exotic* also implies "different" or "strange" and hence not understandable. At the very least, it means "something unlike me."

Thus far, the *D*s of Difference sound very negative, but they are natural human tendencies. It is natural to feel uncomfortable in an unfamiliar situation, and we naturally respond by trying to decrease that discomfort. As we saw in Chapter 6, it is not bad that we have

discovery The fifth of Harrell's Five *D*s of Difference; appreciating the difference between oneself and another, seeing how enriching that difference may be, and seeking out opportunities to gain familiarity.

stereotypes, but it is bad when we let them negatively affect our relationships with others. The same is true of the *D*s of Difference: we must be aware of the feelings, acknowledge them, and then take action to prevent them from negatively affecting our interactions.

Discovery

The last *D* of Difference, **discovery**, is a positive experience. Encounters with people from different backgrounds are opportunities for discovery. Discovery means embracing and seeking greater familiarity with difference (Harrell, 1995). It involves working through the discomfort and anxiety, rather than avoiding it. It means experiencing differences as challenges and opportunities for learning and growth.

An attitude of discovery means being willing to stretch and get outside our comfort zones. It means taking risks and feeling uncomfortable sometimes. It means keeping an open mind and being open to new experiences, new places, new things, and new people. By doing so, we enrich our own lives and the lives of others. The negative feelings associated with difference are natural. We all experience them. Their purpose is to protect us. We will not be able to eliminate those negative feelings, but with them comes the opportunity for personal growth and improved interpersonal and intergroup relations.

Katie, a European-American student, illustrates the benefits of discovery:

> I had the opportunity to go to a community in Mexico to fellowship with the people there. The first year I did not go because ultimately the language barrier made me feel uncomfortable. I kept focusing on the fact that I would be in a community of people for an entire week and I could not say anything but *hola* and *adiós*. I was scared of social

Experiencing other cultures can be an enriching experience.

situations. I did not want to have to face the "awkwardness" of not understanding someone in conversation. In the five Ds of difference, I was distancing myself from a situation that was unfamiliar to me. However, the next three years in a row, I decided to go, and I experienced discovery there. I realized just how quickly one could pick up a language when they are immersed in it for a period of time. I was able to make lasting friendships, and to think I never would have had the blessing of experiencing such friendships . . . all because I was afraid of something that was unfamiliar to me.

I have realized and encouraged others to realize that staying in one's comfort zone is, well, comforting, but it's not nearly as rewarding as stepping out of it to find so much more about other people, and even oneself.

—*Katie, 20+-year-old European-American student*

Katie comes from a predominantly European-American background. At first, she distanced and turned down the opportunity to volunteer in Mexico due to her anticipated discomfort at encountering people who spoke a different language. However, the next year she worked up the courage and took on an attitude of discovery. She opened her mind, took a risk, got out of her comfort zone, and took advantage of the opportunity to learn and experience something new.

Discovery can also be fun if you can fight through your initial desire to distance yourself from the situation. Rayanne discovered this in a tasty way:

Since it was around Christmas and I was meeting new people, I decided to get dressed up. Around the holidays my family always gets dressed up when they get together—nothing too fancy, maybe a nice sweater or blouse. Besides that, I wanted to look cute, after all I was meeting my boyfriend's family for the first time. Unfortunately, I looked too nice—in fact, I stood out from everyone else. Since his family was making tamales, which are very messy, his family was dressed in old jeans and sweatshirts. On top of being the new girl, they looked at me funny for wearing a skirt to make tamales.

After a couple of minutes, I was no longer uncomfortable by my appearance. It was a long night of making tamales, but I enjoyed the time I spent with them. When we left, they invited me back to eat the tamales with them on Christmas Eve. So, the next night I went back and enjoyed the food we worked so hard to make the night before.

It was very interesting to observe his family's traditions. Every year his family does the same thing around Christmas. . . . I've discovered that other Hispanic families do the same thing around Christmas. They go to a relative's house to make tamales the day before Christmas Eve and then come back on Christmas Eve to eat them and open presents up at midnight. At first, I compared my family to his and made remarks like, "That's not what my family does," but now I embrace our differences.

—*Rayanne, 20+-year-old European-American student*

The Ds of Difference are useful in increasing awareness of your own attitudes and beliefs regarding cultural issues. They help you understand your desire to stick with situations and groups that are familiar and how you react when you encounter people, things, or situations that are different or unfamiliar. You can also increase your cultural competence by becoming more aware of your attitudes and beliefs about other cultures.

Increased awareness includes examining your own biases, prejudices, and stereotypes. In Chapter 6, we mentioned that biases, prejudices, and stereotypes by themselves are not necessarily bad. We naturally develop them as human beings. Stereotypes help us summarize

Stepping outside one's comfort zone can lead to discovery about oneself.

and organize all the millions of bits of information our senses and brains are bombarded with every day. Biases and prejudices are a natural outcome of growing up in a society built on them.

The Museum of Tolerance in Los Angeles has an exhibit with two doors. One is marked Racist; the other, Non-Racist. You must pass through one of these doors to continue to the next section of the museum. The only problem is that the door marked Non-Racist is locked, which forces everyone to go through the door marked Racist. The point is obvious: we all harbour racist thoughts and ideas. These thoughts and ideas become bad when we allow them to negatively affect our relationships with others. Even if we are not aware we have them, they still have an effect on us. The goal is to be aware of our racist thoughts and ideas so we can better control them, challenge them, and prevent them from negatively affecting our interactions.

10.3 Learning about Your Own Culture

Self-awareness also involves learning about your own culture and its effect on your personal attitudes and beliefs. As we discussed in Chapter 7, your personal perceptions and feelings about your own culture are an important part of your ethnic identity. These feelings may be positive, negative, or mixed. It is important to become aware of your thoughts, feelings, and behaviours as they relate to people of your own group.

Students of colour are not the only ones who can benefit from exploring their own culture. Some of you, especially those of you from a White-European background, may be saying, "I don't have a culture." Students often say things like, "Whenever we start talking about culture in class, I feel left out because I don't really have a culture." Or, "I'm boring. I'm just White." We hope you now understand that everyone has a culture. The statement "I have no culture" is very ethnocentric. It implies that your own culture is the norm and that everything else is different or abnormal. It means that you use your own culture as the standard against which all others are measured. Once you do that, you risk the pitfalls described as the Ds of Difference, such as devaluing other cultures.

Many of you identify with being Canadian. Whether you identify as Anglo Canadian, French Canadian, African-Caribbean Canadian, Latino Canadian, or Arab Canadian, Canadian is still part of your identity. But what does it mean to be a Canadian? Ricardo Larrivée, a Montreal-based television host and food writer, shares his definition:

> To me, being Canadian means the beauty of having friends who don't all think the same way. It is having the restraint to not hurt others in a political, economic, or religious conversation. . . . Canada has a sense of community that can be intimidating to those who haven't had the chance to experience the power of its vision of justice and social equality.
> —*Ricardo Larrivée, a Montreal-based television host and food writer*
> *(Larrivée, 2019, paras. 6–8)*

In this excerpt, Ricardo reflects on the freedom that he feels exists in Canada. He mentions the ability to express himself politically, culturally, religiously—freely and without fear. Ricardo also emphasizes the sense of community and unity that he has experienced.

Alternatively, Roshaan reflects on her identity as a Canadian. She immigrated to Canada from Pakistan at 11 years old and found the adjustment to Canadian society to be very difficult:

> . . . being Canadian may mean different things to different people. For some, being Canadian may mean having been born and raised in Canada. For others, being Canadian may mean moving to a new community and becoming acclimated to a new home. Being Canadian may also mean facing the trauma of oppression, displacement, and disenfranchisement. Being Canadian may mean all of these things or none of these things, but it most definitely means coming together as a country and listening to the voices of everyone.
> —*Roshaan, a Pakistani immigrant to Canada to (Pathways to Education, 2020, para. 12)*

Throughout her childhood and new Canadian upbringing, Roshaan faced many hardships and difficulties, trying to accommodate both her Pakistani identity and her Canadian identity, wondering if she could truly have both (Pathways to Education, 2020). That is why she explains that being Canadian means different things for each person. Some people may have lived in Canada their whole lives, and to them, Canada is home, but others may have struggled in trying to make Canada their home (Pathways to Education, 2020).

Canada is a country made up of many different cultural groups. One person's definition of what it means to be Canadian may be different from another's. For example, for Ricardo, a French Canadian, to be different is to be Canadian; for Roshaan, however, there is no singular Canadian identity. Being Canadian may mean acceptance to some and struggle to others; no two experiences are the same, and all these experiences are valid. An important part of cultural competence is first increasing your knowledge about your own group. Even something as simple as exploring the food of your culture can be a method for learning about your own group. Another place to start is with your family: interview your parents, grandparents, and other relatives. Ask them to tell you about family stories, traditions, and personalities, and record the

People have different values when it comes to their national identity. How do you define your Canadian identity?

interview. Begin working on a family tree. Take classes that focus on Canada. Attend cultural events and celebrations. Read books.

While it may not always be feasible for first- or second-generation immigrants to return to their homeland, incorporating their family's heritage and traditions into their lives, taking classes, reading books, watching films and television programs, and attending cultural events and celebrations are something that can enhance people's connection to their ancestry. Knowledge about your own group provides a springboard for learning about other groups. Knowing yourself gives you the confidence to go out and learn about others who are different from you.

We have spent a large portion of this chapter discussing the first area of cultural competence: awareness of your own cultural values and biases. That is because self-awareness is arguably the most important part of cultural competence. Knowing yourself gives you the strength and the confidence to learn about other cultures and provides you with a foundation on which to build the other aspects of cultural competence. Let us turn now to the second part of cultural competence: understanding other world views.

10.4 Understanding Other World Views

Although knowing and understanding your own culture is vital to cultural competence, it is also important to learn about other cultures. Part of cultural competence is obtaining basic knowledge about different groups. Although each person within a culture is unique, there are some general facts about each cultural group that are helpful to know, such as the group's history, current socio-political concerns, and knowing the group's core values and beliefs.

Learning Key Historical Events

Just as it is important to know your own history, it is important to know the key historical events that influenced other groups. For example, to truly understand Indigenous culture, you must study the history of colonization and its continued impact on Canadian culture. In particular, understanding the lasting consequences of residential schools on Indigenous communities is crucial. In an attempt to assimilate Indigenous Peoples into European-Canadian culture, Indigenous children were forcefully taken from their homes and stripped of their native language and culture. This resulted in many Indigenous children losing their sense of self, as they felt as though they did not belong to either the Indigenous or settler society (Miller, 2012). Although the last residential school closed in 1996 (Miller, 2012), the impact of these schools is intergenerational. Residential schools caused a general loss of language and culture, which brings forth feelings of alienation, shame, and anger that are still felt by many Indigenous Peoples to this day (Manitoba Trauma Information and Education Center, 2020).

It is also important to know the history of the different immigrant groups. As we discussed in Chapter 5, there is a difference between groups who immigrate voluntarily, such as those who come looking for a better education and better job opportunities, and refugees who come involuntarily, escaping war or political or religious persecution.

Becoming Aware of Socio-political Issues

Becoming aware of current socio-political issues affecting various cultural groups is also key to cultural competence. For example, the United Nations (UN, 2020) reports that people fleeing their country of birth due to conflict, fear of persecution, or natural disasters (e.g., floods, hurricanes, earthquakes) is a global crisis in the twenty-first century. In 2018, 57 per cent of UN refugees came from only three countries: Syria, Afghanistan, and South Sudan (UN, 2020). The majority of refugees (80 per cent) end up living in their neighbouring countries, and the top refugee-hosting countries are Turkey, Pakistan, Uganda, Sudan, and Germany (UN, 2020). Such large-scale displacement creates challenges for both refugee groups and their host countries. Being aware of socio-political issues surrounding factors that force people to be displaced and paying attention to characteristics of the societies and communities that refugees have to adjust to are important in creating a harmonious relationship between people from different cultural backgrounds. Recognizing the enormous challenges that children of refugees, women, and youth encounter is a critical step in the path of protecting this vulnerable and heterogeneous group.

After the war that created the State of Israel in 1948, many Palestinian families were forced to settle in refugee camps in the West Bank or the Gaza Strip (Amnesty International, 2019). These areas are incredibly dense and overcrowded, with some of the highest numbers of refugees in the world (Amnesty International, 2019). The West Bank and Gaza Strip are surrounded by concrete walls eight metres high and military watchtowers, with checkpoints that are controlled by the Israeli military (Amnesty International, 2019). Moreover, the Israeli government restricts the movement of Palestinian refugees. The Al Jawarash family has lived in the Aida Refugee Camp in occupied Palestine for many years (Amnesty International, 2019). For this family, the movement restrictions mean not seeing their hometown of Al Malha (Amnesty International, 2019). Thair, the father, describes dreaming of the day they can go back to their home:

> I am going to go back to my land. I am suffocated in this camp, but I am going to stay until I can go back to my land. I am a man of the land. Our right to return is the most important thing to our resistance. Whether it is in one, two, or even ten more years . . . it doesn't matter; we will return to our land. I will die in this camp until then. We are not going to give up being refugees because we want our right to return. Yes, the occupation is harsh, but the tear gas has not killed us. The bullets have not killed us. The tanks have not killed us. All of this and we still have not lost our dignity. The Palestinian people are still living, and I am not leaving. (Amnesty International, 2019, para. 13)

Within the refugee camps, protests and demonstrations by the Palestinian people against the Israeli occupation occur frequently (Amnesty International, 2019). These protests are often broken up by the military using tear gas and rubber bullets (Amnesty International, 2019). One study asked 236 Aida Refugee Camp residents if they had been exposed to tear gas as a result of the Israeli military raids in 2017, and how often (Haar & Ghannam, 2018). The results showed that 100 per cent of the 236 residents surveyed had been exposed to tear gas in 2017, and some respondents were reported to have been exposed to tear gas up to three times a week (Haar & Ghannam, 2018). For the Al Jawarash family, tear gas has greatly impacted every member of the family. One of the daughters, Sileen, had her first experience with tear gas at four months old, when a canister was thrown into her home by the Israeli army to disperse nearby protests against the occupation (Amnesty International, 2019). The gas had entered the room where Sileen was sleeping. By the time the paramedics were called, Sileen had fallen unconscious and was thought to be dead but was later resuscitated on her way to the hospital (Amnesty International, 2019). Her mother recounts the events and describes the reckless use of tear gas:

> The Israeli army was firing tear gas at the whole camp; it was not just focused on our house. The jeeps can shoot hundreds of tear gas canisters at a time and the camp is so small that it reaches everyone. No matter where you go, you are suffocated in this camp. Where are we supposed to go? You close the door, and the gas comes. You close the windows and it's the same. It doesn't matter. (Amnesty International, 2019, para. 10)

Being a refugee in your own country and never being able to return to your home is the reality for thousands of Palestinians in the West Bank and the Gaza Strip (Amnesty International, 2019). A 2016 survey of Palestinian families living in the Gaza Strip found that over 16,000 families that were displaced to the Gaza Strip were living in desperate conditions (UN Office for the Coordination of Human Affairs, 2016). The survey results showed that 80 per cent of these families had to borrow money to pay for living expenses in the past year, and 85 per cent

Graffiti by British artist Banksy, in Palestine. Banksy's art on the wall surrounding the Gaza Strip has contributed to a global awareness of the Israel-Palestine conflict.

had purchased most of their food on credit. As well, 40 per cent of families had decreased their consumption of food due to lack of funds and 50 per cent feared eviction from their already inadequate accommodations (UN Office for the Coordination of Human Affairs, 2016). The 2019 Human Rights Watch Report for Israel and Palestine highlighted that for the over 17,000 people who were displaced during the Israeli occupation, most remain in inadequate housing and conditions (Human Rights Watch, 2019). The families living in Gaza also face limited access to electricity, hospital operations, clean water, and sewage treatment as a result of disputes and limits on resources set by the Israeli army and government (Human Rights Watch, 2019). As explained by the Al-Jawarash family, conflicts like these have massive impacts on the families caught in the middle and affect the quality of life for the thousands involved.

Knowing Basic Values and Beliefs of Other World Views

Aside from factual knowledge about different cultural groups, understanding other world views also involves knowing the basic values and beliefs of these groups. In Chapter 3, we compared and contrasted the world views of different cultural groups. We emphasized that although each individual is unique, there are broad concepts that characterize each group. Knowing something about an individual's culture helps you formulate hypotheses that can be explored in your interactions with that person.

For example, it is helpful to know that Latino culture tends to be patriarchal, with more traditional gender roles. In Latin America, women are expected to be subordinate, self-sacrificing, chaste, and virgins until marriage (Castillo, et al., 2010; Gibbons & Luna, 2015). Therefore, it is possible that female Latino students encounter unique challenges being in university compared to other female students. They may have more family responsibilities at home, such as taking care of younger siblings, and these may be seen as a higher priority than their studies. One female Latina student said, "My family is always asking me when I'm going to get married and have babies." However, we cannot assume that this is the case for all Latino students because it is not, but such information helps us to know basic values and beliefs of a particular cultural group.

Understanding Cultural Practices

It is also helpful to know and understand cultural practices. These are behaviours that may be normal and expected and have a particular meaning in a culture. The following quote highlights differences between Ghanaian and Canadian culture and the importance of knowing about the values, beliefs, and practices of such different groups in order to increase your level of cultural competence.

> From my culture in Ghana, all family members live in the same big house. This is fathers, mothers, aunties, uncles, siblings, and sometimes even friends can come and live with you without paying any money. What surprised me [about Toronto] was that you cannot even get a place to stay without paying rent. Even if a friend allows you to come live with [them], you still have to pay rent. This was something that really stood out for me. . . . I came to live with friends who I knew very well in Ghana and the person had lived with me in my house for free before [in Ghana]. When I came [to Toronto], after the first month he started charging me for rent. This means there is no free stuff in Canada even if they are your family members.
> —Ghanaian man who moved to Toronto, Canada (Mensah & Williams, 2014, p. 450)

Knowing the Dynamics of Racism, Discrimination, and Stereotyping

Another aspect of understanding other world views is knowledge of the dynamics of racism, oppression, discrimination, and stereotyping. We discussed each of these concepts in detail in Chapter 6, so it is not necessary to explain them again here. However, it is important to understand how these forces affect people in their everyday lives. A student who was active in an on-campus gay/lesbian community said that one of the main factors influencing formation of a gay/lesbian community was the oppression and discrimination experienced by members of their group. They bonded because they had common sexual orientations but also because they had a common "enemy" and came together for protection and support.

In Chapter 7, we discussed one of the early studies by Clark and Clark (1939) in which African-American children preferred White dolls to Black dolls. The researchers concluded that Black children had lower self-esteem because of the racism and discrimination experienced by their group and because of the negative portrayals of Black people in the media. Remember our discussion of identity development in Chapter 7? All individuals from a diverse background must resolve their status in relation to the dominant culture and how their own group is perceived and treated by the dominant group. This also relates to the discussion of similarity in this chapter, in which students sought out members of their own group after having negative experiences with members of the dominant group. These examples illustrate how racism, discrimination, oppression, and stereotypes have an impact on individuals and on their development, personality, and behaviour. It is important to understand these forces and their impact on your interactions with others.

10.5 Developing Culturally Appropriate Interpersonal Skills

The first two dimensions of cultural competence involve awareness—of your own cultural attitudes and of other world views. You might be wondering, "Once I become aware of all these things, what do I do?" It is true that awareness is essential, but it is not enough. You must act on that awareness and take concrete steps toward building positive relationships with people from different backgrounds. That is where part three of cultural competence comes in—developing culturally appropriate interpersonal skills.

A skill is the ability to do something well, or the ability to do something with accuracy and ease. Skills are developed through training, experience, and practice (Warren, 1995). Cultural competence is an interpersonal skill. It is the ability to interact effectively with others who are different from you. To achieve this, you must have education, training, experience, and practice in working with people from different groups. This section describes specific strategies for increasing your level of cultural competence.

Participating in Education and Training

A skill is developed through education and training. Reading this book and taking this class are significant steps toward your cultural education and training. From them, you gain knowledge that can serve as a foundation for developing further competence. You can take more classes and attend lectures, workshops, seminars, and retreats that focus on cultural issues. For example, you can take a class that focuses on a specific cultural group, such as a women's studies course or a course on a particular religion. That will allow you to learn in more depth about some of the topics covered in this class. Or you can learn another language. Learning how individuals from another culture communicate is a great way to understand the culture better, and knowing another language opens the door to many opportunities. See Table 10.2 for a list of things to do to increase your cultural competence.

TABLE 10.2 Concrete Things to Do to Increase Your Cultural Competence

- Take more classes and attend lectures, workshops, seminars, and retreats on cultural issues.
- Read books, magazines, and journals on cultural issues.
- Watch relevant films, television shows, and videos on diverse issues.
- Listen to music and attend plays, concerts, and other cultural events and celebrations.
- Research issues related to diversity.
- Develop relationships with people from diverse backgrounds.
- Get involved in cultural organizations.
- Develop the ability to say "I don't know" and to ask questions. You cannot possibly know everything, so allow others to help you develop your knowledge.
- Travel to experience different cultures directly.
- Be an ally and speak up on behalf of others.
- Speak up on behalf of yourself and your group.
- Develop a level of comfort discussing difficult issues.
- Have an attitude of discovery and be open to new experiences.
- Have the courage to take risks and step outside your comfort zone.
- Develop empathy for others, their experiences, and their perspectives.

You can also attend lectures, seminars, and workshops offered on your campus. College and university campuses offer a wealth of opportunities for cultural education. Programs are usually available throughout the year, but a particularly good time is during cultural emphasis months, such as Black History Month, Women's Herstory Month, and LGBTQ2+ Month. If your campus does not offer diversity retreats or something similar, look for organizations in your area that do. For instance, there is a Canadian Multiculturalism Day (27 June), which enables individuals to celebrate cultural diversity and appreciate the contribution of multicultural groups to Canada (Government of Canada, n.d.). There are also educational opportunities for multiculturalism and multicultural competence. For example, the Canadian Multicultural Education Foundation (CMEF) regularly hosts workshops on racism, conferences, and exhibits across Canada and offers opportunities for individuals to volunteer (Canadian Multicultural Education Foundation, n.d.). In the past, CMEF has hosted seminars that discuss the Syrian-Refugee Crisis and a heritage exhibition of wedding gowns, photos, and stories of nine multicultural families in Edmonton, Alberta (CMEF, n.d.). The foundation's mission is to strengthen the sense of multiculturalism in Canada through educational and community programs (CMEF, n.d.).

Local museums are another source of cultural education. Museums often host exhibits, lectures, and other programs related to cultural issues. Some museums focus on a particular culture. In Canada, there are numerous museums that highlight the cultural diversity of Indigenous groups in Canada. Most notably, the *Musée Canadien de L'histoire* (Canadian Museum of History) in Quebec is a popular museum for learning about the history of the First Nations, Métis, and Inuit peoples (Musée Canadien de L'histoire, n.d.). Online exhibits in the summer of 2020 covered such moments in Canadian history as the history of voting, the history of Indigenous Peoples, the Yukon dog sled postal service, and others (Musée Canadien de L'histoire, n.d.). Another example is the Apartheid Museum in Johannesburg, South Africa, which is well-known for teaching about the prevalent social oppression in that country's history. The museum's permanent exhibitions include those on race classification, segregation, political executions, Mandela's release, and more (Apartheid Museum, n.d.).

You can also further your cultural education by reading books and journals. Literature provides a wonderful window into different worlds. You gain access to the words, private thoughts, and experiences of individuals from different backgrounds. Other suggestions for cultural education and training include watching relevant films, television shows, or videos, doing online research, listening to music, and attending plays, concerts, and other cultural events and celebrations.

Laryssa Gorecki is a high school teacher who arranged for her students to participate in a YMCA student exchange program in Thunderchild First Nation in Northern Saskatchewan. In the following quote, she explains how participating in an exchange program requires a lot of preparation in order to be a rewarding experience for everyone involved:

> [My] students had all taken the English: Understanding Contemporary First Nations, Métis, and Inuit Voices course I teach at James Cardinal McGuigan (JCM) high school—a course designed to honour Indigenous voices. But I wanted to push that education further by having my students participate in authentic experiential learning: being immersed in a First Nations community, engaging in rich discussion with the youth and Elders, and forming relationships that would bridge the gap between our cultures.
>
> The project required an enormous amount of preparation—both logistically and emotionally. We explored stereotypes and learned about how to respectfully enter into an Indigenous community. We participated in a workshop . . . that teaches about the impacts of colonialism and connects participants to the historical facts in a heart-based way.

Museums, such as the Canadian Museum of History pictured here, are good sources of cultural education.

> When we arrived at Piyesiw Awasis school [at the Thunderchild First Nations Reserve], we were graciously greeted in a welcoming ceremony by all 250 students and teachers, who shook each of our hands, saying, "*Tansi*" (welcome). My students formed immediate relationships with the host students. They played co-operative games and volleyball, . . . listened to music, and watched movies together. They talked about social media, family, traditions, and hobbies.
>
> They were so alike and so eager to learn about one another. At the end, the students participated in a sharing circle where they were able to openly and honestly express their thoughts and feelings regarding their newfound relationships. It was moving for me to see such a wonderful example of trauma-informed and anti-colonial relationship-building.
>
> Over the course of the week, my students engaged in land-based learning activities, including teepee-building, hide-stretching, fire-building, and hiking. They visited historic sites and museums in neighbouring communities. A lucky few were even able to participate in a Sweat Lodge ceremony. Thunder-child shared their teachings, traditions, languages, artwork, and dance. Students met with Elders, watched a traditional powwow demonstration, and participated in a round dance. (Adapted or reprinted in part with permission from Gorecki, L., 2020. Connecting through cultural exchange. Education Canada. https://www.edcan.ca/articles/cultural-exchange/. Copyright [2020] *Education Canada* magazine.)

Laryssa describes the necessity of confronting stereotypes and educating students about Indigenous culture prior to the exchange to ensure that they were informed and respectful. Students learned about Indigenous culture first-hand by participating in traditional events and learning directly from Indigenous elders. This type of learning, as well as the preparation the students underwent before the exchange, allowed them to have a valuable and respectful experience.

Gaining Experience and Practice

The more education and training you have in cultural issues, the more experience you accumulate and the more opportunities you have to practise your newfound skills. Practice is necessary to perform any new skill with accuracy and ease. You can gain more experience and practise your culturally appropriate interpersonal skills by seeking out opportunities to interact with people who are different from you. Reach out and develop relationships with people from diverse backgrounds. Start a conversation with people sitting next to you in class. Volunteer to work with them on a group project, or invite them to study, go to lunch, or have a cup of coffee with you.

You can also get involved with cultural organizations on your campus. Some campuses have cultural centres, one for each of the major cultural groups. We encourage students to get involved with their own centre, as well as others. Cultural centres often put on programs highlighting cultural heritage, and they appreciate individuals of all cultures who are willing to serve on planning committees.

Saying "I Don't Know" and Asking Questions

Two related skills that are important to learn when reaching out to others from different cultures are the ability to say "I don't know" and the ability to ask questions. It is impossible to learn everything from taking a class or reading a book. Individual people are an invaluable source of information. People are often hesitant to admit they don't know something because they don't want to look ignorant, stupid, or insensitive, and they are afraid to ask because they don't want to offend. However, it is better to ask a question than to remain ignorant. You run a greater risk of offending someone if you interact with them on the basis of assumptions and stereotypes that may be incorrect, as the following story illustrates:

> People assume that I don't speak English, that I speak Spanish first, so they'll . . . say "*Hola*." When people find out that I'm not from Central or South America, [when] they find out that I'm [Indigenous], they often assume that I'm from the North and [that I must] have a harder time understanding what people are saying or what we are discussing.
>
> —Indigenous undergraduate student in Canada (Clark et al., 2014, p. 118)

This student has had negative experiences from assumptions people have made based on this student's skin colour and Indigenous background. This example demonstrates why cultural competence is important. Instead of making assumptions, this student's peers should have asked questions in order to get to know the student better, which is less likely to leave the student feeling hurt or offended. Most people will not be offended if you ask questions in a respectful and caring manner. It shows them that you are genuinely interested in getting to know them and their culture, and they will likely appreciate your interest and effort.

Travelling

Another strategy for building culturally appropriate interpersonal skills is travelling. St Augustine wrote, "The world is a book, and those who do not travel read only one page." Travelling to other countries opens up the world to you and changes your perspective. When you travel, you interact with people from another culture. You see them in their daily lives as they work, play, and love. You experience their food, music, language, sights, and sounds.

Travel helps you learn about others, as well as yourself. There are lessons learned and skills obtained when you travel that are hard to gain any other way. We cannot overstate the benefits of experiencing another culture first-hand.

Travelling is a great way to develop communication skills and discover alternative world views. You don't have to travel far to learn about another culture. Most cities have cultural centres or neighbourhoods where people of one particular culture tend to gather and live. These neighbourhoods often have names that reflect that culture, such as Chinatown or Little Tokyo. You can learn a lot by visiting these cultural centres, walking the streets, eating at the restaurants, shopping at the stores, visiting the churches, and talking to the residents. With technology, we are able to travel the world and learn about other cultures without even leaving our homes. We can use the internet to learn about and virtually experience other cultures.

Speaking Up for Others: Being an Ally

Another important interpersonal skill is learning to be an ally. (Recall our discussion in Chapter 6.) An ally is someone from a privileged group who speaks up for and supports individuals from oppressed minority groups. For example, if you are heterosexual, you can speak up when you hear someone make a negative comment about LGBTQ2+ people. If you are in a class and hear someone make a comment based on stereotypes, you can point that out. Supporting individuals from oppressed or marginalized groups relieves them of some of the burden they carry every day. Often, individuals feel the pressure of having to represent their entire ethnic group in their classes. If you see that happening in a class, you can speak up in support of that person.

When we speak up on behalf of others, we teach important lessons, as illustrated by the following story:

> Playing by the rules to be part of the "model minority" allowed me [a Chinese-Canadian woman] to be "White-adjacent": I wasn't White, but I was seen by some White people as less "offensive" than other ethnicities. I had the great privilege to not have to grow up being scared of authorities such as police officers, unlike people who are Black or Indigenous.
>
> In reality, the "model minority" concept is really about having implicit rules of engagement to make Asians stay silent about the White power structure that's more overtly racist of other racialized and minority groups. My entire extended family, partly based on their own previous experiences of overt racism, all bought into the "model minority" requirement that allowed us to be "accepted," albeit on the White power structure's terms. Thus, my family and I have been complicit in anti-Black racism as Chinese Canadians.
>
> I've been complicit in perpetuating anti-Black racism by not calling out obviously racist comments that I heard in my Chinese community, and by striving to maintain the benefits I received by being a "model minority." This is personally painful.

I now own my part in holding up racist structures while also acknowledging my privilege as a physician. It took me many years to embrace that I have a duty to use my areas of privilege for good to speak out against racism and injustice.

We may not have White privilege, but we'll use the privilege we do have to speak up for the human rights of those people who can't. This is what we can do as anti-racist allies. We will not opt-out. As Ibram Kendi states in his book How to be an Anti-Racist, *anti-racism involves actively fighting racist policies and ideas that lead to racial inequity. There is no "neutral" in this space, so it's not possible to be "not racist."*

—Amy Tan, a Chinese-Canadian physician and academic (Tan & Roach, 2020, paras. 13–16, 22)

Amy discusses the necessity of being an ally to Black Canadians. Even as a Chinese Canadian who has experienced racism herself, she discusses the difference between the racism she experiences and the racism that Black Canadians experience, highlighting that it is not the same. Although she may not be White, she still experiences privileges that Black Canadians do not. Amy explains that being an ally for Black Canadians means being actively anti-racist and openly calling out racism and racist policies wherever they may occur, including within your own communities.

It is ironic how quickly many Asians living in the West became the target of racial slurs, physical distancing, and even violence in the wake of the COVID-19 pandemic (Hosseini-Nezhad et al., in press). Anti-Asian sentiment spread quickly, particularly when COVID-19 was labelled the "Chinese virus" by some politicians. This indicates how the nature of stereotypes and racism changes across time and space.

Speaking Up for Oneself: Comfort with Difficult Dialogues

Part of cultural competence is speaking up on behalf of others, otherwise known as being an ally. Knowing how to speak up for oneself is also an important skill.

It can be difficult to know whether to directly address a cultural issue. In Chapter 6, we discussed the double bind that racial microaggressions cause. On the one hand, if you speak up, you take a risk regarding the reaction you get from the other person. On the other hand, if you keep silent, the internalized anger, stress, and frustration also take a toll. In fact, it is not necessary, or healthy, to speak up in every situation; another critical skill is knowing how to pick your battles. It should also be acknowledged that some people believe speaking up is a bad thing.

Discussing racism and becoming enlightened about it may be seen by some as a double-edged sword. While education, knowledge, and self-awareness may lead to more tolerance and empathy as described in Amy's quotation, overzealousness to the point of being consumed by the issue may lead to further division and emphasis on the differences between people rather than on their

Viola Desmond, who fought segregation in Canada by sitting in the "White Only" section of a movie theatre in 1946, is featured on the Canadian $10 bill. In 2018, the bill was named the International Bank Note Society's Banknote of the Year.

commonalities. On the one hand, does talking about racism, stereotypes, ethnic identity, and other cultural issues perpetuate the problem? On the other hand, taking direct action by speaking up for oneself and others can be an empowering, positive outlet and a motivator for change.

It is helpful to develop a level of comfort discussing difficult issues, such as racism, sexism, and heterosexism. These are emotional topics and many people are afraid to discuss them. Ethnicity, gender, sexual orientation, and religion are all core parts of a person's identity. Because these topics have such high personal relevance, people are sensitive when they are discussed. People may also have painful experiences related to these parts of their identity, and talking about these topics brings up that pain. Others may react with anger to what they perceive to be the ignorant, insensitive, or offensive remarks of others; those witnessing such pain or anger may feel uncomfortable or afraid. These are difficult emotions to handle, and it is easy to be overwhelmed by them, but they should not be avoided. Instead, they must be brought out in the open, acknowledged, validated, and worked through. The film *Indian Horse* (based on a 2012 novel) (Campanelli, 2017) follows the experiences of Indigenous Peoples in the Canadian residential school system. The story follows a young hockey player who struggles between the tensions of his Indigenous culture and the residential school system. Books and movies that address topics of colonialism, racism, and trauma are important for educating larger audiences on the realities of cultural discrimination. It takes courage and skill to discuss these difficult topics in a meaningful and beneficial manner, but doing so builds cultural competence.

Developing an Attitude of Discovery and Courage

Perhaps the two most important skills you need in order to increase your level of cultural competence are an attitude of discovery and courage. *Discovery* was defined earlier as openness to new experiences and a willingness to step out of your comfort zone. Doing that takes courage. As we said, encountering people and situations that are different naturally makes us feel frightened and uncomfortable. Courage is moving forward despite such negative feelings. If you do, you will reap the rewards.

Putnam (2007) conducted a series of research studies in the US that show that as communities become more diverse, people become more isolated from one another. Such diversification has the effect of increasing mistrust, even among our own ethnic group, and disrupting prosocial behaviours and community co-operation. Because of these short-term costs, many find it difficult to see the long-term economic, cultural, and developmental benefits of diversity (Putnam, 2007). Similarly, other research conducted in the United States has consistently found that ethnic heterogeneity decreases social cohesion (Putnam, 2007; Savelkoul et al., 2015). On the other hand, studies in Canada, Australia, and New Zealand have found little evidence of this negative relationship (Meer & Tolsma, 2014). Despite being a traditional immigration country, the United States reacts negatively to diversity (Meer & Tolsma, 2014), whereas Canada takes pride in being a multicultural nation. Furthermore, Kesler and Bloemraad (2010) suggest that diversity is more likely to have a negative effect in countries like the United States, where multicultural policies are not in place.

Likewise, Putnam (2007) argues that the obstacles to prosocial behaviour can be overcome with deliberate, organized, concerted efforts on individual, organizational, societal, and cultural levels. Putnam believes the answer lies in creating shared social identities, or providing opportunities for lines between groups to become blurred, which fosters a sense of shared citizenship. Examples include developing programs that bring groups together at churches, schools, community centres, and athletic fields. Such local programs should receive public, national support.

Thus, Putnam (2007) believes that society can be advanced if we make conscious efforts to increase meaningful interactions between diverse groups. Reaching out to others who are different from you is a critical step in this process. However, we should warn you that it will not be easy. Any time you learn a new skill, you will make mistakes. Remember learning how to ride a bike? How many times did you fall down before you learned to stay up? Did you give up? Chances are you kept trying until you were peddling your way freely down the block. And once you learned, you never forgot how. It became automatic.

The same is true of cultural competence. In the beginning, you will have some falls, but just get up and keep trying. The more you practise, the easier it will become, and the more effective you will be at interacting with others who are different from you. After you learned to ride a bike, you probably still had a spill from time to time. The same will be true of your cultural interactions. There will always be the awkward moments, the uncomfortable situations, the statements or actions that are misunderstood. Not everyone will be receptive when you reach out. Making mistakes is part of the process. We have a responsibility to reach out, so be willing to admit your mistakes and learn from them. It will only help you further along the road to cultural competence.

Rebecca Belmore (2020) is an internationally recognized multidisciplinary Anishinaabekwe artist. Her work is an expressive connection between body, land, and language, which captures the political and social realities of Indigenous Peoples in Canada. For instance, her performance *Vigil* commemorates the lives of missing and murdered Indigenous women of Vancouver's Downtown Eastside. In an interview with writer Leanne Betasamosake Simpson, Belmore explains, "I am the artist amongst my people. Every society has its own artists, and we have the responsibility to speak about how we are collective, at this moment in time" (Simpson, 2018, para. 20).

We challenge you to step out of your safe house and venture along the road of discovery. Sometimes the road will be rough and at other times easy, but rich rewards await you along the way.

Developing Empathy

We have many sayings in our culture to depict empathy: "Walk a mile in someone's shoes," "See the world through someone else's eyes," "Climb inside someone's skin," and so on. *Empathy* means genuinely understanding another person's perspective or experience. Empathy makes us more sensitive to and understanding of the experiences of others and thus builds cultural competence.

Cultural competence involves learning about your own culture, as well as other cultures. The strategies described here can be used to learn more about yourself and others. We have given only a few suggestions here for how to develop culturally appropriate interpersonal skills. If you act on these suggestions, you may find that these activities can be fun and enriching, as well as important. There are many other things that you can do, as well. We hope these get you started.

10.6 A Change in World View

Often students who take this class and read this book make statements such as, "I never saw it that way," "This gave me a new perspective," and "I'm noticing things I never did before." You have read similar statements in the narratives in this chapter and throughout this book. Perhaps you have said similar things or had similar thoughts. Such statements reflect a change in world view.

Previously, we defined *world view* as a psychological perception of the environment that determines how we think, behave, and feel. World view is influenced by past experiences and influences how we perceive, define, and interact with our environments. It is the filter through which we see and interpret the world around us. A change in world view means you now see and understand things in a different way. As a result of taking this class and reading this book, you most likely see things in a different way.

Liberation of consciousness is one of the primary goals of cultural psychology (Sue et al., 1996) and it refers to going beyond one's individual experience to consider underlying cultural factors that influence the situation. It means expanding one's personal perspective to consider that others have differing experiences and opinions that are just as real and valid. It means breaking out of old patterns of thinking and developing new ones. It means being flexible, creative, critical, and open.

According to Freire (1973), critical consciousness goes beyond simply perceiving things in new ways; it also involves action. This reflects the action-oriented side of multiculturalism. Multiculturalism stands for values such as justice, equity, and sensitivity, but it also means seeing these values as goals and taking active steps to achieve these goals. In other words, when you see a wrong, you work to make it right. This is social justice.

We would like to close with a quote from the United Nations Secretary-General António Guterres, who was appointed to a five-year term starting on 1 January 2017, to sum up the importance of cultural competency and why people everywhere should continue to educate themselves on issues of diversity and culture:

> We still have a long way to go before we end the discriminatory attitudes, actions, and practices that blight our world. . . . Let us work to eliminate messages of hatred—the concept of "us" and "them"; the false attitude that we can accept some and reject and

United Nations Secretary-General António Guterres (five-year term, appointed 1 January 2017).

> exclude others simply for how they look, where they worship, or who they love. And let us keep in mind the grave consequences of racist thinking—discrimination, slavery, and genocide. . . . The answer is to preach and practise tolerance, inclusion, and respect for diversity. This is achieved through greater debate and openness, and the exchange of different views, experiences, and perspectives. And it is achieved through leadership—the kind of leadership admirably shown by Nelson Mandela. Leadership that is courageous enough and principled enough to counter intolerance, racism, and discrimination in all its forms. (Guterres, 2018, paras. 6–8)

Summary

In our increasingly diverse and global society, we come into contact with people who are different from us every day. Sometimes that makes us feel uncomfortable. Our natural tendency is to stick to what is familiar because it is easy and helps us feel good about ourselves. However, if we are to truly benefit from all the world has to offer, it is to our advantage to become skilled at interacting with people from different backgrounds. That is cultural competence.

The three areas of cultural competence are (1) awareness of your own culture, (2) understanding other world views, and (3) development of culturally appropriate interpersonal skills. Development in these three areas will help you learn to interact effectively with others from different cultural backgrounds. These are important skills in today's world.

Cultural competence is characterized by openness to the other. This means being open to people, situations, experiences, values, and beliefs different from one's own. People who embody openness to the other embrace the basic values of multiculturalism discussed in Chapter 1, such as inclusion, sensitivity, respect, and social justice. They engage in self-exploration and self-critique, are open to differing perspectives, actively question their own, engage in meaningful dialogue with others from differing backgrounds, and are willing to be transformed by this process. It is through openness to others that we have the opportunity to learn and grow. Building cultural competence is a lifelong educational process where individuals continuously seek knowledge and cultivate habits that make cultural competence second nature.

Cultural competence is about applying the things you have learned in this book to your life, your work, and your interactions with others. The theories, concepts, and research covered in this book should increase your self-awareness, your understanding of how your own cultural background influences you. They should increase your understanding of and empathy for people from other groups. This increased understanding of self and others should ultimately improve your interactions with others in school, at work, and in your personal life. If you open yourself up to new knowledge and new experiences, if you take the risk and accept the challenge, your life will be enriched. We are all different; no two people are alike. Our lives are enriched when we adopt an attitude of discovery, when we open our minds and hearts to the experiences of others, and when we openly share our experiences with them. If each of you reading this book takes what you have learned and applies it to your own life, the world will be a better place.

> Without taking some action, learning is more difficult and less efficient because it is not grounded in real experience. (Pfeffer & Sutton, 2000, p. 7)

> ## FOOD FOR THOUGHT
>
> When one of the authors of this book, Jeffery Scott Mio, went to graduate school, it was the first time he had ever lived for an extended period of time outside his home state in the US. He encountered people from various places of the country in an intensive environment. He sees that time as one of the greatest periods of growth in his life. Another one of the authors, Saba Safdar, discovered how enriching it was for her to travel outside Canada. She learned to understand herself and her culture (Iranian Canadian) better through the eyes of people from other cultures. Think back to when you met someone quite different from you. What did you learn from that person? What did that person learn from you? What you learned from one another is what Joe White calls mutual enrichment. Now think back to all of those who seemed quite different from you. This number may be far beyond what you can recall. However, if you conceptualize each of those interactions as being mutually enriching, you will get a sense of just how enriched your life has become from those encounters.

Critical Thinking Questions

1. Have you ever been to a foreign country and felt out of place? Have you ever been to another part of the country and felt out of place? Have you ever been to a different area of the city you live in that made you feel out of place? How did you handle those situations?
2. Have you ever found yourself distancing yourself from the uncomfortable situations posed in the previous question? Have you ever denied that you felt uncomfortable when on reflection you actually did feel uncomfortable? Did you ever find yourself being defensive about the differences? Did you ever devalue what was different from your areas of comfort? Did you ever discover something about yourself or discover something new and exciting when you were in a situation of difference?
3. Did you ever go back to situations of comfort because they made your life simpler? Did you find such situations to be safer? Did these situations make you feel sane?
4. Has learning about the values and beliefs of others ever made you re-examine your own values and beliefs? Did that make you feel more enriched?
5. Have you ever advocated for people or groups with demographic characteristics different from yours? What were those experiences like?
6. Has anyone ever said something offensive or insensitive in front of you? Was it about you? Was it about someone else? Did you speak up and confront the person who made the offensive comment? Why or why not? What might you do the next time you hear someone make such a comment?
7. How has your perspective changed since reading this book and taking this class? What are some ideas, beliefs, or opinions you had before that were challenged by what you learned? What will you do now that you have this new perspective?

Glossary

acculturation Experiences and changes that groups and individuals undergo when they come in contact with a different culture.

acculturative stress Behavioural and psychological reactions, characterized by uncertainty, anxiety, and depression, resulting from contact between different cultures.

additive bilingualism The acquisition of a second language that does not replace the native language.

administration bias A bias that occurs when challenges during data collection, such as ambiguous instruction and communication problems, affect a group's response.

affect Feelings or emotions.

allies Individuals who are on the upside of power who cross a demographic boundary to advocate for those on the downside of power.

allocentric values Values based on interpersonal achievement and collective goals and tendencies that reside within an individual.

anorexia nervosa An eating disorder marked by extreme weight loss, intense fear of gaining weight, and a distorted body image.

appreciation stage The stage or status in which young people begin to broaden their perspective to include the ethnicity not initially selected for their identity.

assimilationist An individual who accepts the host society values but rejects the values of their heritage culture.

asylum seekers A special class of refugees whose refugee claims have not been decided on by the country in which the claim is submitted.

attribution theory A theory that attempts to determine the cause of a behaviour. Two major dimensions are internal–external and stable–unstable.

autonomy status The status in which White-European people are comfortable with their European identity, understand that racism is connected with other forms of oppression, and work to address all forms of oppression.

availability heuristic A mental shortcut whereby the importance, frequency, or credence of something is exaggerated because it comes to mind easily.

aversive racism Covert, unintentional discriminatory behaviour practised by individuals who hold both egalitarian values and negative views toward minority groups.

barriers One of the areas of analysis of the health-belief model that refers to obstacles that reduce the likelihood of engaging in a new behaviour.

benefits One of the areas of analysis of the health-belief model that refers to advantages gained from a behaviour.

bias A factor that reduces the validity of the measurements that are used in different cultures.

bias in the usage A bias introduced when a test is used in an inappropriate manner that disadvantages the test taker.

bias of the user A bias in the interpretation of a test when the test user has a particular perspective or bias that influences the interpretation of the test results.

binge-eating disorder An eating disorder marked by consumption of large amounts of food in one sitting, accompanied by feelings of lack of control, embarrassment, disgust, depression, and guilt, along with rapid eating, eating until uncomfortably full, and eating large amounts when not hungry.

biological definition of race A group of people who share a specific combination of physical, genetically inherited characteristics that distinguish them from other groups.

biopsychosocial model A model of human behaviour that takes into consideration biological, cognitive-affective, social-interpersonal, social institutional, and cultural factors.

bulimia nervosa An eating disorder marked by the consumption of a large amount of food in one sitting—called a binge—followed by the purging of that food, most typically through vomiting but also through extreme exercise or the use of laxatives.

causal stage An emotional stage when the individual accepts the negative labels attached to a Latino identity and feels humiliated and traumatized by these labels.

choice of group categorization stage The stage in which a young person is forced to choose one identity over another.

cognitions Thoughts and all basic mental processes, such as memories, perceptions, and beliefs.

cognitive dissonance theory When two cognitions are in conflict, a person will be motivated to change one of them to reduce the unsettled feelings caused by the discrepancy.

cognitive stage The belief that maintaining a Latino identity necessarily means being poor and the assumption that success in life can be attained only through assimilation to the mainstream culture.

collectivistic countries Countries that place collective rights over the rights of the individual.

colour-blind The stance that everyone is the same and that there is no need to acknowledge ethnic or skin-colour differences.

colour-blind racial ideology An attempt to pretend that race and racism will not exist if people ignore race or ethnicity. This ideology has two components: colour evasion and power evasion.

coming out The process by which non-heterosexual individuals openly express their sexual orientation.

common-sense model A theoretical framework used to explain how patients perceive an illness, cope with that perception, evaluate their coping, and integrate feedback and experiences into revising their perceptions and their coping.

conceptual equivalence A term or phrase that has equivalent meanings in different cultures.

conformity stage The stage in which individuals show preference for the values, beliefs, and features of the dominant culture over their own values and beliefs.

consequence stage Rejection of Latino heritage because of the sense that negative attributes are associated with being Latino.

construct bias The construct being studied across cultures is not identical.

contact cultures Cultures that encourage touching and closer proximity.

contact status The status in which White Europeans are uninformed about the realities of racism and privilege.

co-operative principle A psycholinguistic term that assumes that we strive to communicate with one another sincerely and effectively when we engage in a conversation.

countercultural individuals Idiocentric individuals residing in a collectivistic culture or allocentric individuals residing in an individualistic culture.

covert, intentional racism Discriminatory behaviour that is intentional but is covered up so that people can deny their racism.

covert, unintentional racism Discriminatory behaviour that is unintentional or well-intended but serves to perpetuate ongoing racist acts or traditions.

cross-cultural psychology The comparative study of psychological functioning in various cultural and ethnocultural groups.

cross-sectional designs Research designs that gather data across different age groups.

cultural competence The ability to interact effectively with individuals who are of a culture different from one's own.

cultural explanations or perceived causes When certain cultural groups attach unique meanings to symptoms or have particular explanations for the etiology of illness or distress.

cultural idioms of distress Specific ways of expressing troubling thoughts, behaviours, and emotions.

cultural psychology The study of human psychological processes within a cultural context based on the assumption that culture and psychological process are deeply connected together and cannot be studied in isolation.

cultural racism The belief that one's own culture is inherently superior to another.

cultural syndromes Clusters of symptoms that tend to occur only in specific cultural groups.

culture The practices of a group of people, expressed through symbols, values, and beliefs and passed down from generation to generation.

culture contact Critical incidents in which people from different cultures come into social contact with one another, either (a) by living and working with one another on a daily basis or (b) through visiting other countries on a temporary basis, such as for business, tourism, or study.

culture shock The experience individuals have when moving to a country in which the culture is very different from their own.

defensiveness The third of Harrell's Five *D*s of Difference; trying to protect oneself from acknowledging the difference between oneself and another to avoid feelings of discomfort or anxiety.

delay of gratification The ability to wait for a more desirable reward instead of taking a less desirable reward immediately.

denial The second of Harrell's Five Ds of Difference; pretending that there is no difference between oneself and another, minimizing the difference's importance, or ignoring the difference altogether.

devaluing The fourth of Harrell's Five Ds of Difference; assessing the difference between oneself and another as deficient or less important.

direct communication Blunt communication that is literal and to the point.

discovery The fifth of Harrell's Five Ds of Difference; appreciating the difference between oneself and another, seeing how enriching that difference may be, and seeking out opportunities to gain familiarity.

discrimination A negative behaviour toward a group or its members based on their categorization.

disintegration status The status in which White Europeans have enough contact with people of colour that their naïveté about racism is shattered.

dissonance stage The stage in which there is a sudden or gradual occurrence that challenges one's belief of inferiority of own's group and superiority of the dominant group.

distancing The first of Harrell's Five Ds of Difference; avoiding situations in which one feels different. Distancing can occur physically, emotionally, or intellectually.

ecological fit or ecological context Similarity of the social and cultural environments between an immigrant's country of origin and new host country.

ecological validity The ability to generalize the results of the study to other settings.

emic approach An attempt to derive meaningful concepts within one culture.

encounter stage The stage or status in which one encounters negative experiences that lead to re-evaluating one's own beliefs about Blackness and race.

enculturation When individuals retain or deepen their learning of their own cultural norms.

enmeshment/denial stage The stage or status in which a young person feels guilty about choosing one ethnicity over the other because of the implicit rejection of the parent whose ethnicity was not chosen.

equality The state of all people having equal access to resources and opportunities and being able to take advantage of them if they choose.

equity The state of all people having equal access to the same resources and opportunities.

ethnicity A combination of race and culture.

ethnic psychology or ethnic minority psychology The study of social classifications and social opportunities of subordinate groups.

etic approach An attempt to build theories of human behaviour by examining commonalities across many cultures.

exosystem A layer of context that includes major societal institutions, such as the media and the government.

explicit bias Conscious attitudes that are deliberate and that influence how people feel, think, and behave.

externalizing Projecting feelings outward and expressing them through overt behaviours.

external validity The generalizability of the results to the study.

face giving/giving face Praising the virtues of another person in public.

fight If escape is not possible, we may attempt to be aggressive to defend against the danger we perceive.

flee An attempt to escape an uncomfortable or potentially dangerous situation.

fourth force Refers to the major influence that this perspective has on the field of psychology.

freeze To stop and try to interpret a situation that may be a potential threat.

fright Feelings of anxiety about a potentially dangerous situation.

functional equivalence The equating of items on a test or a survey functionally as opposed to literally.

fundamental attribution error or correspondence bias The tendency to overestimate dispositional (internal, stable) causes of behaviours and to underestimate external causes of behaviours.

guilt A negative emotion that involves an individual's sense of personal regret for having engaged in a negative behaviour.

health A complete state of physical, mental, and social well-being, not merely the absence of disease or infirmity.

health behaviours Behaviours undertaken by people to enhance or maintain their well-being.

health-belief model A set of assumptions that suggests that one's health behaviour is affected by one's perception of a personal health threat, as well as by how a particular health practice would be effective in reducing the personal health threat.

health-care disparities Differential access to health care or treatment by health-care providers at the institutional or patient–provider level.

health disparities Systematic differences in illness, mortality, disability, and injury that marginalized groups experience in comparison with their privileged counterparts.

health inequality Health differences that are associated with age, gender, and socio-economic status.

health inequity Systematic differences in health inequalities that stem from social and economic inequalities.

health psychology The study of psychological influences on how people stay healthy, why they become ill, and how they respond when they do get ill.

healthy immigrant effect (HIE) The paradox where immigrants tend to have better health than the native-born despite having a lower socio-economic status compared to non-immigrants. (See also *immigrant health paradox*.)

high-context communication (HC) Communication in which the context conveys much of the meaning.

human activity dimension The distinction among being, being and in becoming, and doing.

identity acceptance The stage or status in which a non-heterosexual individual fully accepts their sexual orientation but expresses those values in limited, specific environments.

identity comparison The stage or status in which non-heterosexual individuals recognize their differences from most same-sex individuals.

identity confusion The stage or status in which gay, lesbian, or bisexual individuals begin to question their sexual identity.

identity pride The stage or status in which a non-heterosexual individual openly expresses their sexual orientation and takes pride in that identity.

identity synthesis The stage or status in which a non-heterosexual individual is able to integrate all aspects of their identities, including ethnicity and gender.

identity tolerance The stage or status in which non-heterosexual individuals fully recognize their non-heterosexual feelings but attempt to hide them from others and from themselves by trying to believe, for example, that it is just a phase they are going through.

idiocentric values Values based on personal achievement and giving priority to personal goals and individualistic tendencies that reside within an individual.

illusory correlation A false perception of associating two events together.

immersion/emersion The stage or status in which a group begins to immerse themselves in and focus on their own identity and culture.

immigrant health paradox The paradox where immigrants tend to have better health than the native-born despite the fact that they have a lower socio-economic status compared to non-immigrants. (See also *healthy immigrant effect*.)

implicit bias Attitudes that are unconscious or involuntary but nonetheless influence how people feel, think, and behave.

implicit racial attitude An idea or opinion about race that people hold but are unaware they hold.

imposed etics The imposition of one culture's world view on another culture, assuming that one's own world views are universal.

incidence The number of new cases of a disorder that occur during a given period of time.

indirect communication Communication that relies on context and the receiver's ability to draw inferences.

individualistic countries Countries that place individual rights and the pursuit of one's own goals over the rights of the collective and the goals of the group.

in-group social support Support provided by members of a person's community, cultural group, and family.

instrument bias A bias that occurs when one cultural group has a larger degree of familiarity with an instrument over another.

integrationists or biculturals Individuals who hold on to their original values while also learning and adopting the values of the host culture.

integration stage The stage or status in which a child/adolescent/adult sees the benefits of embracing both ethnicities.

integrative awareness stage The stage in which individuals find a greater sense of cultural security, become aware of themselves as individual and cultural beings, and recognize differences among cultural groups, both positive and negative.

internalization The stage or status in which one feels comfortable with one's identity. This allows one to express acceptance of other cultures.

internalized oppression People who are colonized and/or oppressed may automatically accept the superiority of the oppressor.

internal validity When procedures in an experiment are designed to help make an inference that a change in procedure leads to a change in behaviour or outcome.

international immigrants People who move into a country other than their country of origin and become residents of the new country.

interrater reliability The degree to which coders agree on a rating system.

intersectionality The meaningful ways in which various social statuses interact (e.g., race, gender, social class) and result in differing experiences with oppression and privilege.

intimate distance The distance between individuals in close relationships.

introspection stage The stage in which individuals tend to educate themselves about their own identity, appreciate their own and other cultural groups, and become less angry at the dominant group.

item bias A bias that occurs when an item has different meanings across cultures.

kinesics Bodily movements in conversations, including hand gestures, facial expressions, and eye contact.

language attrition Equivalent to subtractive bilingualism.

language brokers People who support translation or interpretation without formal training for this task.

linguistic equivalence The translation of a term based on similarity of linguistic features by evaluating grammatical accuracy and lexical similarity.

locus of control A psychological concept referring to the perception of having control over outcomes of one's life, be it internal or external control.

locus of responsibility A psychological concept referring to the perception of having responsibility for one's position in life, be it internal feelings of responsibility or external, societal responsibility.

logical positivism Scientific approach that attempts to measure "truth" or real phenomena through methods of numbers and statistical analyses.

longitudinal design Research designs that follow a certain set of individuals over time.

loose cultures Those cultures with weak social norms where transgression of norms is permissible.

losing face To lose respect and to suffer humiliation because of one's behaviour.

low-context communication (LC) Language-dependent communication in which the words carry most of the meaning and context plays a lesser role.

macrosystem A layer of context that includes the cultural norms and societal rules that determine rules of conduct.

male privilege Systematic advantages that society provides to men based on their gender. It also refers to the unearned advantages associated with being male.

marginalist An individual who rejects the host society's values and also rejects the heritage culture values.

marginalized groups People who are disadvantaged because of their ethnicity, socio-economic status, disability, age, gender, sexual orientation, geographic location, special health-care needs, or need for end-of-life care.

masculine–feminine dimension A continuum of authority from hierarchical (masculine) to egalitarian (feminine), also known as power distance by Hofstede (1980).

maxim of manner A communicative presumption that suggests that we be clear in our language, avoid ambiguity, and pay attention to standards of conversation that are the norm in a particular context.

maxim of quality A communicative presumption that suggests that we tell each other the truth when we engage in a conversation.

maxim of quantity A communicative presumption that suggests that we contribute an appropriate amount of talk when we engage in a conversation.

maxim of relevance A communicative presumption that suggests that our discussion remains relevant to the conversation.

mesosystem A layer of context that includes relationships in the immediate area outside the family, such as schools, work, the extended family, and the community in which one lives.

method bias Refers to three biases: sample bias, instrument bias, and administration bias.

metric equivalence Patterns of numerical scores and psychometric properties across cultures.

microaggression A small slight or offence that may be intentional but is mostly unintentional and does not harm the target of the offences in any major way but can accumulate to be burdensome over time.

microassault A blatant verbal, non-verbal, or environmental attack that is intentionally discriminatory or biased.

microinsult An unintentional behaviour or verbal comment conveying rudeness or insensitivity.

microinvalidation An action that excludes, negates, or dismisses the perceptions of the target person.

microsystem A layer of context that includes relationships among family members living within one household.

migration The movement of persons away from their place of usual residence.

migration phase The period when individuals are migrating from their country of origin to a host country. This includes the period immediately before the migration and the process of departure.

multicultural competence The awareness of one's own culture, the ability to learn about other cultures, and the development of a culturally appropriate set of skills to work effectively with diverse groups.

multicultural model The multicultural model involves cultures with distinct identities joined together within a social structure.

multicultural psychology Refers to research conducted on different ethnic groups or on people with different cultural backgrounds who live in a pluralistic nation.

native bilingualism The ability to speak two languages from birth, acquired because both languages are spoken in the household.

outgroup social support Support provided by members of the larger society, including both informal and formal support.

overt racism Discriminatory behaviour in which people in the majority engage in open, hostile acts of aggression against racial minorities.

paradigm shift Refers to a major change in the way people think about human behaviour.

paralanguage Non-verbal vocal cues in conversation, such as loudness of voice, silences, and rates of speech.

people/nature relationship Refers to how people relate to nature and includes subjugation to nature, harmony with nature, and mastery over nature.

personal distance The distance between individuals who are friends.

personal identity stage The first stage of identity development in which children base their identity on personal factors, such as self-esteem, instead of on ethnicity.

population validity The ability to generalize the results of the study to other populations.

post-migration phase The continued stress experienced by immigrants, specifically related to new societal and cultural contexts.

pre-encounter stage The stage or status in which one is influenced by the dominant Eurocentric values of Blackness and may devalue one's own Blackness.

prejudice (Mostly) a negative judgment about a group or its members based on their categorization.

pre-migration phase The time before individuals leave their country of origin.

prevalence The rate of a particular disorder at a given point in time.

proxemics Personal space in conversations.

pseudo-independence status The status in which White Europeans begin to acknowledge the realities of racism but believe that it is Blacks who should change, not Europeans.

psychology The systematic study of behaviour, cognition, and affect.

qualifiers Words or phrases that soften statements and affect the certainty of a statement.

racial and cultural identity development model (R/CID) A general model that covers all forms of cultural identity and addresses how one relates to oneself, to others of the same culture, to others of different cultures, and to the dominant cultural group.

racial salience The extent to which one's ethnicity is relevant in self-concept in a particular situation.

racism Discriminatory behaviour that is backed by institutional power.

refugees Those who are forced to flee from their birth countries due to conflict, environmental disaster, or fear of persecution.

reintegration status The status in which White Europeans retreat to their comfort zone within their European communities, which actively or passively support European superiority.

relations with conversational partner A communicative presumption that suggests that we use our previous relationship with our conversational partner so that we do not have to repeat shared experiences.

resistance and immersion stage The stage in which individuals become immersed within their own cultural group and reject the dominant culture with feelings of anger and guilt for their initial preference of the dominant culture and rejection of their own culture.

response style bias A bias that occurs when a culture has the tendency to agree rather than disagree with a statement and to use the endpoint of a scale.

rule violations A communicative presumption that suggests that we signal our conversational partners when we are about to engage in a violation of one of the other maxims.

sample bias A bias that occurs when samples that are not equivalent and have different characteristics are compared.

saving face To avoid humiliation and losing respect by adopting social skills and strategies.

separationist An individual who rejects the host society values and only accepts the values of the heritage culture.

sequential design Sequential design refers to a combination of the cross-sectional and longitudinal designs.

severity One of the areas of analysis of the health-belief model that refers to intensity of negative outcome.

shame A negative emotion that involves an individual's sense of regret for having engaged in a negative behaviour that reflects badly on that individual's family.

social distance The distance between individuals during formal interactions.

social relations dimension The distinction among lineal, collateral, and individualistic. Lineal orientation is a respect for the hierarchy within one's family. Collateral orientation is essentially the same as collectivism, and individualistic orientation is the same as individualism.

socio-cultural concept of race The perspective that characteristics, values, and behaviours that have been associated with groups of people who share different physical characteristics serve the social purpose of providing a way for outsiders to view another group and for members of a group to perceive themselves.

stereotype An overgeneralization about a group or its members based on their categorization.

stereotype threat A fear that one will confirm the negative stereotype of a group to which one belongs.

structural introspection The method that structuralists used to examine the contents of people's minds in which people reported on their own mental experiences.

structuralism The early formal approach to psychology that attempted to examine the contents of people's minds.

subtractive bilingualism The acquisition of a second language that replaces the native language.

successful resolution stage The final stage, when the Latino identity is integrated into one's own identity and there is a sense of acceptance and positive Latino identity.

susceptibility One of the areas of analysis of the health-belief model that refers to the likelihood of acquiring a disease or being impacted by an illness-producing stimulus.

symbolic racism An attempt and affect that is not overtly racist but is motivated to reject others based on their ethnicity and skin colour.

tag questions Questions added to a statement of assertion, such as "This is good, don't you think?"

tight cultures Cultures with strict social norms where transgression of norms is punishable.

time focus An orientation that values a particular time perspective. Some cultures value the past, some value the present, and some value the future. Although all cultures value all three, some cultures value one of these perspectives more than do other cultures.

tripartite model of personal identity The understanding that personal identity is made up of three components: individual, group, and universal levels.

ultimate attribution error The tendency to ascribe the cause of a behaviour to dispositional characteristics of the group rather than to an individual member.

White ethnics Individuals whose families have either recently emigrated from Europe or held on to their European origin identification.

White privilege The socio-economical advantages that Caucasians receive in society.

working-through stage A stage when individuals feel distress because of alienation from their Latino community and are therefore motivated to integrate their Latino identity into a sense of self.

world view A psychological perception of the environment that determines how we think, behave, and feel.

References

Chapter 1

Accessibility for Ontarians with Disabilities Act, Statutes of Ontario (2005, c. 11). Retrieved from Ontario Law website: https://www.ontario.ca/laws/statute/05a11

American Psychiatric Association. (1987). *Diagnostic and statistical manual of mental disorders* (3rd ed., revised). American Psychiatric Press.

Angier, N. (2000, August 22). Do races differ? Not really, DNA shows. *The New York Times*, p. F1.

Associated Press. (2004, May 12). David Reimer, 38, subject of the John/Joan Case. *The New York Times*. https://www.nytimes.com/2004/05/12/us/david-reimer-38-subject-of-the-john-joan-case.html

Atkinson, D. R. (2004). *Counseling American minorities* (6th ed.). McGraw-Hill.

Backenroth, G. (1998). Multiculturalism and the deaf community: Examples given from deaf people working in bicultural groups. In P. Pedersen (Ed.), *Multiculturalism as a fourth force* (pp. 111–46). Brunner/Mazel.

Banks, J. A. (2010). *Multicultural education: Goals and dimensions*. Center for Multicultural Education, College of Education, University of Washington. https://education.uw.edu/cme/view

Banks, J. A., & Banks, C. A. M. (Eds.). (2004). *Handbook of research on multicultural education* (2nd ed.). Wiley.

Beck, A. T. (1967). *Depression: Causes and treatment*. University of Pennsylvania Press.

Beck, A. T. (1970). Cognitive therapy: Nature and relation to behavior therapy. *Behavior Therapy, 1*, 184–200.

Begley, S. (1995, February 13). Three is not enough: Surprising new lessons from the controversial science of race. *Newsweek*, pp. 67–69.

Berry, J. W. (2019). *Acculturation, a personal journey across cultures*. Cambridge University Press. doi:10.1017/9781108589666.

Berry J. W., & Dalal, A. (1996). *Disability attitudes, beliefs and behaviours: Final report*. Kingston: International Centre for the Advancement of Community-Based Rehabilitation.

Berry, J. W., Poortinga, Y. H., Pandey, J., Dasen, P. R., Saraswathi, T. S., Segall, M. H., & Kagitcibasi, C. (Eds.). (1998). *Handbook of cross-cultural psychology*. Allyn & Bacon.

Berry, J. W., Poortinga, Y. H., Segall, M. H., & Dasen, P. R. (1992). *Cross-cultural psychology: Research and applications*. Cambridge University Press.

Bhatt, G., Tonks, R. G., & Berry, J. W. (2013). Culture in the history of psychology in Canada. *Canadian Psychology/Psychologie Canadienne, 54*(2), 115–23.

Blumenbach, J. F. (1775/1795/1865). *The anthropological treatises of Johann Friedrich Blumenbach*. Longman, Green, Longman, Roberts, and Green. http://www.archive.org/details/anthropologicalt00blumuoft

Bochner, S. (1999). Cultural diversity within and between societies: Implications for multicultural social systems. In P. Pedersen (Ed.), *Multiculturalism as a fourth force*. Taylor & Francis.

Bond, M. H. (2019). Travelling from the past into the future of cross-cultural psychology: A personal-scientific journey. In D. Matsumoto & H. C. Hwang (Eds.), *The handbook of culture and psychology*. Oxford University Press.

Brown, L. S. (2011). *Queer mentoring—it's not about coming out any more (and it is)* [Invited presentation]. Western Psychological Association Annual Convention, Los Angeles, CA.

Canada Population 2020. (2019, October 16). Retrieved February 4, 2020, from http://worldpopulationreview.com/countries/canada-population/

Canadian Psychological Association. (1982). *Discrimination on sexual orientation*. https://cpa.ca/aboutcpa/policystatements/#orientation

Canadian Psychological Association. (2000). *Canadian code of ethics for psychologists* (3rd ed.). https://cpa.ca/cpasite/UserFiles/Documents/Canadian%20Code%20of%20Ethics%20for%20Psycho.pdf

Canadian Psychological Association. (2017a). *Canadian code of ethics for psychologists* (4th ed.). https://cpa.ca/docs/File/Ethics/CPA_Code_2017_4thEd.pdf

Canadian Psychological Association. (2017b). *Ethical guidelines for supervision in psychology: Teaching, research, practice, and administration*.

Canadian Psychological Association. (2017c). *Guidelines for non-discriminatory practice*. https://cpa.ca/docs/File/Ethics/CoEGuidelines_NonDiscPract2017_Final.pdf

Canadian Psychological Association. (2018). *Health and well-being needs of LGBTQI people*. https://cpa.ca/aboutcpa/policystatements/#Health-LGBTQI

Canadian Race Relations Foundation. (2015). *CRRF glossary terms*. https://www.crrf-fcrr.ca/en/resources/glossary-a-terms-en-gb-1?start=50

Casas, J. M. (1984). Policy, training, and research in counseling psychology: The racial/ethnic minority perspective. In S. D. Brown & R. W. Lent (Eds.), *Handbook of counseling psychology* (pp. 785–831). Wiley.

Clymer, E. C. (1995). The psychology of deafness: Enhancing self-concept in the deaf and hearing impaired. *Family Therapy, 22*(2), 113–20.

Cohen, A. B., Wu, M. S., & Miller, J. (2016). Religion and culture. *Journal of Cross-Cultural Psychology, 47*(9), 1236–49.

Colapinto, J. (2000). *As nature made him: The boy who was raised as a girl*. Harper Collins.

Colapinto, J. (2004). *Gender gap: What were the real reasons behind David Reimer's suicide?* Slate. https://slate.com/technology/2004/06/why-did-david-reimer-commit-suicide.html

Cole, M. (1996). *Cultural psychology: A once and future discipline*. Harvard University Press.

Comas-Diaz, L. (2006). Latino healing: The integration of ethnic psychology into psychotherapy. *Psychotherapy: Theory, Research, Practice, Training, 43*(4), 436–53.

Comas-Díaz, L. (2009). Changing psychology: History and legacy of the Society for the Psychological Study of Ethnic Minority Issues. *Cultural Diversity and Ethnic Minority Psychology, 15*(4), 400–8. doi:10.1037/a0017560

Crenshaw, K. (1989). Demarginalizing the intersection of race and sex: A Black feminist critique of anti-discrimination doctrine, feminist theory, and anti-racist politics. *University of Chicago Legal Forum*, 1989, 139–67.

Darwin, C. R. (1871). *The descent of man, and selection in relation to sex. The complete work of Charles Darwin online*. http://darwin-online.org.uk/converted/pdf/1889_Descent_F969.pdf

Diamond, J. (1997). *Guns, germs, and steel: The fates of human societies*. Norton.

Drescher, J. (2015). Queer diagnoses revisited: The past and future of homosexuality and gender diagnoses in DSM and ICD. *International Review of Psychiatry, 27*(5), 386–95.

Early, G. (1996). Understanding Afrocentrism: Why blacks dream of a world without Whites. In G. C. Ward & R. Atwan (Eds.), *The best American essays 1996* (pp. 115–35). Houghton Mifflin Company.

Engel, G. L. (1977). The need for a new medical model: A challenge for biomedicine. *Science, 196*, 129–36.

Fish, J. M. (2002). A scientific approach to understanding race and intelligence. In J. J. Fish (Ed.), *Race and intelligence: Separating science from myth* (pp. 1–28). Erlbaum.

Fowers, B. J., & Davidov, B. J. (2006). The virtue of multiculturalism. *American Psychologist, 61*(6), 581–94. doi:10.1037/0003-066X.61.6.581

Franklin, A. J. (2009). Reflections on ethnic minority psychology: Learning from the past so the present informs our future. *Cultural Diversity and Ethnic Minority Psychology, 15*(4), 416–24. doi:10.1037/a0017560

Gelfand, M. (2020, March 13). *To survive the coronavirus, the United States must tighten up*. https://6df1098c-05f3-4ab1-a049-b59ba7f3ecfe.usrfiles.com/ugd/6df109_6da2e95a748c49adb1fefdc34d966569.pdf

Gilligan, C. (1982/1993). *In a different voice: Psychological theory and women's development*. Harvard University Press.

Goldstein, E. B. (2005). *Cognitive psychology: Connecting mind, research, and everyday experience*. Wadsworth.

Gopaldas, A. (2013). Intersectionality 101. *Journal of Public Policy and Marketing, 23*(Special Issue), 90–4.

Gorski, P. C. (2010). *The challenge of defining multicultural education*. Multicultural Education Pavilion. https://studylib.net/doc/6885865/i.-the-challenge-of-defining-multicultural-education-

Great chain of being. (2011). In *Wikipedia*. http://en.wikipedia.org/wiki/Great_chain_of_being

Guthrie, R. V. (1998). *Even the rat was white: A historical view of psychology*. Allyn & Bacon.

Haddon, A. C. (1910). *History of anthropology*. Putnam.

Hall, C. C. I. (2014). The evolution of the revolution: The successful establishment of multicultural psychology. In F. T. L. Leong, L. Comas-Díaz, G. C. N. Hall, V. C. McLoyd, & J. E. Trimble (Eds.), *APA handbook of multicultural psychology, Vol. 1. Theory and research* (pp. 3–18). American Psychological Association. doi:10.1037/14189-001

Hamburger, C., Sturup, G. K., & Dahl-Iverson, E. (1953). Transvestism: Hormonal, psychiatric and surgical treatment. *JAMA, 12*, 391–6.

Heine, S. J., & Ruby, M. B. (2010). *Cultural psychology*. Wiley. https://doi.org/10.1002/wcs.7

Helms, J. E., Jernigan, M., & Mascher, J. (2005). The meaning of race in psychology and how to change it: A methodological perspective. *American Psychologist, 60*(1), 27–36.

Herskovits, M. J. (1948). *Man and his works: The science of cultural anthropology*. Knopf.

Heywood, A. (2007). *Political ideologies* (4th ed.). Palgrave MacMillan.

Hill, A. (2019, February 8). *Gerald Stanley trial: Jury delivers not guilty verdict in death of Colten Boushie*. https://thestarphoenix.com/news/local-news/gerald-stanley-trial-jury-delivers-not-guilty-verdict-in-murder-of-colten-boushie

Historical definitions of race. (2011). In *Wikipedia*. http://en.wikipedia.org/wiki/Historical_definitions_of_race

Hofstede, G. (1980). *Culture's consequences: International differences in work-related values*. SAGE.

Hofstede, G. (2001). Dimensionalizing cultures: The Hofstede model in context. *Online readings in psychology and culture, 2*(1), 1–26.

International Work Group for Indigenous Affairs. (2020). *Indigenous peoples in Canada*. https://www.iwgia.org/en/canada.html.

Jahoda, G. (1970). *The psychology of superstition*. Penguin.

Jorde, L. B., & Wooding, S. P. (2004). Genetic variation, classification and "race." *Nature Genetics, 36*, S28–S33.

Kagitcibasi, C., & Berry, J. W. (1989). Cross-cultural psychology: Current research and trends. *Annual Reviews of Psychology, 40*, 493–531.

Keith, K. D. (2013). *The encyclopedia of cross-cultural psychology*. Wiley.

Kivanc, J. (2016, April 18). *Immigrants explain what shocked them the most about Canadian culture*. https://www.vice.com/en_ca/article/qbx7z5/immigrants-explain-what-shocked-them-the-most-about-canadian-culture

Kohlberg, L. (1968). The child as a moral philosopher. *Psychology Today, 2*, 25–30.

Kohlberg, L. (1976). Moral stage and moralization. In T. Lickona (Ed.), *Moral development and behavior* (pp. 31–53). Holt.

Kranich, N. (2005). *Equality and equity of access: What's the difference?* American Library Association. http://www.ala.org/advocacy/intfreedom/equalityequity

Kroeber, A. L., & Kluckhohn, C. (1952/1963). *Culture: A critical review of concepts and definitions*. Vintage Books.

Latter, B. (1980). Genetic differences within and between populations of the major human subgroups. *The American Naturalist, 116*, 220–37.

Leong, F. T. L., Leung, K., & Cheung, F. M. (2010). Integrating cross-cultural psychology research methods into ethnic minority psychology. *Cultural Diversity and Ethnic Minority Psychology, 16*(4), 590–7.

Lonner, W. J., Keith, K. D., & Matsumoto, D. (2019). Culture and the psychology curriculum: Foundations and resources. In D. Matsumoto & H. C. Hwang (Eds.) *The Handbook of culture and psychology*. Oxford University Press.

Louwagie, P. (2016, July 8). Falcon Heights police shooting reverberates across the nation. Gov. Dayton, seeing racial bias, calls for federal inquiry into deadly police shooting. *Star Tribune*. http://www.startribune.com/falcon-heights-police-shooting-reverberates-across-the-nation/385861101/

Mann, B. (2014). Equity and equality are not equal. *The Equity Line*. https://edtrust.org/the-equity-line/equity-and-equality-are-not-equal/

Mannix, A. (2016, July 12). Police audio: Officer stopped Philando Castile on robbery suspicion. Police recording doesn't cover shooting itself. *Star Tribune*. http://www.startribune.com/police-audio-officeer-stopped-philando-castile-on-robber-suspicion/386344001/#1

Markus, H. R., & Kitayama, S. (2010). Cultures and selves. *Perspectives on Psychological Science, 5*(4), 420–30.

Matsumoto, D., & Hwang, H. C. (2019). *The handbook of culture and psychology*. Oxford University Press.

Matsumoto, D., & Juang, L. (2008). *Culture and psychology* (4th ed.). Belmont, CA: Thomson/Wadsworth.

Mio, J. S., & Awakuni, G. I. (2000). *Resistance to multiculturalism: Issues and interventions*. Brunner/Mazel.

Moghaddam, F. M. (1987). Psychology in the three worlds: As reflected by the crisis in social psychology and the move toward indigenous third-world psychology. *American Psychologist, 42*(10), 912–20. https://doi.org/10.1037/0003-066X.42.10.912

Morning, A. 2011. *The nature of race: How scientists think and teach about human difference*. University of California Press.

Munroe, R. L., Munroe, R. H., & Whiting, B. B. (Eds.). (1981). *Handbook of cross-cultural human development*. Garland.

Parekh, B. (2000). *Rethinking multiculturalism: Cultural diversity and political theory*. Macmillan Press.

Pedersen, P. (1985). Handbook of *cross-cultural counseling and therapy*.

Pedersen, P. (1990). The multicultural perspective as a fourth force in counseling. *Journal of Mental Health Counseling, 12*, 93–5.

Pedersen, P. (1991). Multiculturalism as a generic approach to counseling. *Journal of Counseling Development: Special Issue on Multiculturalism as a Fourth Force, 70*, 6–12.

Pedersen, P. (1999). *Multiculturalism as a fourth force*. Brunner/Mazel.

Phinney, J. S. (1996). When we talk about American ethnic groups, what do we mean? *American Psychologist, 51*, 918–27.

Ponterotto, J. G. (2010). Learning from voices of wisdom: Reflections on multicultural life stories. In Ponterotto, J. G., Suzuki, L. A., Casas, M. J., & Alexander, C. M. (Eds.), *Handbook of multicultural psychology* (3rd ed.). SAGE.

Ratner, C. (2008). *Cultural psychology, cross-cultural psychology, Indigenous psychology*. Nova Science Publishers.

Richeson, J. A., & Sommers, S. R. (2016). Toward a social psychology of race and race relations for the twenty-first century. *Annual Review of Psychology, 67*, 439–63.

Roberts, T. (2009). *Lessons from Little Rock*. Butler Center Books.

Rohner, R. P. (1984). Toward a conception of culture for cross-cultural psychology. *Journal of Cross-Cultural Psychology, 15*, 111–38.

Rose, M. H. (1995). Apprehending deaf culture. *Journal of Applied Communication Research, 23*(2), 156–62.

Rosenzweig, M. R., Holtzman W. H., Sabourin, M, & Bélanger, D. (2000). *History of the International Union of Psychological Science*. Psychology Press.

Ryder, A., Berry, J. W., Safdar, S., & Yampolsky, M. (2020, May). *"Psychology works" fact sheet: Why does culture matter to COVID-19?* https://cpa.ca/docs/File/Publications/FactSheets/FS_CultureAndCOVID-19.pdf

Saini, A. (2019). *Superior: The return of race science*. 4th Estate.

Schwartz, G. E. (1982). Testing the biopsychosocial model: The ultimate challenge facing behavioral medicine. *Journal of Consulting and Clinical Psychology, 50*, 1040–53.

Schwartz, S. H. (2014). Rethinking the concept and measurement of societal culture in light of empirical findings. *Journal of Cross-Cultural Psychology, 45*(1), 5–13. doi:10.1177/0022022113490830

Segall, M. H., Lonner, W. J., & Berry, J. W. (1998). Psychology as a scholarly discipline on the flowering of culture in behavioral research. *American Psychologist, 53*(10), 1101–10.

Stahl, J. (2017, June 16). *Philando Castile's killer acquitted despite forensics that contradicted his case*. Slate. http://www.slate.com/blogs/the_slatest/2017/06/16/philando_castile_s_killer_acquitted_despite_forensics_that_contradicted.html

Statistics Canada. (2017). *Immigration and diversity: Population projections for Canada and its regions, 2011 to 2036 immigration and diversity*. https://www150.statcan.gc.ca/n1/pub/91-551-x/91-551-x2017001-eng.htm

Sue, D. W., Carter, R. T., Casas, J. M., Fouad, N. A., Ivey, A. E., Jensen, M., . . . Vasquez-Nuttal, E. (1998). *Multicultural counseling competencies: Individual and organizational development*. SAGE.

Sue, D. W., Ivey, A. E., & Pedersen, P. B. (1996). *A theory of multicultural counseling and therapy*. Brooks/Cole.

Sue, S. (1977). Community mental health services to minority groups: Some optimism, some pessimism. *American Psychologist, 32*, 616–24.

Sullivan, T. J., & Thompson, K. S. (1994). *Introduction to social problems* (3rd ed.). Macmillan.

Triandis, H. C. (1996). The psychological measurement of cultural syndromes. *American Psychologist, 51*(4), 407–15. https://doi.org/10.1037/0003-066X.51.4.407

Triandis, H. C., Lambert, W. W., Berry, J. W., Lonner, W. T., Heron, A., Brislin, R., & Draguns, J. (Eds.). (1980). *Handbook of cross-cultural psychology* (Vols. 1–6). Allyn & Bacon.

Tutu, D. (2012). *Moving beyond tolerance to understanding.* http://www.tutufoundationusa.org/2012/04/05/tolerance-versus-understanding/

Wade, C., & Tavris, C. (2003). *Psychology* (7th ed.). Prentice Hall.

Wear, D. (2003). Insurgent multiculturalism: Rethinking how and why we teach culture in medical education. *Academic Medicine, 78*(6), 549–5.

White, J. (2001). My story. In D. W. Sue (Chair), *Surviving racism: Lessons we have learned.* Symposium presented at the National Multicultural Conference and Summit II—The psychology of race/ethnicity, gender, sexual orientation, and disability: Intersections, divergence, and convergence, Santa Barbara, CA.

Williams, J. E., & Best, D. L. (1990). *Cross-cultural research and methodology series: Vol. 13. Sex and psyche: Gender and self viewed cross-culturally.* SAGE Publications.

The World Population Review (2019). https://worldpopulationreview.com/countries/canada-population

Zuckerman, M. (1990). Some dubious premises in research and theory on racial differences: Scientific, social, and ethical issues. *American Psychologist, 45*, 1297–303.

Chapter 2

Abdulla, F., & Kasese-Hara, M. (2020). Care worker perspectives on the socio-emotional adjustment of orphans in residential homes. *Vulnerable Children and Youth Studies, 15*(1), 77–84. doi:10.1080/17450128.2020.1719250

Acevedo-Polakovich, I. A., Reynaga-Abiko, G., Garriott, P. O., Derefinko, K. J., Winsett, M. K., Gudonis, L. C., & Brown, T. L. (2007). Beyond instrument selection: Cultural considerations in the psychological assessment of U.S. Latinas/os. *Professional Psychology: Research and Practice, 38*, 375–84.

Armour-Thomas, E. (2003). Assessment of psychometric intelligence for racial and ethnic minorities: Some unanswered questions. In G. Bernal, J. E. Trimble, A. K. Burlew, & F. T. L. Leong (Eds.), *Handbook of racial and ethnic minority psychology* (pp. 357–74). SAGE.

Bandura, A. (1977). *Social learning theory.* Prentice Hall.

Bandura, A. (1986). *Social foundations of thought and action: A social cognitive theory.* Prentice Hall.

Bandura, A. (1997). *Self-efficacy: The exercise of control.* Freeman.

Beaird, G., Baernholdt, M., & White, K. R. (2020). Perceptions of interdisciplinary rounding practices. *Journal of Clinical Nursing 29*(7–8), 1141–1150. doi:10.1111/jocn.15161

Binet, A., & Simon, Th. (1905). Méthodes nouvelles pour le diagnostic du niveau intellectuel des anormaux. *Année psychologique, 11*, 191–244.

Brislin, R. W. (1986). The wording and translation of research instruments. In W. J. Lonner & J. W. Berry (Eds.), *Field methods in cross-cultural research* (pp. 137–64). SAGE.

Brislin, R. W., Lonner, W. J., & Thorndike, R. M. (1973). *Cross-cultural research methods.* Wiley.

Campbell, D. T., & Stanley, J. C. (1963). *Experimental and quasi-experimental designs for research.* Rand McNally College.

Ceballo, R. (2017). Passion or data points? Studying African American women's experiences with infertility. *Quantitative Psychology, 4*(3), 302–14.

Cheung, F. M. (1985). Cross-cultural consideration for the translation and adaptation of the Chinese MMPI in Hong Kong. In J. N. Butcher & C. D. Spielberger (Eds.), *Advances in personality assessment* (Vol. 4, pp. 131–58). Erlbaum.

Chiu, C.-Y., Gelfand, M. J., Yamagishi, T., Shteynberg, G., & Wan, C. (2010). Intersubjective culture: The role of intersubjective perceptions in cross-cultural research. *Perspectives on Psychological Science, 5*, 482–93.

Chooi, W.-T., Long, H., & Thompson, L. (2014). The Sternberg Triarchic Abilities Test (Level-H) is a measure of g. *Journal of Intelligence, 2*(3), 56–67. doi:10.3390/jintelligence2030056.

Clarke, V., Ellis, S. J., Peel, E., & Riggs, D. W. (2010). *Lesbian, gay, bisexual, trans and queer psychology: An introduction.* Cambridge University Press.

Cocodia, E. A. (2014). Cultural perceptions of human intelligence. *Journal of Intelligence, 2*(4), 180–96. doi:10.3390/jintelligence2040180.

Cole, M., Gay, J., Glick, J., & Sharp, D. W. (1971). *The cultural context of learning and thinking.* Basic Books.

Coles, R., & Swami, V. (2012). The sociocultural adjustment trajectory of international university students and the role of university structures: A qualitative investigation. *Journal of Research in International Education, 11*(1), 87–100. https://doi.org/10.1177/1475240911435867

Culross, R., & Winkler, D. (2011). Review of the essential Sternberg: Essays on intelligence, psychology, and education [Review of the book *The essential Sternberg: Essays on intelligence, psychology, and education*, by J. C. Kaufman & E. L. Grigorenko, Eds.]. *Psychology of Aesthetics, Creativity, and the Arts, 5*(2), 194–5. doi:10.1037/a0020107

Diener, E., & Biswas-Diener, R. (2020). The replication crisis in psychology. In R. Biswas-Diener & E. Diener (Eds.), *Noba textbook series: Psychology.* DEF publishers. http://noba.to/q4cvydeh

Dolnicar, S., & Grun, B. (2007). Cross-cultural differences in survey response patterns. *International Marketing Review, 24*(2), 127–43.

Dorfman, D. D. (1978). The Cyril Burt question: New findings. *Science, 201*, 1177–86.

Duarte, M. E. (2018). Life design paradigm: A perspective and practice for career counseling in the twenty-first century. In K. Shigemasu, S. Kuwano, T. Sato, & T. Matsuzawa (Eds.), *Diversity in harmony—Insights from psychology: Proceedings of the 31st International Congress of Psychology* (pp. 255–67). John Wiley & Sons. https://doi-org.subzero.lib.uoguelph.ca/10.1002/9781119362081.ch13

Educational Testing Service. (2020). *The content and structure.* ETS GRE. https://www.ets.org/gre/revised_general/about/content/

Ejiade, O. O., & Salami, K. K. (2018). Conducting social research with elderly: Methodological concerns for researchers and older people in Southwestern Nigeria. *Journal of Aging and Geriatric Medicine, 2*(2). doi:10.4172/2576-3946.1000116

Eron, L. D. (2000). A psychological perspective. In V. B. Van Hasselt & M. Hersen (Eds.), *Aggression and violence: An introductory text* (pp. 23–39). Allyn & Bacon.

Eron, L. D., Huessman, L. R., Lefkowitz, M. M., & Walder, L. O. (1996). Does television violence cause aggression? In D. F. Greenberg (Ed.), *Criminal careers: Vol. 2. The international library of criminology, criminal justice and penology* (pp. 311–21). Dartmouth.

Eron, L. D., Walder, L. O., & Lefkowitz, M. M. (1971). *The learning of aggression in children.* Little, Brown.

Fields, A. J. (2010). Multicultural research and practice: Theoretical issues and maximizing cultural exchange. *Professional Psychology: Research and Practice, 41,* 196–201.

Flynn, D., Gillespie, C., Joyce, M., & Spillane, A. (2020). An evaluation of the skills group component of DBT-A for parent/guardians: A mixed methods study. *Irish Journal of Psychological Medicine.* https://doi-org.subzero.lib.uoguelph.ca/10.1017/ipm.2019.62

Funderburk, J. S., Levandowski, B. A., Wittink, M. N., & Pigeon, W. R. (2020). Team communication within integrated primary care in the context of suicide prevention: A mixed methods preliminary examination. *Psychological Services, 17*(1), 110–7. doi:10.1037/ser0000287

Galton, F. (1883). *Inquiries into human faculty and its development.* Macmillan.

Gardner, H. (1983). *Frames of mind: The theory of multiple intelligences.* Basic Books.

Gardner, H. (1993). *Multiple intelligences: The theory in practice.* Basic Books.

Gardner, H. (1999). *Intelligence reframed.* Basic Books.

Gillie, D. (1977). The IQ question. *Phi Delta Kappan, 58,* 469.

Gilligan, C. (1982/1993). *In a different voice: Psychological theory and women's development.* Harvard University Press.

Hales, A. H. (2016). Does the conclusion follow from the evidence? Recommendations for improving research. *Journal of Experimental Social Psychology, 66,* 39–46. doi:10.1016/j.jesp.2015.09.011

Hays, P. A. (1996). Culturally responsive assessment with diverse older clients. *Professional Psychology: Research and Practice, 27,* 188–93.

Hays, P. A. (2007). *Addressing cultural complexities in practice: Assessment, diagnosis, and therapy* (2nd ed.). American Psychological Association.

Hays, P. A. (2009). Integrating evidence-based practice, cognitive-behavioral therapy, and multicultural therapy: Ten steps for culturally competent practice. *Professional Psychology: Research and Practice, 40,* 354–60.

Hays, P. A. (2016). *Addressing cultural complexities in practice* (3rd ed.). American Psychological Association.

He, J., & van de Vijver, F. (2012). Bias and equivalence in cross-cultural research. *Online Readings in Psychology and Culture, 2*(2). doi.org/10.9707/2307-0919.1111

Hesse-Biber, S. N., & Leavy, P. (Eds.). (2003). *Approaches to qualitative research: A reader on theory and practice.* Oxford University Press.

Hesse-Biber, S. N., & Yaiser, M. (Eds.). (2003). *Feminist perspectives on social research.* Oxford University Press.

Holder, A. M. B., Jackson, M. A., & Ponterotto, J. G. (2015). Racial microaggression experiences and coping strategies of Black women in corporate leadership. *Qualitative Psychology, 2*(2), 147–63.

Jones, J. (1993). The concept of race in social psychology. In L. Wheler & P. Shaver (Eds.), *Review of personality and social psychology* (Vol. 4, pp. 117–50). SAGE.

Kamin, L. (1974). *The science and politics of IQ.* Erlbaum.

Kearns, L. L. (2011). High-stakes standardized testing and marginalized youth: An examination of the impact on those who fail. *Canadian Journal of Education, 34*(2), 112–30.

Kim, S. C. (1997). Korean American families. In E. Lee (Ed.), *Working with Asians: A guide for clinicians* (pp. 125–35). Guilford Press.

Korchin, S. J. (1980). Clinical psychology and minority problems. *American Psychologist, 35,* 262–9.

Labouvie-Vief, G. (1985). Intelligence and cognition. In J. E. Birren & K. W. Schaie (Eds.), *Handbook of the psychology of aging* (2nd ed., pp. 500–30). Van Nostrand Reinhold.

Lentz, T. F. (1938). Acquiescence as a factor in the measurement of personality. *Psychological Bulletin 35,* 659.

Lin, M., Bieda, A., & Margraf, J. (2020). Short form of the Sense of Coherence Scale (SOC-L9) in the US, Germany, and Russia: Psychometric properties and cross-cultural measurement invariance test. *European Journal of Psychological Assessment 36*(5), 796–804. doi:10.1027/1015-5759/a000561

Lonner, W. J. (1979). Issues in cross-cultural psychology. In A. J. Marsella, R. Tharp, & T. Ciborowski (Eds.), *Perspectives on cross-cultural psychology* (pp. 17–45). Halstead Press.

Luria, A. R. (1976). *Cognitive development: Its cultural and social foundations.* Harvard University Press.

Marsella, A. J. (1980). Depressive experience and disorder across cultures. In H. C. Triandis & J. G. Draguns (Eds.), *Handbook of cross-cultural psychology: Vol. 6. Psychopathology* (pp. 237–89). Allyn & Bacon.

Meisenberg, G. (2008). How universal is the negative correlation between education and fertility? *Journal of Social, Political, and Economic Studies, 33*(2), 205–27.

Meuter, R. F., Gallois, C., Segalowitz, N. S., Ryder, A. G., & Hocking, J. (2015). Overcoming language barriers in healthcare: A protocol for investigating safe and effective communication when patients or clinicians use a second language. *BMC Health Services Research, 15*(1), 371. doi:10.1186/s12913-015-1024-8

Milfont, T. L, & Klein, R. A. (2018). Replication and reproducibility in cross-cultural psychology. *Journal of Cross-Cultural Psychology, 49*(5), 735–50. 10.1177/0022022117744892

Miller, C., & Stassun, K. (2014). A test that fails. *Nature, 510,* 303–4. https://doi.org/10.1038/nj7504-303a

Minocha, Sh., Hartnett, E., Dunn., K., Evans, Sh., Heap, T., Middup, Ch. P., Murphy, B., & Roberts, D. (2013). Conducting empirical research with older people. In *Designing for—and with—vulnerable people*. http://oro.open.ac.uk/36592/1/Minocha_DFWVP2013.pdf

Mio, J. S. (2002). Narrative as exemplar: In search of culture [Review of the book *Culture in psychology*]. *Contemporary Psychology: APA Review of Books*, 47, 506–8.

Momani, R. T., & Gharaibeh, S. A. (2017). Investigating the construct validity of Sternberg's triarchic abilities test level-H (Arabic version). *International Journal of Advanced and Applied Sciences*, 4(11), 28–34. doi:10.21833/ijaas.2017.011.005

Mupinga, E. E., & Mupinga, D. M. (2005). Perceptions of international students toward GRE. *College Student Journal*, 39(2), 402–8.

Ndengeyingoma, A., Montigny, F. D., & Miron, J. M. (2014). Development of personal identity among refugee adolescents: Facilitating elements and obstacles. *Journal of Child Health Care*, 18(4), 369–77. doi:10.1177/1367493513496670

Nesselroade, J. R., & Labouvie, E. W. (1985). Experimental design in research on aging. In J. E. Birren & K. W. Schaie (Eds.), *Handbook of the psychology of aging* (2nd ed., pp. 35–60). Van Nostrand Reinhold.

Neubert, J. C., Mainert, J., Kretzschmar, A., & Greiff, S. (2015). The assessment of 21st-century skills in industrial and organizational psychology: Complex and collaborative problem solving. *Industrial and Organizational Psychology*, 8(2), 238–68.

Ngaage, M., & Agius, M. (2016). Does the increased rate of schizophrenia diagnosis in African Caribbean men in the UK shown by the AESOP study reflect cultural bias in healthcare? *Psychiatria Danubina*, 28(1), 25–30. https://pdfs.semanticscholar.org/8155/97cbadf7651f6ac5d7b24beb77bb-bc96c1c8.pdf

Oishi, S., Graham, J., Kesebir, S., & Galinha, I. C. (2013). Concepts of happiness across time and cultures. *Personality and Social Psychology Bulletin*, 39(5), 359–77. doi:10.1177/0146167213480042

Open Science Collaboration. (2012). An open, large-scale, collaborative effort to estimate the reproducibility of psychological science. *Perspectives on Psychological Science*, 7(6), 657–60. 10.1177/1745691612462588

Open Science Collaboration. (2015). Estimating the reproducibility of psychological science. *Science*, 349(6251), aac4716. doi:10.1126/science.aac4716

Organisation for Economic Co-operation and Development. (2013). *PISA 2012 assessment and analytical framework: Mathematics, reading, science, problem solving and financial literacy*. OECD Publishing. doi:10.1787/9789264190511-en

Organisation for Economic Co-operation and Development. (2017). *PISA 2015 results (volume V): Collaborative problem solving*. OECD Publishing. http://dx.doi.org/10.1787/9789264285521-en

Paniagua, F. A. (2001). *Diagnosis in a multicultural context* (2nd ed.). SAGE.

Paniagua, F. A. (2014). *Assessing and treating culturally diverse clients: A practical guide* (4th ed.). SAGE.

Roth, B., Becker, N., Romeyke, S., Schäfer, S., Domnick, F., & Spinath, F. M. (2015). Intelligence and school grades: A meta-analysis. *Intelligence*, 53, 118–37. doi:10.1016/j.intell.2015.09.002

Seale, C., Gobo, G., Gubrium, J. F., & Silverman, D. (Eds.). (2004). *Qualitative research practice*. SAGE.

Smith, P. B., & Fischer, R. (2008). Acquiescence, extreme response bias and culture: A multilevel analysis. In F. J. R. van de Vijver, D. A. van Hemert, & Y. H. Poortinga (Eds.), *Multilevel analysis of individuals and cultures* (pp. 285–314). Taylor & Francis Group/Lawrence Erlbaum Associates.

Spearman, C. (1927). *The abilities of man*. Macmillan.

Spearman, C. S. (1904). "General intelligence," objectively determined and measured. *American. Journal of Psychology*, 15, 201–93.

Stedman, J. M., Kostelecky, M., Spalding, T. L., & Gagné, C. (2016). Scientific realism, psychological realism, and Aristotelian-Thomistic realism. *The Journal of Mind and Behavior*, 37(3), 199–218. https://www.jstor.org/stable/44631770

Stern, P., & Carstensen, L. (Eds.) (2000). *The aging mind: Opportunities in cognitive research*. National Academy Press.

Sternberg, R. (2018). Speculations on the role of successful intelligence in solving contemporary world problems. *Journal of Intelligence*, 6(1), 4. doi:10.3390/jintelligence6010004

Sternberg, R. J. (2002). Successful intelligence: A new approach to leadership. In R. E. Riggio, S. E. Murphy, & F. J. Pirozzolo (Eds.), *Multiple intelligences and leadership* (pp. 9–28). Erlbaum.

Sternberg, R. J. (2012). Intelligence in its cultural context. In M. J. Gelfand, C.-Y. Ciu, & Y.-Y. Hong (Eds.), *Advances in culture and psychology* (Vol. 2, pp. 205–48). Oxford University Press.

Sternberg, R. J. (2014). Teaching about the nature of intelligence. *Intelligence*, 42, 176–9.

Sternberg, R. J., Ferrari, M., Clinkenbeard, P. R., & Grigorenko, E. L. (1996). Identification, instruction, and assessment of gifted children: A construct validation of a triarchic model. *Gifted Child Quarterly*, 40, 129–37.

Sternberg, R. J., Grigorenko, E. L., Ferrari, M., & Clinkenbeard, P. (1999). A triarchic analysis of an aptitude-treatment interaction. *European Journal of Psychological Assessment*, 15, 1–11.

Sternberg, R. J., Rayner, S., & Zhang, L.-F. (2013). An intelligent analysis of human intelligence. *American Journal of Psychology*, 126, 505–9.

Sue, D. W. (1981). *Counseling the culturally different: Theory and practice*. Wiley.

Sue, D. W., & Sue, D. (1990). *Counseling the culturally different: Theory and practice* (2nd ed.). Wiley.

Sue, D. W., & Sue, D. (1999). *Counseling the culturally different: Theory and practice* (3rd ed.). Wiley.

Sue, D. W., & Sue, D. (2003). *Counseling the culturally diverse: Theory and practice* (4th ed.). Wiley.

Sue, D. W., & Sue, D. (2008). *Counseling the culturally diverse: Theory and practice* (5th ed.). Wiley.

Sue, D. W., & Sue, D. (2013). *Counseling the culturally diverse: Theory and practice* (6th ed.). Wiley.

Sue, D. W., & Sue, D. (2016). *Counseling the culturally diverse: Theory and practice* (7th ed.). Wiley.

Sue, S. (1999). Science, ethnicity, and bias: Where have we gone wrong? *American Psychologist, 54*, 1070–7.

Sung, K. (1991). Family-centered informal support networks of Korean elderly: The resistance of cultural traditions. *Journal of Cross-Cultural Gerontology, 6*, 431–47.

ten Have, P. (2004). *Understanding qualitative research and ethnomethodology*. SAGE.

Thorndike, R. L., Hagen, E. P., & Sattler, J. M. (1986). *Technical manual for the Stanford–Binet Intelligence Scale* (4th ed.). Riverside.

Trafimow, D., Triandis, H. C., & Goto, S. G. (2009). Some tests of the distinction between the private self and the collective self. In P. B. Smith & D. L. Best (Eds.), *Cross-cultural psychology: Vol. 1. Basic issues* (pp. 321–33). SAGE.

Treffert, D. A. (2006). *Extraordinary people: Understanding savant syndrome*. iUniverse.

Triandis, H. C. (1989). The self and social behavior in differing cultural contexts. *Psychological Review, 96*, 506–20.

Triandis, H. C., Bontempo, R., Betancourt, H., Bond, M., Leung, K., Brenes, A., . . . de Montmollin, G. (1986). The measurement of etic aspects of individualism and collectivism across cultures. *Australian Journal of Psychology, 38*, 257–67.

Triandis, H. C., Bontempo, R., Villareal, M. J., Asai, M., & Lucca, N. (1988). Individualism and collectivism: Cross-cultural perspectives on self-ingroup relationships. *Journal of Personality and Social Psychology, 54*, 323–38.

van de Vijver, F. (2009). Meta analysis of cross-cultural comparisons of cognitive test performance. In P. B. Smith & D. L. Best (Eds.), *Cross-cultural psychology: Vol. 1. Basic issues* (pp. 212–39). SAGE.

van de Vijver, F. (2015). Methodological aspects of cross-cultural research. In M. Gelfand, Y. Hong, & C. Y. Chiu (Eds.), *Handbook of advances in culture & psychology* (Vol. 5, pp. 101–160). Oxford University Press.

van de Vijver, F. J. R., & Meiring, D. (2011, March). *Social desirability among Blacks and Whites in South Africa*. Paper presented at Cross-Cultural Psychology Symposium at Tilburg University, the Netherlands.

van de Vijver F. J. R., & Tanzer, N. K. (2004). Bias and equivalence in cross-cultural assessment: An overview. *European Review of Applied Psychology, 54*(2), 119–35.

Wagner, R. K. (2000). Practical intelligence. In R. J. Sternberg (Ed.), *Practical intelligence in everyday life*. Cambridge University Press.

Wechsler, D. (1991). *Manual for the Wechsler Intelligence Scale for children* (3rd ed.). Psychological Corporation.

Wilson, J., Gabriel, L., & James, H. (2014). Observing a client's grieving process: Bringing logical positivism into qualitative grief counselling research. *British Journal of Guidance & Counselling, 42*(5), 568–83. https://doi-org.subzero.lib.uoguelph.ca/10.1080/03069885.2014.936823

Yoon, E., Adams, K., Clawson, A., Chang, H., Surya, S., & Jérémie-Brink, G. (2017). East Asian adolescents' ethnic identity development and cultural integration: A qualitative investigation. *Journal of Counseling Psychology, 64*(1), 65–79. https://doi.org/10.1037/cou0000181

Chapter 3

Adair, W. L., Hideg, I., & Spence, J. R. (2013). The culturally intelligent team: The impact of team cultural intelligence and cultural heterogeneity on team shared values. *Journal of Cross-Cultural Psychology, 44*, 941–62. doi:10.1177/0022022113492894

Afifi, T. O., Sareen, J., Fortier, J., Taillieu, T., Turner, S., Cheung, K., & Henriksen, C. A. (2017). Child maltreatment and eating disorders among men and women in adulthood: Results from a nationally representative United States sample. *International Journal of Eating Disorders, 50*(11), 1281–96. doi:10.1002/eat.22783

Alter, C. (2018, April 2). The young and the relentless: Adults have failed to stop school shootings. Now it's the kids' turn to try. *Time, 191*(12), pp. 24–31.

Anonymous. (2016). *Life ended when my parents found out about my secret relationship*. The Tempest. https://thetempest.co/2016/07/20/life-love/when-my-parents-found-out-about-my-secretrelationship/

Aquino, K. (2016). Anti-racism "from below": Exploring repertoires of everyday anti-racism. *Ethnic and Racial Studies, 39*(1), 105–22. https://doi.org/10.1080/01419870.2016.1096408

Arnett, J. J. (2008). The neglected 95 per cent: Why American psychology needs to become less American. *American Psychologist, 63*(7), 602–14.

Ball, L. C., Cribbie, R. A., & Steele, J. R. (2013). Beyond gender differences: Using tests of equivalence to evaluate gender similarities. *Psychology of Women Quarterly, 37*(2), 147–54. 10.1177/0361684313480483

Batalha, L., Reynolds, K. J., & Newbiggin, C. A. (2011). All else being equal: Are men always higher in social dominance orientation than women? *European Journal of Social Psychology, 41*(6), 796–806. 10.1002/ejsp.829

BBC News. (2021, January 25). *Biden overturns Trump transgender military ban*. https://www.bbc.com/news/world-us-canada-55799913

Bendahan, S., Zehnder, C., Pralong, F. P., & Antonakis, J. (2015). Leader corruption depends on power and testosterone. *The Leadership Quarterly, 26*(2), 101–22.

Bernal, G., Cumba-Aviles, E., & Rodriguez-Quintana, N. (2014). Methodological challenges in research with ethnic, racial, and ethnocultural groups. In F. T. L. Leong, L. Comas-Díaz, G. C. N. Hall, V. C. McLoyd, & J. E. Trimble (Eds.), *APA handbook of multicultural psychology*: Vol. 1. Theory and research (pp. 105–23). American Psychological Association.

Bernal, G., & Domenech Rodriguez, M. M. (2012). *Cultural adaptations: Tools for evidence-based practice with diverse populations*. American Psychological Association.

Berry, J. W. (1969). On cross-cultural comparability. *International Journal of Psychology*, *4*, 119–28.

Berry, J. W., Poortinga, Y. H., Segall, M. H., & Dasen, P. R. (1992). *Cross-cultural psychology: Research and applications*. Cambridge University Press.

Bhui, K., Halvorsrud, K., & Nazroo, J. (2018). Making a difference: Ethnic inequality and severe mental illness. *The British Journal of Psychiatry: The Journal of Mental Science*, *213*(4), 574–8. 10.1192/bjp.2018.148

Bissinger, B. (2015, June 15). Caitlyn Jenner: The full story. *Vanity Fair*. https://www.vanityfair.com/hollywood/2015/06/caitlyn-jenner-bruce-cover-annie-leibovitz

Boesveld, S. (2017, July 21). It's been six months since the Women's March. *Maclean's*. What's changed? https://www.macleans.ca/society/its-been-six-months-since-the-womens-march-whats-changed/

Boylan, J. J., Jennings, J. R., & Matthews, K. A. (2016). Childhood socioeconomic status and cardiovascular reactivity and recovery among Black and White men: Mitigating effects of psychological resources. *Health Psychology*, *35*(9), 957–66.

Brenner, C. (1982). *The mind in conflict*. International Universities Press.

Bridges, T. (2017, February 1). *Just how big was the 2017 Women's March?* Huffington Post. https://www.huffpost.com/entry/just-how-big-was-the-2017-women-march_b_588fb282e4b-04c35d58350e1

Brislin, R. W. (1980). Translation and content analysis of oral and written materials. In H. C. Triandis & J. W. Berry (Eds.), *Handbook of cross-cultural psychology: Vol. 2. Methodology* (pp. 389–444). Allyn & Bacon.

Buyantueva, R. (2018). LGBT rights activism and homophobia in Russia. *Journal of Homosexuality*, *65*(4), 456–83. doi:10.1080/00918369.2017.1320167

Calvez, S. S. (2008). *Exploring knowledge of Canadian values and social axioms in international and landed immigrant students' adaptation to Canada* [Unpublished master's thesis]. University of Saskatchewan.

Calvez, S. S. (2014). *Understanding the understanding through intervention: Assessing the effect of learning knowledge about Canadian values and social axioms for newcomers' adapting to Canada* [Unpublished PhD dissertation]. University of Guelph.

Campuzano, M. V. (2019). Force and inertia: A systematic review of women's leadership in male-dominated organizational cultures in the United States. *Human Resource Development Review*, *18*(4), 437–69. doi:10.1177/1534484319861169

Canadian Blood Services. (2019). *About men who have sex with men*. https://blood.ca/en/blood/am-i-eligible/about-msm

Canadian Women's Foundation. (n.d.). *The facts: The #MeToo movement and its impact in Canada*. https://canadianwomen.org/the-facts/the-metoo-movement-inPrince/

CBC (2013). *A Look Back At Canada's Tainted Blood Scandal*. https://www.cbc.ca/strombo/news/canadas-tainted-blood-scandal

Chen, Y.-Y., & Hong, Y.-Y. (2015). Different ways to resolve discrepancy between descriptive and injunctive norms across cultures. *Journal of Cross-Cultural Psychology*, *46*(10), 1316–19. 10.1177/0022022115600265

Chetty, R., Stepner, M., Abraham, S., Lin, S., Scuderi, B., Turner, N., . . . Cutler, D. (2016). The association between income and life expectancy in the United States, 2001–2014. *JAMA: Journal of the American Medical Association*, *315*(16), 1750–66.

Cheung, F. M., & Tang, C. S. K. (2017). Women's lives in contemporary Chinese societies. In C. M. Brown, U. P. Gielen, J. L. Gibbons, & J. Kuriansky (Eds.), *Women's evolving lives: Global and psychosocial perspectives* (pp. 19–38). Springer International Publishing. https://doi.org/10.1007/978-3-319-58008-1_2

Clark, A. E., D'Ambrosio, C., & Ghislandi, S. (2016). Adaptation to poverty in long-run panel data. *Review of Economics and Statistics*, *98*(3), 591–600.

Cleveland, M., Erdoğan, S., Arıkan, G., & Poyraz, T. (2011). Cosmopolitanism, individual-level values and cultural-level values: A cross-cultural study. *Journal of Business Research*, *64*, 934–43. doi:10.1016/j.jbusres.2010.11.015

Colquhoun, G. (2002). *Playing God*. Auckland, New Zealand: Publishing Press.

Coogler, R. (Director). (2018, January 29). *Black Panther* [Film]. Marvel Studios.

Crawford, M. (2003). Gender and humor in social context. *Journal of Pragmatics*, *35*, 1413–30.

Daley, L. P., Travis, D. J., & Shaffer, E. S. (2018). *Sexual harassment in the workplace: How companies can prepare, prevent, respond, and transform their culture*. Catalyst. https://www.catalyst.org/research/sexual-harassment-in-the-workplace-how-companies-can-prepare-prevent-respond-and-transform-their-culture/

Danylova, T. (2014). Approaching the east: Briefly on Japanese value orientations. *International Journal of Social Science & Management*, *2*(8). https://www.researchgate.net/profile/Dr_Arup_Barman/publication/262818455_HRD_Climate_and_Knowledge_Management_PracticesEmpirical_investigation_in_Veterinary_Sector_Offices_in_Assam/links/5506b0ed0cf21de077859b9/HRD-Climate-and-Knowledge-Management-Practices-Empiricalinvestigation-in-Veterinary-Sector-Offices-in-Assam.pdf#page=9

Dhillon, A. K. (2016). *Lighten up: Exploring skin lightening practices among Canadian South Asian women*. http://hdl.handle.net/10315/33448

Dickenson, R., & Martin, L.-A. (2020). Turning the page on the politics of inclusion and exclusion, 30 years on. *C Magazine*, *144*. https://cmagazine.com/issues/144/turning-the-page-on-the-politics-of-inclusion

Dobrow, J., Gidney, C., & Burton, J. (2018, March 7). *Why it's so important for kids to see diverse TV and movie characters*. The Conversation. https://theconversation.com/why-its-so-important-for-kids-to-see-diverse-tv-and-movie-characters-92,57692,576?fbclid=IwAR2kRETnpAgaDLch_WV3cXJ5mdb9UiQjLmj4vPtZZrX_XsqwuYVgeUsNLM

Dominko, M., & Verbič, M. (2020). The effect of income and wealth on subjective well-being in the context of different welfare state regimes. *Journal of Happiness Studies*. https://doi.org/10.1007/s10902-020-00225-9

Dubowitz, T., Ncube, C., Leuschner, K., & Tharp-Gilliam, S. (2015). A natural experiment opportunity in two low-income urban food desert communities: Research design, community engagement methods, and baseline results. *Health Education & Behavior*, *42*(1, Suppl.), 87S–96S.

Eagly, A. H. (2009). The his and hers of prosocial behavior: An examination of the social psychology of gender. *American Psychologist*, *64*, 644–58.

Erigha, M. (2016). Do African Americans direct science fiction or blockbuster franchise movies? Race, genre, and contemporary Hollywood. *Journal of Black Studies*, *47*(6), 550–69.

Feather, N. T. (1986). Cross-cultural studies with the Rokeach Value Survey: The flinders program of research on values. *Australian Journal of Psychology*, *38*, 269–83. doi:10.1080/00049538608259014

Felsenthal, E. (2017, December 18). The choice. *Time*, *190 (25)* pp. 30–3.

Ford, T. E., Boxer, C. F., Armstrong, J., & Edel, J. J. (2008). More than "just a joke": The prejudice-releasing function of sexist humor. *Personality and Social Psychology Bulletin*, *34*, 159–70.

Ford, H., & Crowther, S. (1922). *My life and work*. Doubleday, Page.

Freeman, B. M. (2019). Promoting global health and well-being of Indigenous youth through the connection of land and culture-based activism. *Global Health Promotion*, *26*(3, Suppl.), 17–25. 10.1177/1757975919831253

Friedel, T. L. (2015). Understanding the nature of Indigenous youth activism in Canada: Idle no more as a resumptive pedagogy. *South Atlantic Quarterly*, *114*(4). 10.1215/00382876-3,157,402

Gigerenzer, G., Galesic, M., & Garcia-Retamero, R. (2014). Stereotypes about men's and women's institutions: A study of two nations. *Journal of Cross-Cultural Psychology*, *45*(1), 62–81. https://doi.org/10.1177/0022022113487074

Greenwood, D., & Long, C. R. (2015). When movies matter: Emerging adults recall memorable movies. *Journal of Adolescent Research*, *30*(5), 625–50.

Hagedorn, G., Loew, T., Seneviratne, S. I., Lucht, W., Beck, M., Hesse, J., . . . Zens, J. (2019). The concerns of the young protesters are justified: A statement by scientists for future concerning the protests for more climate protection. *Gaia*, *28*(2), 79–87. https://doi.org/10.14512/gaia.28.2.3

Halpern, D. F., Benbow, C. P., Geary, D. C., Gur, R. C., Hyde, J. S., & Gernsbacher, M. A. (2007). The science of sex differences in science and mathematics. *Psychological Science in the Public Interest*, *8*(1), 1–51).

Halpern, D. F., & Cheung, F. M. (2008). *Women at the top: Powerful leaders tell us how to combine work and family*. Wiley-Blackwell.

Han, K.-H. (2016). The feeling of "face" in Confucian society: From a perspective of psychosocial equilibrium. *Frontiers in Psychology*, *7*. doi:10.3389/fpsyg.2016.01055

Hancock, K. A. (2003). Lesbian, gay, and bisexual psychology: Past, present, and future directions. In J. S. Mio & G. Y. Iwamasa (Eds.), *Culturally diverse mental health: The challenges of research and resistance* (pp. 289–307). Brunner-Routledge.

Henrich, J., Heine, S. J., & Norenzayan, A. (2010). The weirdest people in the world? *Behavioral and Brain Sciences*, *33*(2–3), 61–135. doi:10.1017/S0140525X0999152X

Henrich, J., Heine, S. J., & Norenzayan, A. (2016). Most people are not WEIRD. In A. E. Kazdin (Ed.), *Methodological issues and strategies in clinical research* (pp. 113–14). American Psychological Association.

Herek, G. (2000). The psychology of sexual prejudice. *Current Directions in Psychological Science*, *9*, 19–22.

Hofstede, G. (1980). *Culture's consequences*. SAGE.

Hofstede, G. (1984). *Culture's consequences: Differences in work-related values*. SAGE Publications.

Hofstede, G. (2001). *Culture's consequences: Comparing values, behaviors, institutions and organizations across nations*. 2nd edition. SAGE Publications.

Hofstede, G. (2011). Dimensionalizing cultures: The Hofstede model in context. *Online Readings in Psychology and Culture*, *2*(1). https://doi.org/10.9707/2307-0919.1014

Hofstede, G., Hofstede, G. J., & Minkov, M. (2010). *Cultures and organizations: Software of the mind* (rev. 3rd ed.). McGraw-Hill.

Hutcherson, L. L. (2017, October 19). *My white friend asked me to explain white privilege, so I decided to be honest*. https://www.opendemocracy.net/en/transformation/my-white-friend-asked-me-to-explain-white-privilege-so-i-decide/

Iwamasa, G. Y., & Bangi, A. K. (2003). Women's mental health research: History, current status, and future directions. In J. S. Mio & G. Y. Iwamasa (Eds.), *Culturally diverse mental health: The challenges of research and resistance* (pp. 251–68). Brunner-Routledge.

Jahoda, G. (1982). *Psychology and anthropology: A psychological perspective*. Academic Press.

Jiang, Z. (2015). Core self-evaluation and career decision self-efficacy: A mediation model of value orientations. *Personality and Individual Differences*, *86*, 450–54. doi:10.1016/j.paid.2015.07.012

Johnson, T. (2018, February 16). Black superheroes matter: Why a Black Panther movie is revolutionary. *Rolling Stone*. https://www.rollingstone.com/movies/news/black-superheroes-matter-why-black-panther-is-revolutionary-w509105

Jones, D. (2010, June 25). A WEIRD view of human nature skews psychologists' studies: Relying on undergraduates from developed nations as research subjects creates a false picture of human behavior, some psychologists argue. *Science*, *328*(5986), 1627. doi:10.1126/science.328.5986.1627

Kantor, J., & Twohey, M. (2017, October 5). Harvey Weinstein paid off sexual harassment accusers for decades. *The New York Times*. https://www.nytimes.com/2017/10/05/us/harvey-weinstein-harassment-allegations.html

Kelmendi, K. (2015). Domestic violence against women in Kosovo: A qualitative study of women's experiences. *Journal of Interpersonal Violence*, *30*(4), 680–702. doi:10.1177/0886260514535255

Kim, U., & Park, Y.-S. (2006). The scientific foundation of indigenous and cultural psychology: The transactional approach. In U. Kim, K.-S. Yang, & K.-K. Hwang (Eds.), *Indigenous and cultural psychology: Understanding people in context* (pp. 27–48). Springer.

Kim, U., & Berry, J. W. (1993). *Indigenous psychologies: Experience and research in cultural context.* SAGE.

Kim, U., Yang, K.-S., & Hwang, K.-K. (2006). Contributions to indigenous and cultural psychology: Understanding people in context. In U. Kim, K.-S. Yang, & K.-K. Hwang (Eds.), *Indigenous and cultural psychology: Understanding people in context* (pp. 3–25). Springer.

Kitayama, S., & Markus, H. R. (1999). Yin and yang of the Japanese self: The cultural psychology of personality coherence. In D. Cervone & Y. Shoda (Eds.), *The coherence of personality: Social-cognitive bases of consistency, variability, and organization* (pp. 242–302). Guilford Press.

Kitayama, S., & Markus, H. R. (2000). The pursuit of happiness and the realization of sympathy: Cultural patterns of self, social relations, and well-being. In E. Diener & E. M. Suh (Eds.), *Culture and subjective well-being* (pp. 113–61).

Kitayama, S., Markus, H. R., Matsumoto, H., & Norasakkunkit, V. (1997). Individual and collective processes in the construction of the self: Self-enhancement in the United States and self-criticism in Japan. *Journal of Personality and Social Psychology, 72*, 1245–67.

Kitayama, S., Snibbe, A. C., Markus, H. R., & Suzuki, T. (2004). Is there any "free" choice? Self and dissonance in two cultures. *Psychological Science, 15*(8), 527–33. doi:10.1111/j.0956-7976.2004.00714.x

Kitayama, S., & Uchida, Y. (2003). Explicit self-criticism and implicit self-regard: Evaluating self and friend in two cultures. *Journal of Experimental Social Psychology, 39*, 476–82.

Kluckhohn, F. R., & Strodtbeck, F. L. (1961). *Variations in value orientations.* Row, Patterson.

Koss, M. P., Goodman, L. A., Browne, A., Fitzgerald, L. F., Keita, G. P., & Russo, N. F. (1994). *No safe haven: Male violence against women at home, at work, and in the community.* American Psychological Association.

Krugman, P. R. (2012). *End this depression now!* Norton.

Kwan, C., Baig, R., & Lo, K. (2018). Stressors and coping strategies of ethnic minority youth: Youth and mental health practitioners' perspectives. *Children and Youth Services Review, 88*, 497–503. https://doi.org/10.1016/j.childyouth.2018.04.002

La Ferle, C., Muralidharan, S., & Kim, E. (Anna). (2019). Using guilt and shame appeals from an Eastern perspective to promote bystander intervention: A study of mitigating domestic violence in India. *Journal of Advertising, 48*(5), 1–14. doi:10.1080/00913367.2019.1668893

Lan, G., Gowing, M., Rieger, F., McMahon, S., & King, N. (2010). Values, value types and moral reasoning of MBA students. *Business Ethics: A European Review, 19*, 183–98. doi:10.1111/j.1467-8608.2010.01587.x

Lee, K. C. (1991). The problem of appropriateness of the Rokeach Value Survey in Korea. *International Journal of Psychology, 26*, 299–310. doi:10.1080/00207599108246855

Leong, F. T. L., Kim, H. H. W., & Gupta, A. (2011). Attitudes toward professional counseling among Asian-American college students: Acculturation, conceptions of mental illness, and loss of face. *Asian American Journal of Psychology, 2*(2), 140–53. doi:10.1037/a0024172

Lim, T.-S. (1994). Facework and interpersonal relationships. In S. Ting-Toomey (Ed.), *The challenge of facework* (pp. 209–29). State University of New York Press.

Lott, B., & Bullock, H. E. (2007). *Psychology and economic justice: Personal, professional, and political intersections.* American Psychological Association.

Lovelock, M. (2017). "My coming out story": Lesbian, gay and bisexual youth identities on YouTube. *International Journal of Cultural Studies, 22*(1), 70–85. https://doi.org/10.1177/1367877917720237

Lyons, S., Duxbury, L., & Higgins, C. (2005). Are gender differences in basic human values a generational phenomenon? *Sex Roles, 53*, 763–78. doi:10.1007/s11199-005-7740-4

Macchia, L., & Whillans, A. V. (2019). Leisure beliefs and the subjective well-being of nations. *The Journal of Positive Psychology, 16*(2), 198–206. 10.1080/17439760.2019.1689413

Maiter, S., Joseph, A., Shan, N., & Saeid, A. (2012). Doing participatory qualitative research: Development of a shared critical consciousness with racial minority research advisory group members. *Qualitative Research, 13*(2), 198–213. https://doi.org/10.1177/1468794112455037.17

Markus, H. R., & Kitayama, S. (1991). Culture and the self: Implications for cognition, emotion, and motivation. *Psychological Review, 98*, 224–53.

Martin, N. G., & Sullivan, E. (2013). Sense of humor across cultures: A comparison of British, Australian and American respondents. *North American Journal of Psychology, 15*(2). https://go-gale-com.subzero.lib.uoguelph.ca/ps/i.do?id=GALE|A331348552&v=2.1&u=guel77241&it=&p=AONE&sw=w

Martin, R. A. (2007). *The psychology of humor: An integrative approach.* Elsevier.

Maslow, A. (1970). *Motivation and personality.* Harper & Row.

Matthews, K. A., Boylan, J. M., Jakubowski, K. P., Cundiff, J. M., Lee, L., Pardini, D. A., & Jennings, J. R. (2017). Socioeconomic status and parenting during adolescence in relation to ideal cardiovascular health in Black and White men. *Health Psychology, 36*(7), 673–81.

McCuaig, K. (2012). *Jamaican Canadian Music in Toronto in the 1970s and 1980s: A Preliminary History* [Unpublished master's thesis]. Carleton University.

McKeon, L. (2015, December 19). *What it's really like to be young and transgender in Canada.* Flare. https://www.flare.com/tv-movies/what-its-really-like-to-beyoung-and-trans-in-canada-now/

McLean, G. N., & Beigi, M. (2016). The importance of worldviews on women's leadership to HRD. *Advances in Developing Human Resources, 18*(2), 260–70.

Michelin, O. (2017, July 24). The hard truth about reconciliation. *Canadian Art Magazine.* https://canadianart.ca/features/the-hard-truth-about-reconciliation/

Mio, J. S. (2009). Metaphor, humor, and psychological androgyny. *Metaphor and Symbol, 24*, 174–83.

Mio, J. S. (2013). Holocultural method. In K. D. Keith (Ed.), *Encyclopedia of cross-cultural psychology* (pp. 663–4). Wiley.

Mio, J. S., & Awakuni, G. I. (2000). *Resistance to multiculturalism: Issues and interventions*. Brunner/Mazel.

Mio, J. S., & Fu, M. (2017). Poverty in the Asian/Pacific Islander American community: Social justice-related community responses. In A. W. Blume (Ed.), *Social issues in living color: Challenges and solutions from the perspective of ethnic minority psychology: Vol. 1. Overview and interpersonal issues* (pp. 75–92). Praeger.

Mio, J. S., & Graesser, A. C. (1991). Humor, language, and metaphor. *Metaphor and Symbolic Activity, 6*, 87–102.

Mio, J. S., & Iwamasa, G. Y. (1993). To do, or not to do: That is the question for white cross-cultural researchers. *The Counseling Psychologist, 21*, 197–212.

Mio, J. S., Koss, M. P., Harway, M., O'Neil, J. M., Geffner, R., Murphy, B. C., & Ivey, D. C. (2003). Violence against women: A silent pandemic. In J. S. Mio & G. Y. Iwamasa (Eds.), *Culturally diverse mental health: The challenges of research and resistance* (pp. 269–87). Brunner-Routledge.

Mio, J. S., & Morris, D. R. (1990). Cross-cultural issues in psychology training programs: An invitation for discussion. *Professional Psychology: Research and Practice, 21*, 434–41.

Mio, J. S., Nagata, D. K., Tsai, A. H., & Tewari, N. (2007). Racism against Asian/Pacific Island Americans. In F. T. L. Leong, A. G. Inman, A. Ebreo, L. H. Yang, L. Kinoshita, & M. Fu (Eds.), *Handbook of Asian American psychology* (2nd ed., pp. 341–61). SAGE.

Mischel, W. (1961). Delay of gratification, need for achievement, and acquiescence in another culture. *Journal of Abnormal and Social Psychology, 62*, 543–52.

Mischel, W. (1958). Preference for delayed reinforcement: An experimental study of a cultural observation. *Journal of Abnormal and Social Psychology, 56*, 57–61.

Mitchell, K. S., Mazzeo, S. E., Schlesinger, M. R., Brewerton, T. D., & Smith, B. N. (2011). Comorbidity of partial and subthreshold PTSD among men and women with eating disorders in the national comorbidity survey–replication study. *International Journal of Eating Disorders, 45*(3), 307–15. doi:10.1002/eat.20965

Mooij, M. D., & Hofstede, G. (2010). The Hofstede model. *International Journal of Advertising, 29*(1), 85–110. doi:10.2501/s026504870920104x

Murphy, E. F., & Anderson, T. L. (2001). A longitudinal study exploring value changes during the cultural assimilation of Japanese student pilot sojourners in the United States. *International Journal of Value-based Management, 16*, 111–29. doi:10.1023/A:1024091521657

Nadal K. L., Whitman, C. N., Davis, L. S., Erazo, T., & Davidoff, K. C. (2016). Microaggressions toward lesbian, gay, bisexual, transgender, queer, and genderqueer people: A review of the literature. *The Journal of Sex Research, 53*(4–5), 488–508. doi:10.1080/00224499.2016.1142495

Nagata, D. K. (1990a). The Japanese American internment: Exploring the transgenerational consequences of traumatic stress. *Journal of Traumatic Stress, 3*, 47–69.

Nagata, D. K. (1990b). *Legacy of injustice*. Plenum Press.

Nagata, D. K. (1993). *Legacy of silence: Exploring the long-term effects of the Japanese American internment*. Plenum Press.

Nagata, D. K. (1998). Internment and intergenerational relations. In L. C. Lee & N. W. S. Zane (Eds.), *Handbook of Asian American psychology* (pp. 433–56). SAGE.

Nagata, D. K., & Takeshita, Y. J. (1998). Coping and resilience across generations: Japanese Americans and the World War II internment. *Psychoanalytic Review, 85*, 587–613.

Okonogi, K. (1979). Japanese psychoanalysis and the Ajase complex (Kosawa). *Psychotherapy and Psychosomatics, 31*, 350–6. https://doi.org/10.1159/000287357

Phillip, N. (2018, June 21). L.G.B.T. couples on holding hands in public for the very first time. *The New York Times*. https://www.nytimes.com/2018/06/21/reader-center/pride-month-gay-queer-expressions.html

Pike, K. L. (1967). *Language in relation to a unified theory of the structure of human behavior*. Mouton.

Rappoport, L. (2005). *Punchlines: The case for racial, ethnic, and gender humor*. Praeger.

Rau, K. (2018). Lesbian, gay, bisexual and transgender rights in Canada. In *The Canadian Encyclopedia*. https://www.thecanadianencyclopedia.ca/en/article/lesbian-gay-bisexual-and transgender-rights-in-canada

Riggio, R. E. (2017, November 3). The minds of powerful sexual predators: How power corrupts: Three factors that propel powerful people to outrageous behavior. *Psychology Today*. https://www.psychologytoday.com/blog/cutting-edge-leadership/201711/the-minds-powerful-sexual-predators-how-power-corrupts

Roberts, M. (2018, February 15). Parkland school shooting 208th since Columbine: The tragic list. *Westword*. https://www.westword.com/news/parkland-to-columbine-school-shootings-list-9,993,641

Rokeach, M. (1973). *The nature of human values*. Free Press.

Rokeach, M. (1980). Some unresolved issues in theories of beliefs, attitudes and values. In H. E. Howe & M. M. (Eds.), *Nebraska symposium on motivation* (pp. 261–304). University of Nebraska Press.

Rokeach, M. (1981). *The three Christs of Ypsilanti*. Columbia University Press.

Rokeach, M., & Cochrane, R. (1972). Self-configuration and confrontation with another as determinants of long-term values change. *Journal of Applied Social Psychology, 2*, 283–92. doi:10.1111/j.1559-1816.1972.tb01280.x

Rokeach, M., & McLellan, D. D. (1972). Feedback of information about the values and attitudes of self and others as determinants of long-term cognitive and behavioral change. *Journal of Applied Social Psychology, 2*, 236–51. doi:10.1111/j.1559-1816.1972.tb01275.x

Rutherford, A. (2018, September 17). What the origins of the "1 in 5" statistic teaches us about sexual assault policy. *Behavioural Scientist*. https://behavioralscientist.org/what-the-origins-of-the-1-in-5-statistic-teaches-us-about-sexual-assault-policy/

Sams, L. B., & Keels, J. A. (2013). *Handbook on body image: Gender differences, sociocultural influences and health implications*. Nova Publishers.

Schwartz, S. H. (1994). Are there universal aspects in the structure and content of human values? *Journal of Social Issues*, *50*, 19–45. doi:10.1111/j.1540-4560.1994.tb01196.x

Schwartz, S. H. (2011). Values: Individual and cultural. In S. M. Breugelmans, A. Chasiotis, & F. J. R. van de Vijver (Eds.), *Fundamental questions in cross-cultural psychology* (pp. 463–93). Cambridge University Press.

Schwartz, S. H. (2012). An overview of the Schwartz theory of basic values. *Online Readings in Psychology and Culture*, *2*, 1. http://dx.doi.org/10.9707/2307-0919.1116

Seligman, M. E. P. (1982). *Helplessness: On depression, development and death*. Freeman.

Shi, X., & Wang, J. (2011). Interpreting Hofstede model and GLOBE model: Which way to go for cross-cultural research? *International Journal of Business and Management*, *6*(5). doi:10.5539/ijbm.v6n5p93

Shon, S. P., & Ja, D. Y. (1982). Asian families. In M. McGoldrick, J. K. Pearce, & J. Giordano (Eds.), *Ethnicity & family therapy* (pp. 208–28). Guilford Press.

Sommers, T. (2012). *Relative justice cultural diversity, free will, and moral responsibility*. Princeton University Press. doi:10.23943/Princeton/9780691139937.001.0001

Statistics Canada. (2019). *Labour force characteristics by industry, annual (x 1,000)*.

Stead, N. (2017, September 8). *Same-sex marriage vote: It's upsetting and hurtful to have people judge our lives*. https://www.smh.com.au/opinion/samesex-marriagevote-its-upsetting-and-hurtful-to-have-people-judge-our-lives-20,170,908gydctl.html?fbclid=IwAR0fzyOUKpSqvek46f34xTCw3LfNJTm93sHTC4b3UPiPfGPRjGb2eJY7w4

Stiglitz, J. E. (2012). *The price of inequality: How today's divided society endangers our future*. Norton.

Stone, M., & Vogelstein, R. (2019). *Celebrating #MeToo's global impact*. Foreign Policy. https://foreignpolicy.com/2019/03/07/metooglobalimpactinternationalwomens-day/

Stonequist, E. V. (1937). *The marginal man*. Scribner.

Sue, D. W. (1978). Eliminating cultural oppression in counseling: Toward a general theory. *Journal of Counseling Psychology*, *25*, 419–28.

Sue, D. W., & Sue, D. (2003). *Counseling the culturally diverse: Theory and practice* (4th ed.). Wiley.

Sue, D. W., & Sue, D. (2008). *Counseling the culturally diverse: Theory and practice* (5th ed.). Wiley.

Sue, D. W., & Sue, D. (2013). *Counseling the culturally diverse: Theory and practice* (6th ed.). Wiley.

Sue, D. W., & Sue, D. (2016). *Counseling the culturally diverse: Theory and practice* (7th ed.). Wiley.

Sue, S., & Sue, D. W. (2000). Conducting psychological research with the Asian American/Pacific Islander population. In Council of National Psychological Associations for the Advancement of Ethnic Minority Interests (Ed.), *Guidelines for research in ethnic minority communities* (pp. 2–4). American Psychological Association.

Sundararajan, L. (2015). *Understanding emotion in Chinese culture: Thinking through psychology*. Springer. doi:https://doi.org/10.1007/978-3-319-18221-6

Tan, E. S.-H., & Visch, V. (2018). Co-imagination of fictional worlds in film viewing. *Review of General Psychology*, *22*(2), 230–44.

Tao, Lin. (2017). Face perception in Chinese and Japanese. *Intercultural Communication Studies*, *24*(1), 151–67.

Tao, V. Y. K., & Hong, Y.-Y. (2014). When academic achievement is an obligation: Perspectives from social-oriented achievement motivation. *Journal of Cross-Cultural Psychology 45*(1), 110–36. doi:10.1177/0022022113490072

Taras, V., Steel P., & Kirkman, B. (2012). Improving national cultural indices using a longitudinal meta-analysis of Hofstede's dimensions. *Journal of World Business*, *47*(3), 329–41.

Ting-Toomey, S. (2005). The matrix of face: An updated face-negotiation theory. In W. B. Gudykunst (Ed.), *Theorizing about intercultural communication* (pp. 71–92). SAGE.

Ting-Toomey, S., & Cocroft, B.-A. (1994). Face and facework: Theoretical and research issues. In S. Ting-Toomey (Ed.), *The challenge of facework* (pp. 307–40). State University of New York Press.

Toppa, S. (2019, March 8). How Pakistani women are using IWD to push for peace with India. *Vice*. https://www.vice.com/en_ca/article/7xnqzd/how-pakistani-women-are-using-iwd-to-push-for-peace-with-india

Toppo, G. (2018, February 22). "Generation Columbine" has never known a world without school shootings. *USA Today*. https://www.usatoday.com/story/news/2018/02/22/generation-columbine-has-never-known-world-without-school-shootings/361656002/

Triandis, H. C., Bontempo, R., Betancourt, H., Bond, M., Leung, K., Brenes, A., . . . de Montmollin, G. (1986). The measurement of etic aspects of individualism and collectivism across cultures. *Australian Journal of Psychology*, *38*, 257–67.

Triandis, H. C. (1995). *Individualism & collectivism*. Westview.

Triandis, H. C., Bontempo, R., Villareal, M. J., Asai, M., & Lucca, N. (1988). Individualism and collectivism: Cross-cultural perspectives on self-ingroup relationships. *Journal of Personality and Social Psychology*, *54*, 323–38.

Trimble, J. E. (2003). Infusing American Indian and Alaska Native topics into the psychology curriculum. In P. Bronstein & K. Quina (Eds.), *Teaching gender and multicultural awareness: Resources for the psychology classroom* (pp. 221–36). American Psychological Association.

UN Refugee Agency Canada. (2019, December 10). *Asylum-seeker in Greece speaks out about the violence that upended her life*. https://www.unhcr.ca/news/asylum-seeker-greece-speaks-violence-upended-life/

van de Vijver, F. J. R, Chasiotis, A., & Breugelmans, S. M. (2011). *Fundamental questions in cross-cultural psychology*. Cambridge University Press.

Watkins, L., & Gnoth, J. (2011). The value orientation approach to understanding culture. *Annals of Tourism Research*, *38*(4), 1274–99. doi:10.1016/j.annals.2011.03.003

Young, S. D. (2012). *Psychology at the movies*. Wiley-Blackwell.

Zacharek, S., Docterman, E., & Edwards, H. S. (2017, December 18). The silence breakers. *Time*, *190*(25), pp. 34–71.

Zane, N., & Ku, H. (2014). Effects of ethnic match, gender match, acculturation, cultural identity, and face concern on self-disclosure in counseling for Asian Americans. *Asian American Journal of Psychology*, *5*, 66–74.

Zane, N., & Yeh, M. (2002). The use of culturally-based variables in assessment: Studies on loss of face. In K. S. Kurasaki, S. Okazaki, & S. Sue (Eds.), *Asian American mental health: Assessment methods and theories* (pp. 123–38). Kluwer Academic/Plenum Press.

Chapter 4

Adams, R. B., Jr., & Nelson, A. J. (2016). Eye behavior and gaze. In D. Matsumoto, H. C. Hwang, & M. G. Frank (Eds.), *APA handbook of nonverbal communication* (pp. 335–62). American Psychological Association.

Adaobi, N. O. (2014). Bilingualism and identity in Etulo. *OGIRISI: A New Journal of African Studies*, *10*(1), 23–35. http://doi.org/10.4314/og.v10i 1.2

Andersen, P. (1999). Cues of culture: The basis of intercultural differences in nonverbal communication. In L. A. Samovar & R. E. Porter (Eds.), *Intercultural communication: A reader* (8th ed., pp. 244–56). Wadsworth.

Andersen, P., Gannon, J., & Kalchik, J. (2013). Proxemic and haptic interaction: The closeness continuum. In J. A. Hall & M. L. Knapp (Eds.), *Handbooks of communication science. Nonverbal communication*, 295–329. https://doi-org/10.1515/9783110238150.295

Annisette, L. E., & Lafreniere, K. D. (2017). Social media, texting, and personality: A test of the shallowing hypothesis. *Personality and Individual Differences*, *115*, 154–8.

Argyle, M. (1975). *Bodily communication*. International University Press.

Ayasreh, A., & Razali, R. (2018). The flouting of Grice's conversational maxim: Examples from Bashar Al-Assad's interview during the Arab Spring. *IOSR Journal of Humanities and Social Science*, *23*, 43–7. http://doi.org/10.9790/08372305014347

Backhouse, J., & Graham, A. (2011). Grandparents raising grandchildren: Negotiating the complexities of role-identity conflict. *Child and Family Social Work*. *17*(3), 306–15. https://doi.org/10.1111/j.1365-2206.2011.00781

Baker, C. (2013). The development of theories of bilingualism and school achievement. In B. J. Irby, G. Brown, R. Laura-Alecio, & S. Jackson (Eds.), *The handbook of educational theories* (pp. 385–94). Information Age.

Ballantyne, P. J., Yang, M., & Boon, H. (2013). Interpretation in cross-language research: Tongue-tied in the health care interview? *Journal of Cross-Cultural Gerontology*, *28*, 391–405.

Basu, S., Zuo, X., Lou, C., Acharya, R., & Lundgren, R. (2017). Learning to be gendered: Gender socialization in early adolescence among urban poor in Delhi, India, and Shanghai, China. *Journal of Adolescent Health*, *61*, 24–9. http://doi.org/10.1016/j.jadohealth.2017.03.012

Bayer, J. B., Ellison, N. B., Schoenebeck, S. Y., & Falk, E. B. (2016). Sharing the small moments: Ephemeral social interaction on Snapchat. *Information, Communication & Society*, *19*(7), 956–77.

Beran, T., Mishna, F., McInroy, L. B., & Shariff, S. (2015). Children's experiences of cyberbullying: A Canadian national study. *Children & Schools*, *37*(4), 207–14. https://doi.org/10.1093/cs/cdv024

Berry, J. W., Poortinga, Y. H., Segall, M. H., & Dasen, P. R. (1992). *Cross-cultural psychology: Research and applications*. Cambridge University Press.

Bialystok, E., & Craik, F. I. M. (2010). Cognitive and linguistic processing in the bilingual mind. *Current Directions in Psychological Science*, *19*, 19–23.

Birdsong, D., & Vanhove, J. (2016). Age of second language acquisition: Critical periods and social concerns. In E. Nicoladis & S. Montanari (Eds.), *Language and the human lifespan series. Bilingualism across the lifespan: Factors moderating language proficiency* (pp. 163–81). American Psychological Association. https://doi.org/10.1037/14939-010

Bogen, K. W., Bleiweiss, K., & Orchowski, L. M. (2018). Sexual violence is #NotOkay: Social reactions to disclosures of sexual victimization on Twitter. *Psychology of Violence*, *9*(1). doi:10.1037/vio0000192

Bolmont, M., Cacioppo, J. T., & Cacioppo, S. (2014). Love is in the gaze: An eye-tracking study of love and sexual desire. *Psychological Science*, *25*(9), 1748–56.

Bond, M. H., & Hwang, K.-K. (1986). The social psychology of Chinese people. In M. H. Bond (Ed.), *The psychology of the Chinese people* (pp. 213–66). Oxford English Press.

Bongiorno, R., Bain, P. G., & David, B. (2014). If you're going to be a leader, at least act like it! Prejudice towards women who are tentative in leader roles. *British Journal of Social Psychology*, *53*, 217–34. http://.doi.org/10.1111/bjso.12032

Brennan, C., & Cook, K. (2015, September 25). Why college students aren't voting (and why it matters). *USA Today*. http://college.usatoday.com/2015/09/25/why-college-students-arent-voting

Bridges, A. (2020). *Q&A: Founder of Black Lives Matter in Canada explains the call to defund police*. CBC News. https://www.cbc.ca/news/canada/saskatoon/question-answer-sandy-hudson-black-lives-matter-defund-police-1.5613280

Brown, P., & Levinson, S. (1978). Universals in language usage: Politeness phenomena. In E. Goody (Ed.), *Questions and politeness* (pp. 56–289). Cambridge University Press.

Bruder, C., Blessing, L., & Wandke, H. (2014). Adaptive training interfaces for less-experienced, elderly users of electronic devices. *Behaviour and Information Technology*, *33*, 4–15.

Carli, L. (1990). Gender, language, and influence. *Journal of Personality and Social Psychology*, *59*, 941–51.

Chen, S. X. (2014). Toward a social psychology of bilingualism and biculturalism. *Asian Journal of Social Psychology, 18*(1), 1–11. https://doi.org/10.1111/ajsp.12088

Christenson, A. M., Buchanan, J. A., Houlihan, D., & Wanzek, M. (2011). Command use and compliance in staff communication with elderly residents of long-term care facilities. *Behavior Therapy, 42*, 47–58.

Clément, R., Noels, K. A., & Deneault, B. (2001). Interethnic contact, identity, and psychological adjustment: The mediating and moderating roles of communication. *Journal of Social Issues, 57*(3), 559–77. https://doi.org/10.1111/0022-4537.00229

Coulmas, F. (2017). *An introduction to multilingualism: Language in a changing world.* Oxford University Press.

Coyne, S. M., Padilla-Walker, L. M., & Holmgren, H. G. (2018). A six-year longitudinal study of texting trajectories during adolescence. *Child Development, 89*(1), 58–65.

DeKeyser, R. (2013). Age effects in second language learning: Stepping stones toward better understanding. *Language Learning, 63*(1), 52–67. https://doi.org/10.1111/j.1467-9922.2012.00737.x

Doley, R., Bell, R., Watt, B., & Simpson, H. (2015). Grandparents raising grandchildren: Investigating factors associated with distress among custodial grandparent. *Journal of Family Studies, 21*(2), 101–19. http://doi.org/10.1080/13229400.2015.1015215

Dolphin, C. Z. (1999). Variables in the use of personal space in intercultural transactions. In L. A. Samovar & R. E. Porter (Eds.), *Intercultural communication: A reader* (8th ed., pp. 266–76). Wadsworth.

Ekman, P. (1972). Universal and cultural differences in facial expression of emotion. In J. R. Cole (Ed.), *Nebraska symposium on motivation, 1971* (pp. 207–83). University of Nebraska Press.

Elliot, S., Scott, M. D., Jensen, A. D., & McDonough, M. (1982). Perceptions of reticence: A cross-cultural investigation. In M. Burgoon (Ed.), *Communication yearbook 5* (pp. 591–602). Transaction Books.

Erikson, E. H. (1950/1963). *Childhood and society* (2nd ed.). Norton.

Erikson, E. H. (1964). *Insight and responsibility.* Norton.

Fang, T., & Faure, G. O. (2011). Chinese communication characteristics: A Yin Yang perspective. *International Journal of Intercultural Relations, 35*(3), 320–33. doi:10.1016/j.ijintrel.2010.06.005

Fang, L., & Huang, Y.-T. (2020). "I'm in between": Cultural identities of Chinese youth in Canada. *Families in Society: The Journal of Contemporary Social Services, 1*–14. https://doi.org/10.1177/1044389419891333

Freynet, N., & Clément, R. (2015). Bilingualism in minority settings in Canada: Integration or assimilation? *International Journal of Intercultural Relations, 46*(C), 55–72. https://doi.org/10.1016/j.ijintrel.2015.03.023

Garcia, O., & Kleifgen, J. A. (2010). *Educating emergent bilinguals: Policies, programs, and practices for English language learners.* Teachers College Press.

Garcia-Penton, L., Fernandex, A.P., Iturria-Medina, Y., Gillon-Downes, M., & Carreiras, M. (2014). Anatomical connectivity changes in the bilingual brain. *NeuroImage, 84*, 495–504. http://dx.doi.org/10.1016/j.neuroimage.2013.08.064

Giles, H., Khajavy, G. H., & Choi, C. W. (2012). Intergenerational communication satisfaction and age boundaries: Comparative Middle Eastern data. *Journal of Cross-Cultural Gerontology, 27*, 357–71.

Gleason, B. (2018). Thinking in hashtags: Exploring teenagers' new literacies practices on Twitter. *Learning, Media and Technology, 43*(2), 165–80.

Goman, C. K. (2016, March 31). Is your communication style dictated by your gender? *Forbes.* https://www.forbes.com/sites/carolkinseygoman/2016/03/31/is-your-communication-style-dictated-by-your-gender/#1375978ceb9d

Government of Canada. (2017). Indigenous peoples and communities. https://www.rcaanc-cirnac.gc.ca/eng/1100100013785/1529102490303

Grice, H. P. (1975). Logic and conversation. In P. Cole & J. L. Morgan (Eds.), *Syntax and semantics*: *Vol. 3. Speech acts* (pp. 41–58). Seminar Press.

Grøver, V., Uccelli, P., Rowe, M., & Lieven, E. (Eds.). (2019). *Learning through language: Towards an educationally informed theory of language learning.* Cambridge University Press.

Gruzd, A., & Mai, P. (2020, July). *The state of social media in Canada 2020.* Ryerson University Social Media Lab. https://doi.org/10.5683/SP2/XIW8EW

Gudowska, M. (2019, February 22). A mother's tongue: The complexity of raising multilingual children. *The Globe and Mail.* https://www.theglobeandmail.com/opinion/article-a-mothers-tongue-the-complexity-of-raising-multilingual-children/

Hall, E. T. (1963). A system for the notation of proxemic behavior. *American Anthropologist, 65*, 1003–26.

Hall, E. T. (1966). *The hidden dimension.* Doubleday.

Hall, E. T. (1976). *Beyond culture: Into the cultural unconscious.* Anchor.

Hall, E. T. (1999). Context and meaning. In L. A. Samovar & R. E. Porter (Eds.), *Intercultural communication: A reader* (8th ed., pp. 45–54). Wadsworth.

Hanafiyeh, M., & Afghari, A. (2014). Gender differences in the use of hedges, tag questions, intensifiers, empty adjectives, and adverbs: A comparative study in the speech of men and women. *Indian Journal of Fundamental and Applied Life Sciences, 4*(S4), 1168–77.

Hayslip, B., Fruhauf, C., & Dolbin-MacNab, M. (2019). Grandparents raising grandchildren: What have we learned over the past decade? *The Gerontologist, 59*(3), 152–63. https://doi.org/10.1093/geront/gnx106

Higgins, C., & Stoker, K. (2011). Language learning as a site for belonging: A narrative analysis of Korean adoptee-returnees. *International Journal of Bilingual Education and Bilingualism, 14*, 299–412.

Holtzen, S. (2011). *Perceived gender-typing of successful managerial characteristics* [Unpublished undergraduate honours thesis]. University of Arkansas.

Huang, B. H. (2015). A synthesis of empirical research on the linguistic outcomes of early foreign language instruction. *International Journal of Multilingualism*, *13*(3), 257–73. https://doi.org/10.1080/14790718.2015.1066792

Idle No More. (2020). *Campaigns and actions*. https://idlenomore.ca/campaigns-actions/

Izadi, A. (2016). Over-politeness in Persian professional interactions. *Journal of Pragmatics*, *102*, 13–23. doi:10.1016/j.pragma.2016.06.004

Izadi, A., & Zilaie, F. (2014). Refusal strategies in Persian. *International Journal of Applied Linguistics*, *25*(2), 246–64. doi:10.1111/ijal.12065

Jackson, J. (2020). *Introducing language and intercultural communication*. Routledge.

Kaiser Family Foundation. (2013). *Health coverage by race and ethnicity: The potential impact of the Affordable Care Act*. http://kff.org/disparities-policy/issue-brief/health-coverage-by-race-and-ethnicity-the-potential-impact-of-the-affordable-care-act

Khalib, F. M., & Tayeh, A. (2014). Indirectness in English requests among Malay university students. *Procedia—Social and Behavioral Sciences*, *134*, 44–52. doi:10.1016/j.sbspro.2014.04.223

Kheirabadi, R., & Aghagolzadeh, F. (2012). Grice's cooperative maxims as linguistic criteria for news selectivity. *Theory and Practice in Language Studies*, *2*(3), 547–53.

Kim, M.-S. (2010). Intercultural communication in Asia: Current state and future prospects. *Asian Journal of Communication*, *20*(2), 166–80. doi:10.1080/01292981003693351

Kim, S., Boyle, M. H., & Georgiades, K. (2017). Cyberbullying victimization and its association with health across the life course: A Canadian population study. *Canadian Journal of Public Health*, *108*(5-6), e468–74. https://doi.org/10.17269/CJPH.108.6175

Kouhpaeenejad, M. H., & Gholaminejad, R. (2014). Identity and language learning from poststructuralist perspective. *Journal of Language Teaching and Research*, *5*(1), 199. https://doi.org/10.4304/jltr.5.1.199-204

Kroll, J. F., Bobb, S. C, & Hoshino, N. (2014). Two languages in mind: Bilingualism as a tool to investigate language, cognition, and the brain. *Current Directions in Psychological Science*, *23*, 159–63.

Kunst, A. (2019, June 18). *Social media usage by platform type in Canada*. Statistia. https://www.statista.com/forecasts/998535/social-media-usage-by-platform-type-in-canada

Lakoff, R. (1975). *Language and women's place*. Harper & Row.

Lambert, W. E. (1967). A social psychology of bilingualism. *Journal of Social Issues*, *23*(2), 91–109.

Lambert, W. E. (1977). The effects of bilingualism on the individual: Cognitive and sociocultural consequences. In P. A. Hornby (Ed.), *Bilingualism: Psychological, social and educational implications* (pp. 15–27). Academic Press.

Lambert, W. E. (1980). The social psychology of language: A perspective for the 1980s. In H. Giles, W. Robinson, & P. Smith (Eds.), *Language: Social psychological perspectives* (pp. 415–24). Pergamon.

Lambert, W. E., & Anisfeld, E. (1969). A note on the relationship of bilingualism and intelligence. *Canadian Journal of Behavioral Science*, *1*, 123–8.

Lebra, T. S. (1976). *Japanese patterns of behavior*. University of Hawai`i Press.

Leeman, J. (2010). Bilingualism and identity: Spanish at the crossroads with other languages. *International Journal of Bilingual Education and Bilingualism*, *13*(2), 262–5. https://doi.org/10.1080/13670050903106802

Lemak, A. (2012). *Silence, intercultural conversation, and miscommunication* [Unpublished master's thesis]. University of Toronto.

Llanes, A., & Muñoz, C. (2013). Age effects in a study abroad context: Children and adults studying abroad and at home. *Learning Language*, *63*(1), 63–90. http://doi.org/10.1111/j.1467-9922.2012.00731.x

Logan, S., Steel, Z., & Hunt, C. (2015). Investigating the effect of anxiety, uncertainty, and ethnocentrism on willingness to interact in an intercultural communication. *Journal of Cross-Cultural Psychology*, *46*(1), 39–52. http://doi.org/10.1177/0022022114555762

Lovell, B. L., Lee, R. T., & Brotheridge, C. M. (2012). Interpersonal factors affecting communication in clinical consultations: Canadian physicians' perspectives. *Journal of Health Care Quality Assurance*, *25*(6), 467–82. https://doi.org/10.1108/09526861211246430

Madibbo, A. (2016). The way forward: African francophone immigrants negotiate their multiple minority identities. *Journal of International Migration and Integration*, *17*(3), 853–66. http://doi.org/10.1007/s12134-015-0437-x

Mahmood, R. K., & Hussein, B. (2019). Functions of nonverbal behavior with reference to refugeeism: A sociopragmatic study. *Journal of Zankoy Sulaimani Part (B - for Humanities)*, *20*(2), 347–62. https://doi.org/10.17656/JZSB.10897

Marche, S. (2019, March 4). *Justin Trudeau lived by social media. Now he's dying by it*. Foreign Policy. https://foreignpolicy.com/2019/03/04/justin-trudeau-lived-by-social-media-now-hes-dying-by-it/

Matsumoto, D. (1991). Cultural influences on facial expressions of emotion. *Southern Communication Journal*, *56*, 128–37.

Matsumoto, D. (2000). *Culture and psychology: People around the world* (2nd ed.). Wadsworth/Thomson Learning.

Matsumoto, D. (2006). Are cultural differences in emotion regulation mediated by personality traits? *Journal of Cross-Cultural Psychology*, *37*(4), 421-437.

Matsumoto, D., & Juang, L. (2012). *Culture and psychology* (5th ed.). Thomson/Wadsworth.

McKay, V. C. (1999). Understanding the co-culture of the elderly. In L. A. Samovar & R. E. Porter (Eds.), *Intercultural communication: A reader* (8th ed., pp. 174–80). Wadsworth.

McKay, V. C. (1989). The grandparent–grandchild relationship. In J. F. Nussbaum (Ed.), *Life-span communication: Normative processes* (pp. 257–82). Erlbaum.

McKay, V. C. (1993). Making connections: Narrative as the expression of continuity between generations of grandparents and grandchildren. In N. Coupland & J. Nussbaum (Eds.), *Discourse and lifespan identity* (pp. 173–85). SAGE.

Mensah, J., & Williams, C. J. (2015). Seeing/being double: How African immigrants in Canada balance their ethno-racial and national identities. *African and Black Diaspora: An International Journal, 8*(1), 39–54. http://doi.org/10.1080/17528631.2014.986024

Menshikova, G. Y., Saveleva, O. A., & Zinchenko, Y. P. (2018). The study of ethnic attitudes during interactions with avatars in virtual environments. *Psychology in Russia: State of the Art, 11*(1), 18–29. https://doi.org/10.11621/pir.2018.0102

Merkin, R. (2015). The relationship between individualism/collectivism: Consultation and harmony needs. *Journal of Intercultural Communication, 39.* http://search.proquest.com/docview/1963405976/

Min, W. (2013). Cultural expectations behind Korean and Chilean social greetings and proxemics. *Korea Open Access Journal. 32,* 37–59. Researchgate.net

Minority Rights Group International. (2007). *World directory of minorities and indigenous peoples—Papua New Guinea.* Refworld. https://www.refworld.org/docid/4954ce47c.html

Moberg, P. J., & Rick, J. H. (2008). Decision-making capacity and competency in the elderly: A clinical and neuropsychological perspective. *NeuroRehabilitation, 23,* 403–13.

Mokuau, N., Brown, C. V., Lana, S., Higuchi, P., Sweet, K. M., & Braun, K. L. (2015). Native Hawaiian grandparents: Exploring benefits and challenges in the caregiving experience. *Journal of Indigenous Social Development, 4*(1), 1–19.

MTM Jr. (2020, January 14). *Teens and social media: Stats and statuses.* Media Technology Monitor Junior. https://mtm-otm.ca/Download.ashx?file=Files/PressReleases/2020-01-14-en.pdf

Muñoz, C. (2008). Age-related differences in foreign language learning. Revisiting the empirical evidence. *International Review of Applied Linguistics, 46*(3), 197–220. https://doi.org/10.1515/IRAL.2008.009

Norman, D. A., & Rummelhart, D. E. (Eds.). (1975). *Explorations in cognition.* Freeman.

Nussbaum, J., & Bettini, L. M. (1994). Shared stories of the grandparent–grandchild relationship. *International Journal of Aging and Human Development, 39,* 67–80.

Oborne, P., & Cooke, M. (2020). Reflections on the Black Lives Matter movement. *The Round Table, 109*(5), 612–13. https://doi.org/10.1080/00358533.2020.1820218

Ohbuchi, K.-I., & Takahashi, Y. (1994). Cultural styles of conflict management in Japanese and Americans: Passivity, covertness, and effectiveness of strategies. *Journal of Applied Social Psychology, 24,* 1345–66.

Paludi, M. A. (1998). *The psychology of women.* Prentice Hall.

Peal, E., & Lambert, W. E. (1962). The relation of bilingualism to intelligence. *Psychological Monographs, 76,* 1–23.

Pennbrant, S. (2013). A trustful relationship—the importance for relatives to actively participate in the meeting with the physician. *International Journal of Qualitative Studies on Health and Well-Being, 8*(1), 20608. https://doi.org/10.3402/qhw.v8i0.20608

Pingree, R. J., Stoycheff, E., Sui, M., & Peifer, J. T. (2018). Setting a non-agenda: Effects of a perceived lack of problems in recent news or Twitter. *Mass Communication & Society, 21*(5), 555–84. doi:10.1080/15205436.2018.1451543

Prado, C. G. (Ed.). (2017). *Social media and your brain: Web-based communication is changing how we think and express ourselves.* Praeger/ABC-CLIO.

Price-Williams, D., & Ramirez, M., III. (1977). Divergent thinking, cultural differences, and bilingualism. *Journal of Social Psychology, 103,* 3–11.

Ramlaul, A., & Vosper, M. (2013). *Patient-centered care in medical imaging and radiotherapy [e-book edition].* Elsevier.

Raynauld, V., Richez, E., & Morris, K. B. (2017). Canada is #IdleNoMore: Exploring dynamics of Indigenous political and civic protest in the Twitterverse. *Information, Communication & Society, 21*(4), 626–42. http://doi.org/10.1080/1369118x.2017.1301522

Romaine, S. (2017). Multilingualism. In M. Aronoff & J. Rees Miller (Eds.), *The handbook of linguistics* (2nd ed., pp. 541–56). John Wiley & Sons. doi:10.1002/9781119072256.ch26

Rossi, E., Cheng, Hu, Kroll, J. J., Diaz, M. T., & Newman, S. D. (2017). Changes in white-matter connectivity in late second language learners: Evidence from diffusion tensor imaging. *Frontiers in Psychology, 8,* 1–15. doi:10.3389/fpsyg.2017.02040

Sharifian, F. (2010). Cultural conceptualisations in intercultural communications: A study of Aboriginal and non-Aboriginal Australians. *Journal of Pragmatics, 42*(12), 3367–76. https://doi.org/10.1016/j.pragma.2010.05.006

Shon, S. P., & Ja, D. Y. (1982). Asian families. In M. McGoldrick, J. K. Pearce, & J. Giordano (Eds.), *Ethnicity & family therapy* (pp. 208–28). Guilford Press.

Singh, N., & Pereira, A. (2005). *The culturally customized web site: Customizing web sites for the global marketplace.* Elsevier.

Smith, P. B. (2011). Communication styles as dimensions of national culture. *Journal of Cross-Cultural Psychology, 42*(2), 216–33. http://doi.org/10.1177/0022022110396866

Snow, C. E. (1983). Age differences in second language acquisition: Research findings and folk psychology. In K. Bailey, M. Long, & S. Peck (Eds.), *Second language acquisition studies* (pp. 141–50). Newbury House.

Snow, C. E. (1987). Relevance of the notion of a critical period to language acquisition. In M. Bornstein (Ed.), *Sensitive periods in development: An interdisciplinary perspective* (pp. 183–209). Erlbaum.

Snow, C. E. (1993). Bilingualism and second language acquisition. In J. B. Gleason & N. B. Ratner (Eds.), *Psycholinguistics* (pp. 391–416). Harcourt, Brace, Jovanovich.

Sorokowska, A., Sorokowski, P., Hilpert, P., Cantarero, K., Frackowiak, T., Ahmadi, K., . . . Pierce, J. D., Jr. (2017). Preferred interpersonal distances: A global comparison. *Journal of Cross-Cultural Psychology, 48*(4), 577–92. https://doi-org./10.1177/0022022117698039

Standish, W., & Jackson, J. T. (2019). Papua New Guinea. *Britannica.* https://www.britannica.com/place/Papua-New-Guinea

Statistics Canada. (2017). *An increasingly diverse linguistic profile: Corrected data from the 2016 Census.* https://www150.statcan.gc.ca/n1/daily-quotidien/170817/dq170817a-eng.htm

Sue, D. W., & Sue, D. (2003). *Counseling the culturally diverse: Theory and practice* (4th ed.). Wiley.

Sue, D. W., & Sue, D. (2008). *Counseling the culturally diverse: Theory and practice* (5th ed.). Wiley.

Sue, D. W., & Sue, D. (2013). *Counseling the culturally diverse: Theory and practice* (6th ed.). Wiley.

Sue, D. W., & Sue, D. (2016). *Counseling the culturally diverse: Theory and practice* (7th ed.). Wiley.

Ting-Toomey, S. (1994). Face and facework: An introduction. In S. Ting-Toomey (Ed.), *The challenge of facework* (pp. 1–14). State University of New York Press.

Tsukayama, H. (2015). Teens spend nearly nine hours every day consuming media. *The Washington Post*. https://www.washingtonpost.com/news/the-switch/wp/2015/11/03/teens-spend-nearly-nine-hours-every-day-consuming-media/?noredirect=on&utm_term=.61cc6c05bc62

Underwood, K. (2010). Interactive remembering: Insights into the communicative competence of older adults. *Journal of Aging Studies*, 24, 145–66.

van Meurs, N., & Spencer-Oatey, H. (2010). Multidisciplinary perspectives on intercultural conflict: The "Bermuda Triangle" of conflict, culture, and communication. In D. Matsumoto (Ed.), *APA handbook of intercultural communication* (pp. 59–77). American Psychological Association.

Verkoeijen, P. P. J. L., Bouwmeester, S., & Camp, G. (2012). A short-term testing effect in cross-language recognition. *Psychological Science*, 23, 567–71.

Von Hippel, C., Wiryakusuma, C., Bowden, J., & Shochet, M. (2011). Stereotype threat and female communication styles. *Personality and Social Psychology Bulletin*, 37(10). 1312–24. http://doi.org/1312-1324.10.1177/0146167211410439

Watson, O. M., & Graves, T. D. (1966). Quantitative research in proxemic behavior. *American Anthropologist*, 68, 971–85.

White, H. D. (2010). Some new tests of relevance theory in information science. *Scientometrics*, 83, 653–67. http://doi.org/10.1007/s11192-009-0138-3

Will, J., Self, P., & Datan, N. (1976). Maternal behavior and perceived sex of infant. *American Journal of Orthopsychiatry*, 46, 135–9.

Williams, J. E., & Best, D. L. (1982). *Measuring sex stereotypes: A multination study*. SAGE.

Williams, J. E., & Best, D. L. (1994). Cross-cultural views of woman and men. In W. Lonner & R. Malpass (Eds.), *Psychology and culture* (pp. 191–6). Allyn & Bacon.

Wood, J. (1994). *Gendered lives: Communication, gender, and culture*. Wadsworth.

Wood, J. T. (1999). Gender, communication, and culture. In L. A. Samovar & R. E. Porter (Eds.), *Intercultural communication: A reader* (8th ed., pp. 164–74). Wadsworth.

Yang, P. (2010). Nonverbal gender differences: Examining gestures of university-educated Mandarin Chinese speakers. *Text & Talk: An Interdisciplinary Journal of Language, Discourse & Communication Studies*, 30(3), 333–57. https://doi.org/10.1515/TEXT.2010.017

Yum, J. O. (1999). The impact of Confucianism on interpersonal relationships and communication patterns in East Asia. In L. A. Samovar & R. E. Porter (Eds.), *Intercultural communication: A reader* (8th ed., pp. 78–88). Wadsworth.

Zhao, Y., Qiu, W., & Xie, N. (2012). Social networking, social gaming, texting. In D. G. Singer & J. L. Singer (Eds.), *Handbook of children and the media* (pp. 97–112). SAGE.

Chapter 5

Alencar, A. (2017). Refugee integration and social media: A local and experiential perspective. *Information, Communication & Society*, 21(11), 1–16. doi:10.1080/1369118X.2017.1340500

Ansari, S. (2018). *Everyone fits in: Inside the Canadian cities where minorities are the majority*. The Guardian. https://www.theguardian.com/cities/2018/sep/04/canadian-cities-where-minorities-are-the-majority-markham-brampton

Berry, J. (1988). *Understanding the process of acculturation for primary prevention (Contract No. 278-85-0024 CH)*. University of Minnesota, National Institute of Mental Health Refugee Assistance Program.

Berry, J. W. (1990). Acculturation and adaptation: A general framework. In W. H. Holtzman & T. H. Bornemann (Eds.), *Mental health of immigrants and refugees* (pp. 90–102). Hogg Foundation for Mental Health.

Berry, J. W. (1991). Understanding and managing multiculturalism: Some possible implications of research in Canada. *Psychology and Developing Societies*, 3(1), 17–49.

Berry, J. W. (1997). Immigration, acculturation, and adaptation. *Applied Psychology: An International Review*. 46 (1). 5–68

Berry, J. W., & Sabatier, C. (2010). Acculturation, discrimination, and adaptation among second generation immigrant youth in Montreal and Paris. *International Journal of Intercultural Relations*, 34(3), 191–207. https://doi.org/10.1016/j.ijintrel.2009.11.007

Bolzman, C., Fibbi, R., & Vial, M. (2006). What to do after retirement? Elderly migrants and the question of return. *Journal of Ethnic and Migration Studies*, 32(8), 1359–75.

Brislin, R. W. (2000). *Understanding culture's influence on behavior* (2nd ed.). Harcourt College.

Bronfenbrenner, U. (1979). *The ecology of human development*. Harvard University Press.

Bronfenbrenner, U., & Morris, P. A. (1998). The ecology of developmental processes. In W. Damon & R. M. Lerner (Eds.), *Handbook of child psychology: Theoretical models of human development* (pp. 993–1028). John Wiley & Sons Inc.

Chadwick, K., & Collins, P. (2015). Examining the relationship between social support availability, urban center size, and self-perceived mental health of recent immigrants to Canada: A mixed-methods analysis. *Social Science & Medicine*, 128, 220–30. https://doi.org/10.1016/j.socscimed.2015.01.036

Chao, M. M., Chen, J., Roisman, G. I., & Hong, Y.-Y. (2007). Essentializing race: Implications for bicultural individuals' cognition and physiological reactivity. *Psychological Science*, 18, 341–8.

Chen, J. M. (2017). Three levels of push and pull dynamics among Chinese international students' decision to study abroad in the Canadian context. *Journal of International Students*, 7(1), 113–35. https://doi.org/10.32674/jis.v7i1.248

Chirkov, V. I., Ryan, & R. M., & Willness, C. (2005). Cultural context and psychological needs in Canada and Brazil testing a self-determination approach to the internalization of cultural practices, identity, and well-being. *Journal of Cross-Cultural Psychology*, 36(4), 423–43. doi:10.1177/0022022105275960

Chiswick, B. R. & Miller, P. W. (2008). Why is the payoff to schooling smaller for immigrants? *Labour Economics*, *15*(6), 1317–40, https://doi.org/10.1016/j.labeco.2008.01.001

Creese, G., & Wiebe, B. (2012). "Survival employment": Gender and deskilling among African immigrants in Canada. *International Migration*, *50*(5), 56–76. https://doi.org/10.1111/j.1468-2435.2009.00531.x

David, E. J. R., Okazaki, S., & Saw, A. (2009). Bicultural self-efficacy among college students: Initial scale development and mental health correlates. *Journal of Counseling Psychology*, *56*, 211–26.

Derwing, T. M., Waugh, E. (2012). Language skills and the social integration of Canada's adult immigrants. *IRPP study*, *31*, 1. https://irpp.org/wp-content/uploads/assets/research/diversity-immigration-and-integration/language-skills-and-the-social-integration-of-canadas-adult-immigrants/IRPP-Study-no31.pdf

Devos, T. (2006). Implicit bicultural identity among Mexican American and Asian American college students. *Cultural Diversity & Ethnic Minority Psychology*, *12*, 381–402.

Díaz Andrade, A., & Doolin, B. (2016). Information and communication technology and the social inclusion of refugees. *MIS Quarterly*, *40*(2), 405–16.

Environics Institute for Survey Research. (2016). *Focus Canada—Fall 2016 Canadian public opinion about immigration and citizenship*. https://www.environicsinstitute.org/docs/default-source/project-documents/focus-canada-2016-survey-on-immigration-and-citizenship/focus-canada-fall-2016-survey-on-immigration-and-citizenship---final-report.pdf?sfvrsn=257d6adc_2

Everri, M., Mancini, T., & Fruggeri, L. (2016). The role of rigidity in adaptive and maladaptive families assessed by FACES IV: The points of view of adolescents. *Journal of Child and Family Studies*, *25*(10), 2987–97. https://doi.org/10.1007/s10826-016-0460-3

Falicov, C. J. (1998). *Latino families in therapy: A guide to multicultural practice*. Guilford Press.

Falicov, C. J. (2005). Mexican families. In M. McGoldrick, J. Giordano, & N. Garcia-Preto (Eds.), *Ethnicity and family therapy* (3rd ed., pp. 229–41). Guilford Press.

Getrich, C. (2019). *Border brokers: Children of Mexican immigrants navigating US society, laws, and politics*. The University of Arizona Press. https://search.lib.virginia.edu/catalog/u7986510

Glăveanu, V. P., Constance de Saint-Laurent, C., & Literat, I. (2018). Making Sense of Refugees Online: Perspective Taking, Political Imagination, and Internet Memes. *American Behavioral Scientists*, *62*(4), 440–457. https://doi.org/10.1177/0002764218765060

Hayashino, D. S., & Chopra, S. B. (2009). Parenting and raising families. In N. Tewari & A. N. Alvarez (Eds.), *Asian American psychology: Current perspectives* (pp. 317–36). Psychology Press.

Hoffman, L. (1981). *Foundations of family therapy*. Basic Books.

Hong, G. K., & Ham, M. D. C. (2001). *Psychotherapy and counseling with Asian American clients: A practical guide*. SAGE.

How, P. C., Lo, P., Westervelt, M., & Ton, H. (2018). Refugees and immigrants. In J. Tse & S. Y. Volpp (Eds.), *A case-based approach to public psychiatry* (pp. 179–86). Oxford University Press.

Immigration, Refugees and Citizenship Canada. (2011). *ARCHIVED—Backgrounder—Facts in Canada's immigration history*. Government of Canada. https://www.canada.ca/en/immigration-refugees-citizenship/news/archives/backgrounders-2011/facts-canada-immigration-history.html

Immigration, Refugees and Citizenship Canada. (2015). *Discover Canada—Canada's history*. Government of Canada. https://www.canada.ca/en/immigration-refugees-citizenship/corporate/publications-manuals/discover-canada/read-online/canadas-history.html

Immigration, Refugees and Citizenship Canada. (2017). *Backgrounder: Growing Canada's economic future*. Government of Canada. https://www.canada.ca/en/immigration-refugees-citizenship/news/2017/11/growing_canada_seconomicfuture.html

Immigration, Refugees and Citizenship Canada. (2019). *2018 Annual report to Parliament on immigration*. Government of Canada. https://www.canada.ca/en/immigration-refugees-citizenship/corporate/publications-manuals/annual-report-parliament-immigration-2018/report.html

International Organization for Migration. (n.d.). Key migration terms. https://www.iom.int/key-migration-terms

Gans, H. J. (2009). First generation decline: Downward mobility among refugees and immigrants. *Ethnic & Racial Studies*, *32*, 1658–70.

Gordon, M. M. (1964). *Assimilation in American life*. Oxford University Press.

Guo, Y. (2012). Diversity in public education: Acknowledging immigrant parent knowledge. *Canadian Journal of Education*, *35*, 120–40. https://www.jstor.org/stable/canajeducrevucan.35.2.120?seq=1#metadata_info_tab_contents

Heelsum, A. V. (2017, June 8). Aspirations and frustrations: Experiences of recent refugees in the Netherlands. *Ethnic and Racial Studies*, *40*(13), 2137–50. https://doi.org/10.1080/01419870.2017.1343486

Hossain, Z., Eisberg, G., & Shwalb, D. (2018). Grandparents' social identities in cultural context. *Contemporary Social Science*, *13*(2), 275–87. https://doi.org/10.1080/21582041.2018.1433315

Hovey, J. D. (2000). Acculturative stress, depression, and suicidal ideation in Mexican immigrants. *Cultural Diversity and Ethnic Minority Psychology*, *6*, 134–51.

Hynie, M. (2018). Canada's Syrian refugee program, intergroup relationships, and identities. *Canadian Ethnic Studies*, 50(2),1–12. https://doi.org/10.1353/ces.2018.0012

Jalaluddin, U. (2018, March 1). The fear of losing culture. *The Star*. https://www.thestar.com/life/relationships/opinion/2018/03/01/the-fear-of-losing-culture.html

Jiménez-García, R., Rodés-Soldevil, B., Chico-Moraleja, R. M., de Burgos-Lunar, C, Martín-Madrazo, C., Del Otero-Sanz, L., ... Gómez-Campelo, P. (2011). The relationship between social support and self-reported health status in immigrants: An adjusted analysis in the Madrid Cross Sectional Study. *BMC Family Practice*, *12*(1), 46. https://doi.org/10.1186/1471-2296-12-46

Killoren, S., Wheeler, L., Updegraff, K., Rodríguez De Jésus, S., & McHale, S. (2015). Longitudinal associations among parental acceptance, familism values, and sibling intimacy in

Mexican-origin families. *Family Process, 54*(2), 217–31. https://doi.org/10.1111/famp.12126

Kim, B. S., & Abreu, J. M. (2001). Acculturation measurement: Theory, current instruments, and future directions. In J. G. Ponterotto, J. M. Casas, L. A. Suzuki, & C. M. Alexander (Eds.), *Handbook of multicultural counseling* (pp. 394–424). SAGE.

Kim, B. S. K. (2009). Acculturation and enculturation of Asian Americans: A primer. In N. Tewari & A. N. Alvarez (Eds.), *Asian American psychology: Current perspectives* (pp. 97–112). Psychology Press.

Kirmayer, L. J., Narasiah, L., Muñoz, M., Rashid, M., Ryder, A. G., Guzder, J., ... Canadian Collaboration for Immigrant and Refugee Health (CCIRH). (2011). Common mental health problems in immigrants and refugees: General approach in primary care. *Canadian Medical Association Journal, 183*(12), E959–67. doi:10.1503/cmaj.090292

LaFramboise, T. D., Coleman, H. L. K., & Gerton, J. (1993). Psychological impact of biculturalism: Evidence and theory. *Psychological Bulletin, 114*, 395–412.

Lam, C. B., McHale, S. M., & Updegraff, K. A. (2012). Gender dynamics in Mexican American families: Connecting mothers', fathers', and youths' experiences. *Sex Roles, 67*(1–2), 17–28. https://doi.org/10.1007/s11199-012-0137-3

Leong, F. T. L. (2001). The role of acculturation in the career adjustment of Asian American workers: A test of Leong and Chou's (1994) formulations. *Cultural Diversity and Ethnic Minority Psychology, 7*, 262–73.

Louis, W. R., Esses, V. M., & Lalonde, R. N. (2013). National identification, perceived threat, and dehumanization as antecedents of negative attitudes toward immigrants in Australia and Canada. *Journal of Applied Social Psychology, 43*(2). https://doi.org/10.1111/jasp.12044

Makwarimba, E., Stewart, M., Simich, L., Makumbe, K., Shizha, E., & Anderson, S. (2013). Sudanese and Somali refugees in Canada: Social support needs and preferences. *International Migration, 51*(5). https://doi.org/10.1111/imig.12116

Man G. C. (2013). Families in the Chinese diaspora: Women's experience in transnational Hong Kong and Mainland Chinese immigrant families in Canada. *International Handbook of Chinese Families*, 157–68. https://doi.org/10.1007/978-1-4614-0266-4_9

Morita, L. (2017). Why Japan needs English. *Cogent Social Sciences, 3*(1), 1–11. https://doi.org/10.1080/23311886.2017.1399783

Morling, B., Kitayama, S., & Miyamoto, Y. (2003). American and Japanese women use different coping strategies during normal pregnancy. *Personality and Social Psychology Bulletin, 29*, 1533–46.

Nasiroglu, S., & Ceri, V. (2016). Posttraumatic stress and depression in Yazidi refugees. *Neuropsychiatric Disease and Treatment, 12*, 2941–8. https://doi.org/10.2147/NDT.S119506.

Nichols, M. P., & Schwartz, R. C. (1998). *Family therapy: Concepts and methods* (2nd ed.). Allyn & Bacon.

Nickerson, A., Liddell, B. J., MacCallum, F., Steel, Z., Silove, D., & Bryant, R. A. (2014). Posttraumatic stress disorder and prolonged grief in refugees exposed to trauma and loss. *BMC Psychiatry, 14*(1), 106.

Picot, G., & Lu, Y. (2017). *Chronic low income among immigrants in Canada and its communities*. Analytical Studies Research Paper Series, Statistics Canada, *397*. https://www150.statcan.gc.ca/n1/pub/11f0019m/11f0019m2017397-eng.htm

Reavell, J., & Fazil, Q. (2017). The epidemiology of PTSD and depression in refugee minors who have resettled in developed countries. *Journal of Mental Health, 26*(1), 74–83. https://doi.org/10.1080/09638237.2016.1222065

Redfield, R., Linton, R., & Herskovits, M. J. (1936). Memorandum on the study of acculturation. *American Anthropologist, 38*, 149–52. https://doi.org/10.1525/aa.1936.38.1.02a00330

Robbins, C. P. (2021, Mar. 17). Exiled: Syrians in Canada look back on 10 years of civil war. *The Globe and Mail*. https://www.theglobeandmail.com/world/article-exiled-syrians-in-canada-look-back-on-10-years-of-civil-war/

Roy, P. E. (2011). *The triumph of citizenship: The Japanese and Chinese in Canada, 1941-67*. UBC Press.

Ryan, D., Dooley, B., & Benson, C. (2008). Theoretical perspectives on post-migration adaptation and psychological well-being among refugees: Towards a resource-based model. *Journal of Refugee Studies, 21*, 1–18.

Safdar, S., Calvez, S., & Lewis, J. R. (2012). Multi-group analysis of the MIDA model: Acculturation of Indian and Russian immigrants in Canada. *International Journal of Intercultural Relation, 36*(2). 200–12.

Safdar, S., Lay, C., & Struthers, W. (2003). The process of acculturation and basic goals: Testing a multidimensional individual difference acculturation model with Iranian immigrants in Canada. *Applied Psychology: An International Review, 52*(4), 555–79.

Safdar, S., Struthers, W., & van Oudenhoven. J. P. (2009). Acculturation of Iranians in the United States, the United Kingdom, and the Netherlands. *Journal of Cross-Cultural Psychology, 40*(3), 468–91.

Sam, D. L., & Berry, J. W. (2010). Acculturation: When individuals and groups of different cultural backgrounds meet. *Perspectives on Psychological Science, 5*(4), 472–81. https://doi.org/10.1177/1745691610373075

Sam, D. L., & Berry, J. W. (2016). In D. Sam & J. Berry (Eds.), *The Cambridge handbook of acculturation psychology* (2nd ed.). Cambridge University Press.

Sanchez-Cao, E., Kramer, T., & Hodes, M. (2013). Psychological distress and mental health service contact of unaccompanied asylum-seeking children: Mental health service contact of asylum-seeking children. *Child: Care, Health and Development, 39*(5), 651–9.

Schock, K., Rosner, R., & Knaevelsrud, C. (2015). Impact of asylum interviews on the mental health of traumatized asylum seekers. *European Journal of Psychotraumatology, 6*(1), 26286. doi:10.3402/ejpt.v6.26286

Schwartz, S. J., Unger, J. B., Zamboanga, B. L., & Szapocznik, J. (2010). Rethinking the concept of acculturation: Implications for theory and research. *American Psychologist, 65*, 237–51.

Scottham, K. M., & Dias, R. H. (2010). Acculturative strategies and the psychological adaptation of Brazilian migrants to Japan. *Identity*, *10*(4), 284–303. https://doi.org/10.1080/15283488.2010.523587

Shavitt, S., & Cho, H. (2016). Culture and consumer behavior: The role of horizontal and vertical cultural factors. *Current Opinion in Psychology*, *8*, 149–54. https://doi.org/10.1016/j.copsyc.2015.11.007

Sierau, S., Schneider, E., Nesterko, Y., & Glaesmer, H. (2019). Alone, but protected? Effects of social support on mental health of unaccompanied refugee minors. *European Child & Adolescent Psychiatry*, *28*(6), 769–80. https://doi.org/10.1007/s00787-018-1246-5

Sládková, J. (2014). "The guys told us crying that they saw how they were killing her and they could not do anything": Psychosocial explorations of migrant journeys to the U.S. *Psychosocial Intervention*, *23*(1), 1–9.

Statistics Canada. (2017). *Education in Canada: Key results from the 2016 Census*. The Daily. https://www150.statcan.gc.ca/n1/en/daily-quotidien/171129/dq171129a-eng.pdf?st=pLH4Qubd

Statistics Canada. (2018). *Canada's population estimates: Total population, July 1, 2018*. The Daily. https://www150.statcan.gc.ca/n1/en/daily-quotidien/180927/dq180927c-eng.pdf?st=sBmcACaz

Statistics Canada. (2019b). *Census profile, 2016 census*. https://www12.statcan.gc.ca/census-recensement/2016/dppd/prof/details/page.cfm?Lang=E&Geo1=CSD&Code1=3519036&Geo2=PR&Code2=35&SearchText=Markham&SearchType=Begins&SearchPR=01&B1=All&GeoLevel=PR&GeoCode=3519036&TABID=1&type=0

Statistics Canada. (2019a). *Canada's population estimates: Age and sex, July 1, 2019*. The Daily. https://www150.statcan.gc.ca/n1/daily-quotidien/190930/dq190930a-eng.htm

Stokes, B., Wike, R., & Poushter, J. (2016). *Europeans face the world divided*. Pew Research Center. https://www.pewresearch.org/global/2016/06/13/europeans-face-the-world-divided/

Tartakovsky, E. (2013). *Immigration: Policies, challenges and impact*. Nova Publishers.

Thomas, D. C., Brannen, M. Y., & Garcia, D. (2010). Bicultural individuals and intercultural effectiveness. *European Journal of Cross-Cultural Competence and Management*, *1*(4), 315–33. https://doi.org/10.1504/EJCCM.2010.037640

Triandis, H. C. (2001). Individualism-collectivism and personality. *Journal of Personality*, *69*(6).

Troper, H. (2013). Immigration in Canada. In *The Canadian Encyclopedia*. https://thecanadianencyclopedia.ca/en/article/immigration.

Tseng, V., & Yoshikawa, H. (2008). Reconceptualizing acculturation: Ecological processes, historical contexts, and power inequities. *American Journal of Community Psychology*, *42*, 355–8.

United Nations High Commissioner for Refugees. (n.d.). *Unaccompanied children*. UNHCR. https://www.unhcr.ca/where-we-work/unaccompanied-children/

United Nations High Commissioner for Refugees. (2018). *What is a refugee?* UNHCR. https://www.unrefugees.org/refugee-facts/what-is-a-refugee/

United Nations High Commissioner for Refugees. (2019a, June 19). *Forced displacement above 68m in 2017, new global deal on refugees critical*. UNHCR. www.unhcr.org/news/press/2018/6/5b27c2434/forced-displacement-above-68m-2017-new-global-deal-refugees-critical.html

United Nations High Commissioner for Refugees. (2019b, January 30). *Six people died each day attempting to cross Mediterranean in 2018*. UNHCR. https://www.unhcr.org/news/press/2019/1/5c500c504/six-people-died-day-attempting-cross-mediterranean-2018-unhcr-report.html

UN Refugee Agency. [@refugees]. (2018, November 5). Syrian immigrant holding Brazilian flag. [Photograph]. *Instagram*. https://www.instagram.com/p/Bp0UJOGgqWC/?hl=en

UN Refugee Agency. [@refugees]. (2019, December 26). Woman and child walking. [Photograph]. *Instagram*. https://www.instagram.com/p/B6iiiFsgV50/

UN Refugees and Migrants. (2020, November 19). https://refugeesmigrants.un.org/definitions

Vinokurov, A., Trickett, E. J., & Birman, D. (2017). Community context matters: Acculturation and underemployment of Russian-speaking refugees. *International Journal of Intercultural Relations*, *57*, 42–56. https://doi.org/10.1016/j.ijintrel.2017.02.002

Vivar, J. (2019, September 26). As a gangster in Toronto, I was drawn to the lure of the gun. I know what it takes to stop it. *The Globe and Mail*. https://www.theglobeandmail.com/canada/article-as-a-gangster-in-toronto-i-was-drawn-to-the-lure-of-the-gun-i-know/

Ward, C. (2013). Probing identity, integration and adaptation: Big questions, little answers. *International Journal of Intercultural Relations*, *37*(4), 391–404. https://doi.org/10.1016/j.ijintrel.2013.04.001

Ward, C., Stuart, J., & Kus, L. (2011). The construction and validation of a measure of ethno-cultural identity conflict. *Journal of Personality Assessment*, *93*(5), 462–73. https://doi.org/10.1080/00223891.2011.558872

Warner, W. L., & Srole, L. (1946). *The social systems of American ethnic groups* (2nd ed.). Yale University Press.

Waters, M. C., & Pineau, M. G. (Eds.). (2015). *The integration of immigrants into American society*. National Academies Press.

Weeks, L. E., Keefe, J., & MacDonald, D. J. (2012). Factors predicting relocation among older adults. *Journal of Housing for the Elderly*. *26*(4). https://doi.org/10.1080/02763893.2011.653099

Wulfes, N., Del Pozo, M., Buhr-Riehm, B., Heinrichs, N., & Kröger, C. (2019). Screening for posttraumatic stress disorder in refugees: Comparison of the diagnostic efficiency of two self-rating measures of posttraumatic stress disorder. *Journal of Traumatic Stress*, *32*(1), 148–55. https://doi.org/10.1002/jts.22358

Yoon, E., Chang, C.-T., Kim, S., Clawson, A., Cleary, S. E., Hansen, M., . . . Gomes, A. M. (2013). A meta-analysis of acculturation/enculturation and mental health. *Journal of Counseling Psychology*, *60*(1), 15–30. doi:10.1037/a0030652

Ysseldyk, R., Talebi, M., Matheson, K., Bloemraad, I., & Anisman, H. (2014). Religious and ethnic discrimination: Differential implications for social support engagement, civic involvement, and political consciousness. *Journal of Social and Political Psychology*, *2*(1), 347–76. http://dx.doi.org/10.23668/psycharchives.1770

Chapter 6

Alter, A. L., Aronson, J., Darley, J. M., Rodriguez, C., & Ruble, D. N. (2010). Rising to the threat: Reducing stereotype threat by reframing the threat as a challenge. *Journal of Experimental Social Psychology*, *46*, 166–71.

Anderson, M. C., & Robertson, C. L. (2011) *Seeing red: A history of Natives in Canadian newspapers*. University of Manitoba Press.

Apfelbaum, E. P., Pauker, K., Sommers, S. R., & Ambady, N. (2010). In blind pursuit of racial equality? *Psychological Science*, *21*, 1587–92.

Apfelbaum, E. P., Sommers, S. R., & Norton, M. I. (2008). Seeing race and seeming racist: Evaluating strategic colorblindness in social interaction. *Journal of Personality and Social Psychology*, *93*, 918–32.

Armenta, B. E. (2010). Stereotype boost and stereotype threat effects: The moderating role of ethnic identification. *Cultural Diversity and Ethnic Minority Psychology*, *16*, 94–8.

Aronson, E. (1990, April). *The return of the repressed: Dissonance theory makes a comeback*. Presidential address presented at the 70th Annual Meeting of the Western Psychological Association, Los Angeles, CA.

Awad, G. H., Cokley, K., & Ravitch, J. (2005). Attitudes toward affirmative action: A comparison of color-blind versus modern racist attitudes. *Journal of Applied Social Psychology*, *33*, 1384–99.

Bailey, T.-K. M., Chung, Y. B., Williams, W. S., Singh, A. A., & Terrell, H. K. (2011). Development and validation of the internalized racial oppression scale for Black individuals. *Journal of Counseling Psychology*, *58*, 481–93.

Baker, J. (2017). Through the looking glass: White first-year university students' observations of racism in St. John's, Newfoundland and Labrador. *Canada. Sociology Inquiry*, *87*(2), 362–84. https://doi.org/10.1111/soin.12165

Bearman, S., Korobov, N., & Thorne, A. (2009). The fabric of internalized sexism. *Journal of Integrated Social Sciences*, *1*, 10–47.

Beatty, M. (2018, September 10). *Colour me right: It's time to end colourism in India*. Al Jazeera. https://www.aljazeera.com/indepth/opinion/colour-time-colourism-india-180906101053056.html

Blaut, J. M. (1992). The theory of cultural racism. *Antipode: A Radical Journal of Geography*, *23*, 289–99.

Boatright-Horowitz, S. L., & Soeung, S. (2009). Teaching white privilege to white students can mean saying good-bye to positive student evaluations. *American Psychologist*, *64*, 574–5.

Bonilla-Silva, E. (2003). *Racism without racists: Color-blind racism and the persistence of racial inequality in the United States*. Rowman & Littlefield.

Bonilla-Silva, E., & Dietrich, D. (2011). The sweet enchantment of color-blind racism in Obamerica. *Annals of the American Academy of Political and Social Science*, *634*, 190–206.

Borrows, J. (2016). Unextinguished: Rights and the Indian Act. *University of New Brunswick Law Journal*, *67*. 3–35. https://link-gale.com.subzero.lib.uoguelph.ca/apps/doc/A472003305/AONE?u=guel77241&sid=AONE&xid=c155a20c

Bregolisse, D. M. (2019, October 30). *UPDATE: B.C. man dies after roadside arrest where RCMP said a taser was used*. Global News. https://globalnews.ca/news/6103003/b-c-man-tasered-by-rcmp-has-died-says-family/

Britton, J. (2015). Muslims, racism, and violence after the Paris attacks. *Sociological Research Online*, *20*(3), 1–6. https://doi.org/10.5153/sro.3736

Brown, L. S. (1986). Confronting internalized oppression in sex therapy with lesbians. *Journal of Homosexuality*, *12*, 99–107.

Bryan, C., & Denov, M. (2011). Separated refugee children in Canada: The construction of risk identity. *Journal of Immigrant & Refugee Studies*, *9*(3), 242–66. https://doi.org/10.1080/15562948.2011.592806

Burrow, A. L., & Hill, P. L. (2012). Flying the unfriendly skies? The role of forgiveness and race in the experience of racial microaggressions. *Journal of Social Psychology*, *152*, 639–53.

Canel-Çınarbaş, D., & Yohani, S. (2019). Indigenous Canadian university students' experiences of microaggressions. *International Journal for the Advancement of Counselling*, *41*, 41–60. https://doi.org/10.1007/s10447-018-9345-z

Carraro, L., Castelli, L., & Macchiella, C. (2011). The automatic conservative: Ideology-based attentional asymmetries in the processing of valanced information. *PLoS One*, *6*(11), e26456. https://doi.org/10.1371/journal.pone.0026456

Casad, B. J., & Merrit, S. M. (2014). The importance of stereotype threat mechanisms in workplace outcomes. *Industrial and Organizational Psychology: Perspectives on Science and Practice*, *7*, 413–19.

Castelli, L., & Carraro, L. (2011). Ideology is related to basic cognitive processes involved in attitude formation. *Journal of Experimental Social Psychology*, *47*(5), 1013–16. https://doi.org/10.1016/j.jesp.2011.03.016

Centre for Race and Culture. (2020). "Where are you REALLY from?"—What is a microaggression? *Centre for Race and Culture*. https://cfrac.com/fact-sheets/where-are-you-really-from-what-is-a-microaggression/

Chao, R. C. L., Wei, M., Good, G. E., & Flores, L. Y. (2011). Race/ethnicity, color-blind racial attitudes, and multicultural counseling competence: The moderating effects of multicultural counseling training. *Journal of Counseling Psychology*, *38*, 72–82.

Choi, I., Nisbett, R. E., & Norenzayan, A. (1999). Causal attribution across cultures: Variation and universality. *Psychological Bulletin*, *125*, 47–63.

Clark, K. B., & Clark, M. P. (1939). The development of consciousness of self and the emergence of racial identification of Negro pre-school children. *Journal of Social Psychology*, *10*, 591–9.

Coates, T. (2017, September 14). The first White president. *The Atlantic*. https://www.theatlantic.com/magazine/archive/2017/10/the-first-white-president-ta-nehisi-coates/537909/

Commission on Systemic Racism in the Ontario Criminal Justice System. (1995). N° catalog: RPT.C73722.1995.

https://www.crrf-fcrr.ca/en/resources/clearinghouse/7-rpt/223-rpt-c73722-1995

Craig, M. A., & Richeson, J. A. (2014). More diverse yet less tolerant? How the increasingly diverse racial landscape affects white Americans' racial attitudes. *Personality and Social Psychology Bulletin, 40*(6), 750–61. https://doi.org/10.1177/0146167214524993

David, E. J. R. (2008). A colonial mentality model of depression for Filipino Americans. *Cultural Diversity and Ethnic Minority Psychology, 14*, 118–227.

David, E. J. R. (2009). Internalized oppression, psychopathology, and cognitive behavioral therapy among historically oppressed groups. *Journal of Psychological Practice, 15*, 71–103.

David, E. J. R. (2010). Testing the validity of the colonial mentality implicit association test (CMIAT) and the interactive effects of covert and overt colonial mentality on Filipino American mental health. *Asian American Journal of Psychology, 1*, 31–45.

David, E. J. R. (Ed.). (2014). *Internalized oppression: The psychology of marginalized groups*. Springer.

David, E. J. R., & Derthick, A. O. (2014). What is internalized oppression, and so what? In E. J. R. David (Ed.), *Internalized oppression: The psychology of marginalized groups* (pp. 1–30). Springer.

David, E. J. R., & Okazaki, S. (2006). Colonial mentality: A review and recommendation for Filipino American psychology. *Cultural Diversity and Ethnic Minority Psychology, 12*, 1–16.

David, E. J. R., & Okazaki, S. (2010). Activation and automaticity of colonial mentality. *Journal of Applied Social Psychology, 40*, 850–87.

de França, D. X., & Monteiro, M. B. (2013). Social norms and the expression of prejudice: The development of aversive racism in childhood. *European Journal of Social Psychology, 43*, 263–71.

Dovidio, J. F. (2001, January). *Why can't we get along? Interpersonal biases and interracial distrust*. Invited address delivered at the National Multicultural Conference and Summit II, Santa Barbara, CA.

Dovidio, J. F., & Gaertner, S. L. (2000). Aversive racism and selection decisions: 1989 and 1999. *Psychological Science, 11*, 319–23.

Dovidio, J. F., & Gaertner, S. L. (2004). Aversive racism. In M. P. Zanna (Ed.), *Advances in Experimental Social Psychology* (Vol. 36, pp. 1–51). Academic Press.

Dovidio, J. F., & Gaertner, S. L. (2008). New directions in aversive racism research: Persistence and pervasiveness. In C. Willis-Esqueda (Ed.), *Motivational aspects of prejudice and racism* (pp. 43–67). Springer Science & Business Media.

Dovidio, J. F., Gaertner, S. L., Penner, L. A., Pearson, A. R., & Norton, W. E. (2009). In J. L. Chin (Ed.), *Aversive racism—How unconscious bias influences behavior: Implications for legal, employment, and health care contexts. Vol. 3. Social justice matters* (pp. 21–35). Praeger/ABC-CLIO.

Duran, E., & Duran, B. (1995). *Native American post-colonial psychology*. State University of New York Press.

Durrheim, K., Okuyan, M., Twali, M. S., García-Sánchez, E., Pereira, A., Portice, J. S., . . . Keil, T. F. (2018). How racism discourse can mobilize right-wing populism: The construction of identity and alliance in reactions to UKIP's Brexit "Breaking Point" campaign. *Journal of Community & Applied Social Psychology, 28*(6), 385–405. https://doi.org/10.1002/casp.2347

Fazio, R. H., & Olson, M. A. (2003). Implicit measures in social cognition research: Their meaning and use. *Annual Review of Psychology, 54*, 297–327.

Festinger, L. (1957). *A theory of cognitive dissonance*. Stanford University Press.

FitzGerald, C., & Hurst, S. (2017). Implicit bias in healthcare professionals: A systematic review. *BMC Medical Ethics, 18*(1), 19. https://doi.org/10.1186/s12910-017-0179-8

Forbes, C. E., & Schmader, T. (2010). Retraining attitudes and stereotypes to affect motivation and cognitive capacity under stereotype threat. *Journal of Personality and Social Psychology, 99*, 740–54.

Freire, P. (1970). *Pedagogy of the oppressed*. Continuum.

Gadacz, R. R. (2006, February 7). First Nations. In *The Canadian Encyclopedia*. https://www.thecanadianencyclopedia.ca/en/article/first-nations

Gaertner, S. L., & Dovidio, J. F. (1986). The aversive form of racism. In J. F. Dovidio & S. L. Gaertner (Eds.), *Prejudice, discrimination and racism* (pp. 61–90). Academic Press.

Gainor, K. A. (1992). Internalized oppression as a barrier to effective group work with Black women. *Journal for Specialists in Group Work, 17*, 235–42.

Gonzalez, J., Simard, E. Baker Demeray, T., & Iron Eyes, C. (2014). Internalized oppression of North American Indigenous peoples. In E. J. R., David (Ed.), *The internalized oppression of marginalized groups* (pp. 31–56). Springer.

Goodwin, R., Kaniasty, K., Sun, S., & Ben-Ezra, M. (2017). Psychological distress and prejudice following terror attacks in France. *Journal of Psychiatric Research, 91*, 111–15. https://doi.org/10.1016/j.jpsychires.2017.03.001

Gorelick, M. (2013, June 27). Discrimination of Aboriginals on native lands in Canada. *UN Chronicle*. https://www.un.org/en/chronicle/article/discrimination-aboriginals-native-lands-canada

Gross, Z., & Rutland, S. (2014). Combatting antisemitism in the school playground: An Australian case study. *Patterns of Prejudice, 48*(3), 318. https://doi.org/10.1080/0031322X.2014.918703

Guinier, L., & Torres, G. (2007). The ideology of colorblindness. In C. Gallagher (Ed.), *Rethinking the color line: Readings in race and ethnicity* (3rd ed., pp. 143–8). McGraw-Hill.

Hamilton, D. L. (1981). *Cognitive processes in stereotyping and intergroup behavior*. Erlbaum.

Hamilton, D. L., Dugan, P. M., & Trolier, T. K. (1985). The formation of stereotypic beliefs: Further evidence for distinctiveness-based illusory correlations. *Journal of Personality and Social Psychology, 48*, 5–17.

Hamilton, D. L., & Gifford, R. K. (1976). Illusory correlation in interpersonal perception: A cognitive basis of stereotypic judgments. *Journal of Experimental Social Psychology, 12*, 392–407.

Hamilton, D. L., & Rose, T. L. (1980). Illusory correlation and the maintenance of stereotypic beliefs. *Journal of Personality and Social Psychology, 39*, 832–45.

Hamilton, D. L., & Sherman, J. W. (1989). Illusory correlations: Implications for a stereotype theory and research. In D. Bar-Tal, C. F. Graumann, A. W. Kruglanski, & W. Stroebe (Eds.), *Stereotyping and prejudice: Changing conceptions* (pp. 59–82). Springer-Verlag.

Hamilton, D. L., & Sherman, J. W. (1994). Stereotypes. In R. S. Wyer, Jr., & T. K. Srull (Eds.), *Handbook of social cognition* (2nd ed., Vol. 2, pp. 1–68). Erlbaum.

Hamilton, D. L., & Sherman, J. W. (1996). Perceiving persons and groups. *Psychological Review, 103*, 336–55.

Hamilton, D. L., & Trolier, T. K. (1986). Stereotypes and stereotyping: An overview of the cognitive approach. In J. F. Dovidio & S. L. Gaertner (Eds.), *Prejudice, discrimination, and racism* (pp. 127–63). Academic Press.

Hanna, F. J., Talley, W. B., & Guindon, M. H. (2000). The power of perception: Toward a model of cultural oppression and liberation. *Journal of Counseling and Development, 78*, 430–46.

Helleiner, J. (2012). Whiteness and narratives of a racialized Canada–US border at Niagara. *Canadian Journal of Sociology, 37*(2), 109–54. https://doi.org/10.29173/cjs10016

Henkel, K. E., Dovidio, J. F., & Gaertner, S. L. (2006). Institutional discrimination, individual racism, and Hurricane Katrina. *Analyses of Social Issues and Public Policy, 6*, 99–124.

Henry, N. L. (2019, May 28). Racial segregation of black people in Canada. In *The Canadian Encyclopedia*. https://www.thecanadianencyclopedia.ca/en/article/racial-segregation-of-black-people-in-canada

Hernandez, P., Carranza, M., & Almeida, R. (2010). Mental health professionals' adaptive responses to racial microaggressions: An exploratory study. *Professional Psychology: Research and Practice, 41*, 202–9.

Hickson, K. (2018). Enoch Powell's "Rivers of Blood" speech: Fifty years on. *Political Quarterly, 89*(3), 352–7. https://doi.org/10.1111/1467-923X.12554

Holoien, D. S., & Shelton, J. N. (2012). You deplete me: The cognitive costs of colorblindness on ethnic minorities. *Journal of Experimental Social Psychology, 48*, 562–5.

Holroyd, J. (2015). Implicit racial bias and the anatomy of institutional racism. *Criminal Justice Matters, 101*(1), 30–2. https://doi.org/10.1080/09627251.2015.1080943

Houshmand, S., Spanierman, L. B., & Tafarodi, R. W. (2014). Excluded and avoided: Racial microaggressions targeting Asian international students in Canada. *Cultural Diversity and Ethnic Minority Psychology, 20*(3), 377–88. https://doi.org/10.1037/a0035404

Hyde, J. S. (2016). Sex and cognition: Gender and cognitive function. *Current Opinions in Neurobiology. 38* 53–56. https://doi.org/10.1016/j.conb.2016.02.007

Ifil, G. (2009). *The breakthrough: Politics and race in the age of Obama*. Doubleday.

Jha, B. (2016). Representation of fair-skin beauty and the female consumer. *IOSR Journal of Humanities and Social Science, 21*(12), 1–12. https://doi.org/10.9790/0837-2112080112

Jones, J. M. (1997). *Prejudice and racism* (2nd ed.). New York, NY: McGraw-Hill.

Jones, M. L., & Galliher, R. V. (2015). Daily racial microaggressions and ethnic identification among Native American young adults. *Cultural Diversity and Ethnic Minority Psychology, 21*, 1–9.

Kelly, H. H. (1967). Attribution theory in social psychology. In D. Levine (Ed.), *Nebraska symposium on motivation* (Vol. 15, pp. 192–240). University of Nebraska Press.

Kelly, H. H. (1973). The process of causal attribution. *American Psychologist, 28*, 107–28.

Killer Cops Canada. (2018, November 2). *Video shows Montreal police shoot Nicholas Gibbs in the back (Black Lives Matter)*. https://killercopscanada.wordpress.com/category/quebec/

Killer Cops Canada. (2019a, November 5). *Clayton Donnelly (38) dies after being tased by RCMP in Malakwa, B.C. (Oct. 28, 2019)*. https://killercopscanada.wordpress.com/

Killer Cops Canada. (2019b, February 26). *Winnipeg police shoot and kill Machuar Mawien Madut: South Sudanese migrant in mental health crisis (Feb. 23, 2019)*. https://killercopscanada.wordpress.com/

Killer Cops Canada. (2020, February 18). *RCMP shoot and kill Brian Kyle Schriver (30) in Blairmore, Alberta (Feb. 11, 2020)*. https://killercopscanada.wordpress.com/

Kivel, P. (1996). *Uprooting racism: How white people can work for racial justice*. New Society.

Klapp, O.E., (1959). Ritual and Family Solidarity. *Social Forces, 37*(3), 212–14.

Knowles, E. D., Lowery, B. S., Hogan, C. M., & Chow, R. M. (2009). On the malleability of ideology: Motivated construals of color blindness. *Journal of Personality and Social Psychology, 96*, 857–69.

Levy, N. (2017). Am I racist? Implicit bias and the ascription of racism. *The Philosophy Quarterly, 67*(268), 534–51. https://doi.org/10.1093/pq/pqw070

Lipsky, S. (1977). Internalized oppression. *Black Re-Emergence, 2*, 5–10.

Lipsky, S. (1987). *Internalized racism*. Rational Island.

Lum, J. (2017). "Familial looking": Chinese Canadian vernacular photography of the exclusion period (1923–1967). *Visual Studies, 32*(2), 111–23. https://doi.org/10.1080/1472586X.2017.1326838

MacDonald, C., & Steenbeek, A. (2015). The impact of colonization and Western assimilation on health and wellbeing of Canadian Aboriginal people. *International Journal of Reginal and Local History, 10*(1), 32–46. https://doi.org/10.1179/2051453015Z.00000000023

MacLeod, G. (2018). The Grenfell Tower atrocity, *City, 22*(4), 460–89. https://doi.org/10.1080/13604813.2018.1507099

Maeder, E. M., Yamamoto, S., & McManus, L. A. (2015). Race salience in Canada: Testing multiple manipulations and target races. *Psychology, Public Policy, and Law, 21*(4), 442–51. https://doi.org/10.1037/law0000057

Mann, R. (2020). Open secularism and the RCMP turban debate. *Social Compass, 67*(1), 18–28. https://doi.org/10.1177/0037768619895152

Marshall, L. R. (2017). *Racial disparities in police stops in Kingston, Ontario: Democratic racism and Canadian racial profiling in theoretical perspective* [Unpublished doctoral dissertation]. University of Toronto.

McGlone, M. S., & Neal, A. (2003, May). *Stereotype threat and the gender gap in political knowledge.* Paper presented at the 83rd Annual Meeting of the Western Psychological Association, Vancouver, Canada.

McIntosh, P. (1988). *White privilege and male privilege: A personal account of coming to see correspondences through work in women's studies* (Working Paper No. 189). Wellesley College.

McIntosh, P. (1995). White privilege and male privilege: A personal account of coming to see correspondences through work in women's studies. In M. L. Andersen & P. H. Collins (Eds.), *Race, class, and gender: An anthology* (pp. 76–87). Wadsworth.

McQueen, S. (Director). (2013). *12 years a slave* [Film]. Fox Searchlight Pictures.

Mikkelson, D. P., & Mikkelson, B. (2005). *Urban legends references pages: Glurge gallery.* Snopes. https://www.snopes.com/fact-check/teddy-bared/

Miller, J. R. (2012, October 10). Residential schools in Canada. In *The Canadian Encyclopedia.* https://www.thecanadianencyclopedia.ca/en/article/residential-schools

Mio, J. S. (2003). Modern forms of resistance to multiculturalism: Keeping our eyes on the prize. In J. S. Mio & G. Y. Iwamasa (Eds.), *Culturally diverse mental health: The challenges of research and resistance* (pp. 3–16). Brunner-Routledge.

Mio, J. S. (2016). Teaching for change: Post-racial or a different form of racism? In L. A. Barker (Ed.), *Obama on our minds: The impact of Obama on the psyche of America* (pp. 75–92). Oxford University Press.

Mio, J. S., & Roades, L. A. (2003). Building bridges in the 21st century: Allies and the power of human connection across demographic divides. In J. S. Mio & G. Y. Iwamasa (Eds.), *Culturally diverse mental health: The challenges of research and resistance* (pp. 105–17). Brunner-Routledge.

Mitra, S. (2017, April 17). *I am a man. I am a feminist. And feminism helped me.* Medium. https://medium.com/allies-for-the-uncertain-futures/i-am-a-man-i-am-a-feminist-and-feminism-helped-me-c521bea28695

Murphy, M. C., Steele, C. M., & Gross, J. J. (2007). Signaling threat: How situational cues affect women in math, science, and engineering settings. *Psychological Science, 18,* 879–85.

Myers, D. G. (2013). *Psychology* (Tenth Edition). Worth Publishers.

Nadal, K. L. (2011). The Racial and Ethnic Microaggressions Scale (REMS): Construction, reliability, and validity. *Journal of Counseling Psychology, 58,* 470–80.

Nadal, K. L., Griffin, K. E., Wong, Y., Hamit, S., & Rasmus, M. (2014). The impact of racial microaggressions on mental health: Counseling implications for clients of color. *Journal of Counseling and Development, 92,* 57–66.

Nagar, I. (2018). The unfair selection: A study on skin-color bias in arranged Indian marriages. *SAGE Open.* https://doi.org/10.1177/2158244018773149

Neil, R., & Carmichael, J. T. (2015). The use of incarceration in Canada: A test of political and social threat explanations on the variation in prison admissions across Canadian provinces, 2001–2010. *Sociological Inquiry, 85*(2), 309–32. https://doi.org/10.1111/soin.12078

Neville, H. A., & Awad, G. H. (2014). Why racial color-blindness is myopic. *American Psychologist, 69,* 313–14.

Neville, H. A., Awad, G. H., Brooks, J. E., Flores, M. P., & Bluemel, J. (2013). Color-blind racial ideology: Theory, training, and measurement implications in psychology. *American Psychologist, 68,* 455–66.

Neville, H. A., Spanierman, L., & Doan, B. (2006). Exploring the association between color-blind racial ideology and multicultural counseling competencies. *Cultural Diversity and Ethnic Minority Psychology, 12,* 275–90.

Niigaanwewidam, J., & Sinclair, S. D. (2016, June 22). Sixties Scoop. In *The Canadian Encyclopedia.* https://www.thecanadianencyclopedia.ca/en/article/sixties-scoop

Ontario Human Rights Commission. (n.d.). *The impact of racial profiling on the Aboriginal community.* http://www.ohrc.on.ca/en/paying-price-human-cost-racial-profiling/impact-racial-profiling-aboriginal-community

Owen, J., Tao, K. W., Imel, Z. E., & Wampold, B. E. (2014). Addressing racial and ethnic microaggressions in therapy. *Professional Psychology: Research and Practice, 45,* 283–90.

Padilla, L. M. (2001). "But you're not a dirty Mexican": Internalized oppression, Latinos, and law. *Texas Hispanic Journal of Law and Policy, 7,* 58–113.

Padilla, L. M. (2004). Internalized oppression and Latino/as. *Diversity Factor, 12,* 15–21.

Palmater, P. (2016). Shining light on the dark places: Addressing police racism and sexualized violence against Indigenous women and girls in the national inquiry. *Canadian Journal of Women and the Law, 28*(2), 253–84. https://doi.org/10.3138/cjwl.28.2.253

Parmer, T., Arnold, M. S., Natt, T., & Jansen, C. (2004). Physical attractiveness as a process of internalized oppression and multigenerational transmission in African American families. *Family Journal, 12,* 230–42.

Pearson, A. R., Dovidio, J. F., & Gaertner, S. L. (2009). The nature of contemporary prejudice: Insights from aversive racism. *Social and Personality Psychology Compass, 3,* 314–38.

Penal Reform International. (2018). *Report of the Commission on Systemic Racism in the Ontario Criminal Justice System (1995).* N° catalog: RPT.C73722.1995. https://www.crrf-fcrr.ca/en/resources/clearinghouse/7-rpt/223-rpt-c73722-1995

Penner, L. A., Dovidio, J. F., West, T. V., Gaeterner, S. L., Albrecht, T. L., Dailey, R. K., & Marcova, T. (2010). *Journal of Experimental Social Psychology, 46,* 436–40.

Perry, J. (2019). "The present of California may prove . . . the future of British Columbia": Local, state, and provincial immigration policies prior to the American Chinese exclusion act and Canadian Chinese immigration act. *BC Studies, 201,* 13–35. http://search.proquest.com/docview/2265666866/

Pettigrew, T. F. (1979). The ultimate attribution error: Extending Allport's cognitive analysis of prejudice. *Personality and Social Psychology Bulletin, 55*, 461–76.

Plaut, V. C., Thomas, K. M., & Goren, M. J. (2009). Is multiculturalism or color blindness better for minorities? *Psychological Science, 20*, 444–6.

Poupart, L. M. (2003). The familiar face of genocide: Internalized oppression among American Indians. *Hypatia, 18*, 86–101.

Prilleltensky, I., & Laurier, W. (1996). Politics change, oppression remains. On the psychology and politics of oppression. *Political Psychology, 17*, 127–48.

Pyke, K. D. (2010). What is internalized racial oppression and why don't we study it: Acknowledging racism's hidden injuries. *Sociological Perspectives, 53*, 551–72.

Ratliff, K. A., & Nosek, B. A. (2010). Creating distinct implicit and explicit attitudes with an illusory correlation paradigm. *Journal of Experimental Social Psychology, 46*, 721–8.

Regner, I., Smeding, A., Gimmig, D., Thinus-Blanc, C., Monteil, J.-M., & Huguet, P. (2010). Individual differences in working memory moderate stereotype-threat effects. *Psychological Science, 21*, 1646–8.

Ridley, C. R. (1995). *Overcoming unintentional racism in counseling and therapy: A practitioner's guide to intentional intervention.* SAGE.

Risen, J. L., Gilovich, T., & Dunning, D. (2007). One-shot illusory correlations and stereotype formation. *Personality and Social Psychology Bulletin, 33*, 1492–502.

Roades, L. A., & Mio, J. S. (2000). Allies: How are they created and what are their experiences? In J. S. Mio & G. I. Awakuni (Eds.), *Resistance to multiculturalism: Issues and interventions* (pp. 63–82). Brunner/Mazel.

Rodenborg, N. A., & Boisen, L. A. (2013). Aversive racism and intergroup contact theories: Cultural competence in a segregated world. *Journal of Social Work Education, 49*, 564–79.

Rope, O., Sheahan, F., & Slade, H. (2018). *Global prison trends 2018.* Penal Reform International.

Rose, L. R. (1996). White identity and counseling white allies about racism. In B. B. Bowser & R. G. Hunt (Eds.), *Impacts of racism on white Americans* (2nd ed., pp. 24–47). SAGE.

Rosenwasser, P. (2002). Exploring internalized oppression and healing strategies. *New Directions for Adult and Continuing Education, 94*, 53–61.

Ross, L. (1977). The intuitive psychologist and his shortcomings: Distortions in the attribution process. In L. Berkowitz (Ed.), *Advances in Experimental Social Psychology* (Vol. 10, pp. 174–221). Academic Press.

Ross, L. E., Doctor, F., Dimito, A., Kuehl, D., & Armstrong, M. S. (2007). Can talking about oppression reduce depression: Modified CBT group treatment for LGBT people with depression. *Journal of Gay and Lesbian Studies, 19*, 1–15.

Sawyer, P. J., Major, B., Casad, B. J., Townsend, S. S. M., & Mendes, W. B. (2012). Discrimination and the stress response: Psychological and physiological consequences of anticipating prejudice in interethnic interactions. *American Journal of Public Health, 102*, 1020–6.

Schmidt, K., & Nosek, B. A. (2010). Implicit (and explicit) racial attitudes barely changed during Barack Obama's presidential campaign and early presidency. *Journal of Experimental Social Psychology, 46*(2), 308–14. https://doi.org/10.1016/j.jesp.2009.12.003

Sciarpelletti, L. (2020, February 12). *Q&A: Author Hadiya Roderique on "fitting in," subtle racism and inclusivity.* CBC News. https://www.cbc.ca/news/canada/saskatchewan/q-a-hadiya-roderique-speaks-on-subtle-racism-inclusivity-1.5461680

Sears, D. O. (1988). Symbolic racism. In P. A. Katz and D. A. Taylor (Eds.), *Eliminating racism: Profiles in controversy* (pp. 53–84). Plenum Press.

Shapiro, J. R. (2013). Stereotype threat. In C. Stangor & C. S. Crandall (Eds.), *Stereotyping and prejudice* (pp. 95–117). Psychology Press.

Shapiro, J. R., Williams, A. M., & Hambarchyan, M. (2013). Are all interventions created equal? A multi-threat approach to tailoring stereotype threat interventions. *Journal of Personality and Social Psychology, 104*, 277–88.

Sherman, J. W., Kruschke, J. K., Sherman, S. J., Percy, E. J., Petrocelli, J. V., & Conrey, F. R. (2009). Attentional processes in stereotype formation: A common model for category accentuation in illusory correlation. *Journal of Personality and Social Psychology, 96*, 305–23.

Smith, M. R., & Alpert, G. P. (2007). Explaining police bias: A theory of social conditioning and illusory correlation. *Criminal Justice and Behavior, 34*, 1262–83.

Son Hing, L. S., Chung-Yan, G. A., Hamilton, L. K., & Zanna, M. P. (2008). A two-dimensional model that employs explicit and implicit attitudes to characterize prejudice. *Journal of Personality and Social Psychology, 94*(6), 971–87. https://doi.org/10.1037/0022-3514.94.6.971

Statistics Canada. (2010). *Adult correctional services, admissions to federal programs.* http://www5.statcan.gc.ca/cansim/a47

Statistics Canada. (2012). *Adult correctional services, admissions to provincial and territorial programs.* http://www5.statcan.gc.ca/cansim/a26

Statistics Canada. (2013). *Number and distribution of the population reporting an Aboriginal identity and percentage of aboriginal people in the population: Canada, provinces and territories, 2011.* http://www12.statcan.gc.ca/nhs-enm/2011/as-sa/99-011-x/2011001/tbl/tbl02-eng.cfm

Steele, C. (2012, April). *Remedying stereotype threat.* Invited address delivered at the 92nd Annual Meeting of the Western Psychological Association, San Francisco, CA.

Steele, C. M. (1997). A threat in the air: How stereotypes shape intellectual identity and performance. *American Psychologist, 52*, 613–29.

Steele, C. M. (2001). *Institutional climate and stereotype threat: Enhancing educational performance and identification in the face of negative group stereotypes.* Keynote address at the Second Biennial National Multicultural Conference and Summit: The psychology of race/ethnicity, gender, sexual orientation, and disability: Intersections, divergence, and convergence, Santa Barbara, CA.

Sue, D. W., Bucceri, J., Lin, A. I., Nadal, K. L., & Torino, G. C. (2007). Racial microaggressions and the Asian American experience. *Cultural Diversity & Ethnic Minority Psychology, 13*, 72–81.

Sue, D. W., Capodilupo, C. M., Torino, G. C., Bucceri, J. M., Holder, A. M., Nadal, K. L., & Esquilin, M. (2007). Racial microaggressions in everyday life: Implications for clinical practice. *American Psychologist, 62*, 271–86.

Sue, D. W., Lin, A. I., Torino, G. C., Capodilupo, C. M., & Rivera, D. P. (2009). Racial microaggressions and difficult dialogues on race in the classroom. *Cultural Diversity & Ethnic Minority Psychology, 15*, 183–90.

Sue, D. W., Nadal, K. L., Capodilupo, C. M., Lin, A. L., Torino, G. C., & Rivera, P. (2008). Racial microaggressions against Black Americans: Implications for counseling. *Journal of Counseling and Development, 86*, 330–8.

Sue, D. W., & Sue, D. (2008). *Counseling the culturally diverse: Theory and practice* (5th ed.). Wiley.

Sue, D. W., & Sue, D. (2013). *Counseling the culturally diverse: Theory and practice* (6th ed.). Wiley.

Szymanski, D. M., & Kashubeck-West, S. (2008). Mediators of the relationship between internalized oppressions and lesbian and bisexual women's psychological distress. *Counseling Psychologist, 36*, 575–94.

Tappan, M. B. (2006). Reframing internalized oppression and internalized domination: From the psychological to the sociocultural. *Teachers College Record, 108*, 2115–44.

Tatum, B. D. (1997). *"Why are all the Black kids sitting together in the cafeteria?" and other conversations about race*. Basic Books.

Thomas, A. J., Speight, S. L., & Witherspoon, K. M. (2005). Internalized oppression among Black women. In J. L. Chin (Ed.), *The psychology of prejudice and discrimination: Bias based on gender and sexual orientation* (Vol. 3, pp. 113–32). Praeger/Greenwood.

Thompson, D., & Wallner, J. (2012). A focusing tragedy: Public policy and the establishment of Afrocentric education in Toronto. *Canadian Journal of Political Science, 44*(4), 807–28. https://doi.org/10.1017/S000842391100076X

Torres-Harding, S. R., Andrade, A. L., & Romero Diaz, C. E. (2012). The Racial Microaggressions Scale (RMAS): A new scale to measure experiences of racial microaggressions in people of color. *Cultural Diversity and Ethnic Minority Psychology, 18*, 153–64.

Tversky, A., & Kahneman, D. (1973). Availability: A heuristic for judging frequency and probability. *Cognitive Psychology, 5*, 207–302.

Tynes, B. M., & Markoe, S. L. (2010). The role of color-blind racial attitudes in reactions to racial discrimination on social network sites. *Journal of Diversity in Higher Education, 3*, 1–13.

Van Rooy, D., Vanhoomissen, T., & Van Overwalle, F. (2013). Illusory correlation, group size and memory. *Journal of Experimental Social Psychology, 49*, 1159–67.

Walton, G.M. & Spencer, S.J. (2009). Latent Ability: Grades and Test Scores Systematically Underestimate the Intellectual Ability of Negatively Stereotyped Students. *Psychological Science, 20*(9), 1132-1139. https://doi.org/10.1111/j.1467-9280.2009.02417.x

Wang, J., Leu, J., & Shoda, Y. (2011). When the seemingly innocuous "stings": Racial microaggressions and their emotional consequences. *Personality and Social Psychology Bulletin, 37*, 1666–78.

Webb, P. T., & Gulson, K. N. (2015). Faciality enactments, schools of recognition and policies of difference (in-itself). *Discourse: Studies in the Cultural Politics of Education, 36*(4), 515–32. https://doi-org.subzero.lib.uoguelph.ca/10.1080/01596306.2015.979577

Whitbeck, L. B., Sittner Hartshorn, K. J., & Walls, M. L. (2014). *Indigenous adolescent development: Psychological, social and historical contexts*. Routledge.

White, R. (2020, February 14). *"Beyond shocked": Questions unanswered for family of man shot dead by police in Blairmore*. CTV News. https://calgary.ctvnews.ca/beyond-shocked-questions-unanswered-for-family-of-man-shot-dead-by-police-in-blairmore-1.4813034

Wise, T. J. (2008). *White like me: Reflections on race from a privileged son*. Soft Skull Press.

Wise, T. J. (Producer and Presenter). (2013). *White like me: Race, racism and white privilege in America* [Film]. Media Education Foundation.

Worthington, R. L., Navarro, R. L., Loewy, M., & Hart, J. (2008). Color-blind racial attitudes, social dominance orientation, racial ethnic group membership and college students' perceptions of campus climate. *Journal of Diversity in Higher Education, 1*, 8–19.

Wortley, S., & Owusu-Bempah, A. (2011). The usual suspects: Police stop and search practices in Canada, *Policing and Society, 21*(4), 395–407. https://doi.org/10.1080/10439463.2011.610198

Wortley, S. (2003). Hidden intersections: Research on race, crime, and criminal justice in Canada. *Canadian Ethnic Studies Journal, 35*(3), 99–118. https://go.gale.com/ps/anonymous?id=GALE%7CA116860854&sid=googleScholar&v=2.1&it=r&linkaccess=abs&issn=00083496&p=AONE&sw=w

Chapter 7

Akbar, N. (1989). Nigrescence and identity: Some limitations. *The Counseling Psychologist, 17*, 258–63.

Akerlund, M., & Cheung, M. (2000). Teaching beyond the deficit model: Gay and lesbian issues among African Americans, Latinos, and Asian Americans. *Journal of Social Work Education, 36*, 279–93.

Atkinson, D. R., Morten, G., & Sue, D. W. (Eds.). (1979). *Counseling American minorities: A cross-cultural perspective*. Brown.

Atkinson, D. R., Morten, G., & Sue, D. W. (1989). A minority identity development model. In D. R. Atkinson, G. Morten, & D. W. Sue (Eds.), *Counseling American minorities: A cross-cultural perspective* (3rd ed., pp. 35–52). Brown.

Atkinson, D. R., Morten, G., & Sue, D. W. (Eds.). (1998). *Counseling American minorities: A cross-cultural perspective* (5th ed.). Brown.

Australian Institute of Health and Welfare. (2018). *Youth detention population in Australia 2018*. Australian Government. https://www.aihw.gov.au/getmedia/55f8ff82-9091-420d-a75e-

37799af96943/aihw-juv-128-youth-detention-population-in-Australia-2018-bulletin-145-dec-2018.pdf.aspx?inline=true

Barker-Hackett, L. (2003). African Americans in the new millennium: A continued search for our true identity. In J. S. Mio & G. Y. Iwamasa (Eds.), *Culturally diverse mental health: The challenges of research and resistance* (pp. 121–40). Brunner-Routledge.

Bauer, G., Boyce, M., Coleman, T., Kaay, M., & Scanlon, K. (2010). Who are trans people in Ontario? *Trans PULSE e-Bulletin*, July 20. http://transpulseproject.ca/research/who-are-trans-people-in-ontario/

Behrens, J. T. (1997). Does the white Racial Identity Attitude Scale measure racial and ethnic identity? *Journal of Counseling Psychology, 44*, 3–12.

Benibgui, M. (2010). *Mental health challenges and resilience in lesbian, gay, and bisexual young adults: Biological and psychological internalization of minority stress and victimization* [Doctoral dissertation]. Concordia University. https://spectrum.library.concordia.ca/979282/

Bonilla-Silva, E. (2017). *Racism without racists: Color-blind racism and the persistence of racial inequality in the United States*. Rowman & Littlefield.

Bowleg, L. (2012). The problem with the phrase women and minorities: Intersectionality—an important theoretical framework for public health. *American Journal of Public Health, 102*(7), 1267–73.

Britton, J. (2013). Researching white mothers of mixed-parentage children: The significance of investigating whiteness. *Ethnic and Racial Studies, 36*(8), 1311–22. https://doi.org/10.1080/01419870.2013.752101

Carter, R. T. (1995). *The influence of race and racial identity in psychotherapy*. Wiley.

Cass, V. C. (1979). Homosexual identity formation: A theoretical model. *Journal of Homosexuality, 4*, 219–35.

Chang, T., & Kwan, K.-L. K. (2009). Asian American racial and ethnic identity. In N. Tewari & A. N. Alvarez (Eds.), *Asian psychology: Current perspectives* (pp. 113–33). Psychology Press.

Charmaraman, L., & Grossman, J. M. (2010). Importance of race and ethnicity: An exploration of Asian, Black, Latino, and multiracial adolescent identity. *Cultural Diversity and Ethnic Minority Psychology, 16*, 144–51.

Cheng, C.-Y., & Lee, F. (2009). Multiracial identity integration: Perceptions of conflict and distance among multiracial individuals. *Journal of Social Issues, 65*, 51–68.

Cheryan, S., & Tsai, J. L. (2007). Ethnic identity. In F. T. L. Leong, A. G. Inman, A. Ebreo, L. H. Yang, L. Kinoshita, & M. Fu (Eds.), *Handbook of Asian American psychology* (2nd ed., pp. 125–39). SAGE.

Church, A., & Katigbak, M. S. (2002). Studying personality traits across cultures: Philippine examples. *Online Readings in Psychology and Culture, 4*(4). https://doi.org/10.9707/2307-0919.1039

Clark, K. B., Chein, I., & Cook, S. W. (2004). The effects of segregation and the consequences of desegregation: A (September 1952) social science statement in the *Brown v. Board of Education of Topeka* Supreme Court case. *American Psychologist, 59*, 495–501.

Clark, K. B., & Clark, M. P. (1939). The development of consciousness of self and the emergence of racial identification of Negro pre-school children. *Journal of Social Psychology, 10*, 591–9.

Collins, P. H. (2000). *Black feminist though: Knowledge, consciousness, and the politics of empowerment*. Routledge.

Corvin, S., & Wiggins, F. (1989). An antiracism training model for white professionals. *Journal of Multicultural Counseling and Development, 17*, 105–14.

Cross, W. E., Jr. (1971). The Negro-to-Black conversion experience. *Black World, 20*, 13–27.

Cross, W. E., Jr. (1991). *Shades of Black: Diversity in African American identity*. Temple University Press.

Cross, W. E., Jr. (1995). The psychology of nigrescence: Revisiting the Cross model. In J. G. Ponterotto, J. M. Casas, L. A. Suzuki, & D. M. Alexander (Eds.), *Handbook of multicultural counseling* (pp. 93–122). SAGE.

Cross, W. E., Jr., Strauss, L., & Fhagen-Smith, P. E. (1999). African American identity development across the life span: Educational implications. In R. H. Sheets & E. R. Hollins (Eds.), *Racial and ethnic identity in school practices: Aspects of human development* (pp. 29–47). Erlbaum.

Cross, W. E., Jr., & Vandiver, B. J. (2001). Nigrescence theory and measurement: Introducing the Cross Racial Identity Scale (CRIS). In J. G. Ponterotto, J. M. Casas, L. A. Suzuki, & C. M. Alexander (Eds.), *Handbook of multicultural counseling* (pp. 371–93). SAGE Publications.

D'Andrea, M. (2003). Expanding our understanding of white racism and resistance to change in the fields of counseling and psychology. In J. S. Mio & G. Y. Iwamasa (Eds.), *Culturally diverse mental health: The challenges of research and resistance* (pp. 17–37). Brunner-Routledge.

Delgado-Romero, E. A. (2001). Counseling a Hispanic/Latino client—Mr. X. *Journal of Mental Health Counseling, 23*, 207–22.

DiAngelo, R. (2016). *What does it mean to be white? Developing white racial literacy*. Peter Lang.

Digman, J. M. (1990). Personality structure: Emergence of the five-factor model. *Annual Review of Psychology, 41*, 417–40. https://doi.org/10.1146/annurev.ps.41.020190.002221

Erikson, E. H. (1950/1963). *Childhood and society* (2nd ed.). Norton.

Ferdman, B. M., & Gallegos, P. I. (2001). Racial identity development and Latinos in the United States. In C. Wijeyesinghe & B. W. Jackson (Eds.), *New perspectives on racial identity development: A theoretical and practical anthology*. New York University Press.

Gabrielson, R., Sagara, E., & Jones, R. G. (2014). *Deadly force in Black and White*. ProPublica. October 10. https://www.propublica.org/article/deadly-force-in-black-and-white

Goff, P. A., Jackson, M. C., Di Leone, B. A. L., Culotta, C. M., & DiTomasso, N. A. (2014). The essence of innocence: Consequences of dehumanizing Black children. *Journal of Personality and Social Psychology, 106*(4), 526–45.

Goldberg, L. R. (1993). The structure of phenotypic personality traits. *American Psychologist, 48*(1), 26–34. https://doi.org/10.1037/0003-066X.48.1.26

Gonzalez, J. & Bennett, R. (2011). Conceptualizing Native Identity with a multidimensional model. *American Indian and Alaska Native Mental Health Research, 17*(2), 22–42.

Greene, B., & Boyd-Franklin, N. (1996). African American lesbian couples: Ethnocultural considerations in psychotherapy. *Women and Therapy, 19*:3 49–60. doi:10.1300/J015v19n03_06

Hall, C. C. I. (1980). *The ethnic identity of racially mixed people: A study of Black Japanese* [Unpublished doctoral dissertation]. University of California, Los Angeles.

Hall, C. C. I. (1992). Please choose one: Ethnic identity choices for biracial individuals. In M. P. P. Root (Ed.), *Racially mixed people in America* (pp. 250–64). SAGE.

Hall, S. (1991). Ethnicity, identity and difference. *Radical America, 23*(4), 9–21.

Hall, S. (2000). Who needs "identity"? In P. du Gay, & J. Evans (Eds.), *Identity: A reader* (pp. 15–30). SAGE Publications.

Hardiman, R. (1982). *White identity development: A process-oriented model for describing the racial consciousness of white Americans* [Unpublished doctoral dissertation]. University of Massachusetts, Amherst.

Hatzenbuehler, M. L. (2011). The social environment and suicide attempts in lesbian, gay, and bisexual youth. *Pediatrics, 127*(5), 896–903. https://doi.org/10.1542/peds.2010-3020

Helms, J. E. (1984). Toward a theoretical explanation of the effects of race on counseling: A Black and White model. *The Counseling Psychologist, 13*, 695–710.

Helms, J. E. (1985). Cultural identity in the treatment process. In P. Pedersen (Ed.), *Handbook of cross-cultural counseling and therapy* (pp. 239–45). Greenwood.

Helms, J. E. (1989). Considering some methodological issues in racial identity research. *The Counseling Psychologist, 17*, 227–52.

Helms, J. E. (1990). *Black and White racial identity: Theory, research, and practice*. Praeger.

Helms, J. E. (1995). An update of Helms's white and people of color racial identity models. In J. G. Ponterotto, J. M. Casas, L. A. Suzuki, & D. M. Alexander (Eds.), *Handbook of multicultural counseling* (pp. 181–98). SAGE.

Horse, P. G. (2012). Twenty-first-century Native American consciousness: A thematic model of Indian identity. In C. L. Wijeyesinghe & B. W. Jackson III (Eds.), *New perspectives on racial identity development: Integrating emerging frameworks* (pp. 121). New York University Press.

Hubbard, R., & Utsey, S. (2015). A qualitative study of biracial identity among Afro-Germans living in Germany. *Identity, 15*(2), 89–112. https://doi.org/10.1080/15283488.2015.1023438

Ibrahim, A. (1999). Becoming Black: Rap and hip-hop, race, gender, identity, and the politics of ESL learning. *TESOL Quarterly, 33*(3), 349–69. https://doi.org/10.2307/3587669

Ibrahim, A. (2008). The new Flaneur: Subaltern cultural studies, African youth in Canada and the semiology of in-betweenness. *Cultural Studies, 22*(2), 234–53. https://doi.org/10.1080/09502380701789141

Israel, T. (2004). What counselors need to know about working with sexual minority clients. In D. R. Atkinson & G. Hackett (Eds.), *Counseling diverse populations* (3rd ed., pp. 347–64). McGraw-Hill.

Jackson, B. W., III. (2012). Black identity development: Influences of culture and social oppression. In C. I. Wijeyesinghe & B. W. Jackson III (Eds.), *New perspectives on racial identity development: Integrating emerging frameworks* (2nd ed., pp. 33–50). New York University Press

Jacobs, J. H. (1992). Identity development in biracial children. In M. P. P. Root (Ed.), *Racially mixed people in America* (pp. 190–206). SAGE.

Johnson, D. J. (1992). Developmental pathways: Toward an ecological theoretical formulation of race identity in Black–white biracial children. In M. P. P. Root (Ed.), *Racially mixed people in America* (pp. 37–49). SAGE.

Keerdoja, E. (1984, November 19). Children of the rainbow: New parent support groups help interracial kids cope. *Newsweek*, pp. 120–2.

Kerwin, C., & Ponterotto, J. G. (1995). Biracial identity development: Theory and research. In J. G. Ponterotto, J. M. Casas, L. S. Suzuki, & C. M. Alexander (Eds.), *Handbook of multicultural counseling* (pp. 199–217). SAGE.

Kich, G. K. (1992). The developmental process of asserting a biracial, bicultural identity. In M. P. P. Root (Ed.), *Racially mixed people in America* (pp. 304–17). SAGE.

Kitano, H. H. L. (1982). Mental health in the Japanese American community. In E. E. Jones & S. J. Korchin (Eds.), *Minority mental health* (pp. 149–64). Praeger.

Kohlberg, L. (1966). A cognitive developmental analysis of children's sex-role concepts and attitudes. In E. Maccoby (Ed.), *The development of sex differences* (pp. 82–172). Stanford University Press.

Korff, J. (2020). *Aboriginal–police relations*. Creative spirits. https://www.creativespirits.info/aboriginalculture/law/aboriginal-police-relations

Krate, R., Leventhal, G., & Silverstein, B. (1974). Self-perceived transformation of the Negro-to-Black identity. *Psychological Reports*, 35, 1071–5.

LaFramboise, T., Coleman, H. L. K., & Gerton, J. (1993). Psychological impact of biculturalism: Evidence and theory. *Psychological Bulletin, 114*(3), 395–412. http://dx.doi.org.subzero.lib.uoguelph.ca/10.1037/0033-2909.114.3.395

Lanzieri, G. (2012). Mixed marriages in Europe, 1990–2010. In D. Kim (Eds.), *Cross-border marriage: Global trends and diversity* (pp. 81–121). Korea Institute for Health and Social Affairs (KIHASA).

Lartey, J. (2015, June 9). By the numbers: US police kill more in days than other countries do in years. *The Guardian*. https://www.theguardian.com/us-news/2015/jun/09/the-counted-police-killings-us-vs-other-countries

Litchmore, R. (2019). *Understanding "Black" identities, youth, and education in Toronto: A post-structural ethnographic approach* [Doctoral thesis]. University of Guelph Library.

Loftsdottir, K. (2011). Negotiating white Icelandic identity: Multiculturalism and colonial identity formations. *Social Identities, 17*(1), 11–25. https://doi.org/10.1080/13504630.2011.531902

Lund, D. E., & Carr, P. R. (2010). Exposing privilege and racism in The Great White North: Tackling Whiteness and identity issues in Canadian education. *Multicultural perspectives, 12*(4), 229–34. https://doi.org/10.1080/15210960.2010.527594

Markus, H., & Kitayama, S. (1991). Culture and self: Implications for cognition, emotion, and motivation. *Psychological Review, 98*(2). 224–53. https://doi.org/10.1037/0033-295X.98.2.224

Markus, H., Uchida, Y., Omoregie, H., Townsend, S., & Kitayama, S. (2006). Going for the gold: Models of agency in Japanese and American contexts. *Psychological Science, 17*(2), 103–12. https://doi.org/10.1111/j.1467-9280.2006.01672.x

McAllister, G., & Irvine, J. (2000). Cross cultural competency and multicultural teacher education. *Review of Educational Research, 70*(1), 3–24. https://doi.org/10.3102/00346543070001003

McCrae, R. R. (2002). Cross-cultural research on the five-factor model of personality. *Online Readings in Psychology and Culture, 4*(4). https://doi.org/10.9707/2307-0919.1038

McCrae, R. R., & Oliver P. J. (1992). An introduction to the five-factor model and its applications. *Journal of Personality, 60*(2), 175–215. https://doi.org/10.1111/j.1467-6494.1992.tb00970.x

Mensah, J. (2010). *Black Canadians* (2nd ed.). Fernwood Publishing.

Murray, H. A., & Kluckhohn, C. (1953). *Personality in nature, society, and culture.* Knopf.

Nadal, K. L. (2004). Pilipino American identity development model. *Journal of Multicultural Counseling & Development, 32*, 45–62.

National Council on Crime and Delinquency. (2007). *And justice for some: Differential treatment of youth of color in the justice system.* National Council on Crime and Delinquency. http://www.nccdglobal.org/sites/default/files/publication_pdf/justice-for-some.pdf

Neville, H. A., Gallardo, M. E., & Sue, D. W. (Eds.). (2016). *The myth of racial color blindness: Manifestations, dynamics, and impact.* American Psychological Association.

Nobles, W. W. (1989). Psychological nigrescence: An Afrocentric review. *The Counseling Psychologist, 17*, 253–7.

Ontario Human Rights Commission. (2018). *A collective impact: Interim report on the inquiry into racial profiling and racial discrimination of Black persons by the Toronto Police Service.* Government of Canada. http://www.ohrc.on.ca/sites/default/files/TPS%20Inquiry_Interim%20Report%20EN%20FINAL%20DESIGNED%20for%20remed_3_0.pdf

Parham, T. A. (1989). Cycles of psychological nigrescence. *The Counseling Psychologist, 17*, 187–226.

Parham, T. A. (2001). Psychological nigrescence revisited: A foreword. *Journal of Multicultural Counseling & Development, 29*, 162–4.

Parham, T. A., & Helms, J. E. (1985a). Attitudes of racial identity and self-esteem of Black students: An exploratory investigation. *Journal of College Student Personnel, 26*, 143–7.

Parham, T. A., & Helms, J. E. (1985b). Relation of racial identity attitudes to self-actualization and affective states of Black students. Journal of Counseling Psychology, 32(3), 431–440. doi:10.1037/0022-0167.32.3.431

Parham, T. A., & Helms, J. E. (1981). Influences of Black students' racial identity attitudes on preferences for counselor race. *Journal of Counseling Psychology, 28*, 250–6.

Parham, T. A., & Williams, P. T. (1993). The relationship of demographic and background factors to racial identity attitudes. *Journal of Black Psychology, 19*, 7–24.

Phinney, J. (1989). Stages of ethnic identity development in minority group adolescents. *The Journal of Early Adolescence, 9*(1–2), 34–49. https://doi.org/10.1177/0272431689091004

Pickren, W. E. (2004). Fifty years on: *Brown v. Board of Education* and American psychology, 1954–2004: An introduction. *American Psychologist, 59*, 493–4.

Ponterotto, J. G. (1988). Racial consciousness development among white counselor trainees: A stage model. *Journal of Multicultural Counseling and Development, 16*, 146–56.

Poston, W. S. C. (1990). The biracial identity development model: A needed addition. *Journal of Counseling & Development, 69*, 152–5.

Potter-Collins, A. (2014). *2011 Census analysis 2011: What does the 2011 Census tell us about inter-ethnic relationships.* Office of National Statistics. https://www.ons.gov.uk/peoplepopulationandcommunity/birthsdeathsandmarriages/marriagecohabitationandcivilpartnerships/articles/whatdoesthe2011censustellusaboutinterethnicrelationships/2014-07-03

Rangel, S. (2019, April 9). Can a nation forgive a reformed neo-Nazi? *Life After Hate.* https://www.lifeafterhate.org/blog/2019/4/9/when-a-nation-wont-forgive-a-former-neo-nazi

Reicher, S. (2004). The context of social identity: Domination, resistance, and change. *International Society of Political Psychology, 25*(6), 921–45. http://www.jstor.org/stable/3792283

Root, M. P. P. (1990). Resolving "other" status: Identity development of biracial individuals. In L. S. Brown & M. P. P. Root (Eds.), *Diversity and complexity in feminist therapy* (pp. 185–205). Haworth.

Root, M. P. P. (1998). Facilitating psychotherapy with Asian American clients. In D. R. Atkinson, G. Morten, & D. W. Sue (Eds.), *Counseling American minorities: A cross-cultural perspective* (6th ed., pp. 214–34). Brown.

Root, M. P. P. (2004, August). *Mixed race identities—Theory, research, and practice implications.* Continuing education workshop presented at the 112th Annual Convention of the American Psychological Association, Honolulu, HI.

Rowe, W., Bennett, S. K., & Atkinson, D. R. (1994). White racial identity models: A critique and alternative proposal. *The Counseling Psychologist, 22*(1), 129–46. https://doi.org/10.1177/0011000094221009

Ruiz, A. S. (1990). Ethnic identity: Crisis and resolution. *Journal of Multicultural Counseling and Development, 18*, 29–40.

Sarbescu, P., & Boncu, A. (2018). The resilient, the restraint and the restless: Personality types based on the Alternative Five-Factor Model. *Personality and Individual Differences, 134*, 81–7. https://doi.org/10.1016/j.paid.2018.06.002

Sellers, R. M., Rowley, S. A. J., Chavous, T. M., Shelton, J. N., & Smith, M. A. (1997). Multidimensional inventory of Black identity: A preliminary investigation of reliability and construct validity. *Journal of Personality and Social Psychology, 73*(4), 805–15. https://doi-org.subzero.lib.uoguelph.ca/10.1037/0022-3514.73.4.805

Sellers, R. M., Smith, M. A., Shelton, J. N., Rowley, S. A. J., & Chavous, R. M. (1998). Multidimensional model of racial identity: A reconceptualization of African American racial identity. *Personality and Social Psychology Review, 2*, 18–39.

Shih, M., & Sanchez, D. T. (2009). When race becomes even more complex: Toward understanding the landscape of multiracial identity and experiences. *Journal of Social Issues, 65*, 1–11.

Statistics Canada. (2016). *Ethnic and cultural origins of Canadians: Portrait of a rich heritage.* https://www12.statcan.gc.ca/census-recensement/2016/as-sa/98-200-x/2016016/98-200-x2016016-eng.cfm

Statistics Canada. (2017). *Same-sex couples and sexual orientation . . . by the numbers.* https://www.statcan.gc.ca/eng/dai/smr08/2015/smr08_203_2015#a3

Statistics Canada (2018). *Mixed unions in Canada.* https://www12.statcan.gc.ca/nhs-enm/2011/as-sa/99-010-x/99-010-x2011003_3-eng.cfm

Statistics Canada. (2019). *Aboriginal group of person.* https://www23.statcan.gc.ca/imdb/p3Var.pl?Function=DECI&Id=246581

Stonewall Cymru. (2017, March). *Coming out: LGBT stories from Wales.* https://www.stonewall.org.uk/system/files/stonewall_cymru_coming_out.pdf.

Sue, D. W. (2001). Multidimensional facets of cultural competence. *The Counseling Psychologist, 29*, 790–821.

Sue, S., & Sue, D. W. (1971). Chinese American personality and mental health. *Amerasian Journal, 1*, 35–49.

Sue, D. W., & Sue, D. (1990). *Counseling the culturally different: Theory and practice* (2nd ed.). Wiley.

Sue, D. W., & Sue, D. (1999). *Counseling the culturally different: Theory and practice* (3rd ed.). Wiley.

Sue, D. W., & Sue, D. (2003). *Counseling the culturally diverse: Theory and practice* (4th ed.). Wiley.

Sue, D. W., & Sue, D. (2008). *Counseling the culturally diverse: Theory and practice* (5th ed.). Wiley.

Suinn, R. M., Ahuna, C., & Khoo, G. (1992). The Suinn–Lew Self-Identity Acculturation Scale: Concurrent and factorial validation. *Educational and Psychological Measurement, 47*, 401–7.

Suyemoto, K. L. (2004). Racial/ethnic identities and related attributed experiences of multiracial Japanese European Americans. *Journal of Multicultural Counseling and Development, 32*, 206–21.

Syed, K., & Hill, A. (2011). Awakening to white privilege and power in Canada. *Policy Futures in Education, 9*(5), 608–15. https://doi.org/10.2304/pfie.2011.9.5.608

Tatum, B. D. (1997). *"Why are all the Black kids sitting together in the cafeteria?" and other conversations about race.* Basic Books.

Telesford, J., Mendoza-Denton, R., & Worrell, F. C. (2013). Clusters of CRIS scores and psychological adjustment. *Cultural Diversity and Ethnic Minority Psychology, 19*(1), 86–91.

Torres, V. (2003). Influences on ethnic identity development of Latino college students in the first two years of college. *Journal of College Student Development, 44*(4), 532–47. https://doi.org/10.1353/csd.2003.0044

Trimble, J E. (1987). Self-understanding and perceived alienation among American Indians. *Journal of Community Psychology, 15*(July), 316–33.

Trimble, J. E. (2000). Social psychological perspectives on changing self-identification among American Indians and Alaska Natives. In R. H. Dana (Ed.), *Handbook of Cross-Cultural and Multicultural Personality Assessment,* (pp. 197–222). Lawrence Erlbaum Associates.

Trimble, J. E., Helms, J., & Root, M. (2002). Social and psychological perspectives on ethnic and racial identity. In G. Bernal, J. Trimble, K. Burlew, & F. Leong (Eds.), *Handbook of racial and ethnic minority psychology* (pp. 239–75). SAGE.

Vandiver, B. J., Cross, W. E., Jr., Worrell, F. C., & Fhagen-Smith, P. E. (2002). Validating the Cross Racial Identity Scale. *Journal of Counseling Psychology, 49*(1), 71–85.

Vandiver, B. J., Fhagen-Smith, P. E., Cokley, K. O., Cross, W. E., Jr., & Worrell, F. C. (2001). Cross's nigrescence model: From theory to scale to theory. *Journal of Multicultural Counseling and Development, 29*(3), 174–200.

Walton, J., Priest, N., Kowal, E., White, F., Fox, B., & Paradies, Y. (2018). Whiteness and national identity: Teacher discourses in Australian primary schools. *Race, Ethnicity and Education, 21*(1), 132–47. https://doi.org/10.1080/13613324.2016.1195357

Wang, Q. (2011). Autobiographical memory and culture. *Online Readings in Psychology and Culture, 5*(2). https://doi.org/10.9707/2307-0919.1047

Worrell, F. C., Cross, W. E., & Vandiver, B. J. (2001). Nigrescence theory: Current status and challenges for the future. *Journal of Multicultural Counseling and Development, 19*(3), 201–13.

Worrell, F. C., & Gardner-Kitt, D. L. (2006). The relationship between racial and ethnic identity in Black adolescents: The Cross Racial Identity Scale (CRIS) and the Multigroup Ethnic Identity Measure (MEIM). *Identity: An International Journal of Theory and Research, 6*(4), 293–315.

Worrell, F. C., Mendoza-Denton, R., Telesford, J., Simmons, C., & Martin, J. F. (2011). Cross Racial Identity Scale (CRIS) scores: Stability and relationships with psychological adjustment. *Journal of Personality Assessment, 93*(6), 637–48.

Worrell, F. C., Vandiver, B. J., Cross, W. E., Jr., & Fhagen-Smith, P. E. (2004). The reliability and validity of Cross Racial Identity Scale (CRIS) scores in a sample of African American adults. *The Journal of Black Psychology, 30*(4), 489–505.

Worrell, F. C., Vandiver, B. J., Schaefer, B. A., Cross, W. E., Jr., & Fhagen-Smith, P. E. (2006). Generalizing nigrescence profiles: A cluster analysis of Cross Racial Identity Scale (CRIS) scores in three independent samples. *The Counseling Psychologist, 34*(4), 519–47.

Worrell, F. C., & Watson, S. (2008). A confirmatory factor analysis of Cross Racial Identity Scale (CRIS) scores: Testing the expanded nigrescence model. *Educational and Psychological Measurement, 68*(6), 1041–58.

Zhu, Y., Zhang, L., Fan, J., & Han, S. (2007). Neural basis of cultural influence on self-representation. *NeuroImage, 34*(3), 1310–16. https://doi.org/10.1016/j.neuroimage.2006.08.047

Chapter 8

Abraído-Lanza, A., Chao, M., & Flórez, K. (2005). Do healthy behaviors decline with greater acculturation?: Implications for the Latino mortality paradox. *Social Science & Medicine, 61*(6), 1243–55. https://doi.org/10.1016/j.socscimed.2005.01.016

Ahmed, S., Shommu, N., Rumana, N., Barron, G., Wicklum, S., & Turin, T. (2016). Barriers to access of primary healthcare by immigrant populations in Canada: A literature review. *Journal of Immigrant and Minority Health, 18*(6), 1522–40. https://doi.org/10.1007/s10903-015-0276-z

Arpey, N. C., Gaglioti, A. H., & Rosenbaum, M. E. (2017). How socioeconomic status affects patient perceptions of health care: A qualitative study. *Journal of Primary Care & Community Health, 8*(3), 169–75. https://doi.org/10.1177/2150131917697439

Beckfield, J., Olafsdottir, S., & Bakhtiari, E. (2013). Health inequalities in global context. *American Behavioral Scientist, 57*(8), 1014–39. http://doi.org/10.1177/0002764213487343

Beiser, M. (2005). The health of immigrants and refugees in Canada. *Canadian Journal of Public Health, 96*(Suppl. 2), S30–44. http://doi.org/10.1007/BF03403701

Best Start Resource Center. (2010). *A child becomes strong: A journey through each stage of the life cycle*. Health Nexus. https://resources.beststart.org/wp-content/uploads/2019/01/K12-A-1.pdf

Blanchet, R, Nana, C. P., Sanou D., Batal, M., & Giroux, I. (2018). Dietary acculturation among black immigrant families living in Ottawa—a qualitative study. *Ecology of Food and Nutrition, 57*(3), 223–45. https://doi.org/10.1080/03670244.2018.1455674

Blumenshine, P., Egerter, S., Barclay, C., Cubbin, C., & Braveman, P. (2010). Socioeconomic disparities in adverse birth outcomes. *American Journal of Preventive Medicine, 39*(3), 263–72. https://doi.org/10.1016/j.amepre.2010.05.012

Branker, R. R. (2017). Labour market discrimination: The lived experiences of English-speaking Caribbean immigrants in Toronto. *Journal of International Migration and Integration, 18*, 203–22. https://doi.org/10.1007/s12134-016-0469-x

Breland, J. Y., Wong, J. J., & McAndrew, L. M. (2020). Are Common Sense Model constructs and self-efficacy simultaneously correlated with self-management behaviors and health outcomes: A systematic review. *Health Psychology Open, 7*(1), 1–13. https://doi.org/10.1177/2055102919898846

Brondolo, E., & Gallo, L., & Myers, H. (2009). Race, racism and health: Disparities, mechanisms, and interventions. *Journal of Behavioral Medicine, 32*. 1–8. 10.1007/s10865-008-9190-3

Burton, J. (2010). *A conceptual framework for action on the social determinants of health*. World Health Organization. https://www.who.int/sdhconference/resources/ConceptualframeworkforactiononSDH_eng.pdf

Bushnik, T., Tjepkema, M., & Martel, L. (2020). Socioeconomic disparities in life and health expectancy among the household population in Canada. *Health Reports, 31*(1), 3–14. https://doi.org/10.25318/82-003-x202000100001-eng

Carpenter, C. J. (2010). A meta-analysis of the effectiveness of health belief model variables in predicting behavior. *Health Communication, 25*(8), 661–9. doi:10.1080/10410236.2010.521906

Castillo, L. G., Brossart, D. F., Reyes, C. J., Conoley, C. W., & Phoummarath, M. J. (2007). The influence of multicultural training on perceived multicultural counseling competencies and implicit racial prejudice. *Journal of Multicultural Counseling and Development, 35*(4), 243–55. doi:10.1002/j.2161-1912.2007.tb00064.x

Chan, L. Batal, M., Sadik, T., Tikhonov, C. Schwartz, H., Fediuk, K., . . . Receveur, O. (2019). *FNFNES final report for eight assembly of First Nations regions: Draft comprehensive technical report*. Assembly of First Nations, University of Ottawa, Université de Montréal. http://www.fnfnes.ca/docs/FNFNES_draft_technical_report_Nov_2__2019.pdf

Chapman, M. V., Hall, W. J., Lee, K., Colby, R., Coyne-Beasley, T., Day, S., . . . Payne, K. (2018). Making a difference in medical trainees' attitudes toward Latino patients: A pilot study of an intervention to modify implicit and explicit attitudes. *Social Science & Medicine, 199*, 202–8. doi:10.1016/j.socscimed.2017.05.013

Chauhan, A., de Wildt, G., Virmond, M., Kyte, D., Galan, N., Prado, R., & Shyam-Sundar, V. (2020). Perceptions and experiences regarding the impact of race on the quality of healthcare in Southeast Brazil: A qualitative study. *Ethnicity & Health, 25*(3), 436–52. https://doi.org/10.1080/13557858.2018.1431206

Chen, E., & Miller, G. E. (2013). Socioeconomic status and health: Mediating and moderating factors. *Annual Review of Clinical Psychology, 9*, 723–49. https://doi.org/10.1146/annurev-clinpsy-050212-185634

Commission on Social Determinants of Health. (2008). *Closing the gap in a generation: Health equity through action on the social determinants of health*. World Health Organization. https://www.who.int/social_determinants/final_report/csdh_finalreport_2008.pdf

Commonwealth Fund. (2017). *International profiles of healthcare systems*. https://www.commonwealthfund.org/publications/fund-reports/2017/may/international-profiles-health-care-systems

Commonwealth Fund. (2020). *International health policy surveys*. https://www.commonwealthfund.org/series/international-health-policy-surveys

Dehlendorf, C., Bryant, A. S., Huddleston, H. G., Jacoby, V. L., & Fujimoto, V. Y. (2010). Health disparities: Definitions and measurements. *American Journal of Obstetrics and Gynecology, 202*(3), 212–13. doi:10.1016/j.ajog.2009.12.003

De Maio, F. G. (2010). Immigration as pathogenic: A systematic review of the health of immigrants to Canada. *International Journal for Equity in Health, 9*, 27. https://doi.org/10.1186/1475-9276-9-27

Dempster, M., Howell, D., & McCorry, N. K. (2015). Illness perceptions and coping in physical health conditions: A meta-analysis. *Journal of Psychosomatic Research, 79*(6), 506–13. doi:10.1016/j.jpsychores.2015.10.006

Domenech Rodríguez, M. M. (2018). Staying woke at the intersections. In L. Comas-Díaz & C. Inoa Vazquez (Eds.), *Latina psychologists: Thriving in the cultural borderlands*. Routledge.

Du Mont, J., & Forte, T. (2016). Perceived discrimination and self-rated health in Canada: An exploratory study. *BMC*

Public Health, 16(1), 742. https://doi.org/10.1186/s12889-016-3344-y

Fadiman, A. (2012). *The spirit catches you and you fall down: A Hmong child, her American doctors, and the collision of two cultures.* Farrar, Straus and Giroux.

First Nations Health Authority. (2020). *Traditional healing.* https://www.fnha.ca/what-we-do/traditional-healing

Foxwell, R., Morley, C., & Frizelle, D. (2013). Illness perceptions, mood and quality of life: A systematic review of coronary heart disease patients. *Journal of Psychosomatic Research, 75*(3), 211–22. doi:10.1016/j.jpsychores.2013.05.003

Friedli, L. (2009). *Mental health, resilience, and inequalities.* World Health Organization. http://www.euro.who.int/__data/assets/pdf_file/0012/100821/E92227.pdf

Gele, A. A., Qureshi, S. A., Kour, P., Kumar, B., & Diaz, E. (2017). Barriers and facilitators to cervical cancer screening among Pakistani and Somali immigrant women in Oslo: A qualitative study. *International Journal of Women's Health, 9*, 487–96. https://doi.org/10.2147/IJWH.S139160

Ghebreyesus, T. A. (2020, January 13). *Urgent health challenges for the next decade.* World Health Organization. https://www.who.int/news-room/photo-story/photo-story-detail/urgent-health-challenges-for-the-next-decade

Global Burden of Disease. (2018). Measuring performance on the Healthcare Access and Quality Index for 195 countries and territories and selected subnational locations: A systematic analysis from the Global Burden of Disease Study 2016. *The Lancet, 391*, 2236–71. https://www.thelancet.com/action/showPdf?pii=S0140-6736%2818%2930994-2

Government of Canada. (2020). *Household food insecurity in Canada: Overview.* https://www.canada.ca/en/health-canada/services/food-nutrition/food-nutrition-surveillance/health-nutrition-surveys/canadian-community-health-survey-cchs/household-food-insecurity-canada-overview.html

Gracey, M., & King, M. (2009). Indigenous health, part 1: Determinants and disease patterns. *The Lancet, 374*(9683), 65–75. https://doi.org/10.1016/S0140-6736(09)60914-4

Greenwald, A. G., McGhee, D. E., & Schwartz, J. L. (1998). Measuring individual differences in implicit cognition: The implicit association test. *Journal of Personality and Social Psychology, 74*(6), 1464–80. https://doi.org/10.1037//0022-3514.74.6.1464

Gunaratnam, P., Heywood, A., McGregor, S., Jamil, M., McManus, H., Mao, L., . . . Guy, R. (2019). HIV diagnoses in migrant populations in Australia: A changing epidemiology. *PLoS ONE, 14*(2). https://doi.org/10.1371/journal.pone.0212268

Hafeez, H., Zeshan, M., Tahir, M. A., Jahan, N., & Naveed, S. (2017). Health care disparities among lesbian, gay, bisexual, and transgender youth: A literature review. *Cureus, 9*(4), e1184. https://doi.org/10.7759/cureus.1184

Hajizadeh, M., Mitnitski, A., & Rockwood, K. (2016). Socioeconomic gradient in health in Canada: Is the gap widening or narrowing? *Health Policy, 120*(9), 1040–50. https://doi.org/10.1016/j.healthpol.2016.07.019

Halseth, R. (2019). *The prevalence of type 2 diabetes among First Nations and considerations for prevention.* National Collaborating Centre for Aboriginal Health. https://www.nccih.ca/docs/health/RPT-Diabetes-First-Nations-Halseth-EN.pdf

Harris, R. B., Stanley, J., & Cormack, D. M. (2018). Racism and health in New Zealand: Prevalence over time and associations between recent experience of racism and health and wellbeing measures using national survey data. *PLoS ONE, 13*(5). https://doi.org/10.1371/journal.pone.0196476

Harris, S., Naqshbandi, M., Bhattacharyya, O., Hanley, A., Esler, J., Zinman, B., & CIRCLE Study Group. (2011). Major gaps in diabetes clinical care among Canada's First Nations: Results of the CIRCLE study. *Diabetes Research and Clinical Practice, 92*(2), 272–9. https://doi.org/10.1016/j.diabres.2011.02.006

Hughes, J. L., Camden, A. A., & Yangchen, T. (2016). Rethinking and updating demographic questions: Guidance to improve descriptions of research samples. *Psi Chi Journal of Psychological Research, 21*(3), 138–51. https://doi.org/10.24839/2164-8204.JN21.3.138

International Federation of Red Cross and Red Crescent Societies. (2011). *Eliminating health inequalities: Every woman and every child counts.* https://www.ifrc.org/Global/Publications/Health/1208600-Health%20inequities%20advocacy%20report-EN-LR%20FINAL.pdf

International Trade Union Confederation. (2020, March 27). *Putting people first: 12 governments show the world how to protect lives, jobs and incomes.* https://www.ituc-csi.org/IMG/pdf/20200327_ituc_covid-19_countryresponses_.pdf

Islam, F. (2013). Examining the "healthy immigrant effect" for mental health in Canada. *University of Toronto Medical Journal, 90*(4), 169–75. http://utmj.org/index.php/UTMJ/article/view/105

Johnson, T. J., Winger, D. G., Hickey, R. W., Switzer, G. E., Miller, E., Nguyen, M. B., . . . Hausmann, L. R. M. (2017). Comparison of physician implicit racial bias toward adults versus children. *Academic Pediatrics, 17*(2), 120–6. doi:10.1016/j.acap.2016.08.010

Jones, C. L., Jensen, J. D., Scherr, C. L., Brown, N. R., Christy, K., & Weaver, J. (2015). The health belief model as an explanatory framework in communication research: Exploring parallel, serial, and moderated mediation. *Health Communication, 30*(6), 566–76. doi:10.1080/10410236.2013.873363

Kam, J. A., Guntzviller, L. M., & Pines, R. (2017). Language brokering, prosocial capacities, and intercultural communication apprehension among Latina mothers and their adolescent children. *Journal of Cross-Cultural Psychology, 48*(2), 168–83. doi:10.1177/0022022116680480

Kickbusch, I. (2013, June 27). Advancing the global health agenda. *UN Chronicle.* https://www.un.org/en/chronicle/article/advancing-global-health-agenda

Kim, L., Carrasco, C., Muntaner, C., McKenzie, K., Noh, S. (2013). Ethnicity and postmigration health trajectory in new immigrants to Canada. *American Journal of Public Health, 103*(4), 96–104. https://doi.org/10.2105/AJPH.2012.301185

Kleinman, A., Eisenberg, L., & Good, B. (1978). Culture, illness, and care: Clinical lessons from anthropologic and cross-cultural research. *Annals of Internal Medicine, 88*(2), 251–8.

Knibbs, L., & Sly, P. (2014). Indigenous health and environmental risk factors: An Australian problem with global analogues? *Global Health Action, 7*(1), 23766. https://doi.org/10.3402/gha.v7.23766

Kobayashi, K. M., & Prus, S. G. (2012). Examining the gender, ethnicity, and age dimensions of the healthy immigrant effect: Factors in the development of equitable health policy. *International Journal for Equity in Health, 11*, 8. https://doi.org/10.1186/1475-9276-11-8

Lago, S., Cantarero, D., Rivera, B., Pascual, M., Blázquez-Fernández, C., Casal, B., & Reyes, F. (2018). Socioeconomic status, health inequalities and non-communicable diseases: A systematic review. *Journal of Public Health, 26*(1), 1–14. https://doi.org/10.1007/s10389-017-0850-z

Lee, D. L., & Ahn, S. (2011). Racial discrimination and Asian mental health: A meta-analysis. *The Counseling Psychologist, 39*(3), 463–89. https://doi.org/10.1177/0011000010381791

Levasseur, J., & Marcoux, J. (2015, October 15). *Bad water: "Third World" conditions on First Nations in Canada*. CBC. https://www.cbc.ca/news/canada/manitoba/bad-water-third-world-conditions-on-first-nations-in-canada-1.3269500

Lewis, N. M., & Wilson, K. (2017). HIV risk behaviours among immigrant and ethnic minority gay and bisexual men in North America and Europe: A systematic review. *Social Science & Medicine, 179*, 115–28. https://doi.org/10.1016/j.socscimed.2017.02.033

Lilly, E., & Kundu, R. V. (2012). Dermatoses secondary to Asian cultural practices. *International Journal of Dermatology, 51*(4), 372–82. https://doi.org/10.1111/j.1365-4632.2011.05170.x

Lundberg, P. C., Thu, T. T. N. (2011). Vietnamese women's cultural beliefs and practices related to the postpartum period. *Midwifery, 27*(5), 731–6. https://doi.org/10.1016/j.midw.2010.02.006

Maina, I. W., Belton, T. D., Ginzberg, S., Singh, A., & Johnson, T. J. (2018). A decade of studying implicit racial/ethnic bias in healthcare providers using the implicit association test. *Social Science & Medicine, 199*, 219–29. doi:10.1016/j.socscimed.2017.05.009

Martin, D., Miller, A., Quesnel-Vallée, A., Caron, N., Vissandjée, B., & Marchildon, G. (2018). Canada's universal health-care system: Achieving its potential. *The Lancet, 391*(10131), 1718–35. https://doi.org/10.1016/S0140-6736(18)30181-8

Masoomi, F., Feyzabadi, Z., Hamedi, S., Jokar, A., Sadeghpour, O., Toliyat, T., & Fakheri, H. (2016). Constipation and laxative herbs in Iranian traditional medicine. *Iran Red Crescent Medical Journal, 18*(12). https://doi.org/10.5812/ircmj.24574

Mestral, C., & Stringhini, S. (2017). Socioeconomic status and cardiovascular disease: An update. *Current Cardiology Reports, 19*(11), 1–12. https://doi.org/10.1007/s11886-017-0917-z

Miller, L. J., & Lu, W. (2019, February 24). *These are the world's healthiest nations*. Bloomberg. https://www.bloombergquint.com/onweb/spain-tops-italy-as-world-s-healthiest-nation-while-u-s-slips

Mustanski, B., & Liu, R. T. (2013). A longitudinal study of predictors of suicide attempts among lesbian, gay, bisexual, and transgender youth. *Archives of Sexual Behavior, 42*(3), 437–48. https://doi.org/10.1007/s10508-012-0013-9

National Collaborating Centre for Aboriginal Health (NCCAH). (2013). An overview of Aboriginal health in Canada. https://www.ccnsa-nccah.ca/docs/context/FS-OverviewAbororiginal-Health-EN.pdf

Ninou, A., Guthrie, E., Paika, V., Ntountoulaki, E., Tomenson, B., Tatsioni, A., ... Hyphantis, T. (2016). Illness perceptions of people with long-term conditions are associated with frequent use of the emergency department independent of mental illness and somatic symptom burden. *Journal of Psychosomatic Research, 81*, 38–45. doi:10.1016/j.jpsychores.2016.01.001

Oosterveer, T. M., & Young, T. K. (2015). Primary health care accessibility challenges in remote indigenous communities in Canada's North. *International Journal of Circumpolar Health, 74*(1). https://doi.org/10.3402/ijch.v74.29576

Oreopoulos, P. (2011). Why do skilled immigrants struggle in the labor market? A field experiment with thirteen thousand resumes. *American Economic Journal: Economic Policy, 3*(4), 148–71. https://doi.org/10.1257/pol.3.4.148

Orji, R., Vassileva, J. M., & Mandryk, R. (2012). Towards an effective health interventions design: An extension of the Health Belief Model. *Online Journal of Public Health Informatics, 4*(3). https://doi.org/10.5210/ojphi.v4i3.4321

Osborn, R., Squires, D., Doty, M. M., Sarnak, D. O., & Schneider, E. C. (2016). In new survey of eleven countries, US adults still struggle with access to and affordability of health care. *Health Affairs, 35*(12), 2327–36. https://doi.org/10.1377/hlthaff.2016.1088

Peiris, D., Brown, A., & Cass, A. (2008). Addressing inequities in access to quality health care for Indigenous people. *CMAJ: Canadian Medical Association Journal, 179*(10), 985–6. https://doi.org/10.1503/cmaj.081445

Phipps, M., Chan, K., Naidu, R., Mohamad, N., Hoh, B., Quek, K., ... Kadir, K. A. (2015). Cardio-metabolic health risks in indigenous populations of Southeast Asia and the influence of urbanization. *BMC Public Health, 15*(1), 47. https://doi.org/10.1186/s12889-015-1384-3

Pollock, G., Newbold, K. B., Lafrenière, G., & Edge, S. (2012). Discrimination in the doctor's office: Immigrants and refugee experience. *Critical Social Work, 13*(2), 60–79. https://pdfs.semanticscholar.org/6cb2/17281e4a150313c1c32cb7096e0ed43f205a.pdf?_ga=2.132984838.987703391.1588917086-1423103957.1538884065

Razzak, J., Khan, U., Azam, I., Nasrullah, M., Pasha, O., Malik, M., & Ghaffar, A. (2011). Health disparities between Muslim and non-Muslim countries/Disparités en matière de santé entre pays musulmans et non musulmans. *Eastern Mediterranean Health Journal, 17*(9), 654–64. https://doi.org/10.26719/2011.17.9.654

Sawchuk, J. (2018). Social conditions of Indigenous peoples in Canada. In *The Canadian Encyclopedia*. https://www.thecanadianencyclopedia.ca/article/native-people-social-conditions

Schneider E. C., Sarnak D. O., Squires D., Shah A., & Doty M. M. (2017). *Mirror, Mirror 2017: International comparison reflects flaws and opportunities for better U.S. health care.* The Commonwealth Fund. https://interactives.commonwealthfund.org/2017/july/mirror-mirror/

Shahid, S., Bleam, R., Bessarab, D., & Thompson, S. (2010). "If you don't believe it, it won't help you": Use of bush medicine in treating cancer among Aboriginal people in Western Australia. *Journal of Ethnobiology and Ethnomedicine, 6*(18). https://doi.org/10.1186/1746-4269-6-18

Smedley, B. D., Stith, A. Y., & Nelson, A. R. (2003). *Unequal treatment: Confronting racial and ethnic disparities in health care.* National Academies Press. https://doi.org/10.17226/10260

Straits, K. J. E. (2010). *Language brokering in Latino families: Direct observations of brokering patterns, parent-child interactions, and relationship quality* [Doctoral dissertation]. https://digitalcommons.usu.edu/etd/722/

Sun, D., Li, S., Liu, Y., Zhang, Y., Mei, R., & Yang, M. (2013). Differences in the origin of philosophy between Chinese medicine and western medicine: Exploration of the holistic advantages of Chinese medicine. *Chinese Journal of Integrated Medicine, 19*, 706–11. https://doi.org/10.1007/s11655-013-1435-5

Suwannaphant, K., Laohasiriwong, W., Puttanapong, N., Saengsuwan, J., & Phajan, T. (2017). Association between socioeconomic status and diabetes mellitus: The National Socioeconomic Survey, 2010 and 2012. *Journal of Clinical and Diagnostic Research, 11*(7). https://doi.org/10.7860/JCDR/2017/28221.10286

Tan, A., & Mallika, P. (2011). Coining: An ancient treatment widely practiced among Asians. *Malaysian Family Physician, 6*(2–3), 97–8.

Taylor, S. E. (2009). *Health psychology* (7th ed.). McGraw-Hill.

Travers, M. (2020, April 22). Which countries are handling the COVID-19 crisis best? New public opinion data offer answers. *Forbes.* https://www.forbes.com/sites/traversmark/2020/04/22/which-countries-are-handling-the-covid-19-crisis-best-new-public-opinion-data-offer-answers/#23334c2d2f4f

Uğurlu, S. (2011). Traditional folk medicine in the Turkish folk culture. *Turkish Studies, 6*(4), 317–27. https://doi.org/10.7827/TurkishStudies.2631

United Nations (UN). (2019). *Indigenous peoples.* Department of Economic and Social Affairs. https://www.un.org/development/desa/indigenouspeoples/mandated-areas1/health.html

Van Geel, M., & Vedder, P. (2010). The adaptation of non-western and Muslim immigrant adolescents in the Netherlands: An immigrant paradox? *Scandinavian Journal of Psychology, 51*(5), 398–402. https://doi.org/10.1111/j.1467-9450.2010.00831.x

Walker, R., St Pierre-Hansen, N., Cromarty, H., Kelly, L., Minty, B., & Walker, R. (2010). Measuring cross-cultural patient safety: Identifying barriers and developing performance indicators. *Healthcare Quarterly, 13*(1), 64–71. https://doi.org/10.12927/hcq.2013.21617

Wallace, M., & Kulu, H. (2014). Low immigrant mortality in England and Wales: A data artefact? *Social Science & Medicine, 120*, 100–9. https://doi.org/10.1016/j.socscimed.2014.08.032

Wang, J., & Geng, L. (2019). Effects of socioeconomic status on physical and psychological health: Lifestyle as a mediator. *International Journal of Environmental Research and Public Health, 16*(2). https://doi.org/10.3390/ijerph16020281

Wong, T. (2019). *Language brokering experiences among young Chinese immigrants in Canada: A narrative study* [Doctoral dissertation]. Fielding Graduate University. ProQuest.

World Health Organization. (1946). *WHO Constitution.* https://www.who.int/about/governance/constitution

World Health Organization. (2008). *Closing the gap in a generation: Health equity through action on the social determinants of health.* https://www.who.int/social_determinants/thecommission/finalreport/en/

World Health Organization. (2010). *Hidden cities: Unmasking and overcoming health inequities in urban settings.* https://apps.who.int/iris/bitstream/handle/10665/44439/9789241548038_eng.pdf?sequence=1&isAllowed=y

World Health Organization. (2013). *Health inequality monitoring: An overview.* https://apps.who.int/iris/bitstream/handle/10665/85345/9789241548632_eng.pdf?sequence=1

World Health Organization. (2017). *Human rights and health.* https://www.who.int/news-room/fact-sheets/detail/human-rights-and-health

World Health Organization. (2019a). *Promoting the health of refugees and migrants.* https://www.who.int/migrants/about/framework_refugees-migrants.pdf

World Health Organization. (2019b). *World health statistics 2019: Monitoring health for the SDGs, sustainable development goals.* https://www.who.int/gho/world-health-statistics

World Health Organization. (2019c). *Ten threats to global health in 2019.* https://www.who.int/news-room/feature-stories/ten-threats-to-global-health-in-2019

World Health Organization. (2019d). *Pandemic influenza preparedness in WHO member states: Report of a member states survey.* https://apps.who.int/iris/bitstream/handle/10665/325411/9789241515962-eng.pdf?ua=1

World Health Organization & the International Bank for Reconstruction and Development/The World Bank. (2017). *Tracking universal health coverage: 2017 global monitoring report.* https://apps.who.int/iris/bitstream/handle/10665/259817/9789241513555-eng.pdf;jsessionid=1FF38987ADC589984B-80612C9832DB59?sequence=1

Chapter 9

Aarts, M., Lemmens, V., Louwman, M., Kunst, A., & Coebergh, J. (2010). Socioeconomic status and changing inequalities in colorectal cancer? A review of the associations with risk, treatment and outcome. *European Journal of Cancer, 46*(15), 2681–95. https://doi.org/10.1016/j.ejca.2010.04.026

Aden, H., Oraka, C. & Russell, K. (2020). *Mental Health of Ottawa's Black Community.* Ottawa Public Health. https://www.ottawapublichealth.ca/en/reports-research-and-statistics/resources/Documents/MHOBC_Technical-Report_English.pdf.

Aglipay, M., Colman, I., & Chen, Y. (2013). Does the healthy immigrant effect extend to anxiety disorders? Evidence from a nationally representative study. *Journal of Immigrant and Minority Health, 15*(5), 851–7. https://doi.org/10.1007/s10903-012-9677-4

American Psychiatric Association. (1994). *Diagnostic and statistical manual of mental disorders* (4th ed.). American Psychiatric Association.

American Psychiatric Association. (2013). *Diagnostic and statistical manual of mental disorders* (5th ed.). American Psychiatric Association.

Arredondo, P., Toporek, R., Brown, S., Jones, J., Locke, D., Sanchez, J., & Stadler, H. A. (1996). Operationalization of multicultural counseling competencies. *Journal of Multicultural Counseling and Development, 24*, 42–78.

Balhara, Y. P. S., Schachi, M., & Kataria, D. K. (2012). Body shape and eating attitudes among female nursing students in India. *East Asian Archives of Psychiatry, 22*(2), 70–4. https://search.informit.com.au/documentSummary;dn=701316014421142;res=IELHEA

Baroud, R. (2020, December 21). The great divider: Covid-19 reflects global racism, not equality. *CounterPunch*. https://www.counterpunch.org/2020/12/21/the-great-divider-covid-19-reflects-global-racism-not-equality/

Boisvert, J. A., & Harrell, W. A. (2012). The impact of spirituality on eating disorder symptomatology in ethnically diverse Canadian women. *International Journal of Social Psychiatry, 59*(8), 729–38. https://doi.org/10.1177/0020764012453816

Breslau, J., Aguilar-Gaxiola, S., Kendler, K.S. Su, M., Williams, D. & Kessler, R.C. (2006). Specifying race-ethnic differences in risk for psychiatric disorder in a USA national sample. *Psychological Medicine, 36*(1), 57–68. doi: https://doi.org/10.1017/S0033291705006161

Bromet, E., Andrade, L. H., Hwang, I., Sampson, N. A., Alonso, J., Girolamo, G., . . . Santabárbara, J. (2020). Prevalence of depression during the COVID-19 outbreak: A meta-analysis of community-based studies. *International Journal of Clinical and Health Psychology, 21*(1). https://doi.org/10.1016/j.ijchp.2020.07.007

Bueno-Notivol, J., Gracia-García, P., Olaya, B., Lasheras, I., López-Antón, R., & Santabárbara, J. (2021). Prevalence of depression during the COVID-19 outbreak: A meta-analysis of community-based studies. International Journal of Clinical and *Health Psychology, 21*(1), 100196–11. https://doi.org/10.1016/j.ijchp.2020.07.007

Canadian Psychological Association. (2020, June 10). *"Psychology works" fact sheet: Why does culture matter to COVID-19?* https://cpa.ca/docs/File/Publications/FactSheets/FS_CultureAndCOVID-19.pdf

Caron, J., & Liu, A. (2010). A descriptive study of the prevalence of psychological distress and mental disorders in the Canadian population: Comparison between low-income and non-low-income populations. *Chronic Diseases and Injuries in Canada, 30*(3), 84–94. https://pubmed.ncbi.nlm.nih.gov/20609292/

Castaldelli-Maia, J. M., Marziali, M. E., Lu, Z., & Martins. S. S. (2021). Investigating the effect of national government physical distancing measures on depression and anxiety during the COVID-19 pandemic through meta-analysis and meta-regression. *Psychological Medicine*, 2021, 1. doi:10.1017/S0033291721000933

Chang, D. F. (2002). Understanding the rates and distribution of mental disorders. In K. S. Kurasaki, S. Okazaki, & S. Sue (Eds.). *Asian American mental health: Assessment theories and methods* (pp. 9–27). Kluwer Academic/Plenum Publishers. https://doi.org/10.1007/978-1-4615-0735-2_2

Chen, A. W., Kazanjian, A., Wong, H., & Goldner, E. M. (2010). Mental health service use by Chinese immigrants with severe and persistent mental illness. *The Canadian Journal of Psychiatry, 55*(1), 35–42. https://doi.org/10.1177/070674371005500106

Chisuwa, N., & O'Dea, J. A. (2010). Body image and eating disorders amongst Japanese adolescents: A review of the literature. *Appetite, 54*(1), 5–15. https://doi.org/10.1016/j.appet.2009.11.008

Chiu, M., Amartey, A., Wang, X., & Kurdyak, P. (2018). Ethnic differences in mental health status and service utilization: A population-based study in Ontario, Canada. *The Canadian Journal of Psychiatry/La Revue Canadienne de Psychiatrie, 63*(7), 481–91. https://doi.org/10.1177/0706743717741061

Chiu, M., Lebenbaum, M., Newman, A. M., Zaheer, J., & Kurdyak, P. (2016). Ethnic differences in mental illness severity: A population-based study of Chinese and South Asian patients in Ontario, Canada. *The Journal of Clinical Psychiatry, 77*(9), 1108–16. https://doi.org/10.4088/JCP.15m10086

Clark, L. A., Cuthbert, B., Lewis-Fernández, R., Narrow, W. E., & Reed, G. M. (2017). Three approaches to understanding and classifying mental disorder: ICD-11, DSM-5, and the National Institute of Mental Health's Research Domain Criteria (RDoC). *Psychological Science in the Public Interest, 18*(2), 72–145. https://doi.org/10.1177/1529100617727266

Collins, S., & Arthur, N. (2010). Culture-infused counselling: A fresh look at a classic framework of multicultural counselling competencies. *Counselling Psychology Quarterly, 23*(2), 203–16. https://doi.org/10.1080/09515071003798204

Comas-Díaz, L. (2014). Multicultural psychotherapy. In F. T. L. Leong, L. Comas-Díaz, G. C. Nagayama Hall, V. C. McLoyd, & J. E. Trimble (Eds.), *APA handbook of multicultural psychology: Vol. 2. Applications and training* (pp. 419–41). American Psychological Association.

Corey, G. (2017). *Theory and practice of counseling and psychotherapy* (10th ed.). Cengage.

Daley, A., Costa, L., & Ross, L. (2012). (W)righting women: Constructions of gender, sexuality and race in the psychiatric chart. *Culture, Health & Sexuality, 14*, 955–69. https://doi.org/10.1080/13691058.2012.712718

Dardas, L., & Simmons, L. (2015). The stigma of mental illness in Arab families: A concept analysis. *Psychiatric and Mental Health Nursing, 22*(9), 668–79. https://doi.org/10.1111/jpm.12237.

Durà-Vilà, G., & Hodes, M. (2012). Cross-cultural study of idioms of distress among Spanish nationals and Hispanic American migrants: Susto, nervios and ataque de nervios. *Social Psychiatry and Psychiatric Epidemiology, 47*(10), 1627–37. https://doi.org/10.1007/s00127-011-0468-3

Dwairy, M. (2006). *Counselling psychotherapy with Arabs and Muslims: A culturally sensitive approach*. Teachers College Press.

Ebigbo, P., Lekwas, E., & Chukwunenyem, N. (2015). Brain fog: New perspectives from case observations. *Transcultural Psychiatry, 52*(3), 311–30. https://doi.org/10.1177/1363461514557064

Freud, S. (1909/1977). *Five lectures on psychoanalysis*. Norton.

Gaebel, W., Stricker, J., & Kerst, A. (2020). Changes from ICD-10 to ICD-11 and future directions in psychiatric classification. *Dialogues in Clinical Neuroscience, 22*(1), 7–15. https://doi.org/10.31887/DCNS.2020.22.1/wgaebel

Gaebel, W., Zielasek, J., & Reed, G. M. (2017). Mental and behavioural disorders in the ICD-11: Concepts, methodologies, and current status. *Psychiatria Polska, 51*(2), 169–95. https://doi.org/10.12740/PP/69660

Gearing, R. E., Schwalbe, C. S., MacKenzie, M. J., Brewer, K. B., Ibrahim, R. W., Olimat, H. S., & Al-Krenawi, A. (2013). Adaptation and translation of mental health interventions in Middle Eastern Arab countries: A systematic review of barriers to and strategies for effective treatment implementation. *International Journal of Social Psychiatry, 59*(7), 671–81. https://doi.org/10.1177/0020764012452349

Gelfand, M. (2020, March 13). *To survive the coronavirus, the United States must tighten up*. https://6df1098c-05f3-4ab1-a049-b59ba7f3ecfe.usrfiles.com/ugd/6df109_6da2e95a748c49adb1fefdc34d966569.pdf

Gelfand, M. J., Raver, J. L., Nishii, L., Leslie, L. M., Lun, J., Lim, B. C., . . . Aycan, Z. (2011). Differences between tight and loose cultures: A 33-nation study. *Science, 332*(6033), 1100–4. http://doi.org/10.1126/science.1197754

Global Burden of Disease. (2018) Global, regional, and national incidence, prevalence, and years lived with disability for 354 diseases and injuries for 195 countries and territories, 1990 2017: A systematic analysis for the Global Burden of Disease Study 2017. *The Lancet. 392*, p. 1789–858 https://www.thelancet.com/action/showPdf?pii=S01406736%2818%2932279-7

Goldin, I., & Muggah, R. (2020, October 9). *COVID-19 is increasing multiple kinds of inequality. Here's what we can do about it*. World Economic Forum. https://www.weforum.org/agenda/2020/10/covid-19-is-increasing-multiple-kinds-of-inequality-here-s-what-we-can-do-about-it/

González-Sanguino, C., Ausín, B., Castellanos, M. A., Saiz, J., López-Gómez, A., Ugidos, C., & Muñoz, M. (2020). Mental health consequences during the initial stage of the 2020 Coronavirus pandemic (COVID-19) in Spain. *Brain, Behavior, and Immunity, 87*, 172–6. https://doi.org/10.1016/j.bbi.2020.05.040

Guarnaccia, P. J., Lewis-Fernandez, R., Martinez Pincay, I., Shrout, P., Guo, J., Torres, M., . . . Alegria, M. (2010). Ataque de nervios as a marker of social and psychiatric vulnerability: Results from the NLAAS. *International Journal of Social Psychiatry, 56*(3), 298-309. https://doi.org/10.1177/0020764008101636

Haque, A. (2010). Mental health concepts in Southeast Asia: Diagnostic considerations and treatment implications. *Psychology, Health, & Medicine. 15*(2), 127–34. https://doi.org/10.1080/13548501003615266

Hansson, E., Tuck, A., Lurie, S., & McKenzie, K. (2009). *Improving mental health services for immigrant, refugee, ethno-cultural and racialized groups: Issues and options for service improvement*. Mental Health Commission of Canada. https://www.mentalhealthcommission.ca/wp-content/uploads/drupal/Diversity_Issues_Options_Report_ENG_0_1.pdf

Herba, C. M., Glover, V., Ramchandani, P. G., & Rondon, M. B. (2016). Maternal depression and mental health in early childhood: An examination of underlying mechanisms in low-income and middle-income countries, *The Lancet Psychiatry, 3*(10), 983–92. https://doi.org/10.1016/S2215-0366(16)30148-1

Hofmann, S. G. (2018). *Clinical psychology: A global perspective*. Wiley Publications.

Jarvis, E. G., Kirmayer, L. J., Jarvis, G. K., & Whitley, R. (2005). The role of Afro-Canadian status in police or ambulance referral to emergency psychiatric services. *Psychiatric services (Washington, DC), 56*(6), 705–10. https://doi.org/10.1176/appi.ps.56.6.705

Jarvis, G. E., Toniolo, I., Ryder, A. G. Sessa, S., & Cremonesse, C. (2011). High rates of psychosis for black inpatients in Padua and Montreal: Different contexts, similar findings. *Social Psychiatry and Psychiatric Epidemiology, 46*, 247–53. https://doi.org/10.1007/s00127-010-0187-1

Karam, E., Friedman, M., Hill, E., Kessler, R., Mclaughlin, K., Petukhova, M., & Koenen, K. (2014). Cumulative traumas and risk thresholds: 12-month PTSD in the World Mental Health (WMH) surveys. *Depression and Anxiety, 31*(2), 130–42. https://doi.org/10.1002/da.22169

Keel P. K., & Klump, K. L. (2003). Are eating disorders culture-bound syndromes? Implications for conceptualizing their etiology. *Psychological Bulletin. 129*(5), 747–69. doi:10.1037/0033-2909.129.5.747. PMID: 12956542.

Kessler, R., & Bromet, E. (2013.). The epidemiology of depression across cultures. *Annual Review of Public Health, 34*(1), 119–38. https://doi.org/10.1146/annurev publhealth-031912-114409

Kessler, R., Sampson, N., Berglund, P., Gruber, M., Al-Hamzawi, A., Andrade, L., . . . Wilcox, M. (2015). Anxious and non-anxious major depressive disorder in the World Health Organization World Mental Health Surveys. *Epidemiology and Psychiatric Sciences, 24*(3), 210–26. doi:10.1017/S2045796015000189

Kidia, K., Machando, D., Bere, T., Macpherson, K., Nyamayaro, P., Potter, L., . . . Murphy-Shigematsu, S. (2015, February). *Day of remembrance panel*. California State Polytechnic University.

Kolapo, T. (2017). Culturally competent commissioning; meeting the needs of Canada's diverse communities: The road map to a culturally competent mental health system for all. *Canadian Journal of Community Mental Health, 36*(4), 83–96. https://doi.org/10.7870/cjcmh-2017-034

Kolar, D. R., Rodriguez, D. L. M., Chams, M. M., & Hoek, H. W. (2016). Epidemiology of eating disorder in Latin America: A systematic review and meta-analysis. *Current Opinion in Psychiatry, 29*(6), 363–71. https://doi.org/10.1097/YCO.0000000000000279

Kumachev, A., Trudeau, M., & Chan, K. (2016). Associations among socioeconomic status, patterns of care, and outcomes in breast cancer patients in a universal health care system: Ontario's experience. *Cancer, 122*(6), 893–8. https://doi.org/10.1002/cncr.29838

Kvrgic, S., Harhaji, S., Mijatovic Jovanovic, V., AC Nikolic, E., Radic, I., Cankovic, S., & Cankovic., D. (2013). Gender differences in mental health among adult population in Vojvodina, Serbia. *Iranian Journal of Public Health, 42*(8), 833–41. http://search.proquest.com/docview/1687347551/

Kwak, K. (2016). An evaluation of the healthy immigrant effect with adolescents in Canada: Examinations of gender and length of residence. *Social Science & Medicine, 157*, 87–95. https://doi.org/10.1016/j.socscimed.2016.03.017

Lai, D. W. L., & Surood, S. (2010). Types and factor structure of barriers to utilization of health services among aging south Asians in Calgary, Canada. *Canadian Journal on Aging, 29*(2), 249–58. https://doi.org/10.1017/S0714980810000188

The Lancet Public Health. (2021). COVID-19—break the cycle of inequality. *Lancet Public Health. 6*(2), E82. https://doi.org/10.1016/S2468-2667(21)00011-6

Latner, J. D., Knight, T., & Illingworth, K. (2011). Body image and self-esteem among Asian, Pacific Islander, and white college students in Hawaii and Australia. *Eating Disorders, 19*(4), 355–68. https://doi.org/10.1080/10640266.2011.584813

Lee, S. (2001). From diversity to unity: The classification of mental disorders in 21st-century China. *Psychiatric Clinics of North America, 24*(3), 421–31.

Lewis-Fernández, R., Gorritz, M., Raggio, G., Peláez, C., Chen, H., & Guarnaccia, P. (2010). Association of trauma-related disorders and dissociation with four idioms of distress among Latino psychiatric outpatients. *Culture, Medicine, and Psychiatry, 34*(2), 219–43. https://doi.org/10.1007/s11013-010-9177-8

Loue, S., & Sajatovic, M. (2012) *Encyclopedia of immigrant health* (Vol. 1). Springer

Markides, K. S., & Rote, S. (2015). Immigrant health paradox. *Emerging trends in the social and behavioral sciences*, 1–15. Wiley. https://doi.org/10.1002/9781118900772.etrds0174

Memon, A., Taylor, K., Mohebati, L., Sundin, J., Cooper, M., Scanlon, T., & de Visser, R. (2016). Perceived barriers to accessing mental health services among black and minority ethnic (BME) communities: A qualitative study in Southeast England. *BMJ Open, 6*(11), 1–9. https://doi.org/10.1136/bmjopen-2016-012337

Mezzich J. E., Salloum I. M., Cloninger, C. R., & Botbol M. (2016). Person-centered integrative diagnosis and its context. In Mezzich J., Botbol M., Christodoulou G., Cloninger C., Salloum I. (Eds.), *Person-centered psychiatry* (pp. 139–55). Springer.

Mio, J. S., Barker-Hackett, L., & Tumambing, J. (2012). *Multicultural psychology: Understanding our diverse communities* (3rd ed.). Oxford University Press.

Mio, J. S., Koss, M. P., Harway, M., O'Neil, J. M., Geffner, R., Murphy, B. C., & Ivey, D. C. (2003). Violence against women: A silent pandemic. In J. S. Mio & G. Y. Iwamasa (Eds.), *Culturally diverse mental health: The challenges of research and resistance* (pp. 269–87). Brunner-Routledge.

Mojtabai, R., Olfson, M., Sampson, N. A., Jin, R., Druss, B., Wang, P. S., . . . Kessler, R. C. (2011). Barriers to mental health treatment: Results from the National Comorbidity Survey Replication (NCS-R). *Psychological Medicine, 41*, 1751–61.

Moitra, E., Duarte-Velez, Y., Lewis-Fernández, R., Weisberg, R. B., & Keller, M. B. (2018). Examination of ataque de nervios and ataque de nervios like events in a diverse sample of adults with anxiety disorders. *Depression and anxiety, 35*(12), 1190–7. https://doi.org/10.1002/da.22853

Morgan, C., Dazzan, P., Morgan, K., Jones, P., Harrison, G., Leff, J., Murray, R., & Fearon, P. (2006). First episode psychosis and ethnicity: Initial findings from the AESOP study. *World Psychiatry, 5*(1), 40–6.

Murphy-Shigematsu, S. (2014). Hikikomori: Adolescence without end. *Culture, Medicine, and Psychiatry, 38*, 512–13. https://doi.org/10.1007/s11013-014-9388-5

Murray, S. B., Nagata, J. M., Griffiths, S., Calzo, J. P., Brown, T. A., Mitchison, D., . . . Mond, J. M. (2017). The enigma of male eating disorders: A critical review and synthesis. *Clinical Psychology Review, 57*, 1–11. https://doi.org/10.1016/j.cpr.2017.08.001

Musaiger, A., Al-Mannai, M., Tayyem, R., Al-Lalla, O., Ali, E., Kalam, F., . . . Chirane, M. (2013). Risk of disordered eating attitudes among adolescents in seven Arab countries by gender and obesity: A cross-cultural study. *Appetite, 60*, 162–7. https://doi.org/10.1016/j.appet.2012.10.012

Nakai, Y., Nin, K., & Noma, S. (2014). Eating disorder symptoms among Japanese female students in 1982, 1992, and 2002. *Psychiatry Research, 219*(1), 151–6. https://doi.org/10.1016/j.psychres.2014.05.018

Nasser, M., Katzman, M. A., & Gordon, R. A. (Eds.). (2001). *Eating disorders and cultures in transition*. Brunner-Routledge.

Nelson, S. E., Browne, A. J., & Lavoie, J. G. (2016). Representations of Indigenous peoples and use of pain medication in Canadian news media. *International Indigenous Policy Journal, 7*(1). https://doi.org/10.18584/iipj.2016.7.1.5

Nelson, S. E., & Wilson, K. (2017). The mental health of Indigenous peoples in Canada: A critical review of research. *Social Science & Medicine, 176*, 93–112. https://doi.org/10.1016/j.socscimed.2017.01.021

Ohtani, A., Suzuki, T., Takeuchi, H., & Uchida, H. (2015). Language barriers and access to psychiatric care: A systematic review. *Psychiatric Services, 66*(8), 798–805. https://doi.org/10.1176/appi.ps.201400351

Olah, M., Gaisano, G., & Hwang, S. (2013). The effect of socioeconomic status on access to primary care: An audit study. *CMAJ: Canadian Medical Association Journal, 185*(6), E263–9. https://doi.org/10.1503/cmaj.121383

Ottawa Public Health (August, 2020) Mental Health of Ottawa's Black Community Research Study. https://www.ottawapublichealth.ca/en/reports-research-and-statistics/resources/Documents/MHOBC_Technical-Report_English.pdf

Palay, J., Taillieu, T. L., Afifi, T. O., Turner, S., Bolton, J. M., Enns, M. W., . . . Sareen, J. (2019). Prevalence of mental disorders and suicidality in Canadian provinces. *The Canadian Journal of Psychiatry/La Revue Canadienne de Psychiatrie, 64*(11), 761–9. https://doi.org/10.1177/0706743719878987

Patten, S. B., Williams, J. V. A., Lavorato, D. H., Wang, J. L., McDonald, K., & Bulloch, A. G. M. (2016). Major depression in Canada: What has changed over the past 10 years?

The Canadian Journal of Psychiatry, 61(2), 8085. https://doi.org/10.1177/0706743715625940

Pedersen, P. (1988). *A handbook for developing multicultural awareness*. American Association for Counseling and Development.

Pike, K. M., & Dunne, P. E. (2015). The rise of eating disorders in Asia: A review. *Journal of Eating Disorders, 3*(33), 2–14. https://doi.org/10.1186/s40337-015-0070-2

Pike, K. M., Hans, H. W., & Dunne, P. E. (2014). Cultural trends and eating disorders. *Current Opinion in Psychiatry, 27*(6), 436–42. doi:10.1097/YCO.0000000000000100

Pizzigati, S. (2021, January 5). In 2021, let's ring a global alarm on inequality that everyone can hear. *CounterPunch*. https://www.counterpunch.org/2021/01/05/in-2021-lets-ring-a-global-alarm-on-inequality-that-everyone-can-hear/

Qian, J., Hu, Q, Wan, Y., Li, T., Wu., M., Ren, Z., & Yu., D. (2013). Prevalence of eating disorders in the general populations: A systematic review. *Shanghai Archives of Psychiatry, 25*(4), 212–23. https://doi.org/10.3969/j.issn.1002-0829.2013.04.003

Rahman, M., Kopec, J., Sayre, E., Greidanus, N., Aghajanian, J., Anis, A., . . . Rahman, M. (2011). Effect of sociodemographic factors on surgical consultations and hip or knee replacements among patients with osteoarthritis in British Columbia, Canada. *The Journal of Rheumatology, 38*(3), 503–9. https://doi.org/10.3899/jrheum.100456

Reed, G. M., Correia, J. M., Esparza, P., Saxena, S., & Maj, M. (2011). The WPA–WHO global survey of psychiatrists' attitudes toward mental disorders classification. *World Psychiatry, 10*, 118–31.

Ristovski-Slijepcevic, S., Bell, K., Chapman, G., & Beagan, B. (2010). Being "thick" indicates you are eating, you are healthy and you have an attractive body shape: Perspectives on fatness and food choice amongst Black and White men and women in Canada. *Health Sociology Review: Food, Ethics and Identity, 19*(3), 317–29. https://doi.org/10.5172/hesr.2010.19.3.317

Rosenfeld, S. (1999). Gender and mental health: Do women have more psychopathology, men more, or both the same (and why)? In A. V. Horwitz & T. L. Scheid (Eds.), *A handbook for the study of mental health: Social contexts, theories, and systems* (pp. 348–60). Cambridge University Press.

Rushe, D. (2020). Coronavirus has widened America's vast racial wealth gap, study finds. *The Guardian* (June 19, 2020). https://www.theguardian.com/us-news/2020/jun/19/coronavirus-pandemic-billioinaires-racial-wealth-gap

Ryder, A. G., Berry, J., Safdar, S., & Yampolsky, M. (2020). "Psychology Works" fact sheet: Why does culture matter to COVID-19? https://cpa.ca/docs/File/Publications/FactSheets/FS_CultureAndCOVID-19.pdf

Safdar, S., & Kosakowska-Berezecka, N. (Eds.). (2015). *Psychology of gender through the lens of culture, theories and applications*. Springer Publisher.

Scull, A. (2013). *Cultural sociology of mental illness: An A-to-Z guide*. SAGE Publications.

Shapiro, E., Levine, L., & Kay, A. (2020). Mental health stressors in Israel during the coronavirus pandemic. *Psychological Trauma, 12*(5), 499–501. https://doi.org/10.1037/tra0000864

Shuttlesworth, M., & Zotter, D. (2011). Disordered eating in African American and Caucasian women: The role of ethnic identity. *Journal of Black Studies, 42*(6), 906–22. https://doi.org/10.1177/0021934710396368

Sikka, A., Vaden-Goad, L. (G.), & Waldner, L. K. (2010). Authentic self-expression: Gender, ethnicity, and culture. In D. C. Jack & A. Ali (Eds.), *Silencing the self across cultures: Depression and gender in the social world* (pp. 261–84). Oxford University Press. https://doi.org/10.1093/acprof:oso/9780195398090.003.0013

Sinacore, A., Borgen, W., Daniluk, J., Kassan, A., Long, B., & Nicol, J. (2011). Canadian counselling psychologists' contributions to applied psychology. *Canadian Psychology/Psychologie Canadienne, 52*(4), 276–88. https://doi.org/10.1037/a0025549

Smink, F., Hoeken, D., & Hoek, H. (2012). Epidemiology of eating disorders: Incidence, prevalence and mortality rates. *Current Psychiatry Reports, 14*(4), 406–14. https://doi.org/10.1007/s11920-012-0282-y

Solmi, F., Hotopf, M., Hatch, S. L., Treasure, J., & Micali, N. (2016). Eating disorders in a multi-ethnic inner-city UK sample: Prevalence, comorbidity and service use. *Social Psychiatry and Psychiatric Epidemiology, 51*(3), 369–81. https://doi.org/10.1007/s00127-015-1146-7

Stafford, M., Newbold, B., & Ross, N. (2010). Psychological distress among immigrants and visible minorities in Canada: A contextual analysis. *International Journal of Social Psychiatry, 57*(4), 428–41. https://doi.org/10.1177/0020764010365407

Stein, D., Lim, C., Roest, A., de Jonge, P., Aguilar-Gaxiola, S., Al-Hamzawi, A., & Scott, K. (2017). The cross-national epidemiology of social anxiety disorder: Data from the World Mental Health Survey Initiative. *BMC Medicine, 15*(1), 1–21. https://doi.org/10.1186/s12916-017-0889-2

Straiton, M., Grant, J., Winefield, H., & Taylor, A. (2014). Mental health in immigrant men and women in Australia: The North West Adelaide health study. *BMC Public Health, 14*(1), 1–15. https://doi.org/10.1186/1471-2458-14-1111

Sue, D., Arredondo, P., & McDavis, R. (1992). Multicultural counseling competencies and standards: A call to the profession. *Journal of Counseling and Development, 70*(4), 477–486. https://doi.org/10.1002/j.1556-6676.1992.tb01642.x

Sue, D. W., Bernier, J. E., Durran, A., Feinberg, L., Pedersen, P., Smith, E. J., & Vasquez-Nuttall, E. (1982). Position paper: Cross-cultural counseling competencies. *The Counseling Psychologist, 10*, 45–52.

Sue, D. W., Carter, R. T., Casas, J. M., Fouad, N. A., Ivey, A. E., Jensen, M., . . . Vasquez-Nuttal, E. (1998). *Multicultural counseling competencies: Individual and organizational development*. SAGE.

Sue, D. W., & Sue, D. (2016). *Counseling the culturally diverse: Theory and practice* (7th ed.). Wiley.

Sue, D. W., & Sue, D. (1999). *Counseling the culturally different: Theory and practice* (3rd ed.). Wiley.

Sue, D. W., Ivey, A. E., & Pedersen, P. B. (1996). *A theory of multicultural counseling and therapy*. Brooks/Cole.

Surhone, L. M., Tennoe, M. T., & Henssonow, S. F. (Eds.). (2010). *The Chinese classification of mental disorders* (3rd ed.). Betascript.

Taylor, D., & Richards, D. (2019). Triple jeopardy: Complexities of racism, sexism, and ageism on the experiences of mental health stigma among young Canadian Black Women of Caribbean descent. *Frontiers in Sociology*, 4, 43. https://doi.org/10.3389/fsoc.2019.00043

Thomas, J., Khan, S., & Abdulrahman A. A. (2010). Eating attitudes and body image concerns among female university students in the United Arab Emirates. *Appetite* 54(3), 595–8. https://doi.org/10.1016/j.appet.2010.02.008

Tortelli, A., Morgan, C., Szoke, A., Nascimento, A., Skurnik, N., de Caussade, E. M., . . . Murray, R. (2014). Different rates of first admissions for psychosis in migrant groups in Paris. *Social Psychiatry and Psychiatric Epidemiology*, 49, 1103–9. https://doi.org/10.1007/s00127-013-0795-7

US Department of Health and Human Services. (2001). *Mental health: Culture, race, and ethnicity—A supplement to mental health: A report of the Surgeon General*. https://pdfs.semanticscholar.org/992b/19cf1c50b30291d1cdb3b83ac-d0e56043a7d.pdf?_ga=2.134499953.1260633549.1591305105-1494096907.1590857865

Wade, T., Keski-Rahkonen, A., & Hudson, J. (2011). Epidemiology of eating disorders. In *Textbook of psychiatric epidemiology* (3rd ed.), pp. 343–60. https://doi.org/10.1002/9780470976739.ch20

Wainberg, M. L., Scorza, P., Shultz, J. M., Helpman, L., Mootz, J. J., Johnson, K. A., . . . Arbuckle, M. R. (2017). Challenges and opportunities in global mental health: A research-to-practice perspective. *Current Psychiatry Reports*, 19(5), 28. https://doi.org/10.1007/s11920-017-0780-z

Williams, D. R., & Harris-Reid, M. (1999). Race and mental health: Emerging patterns and promising approaches. In A. V. Horwitz & T. L. Scheid (Eds.), *A handbook for the study of mental health: Social contexts, theories, and systems* (pp. 295–314). Cambridge University Press.

World Health Organization. (2017). *Depression and other common mental disorders: Global health estimates*. https://www.who.int/mental_health/management/depression/prevalence_global_health_estimates/en/

World Health Organization. (2020). *WHO Director-General's opening remarks at the media briefing on COVID-19—11 March 2020*. https://www.who.int/dg/speeches/detail/who-director-general-s-opening-remarks-at-the-media-briefing-on-covid-19---11-march-2020

World Health Organization WMH-CIDI. (2020). *About the WHO WMH-CIDI*. https://www.hcp.med.harvard.edu/wmhcidi/about-the-who-wmh-cidi/

Yeung, B. (2018). *A qualitative exploration of second-generation Asian Canadian bicultural women's stories about counselling and gender-based violence* [Master's thesis]. University of Ottawa.

Chapter 10

Amnesty International. (2019). *Seventy+ years of suffocation*. https://nakba.amnesty.org/en/chapters/west-bank-gaza/#the-al-jawarash-family

Apartheid Museum. (n.d.). *Permanent exhibition*. https://www.apartheidmuseum.org/permanent-exhibition

Belmore, R. (2020). *Rebecca Belmore*. https://www.rebeccabelmore.com/

Betancourt, J., & Green, A. (2010). Commentary: Linking cultural competence training to improved health outcomes: Perspectives from the field. *Academic Medicine: Journal of the Association of American Medical Colleges*, 85(4), 583–5. https://doi.org/10.1097/ACM.0b013e3181d2b2f3

Bracha, H. S., Ralston, T. C., Matsukawa, J. M., Matsunaga, S. M., Williams, A. E., & Bracha, A. S. (2004). Does "fight or flight" need updating? *Psychosomatics*, 45, 448–9.

Campanelli, S. (Director). (2017). *Indian horse* [Film]. Elevation Pictures.

Canadian Multicultural Education Foundation (CMEF). (n.d.). *About us*. https://www.cmef.ca/about/#pastHighlights

Castillo, L. G., Perez, F. V., Castillo, R., & Ghosheh, M. R. (2010). Construction and validation of the Marianismo Beliefs Scale. *Counseling Psychology Quarterly*, 23, 163–75. https://doi.org/10.1080/09515071003776036

Clark, A. D., Kleiman, S., Spanierman, L. B., Isaac, P., & Poolokasingham, G. (2014). "Do you live in a teepee?" Aboriginal students' experiences with racial microaggressions in Canada. *Journal of Diversity in Higher Education*, 7(2), 112–25. https://doi.org/10.1037/a0036573

Clark, K. B., & Clark, M. P. (1939). The development of consciousness of self and the emergence of racial identification of Negro pre-school children. *Journal of Social Psychology*, 10, 591–9.

Freire, P. (1973). *Education for critical consciousness*. Continuum.

Gibbons, J. L., & Luna, S. E. (2015). For men life is hard, for women life is harder: Gender roles in Central America. In S. Safdar & Kosakowska-Berezecka, N. (Eds.), *Psychology of gender through the lens of culture, theories and applications*. Springer Publisher.

Gorecki, L. (2020, March 5). *Connecting through cultural exchange*. Education Canada. https://www.edcan.ca/articles/cultural-exchange/

Government of Canada. (n.d.). *Canadian Multiculturalism Day*. https://www.canada.ca/en/canadian-heritage/campaigns/multiculturalism-day.html

Guterres, A. (2018). *Inclusive efforts must target persistent racial discrimination plaguing communities worldwide, Secretary-General says on International Day*. United Nations. https://www.un.org/press/en/2018/sgsm18942.doc.htm

Haar, R. & Ghannam, J. (2018). *No safe space: Health consequences of tear gas exposure among Palestine refugees*. Human Rights Center, UC Berkeley School of Law.

Harrell, S. P. (1995, August). *Dynamics of difference: Personal and sociocultural dimensions of intergroup relations*. Paper presented at the 103rd Annual Convention of the American Psychological Association, New York.

Harrell, S. P. (2014). Compassionate confrontation and empathic exploration: The integration of race-related narratives in clinical supervision. In C. A. Falender, E. P. Shafranske, & C. J. Falicov (Eds.), *Multiculturalism and diversity in clinical supervision: A competency-based approach* (pp. 83–110). American Psychological Association. https://doi.org/10.1037/14370-004

Hosseini-Nezhad, S., Safdar, S., Hosseini-Nezhad, P., & Nguyen Luu, L. A. (in press). Psychological Perspectives on COVID-19. In N. Faghih and A. Forouharfar (Eds.), *Comprehensive global studies of COVID-19 aftermath: Multidisciplinary studies of the consequences and repercussions.* Springer.

Human Rights Watch. (2019). *Israel and Palestine: Events of 2018.* Human Rights Watch. https://www.hrw.org/world-report/2019/country-chapters/israel/palestine#

Jon, J. (2013). Realizing internationalization at home in Korean higher education: Promoting domestic students' interaction with international students' intercultural competence. *Journal of Studies in International Education, 17*(4). https://doi.org/10.1177/1028315312468329

Juric, S. (2020, June 6). *Want to be an ally to black, Indigenous and people of colour? Here's what you need to know.* CBC News. https://www.cbc.ca/news/canada/prince-edward-island/pei-what-it-means-to-be-an-ally-1.5594973

Kesler, C., & Bloemraad, I. (2010). Does immigration erode social capital? The conditional effects of immigration-generated diversity on trust, membership, and participation across 19 countries, 1981–2000. *Canadian Journal of Political Science, 43*(2), 319–47. https://doi.org/10.1017/S0008423910000077

Larrivée, R. (2019). What does it mean to be Canadian? *The Star.* https://www.thestar.com/life/2019/06/30/what-does-it-mean-to-be-canadian.html

Manitoba Trauma Information and Education Centre. (2020). Residential schools. https://trauma-informed.ca/trauma-and-first-nations-people/residential-schools/

Meer, T., & Tolsma, J. (2014). Ethnic diversity and its effects on social cohesion. *Annual Review of Sociology, 40*(1), 459–78. https://doi.org/10.1146/annurev-soc-071913-043309

Mensah, J., & Williams, C. J. (2014). Cultural dimensions of African immigrant housing in Toronto: A qualitative insight. *Housing Studies, 29*(3), 438–55. http://dx.doi.org/10.1080/02673037.2014.848266

Miller, J. R. (2012). Residential schools in Canada. In *The Canadian Encyclopedia.* https://www.thecanadianencyclopedia.ca/en/article/residential-schools#:~:text=Residential%20schools%20were%20government%2Dsponsored,to%20schools%20established%20after%201880

Musée Canadien de l'Histoire. (n.d.). *Exhibitions.* https://www.museedelhistoire.ca/expositions/

Parham, T. A., white, J. L., & Ajamu, A. (1999). *The psychology of Blacks* (3rd ed.). Prentice Hall.

Pathways to Education. (2020). *What being Canadian means to me.* https://www.pathwaystoeducation.ca/story/what-being-canadian-means-to-me/

Pfeffer, J., & Sutton, R. (2000). *The knowing–doing gap.* Harvard Business School Press.

Putnam, R. C. (2007). E pluribus unum: Diversity and community in the twenty-first century. The 2006 Johan Skytte Prize Lecture. *Scandinavian Political Studies, 30,* 137–74.

Ratts, M. J., Singh, A. A., Nassar-McMillan, S., Butler, S. K., & McCullough, J. R. (2015). *Multicultural and social justice counseling competencies.* https://www.counseling.org/docs/default-source/competencies/multicultural-and-social-justice-counseling-competencies.pdf?sfvrsn=14

Savage, J. M. (2020). *My job is talking about race, and yet I dread talking about it at work. Here's why.* HuffPost. https://www.huffpost.com/entry/racial-discrimination-at-work-equal-employment-opportunity-officer_n_5ef3b724c5b66c312681825d

Savelkoul, M., Hewstone, M., Scheepers, P., & Stolle, D. (2015). Does relative out-group size in neighborhoods drive down associational life of Whites in the U.S.? Testing construct, conflict and contact theories. *Social Science Research, 52,* 236–52. https://doi.org/10.1016/j.ssresearch.2015.01.013

Simpson, L. B. (2018). *I am the artist amongst my people.* Canadianart. https://canadianart.ca/features/i-am-the-artist-amongst-my-people/

Sue, D. W. (2001). Multidimensional facets of cultural competence. *The Counseling Psychologist, 29,* 790–821.

Tan, A., & Roach, P. (2020, June 9). *Ways to be an ally, from two lifetimes of learning.* The Tyee. https://thetyee.ca/Analysis/2020/06/09/Ways-To-Be-An-Ally/

Undi, C. (2020, June 6). *No single right way to be an effective ally, says Black Lives Matter activist—but there is a wrong way.* CBC News. https://www.cbc.ca/news/canada/manitoba/opinion-black-lives-matter-winnipeg-how-to-be-an-ally-1.5600498

United Nations (UN). (2020). *Refugees.* https://www.un.org/en/sections/issues-depth/refugees/index.html

United Nations (UN) Office for the Coordination of Human Affairs. (2016). *UN survey finds displaced Palestinian families in Gaza Strip live in desperate conditions.* UN News. https://news.un.org/en/story/2016/04/526452-un-survey-finds-displaced-palestinian-families-gaza-strip-live-desperate

Warren, R. (1995). *The purpose-driven church.* Zondervan.

Index

Page references followed by "*f*" indicate a figure and "*t*" a table.

Aboriginal Australians, 106, 183, 225
Accessibility for Ontarians with Disabilities Act (Ontario, 1990), 15
acculturated, 142
acculturation: definition and description, 137–8; of host culture, 137; impact, 132–3; models, 138–44, 139*t*, 141*t*
acculturative stress, 130
Acevedo-Polakovich, I. A., and colleagues, 48
additive bilingualism, 114
ADDRESSING model of inquiry, 43
administration bias, 46
affect, 21
affirmative action, 164
African Americans, 31, 60, 153, 154; *See also* Black people
"Africentric" education, 163
Afro-Caribbean and African Canadians: identity, 40–1, 182–3; and mental health, 243–4, 249–50; microinvalidation, 173; patterns of communication, 104–5; as population, 182
age: in experimental research designs, 37–8, 39*f*; and world views, 84–6
Aida Refugee Camp, 280
AIDS epidemic, 81–2
air pollution mortality, 216*t*
Ajase complex, 61–2
allies: being an ally, 287–8; definition and description, 177–8, 287; fair-weather allies, 272
allocentric values, 66
allocentrism, 66–8
Almeida, R., 173–4
alternation, in acculturation, 142
American Psychiatric Association (APA), and sexual identity in DSM, 26–7
amok, 259
analytic intelligence, 53
anorexia nervosa, 260, 262
anxiety disorders, rates, 242
appreciation stage, 198
Arab Canadians, in mental health research, 245–6
Arab populations, and proxemics, 96–7
Armour-Thomas, E., 51
Aronson, E., 158
Arthur, N., 255, 256*f*
Asian Americans, and loss of face, 69
Asian Canadians, 105, 239, 256–7, 261
Asian immigration to Canada, 129
Asians, and identity, 40, 184, 195–6
al-Assad, Bashar, 91
assimilationist, 139–40, 141–2
asylum seekers, 124
ataque de nervios, 259

Atkinson, Dwight, 5, 8, 202
Atkinson,ttt, 2
attachment to objects, 71–2
attribution theory, 149–50, 150*t*
Australia, 159, 225
autonomy status, 193
availability heuristic, 157
aversive racism, 167–9, 168*t*, 271–2
aversive sexism, 169
Awakuni, G. I., 17

Backenroth, G., 4
back translation, 47
Baker, Lori A., 102
Banks, James, 199
Banks' Typology of Ethnic Identity, 199
Banksy, 109*f*, 281*f*
barriers, 211
Beatty, Muna, 170–1
Beck, Aaron, 22
behaviour (human), 20, 149
behavioural expressiveness, 251
Belmore, Rebecca, 290
benefits, 211
Berry, John W.: on acculturation, 138; acculturation model, 139–41, 139*t*, 142–3; refugee careers, 126–7, 126*t*
Berry, J. W., and associates, 3, 11
Best, Deborah, 26
bias: in cross-cultural research, 31, 45–7; definition and description, 45; in health, 221; and psychologists, 16
bias in the usage, 46–7
bias of the user, 46
bicultural competence model, 199
bilingualism: acquisition and types, 113–14; cognitive consequences, 114–16; social consequences, 116–17
Binet, Alfred, 50
binge-eating disorder, 260, 262
biological definition of race, 8, 9
biological level, in biopsychosocial model, 21, 23
biopsychosocial model, 22*f*; definition, 20; description, 20, 21–4; levels in, 21–3, 22*f*, 174; and racism, 174–6
BIPOC, and mental health services, 248; *See also* people of colour
biracial identity development, five-stage model, 197–9
birthing practices, 230
Black Americans. *See* African Americans
Black Canadians. *See* Afro-Caribbean and African Canadians
Black Identity Development Model, 188
#BlackLivesMatter (BLM) campaign, 110
Black Lives Matter (BLM) movement, 272, 273*f*

Black Panther (film), 60, 78*f*
Black people: activism, 272; aversive racism, 167, 168*t*; eating disorders in women, 260; as ethnicity, 9; identity development, 182-3, 187-9, 282; identity formation, 205-6; and mental-health services, 237; police killings and brutality, 7, 158-9, 183; psychosis diagnosis, 239; racial profiling, 157, 159; racism from other minorities, 287-8; racism in education, 163; and superheroes, 78; as youth, 182-3
blood donations, 82
Blumenbach, Johann Friedrich, 8
Blumenbach's five races, 8, 9*f*
Bochner, S., 13
body image, 260, 261
body shame, 261
Boushie, Colten, shooting of, 7
brain, and language, 115
Britain, racism in, 159-60, 166-7
British Columbia, access to mental health services, 248
Bronfenbrenner, U., 143, 143*t*
Brown v. Board of Education decision, 187
Buchanan, Stacy-Ann, 249, 250*f*
bulimia nervosa, 260, 262
bullying online, 110
Burt, Cyril, 50

Callingbull, Ashley, 13*f*
Campbell, D. T., 33
Canada: Canadian identity, 277; diversity in, 13; ethnic *vs.* majority groups, 76; foreign-sounding names and employment, 223-4; and health-belief model, 212; health disparities, 214-15; history of immigration, 122, 129; and homosexuality, 81; identification with, 104; language at home and mother tongue, 116; and LGBTQ2+, 81; male-dominated industries, 65; multi-ethnicity, 197; rate and role of immigration, 122, 136; Syrian refugees, 124, 125; $10 bill, 288*f*; value priorities, 74
Canadian, as identity, 277
Canadian Code of Ethics for Psychologists, and LGBTQ2+, 28
Canadian Multicultural Education Foundation (CMEF), 284
Canadian Museum of History, 284, 285*f*
Canadian Psychological Association (CPA): code of ethics, 17, 18*t*, 28; impact of COVID, 263; and LGBTQ2+, 27-8; and multiculturalism, 16-17
Canadian Race Relations Foundation, 9
Carr, P. R., 194
Carranza, M., 173-4
Carter, R. T., 17
Cass, V. C., 200-1
Castile, Philando, shooting of, 7, 8*f*
Caucasians. *See* White people
causal inference, 32-3, 38
causal stage, 195
Cheung, F. M., 64-5
children: characters in TV and movies, 78-9; collaborative problem solving, 49; cyberbullying, 110; and grandparents, 107; as language brokers, 225; obesity, 216*t*; as refugees, 127
Chileans, patterns of communication, 105
China, 239, 263-4
Chinese Canadians, 129, 239, 244, 248
Chinese Classification of Mental Disorders, 239
Chinese culture, and gratification, 61
Chinese head tax and immigrants, 129

choice of group categorization stage, 198
Clark, Kenneth and Mamie, 187
Clarke, V., and colleagues, 41
class-bound values, as barrier to mental health treatment, 253
climate change, activism, 85-6
Cocodia, E. A., 51
codes of ethics: of CPA, 17, 18*t*, 28; and LGBTQ2+, 28; purpose, 17*f*
cognitions, 21
cognitive-affective level, 21-2, 174
cognitive dissonance theory, 158
cognitive stage, 195
coining technique, 210
Cole, M., and colleagues, 11, 53
Coles, R., 39-40
collaborative problem solving, 49-50
collectivism: and horizontal-vertical dimension, 66-8, 67*f*, 132; and values, 66
collectivistic countries/societies: definition and tendencies, 62; differences in countries, 66; face giving, 69-70; and "fitting in," 61; and immigration, 131-2; and kinesics, 99; self-reliance, 42
Collins, Patricia Hill, 189
Collins, S., 255, 256*f*
colour-blind, 192
colour-blind racial ideology, 169-70
colour evasion, 169, 170
Colquhoun, Glenn, 59
Comas-Diaz, L., 12, 19
coming out, 200, 202
Common Schools Act (Ontario, 1850), 163
common-sense model (of health), 211, 211*f*
Commonwealth Fund survey and program, 227, 228-9, 229*t*
communication: bilingual communication, 113-17; direct *vs.* indirect, 102-3; and distance, 92-3, 93*f*, 94*f*, 96; gender differences, 111-13; high- *vs.* low-context, 101-2; non-verbal aspects, 95-101; patterns in elderly and young adults, 107-8; patterns in ethnic minority populations, 104-6, 252-3; social media's role, 108-11
Composite International Diagnostic Interview (CIDI), 246
conceptual equivalence, 47
conformity stage, 202
consequence stage, 195
construct bias, 45
contact cultures, 96, 105
contact status, 192
control group, 31-2, 31*f*, 33, 37
control over (own) lives, 74-5
conversational rules, 90-5, 90*t*
Coogler, Ryan, 78
Cooper, Nick, 193-4
co-operative principle: definition and description, 90; and maxims, 90-5
correlational research, 35-6, 35*f*, 38
correspondence bias (or fundamental attribution error), 150
countercultural individuals, 66
covert, intentional racism, 164
covert, unintentional racism, 165-6
covert racism: description, 163-4; examples, 165-6; *vs.* overt, 163-7
COVID-19 pandemic: and culture, 6-7; and inequalities, 264-5; and mental health, 242, 263-4; and racism, 288; resources for, 232
creative intelligence, 53

criminal justice system, racism in, 162–3, 183
Cross, William, 187, 204–5
cross-cultural psychology: and culture, 12; description and aim, 11–12; historical background, 24–8
cross-cultural research: biases in, 31, 45–7; equivalence of measures, 47–8; historical background, 24–5
cross-sectional designs, 37–8
cultural attitudes, self-awareness for, 269–76
cultural awareness, 255, 256f
cultural centres on campus, 286
cultural competence: areas of, 268–9, 292; definition, description, and as skill, 268–9, 292; development and education in, 283–7, 283t, 292; discovery and empathy in, 289–90; importance, 291–2; as interpersonal skill, 283; practice for, 286, 290; for psychologists, 268; self-awareness, 269, 276–9; and speaking up, 287–9; and understanding other world views, 279–82; *See also* bicultural competence model; multicultural competence
cultural concepts of distress in DSM-5, 239, 258–60
cultural explanations or perceived causes, 239
cultural identity development. *See* identity development
cultural idioms of distress, 239
cultural level, in biopsychosocial model, 22–3
culturally appropriate strategies, 255
culturally deprived, 175
culturally sensitive working alliance, 255, 256f
cultural practices, understanding of, 282
cultural psychology, 12; *See also* cross-cultural psychology; multicultural psychology
cultural racism, 175
cultural sensitivity, in therapeutic approaches, 254–7
cultural syndromes, 239, 259, 262
culture: in cross-cultural and cultural psychology, 12; definitions, 2, 3–5; description and uses of term, 2–4, 8; and diagnostic manuals, 237–40, 258–60; differences from within, 62–3; education in, 283–6; influence of, 20; investigative approaches, 59–70; self-awareness, 276–9; as standard against others, 277; and world views, 6–8; *See also* specific topics
culture-bound values, as barrier to mental health treatment, 250–3, 250t
culture contact, 13–14
culture shock, 123–4
cyberbullying, 110

Dayton, Mark, 7
deaf community, as culture, 4
decision-making, emic differences in, 62
defensiveness, 271–2
delay of gratification, 60, 61
denial, 271
Denim Day, 65f
dependent variables, 36
depression, 21–2, 241, 242, 243, 247–8
Derwing, T. M., 130
Desmond, Viola, 288f
devaluing, 272–4
Dhillon, Baltej Singh, 164–5, 164f
diabetes, and Indigenous Peoples, 218
Diagnostic and Statistical Manual of Mental Disorders. *See* DSM
diagnostic classification systems, 240
diagnostic criteria, and culture, 239, 244

diagnostic manuals, and culture, 237–40, 258–60; *See also* specific manuals
difference: five Ds, 270–6, 270t; reactions to, 270
dimensions, in value orientation models, 71, 71t
direct communication, 102–3
disabilities (people with), and inclusion, 15
discovery: as attitude, 289–90; definition and description, 274–6
discrimination: definition and description, 151, 152; dynamics, 282; and ethnic groups, 76; in health care, 226–7; immigrants and refugees, 128–9, 134, 135–6; Indigenous Peoples in Canada, 161–2; LGBTQ2+, 81, 82
disintegration status, 192
displacement of populations, 127, 279–81
dispositional attributions, 149–50
dissonance stage, 202–3
distance, and communication, 92–3, 93f, 94f, 96
distancing, 270–1
distress, cultural concepts in DSM-5, 239, 258–60
diverse, use as term, 32
diverse populations: and acculturation, 141–3; guidelines for ethical practice, 18t
diversity: impact on communities, 289; increase in, 13, 268
Domenech Rodríguez, Melanie, 136, 220
Donnelly, Clayton, 158
Dovidio, J. F., 167, 168t
dress code regulations in RCMP, 165
DSM (*Diagnostic and Statistical Manual of Mental Disorders*): and culture, 237–8, 246–7, 258–9; depressive symptoms, 241; description and editions, 26, 237, 238; and sexual identity, 26–7
DSM-I and *DSM-II*, 26–7
DSM-III and *DSM-III-R*, 27
DSM-IV, 238
DSM-V or *DSM-5*, 27, 239

East Asia: communication orientations, 103t; eye contact and gaze, 97–8; face giving, 70; medical traditions, 230
Easterlin paradox, 72
eating disorders, 79, 260–3
Eckford, Elizabeth, 154f
ecological fit or ecological context, 143
ecological model, 143–4, 143t
ecological validity, 33
education: for cultural competence, 283–6, 283t; and health disparities, 214, 215; immigrants and refugees, 135–6; racism in, 163
Einsenberg, L., 213
Ejiade, O. O., 44
elderly. *See* older populations
emersion/immersion, 187, 193
emic approach, 59
emic differences, 62–3
empathy, and cultural competence, 290
employment: aversive racism, 167, 168t; and foreign-sounding names, 223–4; and health, 223; immigrants and refugees, 134–5, 136
empowerment, in multiculturalism, 16
encounter stage, 187
enculturation, 138
enmeshment/denial stage, 198
epidemiologic studies in ethnic groups, 243–7
equality, 15

equity, 15
equivalence of measures, in cross-cultural research, 47–8
Espine, Marc d', 238
ethics, guidelines for diverse populations, 18t; *See also* codes of ethics
ethnical psychology, 24
ethnic counselling, 12
ethnic groups: and discrimination, 76; epidemiologic studies, 243–7; health outcomes, 216–19; *vs.* majority groups, 76; mental disorders prevalence, 242–4, 243t, 247; and stereotypes, 104; world views differences, 76–9, 78f, 281–2; *See also* specific groups
ethnic identity: development, 186–96; experiences and examples, 186, 190, 193–4, 197; multi-ethnic identity development models, 196–9
ethnicity: description and use of term, 10–11; and health disparities, 214–15; *See also* race
ethnic minority populations: bias in research, 31; HIV risk in men, 231–2; language learning, 116; and mental health, 237; patterns of communication, 104–6, 252–3; police and imprisonment, 158–9; and White European standard, 32; *See also* visible minorities
ethnic psychology (or ethnic minority psychology), 12–13
etic approach, 59–60
European Americans. *See* White people
exosystem, 143
experimental designs, in quantitative research, 36–8, 39f
experimental group, 31–2, 31f, 33
explicit bias, 221
externalizing, 257
external validity, 32–4
eye contact, 97–8

face giving/giving face, 69–70
face saving, 69, 102
facial expressions, 99
Fahmy, Rania, 64
families: gender differences, 65, 113; hierarchy in, 131–3; roles in, 133–4
Farage, Nigel, 160
Farr, William, 238
feminine countries, 66
Fields, A. J., 48
Filipinos, identity development, 195–6
films, and world views, 77, 78f, 79
first asylum of refugees, 127
First Nations, 3, 196, 218; *See also* Indigenous Peoples in Canada
first-world psychology, 11
five Ds of difference, 270–6, 270t
five-factor model (FFM) of personality across cultures, 186
five-stage model of biracial identity development, 197–9
flee, 269
flight, 269
flight of refugees, 126–7
Floyd, George, 272
Fontaine, Tina, 163
food, and Indigenous Peoples, 218
forces, in psychology, 19, 19t
foreign-sounding names, and employment, 223–4
four F reactions, 269–70
fourth force, 19
France, racism in, 159

freeze, 269
French-speaking immigrants, 104
Freud, Sigmund, 251
Fridays for Future campaign, 85–6
fright, 269
functional equivalence, 47
fundamental attribution error (or correspondence bias), 150
fusion, in acculturation, 142

Gaertner, S. L., 167, 168t
Galton, Francis, 50
Garcia, O., 116
Gardner, H., 53–5
gayness, and emic differences, 62–3
gaze duration, 97–8
Gelfand, M., 7
gender: and culture, 26; in DSM as mental disorder, 27; and power differentials, 63; qualitative approaches, 42; *vs.* sexual orientation, 231; and socialization, 113
gender-based violence, 64, 79–80
gender differences: characteristics and stereotypes, 111–12, 113; in collaborative problem solving, 49; and communication, 111–13; and families, 65, 133; inclusion in psychology, 26; and mental disorders, 257–8; in moral reasoning, 25–6, 42; stereotype threat, 153; at work, 64–5; and world views, 63–5, 79–80
gender dysphoria, 28
gender identity, changes towards, 27
general intelligence, 50
genetics, and racial groups, 9, 10
Gibbs, Nicholas, 158
Gilligan, Carol, 25, 26, 42
giving face/face giving, 69–70
globalization, and immigration, 124
global village, 268
glossary, 294–300
Gonzalez, John, 171
Good, B., 213
Gorecki, Laryssa, 284–5
Graduate Record Examinations (GRE), 51
grandparents and grandchildren, 107
Great Chain of Being, 9
Great White North project, 194
greetings, 67, 105
Grenfell Tower fire, 166–7, 166f
Grice, Paul, 90, 90t
group level of identity, 184–5, 184f
group-oriented societies. *See* collectivistic countries
Gudowska, Malwina, 114
Guidelines for Non-Discriminatory Practice (CPA), 17, 18t
guilt, 68–9
Gunaratnam, P., and colleagues, 231–2
Guterres, António, 291–2, 291f
Guthrie, Robert, 24

Haddon, A. C., 24
Hall, E. T., 101
Hamilton, D. L., and colleagues, 156
Harrell, S. P., 270, 270t
Hawaiians (native), 107
Hayles, Adrian, 77f

Hays, P. A., 43
health: and culture, 213; definition and description, 209–10; diversity in approaches, 230–1; as human right, 209, 232; link with racism and poverty, 223–4; overview, 209–10, 234; psychological models, 211–13; World's Healthiest Country Index, 228
health behaviours, 210
health-belief model, 211–12
health care and health-care system: access, 209, 210, 224–30, 229t; change and challenges, 232–4; and communication, 107; costs, 220, 228, 229t; deficiencies in Canada, 227; discrimination in, 226–7; expenditures, 228; global rankings, 227–9
health-care disparities, 210
health-care workers, and health disparities, 216t
health disparities: in Canada, 214–15; causes, 219–23; definition and description, 210, 232; globally, 215–16, 216t, 229t; and income, 214, 215, 220, 227; in LGBTQ2+, 231–2; obscure disparities, 231–2; and racism, 221–3
health inequality, 213–14
health inequity, 213–14
health outcomes, 216–19, 220
health professionals: for Indigenous Peoples, 224–5; multicultural competence training, 254–7; trust in, 219–20, 249
health psychology, 211
health threats, 219
healthy immigrant effect (HIE), 244; *See also* immigrant health paradox
Helms, Janet, and model of White identity development, 191, 192–4
Helms, J. E., 189–90
herbal medicines, 230–1
Hernandez, P., 173–4
Herskovits, Melville J., 4, 5
high-context communication (HC), 101–2
historical knowledge of others, 279
HIV (human immunodeficiency virus), and health disparities, 216t, 231–2
hoarding, and culture, 7
Hofstede, Geert, 4, 5, 60
homosexuality, 26–7, 62–3, 81–2; *See also* LGBTQ2+
Hong, Y.-Y., 61
horizontal–vertical dimension, 66–8, 67f, 132
host culture, acculturation of, 137
households, and gender differences, 65
human activity dimension, 71
human culture, 5
human values theory, 72–4, 73f
humour, 80
Hussein, B., 96–7

Ibrahim, Sahar, 172–3
ICD. *See* International Classification of Diseases and Related Health Problems
identity: formation, 182, 205–6; and language, 116–17; and mentalities, 191–2; multiple identities, 9–10, 205–6; self-description, 183–4; simultaneous identities, 9–10; *See also* ethnic identity
identity acceptance, 201
identity comparison, 200–1
identity confusion, 200
identity development: Asian/Filipino identity, 195–6; Black identity, 182–3, 187–90, 282; Chicano/Latino identity, 194–5; critiques of models, 204–5; ethnic identity, 186–96; independent and interdependent self, 183–4; Indigenous identity, 190, 196; multi-ethnic identity, 196–9; overview, 182–3; personality models, 184–5; racial and cultural identity development model (R/CID), 202–4; self-identification, 207; sexual identity, 200–2, 205; White identity, 190–4
identity models, 206; *See also* specific models
identity pride, 201
identity synthesis, 201
identity tolerance, 201
idiocentric values, 66
idiocentrism, 66–8
Idle No More, 85, 110, 111f
"I don't know" statement, 285
illness, contributing factors to, 20
illusory correlation, 156–7
immersion/emersion, 187, 193
immigrant health paradox, 216–17, 244
immigrants: acculturation, 137–41; barriers to health-care system, 225–6; definition, 123; discrimination and exclusion, 128–9, 134, 135–6; experiences of, 123–4, 129–37, 144; health, 216–17; identity formation, 205–6; integration, 141; and labour market, 223–4; and language, 104, 116; language barriers, 129–30, 135, 225; migration phases, 125–6; origin in Canada, 13; overview, 122–4; and qualitative research methods, 40–1; selection process, 164; self-awareness on culture, 278
immigration: historical background for Canada, 122, 129; rate in Canada, 122; reasons for, 134; role in Canada, 136; symbolic racism, 164
Implicit Associations Test (IAT), 221, 222
implicit attitudes, 222–3
implicit bias (in health), 221–2
implicit racial attitudes, 175
imposed etics, 59–60
imprisonment, and minorities, 159, 162, 183
incidence, 241
inclusion, 15
income: and happiness, 72; and health disparities, 214, 215, 220, 227
independent self, 183–4
independent variables, 36
India, and skin colour, 170–1
Indian Act (1876), 161
Indian Horse (movie), 289
Indigenous Peoples globally: access to health-care system, 225; health, 217–18; life expectancy and diet, 218; patterns of communication, 106; silences in conversations, 100; tenure at universities, 152–3
Indigenous Peoples in Canada: access to health-care system, 224–5; activism and advocacy, 85, 110, 161f, 162f; in art, 77–8; culture of, 3; description and terminology, 3, 106, 196; discrimination, 161–2; distancing from by non-Indigenous, 270–1; education on for non-Indigenous, 279, 284–6; health and health disparities, 215, 218–19; health care, 210, 224–5; identity development, 190, 196; imprisonment, 161; internalized oppression, 171; in mental health research, 244–5; microinvalidation, 173; racial profiling, 157–8; racism towards, 160–3; value orientation models, 70–1
indirect communication, 102–3
individualism: and horizontal–vertical dimension, 66–8, 67f, 132; and values, 66
individualistic countries/societies: definition and tendencies, 62; differences in countries, 66; and immigration, 131–2; individuation, 251; and kinesics, 99; self-reliance, 42

individuation, as orientation, 251
infectious diseases, and health disparities, 216t
in-group social support, 131, 134
insight, 251–2
institutional racism, 175
instrument bias, 45–6
integrationists, 141, 142
integration stage, 198
integrative awareness stage, 204
intelligence: alternative conceptions, 53–5; components, 53; and context, 52; and cultural knowledge, 50–1, 55; types, 53–5, 55t
intelligence testing, 50–5
interdependent self, 183–4
inter-ethnic group marriages, 197
internalization, 187, 189, 257
internalized oppression, 170–1
internal validity, 32–4
International Classification of Diseases, Injuries, and Causes of Death (ICD-6), 238
International Classification of Diseases and Related Health Problems (ICD) and ICD-11, 237, 238, 259
International Congress of Psychology, 17
international immigrants, 123
International List of Causes of Death, 238
international students, and microaggression, 172
International Union of Psychological Science (IUPsyS), 17
internment during World War II, 75, 251
interpersonal distances, 92, 94f
interrater reliability, 36–7
intersectional identity development, 189
intersectionality, 11
intersubjective approach, 41
intimate distance, 92, 94f
introspection stage, 203–4
Irish immigration to Canada, 122
isms, as practice, 152, 174
Israel, and Palestinians, 280–1
item bias, 46
Ivey, A. E., 3

Ja, D. Y., 68
Jackson, Bailey W., 188–9
Jahoda, Gustav, 11
Jalaluddin, Uzma, 139
Jamaican music in Canada, 78
Japanese Americans, internment, 75
Japanese culture, 61–2, 102, 251
Japanese immigrants, 129
Al Jawarash family, 280, 281
Jones, J., 32
Jorgensen, George/Christine, 27
journals and books, in cross-cultural research, 25
Juang, Linda, 5
Judd, Ashley, 64
jurors, and aversive racism, 168–9

Kagitcibasi, C., 11
Kahneman, Daniel, 157
Kasky, Cameron, 86
kinesics, 97–9, 98f
Kitayama, S., 183–4
Kleifgen, J. A., 116
Kleinman, A., 213
Kluckhohn, C., 3
Kluckhohn, F. R., 71–2
knowledge transfer, 107
Kohlberg, Lawrence, 25, 26
Korchin, S. J., 31
Kosovo, gender differences in, 65
Kpelle tribe, 53
Kroeber, A. L., 3
kufungisisa (or "thinking too much"), 259
Kurdi, Alan, 125
Kurdish populations, and proxemics, 96–7

labour market, 65, 223–4
Labouvie-Vief, G., 52
LaFramboise, T. D., and colleagues: acculturation model, 141–3, 141t; bicultural competence model, 199
language: and brain, 115; and identity, 116–17; and immigrants, 104, 116; learning, 115–16; non-verbal aspects, 95–101; *See also* bilingualism
language attrition, 114
language barriers: in cross-cultural research, 47–8; immigrants and refugees, 129–30, 135, 225; in mental health treatment, 253–4
language brokers and brokering, 225–6
Larrivée, Ricardo, 277
Latin America, diagnostic manual for, 240
Latin American Guide for Psychiatric Diagnosis (GLADP), 240
Latino people, 105, 194–5, 281–2
Laure, Virginie, 64
law enforcement, as institution, 159
laws and legislation: aversive racism, 168–9; covert racism, 165–6; discrimination in, 161; and homosexuality, 81, 82
learned helplessness, 75
Leong, F. T. L., and colleagues, 69
LGBTQ2+ (lesbian, gay, bisexual, transgender, queer, and two-spirit): discrimination and microaggressions, 81–3; health disparities, 231–2; historical changes in, 26–7; inclusion in psychology, 27–8; and suicide, 201; world views, 80–3
LGBTQQIP2SAA, 200
liberation of consciousness, 290
life expectancy, and health disparities, 216t, 218
lifetime incidence, 241
linguistic equivalence, 47
Litchmore, R., 206
locus of control, 74, 74f
locus of responsibility, 74, 74f
logical positivism, 35
longitudinal design, 38
long-term orientation, 60–2
Lonner, W. J., and colleagues, 24–5
loose cultures, 7, 263
losing face, 69
low-context communication (LC), 101–2
low-paid occupations, and COVID, 264–5
Lund, D. E., 194
Luria, A. R., 52

McKenna, Catherine, 107–8
macrosystem, 143, 144
Madut, Machuar Mawien, 158
Mahmoud, R. K., 96–7
Maiter, S., and colleagues, 76
major depressive episodes (MDE), 243
male privilege, 176
Manual for North African Practitioners, 239–40
marginalist, 140–1
marginalized groups, 210, 264–5
Markham (ON), 137
Markus, H., 183–4
masculine countries, 66
masculine–feminine dimension, 66
maternity and pregnancy, and health disparities, 216t
Matsumoto, David, 5, 99
maxim of manner, 90, 92–4, 95
maxim of quality, 90–1
maxim of quantity, 90, 91
maxim of relevance, 90, 91–2
maxims, and co-operative principle, 90–5
MCT. *See* multicultural counselling and therapy
media, and news values, 90
mediational common-sense model, 211f
Medical College Admission Test (MCAT), 56
medicine: diverse approaches, 230–1; and world views, 59, 60
Melanesians, 106
melting pot notion, 142
Memon, A., and colleagues, 237
men, *vs.* women. *See* gender differences
Menshikova, G. Y., and colleagues, 96
mental and physical functioning, 252
mental disorders: culture-specific disorders, 258–63; and gender differences, 257–8; prevalence in ethnic groups, 242–4, 243t, 247; rates and cultural differences, 241–7; sexual identity and gender as, 26–7
mental health: access to services, 247–8; access to treatment, 237, 248–54; and COVID-19 pandemic, 242, 263–4; and cultural sensitivity, 254–7; and culture, 237, 240, 247–8; data collection, 246; diagnostic manuals, 237–40; and multicultural competence, 254–7; in women, 79
mental health professionals: and culture, 237; multicultural competence training, 254–7
mesosystem, 143
method bias, 45
#MeToo campaign/movement, 64, 110
metric equivalence, 47
Meuter, R. F., and colleagues, 48
microaggression, 81, 172–4, 288
microassault, 172
microinsult, 172
microinvalidation, 173
microsystem, 143
migrants, vilification of, 164
migration, 122
migration phases, 125–6
Miller, C., 51
Min, W., 105
Minocha, Sh., and colleagues, 45

minority identity development model, 202
Mio, J. S., 17, 41, 87, 96, 173
Mio, J. S., and colleagues, 254
Miron, J. M., 40–1
Mischel, Walter, 60
miscommunication, 48
missing and murdered Indigenous women and girls, 163
Mitra, Sudhamshu, 178
mixed unions, 197
"model minority" concept, 287
Mojtabai, R., and colleagues, 249
Money, John, 20, 22
Montigny, F. D., 40–1
moral reasoning, gender differences in, 25–6, 42
Morris, P., 143
Morten, G., 202
movies, and world views, 77, 78f, 79
multicultural competence, 254–7
multicultural counselling and therapy (MCT), 250–4, 250t
multiculturalism: assumptions, 14–16, 14t; code of ethics, 17, 18t; education in, 284; as fourth force, 19, 19t; as philosophy, 14–16; and psychology, 16–17; resistance to, 17, 19; rise of, 16–17, 19
multicultural model, 142
multicultural psychology, 13–14, 19
multi-ethnic identity development models, 196–9
multiple identities, 9–10, 205–6
Museum of Tolerance, 276
museums, 284
Muslim countries, 215
Muslims, and racism, 159
Muslims in Canada, 135–6
Myers,ttt, 151

Native Americans, 70–1, 106, 171, 230; *See also* Indigenous Peoples globally
native bilingualism, 114
natural responses to threats, 269–70
Ndengeyingoma, A., 40–1
negative stereotypes, 155–8
news values, 90
"nigrescence" process, 187
non-communicable diseases, and health disparities, 216t
non-contact cultures, 96
non-verbal communication, 95–101
Norman, D. A., 90t, 94
North Africa, diagnostic manual for, 239–40
North America, 99, 103t, 264
Northern Canada, access to health care, 224–5
Nosek, Brian, 48
#NotOkay, 110
nuclear wars, 85
Nunavut, and health disparities, 215
Nyong'o, Lupita, 177, 177f

Obama, Barack, 164
obesity in children, 216t
OCEAN acronym, 185
Oedipal complex, 61–2
Ohtani, A., and colleagues, 253–4

older populations: as immigrants, 129–30, 133; intelligence, 52; patterns of communication, 107; qualitative approaches to, 43–5
Ontario: mental health and disorders, 239, 243–4, 243t, 248; people with disabilities, 15; police and Blacks, 183; racism, 163
Open Science, 48–9
Oreopoulos, Philip, 223
Organisation for Economic Co-operation and Development (OECD), on collaborative problem solving, 49
orientation, long- and short-term, 60–2
Orji, R., and colleagues, 212
outgroup social support, 131
overt racism: vs. covert, 163–7; definition and description, 163; examples, 159–60, 162–3, 165

Palestinians, 280–1
Paquette, Adam, 3f
paradigm shift, 19
paralanguage, 100
parents in education, 136
Parham, T. A., 189–90
participants, and research methodology, 31–2, 31f, 33
Pedersen, P., 3, 19
people/nature relationship, 71
people of colour: mental health services, 248; negative stereotypes, 156; police killings and brutality, 7, 158–9, 183; world views, 7, 76–7
people with disabilities, and inclusion, 15
Persian culture, and high-context communication, 102
personal distance, 92, 94f
personal identity, levels in, 184–5
personal identity stage, 197–8
personality models, 184–5
personal life stories, use in psychology, 2
personal space, 92, 93f, 96
person-centred medicine (PCM), 240
Philippines, 62–3, 185
Phinney, J., 195–6
physical and mental functioning, 252
pity, 270
police in Canada, and racial profiling, 157, 159
police killings and brutality, 7, 158–9, 183
politicians, and social media, 107–8
population validity, 33
post-migration phase, 126
Poston, W. S. C., 197–8
poverty, 84, 220, 223–4, 253
Powell, Enoch, 159–60
power evasion, 169, 170
practical intelligence, 53
pre-encounter stage, 187
preferred space. See personal space
pregnancy, and health disparities, 216t
"pregnant pause", 100
prejudice, 151, 152, 174
pre-migration phase, 125
prevalence, 237, 241
Primordial Qi theory, 230
privilege, 179
PROGRESS and health inequity, 214

provinces and territories, and health disparities, 214–15
proxemics, 96–7
pseudo-independence status, 193
psychological treatment, and access to mental health, 237, 248–54
psychologists: bias and objectivity, 16; cultural competence, 268; as WEIRD, 70
psychology: cultural approaches to, 252; definition, 11; ethnocentricity of, 11, 16; forces in, 19, 19t; magnetic resonance imaging use, 154–5; multiculturalism in, 16–17; origin, 24; replication in, 48–9; sub-fields, 11; union for, 17; See also specific types of psychology
psychosis, 240
psychosis diagnosis, 239
psychotherapy, and culture, 250–1
publications, in cross-cultural research, 25
Putnam, R. C., 289–90

qualifiers, 112–13
qualitative methods, in cultural psychology, 12
qualitative research: approaches in, 42–5; description, 39–42; vs. quantitative research, 41–2; types, 39
quantitative methods, in cross-cultural psychology, 12
quantitative research: approaches in, 35–6; description, 35, 38; example, 34–5, 39; experimental designs, 36–8, 39f; vs. qualitative research, 41–2
questions: asking questions, 286; and hierarchy, 92–4

race: as biological concept, 8–9; description and use of term, 8; and genetics, 9, 10; as socio-cultural concept, 9–10; as sociological concept, 9–10; See also ethnicity
racial and cultural identity development model (R/CID), 202–4, 203t, 205
Racial Identity Attitude Scale, 189–90
racial inferiority, 9
racial microaggression, 172–4
racial prejudice, 174
racial profiling, 157–8, 159
racial salience, 206
racism: allyship example, 287–8; and biopsychosocial model, 174–6; defensiveness of White people, 271–2; definition and description, 151–2; dynamics of, 282; in education, 163; examples, 159–60; and health disparities, 221–3; and Indigenous Peoples in Canada, 160–3; link with health and poverty, 223–4; modern complexities, 167–71; by other minorities, 287–8; from police, 158–9; responses from racists, 172, 176, 271–2; roots and history, 175; self-awareness, 276; speaking up against, 287–9; systematic racism in society, 158–63; and world views, 74–7; See also specific types of racism
Rage against Colonialism, 161f
random sampling, 36
Razzak, J., and colleagues, 215
R/CID. See racial and cultural identity development model
RCMP, and uniform vs. turban debate, 164–5
refugee careers, 126–7, 126t
refugees: acculturation, 137; definition, 123, 124; discrimination, 128–9; experiences of, 124–5, 129–37, 144; overview, 122–3, 124–5; proxemics, 96; screening, 164; as socio-political issue, 279–81; stages of journey and "careers," 126–8; trauma, 127
Reimer, David, 20–1, 21f, 22–3
reintegration status, 193

relations with conversational partner, 94–5
religion, and health, 215
replication, in psychology, 48–9
researchers as WEIRD, 70
research methodology (in psychology): and correlations, 35–6, 35*f*, 38; general model, 31–2; internal and external validity, 32–4; participants and groups, 31–2, 31*f*, 33; principles of research, 48–9; and White European standard, 32
residential school system, 161, 279, 289
resistance and immersion stage, 203
response style bias, 46
Roberts, Terrence, 2
Roderique, Hadiya, 165–6
Rohner, Ronald, 4, 5
Root, M. P. P., 198–9
Rowe, W., and colleagues, 191–2
Ruiz, A. S., 194–5
rule violations, 95
Rummelhart, D. E., 90*t*, 94
Russia, 82, 96

Salami, K. K., 44
same-sex marriage, 82–3
sample bias, 45
Savage, Jodi M., 272
saving face, 69, 102
schools in US, and mass shootings, 86
Schriver, Kyle, 158
Schwartz, Shalom, 4–5, 72–4, 73*f*
scientific empiricism, 252
"selective enforcement of scientific principles," 33
self-disclosure, 252
self-reliance, 42, 62
Sellers, R. M., and colleagues, 206
separationist, 140
sequential design, 38
severity, 211
sexism, 79, 111
sexual abuse and harassment, 64, 79–80
sexual identity: development, 200–2, 205; as mental disorder, 26–7
sexual orientation, *vs.* gender identity, 231
shadeism, 79
shallowing hypothesis, 109
shame, 68–9
Shon, S. P., 68
shoplifting, and negative stereotypes, 156, 157
short-term orientation, 60–2
sign language at conference, 87
Sikh Canadians, 164–5
silences in conversations, 100
simultaneous identities, 9–10
Singh, Jagmeet, 165*f*
Sixties Scoop, 161
skin colour, 170–1, 173, 177
smiling, 99
Snapchat, 109
social categorizations, 151–3
social change, 16
social class, 84–5, 253
social determinants of health, 213
social distance, 92, 94*f*
social dominance orientation (SDO), 80
social hierarchy, 8
social institutional level, 22, 175
social institutions, 22, 175
social-interpersonal level, 22, 174–5
social justice, 16, 110
social media: activism and allyship, 272; role in communication, 108–11; use of, 107–8
social mistakes, 69
social relations dimension, 71
social support, for immigrants and refugees, 123, 130–1, 134
societal expectations, and world views, 79
socio-cultural concept of race, 9–10
socio-economic status, 220, 223, 253
sociological concept of race, 9–10
socio-political issues, awareness in, 279–81
somatization, 241
Sorokowska, A., and colleagues, 92
South Asians in Canada, and mental health, 243, 248
South Koreans, patterns of communication, 105
speaking up, and cultural competence, 287–9
Stanley, Gerald, 7
Stanley, J. C., 33
Stassun, K., 51
Statistical Classification of Diseases, Injuries, and Causes of Death, 238
statistics, as system, 35
status for First Nations, 196
Steele, Claude M., 153, 154–5
stereotypes: definition and description, 151, 152, 174; development, 155–8; dynamics of, 282; and ethnic groups, 104; gender differences, 112, 113
stereotype threat, 153–5
stereotyping, 282
Sternberg, R., and colleagues, 53
Stiglitz, Joseph, 84
stress, and health, 223
Strodtbeck, F. L., 71–2
structural introspection, 24
structuralism, 24
subtractive bilingualism, 114
successful resolution stage, 195
Sue, D. (David): barriers to MCT, 250–4, 250*t*; on culture-bound values, 250–2; on "different" as word, 32; on emic differences, 62; and MCT, 254; and R/CID, 202; tripartite model of personal identity, 184
Sue, D. W. (Derald Wing): barriers to MCT, 250–4, 250*t*; on culture-bound values, 250–2; on "different" as word, 32; on emic differences, 62; and MCT, 254; and R/CID, 202; tripartite model of personal identity, 184, 184*f*; world view model, 74–5, 74*f*
Sue, D. W., and associates, 3, 17, 172
Sue, S. (Stanley), 6, 31, 34
suicide, 201, 216*t*
Sundararajan, Louise, 61
support networks, for immigrants and refugees, 123, 130–1, 134
susceptibility, 211
Swami, V., 39–40
sweat-lodge ceremony, 3*f*
symbolic racism, 164
symptoms of disorders, 241

Syrian refugee crisis, 124–5
systematic racism in society, 158–63

tag questions, 112
talking cure (or talk therapy), 251
Tam, Theresa, 176*f*
Tan, Amy, 288
Tang, C. S. K., 64–5
Tao, V. Y. K., 61
Tatum, Daniel, 182, 183
teachers, influence on students, 148–9
Teddy Stoddard story, 148–9, 150
teenagers. *See* youth
television (TV), and world views, 78
$10 bill in Canada, 288*f*
tenure process, 152–3
terrorist attacks in Paris (France, 2015), 159
therapeutic approaches, and cultural sensitivity, 254–7
Thunberg, Greta, 85*f*, 86
Thunderchild First Nation, 284–5
tight cultures, 7, 263–4
time focus, 71
tolerance, in multiculturalism, 14
Toronto Police Service, and Blacks, 183
Toronto schools, and Blacks, 163, 206
traditional values, and gender differences, 65
Trafimow, D., and colleagues, 36–7
training, for cultural competence, 283–6, 283*t*
transgender identity, changes towards, 27
trauma and PTSD, in refugees, 127
travel, as education, 287
Triandis, H., and associates, 62
Triandis, Henry, 4, 5, 36, 66–8, 67*f*
Trimble, J. E., 71–2, 97–8
tripartite model of personal identity, 184–5, 184*f*, 255
Trump, Donald, 63
turban debate at RCMP, 164–5
Tutu, Desmond, on tolerance, 14
Tversky, Amos, 157
type 2 diabetes, and Indigenous Peoples, 218
Typology of Ethnic Identity, 199

ultimate attribution error, 150
unaccompanied youth, as refugees, 127
United States (US): and COVID, 7; health-care access, 228, 229; immigration to Canada, 122; impact of diversity, 289; mass shootings, 86; mental disorders prevalence, 244; same-sex relations, 82–3; segregation in schools, 187
universities, tenure process at, 152–3

value orientation models, 71–4, 71*t*
values: in collectivism and individualism, 66; in culture and psychology, 16; human values theory, 72–4, 73*f*; importance in society, 70–1; in multiculturalism, 14–16; in other world views, 281–2; priorities in Canada, 74
van de Vijver, F., 55
Van Ness, Jonathan, 82*f*
variables: and correlation, 35–6, 35*f*; experimental designs, 36, 38

verbal/emotional/behavioural expressiveness., 251
Vietnamese medicine, 230
vilification, 164
visible minorities, 13, 76; *See also* ethnic minority populations
Vivar, Jose, 140

Wallen, Donna, 159
water contamination, and Indigenous Peoples, 218–19
Waugh, E., 130
wealth gap, 84
Weinstein, Harvey, 64
WEIRD (Western, Educated, Industrialized, Rich, and Democratic), 70
Welcome Refugees program, 125
well-being, 72
West Bank and Gaza Strip, 280–1, 280*f*
Western countries, and eating disorders, 260, 261–2
Western medicine, 230
Wet'suwet'en peoples, 162*f*
White, H. D., 92
White ethnics, 76
White European standard, 32
White people (Euro-Americans): attitudes towards race and racism, 191–2; and aversive racism, 167, 168*t*; cultural superiority, 175; defensiveness with racism, 271–2; and early psychology, 24–5; identity development, 190–4; as immigrants, 76; and killings of people of colour, 7; mental health in Ontario, 243; self-awareness of own culture, 276–7; as standard in research, 32; stereotype threat, 154
White privilege, 78, 176–8
White supremacy movement, 160*f*
WHO (World Health Organization), 209, 213–14, 232, 238
WHO-WMH Survey Initiative, 243, 246
Williams, John, 26
Wilson-Raybould, Jody, 176*f*
women: body image, 260; eating disorders, 260–2; exclusion in psychology, 26; *vs.* men (*see* gender differences); and mental health issues, 79; stereotype threat, 153; violence against, 64, 79–80; world views, 64–5, 79–80
Women's March, 63–4, 63*f*
working-through stage, 195
World's Healthiest Country Index, 228
world views: changes in, 290–2; and culture, 6–8; definitions and description, 6, 290–1; ethnic groups differences, 76–9, 78*f*, 281–2; example of differences in, 59; and gender differences, 63–5, 79–80; LGBTQ2+, 80–3; of mental health professionals, 255; model of D. W. Sue, 74–5, 74*f*; and racism, 74–7; in social class and age, 84–6; understanding of others' world views, 279–82; and value orientation, 71; of women, 64–5, 79–80
Wundt, Wilhelm, 24

Yoon, E., and colleagues, 40
young adults, and social media, 107, 108, 109
youth: Blacks as, 182–3; health disparities for LGBTQ2+, 231; as immigrants, 129–30, 133, 135–6; as refugees, 127; and social media, 108–11; world views, 85–6
Yum, ttt, 103

Zuckerman, M., 8